Translations from the Asian Classics

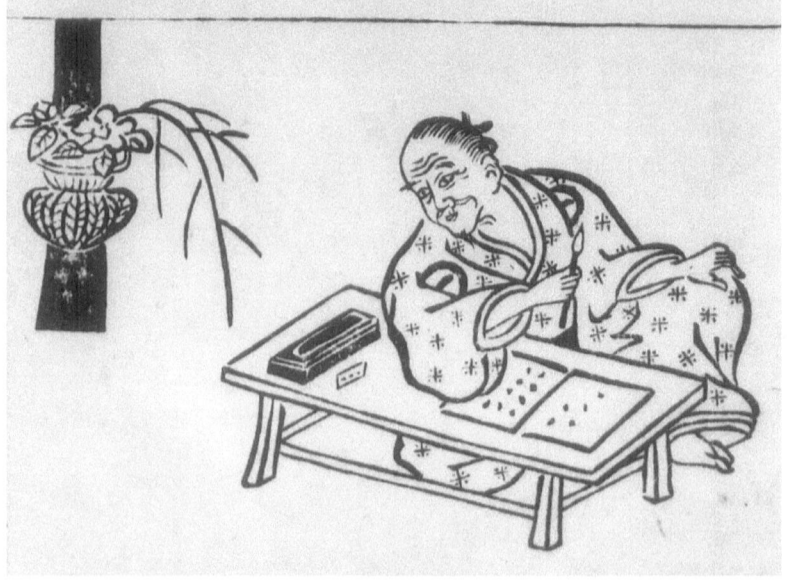

Chikamatsu portrait from the book *Naniwa miyage* (1738). *(Waseda Theater Museum.)*

Chikamatsu
5 Late Plays

Translated and annotated by C. Andrew Gerstle

Columbia University Press
New York

TRANSLATIONS FROM THE ASIAN CLASSICS

Editorial Board

Wm. Theodore de Bary, Chairman
Paul Anderer
Irene Bloom
Donald Keene
George A. Saliba
Haruo Shirane
David D. W. Wang
Burton Watson

 COLUMBIA UNIVERSITY PRESS
Publishers Since 1893
New York   Chichester, West Sussex
Copyright © 2001 Columbia University Press
All rights reserved

Columbia University Press wishes to express its appreciation for funds given by the Japan Foundation toward the cost of publishing this volume.

Library of Congress Cataloging-in-Publication Data
Chikamatsu, Monzaemon, 1651–1725.
  [Selections. 2001]
  Chikamatsu : five late plays / translated and annotated by C. Andrew Gerstle.
     p. cm.
  Includes bibliographical references.
  ISBN 978-0-231-12166-8 (cloth) — ISBN 978-0-231-12167-5 (pbk.)

  I. Gerstle, C. Andrew, 1951– II. Title.
PL793.4 .A6 2001
895.6'232—dc21

00-052361

Contents

Acknowledgments   vii

Abbreviations in the Bibliography and Notes   ix

Maps   xi

Introduction   1

Twins at the Sumida River   36
  (*Futago sumidagawa*, 1720)

Lovers Pond in Settsu Province   118
  (*Tsu no kuni meoto ike*, 1721)

Battles at Kawa-nakajima   202
  (*Shinshū kawa-nakajima kassen*, 1721)

Love Suicides on the Eve of the Kōshin Festival   278
  (*Shinjū yoigōshin*, 1722)

Tethered Steed and the Eight Provinces of Kantō   325
  (*Kanhasshū tsunagi-uma*, 1724)

Notes   429

Bibliography   513

Glossary of Terms   523

Acknowledgments

This project has been ongoing for many years, and its completion would not have been possible without the support of many individuals and institutions. I am grateful to all who helped me along the way. Two research fellowships to spend time in Japan were invaluable in giving me access to both specialists and sources. I am grateful to the National Institute of Japanese Literature in Tokyo and the Faculty of Letters, Kyoto University, for grants and hospitality. Numerous individuals have offered assistance. Professors Takei Kyōzō, Uchiyama Mikiko, Matsuzaki Hitoshi, Hara Michio, Ōhashi Masatoshi, Kasaya Kazuhiko, and Wada Osamu all participated in a series of seminars on Chikamatsu at the National Institute of Japanese Literature and offered help with the translations. Professors Hino Tatsuo, Kida Akiyoshi, and Ōtani Yoshio made my stay at Kyoto University most pleasant and fruitful. I also want to thank the graduate students, in particular Kubori Hiroaki and Kawashima Tomoko, who participated in the seminar I led at Kyoto University in which we read several of the plays translated in this book. I received a grant from the Japan Foundation Endowment Committee (UK) for a short research trip to Japan to work on the translations with Professor Torigoe Bunzō at the Waseda University Theater Museum. Professor Nishino Haruo offered advice on the references to nō plays. I would also like to express my gratitude to (the late) Professor Matsudaira Susumu and Professor Mizuta Kayano of the Chikamatsu Research Center at Sonoda Gakuen Joshi University. Professor Susan Matisoff and Jonathan Mills read a draft manuscript and offered important comments and corrections. Professor Hugh Baker of the School of Oriental and African Studies (SOAS) at the University of London kindly checked my Chinese references, and Andrew Lo and Bernard Fuehrer, also of SOAS, offered advice on translations of Chinese works. Others, who helped with the illustrations are Sugai Yayoi of the Shōchiku Ōtani Library, Aoki Shinji of the Osaka National Bunraku Theater, Suzuki Yoshio of the Waseda Theater Museum, Nakamura Ganjirō III and his staff, and, particularly, Kawashima Akira, and Glenn Ratcliffe of SOAS. Cynthia Daugherty, Meri Arichi, and Irene Cummings read parts of this book in draft stages. Roma Beaumont and Carolyne Megan prepared the maps. I would especially like to thank Diana Matias, who helped prepare the final draft. I am also grateful to the anonymous readers for Columbia University Press for their suggestions, and to Margaret B. Yamashita, who edited the book for publication. Finally, I would like to dedicate this book to my late father, who gave me the opportunity to pursue Japanese studies.

Abbreviations in the Bibliography and Notes

CJS: *Chikamatsu jōrurishū* (see Matsuzaki Hitoshi et al., eds., 1995)
CZ: *Chikamatsu zenshū*
IKKB: *Iwanami kōza: kabuki, bunraku* (see Torigoe Bunzō et al., eds., 1997)
NKBT: Nihon koten bungaku taikei
NKBZ: Nihon koten bungaku zenshū
NSBSS: *Nihon shomin bunka shiryō shūsei*
SKT: Shinshaku kanbun taikei
SNKBT: Shin Nihon koten bungaku taikei
TS: *Tsūzoku sangokushi* (see Ōhashi Shintarō, ed., 1893)
YTK: *Yōkyoku taikan* (see Sanari Kentarō, ed., 1927)

Maps

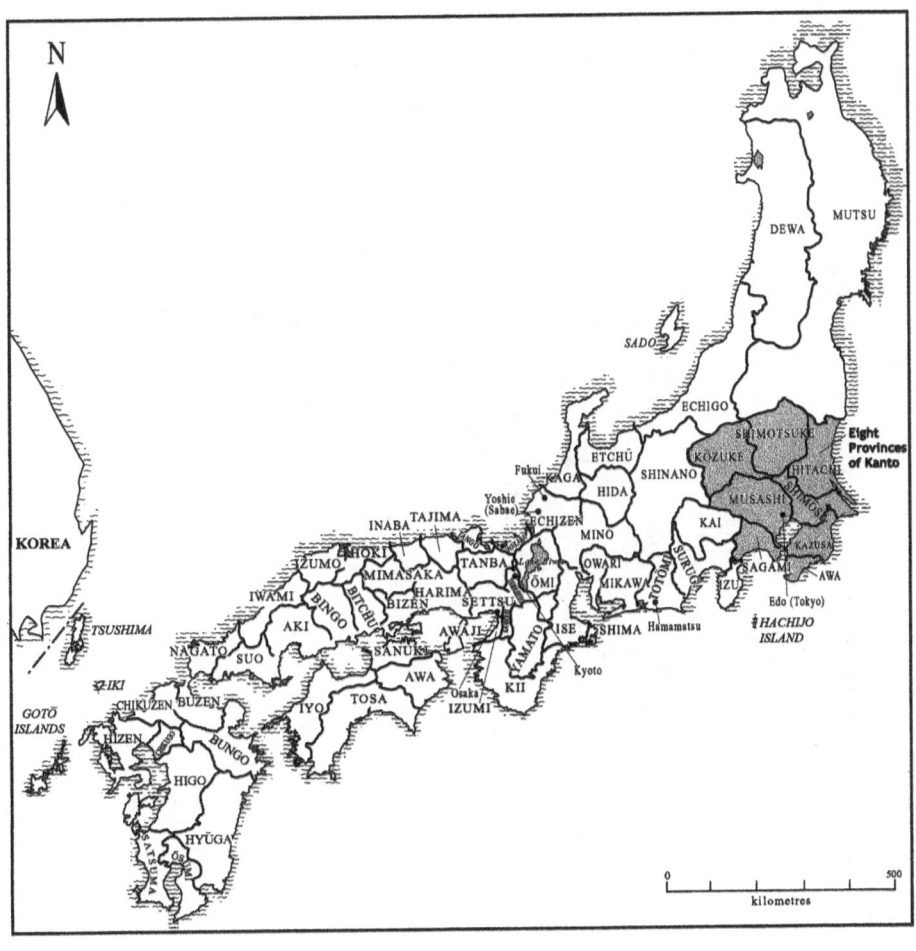

Pre-1868 Japan.

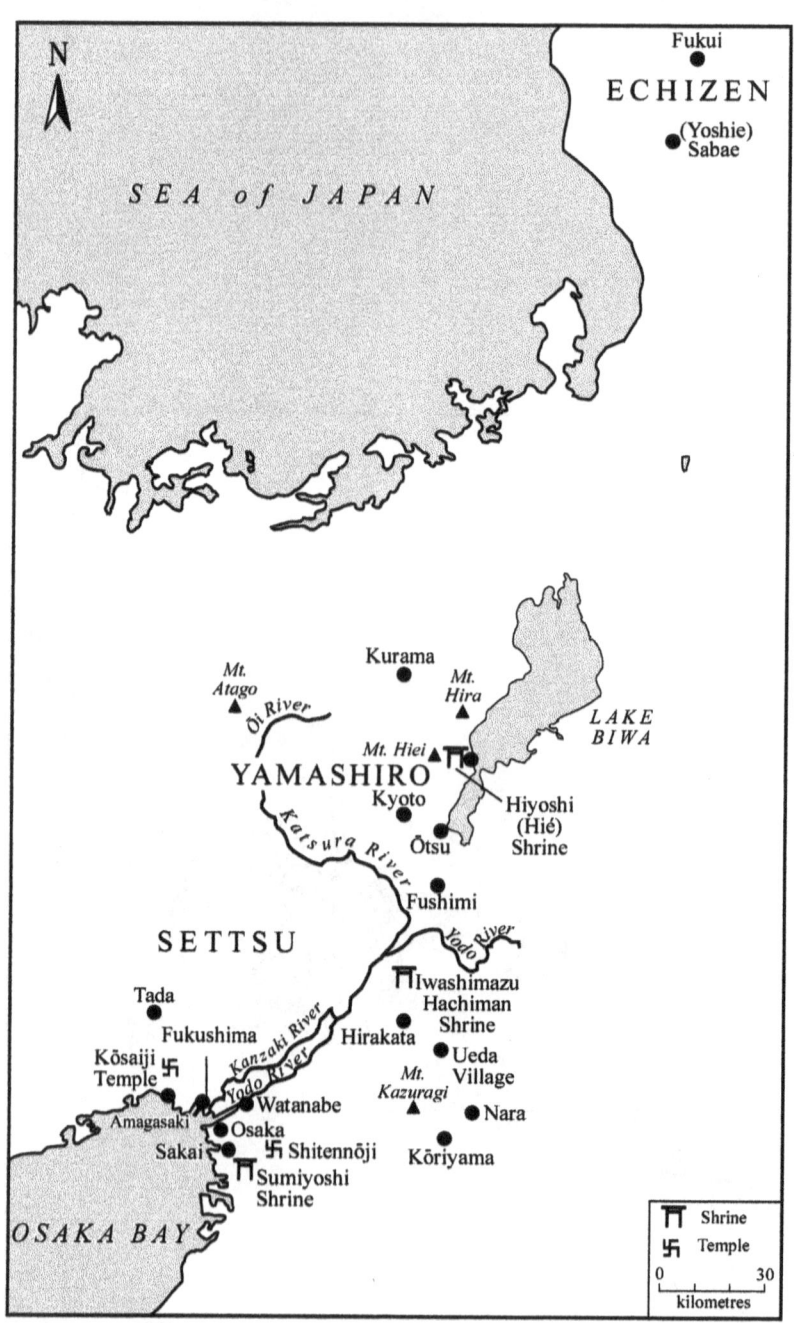

Kyoto and Osaka area.

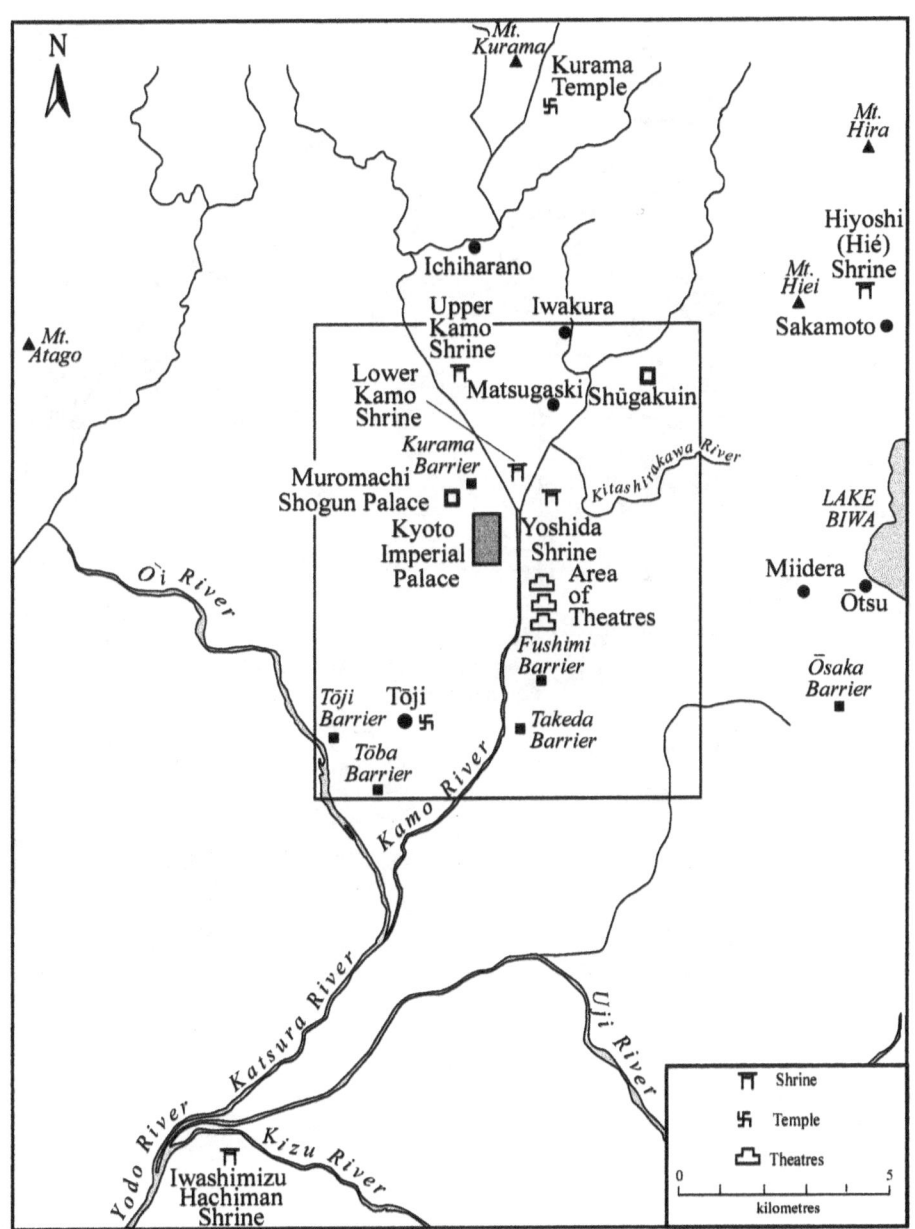

Kyoto and surrounding area.

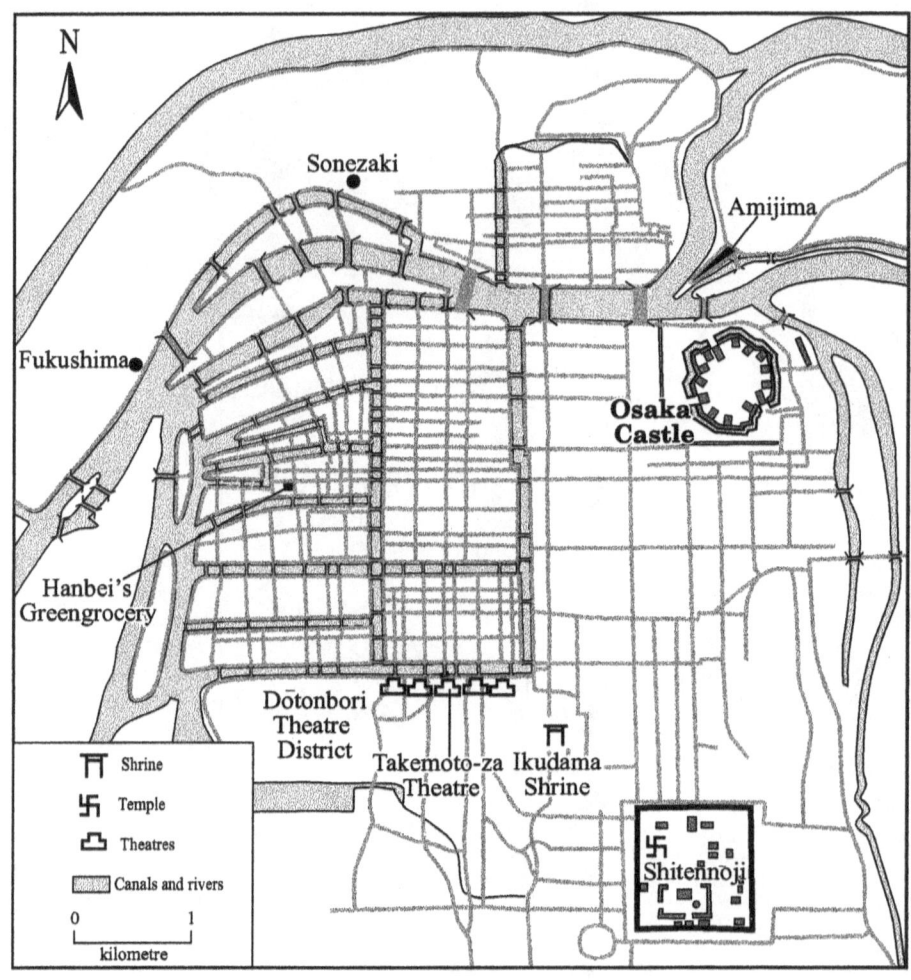

Osaka City.

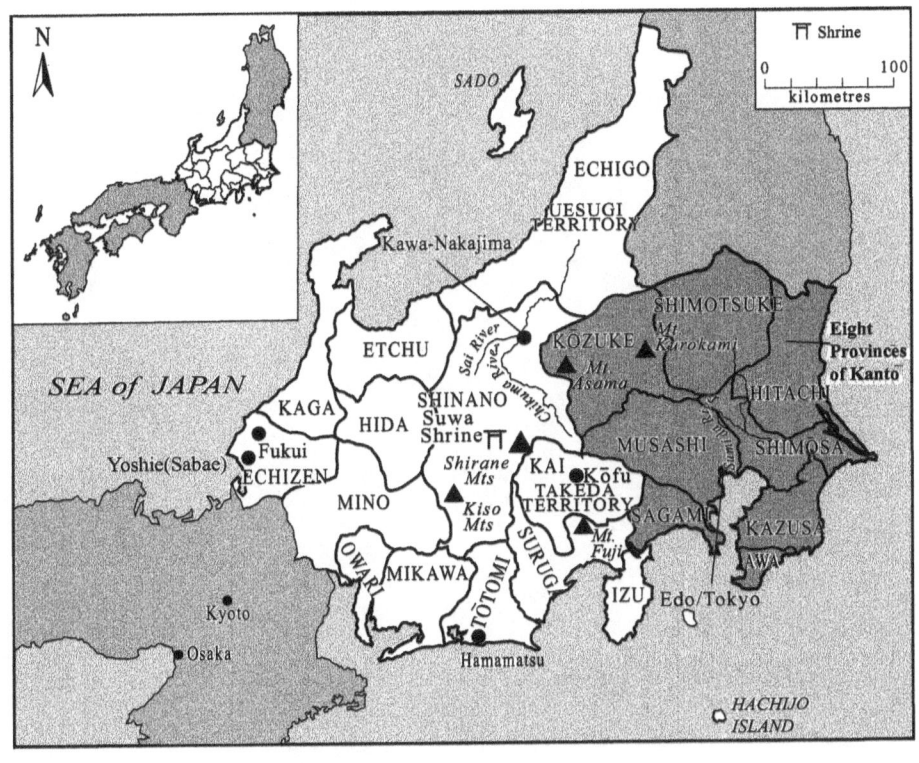

Central and eastern Japan, and the "Eight provinces of Kantō."

Chikamatsu

Introduction

Chikamatsu Monzaemon (1653–1725), Japan's most famous playwright, produced more than one hundred works during a career of about forty-five years spent writing for the jōruri (bunraku) and kabuki theaters in Kyoto and Osaka. Several "collected works" of his plays, most of which filled a complete day of theater, were published in the twentieth century, most recently in seventeen volumes.[1]

Ogyū Sorai (1666–1728), a famous philosopher and contemporary of Chikamatsu, left a succinct comment on the quality of his writing: "Chikamatsu's style can be seen clearly in the opening lines of the *michiyuki* journey section of *Love Suicides at Sonezaki*.[2] One can judge his brilliance as a writer from these lines alone."[3] Sorai, Japan's most celebrated scholar of Chinese thought, is also well known for his interest in literature. Thus his comment is significant because in general, Confucian thinkers considered jōruri and other commercial performing arts to be detrimental to popular morals.

All of Chikamatsu's plays were written under contract for commercial theaters and specific performers. As published books, they were also used as practice texts for the popular hobby of amateur chanting and were read as dramatic literature from the late seventeenth century into the modern era. Editions appeared in relatively large (woodblock) print formats with seven or eight lines to a page, as well as in smaller formats with ten or more lines to a page; all contained the chanter's code of notation. Extant large-format, special editions are known to have been presented to Kyoto aristocrats and others in high positions.

The eleven translations by Donald Keene in *Major Plays of Chikamatsu* have for almost forty years provided the English-speaking world with a wide range of Chikamatsu's plays, particularly the contemporary-life (*sewamono*) works.[4] In Keene's volume, Chikamatsu's mature history or period (*jidaimono*) plays are, however, represented only by *The Battles of Coxinga* (1715), a spectacular success on the stage but in some ways different from the period plays that followed in the last phase of Chikamatsu's writing when he increasingly incorporated elements of complex character portrayal from the contemporary-life works into the period dramas, often exploring similar themes from different angles in each subgenre.[5]

Chikamatsu's twenty-four contemporary-life plays, conceived as one-act dramas equivalent to the intense third act of a five-act period play, maintain a tight unity of place and time, and they are usually realistic, without any of the fantastic elements of the period dramas. This temporal and spatial unity, together with the realism, has earned praise in modern times for *sewamono*, in both Japan and the West. Chikamatsu's more than seventy period plays, with their multiple plots and supernatural elements often taking place over vast areas of time and space, were until recently, however, less favorably received as literature in the twentieth century because of this perceived lack of unity. But the attraction of these plays lies precisely in their abundant variety over a day of theater. The third act—as long as many of the one-act, three-scene *sewamono*, which last for several hours in performance—is usually tightly structured and realistically acted. The action depicted on stage is usually no longer than one day, but this act is part of a long, epic-like drama full of picaresque adventure, and it must contrast with acts 2 and 4 around it. The two genres are distinct and are built on entirely different premises and theatrical conventions.[6] Whereas *sewamono* engage with contemporary society directly through depictions of an actual incident of the time, *jidaimono* use complex interaction and dialogue with an array of texts from both the Japanese and Chinese traditions to portray contemporary politics.

"History," then, is the vehicle for a perspective on the present. Contemporary-life plays tend to focus on the private lives of average folk, while period pieces focus on an individual's interaction with the public, political sphere. Chikamatsu's mature period-dramas present a tense balance between the "private" and "public" spheres of society, usually with the climactic third act emphasizing the private consequences of conflict with the public world of politics. These works are better viewed as parables of the contemporary world than as "history" plays.

Four of the five works in this collection are period plays, and the other is Chikamatsu's final contemporary-life play. This selection complements Keene's *Major Plays of Chikamatsu* in introducing a wider range of mature period works, as well as the final love-suicide play. *Twins at the Sumida River* (1720) and *Lovers Pond in Settsu Province* (1721), both with murderer-heroes, were composed around the time of Chikamatsu's famous contemporary-life works, *Love Suicides at Amijima* (1721) and *Woman-Killer and the Hell of Oil* (1721),[7] and depict human (particularly male) weakness and the consequences of crime. The last three—*Battles at Kawa-nakajima* (1721), *Love Suicides on the Eve of the Kōshin Festival* (1722), and his final work, *Tethered Steed and the Eight Provinces of Kantō* (1724)—show a distinctive shift of theme away from weak figures to the portrayal of strong men and women confronting crisis. These last three plays present a development in Chikamatsu's career hitherto unappreciated outside Japan. An interesting aspect of these final few years of his career is the pattern in both the period and contemporary-life plays of focusing on similar themes from different perspectives. In this introduction, I outline Chikamatsu's career, emphasizing the many figures that he worked for and their ideas. It is clear that he learned his craft from performers, both jōruri chanters and kabuki actors, and continued to collaborate with them over his entire career. Because readers will want to devise their own analyses and interpretations of the plays, my intention here is to provide insights into the context in which the plays were written and into the reception they have received in Japan.

Status as a Playwright

SOON AFTER HIS death, Chikamatsu came to be revered as the "god of writers," particularly in the dramatic tradition, an assessment that remained constant throughout the Tokugawa era: "Chikamatsu Monzaemon is the god of writers. During his lifetime he wrote more than one hundred Jōruri plays and although on the stage some were popular and others not, when you read through them, none is without merit. All the playwrights today take Chikamatsu as their model when composing plays."[8]

Thereafter it was often said that reading Chikamatsu's plays gave one a knowledge of Buddhism, Confucianism, and Shinto. A testament from the Confucian scholar Hozumi Ikan (1692–1769) in his *Naniwa miyage*

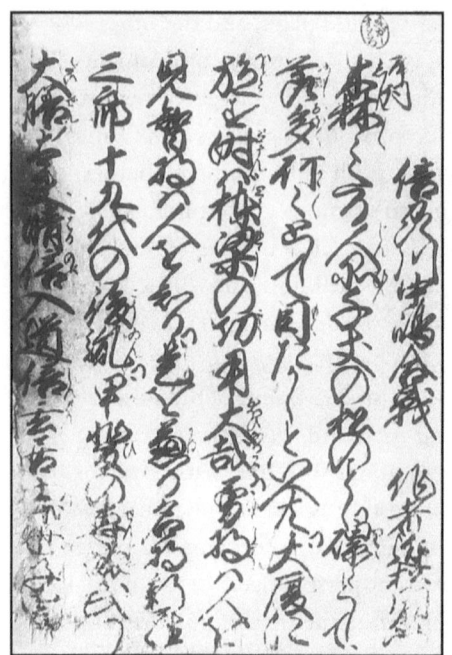

FIGURE 1 The first page of the original text of *Battles at Kawa-nakajima* (1721), with the author's name in the lower right-hand corner.

(*Souvenir from Naniwa*, 1738), which also contains Chikamatsu's famous short essay on the essence of playwriting, presents the following striking image:

He was a warm and upright man who even at seventy was full of youthful vigor. Everyone who met him was struck by his depth of heart. He read with a clear mind a myriad books, and in his plays mixed skillfully the language of the sages with popular songs. At the touch of his brush even ordinary words gain the power to take our breath away.[9]

In the preface to this work Ikan comments further:

Chikamatsu began writing original jōruri plays in the 1680s for the chanter Takemoto Gidayū [1651–1714] whose magnificent voice went straight to the hearts of the audience. Many of them secretly sought out the texts and discovered that the style was outstanding and showed a thorough understanding of Confucianism, Buddhism, and Shinto. Metaphors and allusions are abundant but do not grate on the ear. His descriptions of the distinctions between the high and the humble, those from the city and those from the country, are precise and ring true to the ear. The lyrical *michiyuki* and other song passages evoke the spirit of the elegant *Tales of Ise* and *The Tale of Genji*, while the sections depicting the language and characteristics of the common folk show a lively sense of humor. The effect is such that even the most elevated figures seem natural and real, as if we could reach out and touch them. He continued writing works of charm, beauty, and power until he became famous, and the reading of jōruri books was no longer considered something to be ashamed of. The popularity of jōruri books is all due to his efforts.[10]

This passage makes clear the low status of jōruri books when Chikamatsu first began writing and how this changed during his lifetime.

As was the practice until the late nineteenth century in that tradition, Chikamatsu's thirty kabuki plays were not published as complete texts but were printed in illustrated summary editions (*e-iri kyōgenbon*). His more than ninety jōruri plays, however, were printed in full at the time of their first performance at Osaka's Takemoto-za puppet theater. These were complete, authorized editions that included the author's name and the senior chanter's endorsement of the text as containing the code of musical notation used by the chanters. Unusually for popular writing of the Edo period (1600–1868), as many as fifty of his major works (including the five translated here) remained "in print" in traditional woodblock format until the change to modern movable type after 1870.[11] This was due primarily to the continuing popularity throughout Japan of jōruri chanting as an amateur hobby which declined only after World War II, when Japanese society altered dramatically in ways that led to the demise of many of its cultural traditions.[12] This tradition of amateur chanting meant that until recently, the readership of his and other jōruri plays was extremely sophisticated in the sense that readers received training in performing the texts orally. It was as if most readers of Elizabethan and Jacobean drama from the seventeenth to the early twentieth century had learned from professional actors or teachers how to recite the works of Shakespeare and others as a private hobby.

The popular fiction writer Ryūtei Tanehiko (1783–1842) was known to have a library of hundreds of jōruri and kabuki plays, including nearly eighty of Chikamatsu's jōruri texts.[13] A quotation from Tanehiko gives a sense of how he read Chikamatsu's plays: "As I chanted [*rōshō*] it aloud by lamplight, I felt exactly as if I were seeing a performance more than one hundred years ago before my very eyes."[14] It was not only writers such as Tanehiko who read this way. Vasilii Golovnin (1776–1831), the Russian ship captain held captive in the remote province of Matsumae in Hokkaido between 1811 and 1813, noted Japanese reading habits:

> The Japanese are extremely fond of reading; even common soldiers when on duty are continually engaged with books. This passion for literature, however, proved somewhat inconvenient to us, as they always read aloud, in a tone of voice resembling singing; much in the same style in which the Psalms are read at funerals in Russia. Before we became accustomed to this, we were unable to enjoy a moment's rest during the night. The history of their native country, the contests which have arisen among themselves, and the wars in which they have been

engaged with neighbouring nations, form the subjects of their favourite books, which are all printed in Japan.[15]

It is clear from the description of the content of the works that these soldiers, in perhaps the most remote province of Japan at the time, were chanting jōruri texts in a manner similar to that described by Tanehiko. The widespread popularity of kabuki, whose repertory is heavily influenced by Chikamatsu and other jōruri playwrights, also helped sustain a broad interest in Chikamatsu's work.

Regardless of Chikamatsu's high stature as the preeminent writer in the theatrical traditions of both bunraku and kabuki, few of his plays were regularly performed after his death. In fact, many were rewritten, and it is clear that his plays were a model for playwrights and later fiction writers, particularly in the early-nineteenth-century popular fiction genres of *yomihon*, *gōkan*, and *ninjōbon*.[16] Today Chikamatsu is considered a major figure in the literary canon, and his plays are performed on kabuki and bunraku stages as well as in modern theater, and since the war, many of his works have been revived. As many as forty-nine films of his plays are known to have been made, thirty-one of them from the silent era.[17] In recent years, the director Wada Ben has produced four plays for NHK Television, including *Love Suicides on the Eve of the Kōshin Festival*, translated here. His plays have also been performed in translation abroad.

Early Life

ASIDE FROM THE huge corpus of published work, only a few of Chikamatsu's other writings have survived, and these are mainly letters. Just ten days before he died, he wrote a short final testament that gives an insight into his background and view of himself.

> Although born into an old samurai family, I left the warrior's life behind. I served in courtier houses but never received any rank. I wandered about in the marketplace but knew no trade. I appeared to be a recluse but wasn't; I was thought to have been clever but wasn't; although considered to have been erudite, I knew nothing. I was good at fooling the world, never afraid to let my brush run along on any topic—Chinese and Japanese classics, religion, philosophy, drama, arts,

crafts, comedies—writing about subjects as if I understood them. After a life of constant writing, now at this crucial moment I should say something significant on the essence of life, but nothing, not a single word, comes to mind. How embarrassing after more than seventy years on this earth. Looking back after all that time, how unsteadily did I walk through life.

Should one ask for my final testament, all I can say is, "well then, afterward, may the fragrance from the cherry blossoms remain."

Yet how foolish to hope that the blossoms will live on. During a life as brief as the moment before a smoldering fire dies out—all those frivolous works I leave behind, withering away like decaying wood.[18]

FIGURE 2 Portrait of Chikamatsu and his final testament (1724). *(Waseda Theater Museum.)*

Although the tone is modest and somewhat cryptic, this is an extremely confident final testament. The words "well then, afterward" (*sate mo sono nochi*) are the traditional beginning of a new scene in the storytelling tradition. The "fragrance of cherry blossoms" (*sakura ga hana shi niowaba*) suggests the cherry-wood blocks used for printing books. Although Chikamatsu hoped his works would continue to be read and performed after his death, it is highly unlikely that he imagined his plays would remain in print over the centuries, let alone be translated into the major languages of the world.

Over the centuries there have been more than six claims to being Chikamatsu's birthplace, but research into his background has now given us the basic facts of his early life, filling in some of the detail hinted at in the preceding testament.[19] Chikamatsu was born in the Echizen castle town of Fukui, but the family moved when he was about two to Yoshie (now called

Sabae), a smaller castle town also in Fukui Prefecture on the Japan Sea side of the country where his father, Sugimori Nobuyoshi (1621–87), was in personal service to the young daimyo of Echizen, a Tokugawa fief. His father's stipend of 300 *koku*[20] indicates that the family was upper-class samurai and relatively well off. Chikamatsu's real name was Sugimori Nobumori. His family traced its lineage back to the Kyoto aristocrat Sanjō Sanetsugu (1301–36) and, during the sixteenth century, had served various lords during that turbulent era. Records show that Chikamatsu lived in Fukui until he was at least twelve, and it is thought that after his father left his position as a samurai, his family moved to Kyoto when Chikamatsu was fourteen or fifteen.[21] His mother's father was the daimyo's doctor with a large stipend of 1,000 *koku*, and her family also had Kyoto connections.

Mori Shū argues that the mother's family connections were crucial to the Sugimori family's success in Kyoto.[22] Chikamatsu's younger brother took his maternal grandfather's surname, and as Okamoto Ippō (1654–1716), is famous as a writer of many books on Chinese medicine.[23] Chikamatsu's mother seems to have had an important influence on him. Records at the Kōsaiji temple in Amagasaki note that in 1716 Chikamatsu had a memorial service held for his mother who had died in the ninth month of that year, and as an offering he presented writings that he (or his mother) had received from aristocrats.[24] We can, therefore, deduce that Chikamatsu had a relatively cultured samurai upbringing, at least until his father left his position. It is reasonable to imagine that he grew up familiar with nō chanting and readings of *The Tale of the Heike* and other martial tales, as well as with some knowledge of the Chinese classics.

The move to Kyoto brought many changes. We know that Chikamatsu was in service to several courtier families. One of these was Ichijō Ekan (Akiyoshi, 1605–72), the son of Emperor Go-Yōzei and younger brother of Emperor Go-Mizunō (1596–1680), for whom Chikamatsu worked until Ekan's death. Emperor Go-Mizunō was extremely active in promoting the imperial court as a cultural center during his long period as a retired emperor from 1629 until his death.[25] Ekan, head of the Ichijō house, was Sesshū Kanpaku, the highest position in the court under the emperor. Through Ekan, Chikamatsu would have witnessed courtier cultural life in the late 1660s and early 1670s. We also know that Chikamatsu had a connection to Emperor Gosai (1637–85; r. 1654–63, son of Emperor Go-Mizunō) because of the writings of Emperor Gosai donated by Chikamatsu to Kōsaiji temple.[26]

The essayist Kanzawa Tokō (1709-95), who worked in the Kyoto bakufu office from the age of eleven as a clerk (*yoriki*), records in his *Okina-gusa* (*Writings of an Old Man*, 1772) that Chikamatsu's works were considered unrivaled masterpieces and mentions that Chikamatsu served in the cultivated courtier house of Ōgimachi Kinmichi (1653–1733), who was the same age as Chikamatsu and later became a famous Shinto thinker and poet.

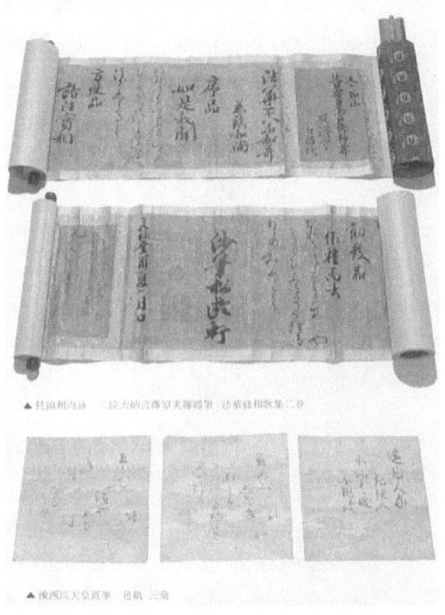

When he was still a young man, Ōgimachi, who liked composing *kyōka* comic poems, wrote plays for the chanter Uji Kadayū [Kaganojō, 1635–1711] as a hobby and used Chikamatsu as a messenger to Kadayū. Since Chikamatsu, too, had talent, he began to help with the writing as well. He gradually learned to write plays, and enticed Kadayū's best disciple, Gidayū [Takemoto Gidayū], to begin his own style of Jōruri, offering to write plays for him.[27]

FIGURE 3 (Top) Scrolls by Fujiwara (Ano) Sanefuji; (bottom) calligraphy by Emperor Gosai, presented to Kōsaiji temple in Amagasaki by Chikamatsu (*Kōsaiji* temple.)

Jōruri was popular among the aristocrats, and Chikamatsu most likely met Kaganojō at one of their houses.[28] Other aristocrats with whom he had contact were Ano Sanefuji (1634–93) and Machigami Kanechika (1662–1742).[29] Chikamatsu's acquaintance with Kyoto's high aristocracy would have been invaluable to his writing, allowing him access to both their way of life and their libraries. The haiku anthology edited by Genrin (1631–72), *Takaragura* (*Treasure Storehouse*), published in 1671, contains a section of poetry by the Sugimori family, including one of Chikamatsu's poems—his earliest extant writing—as well as several by his father, and one each by his grandfather, mother, and one of his brothers.[30] This collection indicates a considerable level of cultural sophistication within his family.

Chikamatsu is thought to have been married twice. His second wife, who was from the Matsuya family in Osaka, died in 1734 at the age of seventy-eight and has graves at both Kōsaiji in Amagasaki and her family's temple Myōhōji in Osaka.[31] Chikamatsu is thought to have had three sons and one daughter: Sugimori Tamon Baishin was a painter (one of his works is extant at Kōsaiji where Chikamatsu is buried); Chikamatsu Keiri had a brief career in the mid-1750s as a playwright; and his other son, Matsuya Taemon (Yūsen, 1701–61), was also a painter; Chikamatsu's daughter died in 1762 at the age of seventy-one.[32]

Apprenticeship and Collaboration

Kaganojō and Gidayū

The jōruri puppet theater in the seventeenth century was the inheritor of the heroic epic storytelling tradition based on the civil wars and sagas of earlier ages as reflected in *The Tale of the Heike* and its spin-offs. From the outset, the chanter (*tayū*) was the star performer, and the puppets were added as accompaniment. During Chikamatsu's time, the puppets were relatively simple, each held by one puppeteer. Later, from about 1734, sophisticated three-man puppets, the type seen on the bunraku stage today, were developed, but for audiences at this early stage, the chanter, who recited all the roles as well as the third-person narration, was the undisputed center of attention. Audiences went to the theater to hear their favorite chanters, who often performed without puppets at private residences. In contrast, kabuki, which had emerged from dance, with the actor's body and voice as the center of attraction, always focused on the here and now of urban life, particularly the pleasure quarters. Chikamatsu wrote for both jōruri chanters and kabuki actors, but as noted earlier, only his jōruri plays were published as complete texts. His experience of writing for both traditions early in his career led to the production of many masterpieces in the last twenty years of his life.

In his mid-twenties, Chikamatsu began writing plays for Uji Kaganojō, and sometime later he started to write kabuki plays as well. During this period, we know from references in the kabuki actors' critique, *Yarō tachiyaku butai ōkagami* (*A Mirror of Kabuki Stage Heroes*, 1687),[33] that Chikamatsu was criticized for publicizing his name as the author of kabuki and jōruri plays. This brought the rejoinder that Chikamatsu "has decided to give his whole life[34] to writing for the theater, and so it is only natural that he wants his name to be known. He has thrown himself into the theatrical world, working backstage at the Mandayū theater and performing with Eitaku as a story-teller [tsurezuregusa no kōshaku] in Sakai."[35] This is followed by praise of Chikamatsu's works for their familiarity with a wide range of Japanese and Chinese writing.

As one who came from a relatively well-off samurai family, served in the households of a member of the imperial family and other culturally active Kyoto aristocrats, and then went on to work for street performers and kabuki actors, officially considered as outcasts (kawara-kojiki, riverbed beggars), Chikamatsu's experience is unprecedented in Edo society with its strict official class system. The preceding quotation defends this cultivated young writer who had decisively chosen to immerse himself in the life of the theater. The late-eighteenth-century work, Ongyoku michishirube, claims that he lived for a period during his twenties in the Karatsu Buddhist temple Konshōji, the characters of which could be read "Chikamatsu-tera," but this is unsubstantiated by contemporary records.[36] It has been suggested that his name derives from this temple, but it was also a name for actors in the kabuki world[37] and is a samurai name as well. Chikamatsu's reference to himself in his final testament as seeming to be a "recluse" has fostered the legend that he spent time in a Buddhist temple.

Chikamatsu did not write his plays in isolation; they were always composed for a particular performer in a commercial theater. His early jōruri and kabuki were written in collaboration with performers, and his later mature works were usually written in consultation with performers and managers. They included Kaganojō, Gidayū, the actors Sakata Tōjūrō (1647–1709) and Kaneko Kichizaemon (d. 1728), and, later, the theater manager and playwright Takeda Izumo I (d. 1747) and the chanter Takemoto Masatayū (Harima no Shōjō, 1691–1744). The first of these is Kaganojō, from whom Chikamatsu learned his trade as an apprentice. Kaganojō was almost twenty years his senior and, for unknown reasons, did not allow Chikamatsu's name to appear as author or coauthor of his plays. Kaganojō was the last of the oral tradition that held the chanter to be the undisputed source of the texts. Jōruri plays were published from the early seventeenth century, but there was little sense of copyright in the content of the tales, all of which were based on well-known earlier legends and stories. Kaganojō's name and seal on the text denoted the book as being his version of the orally transmitted tale and

FIGURE 4 Portrait of Kaganojō (reprinted in *Seikyoku ruisan*, 1847). *(Waseda Theater Museum.)*

authenticated the code of musical notation as an accurate record of his and his troupe's performance. Until the 1680s, the text was considered to be a representation of a particular chanter's performance. Chikamatsu's success as a playwright was to alter this view.

For a time, Kaganojō was also a teacher and employer of Takemoto Gidayū and a crucial figure in the development of jōruri theater. In 1678, he published his best pieces as *Takenokoshū* (*A Collection of Bamboo Shoots*). It included the chanter's notation and was issued as a practice text for amateur chanters. The preface contains an "apologia" for the art of jōruri, in which Kaganojō explains the hitherto "secret" musical notation and principles of the tradition, as well as its lineage.[38]

This important short treatise on the art must have influenced the young Chikamatsu, who was being paid to write for Kaganojō as well as Gidayū. In it, Kaganojō claims nō drama as jōruri's parent. He describes jōruri as fundamentally musical drama with a structure of acts, each with a distinctive musical mood: auspicious (*shūgen*), elegant (*yūgen*), amorous (*renbo*), and tragic (*aishō*). Most of Kaganojō's theoretical ideas came from the Edo-period nō treatise known as the *Hachijō kadensho*. He drew out the musical rather than the dramatic elements of this treatise to emphasize that the plays were organized as musical dramas.

Kaganojō's interest in nō (he had tried to become a professional in that tradition but failed because of its closed family system) and the patronage of courtiers he enjoyed correspond closely to Chikamatsu's early experience of working in the households of cultured aristocrats. Most of the plays thought to be the result of their collaboration in the late 1670s and early 1680s drew on nō drama and other classical Japanese sources.

The earliest work that is definitely attributed to Chikamatsu is *Yotsugi Soga* (*The Soga Successor*, 1683), performed first by Kaganojō and then a year later by Gidayū. This pattern of composing plays, often rewriting them slightly, for both chanters, one working in Kyoto and the other in Osaka, continued during the 1680s. But Chikamatsu's life changed after he began to write for Gidayū, who was only two years his senior.

Gidayū, from the Tennōji area of Osaka, was initially an apprentice of Kaganojō and performed in Kyoto, where he would have met Chikamatsu. Gidayū then broke away from Kaganojō and established his Takemoto-za theater in Osaka in 1684. The collaboration of Chikamatsu and Gidayū, which continued on and off until Gidayū's death in 1714, produced a new age of jōruri writing and many of Chikamatsu's masterpieces.

Gidayū's first published collection of pieces—with a preface in the mode of Kaganojō—was issued in 1686 and titled auspiciously (and ambitiously) *Chihiroshū* (*A Collection a Thousand Fathoms Deep*). This was a significant moment for Gidayū, after several years of failures and struggles touring the countryside. The year before its publication, Kaganojō had provocatively brought his troupe to Osaka and competed for audiences alongside Gidayū. It was about this time that Gidayū wooed Chikamatsu away from Kaganojō and took the decisive step of having Chikamatsu claim authorship for himself. The famous poet and novelist Ihara Saikaku (1642–93) filled the gap left by Chikamatsu and in 1685 wrote two works for Kaganojō for the Osaka audience. The second work at least seems to have met with some success, but Kaganojō's theater burned to the ground, and Kaganojō returned to Kyoto, leaving Gidayū (with Chikamatsu) seemingly the undisputed victor in Osaka.[39]

The precise reason that Kaganojō took the risk of going to Osaka to challenge Gidayū when he was well established in Kyoto is not clear, but it was

FIGURE 5 Portrait of Takemoto Gidayū. *(Tokyo University, Komaba Library.)*

most likely because of the thirty-five-day ban on performances in Kyoto after the death of the retired emperor Gosai in the second month of 1685. In accordance with usual practice, the ban lasted only about ten or twelve days in Osaka and even less in Edo.[40] The impression that emerges is of a tremendously competitive and lively atmosphere, with Osaka host to a battle between two famous chanters, one backed by the most famous popular writer of the age and the other by a new talent. Ironically, the Osakan Saikaku was writing for the Kyotoite Kaganojō, while Kyotoite Chikamatsu wrote for Osakan Gidayū—a rivalry between the established older generation and a rising younger one and between different styles and cities.

Gidayū, like Kaganojō, is bold in his first statement to the world. (The preface to Chihiroshū is signed by an otherwise unknown person, Josui, but it represents sentiments and attitudes echoed in Gidayū's later writings.)

> These days those who chant at the crossroads are either descendants of Kanze nō or in the Kōwaka-mai school. . . . Here we have a new style founded by Takemoto Gidayū which is neither too strong nor too weak. . . . Above, the voices mix with the courtiers in their tall hats, sitting in a row chanting *waka* poetry in thirty-one syllables; below, he and his followers learn from those poor folk who sing songs as they wander about peddling their wares. There are none he does not learn from.[41]

In subsequent prefaces, Gidayū is forthright and confident. He makes fun of contemporary entertainers who claim ancient or august lineage. Tradition is useful only if it can teach you something practical.

Gidayū's most important treatise is his *Sixteen Eighty-Seven Collection of Jōruri Scenes* (*Jōkyō yonen Gidayū danmonoshū*).[42] His prefaces were often quoted, and his individualistic ideology formed the foundation for jōruri performers until the modern age.[43] It begins:

> The courtiers of the palace decorate their hair and hats with blossoms at their leisure as they enjoy spring's glorious beauty. Each person has his own preferred aesthetic pleasures, and Jōruri, too, can be ranked alongside the flowering arts of the nobility. However, even among flowers and plants, there are old trees as well as young ones. The blossoms of young cherry trees have an abundance of bright colors and delightful fragrance around which butterflies, birds, and passersby happily frolic.[44]

Here Gidayū is promoting jōruri as the young but mature cherry tree in full bloom, an art comparable to those of the past and of the aristocracy. He offers his "secret teachings" and comments directly on Kaganojō's writings.

> Recently, on a certain evening, an old and intimate friend came to visit, and asked me to instruct him in the secret teachings of the art of Jōruri. I answered in the following manner. Essentially, since the art is modern, there are no traditional teachings to be learned from anyone. The music is restricted to a five-tone and twelve-note scale. The traditional songs and melodies of Kagura sacred music, popular songs, folk songs, Kōwaka-mai ballad drama, Nō, and Heike recitation are all incorporated into Jōruri; this is the tradition. If an artist performs well, is praised by others, and is then acknowledged by the world as a master, his words will certainly become secret teachings. However, if he slanders others while saying that only he himself is good, in the hope that he will be considered a great artist, then for such a person there is the refined treatise, *Kadensho*, by the sage of Nō, which contains the secret precepts of the tradition, handed down from generation to generation. . . .
>
> It is only natural that those who teach others about the art, or are acknowledged by the world as accomplished artists, must be familiar with these matters. However, to use quotations from the *Kadensho* in order to flaunt one's authority in a pompous manner is distasteful. Those who skip their practice sessions and try to learn solely from secret teachings will never learn to perform well. Reading books on theory will neither help one's mouth to move smoothly nor one's voice to improve and become entertaining for the audience. . . . Although at the lofty Emperor's Court there are disputes about theories of art, even there, the closely-guarded secret teachings of poetry are of little use when composing poems; they

can only give confidence to one's heart, as Konoe Motohiro of the court has said.⁴⁵

Gidayū is consistent: each individual can become a master, but only through constant struggle to improve. One can also hear in this the sure voice of Chikamatsu with his experience of culture in the court and samurai worlds.

Gidayū's most important contribution in this treatise is his outline of the structure of a five-act play. This is crucial background for understanding the four period plays translated in this book. Gidayū's ideas evolved from the structure of a seventeenth-century program of nō theater, but in this case they refer to a single play, the performance of which covers a whole day from morning to dusk. The following is a summary of his outline:

Act One: The theme is "Love": one must entice the feelings of the audience through pleasant melodies and appearances. The opening must be auspicious (*sanbasō*). While your heart must be strong, the words should be light, and your spirit gentle. The metaphor is the "silk fabric of a kimono."

Act Two: The theme is "Warriors and Battles" (*shura*). The mood is light with vigorous rhythms and fast beats. "You should chant with speed and force so that the audience listens tensely without relaxing their clenched fists." The metaphor is the "silk lining."

Act Three: The theme is "Pathos, tragedy." It is the climax of the play. "When chanting scenes of grief and sorrow, you must not disregard reality. While chanting this act, you must hold the essence of the entire play within your chest." The metaphor is the "pattern, color, and embroidery of the kimono."

Act Four: The theme is a "Travel Song" (*michiyuki*). "In this act the entire play begins to come together as a whole, but since the emotions of the audience are exhausted after the third act, you must be careful not to tire them further. The melody is the most important aspect of the *michiyuki* scene." The metaphor is the "cotton padding" of the kimono.

Act Five: The theme is an "Auspicious Conclusion." "The mood of the act is auspicious." The metaphor is the "tailoring of the kimono."⁴⁶

From this and later works on jōruri, we can see how the playwright, performers, and audience viewed the structure of a five-act play. In particular, the final scene of act 3 was always the climax of the play and performed by the star chanter. Next in importance were the final scenes of acts 4, 2, and 1, respectively. Act 5 was always short and an auspicious resolution of the play's crisis. In general, this structure is based on the musical formula of *jo-ha-kyū*—a slow, auspicious beginning, an increase in tempo and intensity over acts 2, 3, and 4, followed finally by a swift conclusion.

Another of Gidayū's metaphors for a play is a stream, with its "rapids and quiet pools," which again relates to the musical and dramatic structure. In contrast to the spatial and tactile metaphor of a kimono, a stream suggests a temporal, narrative sense, the journey through a day of theater. Like ancient Greek drama or more recent European opera, the action is carried forward by different types of language and presentation, marked by lively, dramatic sections and intense, lyrical moments of high passion. Gidayū saw the rapids (*kawase*) as the dramatic moments (*jigoto*), in which the dialogue and action are quick and lively; in contrast, the quiet, deep pools (*fuchi*) are the songs (*fushigoto*), where the action stops and depth is achieved through lyrical and melodic power.[47] This bipolar structure is also evident in the dramatic sections in the contrast of delivery styles used by chanters. The translations in this volume include the major notations used as a code by chanters (explained in detail later).

The basic principle is that a chanter moves between and among a relatively realistic declamatory "spoken" style with no musical accompaniment, and various levels of "song" style accompanied by the shamisen. As the reader will quickly notice, this is evident in both the dialogue and narrative sections. This rhetorical technique of constantly shifting between lyrical and dramatic voices for emphasis and effect is the essence of jōruri chanting. The notations also mark musical cadences that signal the end of paragraph-like units in the dramatic structure of each scene. Since the notation code was inserted by the chanter for whom the play was written, we may consider this as a guide to the first reading and interpretation of Chikamatsu's text. The chanter had to choose which lines to sing, which to declaim, where to make the high notes of musical and dramatic climax, and where to break the text with cadences. The notation reveals the rhetorical strategy of the performers for whom Chikamatsu composed his plays.

Gidayū's ideas on the structure of a five-act play, expressed as early as 1687, remained fundamental to Chikamatsu's method, in particular to his period plays written after the Gidayū's death in 1714. One important work from the 1690s available in English translation is *Semimaru*, thought to date from the early years of that decade.[48] Chikamatsu continued to write for Gidayū and Kaganojō, but from the actors' critique just cited, we know that he was also writing for kabuki by about 1685. This work came to predominate from the mid-1690s until his final kabuki play of 1705, during which time most of his more than thirty surviving kabuki plays were produced. This experience was crucial to his later development as a jōruri playwright.

Apprenticeship and Collaboration

Sakata Tōjūrō and Kaneko Kichizaemon

The Actors' Analects (*Yakusha rongo*), a collection of fascinating essays on kabuki from around the turn of the eighteenth century, gives a clear idea of the theatrical world for which Chikamatsu was writing in the 1690s.[49] In particular, the ideas about acting as expressed by Sakata Tōjūrō were essential to Chikamatsu, whose surviving kabuki plays were written mostly for him. The recent discovery of one year (1698) of the diary of the comic actor and playwright Kaneko Kichizaemon has given further insight into Chikamatsu's career, showing the extent of his collaboration with Kichizaemon in composing plays.[50] At this time, writers for kabuki were not highly regarded, and only a few theaters had playwrights on their staff.

Sakata Tōjūrō, who became a star actor in the 1690s, is known to have considered playwriting important to his success, and his relationship with Chikamatsu was obviously one of mutual respect. From 1693 until 1702, Chikamatsu wrote almost exclusively for Tōjūrō, who is famous as the creator of the Kyoto-Osaka *wagoto* (soft) style of acting, focused on young men of good background who have fallen on hard times. The showpiece was the *yatsushi* (disguise) section in which the hero, formerly the heir of a samurai or high merchant house, is in disguise as a poor, destitute figure, having lost his position due to either his own profligacy or the machinations of a younger brother or disloyal retainer.

FIGURE 6 The actor Sakata Tōjūrō, from *Ogakuzu* (1699). *(Waseda Theater Museum.)*

Tōjūrō was known for his long monologues in which he expresses the character's thoughts and feelings and for his emphasis on realism (*jitsu*) in his acting style. Realism was a fundamental tenet of Kyoto-Osaka kabuki and is explained in various ways in *The Actors' Analects*. The climactic scene was often set in the pleasure quarter where Tōjūrō has an encounter with his courtesan lover. Commentators have made the point that Tōjūrō's interest in monologues and character psychology harmonized well with Chikamatsu's experience of writing for jōruri, with its emphasis on tragedy.

Some time in the 1690s, Tōjūrō made Chikamatsu the staff playwright at his Miyako-za theater, giving him financial security for perhaps the first time in his life. Chikamatsu's experience of writing five-act jōruri plays with integrated plots provided the framework for his kabuki plays, which were usually in three acts made up of different scenes. The *Kaneko Kichizaemon Diary* documents the extent of Chikamatsu's collaboration with actors in the composition of plays, suggesting that they perhaps should be considered joint productions. In retrospect, one can view the period up until about 1705, when Chikamatsu was invited to be staff playwright at the Takemoto-za theater in Osaka, as his long apprenticeship in writing for the stage. The success of the topical, one-act *Love Suicides at Sonezaki*[51] in 1703, Chikamatsu's

FIGURE 7 The actor Sakata Tōjūrō, from *Yakusha mannen goyomi* (1700). *(Waseda Theater Museum.)*

earliest *sewamono* (contemporary-life) jōruri, obviously inspired by his period of writing kabuki, is the first fruit of his maturity. In the last eighteen years of his career, he wrote about seventy-five jōruri, twenty-four of which were *sewamono*, a tremendous burst of creativity after he had passed fifty, which at the time was considered the age for retirement.

Collaboration and Maturity

Takemoto Gidayū and Takeda Izumo

Love Suicides at Sonezaki is a crucial landmark in the history of Japanese theater and Chikamatsu's own career. Its success was unexpected and restored the Takemoto-za to profit and, furthermore, spurred other changes in jōruri drama as it strove to compete with kabuki's live actors for audiences in theaters that sat side by side in the Dōtonbori entertainment district in south

FIGURE 8 The actor and playwright Kaneko Kichizaemon, from *Yakusha mannen goyomi* (1700). *(Waseda Theater Museum.)*

Osaka. Two changes were discontinuing the skits and interludes between acts and introducing short, topical one-act pieces made up of three scenes—under the influence of kabuki practice—after a longer five-act period play.

After the success of *Sonezaki*, Gidayū expressed his desire to retire from the stage, exhausted by managing a theater while being its star performer as well. This made way for the debut of Takeda Izumo as the new manager, leaving Gidayū to concentrate solely on performance. Izumo came from a different puppet tradition, the Takeda Ōmi style of mechanical and trick (*karakuri*) puppets, which had connections with Gidayū's theater but also competed with jōruri and kabuki in Dōtonbori.[52] His older brother had inherited control of the Takeda troupe after the death of their father in 1704, and Izumo moved to the Takemoto-za. It is thought that he also brought funds to invest in improving the productions. Izumo took the decisive step of inviting Chikamatsu to be the Takemoto-za's staff playwright. Tōjūrō had retired in 1702 because of ill health, and so early in 1706, Chikamatsu left Kyoto to live

FIGURE 9 The theater manager and playwright Takeda Izumo I. *(Waseda Theater Museum.)*

the last years of his life in Osaka writing solely for the Takemoto-za.

Izumo himself brought a new element to the partnership of Gidayū and Chikamatsu. With the production and tremendous success of the period play *Yōmei tennō no shokunin kagami (Emperor Yōmei and the Mirror of Craftsmen)* in the last month of 1705, the first under Izumo as the Takemoto-za's manager, came increasingly elaborate stage props and more extravagant stage tricks with puppets. It is from around this time that the puppeteer Tatsumatsu Hachirōbei won fame for his depiction of female characters. Chikamatsu's work with kabuki actors had involved him deeply in stage practice and realistic character portrayal. Izumo then encouraged him to exploit the potential of puppets further and to create scenes with spectacular stage action and sophisticated props, thereby heightening the theatricality of his work.

Izumo's theatrical genius is acknowledged in *Imamukashi ayatsuri nendaiki (Chronicle of Puppet Theater Current and Past)* for the unprecedented success of *The Battles of Coxinga* in 1715, suggesting that he collaborated closely with Chikamatsu in the production of plays.[53] We can see the fruits of this cooperation particularly in acts 2 and 4 of the plays translated in this volume, which demand innovative, elaborate staging and theatrics. Moreover, the reduction of interludes between acts spurred Chikamatsu to expand the five acts to fill the extra time, including more comic scenes for contrast, exploiting his talents to the full to compose plays that filled a whole day.

From 1705 on, period plays were at least twice as long as those earlier. While kabuki pushed Chikamatsu toward the increasingly realistic depiction of character in contemporary-life plays, Izumo pulled him in the direction of spectacular theatricality in acts 2 and 4 of period plays. The mature period plays thrive on the tension between fantastic spectacle and theatricality in acts

2 and 4 and the intensely realistic tragedy of act 3. Chikamatsu's collaboration with various performers over the years continually drove him to produce new and innovative works, in both theatricality and character depiction.

Collaboration and Maturity

Takeda Izumo and Takemoto Masatayū

The death in 1714 of Takemoto Gidayū, the most famous jōruri performer of the time, was a blow to the theatrical world in general and to the Takemoto-za and Chikamatsu in particular. As the staff playwright, Chikamatsu suddenly became the senior member of the Takemoto-za, with increased responsibility for its commercial viability. The unprecedented seventeen-month run of *The Battles of Coxinga* in late 1715 ushered in a golden age of jōruri writing that lasted until the end of the century. The play was immediately performed in kabuki theaters around the country, and it has remained in the repertoires of both traditions. Its success made it the classical model for later *jidaimono*. Chikamatsu was then given a rest by Takeda Izumo and did not produce a new play until early in 1717, and so this would have been the first time since his early life that he had time to reflect and relax. In 1716, both his mother and his younger brother Okamoto Ippō died. It was also the year that Tokugawa Yoshimune, who initiated the wide-ranging Kyōhō Reforms, became shogun.

According to Uchiyama Mikiko, after about 1714 Chikamatsu commented increasingly on contemporary politics in his works, as is evident in the plays translated in this volume.[54] This last period, from 1717 until he fell ill in early 1722, was witness to another burst of playwriting, resulting in the production of twenty-one plays, among them many of his masterpieces: in other words, a prodigious average of four long dramas a year. After a break of a year and a half, Chikamatsu completed his final play, *Tethered Steed and the Eight Provinces of Kantō* in 1724, translated here. He then died on the twenty-second day of the eleventh month of that year, which on the solar calendar is early 1725.

Just before his death, Gidayū, who was renowned for his powerful voice, named as his successor the young Takemoto Masatayū, only twenty-four at the time and known to have a smaller voice, over Takemoto Tanomo, a more senior chanter famous for his beautiful voice. Masatayū came to be the main chanter of the tragic act 3, and Tanomo was the star of the more lyrical act 4. Masatayū emphasized the importance of chanting with deep feeling the characters' emotions (*jō o fukaku kataru*) and insisted that chanters ask the playwright to clarify the meaning of difficult passages.[55] He was famous for his exacting portrayal of the characters' psychology. After Gidayū, Chikamatsu still wrote for particular performers, but as the most experienced member, he was in a commanding position in the troupe.

Three themes are evident in this last decade of writing. One is the probing of the psychology of characters who commit a crime of one kind or another, from lovers eloping and committing suicide, to theft, smuggling, adultery, and murder—in both contemporary-life and period plays. The second is the criticism of corruption among those in positions of power and authority. The third, developed in the last three plays translated here, is the depiction of the demanding ideals of honor and nobility in those in power. I have called the first theme "crime and responsibility." The third acts of *Twins at the Sumida River* and *Lovers Pond in Settsu Province*, with their focus on murderers as tragic heroes, exemplify this theme. The overall theme of *Lovers Pond* is also a condemnation both of the corruption of powerful men and of the ministers who do not admonish them. The last two period plays in this volume shift the focus to the demands on those in positions of power, and *Love Suicides on the Eve of the Kōshin Festival* portrays a strong male lead caught in a web of conflicting duties.

In the final years of his career, Chikamatsu probes from different angles the nature of heroic honor, presenting a complex ideal of strong individuals and rulers. Although set in the past, his period plays are invariably about the contemporary Tokugawa regime. His view of the government was distinctive, as he himself, as has been said, had been brought up as a samurai in the castle town of Yoshie, Echizen, a Tokugawa-family fief, in which Shogun Yoshimune (1684–1751; r. 1716–45) was daimyo for several years from 1697 (although he did not reside there) before becoming shogun. Moreover, Chikamatsu's experience of Kyoto court culture as well as of theater and merchant life gave him a critical view of the dominant samurai culture, which is evident in his mature works. His criticisms reflect his experience of the Tokugawa bakufu during his lifetime. His first theme, arising from his experience of rule under Shogun Tsunayoshi (r. 1680–1709) is the abuse or arbitrariness of power; the second is unstable government, as witnessed during the short eras of two shoguns, one of them a child, from 1709 until the appointment of Yoshimune in 1716; and the third is the overregulation and intrusiveness of government under Yoshimune.[56] Chikamatsu's plays were always written for a popular audience in a commercial theater, but it also is clear that he hoped they would be read widely, even by those in the highest echelons of power, like Ogyū Sorai, quoted earlier, who was adviser to various shoguns. Today they offer a rich and complex view of a wide range of individuals from all levels of society, their daily life as well as their feelings, attitudes, and ideals.

Art: The Slender Margin Between the Real and the Unreal

BECAUSE HE WAS writing for a puppet theater in which the lines were usually recited by a single performer, Chikamatsu had to compose words with the power to bring the wooden figures to life on the stage. Unlike the nō performer and playwright Zeami (1363–1443), Chikamatsu did not leave a treatise on his methods or ideals, perhaps because of the demands of a commercial theater for which he continued to write plays until the very end of his life. We do, however, have some sense of his ideas on the art of playwriting. Hozumi Ikan, mentioned earlier for his comments on Chikamatsu's plays, records in the preface to *Naniwa miyage* (1738) a conversation with Chikamatsu on the art of jōruri.[57] Chikamatsu begins with a reflection on the difficulties of writing for puppets instead of actors:

> *Jōruri* differs from other forms of fiction in that, since it is primarily concerned with puppets, the words should all be living things in which action is the most important feature. Because *jōruri* is performed in theatres that operate in close competition with those of *kabuki*, which is the art of living actors, the author must impart to lifeless wooden puppets a variety of emotions, and attempt in this way to capture the interest of the audience.

His attention to detail in character portrayal in both narrative description and dialogue produced a literary style that came to be considered the predominant model by later popular writers. Chikamatsu then offers an example of the power of language:

> Once, when I was young and reading a story about the court, I came across a passage which told how, on the occasion of a festival, the snow had fallen heavily and

piled up. An order was then given to a guard to clear away the snow from an orange tree. When this happened, the pine tree next to it, apparently resentful that its boughs were bent with snow, recoiled its branches. This was a stroke of the pen which gave life to the inanimate tree.

In describing his method of giving life to inanimate puppets, Chikamatsu uses a key term, *jō* (feeling or passion), several times and considers it "the basis of writing." This term is also fundamental to Confucian thought which places human passions and feelings in conflict with the rules and morals of a civilized society. Many have commented that Chikamatsu's true genius is his masterful depiction of the depths of the passions, obsessions, and irrationality of the human heart. Chikamatsu notes further that jōruri "is basically a musical form, and the length of the lines recited is therefore determined by the melody." As in opera, the essence of human feeling, particularly sadness, is expressed by words in song riding the high notes of the music.

Perhaps because he wrote for puppet theater, Chikamatsu emphasized the need for realism (*jitsu, jitsuji*) in the depiction of characters; that is, their words must suit their station and rank. He nevertheless distinguishes between the exact representation of reality on the stage and the presentation of reality as art. In response to a comment that his contemporary audiences demand realism, Chikamatsu answers with perhaps the most famous passage of this essay:

> Art is something which lies in the slender margin between the real and the unreal. Of course it seems desirable, in view of current taste for realism, to have the chief retainer in the play copy the gestures and speech of a real retainer, but in that case should a real chief retainer of a daimyō put rouge and powder on his face like an actor? Or, would it prove entertaining if an actor, on the grounds that real chief retainers do not make up their faces, were to appear on the stage and perform, with his beard growing wild and his head shaven? This is what I mean by the slender margin between the real and the unreal. It is unreal, and yet it is not unreal; it is real, and yet it is not real. Entertainment (*nagusami*) lies between the two.

Therefore, one must add extra elements (*shukō*) of stylization to create art that gives pleasure to the audience or reader.

Two other terms essential to Chikamatsu's discussion are *urei* and *aware*. Both words mean "pathos," and in the context of jōruri, they refer to tragic climactic moments. Chikamatsu is straightforward on the method of portraying pathos: he places *giri*, translated by Keene as "restraint," as the agent of tragedy. *Giri* (rational principles, proper behavior) was a technical term for Confucian thinkers such as Hozumi Ikan, Chikamatsu's friend who recorded his ideas. In the context of Chikamatsu's plays, I think that it is useful to see the opposition of *jō* and *giri* as that between "desire" and "reason," between our natural, "animal-like" instincts and our rational, "civilized" mind with its rules, morals, and responsibilities inculcated by society. Chikamatsu's works are distinguished by a persistent view (somewhat unorthodox for the time and perhaps in the humanistic vein of the Kyoto philosopher Itō Jinsai, 1627–1705) of human desires as natural and essentially good. Without the tempering of ethics, however, excessive passion inevitably leads to tragedy.

The period plays translated here contain scenes of exacting realism as well as scenes dominated by supernatural action in the mode of the pine tree that Chikamatsu described earlier, which comes alive with the strokes of the author's brush as it shakes off the snow from its branches. The effect of the totality of the five acts is a fantastic, imaginative, and cyclical journey from a world seemingly in peaceful harmony at the outset, to a fall into chaos through the passions of love and greed for power, followed by adventure, tragedy, and battles, leading in the end to a return to order and hope for an auspicious future. Chikamatsu intended that the words would have the power to strike our hearts and stimulate our minds to imagine the scenes and feel the characters come alive. In addition, as Chikamatsu said, jōruri is a musical form, and the words ride the melodies and cadences of the chanter's voice accompanied by the shamisen. This is important not only in the song and dance sections but also in the dramatic parts when the emotions of the characters rise to crescendos of lyrical expression in song. The musical notation in the text helps show how it was traditionally read and performed, and I hope will also help the reader of today imagine how it appeared on the stage.

Musical Notation and Structure: Shallow Rapids and Deep Pools

Jigoto *Rapids*

Most scenes of a jōruri play are performed by one chanter who takes all the roles and the third-person narration. When performed as kabuki, the plays usually have a narrator who takes the narrative parts and sometimes sings the lyrical voice of the actor in order to allow him to mime or dance the action. Takemoto Gidayū's metaphor of a stream for jōruri drama was mentioned earlier. He extended the analogy by describing the active, dramatic parts of the drama as the rapids and, in contrast, the song sections as quiet pools where the flow of the drama slows and we get a deeper insight into the story and the characters.

Most of the play comprises the flowing, dramatic sections in which the story moves along through dialogue and action. These *jigoto* sections are made up of musical paragraphs marked by a concluding cadence notation *fushi*, translated as "cadence."[58] A new paragraph usually begins with a sung line designated by *ji* or *ji-iro*, translated as "sung." The chanter generally shifts voice into declamation without shamisen accompaniment, marked as *kotoba* and translated as "spoken." These paragraphs are the chanter's building blocks on which he creates his performance. Each paragraph begins slowly and rises to an intensity and then relaxes in the cadence, only to begin again in the following paragraph, drawing the audience further into the flow of the drama, leading to the climax of the particular scene. The chanter paces his performance through the rhetorical technique of tightening the tension and releasing it briefly before guiding the audience again into the intensities of the scene, leading eventually to the climaxes in the concluding scenes of each act. The voice constantly shifts back and forth between the quick-paced "spoken" voice of each character to the more lyrical "song" voice in which emotion is expressed through the music of both voice and shamisen.

This competitive interaction of delivery style, shamisen, and puppets is the essence of the art of jōruri performance. One can either ignore the notation in the text or see it as a guide to the play's structure and performance technique, the original stage directions of the first production. The notations also reinforce the fact that Chikamatsu's plays are musical dramas that exploit histrionic techniques and conventions similar to those of opera and other musical theater. The high note designated in the text by *kami* (translated as "high pitch" or "highest pitch") is used sparingly in performance and signals that here we are striving for the heights of aria-like intensity, a lyrical expression of the emotional pain of tragedy. The essence of the chanter's art is to maintain a continuing contrast back and forth between a quick, dramatic voice and a lyrical song voice.

Fushigoto *Pools*

Most scenes have a *fushigoto* ("song") section that is performed as a short song, as in Shakespeare; or a whole scene of an act is a lyrical dance piece, such as the *michiyuki* journeys. These sections are usually in verse and contain some of the best writing in the Japanese tradition. Their literary complexity, in both wordplay and allusion, makes them a considerable challenge to translate. In these songs, Chikamatsu engages the Chinese and Japanese literary traditions through allusion. Readers will notice that the footnotes tend to be bunched in these lyrical passages, as if they themselves were caught in the deep pools.

While analyzing the plays, I began to wonder whether Chikamatsu also considered this "river" analogy to have another significance. Each play tends to have a cluster of metaphors and themes that resonate throughout, reinforced by allusions during crucial lyrical moments. The language is usually complex in such passages, with references that nearly always bear directly on one or another of the main themes flowing through the play. Sometimes the quotation, as seen in its original context, suggests an ironic comment on the surface meaning. One can imagine these clusters of allusions as an undercurrent that occasionally rises to the surface during lyrical song moments and carries the themes and major metaphors of the play.

This point is well illustrated in the passage from act 2, scene 2, of *Twins at the Sumida River* which begins:

> (*sung*) The punt drifts among a brocade of lotus blossoms.
> A marvelous moment—pristine in its beauty.
> Spring flowers have withered;
> the summer day is hot,
> hot as walking through a burning forest,
> but a gentle breeze over cool currents clears away the heat.
> How refreshing!

and ends with the lines:

> (*sung*) Look, look, the carp and goldfish dance and play among the lotus blossoms, petals worn as hats. How charming! Even spotted turtles stamp their feet in rhythm. Eels and catfish, too, strut fashionably. Look, look! (*song*) Even a familiar sight seen morning and night alters with

each season, with each change in weather seen up close or from a distance. The pair let the boat float where it will (*cadence*) in pursuit of (*highest pitch*) beautiful lotus blossoms around the lake.

Lord Yoshida is taking the beautiful Lady Hanjo for a boat excursion in a grand garden pond full of blossoming lotus flowers. At this point in the action, a curse has caused Yoshida to kill his wife in error, and his son Matsuwaka has been stolen by a goblin. Just before this passage, Hanjo has been compared favorably with Yang Guifei, the famous Chinese beauty; and the "lotus blossom" is an erotic image of these women. This is performed as an elegant song and dance mini-scene. As the textual notes to the following translation show, Chikamatsu alludes to the nō plays *Obasute*,[59] *Kinuta*,[60] *Tokusa*, and *Taema*. The references suggest a dark undercurrent in this portrait of Yoshida's paradise-like garden.

On the surface, we witness a lyrical love scene, but as the notes show, through clever allusion, Chikamatsu is taking the boat on a different sort of imaginative journey. He consistently organizes these songs into five parts based on the principles of *jo-ha-kyū* (introduction, three-part intense section, finale). Here the references suggest a circular pattern. The opening is an image of Amida's Western Paradise, but only in the imagination of a woman (*Obasute*) abandoned to die, who can never get there because of her obsessive passion for life. The second is the reference to *Kinuta*, taking us into the world of erotic passion that is transformed into obsessive desire leading one into hell. The third is the reference to the obsessive love of a father insane with grief for a lost son (*Tokusa*) who, when they are reunited, builds a temple with him at their home. The fourth is Chūjōhime (*Taema*), an abandoned daughter who finds relief in Buddhism and eventually rejects her own father, leading us to a mention of the Chinese priest Huiyuan and the lotus image as the saving grace of Amida Buddha. Finally we return to paradise, where all of nature plays in idyllic harmony, with the realization that our vision of a familiar scene is altered by the experience of art, leading us a step closer to enlightenment. The lotus is transformed from a metaphor for erotic beauty to a symbol of a pure heart unsullied by the murky world. The imagination travels down into the depths of hell beneath the pond but returns to the surface to witness a final auspicious portrait of paradise. This quiet pool in the drama is followed immediately by a rush of action, resulting in Yoshida's death; the disappearance of his other son, Umewaka; and the crisis of the Yoshida estate. Chikamatsu's song passages usually reward a close reading.

Musical Notation Code

THE FOLLOWING IS a list of the major notations inserted into the translation at approximately the same point as in the original. The list gives both the original Japanese term and a brief description of it. Although the terms refer to particular musical styles and melodies in current bunraku theater, they also can be seen as general musical principles.

cadence	*fushi* (concludes a musical paragraph)
emotional cadence	*suete* (concludes a highly emotional paragraph)
exit cadence	*okuri* (concludes a scene after which a character exits)
high pitch	*gin* or *kami-u* (used at a climactic moment of intense emotion)
highest pitch	*kami* (used at a climactic moment of intense emotion)
nō chanting	*utai* (nō-style chanting)
prelude	*jo* (opening song of a play)
scene cadence	*sanjū* (concludes a scene after which the setting changes)
song	*uta* (a melody from a song incorporated into the chanting)
spoken	*kotoba* (declamation style without musical accompaniment)
sung	*ji* or *ji-iro* (chanted to a melody, with accompaniment)
threatening melody	*kowari* (a style signaling danger)

After composing a new play, Chikamatsu would read it aloud to the entire troupe, who would make comments. Then the senior chanter(s) would insert the notation in the text as an indication of the delivery styles, composing the music for the voice. This notation then formed part of the published text issued when it was first performed on the stage. The notation code therefore can be considered an indication of the first professional reading and interpretation of Chikamatsu's text, the one that would serve as a guide for later performers and readers.

FIGURE 10 *Nai-yomi* (first internal reading, top) and *so-hon'yomi* (reading before the whole troupe), showing the playwright reading his work before members of the troupe, from *Shibai gakuya zue* (1802). *(Waseda Theater Museum.)*

The translations include the major notations (more exist designating pitch levels or particular singing styles, etc.). They can be viewed as a relatively detailed code of stage directions and as a guide to what Chikamatsu called the "musical form" of jōruri. The fundamental musical-dramatic paragraph or unit is marked by the "cadence" notation (or by one signaling the end of the scene).[61] Usually the paragraph begins with a "sung" line, which is then followed by alternating "spoken" and "sung" lines chanted for rhetorical effect. Each paragraph builds up to a climax of intensity, after which the tension is relaxed in the cadence. For example, if a scene has ten such paragraphs, the dramatic tension will increase with each paragraph as the chanter tightens and loosens the reins, drawing the audience into the intensity of the story. In the seventh paragraph, the climax of the scene will perhaps be reached, and the remaining paragraphs will express its consequences. The intensities will be strongest in the final scenes of each act (where the "high" or "highest pitch" is found), with the peaks in acts 3 and 4.

Texts and Annotation

I BEGAN WORKING on the four period plays several years ago, initially from a prewar "collected works," *Chikamatsu zenshū* (1923), edited by Fujii Otoo, and then later from the new Iwanami *Chikamatsu zenshū* (*CZ*). Neither has annotations for these works. The texts used for the translations are in *Chikamatsu jōrurishū* (*CJS*) II, in the Shin Nihon koten bungaku taikei (SNKBT) series published by Iwanami shoten in 1995. In particular, the annotations of the editors Matsuzaki Hitoshi, Hara Michio, Iguchi Hiroshi, and Ōhashi Tadayoshi of the four period plays, for the first time, has made possible the task of completing the translations. I am most grateful for their pioneering efforts. Many years ago, I wrote a draft translation of *Love Suicides on the Eve of the Kōshin Festival* based on the text in volume 2 of *Chikamatsu Monzaemonshū*, edited by Torigoe Bunzō, in the Nihon koten bungaku zenshū (NKBZ) series (Shōgakkan, 1975); I have completed the translation using the text in Matsuzaki et al., *CJS* II (1995). Since we have authorized first editions of the plays, there are no major textual problems.

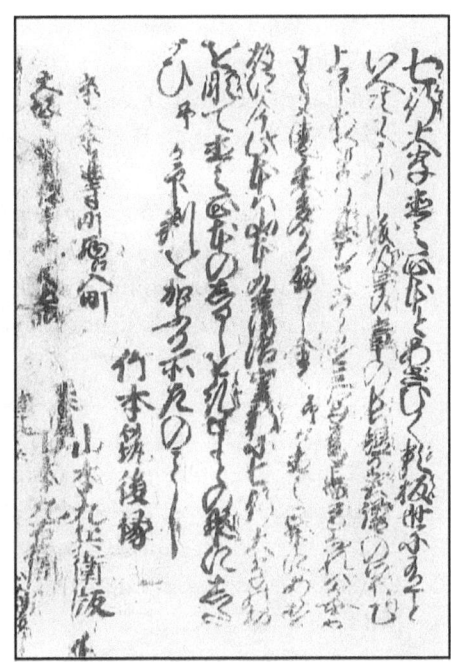

FIGURE 11 Final page of the original text of *Battles at Kawa-nakajima* (1721), which has both the senior chanter's note on the authenticity of the notation in this edition and the publisher's details (see the end of *Twins at the Sumida River* for a translation of this page.)

Chikamatsu's period plays, in particular, engage in what we would now call "intertexuality." His method was to decide on a specific story and source for the basic plot and setting. This would then lead to other, related stories in classical Japanese or Chinese from which he would weave in quotations, usually only a name, a few words, or a line. The work of the four editors just named provided the clues that enabled me to explore each allusion, examine its context, and determine its significance. The results have been fascinating. A comparison of the major sources and Chikamatsu's plays shows how he alters the story to create his own drama with its particular themes and aims. Furthermore, an analysis of the allusions reveals his method of supporting the themes through association with other works that have related themes. Virtually all the references add a dimension to the work's overall themes.

The introduction to each play here notes its major sources and outlines the themes. The notes offer more extensive commentary on the allusions, their context, and their significance. The plays demand that the reader engage with Chikamatsu in a lively dialogue with both the historical and the literary traditions. His works, however, are fiction, not history, and were understood conventionally by his audience and readers to be narratives about contemporary government and social life, even though they were set in the distant past.

The bibliography gives full information about the sources, in the original Japanese or Chinese and in English translations when they exist. Work on the literary sources and allusions to Chikamatsu's period plays has only just begun. We still have little sense of what books he read that gave him access to such a vast array of references to classical Chinese and Japanese, as well as to contemporary social and political life.[62]

Chikamatsu's language is considered by all (both scholars and performers) to be extremely difficult, with a range of vocabulary, styles, and subject matter perhaps unparalleled in the Japanese tradition. The original woodblock-print text does not give the names of characters to indicate that they are speaking dialogue, nor does it mark the narrator's voice. In the translation, I have noted the roles of both the narrator's and the individual characters' voices. My aim has been to make the English as fluid and lively as possible to suit the particular character and action. The chanter's notation has been an important indicator for me of the text's "rhythm" and flow. I hope that the translation conveys some of the enjoyment and depths that I have found in these plays.

Chikamatsu hoped that his plays would live on as both books and performances on the stage. The relatively realistic contemporary-life works have been performed outside Japan with some success. An adaptation of his period plays, however, would offer considerable challenges to a modern Western theater director and producer. One would need to incorporate into one production the conventions of formal acting in the Shakespearean mode, realistic and lively dialogue scenes, as well as elements of opera, musicals, and dance drama and ballet. A recent, successful National Theatre production at the Cottesloe Theatre on the South Bank, London, of Chikamatsu's period play *Fair Ladies at a Game of Poem Cards*, originally written in 1714, has shown that it is possible.[63] The translations of his late works in this volume, particularly the period plays, will, I hope, add another dimension to the English-speaking world's understanding of this extraordinary playwright and the society for which he was writing.

Twins at the Sumida River

(*Futago sumidagawa*)

Long before this play was first performed in the eighth month of 1720, the "Sumida River" theme or "world" (*sekai*) had expanded greatly from the narrow confines of the lyrical nō drama, with its focus on a mother searching for a stolen child, to include a large group of characters and plots in an epiclike narrative.[1]

Nō theatre often takes its source from a longer tale or legend and concentrates on what is perceived to be the essence of the story or character, usually a particular emotion emanating from a specific incident. The later storytelling genres (*sekkyō*, "religious or miracle tales," and *ko-jōruri*, "early jōruri drama"), which flourished in the vibrant oral narrative era of the sixteenth and seventeenth centuries, contain intense, lyrical moments, but these are set in the context of long complex plots. In the Tokugawa era in particular, the conventional framework for many jōruri and kabuki narratives is the *oiesōdō* (crisis in a grand household) genre. These tales center on a daimyo's fief or some large established household in which a crisis occurs, threatening its existence or opening it to usurpation by nonlegitimate "evil" forces. This is the conventional framework for many of Chikamatsu's period plays, including *Twins at the Sumida River*.

Three articles by Japanese scholars give us a relatively full guide to the sources Chikamatsu drew on when composing this play.[2] These fall into two main categories: texts from nō (*Sumida River*,[3] *Hanjo*[4]) and *sekkyō jōruri* (*Sumidagawa monogatari*) which are the basis of pre-Chikamatsu jōruri "Sumida" plays; and Edo kabuki. Shirakata Masaru focuses on the *hito-kai* (slave trading) theme and traces the Umewaka legend, emphasizing the traditional tales of stolen aristocratic children (in the mode of the famous *Sanshō dayū* versions)[5] while acknowledging Edo kabuki as an important background to this theme. Hirata Sumiko concentrates on a detailed analysis of the Edo kabuki "Sumida" plays to demonstrate how well developed the murderer-figure prototype was. By 1710, it was a well-established practice in Edo kabuki to include the figure of a former retainer who begins enslaving children to raise money for his former master and unwittingly kills a child he later learns is in fact his master's son. In Chikamatsu's *Twins at the Sumida River*, Sarushima no Sōta, a former retainer of the Yoshida house, has fallen on hard times after being dismissed for stealing money from his lord and sells kidnapped children in order to make a living. During a fit of rage, he kills a boy whom he had hoped to sell for a good price, unaware that the child is in fact the son of his former lord. Chikamatsu places the murderer Sōta in the "hero" role in the climactic third act of the play.

The earliest extant work that is the bridge between the nō and Chikamatsu is *Sumidagawa monogatari* (1656). Although it is in a popular fiction format (*kanazōshi*), it is considered to be an accurate version of the plays performed around the middle of the century.[6] By the second half of the seventeenth century, the basic elements of the tale were in place: Yoshida had two sons, Umewaka and Matsuwaka, and Hanjo is the mother of one. Matsuwaka is stolen by goblins (*tengu*), and Umewaka dies at the hand of a slave trader at Sumida River. Later, in the mid- to late-1680s, pre-Chikamatsu jōruri plays build on this tale, adding some details and changing others. Two new developments are that Hanjo does not die but is reunited with Matsuwaka at the end and that the villain slave-trader role has become more important.[7]

Shirakata outlines in some detail what he believes were Chikamatsu's innovations. Fundamentally, Chikamatsu seems to have taken an already well-developed and complex tale and integrated the various subplots into a coherent narrative. Shirakata argues that one significant change is Chikamatsu's shift of emphasis: in kabuki the crime of the "Sōta" figure is seen only as a *shu-goroshi* (the killing of one's own lord), whereas Chikamatsu depicts it as both slavery and the murder of one's lord. The tragedy as well, Shirakata contends, is no longer simply coincidence or fate but the direct consequence of causes emanating from Sōta's actions.[8] Hara Michio emphasizes the way that Chikamatsu used the conventional framework of the *oiesōdō* play—its overall plot being the crisis, near destruction, and final restoration of an estate. This type of play was basic to popular theater, both jōruri and kabuki, especially period drama.

Chikamatsu innovates in two distinctive ways. First, he adds new elements to the plot and integrates these into the existing framework to fashion a tightly knit narrative with a consistent cause and consequence. Second, he uses allusion and association to develop his themes. His choice of the setting for the opening scene and for the abode of the *tengu* goblin suggests his method. Umewaka, the young boy of the Sumida story, was thought to have been abducted by slave traders at Sakamoto, near Lake Biwa, at the foot of Mount Hiei. This association leads Chikamatsu to set the opening at the Hiyoshi (Hie) Shrine, the protector of Mount Hiei from evil forces, the guardian of the imperial court and, by extension, of Japan itself. Hiyoshi Shrine is the "demon gate" (*kimon*) at the northeast point on the compass from Kyoto. Mount Hira, known from early times as being inhabited by *tengu* demons, lies farther north. Chikamatsu has the villain characters plot to take sacred cedar timber from Mount Hira (Yoshida land) to build new *torii* (gates) at the Hiyoshi Shrine, with the expectation of invoking the *tengu*'s wrath and curse on the Yoshida house.[9] Monkeys are the messengers of the powerful protective god Sannō Gongen at Hiyoshi. This association leads Chikamatsu to use the metaphor of "monkey" for Sarushima (Monkey Island) no Sōta, who is both the beastly murderer of Umewaka in act 3 and the savior (after he becomes a *tengu*) of Umewaka's twin Matsuwaka in act 4. The themes of "madness" (*monogurui*) and "love of parent and child" are developed through allusion to as many as twenty-five nō and three kyōgen plays. I comment on their significance in the notes to the text. His portrayal of such madness (Hanjo for her children, and Sōta, initially in pursuit of a courtesan and later in his quest for money) is different from that in nō or earlier works in that it is more realistic. Chikamatsu was interested in individual personality and the causes and consequences of madness and crime, and so Hanjo and Sōta are fully developed, complex figures.

We can see how attractive this "Sumida" theme was for Chikamatsu, who had been exploring the nature of crime, evil, and responsibility in his dramas for two to three years before *Twins at the Sumida River*.[10] It was, nevertheless, a critical leap within the jōruri genre to make the traditional villain character, the slave trader who kills his master, into the hero. Edo kabuki was almost certainly Chikamatsu's inspiration. From its origins, Edo kabuki has focused on "outlaw" hero types, whereas jōruri (especially *jidaimono*), with its sources in popular Buddhistic narrative, was more overtly moralistic: good was good and evil was evil. In *Twins at Sumida River*, Chikamatsu, who wrote for both

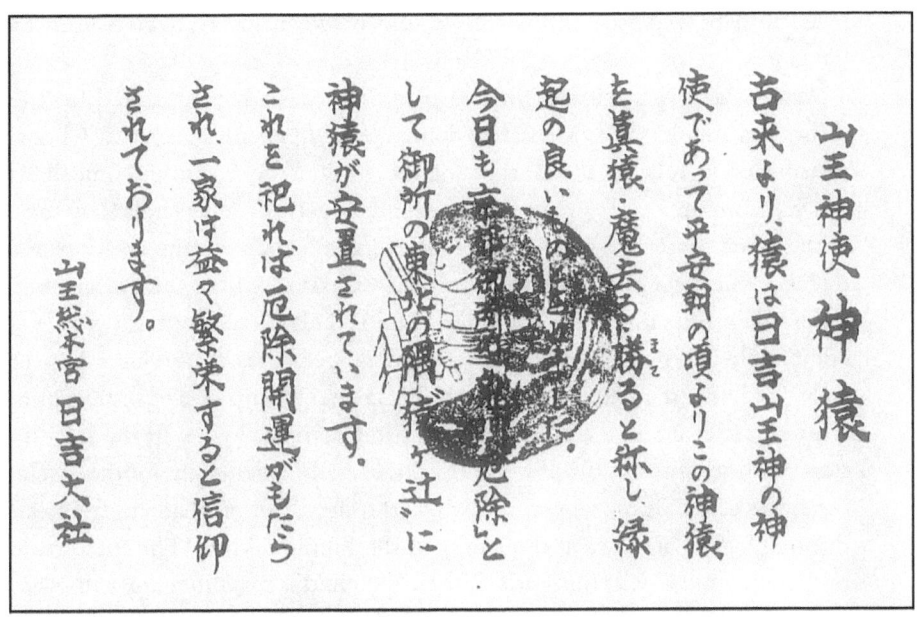

FIGURE 12 Modern Hiyoshi (Hie) Shrine talisman, with a monkey image in the middle and text explaining the role of monkeys as messengers of the deity and as guardians against demons.

kabuki and jōruri, uses the Edo kabuki outlaw figure to great effect by setting him within the jōruri moralistic world and analyzing the nature of his crime. Takemoto Harima no Shōjō (Masatayū, 1691–1744), Gidayū's disciple who performed the third act, offered the following advice for success: "While being careful to portray distinctly Umewaka's aristocratic bearing, Takekuni's anger, and Sōta's regrets, a performer must have the resolve and bravery in his heart somehow to become a supernatural demon."[11]

Harima no Shōjō is thought to have performed in all of Chikamatsu's plays from 1715 onward. Another of his teachings—that the chanter "must bring out the essence of the text and consult the playwright when necessary"—conveys the sense that his views represent the author's as well.[12] Sōta represents the theme of an individual's confrontation with the full force of his own villainy and his heroic will to pay for his crime. This theme is set within the larger theme of the causes and consequences of obsessive love, both between parent and child and between lovers, which leads to "madness."

Act 4 is a new version of the nō play *Sumida River*, refashioned for the jōruri and kabuki stages as a dance drama. A comparison shows that Chikamatsu closely follows the outline of the nō and even quotes some lines exactly from the original, but he has essentially written an entirely new text, with several twists and turns that fit his overall plot. One is the creation of a direct connection between the "ferryman" Karaito (wife of the murderer of Umewaka) and Umewaka's mother Hanjo. This clever shift allows for a completely different attitude toward the deranged woman searching desperately for her lost child. Chikamatsu also creates Hanjo as a realistic figure who expresses a range of feelings far greater than is allowed in the nō version, with its convention of restraint. She is truly a desperate mother seeking her lost child; moreover, we know the details of all that she has been through before arriving at the banks of the Sumida River. The final scene of the encounter with the spirit of the dead child is magnificently achieved, with a concluding twist in which Umewaka is replaced by his twin brother Matsuwaka, who is saved from the *tengu* demons and brought to Hanjo by a *tengu*, the spirit of Sōta, the murderer of Umewaka.

The audience would have been well acquainted with the original nō, as well as with the other versions of this tale as it was told and performed in the Edo period. Chikamatsu expected this knowledge to enhance the experience of this act, giving us both the tragedy of the loss of a child and the recovery of his twin, who was thought to be lost forever. Act 4, as is the convention, ends on a note of hope for the restoration of the Yoshida house.

The play (primarily act 3) was performed regularly in the puppet theater during the Edo period after a revival in 1772 until 1867. Elements of this play were rewritten in kabuki, with the figure Hōkaibō, in particular, becoming an important role in Edo kabuki. Acts 3 and 4 were revived in 1973 on the bunraku stage. Nakamura Ganjirō and his Chikamatsu-za troupe, and Ichikawa Ennosuke revived the whole play on the kabuki stage in the 1980s. The text is listed as being in print in *Gidayū-bon kosō ikken* (1833).[13] Interest in amateur bunraku chanting continued to increase throughout Japan until well into the twentieth century and created a sophisticated reading public for the works of Chikamatsu and other playwrights.

Twins at the Sumida River
(Futago sumidagawa)

CAST OF CHARACTERS

Yoshida Household

Yoshida (Yoshida no Shōshō Fujiwara no Ason Yukifusa): head of the Yoshida household, an aristocrat, highly placed in the Heian court. He is portrayed as elegant and aesthetically sophisticated, as well as effete and selfish.

Lady Yoshida: wife of Yoshida, who becomes the focus of the demon's curse; younger sister of Momotsura.

Lady Hanjo: mistress of Yoshida and mother of the twins Umewaka and Matsuwaka. She was formerly a courtesan with whom Yoshida fell in love and who bore him twin sons.

Umewaka: Yoshida's son and heir and twin of Matsuwaka, about twelve years old. His natural mother is Hanjo, although he was raised as the son of Lady Yoshida. He is kidnapped by slave traders.

Matsuwaka: son of Lady Hanjo, twin of Umewaka. He is captured by *tengu* goblins.

Yoshida Retainers

Kanenari (Awaji no Zenji Kanenari): loyal senior councillor in the Yoshida household, father of Sōta.

Takekuni (Shikken Agata Gon on Kami Takekuni): Yoshida's senior councillor, a brave, upright, and loyal figure.

Gunsuke: a lowly retainer of Yoshida, brave, strong, and loyal, a flamboyant, no-nonsense, brash figure.

Hitachi Household

Momotsura (Hitachi no Daijō Momotsura): Yoshida's brother-in-law, elder brother of Lady Yoshida. Also highly placed in the Heian court, he is the grand villain of the play, scheming to have his own son become heir to the Yoshida house. The Daijō (Hitachi no Daijō) were an important samurai family, tracing their lineage to the Taira family who claim Emperor Kanmu as their ancestor. The Daijō base was originally in eastern Japan. Momotsura is presented as an ambitious, ruthless, and uncouth samurai, in contrast to the courtier Yoshida.

Kageyu (Kageyu Hyōe Kagehaya): a retainer in Yoshida's household who is really Momotsura's right-hand man and a villain figure, in contrast to Takekuni.

Sōta the Slave Trader's World

Sōta: formerly known as Awaji no Shichirō Toshikanu when he was a retainer in the Yoshida house. He has squandered ten thousand gold pieces of Yoshida money in pursuit of a courtesan, but his life has been spared and he has been exiled to eastern Japan where he lives as a trader in child slaves. He is the protagonist in act 3.

Karaito: wife of Sōta, known only as his wife in act 3 but as Karaito in acts 4 and 5. She is the courtesan with whom Sōta fell in love and on whom he squandered a fortune. She plays the ferryman in act 4.

Hōkaibō: a *tengu* goblin who takes the form of a *yamabushi* mountain priest to help Hanjo in act 4. This character is really Sōta, whose spirit after his suicide becomes a *tengu* in order to find Matsuwaka and save the Yoshida house.

Act 1

—Scene 1
Reign of Emperor Horikawa (1086–1107), on the shore of Lake Biwa in Shiga

NARRATOR: (*prelude*) Jiang Yi replied to Emperor Xuan Wang of Chu:[1]

"Borrowing the majesty of the tiger, the fox stands tall.
Standing behind, the tiger believes the animals bow to the fox."[2]

Lords and retainers of all times must beware the wiles of the fox. If a ruler is sharp and farsighted, his officials will be honest and upright, as in the reign of Emperor Horikawa, the seventy-third in the imperial line. His Highness has had a dream and has ordered the construction of twenty-one grand *torii*[3] for the twenty-one shrines at the Hie Sannō Gongen Shrine[4] complex at Ōtsu. To launch the construction of the *torii*, all the officials have gathered on the shores of Lake Biwa in Shiga for the "first cut of the adze"[5] ceremony to ensure a safe and successful completion to the enterprise. (*cadence*) The gods and the emperor shower blessings on the people of the realm.

(*sung*) Lord Yoshida no Shōshō Fujiwara no Ason Yukifusa, who is responsible for the project, sits at the head of a row that includes his heir Umewaka and his senior councillor, Shikken Agata Gon on Kami Takekuni. A temporary building has been erected at the construction site on the shore of Lake Biwa along Shiga Beach at Sasanami. The best timber and materials have been assembled from Ibuki, Makimoku, Kiso, and Shigaraki.[6] Yoshida's brother-in-law Hitachi no Daijō Momotsura,[7] who is in charge of overseeing the construction, sits among the group too. (*spoken*) Takekuni has been requested to speak to the carpenters. He turns toward their hut.

TAKEKUNI: Please begin the "first cut of the adze" ceremony to set this construction in progress.

NARRATOR: (*sung*) The two chief carpenters come forward in their court hats and formal costumes with their crests boldly displayed. They tie back their great sleeves with a cord and offer greetings to the official

FIGURE 13 Opening scene at the construction site. (*Futago Sumidagawa*, 1720, National Diet Library.)

party. They make offerings of sacred saké and rice and carry the tools on sacred, ceremonial paper. They sing a ballad auspicious to the occasion.

>(*ballad style*) Let the heavens be clear[8]
>and the earth firm.
>Since Izanagi and Izanami[9]
>spoke the first words of marriage,
>the Way of yin and yang
>has flowed through the ages.
>The *torii* gates lead to
>the shrines where gods dwell.
>Two pillars:[10]
>They teach us
>that man cannot stand alone.
>In the heavens
>two pillars rise,

the sun and moon,
night and day.
Men have two eyes.
Pine trees have paired needles, evergreen.
Ever frail in the face of a storm
are the single stems of the
suzuki pampas grass.
Accordingly, the great Shakyamuni
taught the two great truths
of karma and of life and death.
Confucianism has its two pillars
of benevolence and justice.
In Japan the gods bless us
with light and peace.
The first strike of the tools
affirms the infinity of heaven,
long life for the earth,
and a thousand years for our sovereign.
The second brings bountiful harvests,
and security for the people.
The third increases the blessings
of Sannō Gongen.
The new gates will bring
to fruition our prayers and wishes,
peace and prosperity,
an auspicious occasion forever more.

The ceremony concludes, and behind the curtains thousands of craftsmen are active as the (*cadence*) banquet begins.
   (*sung*) But Momotsura bellows out.
MOMOTSURA: (*spoken*) Wait! Before you begin the banquet, stop! Today's ceremony is inappropriate and will surely hinder the completion of the twenty-one *torii*. As the magistrate in charge, I am also at fault. (*sung*) This must be reported to the court immediately. I must resign my post.
NARRATOR: He gets up to leave the temporary headquarters. Yoshida is shocked.

YOSHIDA: (*spoken*) How impolite, Lord Momotsura! If something displeases you, as one of us these concerns should properly be confided privately—especially as my wife is your younger sister. You are the uncle of young Umewaka here. If you know of something wrong, there are channels for conveying such anxieties. (*sung*) Let me hear your criticisms of my negligence.

NARRATOR: He presses Momotsura.

MOMOTSURA: (*spoken*) Yes, because we are brothers-in-law, I have warned you time and again, haven't I? This project is extremely important and reflects on the honor of our family. I told you to take care to choose the best timber. On your land at Mount Hira,[11] mature cedars are found in abundance. They are stirred by the winter snowstorms until the fourth or fifth months and grow into firm, fine timber. You ignored my suggestion to take trees from that magnificent mountain forest. Haven't you examined the logs assembled here carefully? (*sung*) The trees come from the dark side of mountains and are waterlogged by the rain, virtually rotten. They won't last even two years as *torii* pillars. (*spoken*) Last year, as governor of Ōshū, gold mining made you the richest of the aristocracy. (*sung*) Your second house has been furnished extravagantly, inlaid with jewels for your mistress Hanjo.[12] You've thrust your mistress's child Matsuwaka up the ranks of the court, no expense spared, treating him as if he were the prime minister's heir. A fraction of your extravagance could've easily funded a rebuilding of the whole shrine complex. (*spoken*) Your senior councillor Takekuni is of good lineage, but his eyes are clouded with the glitter of personal greed. He can't admonish his lord; (*sung*) he's no better than a shop clerk.

NARRATOR: (*cadence*) His outburst comes in a torrent. (*sung*) Takekuni is unable to restrain his anger.

TAKEKUNI: (*spoken*) I appreciate that Lord Momotsura is the overseer of this construction project. But there's no call for you to oversee the private affairs of Lord Yoshida's household or his women. It's amazing that with all your many duties, you've found the time to look for rotting timber among these piles of fine logs. It is up to us alone whether or not to fell trees on Mount Hira, and after careful consideration we have decided against that course. As everyone knows, the mountain is under the spell of black magic and inhabited by *tengu* goblins. From ancient times, no woodsmen have ever gone into its forests. If even one leaf of a single tree were torn, (*sung*) the mountain spirits would run wild and cause havoc, bringing untold suffering to the country. The *torii* are being built at the command of His Highness for the everlasting peace and security of the sovereign and his subjects. I could not ignore the importance of this auspicious project and risk a curse by felling timber from a haunted forest. (*spoken*) My colleague, Kageyu Hyōe Kagehaya, also responsible for the construction, argued strongly that we should use trees from Mount Hira, but I disagreed. We disputed this point. Perhaps because he is angry that I ignored his views, he has been ill for several days, and he hasn't appeared again today. Lord Yoshida is unaware of the decision not to fell trees from the peak of Mount Hira. I alone am responsible. I have no objection to your reporting this to His Highness and the other court officials.

NARRATOR: His retort is forthright and measured, (*cadence*) his manner brusque, as if he were throwing logs at him. (*sung*) Momotsura mumbles, apparently wanting to speak, but just then the refrain "*ei yara yaa*" of the woodsmen's song is heard as they drag up a cart full of logs, their rhythm keeping time with the waves lapping along the shore. The earth rumbles under the pounding of so many workers' feet, and in no time a load of great cedar logs is delivered at the site. Kageyu kneels before Lord Yoshida.

KAGEYU: (*spoken*) Following the wishes of Lord Momotsura, the overseer of this project, I sent woodsmen up to the peak of Mount Hira and had them fell several hundred great cedars to be delivered urgently, so as to be in time for today's ceremony.

NARRATOR: (*sung*) Both Yoshida and his son are aghast at the turn of events (*cadence*) and are unable to respond. (*spoken*) Kageyu reiterates.

KAGEYU: Lord Yoshida is concerned, I'm sure. His face shows that he is afraid he will be cursed for felling trees from a haunted forest. There's no need to worry. On my own, I could never make a decision concerning the Yoshida household without careful consideration. (*sung*) I have taken it upon myself to pray to the god of Mount Hira to lift the curse and allow the use of the timber for the commonweal. I vowed that if blame must fall, then I alone will be clawed to pieces by the talons of the *tengu* demons. I pledged my life when I picked out a sacred oracle at the shrine, and I received a favorable reply, showing that the god had acquiesced to my request. (*spoken*) Only then did I have the trees cut down. If a curse falls, I alone shall suffer at the hands of the *tengu*. (*sung*) Therefore, rest assured that our lord has nothing to worry about.

NARRATOR: His reasoning seems impeccable. Momotsura, who is in league with Kageyu, speaks up.

MOMOTSURA: (*spoken*) What a loyal official, willing to give his life for the welfare of the people, a model retainer! The god's blessing offers us comfort that there'll be no curse from the *tengu*. (*sung*) Lord Yoshida, it seems that you have excellent councillors in Mr. Gon no Kami Takekuni and Kageyu. It all bodes well for Umewaka's future.

NARRATOR: (*spoken*) His provocatively faint praise pushes Takekuni beyond endurance. He jumps up to confront Momotsura.

TAKEKUNI: Leave me off your list of praise. Just a moment ago, didn't you say my eyes were clouded with the glitter of personal greed and that I'm unable to admonish my lord? I don't need to hear your answer. (*sung*) I wasn't good at sending woodsmen into a mountain forest where *tengu* live, but I'm a master woodsman when it comes to cutting down the demon that lives inside Lord Momotsura's head.

NARRATOR: He reaches for his sword.

MOMOTSURA: (*spoken*) What impudence! Go on, then, draw your sword. I'll smash it with my foot.

NARRATOR: He leaps up, but Yoshida intervenes.

YOSHIDA: Umewaka, you restrain Takekuni. Listen, Lord Momotsura. It is not proper for a high official to confront a retainer. At a public ceremony, especially, it is an offense against the Crown to introduce a private squabble. This conflict is all my fault. (*sung*) Please forgive me.

NARRATOR: He calms Momotsura.

YOSHIDA: Takekuni, you, too, please accept my apologies. For the rest of this royal enterprise, I ask that you take charge in my place. I relieve you of service to me until its completion. Stay here at this shrine, and make sure the project succeeds. Kageyu, I ask that you also remain and help Takekuni with this task. So, let us bring the opening ceremony to an auspicious close. All the lords and officials can rejoice that it has been done. Now we must return to the capital to report to His Highness.

NARRATOR: At these words of reconciliation, Momotsura responds.

MOMOTSURA: I shall accompany you to the capital.

YOSHIDA: Then let us depart together.

NARRATOR: They rise. Although we can distinguish between good and evil, we cannot always name one as right, the other wrong. Yoshida lays no blame on either side, and the pair stand tall, like the strong pillars of the *torii*, (*scene cadence*) firm and stable, supporting the vast realm.

—*Scene 2*
Yoshida residence in Kyoto, a few days later in the evening

NARRATOR: (*sung*) Forces above us can affect our lives. Lady Yoshida, wife of Lord Yoshida, has been struck by a rare affliction. Every day in the late afternoon, a double of her exact likeness appears, and no one can distinguish the true form. Some wonder whether a spirit has possessed her. Neither medicine nor acupuncture has been effective, (*cadence*) and prayers to all the gods in the heavens have been fruitless.
   (*sung*) From beyond the sliding door a voice is heard.
KANENARI: The senior counselor Awaji no Zenji Kanenari to see her Ladyship.
NARRATOR: He opens the door and enters the room.
KANENARI: (*spoken*) I was just preparing to come to inquire after your Ladyship when your summons arrived. How are you feeling today?
NARRATOR: Kanenari bows deeply.
LADY YOSHIDA: I wanted to show you a much improved countenance. I also have something to ask of you. You must be exhausted after your duties, which keep you busy day and night. You are being too formal for your venerable age. Please relax.
KANENARI: As I have told you before, my son, Awaji no Shichirō Toshikanu,[13] deceived Lord Yoshida and wasted a fortune in gold in the mad pursuit of a courtesan.[14] He should have been hanged or beheaded, (*sung*) but you intervened because of our family's many generations of service to the Yoshida house. His life was spared, and he was exiled to a far province.[15] We owe his life to your mercy. I must serve loyally for two lives, one of them to make amends for his profligacy. Even if my body were crushed into a hundred, a thousand pieces, I could never repay my debt to you. (*spoken*) You are too kind to use the words "ask of you." I am willing to die any time at your command. Let me know your wish.

NARRATOR: (*cadence*) He lowers his shiny, kumquat-like head to the floor.
LADY YOSHIDA: (*spoken*) Thank you. The matter is not of any great concern. I understand that Lady Hanjo in the second house has a son, Matsuwaka, (*sung*) but I have never met him. I think about him night and day. I want so much for Umewaka and Matsuwaka to meet. I have asked Lord Yoshida time and again, but he puts it off, saying that we must wait for the proper moment. (*spoken*) The other two senior councillors are away at the Sannō *torii* construction. The master, too, is in attendance at court, and this seems to be a good opportunity. Please serve as my messenger (*sung*) and arrange for Lady Hanjo and Matsuwaka to be called here to meet me.
NARRATOR: (*spoken*) At her words Kanenari studies her expression carefully.
KANENARI: Yes, your Ladyship is a most intelligent woman. Until now we have avoided this meeting for fear that you would be jealous. (*sung*) For the future of the Yoshida house, it is most important that there should be a reconciliation. I shall bring them both here immediately.
NARRATOR: (*cadence*) Joy puts a spring into his step. (*sung*) Lady Yoshida is in exceptionally good spirits.
LADY YOSHIDA: Maids, everyone, Lady Hanjo and Matsuwaka are coming, and I want them to be treated with utmost respect. They are my personal guests, and I shall not accept any kind of rudeness. But no one is to report their visit to my brother Lord Momotsura. This must be kept completely secret.
NARRATOR: But even before her sentence ends, a servant announces the arrival of Lord Momotsura.
LADY YOSHIDA: What a nuisance! Why does he have to come to visit me just now? Ah, clouds always appear when one wants to see the moon.
NARRATOR: Weighed down by her bedclothes and a heavy heart, (*cadence*) she lies down in despair.
   (*sung*) Momotsura enters her bedroom.
MOMOTSURA: (*spoken*) Dearest sister, I heard that you were not well, but I was tied up with the court's Sannō *torii* project. Forgive me for not having come earlier. What are you ill with? Have you eaten something strange?
NARRATOR: (*sung*) Her voice is feeble in response.
LADY YOSHIDA: I know that you have been busy, and I did not expect a visit. Talking makes me feel unwell. If anything changes, I will make

sure that you are informed immediately, so there is no need for you to stay.

MOMOTSURA: (*spoken*) No, I could not leave seeing you in such a weak state. If you feel unwell, don't worry about me. I won't disturb you. I'll wait in another room until Yoshida returns from his business at court. (*sung*) Then we'll discuss which doctor to consult.

NARRATOR: He goes into another room, but rather than being encouraged, (*cadence*) she is even more despondent and collapses after the sliding door is closed.

(*sung*) From a side door a young voice is heard.

MATSUWAKA: I offer greetings to Her Ladyship. Is anyone about who can convey my greetings?

NARRATOR: A young boy of about twelve appears holding a bunch of flowers in a basket, (*cadence*) his beauty outshining the floral display. (*sung*) Nagao, a lady-in-waiting, inquires who it is and opens the door.

NAGAO: (*spoken*) How silly of you, Master Umewaka, to act as if you are a stranger. Are you trying to make fun of me? I won't let you get away with it. (*sung*) Actually, I'll announce that there is a young man to see Her Ladyship, and then the joke will be on you.

NARRATOR: She stands up to leave.

MATSUWAKA: (*spoken*) Please listen, madam. You are mistaken to think that I am Umewaka. My name is Matsuwaka.

NAGAO: You still carry on with your joke! How could I not know Umewaka whom I see every day and night? You can't deceive me. (*sung*) Since when have you become such a naughty boy?

NARRATOR: She starts to leave the room, but Matsuwaka clings to her skirts.

MATSUWAKA: (*spoken*) This is all very upsetting. Take a closer look at me. I have never been here, and although you have never seen me before, you must have heard the name Matsuwaka. My mother Hanjo will be coming soon after me. (*sung*) These flowers are for Lady Yoshida, who is ill. Please take them to her for me. Please.

NAGAO: (*spoken*) Then you are in fact Matsuwaka! You look exactly the same as Umewaka. Anyone would take you to be Umewaka. The two of you are like two halves of a melon!

NARRATOR: (*sung*) She is shocked, and behind her Umewaka himself appears. Nagao turns and sees him. Without realizing who he is, she speaks.

FIGURE 14 (Right) Momotsura behind a bamboo screen and the twins Umewaka and Matsuwaka in front; (left) Lord Yoshida confronted by two Lady Yoshida figures. (*Futago Sumidagawa*, 1720, National Diet Library.)

NAGAO: (*spoken*) Now, now, Master Matsuwaka, how did you get over here so fast? How quick your feet are! (*sung*) Please wait here while I announce you.

UMEWAKA: (*spoken*) What? Nagao, you are mistaken. I am Umewaka, not Matsuwaka.

NAGAO: What are you teasing me for! How could I forget Matsuwaka's face so quickly?

UMEWAKA: You are still confused. (*sung*) Matsuwaka is over there.

NARRATOR: More flabbergasted than ever, she stares at the matching pair.

NAGAO: (*spoken*) Yes, it is true. No need to split any melons! You two are mirror images.

NARRATOR: (*sung*) She goes into the next room totally confused. (*cadence*) The boys left behind give a sigh as their eyes meet.

UMEWAKA: (*sung*) Are you really Master Matsuwaka? I am Umewaka. I've wanted to meet you for a long time. Come closer.

NARRATOR: They take each other's hands.

MATSUWAKA: (*spoken*) I had heard that my elder brother lived in the main house. My mother Hanjo said that she would try to have us meet some time. (*sung*) You must have been very brave not to want to show your face (*emotional cadence*) to your younger brother.

NARRATOR: He breaks down in tears.

UMEWAKA: (*spoken*) Everyone has some people they care about. But of all the millions of people in the world, there's only one can call me brother, and I am glad to be able to call you my brother. (*sung*) It's terrible that we've been kept apart for this long!

NARRATOR: They embrace each other warmly, like two branches from the same tree pulled apart now overlapping once again. (*cadence*) They weep for joy, an admirable sight.

NARRATOR: (*sung*) From the inner room Lady Yoshida's angry voice is heard.

LADY YOSHIDA: Where is that imp Matsuwaka?

NARRATOR: The sliding door is flung open to reveal a flushed Lady Yoshida, carrying the basket of flowers, her body shaking. Her ladies follow after.

LADY YOSHIDA: (*spoken*) Are you the one called Matsuwaka? Raise your head so that I can see you. If your face didn't resemble Umewaka so exactly, I wouldn't care very much. The more I see that you look alike, the more furious it makes me. What did you come here for? As I thought, your mother Hanjo is a courtesan from a house in Nogami[16] in Mino Province. I can just imagine her arrogant expression: "I gave birth to Lord Yoshida's child!" (*sung*) The flowers in this basket are wild scarlet lilies. Their color is beautiful but so terrifying! It shows up that wanton Hanjo as a demon tiger-lily. I'm scared even to touch these filthy things, they're disgusting!

NARRATOR: She tosses them back at him. Her words are like the sting of a mountain wasp that sucks the dew from flowers. Matsuwaka bursts into tears. The ladies, too, are shocked at their lady's harshness (*cadence*) but are unable to say a word.

(*sung*) Umewaka speaks gently.

UMEWAKA: (*spoken*) Dear mother, Matsuwaka and I have the same father,

Lord Yoshida. One must be even more considerate to him than to those in a family who are not related by blood. It is only natural that I should want him to be . . .

NARRATOR: But his words are interrupted.

LADY YOSHIDA: Do you think that I am not aware of that? Umewaka, be quiet. But be aware that behind this door sits Lord Momotsura, my brother. (*sung*) Have Matsuwaka removed at once. If he resists, then have him beaten. Maids, all of you, come here at once!

NARRATOR: Lady Yoshida takes Umewaka's hand and leads him weeping into the inner room. Nagao stands up.

NAGAO: (*spoken*) Listen, Master Matsuwaka, I did as Lady Yoshida ordered, but I will not hit you. Stop crying and get away. (*sung*) This anger of Her Ladyship is out of character. She's never been like this before. How frightening it is!

NARRATOR: Mumbling to herself, (*scene cadence*) she leads all the servants to the inner rooms.

(*sung*) Matsuwaka wipes his tears.

MATSUWAKA: Her saying she wanted to see me was a lie. (*spoken*) Mother and I must have been tricked into coming here to be killed. I, too, am a son of Lord Yoshida and won't die that easily. (*sung*) I'll strike that old woman with my sword first.

NARRATOR: He runs after Lady Yoshida, only to return.

MATSUWAKA: What is keeping mother?

NARRATOR: The frightened young boy worries, wondering what to do, when he hears someone in the next room. (*spoken*) Matsuwaka runs to his mother Hanjo.

MATSUWAKA: Dear mother, we have been summoned here today to be killed. It's all a plot by Her Ladyship. She said that I should be beaten and spoke all sorts of abuse.

NARRATOR: (*sung*) Hearing this, Hanjo despairs more than ever. Her heart is anxious, and she is unable to answer. She stands for a moment looking toward the inner room; tears stream down her cheeks.

HANJO: (*spoken*) I am, of course, a lowly woman and am nothing to a court lady. The main wife and a concubine are certainly different, but for all that, I, too, am a wife of Lord Yoshida. (*sung*) Yet a woman must know her place and duty. Even when I took a brief nap, (*cadence*) out of deference, I never once slept with my feet toward the main house. (*sung*) I have heard it rumored at the main house that Her Ladyship's illness is due to a curse of mine, because I want Matsuwaka to become the heir. How it hurts to hear such spite. To prove that my heart holds no deceit, I'll do something to dispel any doubt.

NARRATOR: She grabs Matsuwaka's hair knot and piteously, in one movement, pulls off the already cropped topknot.[17] She holds his soft young locks in her hand, discarded spring grasses.

HANJO: What a shame it is even to have cut a single strand![18] (*highest pitch*) How I cherished each precious hair every time I brushed it. Why must I cut it all off? (*high pitch*) Why make you become a monk? Although I had no hopes for your success in this house, when I was summoned, I succumbed to the desire to have you meet Lady Yoshida and Umewaka at least once. How insulting that he was invited only to be killed. There is no need to ask anyone else to do the deed. He'll die by his own hand. (*spoken*) Listen, Matsuwaka, rather than shame yourself by showing regret, die as a brave young man.

MATSUWAKA: (*sung*) Yes, mother.

NARRATOR: Even before she can hand over the sword, he pulls it to his chest. As he says, "Hail to the Buddha," the sliding door behind opens and Lady Yoshida rushes in.

LADY YOSHIDA: Please, please, wait, wait! Everyone listen. (*spoken*) I swear before the Buddha and the gods in heaven that my reasons for inviting you are just as I explained them to Senior Councillor Kanenari. My intentions have not changed, but unfortunately my elder brother Momotsura arrived unexpectedly. He could hear me from the adjoining room. I was so happy when I heard that Matsuwaka had arrived (*sung*) but could not show my joy because my irritable brother might make a fuss and get angry. Instead I tried to fool him by purposely being rude and nasty. I feel terrible that his young heart took my words as truth. (*cadence*) I am ashamed. (*sung*) My feelings are as true as the sea is deep and the mountains high. Even in lives to come, no matter what I am reborn as, I will not forget you. To help you be calm and to clear doubts long held, let me confess a secret held deep in my heart. (*spoken*) Listen carefully.

NARRATOR: She lowers her voice.

LADY YOSHIDA: You thought that you gave birth only to Matsuwaka, but Umewaka, too, is your child.

HANJO: Impossible! I have given birth only once in my life.

LADY YOSHIDA: That is true. Twelve years ago on the seventh day of the second month, your labor was difficult, and you don't remember what happened. You gave birth to twins, two boys.[19]

HANJO: What?

LADY YOSHIDA: Yes, you must be shocked. We intended to tell you, but the delivery was so difficult that we were afraid for your sanity. And so we secretly kept one of the babies, whom I then brought up and named Umewaka. Since it's considered a bad omen to have twins,[20] *(sung)* we let it be known that Umewaka was adopted. Only Lord Yoshida and myself and the senior councillor Takekuni know the truth. No one else knows about this. All these months and years I have cherished Umewaka more than if he were my own. If I were jealous and hated you, would I have so loved Umewaka, *(cadence)* who was born from the same womb as Matsuwaka? *(sung)* Like pairs of wheels, of wings, like the sun and moon, these two are brothers. I beg of you, as long as I live, do not consider making Matsuwaka a monk. Don't be angry.

NARRATOR: Lady Yoshida bares her soul before Hanjo.

HANJO: Your Ladyship's kindness has enabled me to know the joy of a second child. How happy I am!

NARRATOR: She folds her hands and bows in gratitude. Lady Yoshida grasps her hands.

LADY YOSHIDA: *(spoken)* We both can rejoice now. Are you still angry with me?

HANJO: How could I be? You have been too kind.

NARRATOR: *(sung)* They both struggle to keep their voices quiet and not to cry, but restraint only *(cadence)* brings forth more tears to wipe away.

LADY YOSHIDA: *(sung)* Wait, Nagao is in the inner room. Wait here for a moment. I'll think of some way to get my brother Momotsura to leave. Until you have a word from me, stay quiet. Follow me.

NARRATOR: She leads them into the next room. Though now separated by a sliding door, their hearts are as one. The bell sounds four o'clock, *(scene cadence)* as dusk *(high pitch)* approaches. *(Lady Yoshida, Hanjo, and Matsuwaka exit.)*

—Scene 3
The same

NARRATOR: (*sung*) Lord Yoshida returns from duties at court. A black cloud descends over a walkway in the garden, darkening the area.[21] He spots a strange creature up in the branches of a pine tree as it bends in the wind. Though only a lowly soldier, his retainer Gunsuke is fearless and strong.

GUNSUKE: (*spoken*) Lord Yoshida, did you see that?

YOSHIDA: Did you see it too? Its mouth was wide, its eyes like a monkey's, and its wings like an eagle's.[22] What a fearsome-looking bird!

GUNSUKE: That was no bird. It's a *tengu* goblin.

NARRATOR: (*sung*) The creature swoops down, breathing torrents of fire. (*cadence*) It flies in a direct line toward Lady Yoshida's bedroom.

GUNSUKE: (*spoken*) It's gone straight in to attack Lady Yoshida. I'll rip it to pieces before it can harm her.

YOSHIDA: (*sung*) Wait, Gunsuke, wait! (*spoken*) You're no match for the ferocious powers of black magic. Seeing the *tengu* has given me an idea. Don't let anyone else in the house hear of this. Now go into the inner room.

GUNSUKE: What a chance to bag a *tengu*! I'd've bet gold on the odds. It'd be a shame to miss this trick.[23]

NARRATOR: (*cadence*) He leaves muttering to himself.

(*sung*) The maids' shrieks are heard from within. MAIDS: It's terrifying! Look, there are two of Her Ladyship! How frightening![24]

NARRATOR: They scurry about in confusion as Yoshida peers into the room. He opens the sliding door, only to see two Lady Yoshidas lying down.

THE TWO LADY YOSHIDAS: How shameful it is to have this happen. My shame is there for all to see in this life.

NARRATOR: One weeps, and the other follows suit. Each mimics the other, their voices alike. No one can tell which is the real lady and which is the apparition. (*cadence*) Everyone is in shock.

(*sung*) After a moment, one Lady Yoshida raises her head.

LADY YOSHIDA (1): (*spoken*) That apparition imitating me comes every day late in the afternoon to torment me. Please, dear husband, drive it away.

NARRATOR: (*sung*) As soon as she finishes speaking, the other raises her head.

LADY YOSHIDA (2): (*spoken*) That apparition imitating me comes every day late in the afternoon to torment me. Please, dear husband, drive it away.

LADY YOSHIDA (1): No, you are the one to be driven out!

LADY YOSHIDA (2): No, you are the one to be driven out!

LADY YOSHIDA (1): How awful! Get it away from me!

LADY YOSHIDA (2): How awful! Get it away from me! It hurts. (*sung*) It hurts!

NARRATOR: Each wails in pain, the faces, figures, voices, all mirror images. Which is the possessed one? (*cadence*) How is the affliction to be cured?

LADY YOSHIDA (1): (*sung*) How upsetting this is, Lord Yoshida. We've been married for more than ten years, and still you cannot tell which one is your wife? How heartless! Can't you kill the enemy who stands before you? (*highest pitch*) I'm in agony!

NARRATOR: She grabs hold of him.

YOSHIDA: You are right. I can see that. (*spoken*) That one is the demon.

NARRATOR: He jumps toward the other and grabs her forearm.

LADY YOSHIDA (2): (*high pitch*) How upsetting this is, Lord Yoshida. We've been married for more than ten years, and still you cannot tell which one is your wife? (*cadence*) How heartless!

YOSHIDA: (*spoken*) Speak no more. Quiet! From the first, you have only imitated what the other said, never spoken first. You're the false one. I can tell the difference.

NARRATOR: (*sung*) He unsheathes his long sword and stabs her in the throat. At a twist of the blade, her hands and feet wither. She emits a sigh and is no more of this world, (*cadence*) her life's breath spent. (*spoken*) Lord Yoshida calls out loudly.

YOSHIDA: I have killed the demon spirit. Is anyone near?

NARRATOR: (*sung*) Hanjo, Umewaka, Matsuwaka, and Kanenari all come running at his cry. He begins to tell the tale of Lady Yoshida's agony and his killing of the *tengu* when Lady Yoshida arises, laughing wildly.

LADY YOSHIDA (1): (*spoken*) Yoshida, you fool. You have murdered your own wife. I am the great *tengu* of Mount Hira. You have chopped down the trees on my mountain. My revenge has only just begun!

NARRATOR: His figure is transformed into a strange bird with wings as big

FIGURE 15 (Right) Lady Yoshida lies dead; (top) a *tengu* steals Matsuwaka; Yoshida and Hanjo aghast; Kamenari committing *seppuku*; (left) Gunsuke holds Inokuma's head as Momotsura flees.(*Futago Sumidagawa*, 1720, National Diet Library.)

as carriage wheels, (*sung*) and in a flash he grabs Matsuwaka, (*cadence*) whisking him away into the clouds.[25]

HANJO: (*sung*) Oh! How terrible! Don't let him get away!

NARRATOR: (*highest pitch*) Hanjo wails her despair and collapses. Kanenari, too, is desperate. Lord Yoshida glares angrily at the sky, his eyes clouded with tears. He cries out, first at the loss of his child and then again at the sight of the dead body. (*high pitch*) With a cry of despair, (*cadence*) he collapses in tears.

(*sung*) The elderly Kanenari alone remains calm.

KANENARI: Even more dangerous than the *tengu* is the troublesome Momotsura in the inner room. If he gets wind of this disaster, it will be the end of everything. If we can at least find a way out of this immediate difficulty, then we can think of a plan later. My lord, you must take Lady Hanjo to the other house. Leave the rest to me.

YOSHIDA: (*sung*) You're right. Hanjo, come with me.

NARRATOR: They slip out the back door (*cadence*) to take refuge in Kita-Shirakawa.

NARRATOR: (*spoken*) At the cry of "Murder, murder!" Momotsura comes running out.

MOMOTSURA: What, the victim is my dear little sister! I thought there was something suspicious going on. It's surely Yoshida. Come out, Yoshida!

NARRATOR: He glares about angrily.

KANENARI: Lord Yoshida is still at court. Lady Yoshida was possessed and an apparition appeared, her mirror image. To save her from her agony, I decided to kill the demon phantom but killed Her Ladyship instead. I am the reckless criminal who has murdered Her Ladyship. Here, cut off my head and exact your revenge.

NARRATOR: (*sung*) He unsheathes his short sword and stabs his stomach, reciting "All hail Amida Buddha" with his last breath, gone forever like an arrow shot from a bow; (*cadence*) his ties to this world are severed.

(*sung*) Momotsura remains unconvinced and roughly kicks aside Kanenari's body.

MOMOTSURA: (*spoken*) What a stupid fool! Your deception has only wasted a life. I'm not one to be duped by a stupid tale of a *tengu* goblin. Listen, men, everyone, find Yoshida and Hanjo, even if you have to tear this house apart.

NARRATOR: (*sung*) A fierce, guardian-demon figure, Inokuma Hachirō, takes command of the men as they ransack the residence, tearing up the floorboards and smashing everything in sight (*cadence*) as they search for the pair. (*sung*) Gunsuke, resting in the barracks, is woken by the disturbance. He comes rushing in, his long, curved sword dangling loosely, the shape of a handle on a pot. His beard as spiky as his sword, he swaggers in.

GUNSUKE: (*spoken*) I'm usually only a footman to my lord, but when he's away, I'm General Gunsuke. Come on out, all you smelly foot soldiers, I'll take care of you!

NARRATOR: With this cry, he enters, only to meet Momotsura who is dragging young Umewaka. Gunsuke grabs Momotsura and twists his arm back.

GUNSUKE: Now where are you going?

MOMOTSURA: Where to? Until we find Yoshida, I'm taking Umewaka as a hostage.

GUNSUKE: Well then, thanks. I'll take care of him.
NARRATOR: He rips Momotsura's hand away.
GUNSUKE: You may be "Lord Momotsura," but you're a two-faced, greedy bastard.
NARRATOR: He grabs Momotsura's wrist, lifts him up, and tosses him to the floor. He pins him down, ready to draw his sword, but Inokuma comes running in and grabs Gunsuke's leg, throwing him to the side. He helps up Momotsura.
INOKUMA: Hurry, let's get out of here.
MOMOTSURA: I'll be careful. Inokuma, you finish off Gunsuke.
NARRATOR: (*cadence*) Giving this order, he flees. (*sung*) Inokuma is a massive giant, far stronger than Gunsuke.
INOKUMA: (*spoken*) You low, sandal-carrying footman, have a taste of my foot!
NARRATOR: He kicks Gunsuke's leg, knocks him down, and punches him. Gunsuke staggers under the blows, but he manages to grab Inokuma by one arm.
GUNSUKE: In the bear dance, we twirl a pole. You seem to want to spin your life away. You like this, do you? Then here we go.
NARRATOR: He holds on to one arm and spins him round and round.
INOKUMA: I'm getting dizzy.
NARRATOR: As Inokuma shouts, Gunsuke uses him as a human pole to knock down the other soldiers.
GUNSUKE: Lucky to have such a handy pole.
NARRATOR: Gunsuke fights fiercely, (*battle-scene cadence*) driving off the soldiers until they all take flight. (*sung*) Gunsuke runs back and pins Inokuma to the ground and tramples him underfoot.
GUNSUKE: (*spoken*) I'll take your head as an offering to the young master.
NARRATOR: He grabs Inokuma's jaw with both hands and before he can utter a grunt, he rips his head off, (*cadence*) easier than a child pinching the head off a dragonfly.
GUNSUKE: (*sung*) We must run from here!
NARRATOR: He lifts Umewaka onto his back, and like his name "Umewaka" [plum blossom], he fills the air with his fragrance.[26] We live only briefly in this life. We must never be less than a flower at the height of its bloom.[27] Don't let your name be any less glorious. Be brave and strong, taut as a bowstring. Shine like the moon. Savor the delights of snow and

the taste of rice cakes[28] and saké. Each is distinct, but the pleasures are the same. Those lowly and those of high rank, drinkers and teetotalers, good and evil, fortune and disaster—all are the same if they are of one mind, like this humble footman, so determined in his defense. He's brave, strong, and handsome, this rough young man, so dashing in his colorful kimono. He flees with Umewaka to the Yoshida residence in Kita-Shirakawa.

Act 2

—Scene 1
Dusk on the same day, Kyōgoku Avenue near Ōgimachi in Kyoto

NARRATOR:
>Bats appear as birds.
>And tadpoles as fish.
>Some have the shape of humans
>but their spirits are bent,
>their hearts dark and twisted.

Kageyu Hyōe Kagehaya, a scheming villain, carries a lantern to find his way on the dark road. On Kyōgoku Avenue, he spots Lord Momotsura on horseback as he crosses Ōgimachi Street.

KAGEYU: (*spoken*) Lord Momotsura, is that you?

MOMOTSURA: Yes, is that Kageyu? I'm just returning from the Yoshida house. (*sung*) Good timing, meeting you here.

NARRATOR: He turns his horse away from his retainers.

MOMOTSURA: I'll speak from the saddle. Come closer.

NARRATOR: They draw close to whisper.

MOMOTSURA: (*spoken*) Things never go as we expect. The *tengu* goblins from Mount Hira have really sent down a curse for cutting their trees, but they attacked my sister instead of Yoshida. They possessed her and created a mirror-image apparition. Just now, Yoshida mistook his wife for the demon and killed her. No use regretting my sister's death, although I thought about making Yoshida pay for this. But Kanenari took the blame for the murder and committed *seppuku*. (*sung*) His action means it's impossible to pursue Yoshida for my sister's death. I was just trying to think of another plan, and I remembered something! (*spoken*) You know about it, too. Yoshida and I have been entrusted to take turns storing the imperial hanging scroll with the painting of the carp by Emperor Wu of the Han dynasty.[1] It's now time to hand it over to Yoshida. (*sung*) I've decided to keep it as bait to harass him. I feel much

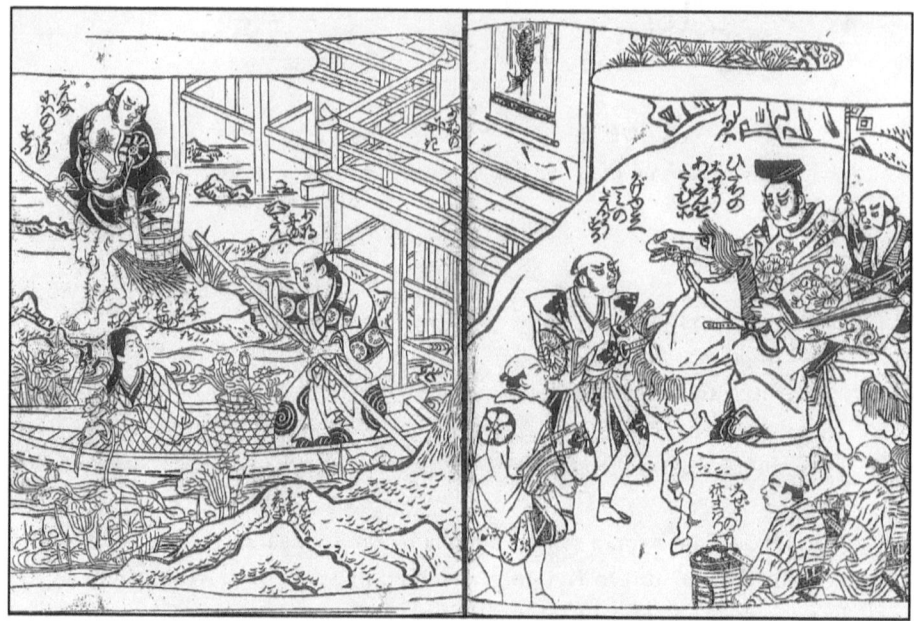

FIGURE 16 (Right) Momotsura and Kageyu plotting against Yoshida; (top) the painting of the carp; (left) Yoshida and Hanjo in a boat watched by Gunsuke. (*Futago Sumidagawa*, 1720, National Diet Library.)

  calmer now with this plan in mind and am on my way home. By the way, where are you returning from?
NARRATOR: Momotsura, still agitated from the excitement of the day, (*cadence*) burns for revenge.
KAGEYU: (*spoken*) Sir, I am surprised at this news. I was ordered by Yoshida to plant one hundred thousand new cedars on Mount Hira for felling timber in the sacred forest. I pretended to agree to his wish (*sung*) but then only went as far as Ōtsu Hatchō and enjoyed myself with the young ladies at the inn. I've been drinking now for four or five days, and I'm just coming home. If I'd been on hand to help you, I might have thought of something. I'm sorry I was away. (*spoken*) Now, this idea about not handing over the carp painting: I find it difficult to agree to that. It originally was an imperial treasure, and you have been asked by imperial decree to store it. If you don't hand it over because of a private quarrel, this will be criticized at court. Instead, Lord Momotsura

will be considered to be in the wrong. Don't worry about taking revenge on Yoshida just now. What if we were to hand over the painting as if nothing were amiss but then wait for an opportunity to steal it? (*sung*) If it's lost while in his possession, then it will be his fault and he will be punished by the palace. He'll lose his position and at least be exiled, if he doesn't lose his head. How about my plan?

NARRATOR: Momotsura is so taken by Kageyu's idea that he leans over too far and falls off his horse. He frowns and rubs his hip.

MOMOTSURA: (*spoken*) Kageyu, I was so taken with your plan that I didn't realize that I had fallen from my horse. (*sung*) I see the wisdom of handing over the painting and then stealing it. What a magnificent idea! Take care of it. I bow to you on this and am counting on your skills. Look, someone is coming from over there. It will not look good for us to be seen together here. You hurry on home. I'm depending on you. The rest of you, come with me.

He pulls in his horse and jumps into the saddle. Kageyu, too, races off, having been praised for his clever plan. (*scene cadence*) They go off in different directions.

—Scene 2

Yoshida's residence at Kita-Shirakawa, on the eastern edge of Kyoto, one hundred days later

NARRATOR: (*sung, highest pitch*) What could surpass the pleasures of this villa along the Shirakawa River? With one sweep of the eye, Lord Yoshida can savor all four seasons (*highest pitch*) in his magnificent garden, fashioned to rival nature's own mountains and rivers.[2] Many great stones piled high to the heavens create a waterfall; from its heights fall ribbons of white like the tangled strings that knot our hearts up with worry, but here troubles dissipate like bubbles on the water. All that delights body and soul, from nature and art, the flowers, moon and snow, together with wine and voluptuous women, is cleverly assembled under the eaves of this palatial paradise (*cadence*) to please and entice the most sophisticated aesthete.

NARRATOR: (*sung*) Here lie Lord Yoshida and Hanjo; not even a breeze wafting from a fan can disturb their intimacy,[3] nor summer's heat invade this haven *(cadence)* where he now lives. *(sung)* Although but a lowly soldier, Gunsuke is a favorite of Lord Yoshida. He has access to the innermost rooms and carefully sweeps every nook and cranny of the garden, picking some flowers along the way to decorate each room, always thinking of how to serve his master. Whether it be preparing the Lotus Pond room, doing menial tasks, serving a formal tea ceremony for lords, or taking the role of valet or footman, *(cadence)* Gunsuke is always conscientious.

(sung) The lotus in the lake have just bloomed, creating a brocade on the water, *(emotional cadence)* so beautiful one is sorry to look away.[4] *(sung)* The morning dewdrops on the lotus blossoms carry the fragrance across the water, enticing Lord Yoshida and Hanjo. (*Yoshida and Hanjo enter.*)

YOSHIDA: *(spoken)* Gunsuke, you are fastidious. I didn't even ask and you have cleaned the garden beautifully. The flowers in this vase, that must be your work, too. You bring delight even to uninspiring spots! I'll call if I need you. For now, relax and take a rest.

NARRATOR: *(sung)* As he speaks, Umewaka enters with Kageyu, who carries a jeweled box containing a hanging scroll.

UMEWAKA: *(spoken)* I have brought the Imperial Carp Painting from Lord Momotsura, Hitachi no Daijō.

NARRATOR: He hands it over to Yoshida, who is delighted.

YOSHIDA: Lord Momotsura has been against me since the death of Lady Yoshida, and I wondered whether he might refuse to hand it over. I am happy that you had no trouble in getting it. You have benefited from our sovereign's glory and performed this task splendidly, young man. Return to your room and rest. *(sung)* You have done well and I'm grateful.

NARRATOR: His face shows his delight as he warmly sends Umewaka to the inner rooms.

YOSHIDA: *(spoken)* Hanjo, you, too, have yet to see this painting. *(sung)* And you, Kageyu, who kindly accompanied Umewaka, let me show you this work as a reward.

NARRATOR: He opens the lid, removes the scroll, and hangs it in the alcove. Everyone comes up for a close look.

EVERYONE: Magnificent! It looks like a real carp. Impossible to think it's a painting. *(cadence)* Wonderful!

NARRATOR: (*sung*) Kageyu has a closer look.

KAGEYU: (*spoken*) I ought to be afraid to criticize this famous masterpiece, but it seems strange that the carp has no eyes.

YOSHIDA: You're sharp to notice the oddity. The work is famous for the lack of an eye. Let me explain its origins. At the time of the Former Han in China, Emperor Wu had a lake called Kunming built for naval training southwest of the capital, Changan. A certain man fished there morning and evening, day after day. One day he caught a carp, but the line snapped before he pulled it in and the fish escaped death, but the hook was stuck in its gills. Emperor Wu had a dream in which an old man told him of his endless suffering with a fishhook caught in his throat. He begged Emperor Wu to remove it. Emperor Wu himself removed the hook and freed the man from his misery. Whereupon the man gave him a marvelous jewel, saying that he lived in Kunming Pond.[5] (*sung*) He promised to protect the imperial throne and at once turned into a carp. Emperor Wu awoke from his dream, and near his pillow was a jewel that glowed in the dark. Right away he painted the image of the carp, but just as he was ready to insert the eye, he noticed the tail move (*spoken*) and realized that if he painted the eye, it would jump off the scroll and into the water. (*sung*) He immediately put down his brush, leaving the painting unfinished, as it has remained, handed down from emperor to emperor. (*spoken*) It happened to come to Japan when my ancestor Shitamichi no Mabi traveled in A.D. 717 with Abe no Nakamaro to Tang China as an emissary of EmperorGanshō. He returned with it as a present to the imperial court from the Chinese emperor. (*sung*) Since then, it has been a (*cadence*) treasure of the imperial household. (*sung*) Therefore, for generations now, the Momotsura and Yoshida households have had the honor of taking turns for three-year periods to store the scroll safely. The Yoshida household has no more precious treasure. You won't have a chance to see it again. Take a closer look. (*spoken*) I've bored everyone with my long tale. Hanjo, look over there, the lotus in full bloom. The Tang poets reveled in the beauty of Yang Guifei, who was said to surpass the exquisite lotus blossoms of Daiye Pond when she bathed in a hot spring.[6] Let me take you out in the boat—(*sung*) your radiant beauty[7] will outshine the lotus blossoms, and your fame will travel as far as China. Let us set off on a pleasure cruise.

NARRATOR: He takes her hand, but Hanjo pushes him away coldly.

HANJO: (*spoken*) It is not yet one hundred days since Lady Yoshida passed away. I'm afraid of imagining her face, and today the winds are strong. This old lake is almost as big as the sea. It's too dangerous today. (*sung*) Instead, have the women pick some of the new lotus blossoms and offer them as a memorial for Lady Yoshida.

NARRATOR: She starts to stand up, but he stops her.

YOSHIDA: (*spoken*) Idle fears. How can you feel reserve toward a dead woman?[8] (*sung*) Kageyu, have the boat prepared. I'll help you aboard, no one else will come. I'll take the oars myself. Nothing will keep me from this pleasure. I won't let you refuse me.

NARRATOR: He forces her into the boat. (*scene cadence*) Never since the time of the gods long ago has such a beautiful sight been seen.[9] He takes the oars in his hands.

> (*sung*) The punt drifts among a brocade of lotus blossoms.[10]
> A marvelous moment—pristine in its beauty.[11]
> Spring flowers have withered;
> the summer day is hot,
> hot as walking through a burning forest,
> but a gentle breeze over cool currents clears away the heat.
> How refreshing!
> Wind through the pines,[12] don't disturb his dream of me!
> Don't scatter my flowers! Never let them fall.
> How loathsome, a shallow vow, thin as a summer robe.[13]
> May your heart be as pure as the lotus blossom, forevermore.[14]
> Pluck the lotus blossoms, save them from becoming soiled.
> Forever keep them safe from the taint of muddy water.
> Waves splash our sleeves.
> (*cadence*) Rumors will float across the waters.
> (*nō chanting*) Pluck the lotus blossoms, save them from becoming soiled.[15]
> (*sung*) Long ago Chūjōhime became a nun
> and wove a mandala from lotus blossom threads,
> dyed in five colors with the Buddha's image in the center.[16]
> The charming cuckoo's call, too, suggests the Buddha.[17]
> The colors of her mandala were made from common indigo dye
> but surpassed all that went before.

The lotus blossom rises from the murky pond
but remains unsullied,
its blossoms auspicious offerings
to our sovereign who rules the land.
Now is the time to pluck them.
The priest Huiyuan[18] long ago near Mount Lu
formed the Pure Lotus Society,
and like the jewels of dew on the blossoms,
his heart remained pure and untouched by the mud of the world.
May the lotus blossom in his enlightened heart illuminate
(*cadence*) our path to Paradise in the next life.

(*sung*) Look, look! The carp and goldfish dance and play among the lotus blossoms, petals worn as hats.[19] How charming! Even spotted turtles stamp their feet in rhythm. Eels and catfish, too, strut fashionably. Look, look! (*song*) Even a familiar sight seen morning and night alters with each season, with each change in weather seen up close or from a distance. The pair let the boat float where it will, (*cadence*) in pursuit of (*highest pitch*) beautiful lotus blossoms around the lake.

NARRATOR: (*sung*) Under orders from Momotsura, to seize his chance, Kageyu watches the pair disappear out of sight and moves quickly to steal the carp painting.

KAGEYU: Lord Momotsura will sing like a thrush when I bring this to him. Yoshida will chirp angrily like a helpless little cricket, only to be food for the thrush.

NARRATOR: So Kageyu thinks to himself as he stealthily approaches the inner room, fearful of every leaf blown in the wind, afraid of being discovered. He opens the door to see the scroll half unrolled, his heart races with suspense when he sees the carp, but he curses when he notices Umewaka. He steps back quickly (*cadence*) but goes on looking at the scroll as if nothing is amiss.

(*sung*) Master Umewaka is unsuspecting.

UMEWAKA: (*spoken*) Hmm, I see that you, too, have come for another look at the painting.

NARRATOR: (*sung*) Kageyu thinks of a plan.

KAGEYU: (*spoken*) Yes, you're right. It is a rare chance to see it again. It really is too marvelous for words and certainly beyond my powers of

70 *Twins at the Sumida River*

FIGURE 17 (Right) Gunsuke pursuing the carp as (left) Umewaka and Kageyu watch. (*Futago Sumidagawa*, 1720, National Diet Library.)

description, but yet that story about the eyes, that if one painted the eyes, it would jump from the canvas into the water, that's surely too fantastic to believe. (*sung*) You've been practicing painting lately, why don't you try yourself and test this myth? Paint in the eye and we'll see whether or not China and Japan have been fooled for two thousand years. You can test the truth of this myth.

NARRATOR: He encourages the youth.

UMEWAKA: (*spoken*) Why such idle doubts? It can't all be a lie. (*sung*) And even if it were a fiction, what's to be gained by proving it?

KAGEYU: (*spoken*) No, you've got it wrong. Some day His Highness is sure to wish to see the eyes painted in, and then, if the carp doesn't move, the Yoshida house will be blamed for losing the real one and substituting a fake; it'll be the demise of the Yoshida estate. Why not just test it with a touch of your brush?

NARRATOR: (*sung*) Clever words prompt Umewaka to deface the painting, (*cadence*) an act that will destroy both father and child.

UMEWAKA: (*spoken*) What you say is true, but if the carp really jumps into the water and doesn't return, then that is even more frightening. I am more terrified of that.

KAGEYU: (*sung*) Even if it jumps into the water, it's really just a painting on a silk canvas. It won't swim off to another lake, and this is only a small pond, its source is a spring. Don't worry. Leave the rest to me. I'll take care of everything. Please, you must paint in the eyes.

NARRATOR: He pushes the ink and brush in front of Umewaka. His cunning words persuade the innocent boy to take up the brush. He dips it into the ink and paints an eye onto the blank space, and suddenly the golden scales begin to flutter and the fins breathe. The tail flaps on the canvas; it squirms off the scroll and flies into the garden lake, (*cadence*) disappearing into its depths.

(*sung*) Master Umewaka turns pale, terrified.

UMEWAKA: (*spoken*) Did you see that! What shall we do? This is a disaster, Kageyu. (*sung*) Please do something!

NARRATOR: He cries out, but nothing can be done to catch the fish.

UMEWAKA: Look, look! There it is. Get it before father returns, please!

KAGEYU: (*spoken*) What a terrible mess. I won't be able to catch it that easily. When Lord Yoshida hears about it, he'll rage as usual and maybe even kill you. Until it's all settled, you had better run somewhere far away and hide. (*sung*) Wait for me to come and get you. This is a catastrophe!

NARRATOR: He frightens the boy even more. Umewaka, never before scolded, is at a loss for words and runs off in tears. He is seen from the boat (*cadence*), but only later does the household learn of his disappearance.

(*sung*) Kageyu screams for help.

KAGEYU: (*spoken*) The carp in the painting has escaped and disappeared. Everyone, come and help!

NARRATOR: (*sung*) The whole household, high and low, are shocked and run out. Yoshida notices the commotion and returns.

YOSHIDA: My God! Who would destroy this masterpiece by painting in the eyes? Everyone knew the consequences. The emperor will be furious. It will bring shame to Japan and be the end of the Yoshida house. This is a disaster. We're ruined!

NARRATOR: He is devastated by the tragedy. A serving girl comes running in.

SERVANT GIRL: (*spoken*) It's awful. Master Umewaka is nowhere to be found. This note was in his room.

NARRATOR: (*sung*) Hanjo grabs the note but is slow to open it, afraid of its contents. She panics before she finishes reading it.

HANJO: Someone, hurry, run after Umewaka. He was talked into painting in the eye. (*highest pitch*) He was terrified of his father's anger and has fled. Where should we look for him?

NARRATOR: She rushes about in alarm until Yoshida stops her.

YOSHIDA: (*spoken*) Come to your senses, Hanjo! Don't you realize this is a national scandal and the demise of the Yoshida house? If we can't restore the painting to its original state, then I'm doomed as well. We've no time to search for Umewaka. (*sung*) There's no hope.

NARRATOR: His hand goes to his sword, but Gunsuke rushes to restrain him.

GUNSUKE: (*spoken*) Suicide is the last resort. The carp has jumped into this pond. We can easily dredge the bottom, drag it with nets, and catch the carp. Senior Councillors, why this stunned panic? Someone help Lady Hanjo. Someone else must search for Master Umewaka. Everyone is so helpless when Takekuni is away!

NARRATOR: (*sung*) He stirs everyone to action, and Kageyu sees his chance to get away.

KAGEYU: I'll go for Umewaka

NARRATOR: (*cadence*) And he runs off as fast as he can. (*sung*) Just then a splash is heard, and the carp's tail is seen.

GUNSUKE: (*spoken*) There it is! I'll catch it. No time to loosen my obi. Off with everything!

NARRATOR: He strips down to his waist, and shifts his short sword around to his back. Taking the shortcut to avoid the garden, he apologizes as he rushes past everyone and dives into the pond. (*sung*) He darts like an arrow across the water after the carp and grabs hold of the huge fish when it leaps out of the water. (*cadence*) He rides it through the water.

(*sung*) The carp's scales rise in anger as it tries desperately to shake off Gunsuke. It flips its tail and water sprays everywhere, (*fight-scene music*) falling like waves of blossom. They grapple through the undergrowth, Gunsuke hanging on, trying to tire the carp by paddling backward. It swims against the current and tries to get away. Then it seeks out the depths. Gunsuke clings on desperately, fighting for his life. They sink and rise back to the surface, again and again, the carp's tail and fins struggling to help it escape the Three Rivers that lead to hell. They fight on against the waves, (*fight-scene cadence*) pitting their strength (*highest pitch*) against each other in deadly battle.[20]

(*sung*) Even an inch-long dragon still wishes to fly the skies. They say a foot-long carp has the strength of a dragon. This giant carp was born from a masterpiece, with the power to scale waterfalls. What it is to see it twist its way up the falls! Never before has such a sight been seen in Japan, a true image of the legendary carp (*cadence*) that climbed the great Dragon Gate Falls of the Yellow River. (*sung*) Gunsuke glares at the carp.

GUNSUKE: (*spoken*) Everyone knows that carp can climb waterfalls. But I'll chase you anywhere.

NARRATOR: (*sung*) He tries to scale the steep cliff, finding stones to step on but nothing to hold on to. Then he grabs at vines but loses his footing and tumbles, only to rise again. He climbs higher and higher.

GUNSUKE: You won't get away from me. I've got you.

NARRATOR: Only his voice can be heard (*cadence*) as he climbs the rocks after the carp. (*sung*) A paragon of loyalty, he climbs up and up the treacherous rocks with seeming ease and leaps to grab hold of the gills, finally able to catch his breath. (*cadence*) His valiant deeds are unsurpassed.

(*sung*) Yoshida's spirits revive.

YOSHIDA: It is said that if one plucks out its eyes, it will return to the canvas. Gunsuke do it, pluck out the eyes!

NARRATOR: Just then Kageyu comes running in, sword drawn. He grabs Yoshida's collar and holds the sword to his chest.

KAGEYU: (*spoken*) You've been tricked. I've promised to carry out Lord Momotsura's request to kill Yoshida and get part of the Yoshida estate as my reward. If you pluck out the eyes, I'll stab Yoshida.

NARRATOR: (*sung*) Gunsuke stops cold, cursing to himself. Lord Yoshida yells out.

YOSHIDA: What a terrible fate, nothing but disaster! You worm of a man, beast! I fell for your treachery, again the curse of the *tengu* demons. If it must be, I'm willing to give my life to save the house. Cut out the eyes, restore the painting, and return it to the emperor. If the Yoshida house is saved, I'll be happy. Don't worry about me. Pluck out the eyes, now!

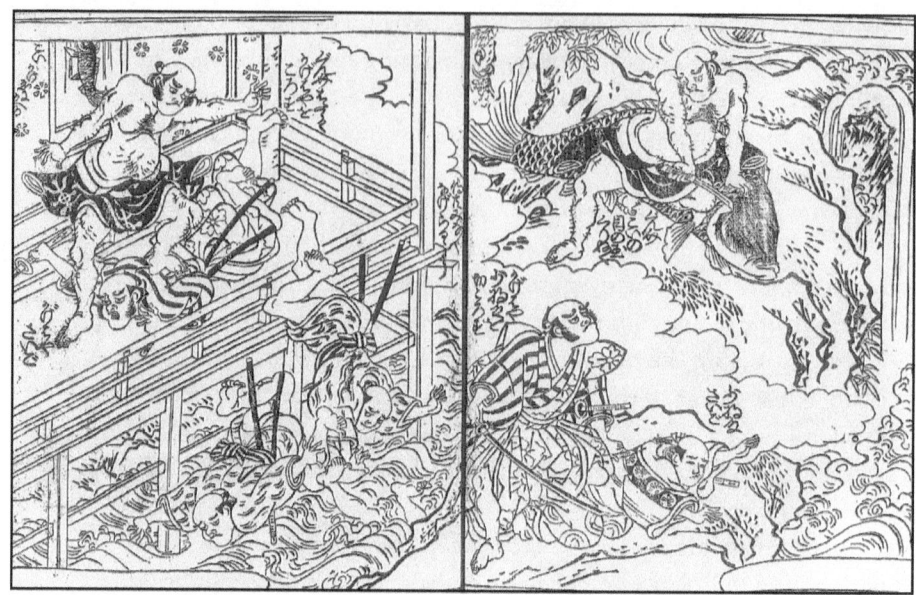

FIGURE 18 (Right) Gunsuke stabs the eye of the carp; (below) Kageyu kills Yoshida; (left) Gunsuke kills Kageyu, and behind him, the carp returns to the painting. (*Futago Sumidagawa*, 1720, National Diet Library.)

KAGEYU: (*spoken*) If you do it, I'll strike.

YOSHIDA: Don't worry about me. Do it now, (*sung*) Gunsuke!

NARRATOR: Loyal to house and sovereign, Yoshida is resolved. But Gunsuke, ever steadfast, cannot act, weighed down by duty to the Yoshida house. He wavers in doubt for a moment but then acts decisively to strike out the eyes, and the carp suddenly disappears and returns to the silk scroll, (*cadence*) truly a miracle, a tribute to the power of the artist's brush.

KAGEYU: (*sung*) If you are so keen to die, then die, you fool!

NARRATOR: He throws down Lord Yoshida and coldly stabs him through the heart.

KAGEYU: Now my dreams are fulfilled. Now, the painting, thank you.

NARRATOR: He rushes to remove the hanging scroll, but Gunsuke runs in from the garden out of breath and grabs Kageyu by his hair knot. He kicks him to the floor.

GUNSUKE: (*spoken*) Shall I stab you in the chest as an offering of vengeance for my master, or shall I let the carp have his revenge and pluck out your eyes? (*sung*) What a pleasant choice!

NARRATOR: He toys cruelly with Kageyu, but just then Momotsura's soldiers (*cadence*) burst into the house.

GUNSUKE: (*spoken*) Well now, it seems my guests haven't yet had enough. Let me show you the full range of the menu.[21]

NARRATOR: He thrusts Kageyu deep under the water and then fends off the other soldiers, throwing each into the pond, making a human raft, a pile of fish salad more or less, layers of *sushi*, their bodies iced in the cold water. Gunsuke's feats are unparalleled; he's a chef capable of mincing some, pickling a few more, (*sung*) and serving the rest as soup, sending everyone home satisfied. Too many chefs, however, have ruined the Yoshida house. Clear the kitchen! Everyone out! Gunsuke's angry eyes drive all away, and then the sorrowful tears flow. The twins have been separated and, like running water, are drifting farther and farther away. Gunsuke's heart will remain in the house, but now his body must say farewell, to search for the young boys.

Act 3

—Scene 1
Outside the gate of the imperial palace, a few days later

NARRATOR:
> (*sung*) Seeking in the distant heavens for one long lost,
> our view is blocked by the clouds of the Shu mountains.[1]
> Searching for his spirit beneath the earth,
> we are carried away by the rushing river of Baling.[2]

Hoping to restore the fortunes of the Yoshida estate, Chief Minister Takekuni carries a petition as he escorts Lady Hanjo, concealed inside a palanquin, to the palace. Takekuni's loyalty unswerving, they stop at the gate (*cadence*) to inquire whether their appeal may be presented. (*sung*) Before Lord Ōe no Masafusa, commander of the palace guards, Takekuni kneels in his full formal attire.

TAKEKUNI: (*spoken*) I am Takekuni, a retainer of the late Yoshida no Yukifusa. Lord Yoshida's untimely death has cast the family into disarray, which could lead to its demise, and so I have brought this humble petition. Although we have as yet been unable to determine the whereabouts of his twin sons, they have committed no offense against the court nor been disinherited by their parents and therefore are their father's rightful heirs. (*sung*) I intend to seek them in the heavens and across the seas. (*spoken*) Until I bring either Umewaka or Matsuwaka home, I would like to request that Lord Yoshida's concubine, the mother of his sons, be made head of the family. I present this humble petition for the palace's wise and merciful judgment. (*sung*) I have brought Lady Hanjo to present this request in person.

NARRATOR: (*emotional cadence*) He bows respectfully to the floor, hands clasped.
   (*spoken*) Lord Masafusa nods approvingly.

MASAFUSA: That is a most reasonable request, but it is late in coming. Lord Momotsura has been eagerly seeking to gain control of the Yoshida estate, coming every day to present his petition. Fortunately, today the judgment is to be handed down. I hear that Momotsura has already

Twins at the Sumida River   77

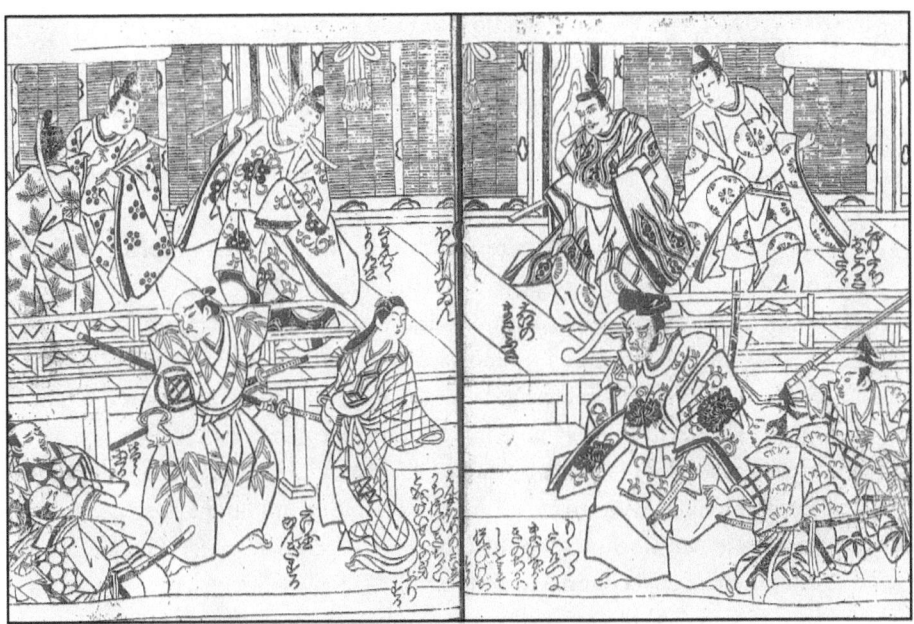

FIGURE 19 Scene at the imperial palace of the judgment between the competing claims of Momotsura and Hanjo to the Yoshida estate. Momotsura is on the right, and on the left, Hanjo, driven mad by stress, begins to act like a courtesan. (*Futago Sumidagawa*, 1720, National Diet Library.)

arrived. You must make your appeal at the Records Office. They should be considered together. (*sung*) Although mercy should be the principle of benevolent government, we cannot bend the truth and favor one side; we must choose justly between the two. (*spoken*) When you present your petition to the court, speak no lies, trust in honesty, and it will be the seed of good fortune.

NARRATOR: (*sung*) Words grave and solemn, fitting for the commander of the palace guards, expert in both martial and ethical affairs. (*cadence*) He departs in his carriage.

TAKEKUNI: (*sung*) Did you hear that? The former mistress's brother Momotsura cannot be trusted. He will use any devious means to wrest control of the estate from you. Today is our once-in-a-lifetime chance and will determine whether we sink or swim in the whirlpools of Naruto. You must be brave.

NARRATOR: He helps Lady Hanjo from the carriage.
HANJO: (*spoken*) We cannot know the outcome, but how frightening just to think of being in the august presence! There may be some who have been beaten or are bound in shackles who will appear before us. (*sung*) If I see something like that, I'll get dizzy and faint. How frightful, awful; my whole body trembles.
NARRATOR: Her voice, too, falters with fear. Just then, an official comes out to summon them to appear for the judgment.
MESSENGER: (*spoken*) Lady Hanjo, widow of Lord Yoshida, and the retainer Takekuni, you are called to appear.
NARRATOR: (*sung*) His piercing cry stuns Lady Hanjo, and she shudders, (*emotional cadence*) barely able to acknowledge the summons.
TAKEKUNI: (*spoken*) How can you lose heart now? Even if Puruna, Buddha's clever disciple,[3] were to be reborn and be your opponent, a twisted, evil mind like Momotsura's would show its true colors. (*sung*) The palace is a mirror that reflects honesty and reason.[4] They will see that Momotsura should be jailed for his treachery.
NARRATOR: His words give her courage.
MESSENGER: Why is the widow of Lord Yoshida late? Quick, come forward.
NARRATOR: Takekuni removes his sword. (*scene cadence*) For the first time ever, they enter through the grand gate and wait outside the court in the area covered with small pebbles.

—Scene 2
At the Palace Records Office

NARRATOR:
> (*sung*) As in China, the Japanese have learned
> never to cut down flourishing fruit trees
> and to cherish wise rulers.[5]

Lady Hanjo and Takekuni arrive at the Records Office. Behind the blinds sits the emperor, and in front sit Lord Ōe no Masafusa and all the highest officials of the imperial government. In the garden stand the guards, each holding ropes and shackles—just like the torturers in Lord Enma's court in hell. (*cadence*) Only the horns are missing. (*sung*) Momotsura, who has been waiting since before dawn, jumps up.

MOMOTSURA: (*spoken*) You deceitful piece of trash! Who are you to enter the palace, heads bowed? I'm the only relative of the Yoshida family. There are no others. And there's the matter of the scandal. Last year, when Lord Yoshida was sent by the court to the gold mines in Mutsu, 10,000 gold pieces were lost. Even now, the Treasury has been unable to cover the loss. At his death, all his extravagances and indiscretions came to light. Fearing the demise of his house and name, I have looked after the affairs and plan to request that my two-year-old son, Yoshida's nephew, become the heir. Today the decision is to be handed down. How dare you burst in and block my petition? Who has put you up to do this? Pretending to be Yoshida's widow! Do you hope to swallow up all the Yoshida estate? You greedy, filthy woman. See those ropes the guards have. Before you become the next guest on the gallows, (*sung*) you'd best leave immediately.

NARRATOR: Hanjo is petrified by the force of his threatening words. Her spirit wilts. (*spoken*) But Takekuni laughs out loud.

TAKEKUNI: Lord Momotsura, the decision on our claim will be determined by the court. You have no authority to tell Lady Hanjo to leave. It is pitiful to witness such a display of low-class bickering over an inheritance. We shall not stoop to argue with such a foul-mouthed, despicable opponent. But I must state that the gold was squandered by Lord Yoshida's retainer, Awaji no Shichirō Toshikanu,[6] who while there on official business, lost his young heart to a courtesan, squandered the money, and fled with her. Lord Yoshida had planned to repay the amount lost and provided for 10,000 *ryō*[7] of gold to be set aside from the inheritance. Today's petition is to enable us to maintain the Yoshida estate. (*sung*) Since his two sons, Umewaka and Matsuwaka, are still alive, there is no need for any appeal from relatives. The essence of our request to the court is that while we search for the sons, Lady Hanjo is to be named head of the Yoshida household.

NARRATOR: He bows to the floor, but Momotsura explodes again.

MOMOTSURA: (*spoken*) You're a liar to say that Yoshida has living male heirs. Matsuwaka was stolen by a *tengu* goblin, and he's surely been ripped to pieces, long dead. Umewaka, as well, is probably strangled or drowned. How can you say that while you search for these elusive phantoms, Lady Hanjo will be head of the house? You scheming bastard! You were with Yoshida in the gold mines in Ōshū, speculating on gold and mountain land, making a mint. (*sung*) You were the one behind it all!

TAKEKUNI: (*spoken*) I know nothing about selling mountains or valleys—but the biggest trick is your getting your snotty two-year-old to be the heir while you control things behind the scenes.

MOMOTSURA: Who are you calling a thief?

TAKEKUNI: Who do you think? You scoundrel!

MOMOTSURA: Where's your proof?

TAKEKUNI: If you want proof, look at your own heart.

NARRATOR: (*sung*) Each pushes harder and harder, like driving nails into fresh wood, like a hammer on metal, neither gives an inch. Like throwing cold water onto hot stones, they push their points louder and louder until the guards intervene with staves to separate them.

GUARDS: Quiet! Quiet down! (*cadence*) You both are out of order!

TAKEKUNI: (*spoken*) Momotsura, if you don't show concern for Lord Yoshida's legacy, I'll jump over there and smash in those fat cheeks.

NARRATOR: (*sung*) He squirms on the white gravel, (*emotional cadence*) gnashing his teeth as he struggles to control his anger.

(*sung*) The blinds are raised halfway, and Lord Yoshinobu is sent forward to speak for the emperor.

YOSHINOBU: (*spoken*) Lord Momotsura is the brother of the first wife of Lord Yoshida. Therefore he is related, but not by blood. Since Lady Hanjo is his second wife and mother of his sons, Umewaka and Matsuwaka, she is an immediate member of the Yoshida household. If we have a precedent that allows a woman to inherit the headship, then she should be allowed to do so. (*sung*) If there is no such precedent, Lord Momotsura's son will inherit the title. The court will consult the records.

NARRATOR: All the lords assembled begin to examine the many records, while down on the ground each party prays fervently—one that there be a precedent, the other that there be none. Hanjo's overwrought nerves, always on edge, make her even more tense, as if her spirit were about to fly out of her body. She can only depend on the records. Will it be good or bad, she frets, as if she were awaiting a doctor's verdict. (*cadence*) She is terrified by the palace's awesome grandeur.

(*sung*) The scholar-officials Nakahara and Kiyohara state the case.

SCHOLARS: We have examined the household records but have not been able to find a suitable precedent.

NARRATOR: Momotsura rises with glee while Takekuni and Lady Hanjo are devastated. Just when they feel all is lost, however, (*spoken*) Lord Masafusa picks up his scepter and addresses the council.

MASAFUSA: We need not seek ancient precedents. We have at hand the examples from the *Nihongi Chronicles*,[8] which all of us know. (*sung*) In the fifteenth imperial reign, after the death of His Highness, Empress Jingū, wife of Emperor Chūai, (*spoken*) succeeded to the throne to inherit all of Japan and beyond. The thirty-sixth empress, Kōgyoku, was the second case. The forty-fifth empress, Jitō, was the wife of Emperor Temmu. She, too, succeeded in inheriting all and ruled from the august throne. His Majesty is all the water in the heavens and four seas. His subjects are the water drops that collect into puddles and streams. (*sung*) Since the emperor rules over the four seas, the ponds and streams, then each must inherit according to his due. Since the precedent is from the imperial line, why should there be any problem about applying it to his subject, the rightful heir of the Yoshida estate? Let her inherit the estate.

NARRATOR: Before he finishes, Hanjo and Takekuni sigh in relief, and thanking him, they bow profusely again and again, drunk with joy. But Momotsura is not flustered.

MOMOTSURA: (*spoken*) Your investigation is not adequate. That woman was originally a courtesan in an inn at Nogami in Mino. She is probably the daughter of a beggar or outcast. She is a filthy woman who has slept with thousands of men. How could you dare to compare her with Empress Jingū or Jitō? It's like comparing a gourd to a temple bell. I cannot accept this unfair judgment.

NARRATOR: (*sung*) But he is ignored.

MASAFUSA: Takekuni, be grateful for this imperial judgment. Now quick, go with Lady Hanjo and take your leave.

NARRATOR: He is delighted.

TAKEKUNI: Lady Hanjo, let us be off, hurry!

NARRATOR: But to his chagrin, Hanjo, timid and fainthearted by nature, seems distraught and unable to move.[9] She was nervous all day, fretting over this judgment. Her emotions are in such confusion that her joy at the result is too much of a shock. As if she were waking from a dream, her eyes glaze over and wander aimlessly, seemingly distracted. She suddenly looks up, eyes wide open, and laughs eerily.

HANJO: (*sung*) Ha, ha, ha. . . . What's so funny?! Ha, ha, ho, ho, over there, there! there! My darling, what have you done? Look at him! He holds a rosary of one hundred and eight beads, (*dance melody*) one foot in flat snow shoes, one in high clogs.[10] Kashiwagi no Emon is in the capital playing football. Hear his cries![11] There, there! Prince Genji catches bream along the shore at Akashi. (*song*) The mountain crone (*high pitch*) carries brushwood along the steep path.[12] This floating world is a mystery, (*spoken*) magnificent to behold.

NARRATOR: (*sung*) Even Takekuni is aghast.

TAKEKUNI: How terrible! Have you gone mad?! At least you could have waited until we left the palace gates. How can you risk losing this chance to restore the Yoshida estate? (*high pitch*) Is this the bad luck of the Yoshidas? How pitiful! You must get back to normal, and we must depart with the proper decorum.

NARRATOR: He pulls her up to her feet.

HANJO: (*spoken*) What, are we to leave? Now, don't be rude. Don't you know who I am? I'm the grand courtesan of the Nogami pleasure quarter at the height of her glory, the most famous along this road and known for refusing customers at her whim. I'm not just a low harlot who's at your beck and call. I know who is behind those curtains. It's our lovely Mr. Emperor I've heard so much about. How naughty of you to hide. You priests over there, won't you arrange for him to come here where I am?[13] Let's go, we're off! Tomorrow's a festival. Festival days are (*song*) special for courtesans.[14] Count the days until the festival. No, I won't be jealous if he visits Nogami often. Ring the bell. Ring the bell and promise never to go; louder and louder—I want the sound to be heard.[15] Bells mean the dawn and in the morning we must part,[16] and I must send you away. Little girls in long sleeves are so sweet. Too bad a kerchief's been left behind; he'll regret its loss.[17] Its tie-dyed red color means it's a gift from another woman. Woven into its edges are a Chinese plum, Chinese pine, Chinese blossoms, Chinese grasses, and Chinese lions,[18] reminding me that my precious children have been lost. Spring flowers and autumn leaves are no comfort; let them scatter as they will. My lost children, if they are still alive, must be in the country.[19] (*sung*) Can't we go there? Isn't he there, (*highest pitch*) over there, there? Give me back my sons.

NARRATOR: She collapses in grief, (*cadence*) weeping hysterically.

(*sung*) The august curtains are quickly lowered. The courtiers recoil at this piteous sight and take their leave. Momotsura is delighted.

MOMOTSURA: She has defiled the palace, have her executed.

NARRATOR: (*cadence*) He yells for a pole or a stick.

(*sung*) As if he, too, had gone mad, Takekuni tries to control Hanjo.

HANJO: (*spoken*) Kill this troubled woman! If it's all right to kill, then kill this one and that one. (*sung*) Where is my child hidden? (*high pitch*) Let me seek out his abode. (*hatsumi melody*) No use asking at any house or inn; no matter how far into the deepest mountains it is, (*cadence*) I'll search. (*sung*) Tigers and wolves, man-eating demons don't frighten me; no fear even for the spirits that roam the heavens. I'll brave the rumbling thunderclouds.[20] (*high pitch*) I'll search every star in the Milky Way. His face is a flower that couldn't wait for autumn storms, falling, falling, our family scattered in the wind.

NARRATOR: His mother is a withered reed in a wintry field.[21] Distraught over her lost husband and children, blown by strong typhoon winds, she wanders aimlessly through the gardens. Rushing madly past chrysanthemums blooming in the wild in fields of bush clover, (*scene cadence*) she's off on a frenzied journey to distant lands.

—Scene 3

Sōta's house on the Sumida River, in the spring of the following year

NARRATOR: (*sung*) Along the banks of the Sumida River in a simple mud house live a poor, struggling couple, birds of an elegant feather, it seems, flown far from the capital.[22] The wife works diligently with her hands, sewing clothes, with no time to worry about her hair. Unable to get rid of (*suete melody*) the dirt of the floating world, (*honbushi melody*) unable to rise up and float easily through life, she now must suffer, her writing brush set aside for knitting needles:[23] a life imagined by poets (*cadence*) who compose on fine decorative paper.

(*sung*) Her husband uses words with skill, wears fine clothes,[24] too fancy for a merchant whose business is to trade in slaves; his name is "Monkey-Island Sōta."[25] Even though he lives in a poor hut, he keeps fine weapons—sharpened spears and swords and even all kinds of gear for torturing children, including steel and wooden poles and a horse's bit. He gets lackeys to do his work and lies around all day sleeping in his hideaway. His base is in Kantō, but he traffics in slaves from the deep north to far Hachijō Island. He is said to be a disciple of the infamous Sanshō Dayū of Tango. (*cadence*) His nickname in these parts is "Fiery" Sōta.[26]

NARRATOR: (*sung*) Sōta lifts up his pillow.

SŌTA: (*spoken*) I say, woman, today is the fifteenth of the third month. It's the arrival day for the Kazusa Bay[27] boat, but we've had no one come to buy anyone, and no one has come to offer us a snotty kid. I get depressed on days like this, with no cash coming in. Stop your sewing and take a walk around the area and kidnap some boy or girl. (*sung*) Then we can celebrate a good day's work.

NARRATOR: She ignores his order but finally speaks.

WIFE: (*spoken*) Every person has a different fate. Some live just by collecting the grains that grow from the seeds that happen to fall between fields. You've caused misery to countless children, and you've certainly collected far more gold than we could ever use, but haven't you thought about the irony of our fate? (*sung*) We have nothing to show for it but a miserable hut. I work my fingers to the bone for nothing. I blame myself for our fate.[28] Things get worse and worse, so I have no mirror, no time to take off my apron or let down my sleeves. Don't you think it's retribution for their suffering? I struggle to make ends meet, but I'm not afraid of even harder trials. But if there's no way we can get rich in this business, why don't you begin thinking of trying something else?

SŌTA: (*spoken*) There you go complaining again. Who likes this kind of work? We were lucky yesterday to sell to Hachijō Island a good-looking, fair-skinned lad who seemed to come from a good family in the capital. If things go well, then we'll get ten gold *ryō*. (*sung*) We'll take the savings, sell off any children left, and leave. Don't you worry about anything, Mrs. Sōta.

NARRATOR: His words are playful, but just then Sajitayū, lord of the flies,[29] brings in a shaven-headed boy of seven or eight in a "monkey" gag.

LORD OF THE FLIES: (*sung*) Here, Mr. Sōta, look at this fine, healthy-looking lad. He was going to his auntie's. You know his auntie, don't you? (*sung*) Can you take him to her?

NARRATOR: Sōta gladly takes up his cue.

SŌTA: (*spoken*) Glad you could come, young fellow. Your auntie's there, over there. (*sung*) See?

NARRATOR: He points and when the boy sees Sōta's wife, he panics and tries to escape.

SŌTA: Think you're clever, do you?

NARRATOR: He hits him three or four times and scowls fiercely, an ape truly more awful than a demon.[30] The poor child, (*emotional cadence*) caught in the gag, weeps in fear but no sound comes out; only his face shows his terror, tears streaming down.

SŌTA: (*spoken*) You've done it again, lord of the flies, what a catch! I'll give you 500 for this lad. If that isn't enough, then I'll throw something else into the bargain. Can we strike a deal?

LORD OF THE FLIES: Well, if that's the case, the boat for Kazusa is leaving today. They need twelve or so good-looking young girls, but I've got only ten. I can get one *kan* of silver for each girlie. We could both make a profit. Got any here?

SŌTA: That's a bit of luck, I've got two girls I want to get rid of. You, "Sixie" and "Watermelon," come here!

NARRATOR: (*sung*) The pair answer yes and come forward. Two lovely gentle-looking girls appear, rosy wildflowers from someone's garden, now wilted. Their expression is serious (*cadence*) and sad.

SŌTA: (*spoken*) Have you been crying again? With their pretty faces, they might fetch 100 *kan*[31] of silver at the pleasure quarters of Ōiso, Koiso, Eguchi, or Kanzaki, but they're not suited for courtesans. They're both faulty products. One has a belly button that protrudes unbelievably—it looks like a huge watermelon was sitting on her tummy. The other has six fingers on her left hand and only three on her right. She's short the usual ten. They're both reject porcelain. They wouldn't suit the customers, would they?

LORD OF THE FLIES: No, so long as their faces are pretty, it doesn't matter if they have three legs or are shaped like a fat vase with no arms. They'll do fine. (*sung*) This is a good deal.

NARRATOR: He claps his hands and says, "Come on girls, let's go" and gets up.
LORD OF THE FLIES: Mrs. Sōta, good-bye and thanks for everything.
NARRATOR: The girls leave weeping, and tears cloud the wife's eyes, too.
WIFE: (*spoken*) Pitiful girls. What is there to thank me for? (*sung*) Young fellow, you come with me.
NARRATOR: (*scene cadence*) She takes his hand, and they go into the back room.

NARRATOR: (*sung*) Sōta laughs to himself at this turn in his fortunes.
SŌTA: If things go on like this, the business of that pale-faced lad from the capital is sure to be settled soon; the ten *ryō* of gold will be mine. How great it'll be to hold those coins in my hands! I can feel the weight already.
NARRATOR: He calculates his fortune in his heart, (*cadence*) delighted at the prospects ahead.
(*sung*) Just then, Yazō the Lasso comes in, dragging the young gentleman by the wrist and flings him inside.
YAZŌ: (*spoken*) Mr. Sōta, after I'd sent him to Hachijō Island, I promised you ten *ryō*, and I expected a bit of profit too. So I worked extra hard to get the boy to agree to go, and just when I thought it was all settled, he started complaining about a stomachache or a backache, all the time. He always looked ready to run whenever he had a chance. No stinging nettles or sour vinegar will force this brat to submit. So I'm returning him. Lucky I hadn't paid you yet. (*sung*) What a waste of effort on this good-for-nothing kid.
NARRATOR: (*cadence*) He glares angrily and takes his leave. (*sung*) Sōta's eyes glisten like gold plate. His angry voice is low and heavy.
SŌTA: (*spoken*) You're just a nasty, rice-eating locust! How dare you defy your parent, you arrogant piece of garbage! I took you to be a good lad, well brought up. Even the child of a king or god will walk a hundred, two hundred leagues and suffer to feed his parent. Your parents have surely been bankrupted or exiled or even worse. You should've been grateful for the food I gave you and been willing to go to Demon Island or even to the bottom of the sea if I sent you. Why did you refuse!? (*sung*) Give me an answer, you lazy good-for-nothing!

NARRATOR: His angry voice fiercely lashes into the boy, terrifying him to his very soul. Master Umewaka had always been loved and gently treated and had never in his life heard a rough word from his parents or anyone. The life in his body shrinks, recoils in fear.

UMEWAKA: Sending me to Hachijō, I would be far from Japan where no one ever visits.[32] Let me at least go somewhere on this same land where my parents live.

NARRATOR: He begs with hands pressed together.

SŌTA: (*spoken*) Don't try to fool me. Why, then, did you refuse to go to Ashikaga[33] with that street entertainer? Ashikaga's still Japan!

UMEWAKA: (*sung*) Ashikaga, I heard, is even farther north than here. Please let me be sent even a mile or a few feet closer to the capital. If I am to die, I want to face my parents in the capital. (*highest pitch*) Master, I shall never forget my debt of gratitude to you for feeding and taking care of me. Please have mercy on me, please!

NARRATOR: His voice pleads to the Buddha above. (*cadence*) Tears fall on his hands, like beads from a broken rosary string.

SŌTA: (*spoken*) Just a scolding will never be enough for a brat like you. You'll only listen to force, to the prick of a sword. (*sung*) This'll change your stubborn bones.

NARRATOR: He unsheathes his dagger and thrusts at the boy.

SŌTA: (*spoken*) Shall I stab your thigh?

UMEWAKA: Yes, yes sir.

SŌTA: Shall I smack your behind?

UMEWAKA: Yes, yes.

SŌTA: Don't move.

UMEWAKA: Yes, sir.

SŌTA: Don't move. If you budge an inch, I'll stab you in the ribs.

UMEWAKA: Yes, yes.

SŌTA: Shall I pluck out your eyes, stab you in the side?

NARRATOR: (*sung*) Threateningly he stalks around the poor boy, who shrinks away shaking in fear, too terrified to cry. No means of escape!

UMEWAKA: (*spoken*) Help! Sir, you're too cruel. If you're going to kill me, then do it quickly. Mrs. Sōta! (*sung*) Please apologize for me, please!

NARRATOR: At his cries, Sōta's wife comes running in.

WIFE: (*spoken*) You're too horrible, too cruel. There are limits to disciplining a child. (*sung*) Who will gain if you scar him?

NARRATOR: She wrestles away the dagger, but he grabs down the bridle and bit and begins to belt the boy with all his strength, all over his back and shoulders. He belts him till he sinks lower and lower, beating his soft skin thinner than the wings shed by a cicada. Afraid that his bones will be broken or his flesh cut, the child lies flat, but then his legs are hit. When he pulls in his hands, his elbows are beaten. He is unable even to cry out, so the wife grabs Sōta's arm.

WIFE: (*spoken*) Our life depends on children. If he's really hurt, we'll have to call doctor after doctor. (*sung*) If you kill him, won't there be retribution?

NARRATOR: She wrestles the bit from Sōta and throws it aside.

SŌTA: (*spoken*) Enough of your complaints, woman. It's fate that he fell into my hands, our karma that by selling him we can eat. I'll beat him till he agrees to go to Hachijō Island.

NARRATOR: (*sung*) He takes up a long rod and holds down the boy with it. The child collapses under the pressure. Sōta bellows as he pounds the boy again and again with the rod. The rod is strong; the body weakens. Finally a blow to the ribs, and the body convulses. (*cadence*) All color is gone; his breath stops.

WIFE: (*sung*) How terrible, pitiful! He's dead!

NARRATOR: She holds him up, rubbing his arms and legs, and hugging him close to her breast. Even Sōta is aghast. (*cadence*) He throws away the rod, unable to speak.

(*sung*) At first, the boy seems to recover, and the wife gets him to swallow a little water from her own mouth.

WIFE: (*spoken*) He's breathing, poor boy. Does it hurt? Are you in pain? Where were you traveling to? (*sung*) Have you a wish? I'll do anything you ask. I saw how terribly you've suffered. It hurt me as much to watch you being beaten. Please, you mustn't die!

NARRATOR: (*emotional cadence*) She pleads tearfully. (*sung*) His eyes are clouded with tears. He puts his hands together in prayer. His voice is weak, panting faintly.

UMEWAKA: (*spoken*) I am from a family of some stature in the Shirakawa district of the capital.[34] I sought to find my father who was said to be in Ōshū, but I became weak and my chest began to hurt. But now before I

FIGURE 20 (Right) Sōta kills Umewaka; (top left) a slave trader abducting children; (below) the arrival of Takekuni. (*Futago Sumidagawa*, 1720, National Diet Library.)

die, one request. (*sung*) The charm around my neck was put there when I was six days old. It contains a clipping of my baby hair, which therefore is the blood of my parents. I treasured this charm as my only protector, never taking it off. I beg of your compassion. (*highest pitch*) Bury me with this charm and (*cadence*) please plant a willow tree over me.

(*sung*) My body will decay, but the baby hair with my parents' blood (*highest pitch*) will give life to the tree, to its hairlike branches. This will be a small offering of gratitude for my parents' love and kindness. Ah, how I long to see the caring expression on my mother's kind face before I die. My lovely, warm mother. How I long to see something of her and my loved ones in the capital. Namu Amida Butsu. All hail Amida Buddha.

NARRATOR: His tongue quivers, then stops; his eyes grow distant. His wounds attack his vital organs; his whole body trembles. Who was it who turned the stick into a sword that killed this child of twelve? (*emotional cadence*) His spirit snaps, all the life gone.

(*sung*) The couple are horrified at his death. Just then a visitor arrives at the door.

TAKEKUNI: (*spoken*) Is this the home of Sōta the slave trader? I am from the capital and would like to make some inquiries.

SŌTA: (*sung*) Strange to see a samurai traveling all alone. No matter who he is, we can't let him see this dead body. Hide the corpse. Get the screen, hurry! Some paper and matting!

NARRATOR: As they scurry about, the visitor calls out again.

TAKEKUNI: Anyone at home, please?

NARRATOR: He steps into the entrance and takes off his large wicker hat. Sōta recognizes him as Takekuni, an officer in the Yoshida house.

TAKEKUNI: (*spoken*) Well now, if it isn't Awaji no Shichirō!

SŌTA: (*sung*) What a pleasant surprise to meet you here. Please come in.

NARRATOR: Invited in, he looks around.

TAKEKUNI: (*spoken*) I asked around for Awaji no Shichirō Toshikanu but was told the only samurai-looking fellow in these parts was Sōta the slave trader. (*sung*) So then, have you been selling people?

NARRATOR: The couple are ashamed and embarrassed.

SŌTA: (*spoken*) No, no, what are you saying! Even if we were starving on the streets and facing death, we would never sell people. Oh yes, I should explain everything. Eleven years ago, I was disloyal because of love for that woman and was thrown out without a job. I was not bad at martial arts but no longer had anyone to do the servant work. So whenever I needed help, I borrowed a servant from a friend. I managed from day to day to get others to work for me and became known as "Sōta the servant poacher." But somehow this was altered jokingly to "Sōta the slave trader," causing me no end of grief. That's right, isn't it, wife?

WIFE: (*sung*) Ah, we have suffered no end because of our master's punishment. We beg of you to intervene and seek our pardon for crimes of long ago so that we can return. Please, kind sir.

NARRATOR: (*cadence*) She breaks down in tears.

TAKEKUNI: (*spoken*) If times were peaceful as they used to be, then a retainer from a loyal family of many generations could be restored to his position. But the Yoshida family has fallen into unexpected difficulties; the estate may fall into the hands of others because there is no head of the family. Had you heard nothing about this?

NARRATOR: (*sung*) Sōta is shocked at this news and can only exclaim (*cadence*) and wonder what has happened.

TAKEKUNI: (*spoken*) You must be shocked at this turn of events. Lady Yoshida's older brother Momotsura plotted with Kageyu to take over the Yoshida estate. Both Lord and Lady Yoshida were killed by unforeseen treachery; the young master (*sung*) Matsuwaka was stolen by a goblin; and Master Umewaka's whereabouts are unknown. Overcome with grief, Lady Hanjo became distraught and left the court in a state of madness. (*spoken*) Furthermore, in trying to save Lord Yoshida, your father Kanenari had to commit suicide as well. I am the only one left who can plan a strategy to save the estate. And so I set out to the north to find Master Umewaka. Would you have any idea where he might be? You last saw him when he was two, and he is now twelve. He's surely worn down by his traveling and darker from the sun, but even in a rough state after being tossed about in the wilds (*sung*) and without the fine garments of the capital, as he was born a flower of the aristocracy, he would still show the refined manners of a courtier and daimyo.[35] Even if his clothes are in tatters and dirty, they're of high quality with the distinctive Yoshida crest. He carries a Yoshida family charm around his neck that contains his baby hair, cut on his sixth day. There is only one like it in all Japan. Have you by any chance seen him or heard anything about him? Tell me what you've heard. One first has to be loyal and then compassionate. (*highest pitch*) I've lost my lord, and yet I have shamelessly gone on living. Take pity and help me.

NARRATOR: As he tells his tale, (*emotional cadence*) he dissolves into tears. (*sung*) But his words strike terror in Sōta's heart. News of his father's suicide strikes deep into his chest and a great stone lodges in his throat, crushing his attempts to speak. His mind wanders about aimlessly, and he catches sight of his wife; their eyes meet. She, too, is burning inside as the hot knife cuts deep. (*cadence*) Neither mind nor body can be still.

(*sung*) Unable to restrain herself, the wife cries out.

WIFE: I was afraid of a disaster like this! (*high pitch*) How terrible!

NARRATOR: (*emotional cadence*) She collapses in a flood of tears. (*sung*) Sōta calms himself before moving forward.

SŌTA: (*spoken*) Listen, Takekuni, what I said before was all a lie. It is true that I, Awaji no Shichirō Toshikanu, am indeed "Sōta the slave trader."

Without realizing that it was my Lord Umewaka, I bought him for three *kan* of silver and sold him for ten *ryō* of gold to Hachijō Island. I got angry at his crying and refusing to go and disciplined him with a stick, which proved to be fatal. He sadly died just a minute ago. (*sung*) Do look at his pitiful body.[36]

NARRATOR: He removes the screen, and Takekuni, as if in a dream, lifts up Umewaka, but his color is gone, (*spoken*) his body cold as ice.

TAKEKUNI: (*sung, high pitch*) Dearest Master Umewaka, Takekuni is here. Even as a spirit, you might recall that masters and servants remain so through three lives. Why, gods, couldn't you have waited just a moment longer (*cadence*) so that I could've been in time? Oh, hateful gods!

NARRATOR: (*sung*) Voice and tears unrestrained in grief. He wipes his tears.

TAKEKUNI: (*spoken*) Listen, Toshikanu, although you didn't know who it was, you are the enemy of my lord. I, too, am now masterless, a good time to die. (*sung*) Die as the enemy of my lord.

NARRATOR: He prepares to draw his sword, but Toshikanu doesn't stir. He bows, wiping his tears.

SŌTA: (*spoken*) My crime of killing my master calls for me to be trampled upon, tied up, and handed over to the outcast villagers for decapitation by a bamboo saw and then crucified upside down.[37] You are most generous to take my life, allowing me honor as a samurai. I am ready for the consequences, but could you wait just a moment? I have a confession to make that even my wife knows nothing about. (*sung*) Witness the results of my past sins.

NARRATOR: He stands up, pulls back his kimono, and lifts up the tatami mats and puts his hand under the floorboards. Out come thirty, fifty gold coins, one hundred, five hundred. He throws out the coins, too many to count. He piles them up into a mountain of gold and sits down in front of it.

SŌTA: (*spoken*) My actions are worse than the monkeys who tried to grasp the moon's reflection in the well and fell in, only to drown—they were just animals.[38] My impossible desires caused such suffering. Humans who hurt other humans are lower than beasts.[39] (*sung*) Awaji no Shichirō Toshikanu is the worst of the lot. I cheated my master of 10,000 gold pieces and have spent my life working to repay the debt. My hope was to regain the trust of the Yoshida family. Whether as a lackey leading the horse of the young master or carrying his sandals, I

FIGURE 21 Nakamura Ganjirō III (Senjaku) as Sōta and Sawamura Tanosuke as his wife, Karaito. From a 1986 kabuki performance. (*Courtesy of Nakamura Ganjirō III.*)

was determined to serve again in the house where my ancestors had long been. I hoped also to give joy to my father through my loyalty and service. I was determined to prove I was a good and dutiful son, (*spoken*) but I knew no trade nor how to cultivate crops. Once I was asked to write out a contract for a slave transaction. Now, today, I realize that this encounter was with the devil (*cadence*) who led me into the dark path of evil.

(*sung*) My wife knew nothing of my plans. I had her wear tattered clothes and eat millet. Like the crane who piles up the grains and the ants that patiently build their mound, for more than ten years (*spoken*) I piled up the dirt to make my mountain of gold—9,990 gold pieces. I was impatient for the last ten and the fulfillment it would bring. At last, after buying the young master, I hurriedly sought a buyer for ten gold pieces. It didn't matter if the child wept or screamed, how could I let that stop me from achieving my goal? (*sung*) To make him agree to go, I struck the child, a blow that was heaven's punishment on me. If only (*highest pitch*) my arm had broken or a cramp set in, then this tragedy might have been averted. Even a billion gold coins reaching to the skies cannot buy a human life. For the sake of just ten *ryō*, a small profit, my eyes were clouded. Revenge wreaks retribution, profits devour profits. Even my own father has been lost. (*cadence*) A miscalculation on Fate's abacus.

(*sung*) Even to tell this tale is to bear a samurai's shame. (*spoken*) Wife, forgive me. You've never had one day of comfort; you've had to bear a life of poverty. My efforts to save and save were not for loyalty or filial duty, (*sung*) no, they were to buy passage for a journey to hell. How pitiful!

NARRATOR: (*high pitch*) In a fit of anger, he kicks the pile of coins, (*emotional cadence*) scattering the gold, and collapses in tears.

(*sung*) His wife, too, can only sigh in despair. After hearing the tale, Takekuni can no longer be angry or bitter; (*cadence*) he chokes in despair and regret for the tragedy.

SŌTA: (*spoken*) No use for regrets. The person who killed Umewaka unwittingly was the slave trader Sōta. From now on, I am Awaji no Shichirō Toshikanu again. If Toshikanu doesn't take his revenge on Sōta the slayer of my master, then my honor as a samurai can't be restored.

NARRATOR: (*sung*) He grabs the sword near him, unsheathes it in a flash and stabs himself in the left side (*spoken*) drawing the blade across to the right. (*sung*) His wife cries out in shock, and Takekuni rushes to his side.

TAKEKUNI: (*spoken*) Toshikanu, why didn't you let me strike the first blow?

TOSHIKANU: You're right to object, but I have a plan. Umewaka is dead, and regret will not bring him back. It will be hard to find Matsuwaka among the *tengu* goblins unless I become a *tengu*. I offer my entrails to heaven. My heart, patient and restrained for eleven years, will enter the realm of black magic and become a demon. (*sung*) I'll search through the mountains, the peaks, the valleys, and the cliffs where demons roam until I find Matsuwaka. I'll bring him back and see the Yoshida family restored.

NARRATOR: He rips out his insides.

TOSHIKANU: (*spoken*) Takekuni, wife! If you don't now avenge your master's death and slay Sōta, then you are not Toshikanu's wife. Don't forget my words. I don't want my body buried or cremated. Let it be exposed

FIGURE 22 (Right) Sōta kills himself and his spirit becomes a *tengu*; (left) Sōta, as a *yamabushi* priest, wrestles with Gunsuke (act 4). (*Futago Sumidagawa*, 1720, National Diet Library.)

in shame along the highway as a criminal who killed his master. This will be my offering to Umewaka. (*sung*) Now, witness Toshikanu's spirit become a demon!

NARRATOR: He thrusts his hand into the wound and (*threatening melody*) grasps his inner organs and throws them up into the heavens. They fly into the sky bursting into a fierce, magical flame, the sign of sorcery.[40] He suffers the three agonies of dragons and serpents.[41] A demon wind, a magic gust from the ground, rises up (*sung*) and up into the treetops, (*climax cadence*) into the clouds.[42]

NARRATOR: (*sung*) In a flash, he is gone. (*cadence*) His body collapses as if into sleep. (*sung*) Takekuni is unable to hold back his tears.
TAKEKUNI: Disloyalty has become loyalty. Although he is a mirror of a true samurai, I cannot break the warrior's code. The enemy of my lord!
NARRATOR: He yells out and strikes off the corpse's left arm.

TAKEKUNI: *(spoken)* Wife of Toshikanu! Remember your husband's words.
NARRATOR: Pushed to complete the promise, *(sung)* she reluctantly unsheathes the sword and cuts slightly into the right shoulder.
TAKEKUNI: Bravely done! You've avenged your master's death.
WIFE: I've done it. How sad that I've struck him.
NARRATOR: *(highest pitch)* She holds tightly the lifeless body and offers her final farewell with tears. Intent on joining him in death, she turns the sword on herself, but Takekuni stops her and tries to console her in her grief. But his thoughts are distracted by the pile of money. He will leave it with the head of the village for later use to aid Matsuwaka's success. Toshikanu's desire will be fulfilled. The children's revival of their parents' estate will release all the dead spirits from the yoke of this world. Half of Toshikanu's spirit is lost in sorcery, but the other half will guide Umewaka safely into the next life.[43] Their bodies will be buried in the same field, memorial stones laid side by side. His charm and baby hair with memories of his parents will be the seed of the willow tree with its flowing hairlike branches. *(high melodic)* They are the many strands of the net from Buddha's hand that saves sinners. The willow branches are a memorial for those long-parted souls who were but dew on the grasses.

Act 4

—Scene 1
Tado Bay in Sanuki Province in Shikoku, less than a year later

GUNSUKE: (*spoken*) Listen up, everyone, this is a daimyo procession, out of the way! Brush everyone aside, clear the path. I'm one of Edo's finest Akasaka *yakko*, a footman, tough and with a *yakko* beard.[1] Swagger and push, lift and carry all day long, our work never done. The *bunbuku* tea kettle sprouted hair;[2] we shaved it with a tea whisk, but it wouldn't come off. Clear the way! No time to stoke the fires, no time for a cup of tea. Out of the way, I say! Leave it all to me.

NARRATOR: (*sung*) "All to me," he sings out as he heads for Sanuki Province and the temple at Mount Konpira.[3] This is Gunsuke with a long, showy sword; he is weathered and rough looking, penniless, and exhausted from his endless search for Master Umewaka. He remembers well the good old days when he wielded the seven accoutrements for accompanying a daimyo on procession.[4] Outside the gates of an inn where an entourage was staying, he would perform the *yakko* dance. At the castle gate, he once pranced in *yakko* style—now all these dances are performed along the streets just to earn a few coppers to get through the day. Gunsuke is weary, his hair in disarray, flying loose like the tall hawk-feather banner as he reaches Tado Bay, (*cadence*) looking a miserable sight.

(*sung*) He attracts the village children with his lively voice, and the crowd presses in.[5]

GUNSUKE: (*spoken*) *Yakko, yakko*, a footman am I, traveling the foothills, flogging sandals, all the price of a copper. (*sung*) Anyone want to see my tricks? (*spoken*) Yes, yes, you're a good lot, want to see my sandals, do you? Leave it to me. In general, we find three principal types and five secret elements.[6] First we have sandals with knots for a bridegroom on his first ceremonial visit to his wife's family and for the father when he visits his son-in-law's home. Then we've got especially fine sandals for gifts at New Years and the summer festival. (*sung*) Young men strut proudly with their girls, and gay boys wiggle their butts. Cherry blossoms are best double-petaled from Nara, the home of fine string sandals.⁷ Today's specials for the ladies have fancy, layered straps and brightly colored ties. I've got sandals for the sea, for mountains and rivers, some in leather, one for every taste. (*spoken*) Right now I'll show you the *yakko* dance. A horse's legs bounce up and down. My shins, too, are springs, up and down. (*cadence*) The sandals have springs, up and down, up and down. (*spoken*) I'll just strut over to the daimyo's gate, swagger like a dandy, legs spread wide, arms up at eye level. Strut here, strut there, and back again, here and there.

NARRATOR: (*sung*) As he moves about, he checks each child's face but doesn't see even a slight resemblance to young Umewaka. This fierce-looking ruffian's beard is wet with the dew of his tears. His arms weaken and his strength wanes; he collapses on the ground crying, "Nothing, nothing again," (*cadence*) a pitiful sight indeed.

(*sung*) The children all clap their hands.

CHILDREN: Look, look, the *yakko* is crying, crying.

NARRATOR: One after another, they all tickle him.

CHILDREN: One more dance. Do another one!

NARRATOR: They pester and tease him.

GUNSUKE: (*spoken*) What a rabble! I've wasted my time on you miserable kids, not even a copper for my song. Your jokes have gone too far. Don't come close, you brats, (*sung*) or you'll get a taste of this spear.

NARRATOR: He spins the spear, and they jump back in surprise.

CHILDREN: (*spoken*) You said you wouldn't dance for us, so now you're a lying *yakko*; we made you dance, you stupid *yakko*, moldy, (*sung*) hairy *yakko*!

NARRATOR: (*cadence*) They roar with laughter as they run home. (*sung*) Gunsuke's legs are weary from his long journey, but even more, his spirit is exhausted by worry. The breeze beckons him to sleep; he dreams with his eyes open.

GUNSUKE: (*spoken*) I'm too sleepy to go on. No date or destination pressing, no money to spend, but at least I can enjoy the benefits of this life and lie down for a nap and sleep until I wake.

NARRATOR: (*sung*) A huge stone covered with ivy serves as his pillow. As comfortable as on Chinese damask, with Kantan's pleasure pillow for his head,⁸ (*cadence*) he starts snoring as soon as he drops off.

(*sung*) Along comes another lone traveler, dressed as a *yamabushi* mountain priest but without his conch-shell horn. He whistles instead.

YAMABUSHI: (*spoken*) What kind of impudent fool have we got here! Sleeping right across a public road. What's he doing sleeping here? I get it. Maybe he's got something there. A sleeping thief is surely on to something. (*sung*) I'm done in after walking so far. I'll join him for a snooze.

NARRATOR: He goes over and snatches up the huge stone pillow with one hand as if it were a feather and lays it down for his bed. He stretches out his legs and falls asleep most contented. (*cadence*) His audacity is awesome.

(*sung*) After losing his pillow, Gunsuke wakes up but is still groggy and rubs his eyes.

GUNSUKE: What! I'll give this country friar a taste of my foot. I'll get the better of him and give him a fright.

NARRATOR: He kicks him aside and takes back the stone pillow, matching the priest's strength. A tree and a stone, both silently stubborn, (*cadence*) each aping the other. (*sung*) The *yamabushi* jumps up and claims the stone.

YAMABUSHI: (*spoken*) You blockhead, low-life scum of a *yakko*, who're you to invade my bedroom where I was peacefully sleeping alone? How dare you bother me without asking my permission! Why should I give this pillow to you?

NARRATOR: He stands up threateningly.

GUNSUKE: How about that? That's a good joke. The owner of this stone is the god of this mountain. I was the first to borrow it for a nap. How come it's yours? Even if you tie it down or pull it off me, you won't have it unless that funny cap of yours touches the ground as you beg for it. In any case, it's crazy of you to ask me to return something that's mine. Why did you take it from me?

YAMABUSHI: (*sung*) Watch this.

NARRATOR: And with a swift move he lifts the stone up over his head, spins it around, and tosses it to Gunsuke with one hand. Gunsuke catches it.

GUNSUKE: (*spoken*) This isn't much better than a child's trick. (*sung*) Over to you.

NARRATOR: He throws it back, and the huge stone goes back and forth, again and again. Like two children playing at shuttlecock or volleyball, they toss the boulder higher and higher, raising echoes that reach the Tsukuba mountain peak.[9] (*cadence*) The stone flies about like ice in a hailstorm.

NARRATOR: (*sung*) Gunsuke suddenly tires and realizes he's no match for the other's might and decides to defeat him with a trick. He puts on a smile and flatters the *yamabushi*.

GUNSUKE: Ha, ha ha. (*spoken*) Now Mr. Pilgrim Priest, I'm impressed. I thought no one in all Japan could keep up with me. But you have proved the better. I give up.

NARRATOR: He approaches, but the *yamabushi* bellows out.

YAMABUSHI: You won't catch me with that trick, Master Yakko. You want a fight? Then get ready.

NARRATOR: (*sung*) He draws his sword. Gunsuke answers, "What a good idea," and the two cross swords. (*fight music*) When Gunsuke strikes to the left, the other replies with the right; to the right, and he parries with the left. He slices across, but the other jumps over the blade. (*sung*) No matter where he strikes, the *yamabushi* is able to defend. Gunsuke, exhausted, panting, and covered with sweat, (*cadence*) is at his wit's end.

YAMABUSHI: (*spoken*) A fellow who draws his sword and doesn't draw blood shouldn't even carry a sword. (*sung*) Have you given up, boy?

NARRATOR: He moves closer, trying to shame him into fighting on.

GUNSUKE: (*spoken*) You're right. You're just too strong for me. Forgive me.

YAMABUSHI: How cowardly to admit defeat, especially for someone who serves at such a noble house. (*sung*) Is a fine man like Gunsuke going to give in so easily? Come on, Gunsuke, have a go at me.

NARRATOR: Gunsuke is shocked to hear his name called and is suspicious.

GUNSUKE: If you know my name is Gunsuke, then you must be the *tengu* goblin I've been seeking. You are the enemy of my lord; I've sworn on Mount Hira to avenge my lord's death. The gods of heaven have brought us together, and I won't let you fly away.

NARRATOR: He lunges and grabs the *yamabushi*'s sword by its hilt.

YAMABUSHI: (*spoken*) Pretty sharp! You're right that I'm one of those long-nosed goblins, but if I were a *tengu* from Mount Hira, do you think I would've wasted my time this long before tearing you to pieces? (*sung*) I don't have anything to do with them. I've seen you searching for your young master, wandering aimlessly all over the land, and decided to take pity and speak to you. Those you are looking for are not in the south or the west or the north, or in Shikoku at all. Hurry up and leave this place. (*high pitch*) You must head east, to Azuma. Now be off, Gunsuke, hurry!

NARRATOR: But Gunsuke doesn't trust him.

GUNSUKE: *(spoken)* You seem genuine enough, but your nose quivers like a liar's. You still must be angry. The young master must be in the west, so you drive me to the east. You won't fool me with your tricks. You don't make sense anyway. *(sung)* If you return the two boys, I'll spare your life. What'll it be?

NARRATOR: The *yamabushi* wrests his sword free; Gunsuke's arm has no strength left and refuses to move.

GUNSUKE: A disgrace! I wanted to tear the feathers from their roots and rip off your nose, but my strength is no match for you. I've failed miserably.

NARRATOR: He grinds his teeth in anger *(highest pitch)* and furiously stamps his feet, *(cadence)* crying his shame aloud.

YAMABUSHI: *(sung)* Oh admirable, most laudable! It is the curse of humans to be suspicious,[10] so you won't believe what I say. My reasoning may appear crooked, but you must be off on the road to the east.

NARRATOR: The more he speaks, the more stubborn Gunsuke becomes. He tries again and again to seize a chance to strike. Obstinate in the face of defeat, he struggles on, *(cadence)* but it is clear that the *tengu* is far too powerful.

YAMABUSHI: *(spoken)* You stubborn fool! Enough is enough. Be on your way.

GUNSUKE: Never! Give up. I'll never go.

YAMABUSHI: Do I really have to get rough before you'll go?

GUNSUKE: What did you have in mind? I like this idea. Show me what you can do.

NARRATOR: He remains defiant.

YAMABUSHI: *(sung)* Then it has to be done.

NARRATOR: The *yamabushi* flies up through the twilight mist into the clouds. *(nōchanting)* In an instant, he travels to the mountains, crushing boulders in his path; *(sung)* he raises a mighty *tengu* wind bending giant old trees in its path. Gunsuke prepares himself for its power and grabs hold of the earth. He clings to bushes, but the roots are upturned. He struggles but is lifted by the twisting wind and flies through the air, off to the east:[11] truly what the world calls a wind-blown tramp, *(scene cadence)*, a rolling stone, a wanderer with no fixed abode.

—Scene 2
"A Madwoman's Journey" to Azuma, the third month

HŌKAIBŌ: (*ballad style*) Shakyamuni performed purification rituals but was also father to his son Ragora.[12] The god Hotei was nurse to children. Enma,[13] guardian of hell, is godfather to demons. Here in the land of the rising sun, our patriarch is En no Gyōja,[14] who was bitter medicine for evil demons and devils. I myself am the famous Hōkaibō, curer of all ills. I conduct all-night rituals on auspicious days, offer prayers to welcome the moon rising on special days each month and services to cheer the god Daikoku[15]—to bring good fortune, long life, and health. I'll stand in for any priest or monk, perform any service, lead any festival. At the Kōshin Festival, your wish is my command.

NARRATOR: The *yamabushi* priest Hōkaibō wanders alone, following the flow of water and clouds, wherever his tired feet will carry him. (*cadence*) He arrives in Azuma,[16] far east of the capital.

HŌKAIBŌ: (*sung*) A pitiful woman, mad with grief for her long-lost child, (*spoken*) travels down the eastern road to Azuma. It hurts to see her in agony. I have accompanied her these last few days. Sometimes she imagines she sees him, falls into a craze, and collapses. I'll wait here and let her ask me about him. Maybe it will calm her heart.

NARRATOR: (*nō chanting*) Is it the mist in the air that brings the spring or the wild spray from racing waterfalls that spreads rumors of her madness?

HANJO: (*spoken*) Excuse me, kind traveler, have you by any chance seen a young boy of twelve or thirteen named Umewaka?[17] What, you haven't seen or heard of him? Even the swallow, nursed by its mother, flies the nest in summer. Although cherished by its mother, she cannot follow after it.[18] (*cadence*) We must not grieve or worry.

NARRATOR: (*sung*) Anxious thoughts, her beautiful long hair in disarray, tossed about like blossoms in strong winds,[19] she grasps a branch of bamboo grass and ties a prayer to it as an offering to the gods.

HANJO: Gods, oh gods, let me find him, please.

NARRATOR: Her prayers well up from the heart where bells chime to waken the gods. She has left the area of Mount Takashi between Mikawa and Ōmi, where the mists are thick, and has left her home far behind. For love of her child, she has braved the waves of the Ōi River.

FIGURE 23 The journey to Azuma; (right) the chanter, Takemoto Tanomo, seated next to the shamisen player, Takezawa Yashichi; (left) the puppets for Sōta as a *yamabushi* priest, and a "mad" Hanjo. The caption notes that this scene was a great success. Sōta was played by Kiritake Kanjūrō; Hanjo by Kiritake Sanemon. (*Futago Sumidagawa*, 1720, National Diet Library.)

(*emotional cadence*) Now deep in delusion, worried for her son, her legs weaken and (*cadence*), like wheels loosened from their bolts, refuse to move.

(*sung*) Hōkaibō has an idea.

HŌKAIBŌ: (*spoken*) The Buddha's teachings will help calm your heart. A heart possessed by the devil may be bewitched by the fox spirit as well. (*sung*) Let me say a prayer.

NARRATOR: He shakes his staff to rouse the gods from slumber.

HŌKAIBŌ:[20] Red *tengu*, white *tengu*, *tengu* with fancy silk, *yūzen*-dyed kimono, you're all marvelous, splendid. You're all invited to join us here. (*nō chanting*) First those from Mount Hiko in Tsukushi, where fervent prayers are answered at Shiō Temple.[21] In Sanuki they come from Matsuyama, (*cadence*) where the snow piles high on Shiro Peak. (*sung*) Next, from Hōki in Tottori, we have Mount Daisen. (*high pitch*) Near Kyoto, Tarōbō lives on Mount Atago.[22] On Mount Hira is Jirōbō. On the famous peak of Mount Hiei, the gods mete out favors to those who pray, giving hope to all that they will stand as tall as the pagoda near Yokawa Stream. On Mount Kazuragi, between Naniwa and Nara, is the highest peak, Mount Kongō, and even higher is Shaka Peak of Mount Ōmine in Yoshino.

NARRATOR: The mendicant monk, trained in ascetic practices,[23] sings his refrain as he dances wildly (*cadence*) and recites incantations.

HANJO: (*sung*) No wind to blow the wisteria. From Fujieda (Wisteria Branch), I drove my self to despair. Can't you see that I'm out on a limb, at my wit's end, (*cadence*) you foolish monk?

NARRATOR: (*sung*)[24] You're a friend used to the road, but to what can you entrust your heart here at Okabe where we seek a night's rest along this narrow, ivy-covered path winding through the Utsu Mountains? Our New Year's auspicious first dream was near Mount Fuji, there's none higher. We skip along the hills and mountains tossing the ball as we pass Mariko (Ball) and the shore at Okitsu (Sea), where kelp bends enticingly with the waves,[25] reminding us that we grow older with each wave as it breaks on the rocks at Yui and Kanbara. Now at Nago Estuary where the waters are deep, no word of him, nor at Hakone where Mount Fuji is hidden, and hidden is the view of my son whom I seek at Ōiso (To Meet), its name a lie, hateful as the town Kakego (Hide the Child). She begs the heavens and implores the earth to relieve her distress.[26]

Hōkaibō can only weep tears that glisten like dew (*cadence*) on his jewel-patterned robe. (*sung*) A heart lost for love thinks not of self or of others or of shame or of peering eyes.[27] Driven to despair, Hanjo falls deeper into madness.

HANJO: Look, my dearest child is there, over there!

NARRATOR: Matching summer kimono and floral-design scabbards suggest plum blossoms (Umewaka). The children dance gracefully, mimicking different things.

HANJO: I'll take a turn at dancing. Mendicant monk, sing the tune.

> Pass through the pines of Mio, through the pines of Mio.
> (*kudoki melody*)[28] The character pine [松] begins with a tree [木].[29]
> How many months and days since I have been a mad woman

able to play clever word games with characters.
No matter how witty, no one listens; it's like wind blowing in a horse's ear.
I look a sight to see, and mountain monk you, too, will be driven mad.
(*high pitch*) No hope for me, the sad heroine in an old tale.
In Naniwa's pleasure quarter we find the Kurumaya house.
I strove to be a courtesan, well respected;
(*high pitch*) my beauty like an angel's, a polished jewel,
many were the hands that pointed when I passed by.
Money we must have and (*high pitch*) tongues will wag.
Rather than fight against the slander, I'll give it all up, give up hope.
(*sung*) I'll give up all hope, (*cadence*) though it hurts me so.

(*song*) If not as far as China or India,

to the east is Tsugaru and the Ezo at Matsumae.
To the west is Kyushu, and the Bay of Satsuma.
To the south is Ki and the Bay of Kumano.
And in the deepest north is the road to Akita and Sado Island.
Shall I search the wilds where tigers sleep.
(*highest pitch*) Oh, my dearest Umewaka, dear Umewaka!

Her burning heart cries out in despair for the loss of her child. Farther east she travels with anxious heart over mountains with the mountain priest and through the young shoots of the Musashi plain, sleeping on the grass, colored deeply with the stain of madness, soaked with endless tears. She stops to rest, (*scene cadence*) to rest for a while.[30]

—Scene 3
Along the Sumida River, fifteenth day of the third month

NARRATOR: (*sung*) In late winter, the plum (*ume*) is the harbinger of spring, with its sweet blossoms peeking through the melting snow. Left alone in this fickle world after the death of her husband, (*cadence*) Karaito is a lonely widow, without even a home to take care of. (*tataki melody*) Cast into the waves, she has grown accustomed to the oar that guides her alone through this harsh life. Her task is to ferry travelers across the

106 *Twins at the Sumida River*

FIGURE 24 Bunraku puppet of Hanjo on her "mad" journey.

Sumida River, so well known in poetry. (*sung*) Her departed husband was taken to the other shore by Buddha's ferryman, but she remains in this world on the shores of the Sumida, which courses the plains of Musashi and Shimōsa.[31] This life and hell are distinct, but her suffering is the same as she ferries back and forth.

KARAITO: Weary pilgrim, let me ferry you across.

NARRATOR: (*cadence*) She guides her boat to the shore. (*sung*) Wandering distraught, searching for her child, Umewaka's mother[32] Lady Hanjo has left the *yamabushi* priest to search alone for her son, though with no idea where to look. A parent will travel to the ends of the earth for love of a child, never able to forget him. Her sleeves stained with tears, (*cadence*) she arrives at the Sumida River.

NARRATOR: (*sung*) The ferryman welcomes the traveler.

KARAITO: What has happened? You look upset. (*spoken*) Have you such worries? How pitiful you look! If you wish to cross the river, I'll gladly row you across. Quick, please come aboard.

HANJO: Though both of this same world, how different are our hearts. I ask you to ferry me to the other shore, but how insensitive you are, ferryman, to say that since I am a mad woman speaking the cadences of a

FIGURE 25 Nakamura Ganjirō III (Senjaku) as Hanjo; Sawamura Tanosuke as Sōta's wife, Karaito. From a 1986 kabuki performance. (*Courtesy of Nakamura Ganjirō* III.)

court lady, you want me to perform some crazy antics for you before you'll take me across. (*sung*) How horrible, you ferryman of the Sumida River. The day is growing dark. Why will you not allow me on board? To refuse is to go against your trade. You bumpkin. I was about to shame you with language of this sort, but you immediately welcome me aboard. Such a gentle person! How delightful. (*nō chanting*) My tortured heart seeks to know if my lost child is alive or dead. But I have no idea where he is, and so if I were to meet him, the cause of my madness would disappear. Your boat is small, but please let me come on board and ferry me across. (*cadence*) I beg of you, kind ferryman.

KARAITO: (*sung*) Indeed, the poet Narihira composed a verse on this spot. "Are you true to your name, Miyako (Capital) bird? (*emotional cadence*) I ask of you, (*high pitch*) is my love alive or no more?" I, too, would like to ask things of someone from the capital, of those I knew long ago, but no one else from Kyoto passes through here. Be careful as you board.

NARRATOR: Karaito helps her on to the boat and casts off. How deep is the link between lord and subject, (*high pitch*) deeper than the oar touching bottom. Little do they know of their past connection (*cadence*) as the boat drifts away from the shore into the current.

HANJO: (*spoken*) May I ask you, woman ferryman, those trees, a pine and a willow, aligned over a memorial tablet. Is there a story attached to it? Please tell me about it.

NARRATOR: The ferryman breaks into tears.

KARAITO: Strange that you don't ask about the other famous sites, that your eyes alight only on the grave. There must be some connection. (*sung*) Let me tell you what I know before we reach the shore. One stone marks the grave of a sinner who died seeking forgiveness. (*emotional cadence*) Please pray for both of the deceased.

(*spoken*) He was a man who lived in this area, although he was originally a samurai who served a courtier family. He lost his heart to a courtesan and went crazy for her, finally stealing money from his lord. He was punished with banishment. (*sung*) He and his wife arrived here in the east hoping to find a new life. They lived near the river, along the other shore. The courtesan knew nothing of weaving or sewing or of cleaning or cooking. Her husband could not make a living as a soldier and knew nothing of commerce or keeping accounts. (*cadence*) Desperate to survive, (*sung*) he, sadly, fell into trafficking in stolen children. How many thousands of parents he must have saddened! As his punishment, the cries of all the parents of the lost children mounted and mounted (*emotional cadence*) and crushed him like the weight of heaven.

(*spoken*) It was last year on the fifteenth of the third month that he finally killed himself, and that pine stands as a memorial at his grave. How our karma comes again to haunt us. (*sung*) Today is the first anniversary of his death. It will be so awful to tell you the story of the grave under the willow. (*spoken*) He was a young boy of eleven or twelve brought up in the capital who was kidnapped by a slave trader, who sold him to another. The poor boy was exhausted from his terrible journey. He was taunted as being a coward, a lazy wastrel, and he finally fell victim to the trader's cane, which cut him to the bone. Was he fated from a former life? Just as it seemed the end, (*song*) he spoke in a feeble voice, hurting from the blows: (*highest pitch*) "I am from the capital but will now become dust far away in Azuma. (*high pitch*) My mother knows nothing of my fate and wastes away pitifully, (*cadence*) anxiously waiting for my return. (*sung*) I long to be in the protective shadow of the arms of those I love in the capital." These were his last words before taking his final rest. His parting wish was for a willow tree to be planted over his grave. (*spoken*) The tragedy of it all is that the slaver who killed him was a former retainer of the child's family. Although he knew nothing of this connection, he committed a crime against heaven, killing his own master, the worst of all crimes. He then took his own life on the spot, and the other grave is his. (*sung*) I am ashamed even to tell this tale, for I was that slaver's wife, (*emotional cadence*) a terrible fate to be the wife of an evil murderer, reviled by everyone.

(*sung*) Compared with this life of misery, to die and trust in Buddha's mercy is my wish. Yet I live on as an insignificant drop of water, a flower on a branch. No one else is left to offer prayers for the souls of my lord, my husband. I offer at least the kindness in my heart to travelers who board my boat seeking the Way, ferrying them across for no charge. My Lady, if you are from the capital, then please offer a prayer at the foot of that willow tree. Oh, I am sorry to have troubled you with such a tragic tale. We have arrived. Please get off with care.

NARRATOR: (*emotional cadence*) Although she speaks strongly, she collapses in grief, (*cadence*) weeping, oblivious of others.
HANJO: (*sung*) Could you tell me the name of the boy in this tale?
KARAITO: (*spoken*) His name was Umewaka.
HANJO: And the boy's father?
KARAITO: Lord Yoshida no Yukifusa.
HANJO: (*sung*) Then that was my son. You said he's buried beneath that mound? I wish to see his face.
NARRATOR: (*scene cadence*) She leaps from the boat as if she had wings and rushes madly to the spot.

—Scene 4
The same, at the grave of Umewaka

NARRATOR: (*sung*) She runs up the bank and hugs the mound.
HANJO: (*highest pitch*) Dearest Umewaka, it's your mother. How could you

leave me alone to suffer in despair for you! Did you hate me? How terrible, yet what a relief to find you again. Is it all just an awful dream?

NARRATOR: She throws herself down at the foot of the willow tree, collapsing in a flood of tears on the mound, (*light cadence*) her cries reaching the heavens.

KARAITO: (*sung, highest pitch*) Then you are his mother, Lady Hanjo. The slave trader was Awaji no Shichirō Toshikanu. I am his wife, Karaito. To pay for his crime, after telling you about Master Umewaka's death, (*highest pitch*) although we were formerly enemies in the last life, let me serve you as my master in this life.

NARRATOR: Lady Hanjo only responds with more tears, (*cadence*) which flow like rain filling the Sumida River.

KARAITO: (*sung*) Your grief is only natural, (*spoken*) but a parent's tears can provoke fires of attachment and destroy the child's merits.[33] Today is auspicious, the anniversary of his death. Say a prayer for the young master's soul. (*sung*) I, too, shall pray for the salvation of my husband's sinful soul. They say the Buddha's light reaches into all corners of the universe and that Amida never casts aside any who pray to him. Prayers to Amida will be the staff that supports us and the pillars of the bridge that will lead them to salvation in the next life.

NARRATOR: She hands Hanjo the bells, but she takes neither bell nor hammer and only stares blankly at the willow tree on the memorial mound.

HANJO: Until now, it was hope of seeing him that gave my heart the strength to search for him far east of the capital in Azuma. Now all I have is his remains, (*emotional cadence*) marked by a willow on a mound. (*sung*) How cruel! Drawn by the specter of death, he left his birthplace and went far away (*highest pitch*) to the east, and now he is just dust on the wayside. Must he be just (*high pitch*) dirt for travelers to kick! Poor Umewaka (*cadence*) won't reach the next life. (*sung*) What a pitiful fate. (*highest pitch*) Such a cruel memorial!

NARRATOR: She pounds the earth, writhing in despair, raising her voice in cries of grief.

KARAITO: This is all because of my husband's crime. Please forgive us.

NARRATOR: Tortured by the truth, (*cadence*) she too falls to the ground and weeps aloud, a sight to pity.

HANJO: (*sung*) For my child's salvation.

NARRATOR: She takes up the hammer and strikes the bell while reciting.
HANJO: May Amida who fills all the universe lead Umewaka to the Western Paradise. (*Both*) Namu Amida Butsu. Namu Amida Butsu, All Praise to Amida. (*low pitch*) Namu Amida Butsu. (*spoken*) Just now, Karaito, didn't you hear the voice of a child faintly chanting? It surely was Umewaka! Didn't you hear it coming from the mound?
KARAITO: It's just as you said, I heard a voice from inside the mound. I'll stop chanting. You chant again alone.
NARRATOR: (*sung*) The wind and waves of the Sumida grow calm.
UMEWAKA: Namu Amida Butsu, Namu Amida Butsu, Namu Amida Butsu.
HANJO: What joy to hear his voice again, my little bird from the capital. Let me hear it once again.
UMEWAKA: (*high pitch*) Namu Amida Butsu, Namu Amida Butsu, Namu Amida Butsu.
NARRATOR: A figure emerges from the shade of the willow, the shadow of a child.
HANJO: (*highest pitch*) Umewaka, is that my child?
NARRATOR: She rushes to hold him, but the shadow fades away. She stops and it steadies, then fades again. They see him again, but he disappears like foam on the Sumida River. (*cadence*) Only the soft sound of the spring wind remains in the willow branches. (*sung*) How pitiful! Lady Hanjo seems to have breathed her last, on the verge of death.
HANJO: If I can never see him alive again, (*highest pitch*) then I will grieve until I see him in the next life. And then I'll grieve no more.
NARRATOR: She goes to the top of the riverbank ready to cast her life away. Just then, a cloud appears and a voice cries out, "Wait, wait a moment!" (*scene cadence*) which strikes her like an arrow.
NARRATOR: (*sung*) A *tengu* goblin appears on the cloud. His right arm holds Matsuwaka whom he leads down from the clouds.
TENGU: You do not know me. I am Awaji no Shichirō Toshikanu, who entered the realm of black magic as my dying wish in order to repay the kindness of my lord. I took the form of a *yamabushi* mountain priest and consoled Lady Hanjo on her journey. (*spoken*) To ease her pain and free her from grief over Umewaka, I had Matsuwaka appear as Umewaka's spirit. As a twin brother, he was the same in your eyes. (*sung*) Rejoice

FIGURE 26 (Right) Karaito ferries Hanjo across the Sumida River; (left) Sōta, as a *tengu*, brings Matsuwaka to Hanjo. (*Futago Sumidagawa*, 1720, National Diet Library.)

> that Matsuwaka is safe; let him console you in your grief for the other. I return Matsuwaka, who was stolen by the great *tengu* of Mount Hira.
>
> NARRATOR: Hanjo wonders whether it is a dream as she runs (*highest pitch*) to embrace him.
>
> HANJO: Is it really Matsuwaka?
>
> MATSUWAKA: Is that mother?
>
> NARRATOR: It's as if he had returned from the dead. As much chance of meeting as a blind turtle finding a floating log or seeing the Indian udumbara blossom[34]—(*cadence*) how deep their ties.
>
> (*sung*) Just then the *tengu* disappears in a roar of fire and smoke over the field.
>
> TENGU: Follow my path. It will lead the way to Master Matsuwaka's success.
>
> NARRATOR: All gaze in the direction of the voice from the sky. Depending on it to guide them, they follow him, setting off again for the capital.

Truly it is as they say: in essence, the devil and the Buddha are the same. The demon's heart is pure and clear[35] as a warrior of unwavering spirit, whose loyalty and duty remain to serve in this world. The young Umewaka, dew on a leaf, has gone before his parent. Alone on the seas, Hanjo and Karaito, their husbands dead, are lost in thoughts that roam with no home in sight. They trust in prayers to Amida, *(high pitch)* "Namu Amida, Namu Amida Butsu." Now only voices of times long past, still heard today through the writer's brush, whose words bring tears to all those who listen to the tale of Sumida River.

Act 5

Autumn of the same year, along the banks of the Kita-Shirakawa River

NARRATOR: (*sung*) Arrogance is the disease of fools; it brings its own calamity. Through clever deceit, Hitachi no Daijō Momotsura has managed to take over the Yoshida estate and guards it with a ruthless and haughty will, afraid of none, an eagle higher than all. Early in autumn, along the shallow Kita-Shirakawa River, he hosts a show of fireworks to light the night sky and paint a Chinese brocade on the river, accompanied by a grand banquet. Canvas walls on the banks blow gently in the wind, enclosing a feast of the best food and wine. Momotsura lords over all, mountain and river, (*cadence*) his expression proud and patronizing. (*sung*) His senior councillor Ban no Tōnai sits to his left, in front of all of Momotsura's allies from near and far. Everyone excitedly awaits dusk and the beginning of (*entrance cadence*) the fireworks display.

(*sung*) With the help of the *tengu* goblin, the Yoshida household has swiftly returned to the capital. As part of the plan to overcome their enemy Momotsura. Lady Hanjo and Karaito disguise themselves as peddlers of fireworks, covering their faces with purple veils (*cadence*) like the gypsy women they saw in Shimōsa in the east.

KARAITO: (*sung*) Fireworks, anyone for fireworks?

NARRATOR: With torches in hand, they brazenly approach the banquet.

HANJO: (*spoken*) This type is called the "Falling Star." It can be thrown into water or into clouds, used in a myriad ways. (*sung*) Let me show you.

NARRATOR: Hanjo inserts the lighted fuse into the rocket but instead of a firework, a bullet shoots straight at the unsuspecting Tōnai, piercing his flesh; (*cadence*) blood splatters among the smoke, and he dies.

(*sung*) Momotsura is shocked.

MOMOTSURA: Kill those villains!

NARRATOR: All the guards draw their swords at once and surround the pair. Into the fray jump Takekuni and Gunsuke.

TAKEKUNI: (*spoken*) We are the family and retainers of the late Yoshida no

FIGURE 27 (Top right) The imperial messenger grants the Yoshida estate to Matsuwaka; (bottom) Momotsura is killed; (left) fireworks display. The text notes that this was a great success. (*Futago Sumidagawa*, 1720, National Diet Library.)

SHŌSHŌ YUKIFUSA. We have imperial sanction to impose punishment on Momotsura. (*sung*) Let no one escape.

NARRATOR: They slash to left and right, (*fight-scene cadence*) (*highest pitch*) cutting down all before them.

TAKEKUNI: (*sung*) Our enemies are vanquished!

NARRATOR: Their faces fill with joy. Then Lord Ōe no Masafusa leads in Matsuwaka.

MASAFUSA: His Highness has decreed that Matsuwaka shall inherit the Yoshida estate.

NARRATOR: All bow their heads in acceptance of the title (*cadence*) and rejoice at their success.

HANJO: (*sung*) Lord Masafusa, (*spoken*) we can never express fully our gratitude for your efforts. Let me at least offer a splendid show of fireworks (*sung*) for your pleasure.

NARRATOR: (*cadence*) She prepares to set off a grand finale of bursting light and sound. (*sung*) First,[36] to celebrate the bountiful "Five Grain Harvest" and peace in the realm, we have the elegant firework "Jeweled Screen," named after Ono no Komachi's poem.[37] Fancy courtier carriages may lead us to dead ends, as in the case of poor gentleman Fukakusa, who failed in his vain pursuit of Komachi for one hundred nights.[38] (*popular song*) Rumors float along the Yodo River where lovers await a rendezvous—where the "Water Wheel" fireworks churn round and round.[39] Up and down, round and round they go. (*sung*) This Floating World is full of jealousy, which turns on the wheels of rumor,[40] powerful as the next firework "Asagao," which blossoms like the morning glory along the bamboo fence, shining amid the dew. (*cadence*) What a magnificent sight to behold!

(*sung*) The firework "Rowing among the Fallen Blossoms" recalls Saigyō's poem and evokes the elegance of "sleeping on the waves."[41] Violet banners grace the deck and orchids line the helm, a brocade of light showers the fireworks boat, glittering in scarlets of deepest hue. All sing in chorus an auspicious ferryman's song. We all are children of the gods at the summer festival.[42] The waves glow with color, and the shores are alight with welcoming lanterns. Festive melodies enliven the crowds and entertain the deities as they are transported to the festival site. Bells and drums beat the rhythm to welcome the god of Tenmangu Shrine. The river's surface, a tapestry of shining colors, highlights the dancers' many turns. Like the opening of a painted fan, the Shirakawa River becomes a delight to the eye, as is young Matsuwaka, now restored as lord of the Yoshida estate. He is youth with its eternal promise, a young pine[43] evergreen, ready to flourish through endless autumns and springs. We conclude with a celebration of peace and prosperity throughout the realm.

(Postscript) *Seven-line, large-print, pirate versions of our jōruri plays have been circulating, published as if they were the Takemoto Theater's authorized editions. Because these are copies, mistakes are numerous, in both the musical notation and the words themselves. Since these are not authorized editions, we have decided to have new blocks carved for the printing of a new edition in the seven-line format by the publisher Yamamoto Kuemon Harushige in Osaka. And responding to the requests of* many, we mark this by the official seal of Takemoto Chikugonojō,[44] representing the Takemoto Theater.

(Name and seal of) *Takemoto Chikugonojō*
Authorized publisher (shōhonya) Yamamoto Kuhei
Yamamoto Kuemon, Kōraibashi Itchōme, Osaka (seal)

Lovers Pond in Settsu Province

(*Tsu no kuni meoto ike*)

First performed in the second month of 1721 when Chikamatsu was sixty-nine years old, *Lovers Pond in Settsu Province*[1] followed three months after what many consider to be his best "contemporary-life" play, *Love Suicides at Amijima*,[2] and six months after his first murderer-hero play, *Twins at the Sumida River*. The title places the tale in the greater Osaka area and refers specifically to act 3. The full title of *Lovers Pond* includes the phrase "chapter 48 of the *Go-Taiheiki*,"[3] which in reality doesn't exist, suggesting to his audience both that Chikamatsu is setting the story in the mid-1500s and that he has written a new fictional chapter to the saga of the final days of the Ashikaga shogunate. His audience understood this convention to mean that the drama was about contemporary Japan. As with *Love Suicides at Amijima*, a major theme is personal responsibility for one's actions. This is evident both in the public sphere of government and, in act 3, at the private level.

Another theme, suggested by the reference to *Go-Taiheiki*, is criticism of corruption and incompetence in rulers and their ministers. The *Go-Taiheiki* is known for its severe condemnation of those in power, blaming them for the fall of the Ashikaga and the civil wars of the sixteenth century that followed. The author's view, as expressed in chapter 41, was extremely bleak after Oda Nobunaga (1534–82) withdrew his support for the last Ashikaga shogun Yoshiaki (1536–65): "If those above are corrupt, then those below will use slander and threats to gain power."[4]

The power of eros—passion and lust—to overwhelm ordinary individuals as well as those in important public positions is a major underlying theme in the dramas of Chikamatsu's mature period.

In *Lovers Pond*, the actions of two men drive the play forward to destructive ends. Some twenty-two years earlier, long before the story begins, a young samurai, Bunjibei, killed his friend in order to marry the friend's wife. His crime was never discovered, and we meet him for the first time in act 3, retired from active service and living in Settsu Province near Osaka Bay with his wife, who has no idea that Bunjibei is the murderer of her former husband. Circumstances force him to admit his crime of long ago, which leads to tragedy. The catalyst is the noble actions of his son and long-lost daughter, who decide to kill themselves after discovering that they are a couple living in incest as brother and sister.

The second man is Shogun Yoshiteru, whom Chikamatsu creates as the epitome of a dissolute and capricious ruler who brings down a dynasty. In act 2, Yoshiteru has become entranced by the charms of the courtesan Ōyodo, whom he brings into his palace to be his official wife, ordering his own wife to be murdered. For Ōyodo's pleasure, moreover, he has his other women cut to pieces before her eyes. His palace reaches frenzies of depravity, culminating in an insurrection led by the supposedly loyal minister Chōkei, who has schemed all along to lead the shogun to lose himself to lust. Yoshiteru and Ōyodo are killed, and the Ashikaga Palace is overrun and razed to the ground. Animal metaphors link the three elements of Bunjibei's murder of his friend, his children's unwitting incest, and Yoshiteru's violent lust.

Chikamatsu refers several times to the *Taiheiki* historical tale and to Chinese sources on the dangers of a ruler's falling under the power of a woman's charms. A particularly important source is book 4 of the *Taiheiki*,[5] which contains a section on the fall of a Chinese dynasty caused by the lust and depravity of the ruler. The section begins with two quotations from the Confucian *Analects*: "The resolute man and the man of virtue do not prize life at the expense of virtue; rather will they destroy their bodies to achieve virtue." "He who sees what is right and fails to act is lacking in manhood."[6] These sentiments echo one of the play's themes: those in service to rulers must speak up and act when wrongs are committed.

In the Tokugawa system, with the shogun (or daimyo within a fief) seen as the supreme figure, beyond criticism, these ideas are crucial to effective governance. In *Lovers Pond*, no one, woman or man, is able to rebuke Shogun Yoshiteru for his actions, and this is the cause of the Ashikaga downfall. Only the loyal but impetuous and lowly figure Kanemori directly confronts the shogun's authority. However, like Umegae in act 2, who is unable to direct her anger at Shogun Yoshiteru, in act 1 even Kanemori is silenced by an admonition from him. In act 4, Kanemori resigns from Yoshiaki's (Keigaku's) service in despair and attacks his former master, demanding that he give up the tonsure and return to restore the Ashikaga shogunate. Although he is a relatively minor character, Kanemori's act of confronting the wrongdoing of those in power occurs at crucial moments in the play. Chikamatsu clearly portrays him as noble and heroic, the kind of brash, no-nonsense figure who is anathema to a bureaucracy.

The second essential section of the *Taiheiki* to which Chikamatsu alludes is from book 37, the tale of three ascetic priests who, despite their reputation for self-discipline, each fall prey to a woman's charm and into dissipation. The overwhelming power of carnal desire affects even older, self-disciplined priests; but its force is even more evident among young men or rulers, who have their choice of any beautiful woman they desire. Although historians consider Yoshiteru to have been a competent shogun at a time when Ashikaga power was weak, Chikamatsu deliberately portrays him as the stereotypical example of the corrupt ruler, blind to all but his own lust. Commentators have noted similarities to the story of the Forty-Seven Rōnin ("Chūshingura") vendetta, especially during the final attack on the villain Chōkei's residence in act 5, which is motivated by personal revenge. Since the Tokugawa considered themselves to be of the same Genji lineage as the Ashikaga shoguns, Chikamatsu is clearly, as in other period plays, discussing the contemporary Tokugawa system with its actual and potential corruption.

As in *Twins at the Sumida River*, allusions throughout the play support the overall themes, with references to at least twenty nō plays; but in contrast to *Sumida River*, *Lovers Pond* also has strong echoes of Chinese philosophy and poetry, as well as Japanese battle tales describing power struggles for political hegemony. Aside from the *Go-Taiheiki* and *Taiheiki*, we see allusions to *The Tale of Heike*, *The Tale of Yoshitsune* (*Gikeiki*), *The Tale of the Soga Brothers*, *The Tale of Genji*, and *Essays in Idleness*, playing on the themes of public and private greed, obsessive desire, and cunning deception. The Chinese references are to *The Analects*, *Chuang Tzu*, *The Book of Odes*, *Tales of Representative Women* (*Lie Nü Zhuan*), *The Book of History* (*Shiji*), and Chinese poems with an overtly political edge. The example of Emperor Zhou (ca. 1100 B.C.), the last of the Yin dynasty—as recorded in *The Book of History*—book 3, is a model for Shogun Yoshiteru. The following is a summary of his reign:

Emperor Zhou was naturally quick witted and sharp, able to judge matters quickly and accurately, a figure superior in talent and physical strength. He was known to kill animals bare-handed and was able to deflect deftly any criticism of his actions. But he was arrogant and thought everyone to be beneath him. He loved his mistress Daji and would do anything to please her. He had wild music composed and performed and overburdened the populace with heavy taxes to support the extravagant orgies held in his fabulous palace. He would have his men and women strip naked in the huge garden and chase each other among the trees. He came to be hated by his subjects, but to control them he made the punishments more severe. One of his minister's daughters came to be his wife but she hated such wild dissipation, and so Zhou killed her and her father, pickling his body in salt. Another minister also chastised Zhou but he, too, was killed and hung up to dry, like meat on a stick. In the end, a successful uprising cornered Zhou, who put on his finest garments and dived into the raging fire. Daji, too, was killed.[7]

The allusions here present an undercurrent of sharp criticism of the political corruption and extravagance that lead to instability and suffering for those below. An important element of this criticism is the demand that ministers act to stop the corruption of those above and that those below take the initiative to rebuke those in positions of power if they abuse their authority.

As with all period plays, the plot moves on two levels: the public and the private. Most of the drama is focused on two historical shoguns, Yoshiteru and Yoshiaki, and their ministers. The tragedy in act 3, however, invariably involves figures from the lower social level and usually bears directly on the development of the play. Here, act 3, the centerpiece and climax of the whole play, has been criticized as not being related to the overall plot.[8] That is, the tragedies of Bunjibei and his wife do not directly affect the drama overall. Rather, the link is at the level of theme: the destructive power of obsessive passion and lust. In this sense, Bunjibei can be usefully considered alongside Sōta, the murderer in *Twins at the Sumida River*. Even after more than two decades, Bunjibei is unable to escape the consequences of his crime, and his story recalls that of Natsume Sōseki's famous novel, *Kokoro* (1914). Six months after *Lovers Pond*, Chikamatsu's third and final murderer-hero work, *Woman-Killer and the Hell of Oil*[9] (1721), was performed, completing his series of three murderer plays.[10]

Lovers Pond was immediately performed in kabuki and was revived later on the jōruri stage as well, but it has not been performed in modern times.

Like the other plays translated in this book, *Lovers Pond* remained in print over the centuries. Act 4 seems to have been a great success for its fantastic theatricality and sophisticated stage props, which recreated the Ashikaga Palace in all its glory in a dreamlike sequence complete with vengeful ghosts. As with act 4 in the other period plays, the text encourages the director to push theatricality to the limits, using all the technical resources available to create a musical-dance drama.

Act 3 is intensely realistic theater which probes individual psychology. The voices of tragedy reach an aria-like crescendo riding the music of the shamisen, but the stage action is almost static and inward; the spectator has to see into the minds of the characters trapped by both circumstance and their own deliberate actions. Act 4, in Gidayū's scheme, has to contrast and to please the eye as well as the ear of the audience, leading them from the depths of tragedy through the hell of vengeance up to the realm of hope in act 5.

Lovers Pond in Settsu Province

(*Tsu no kuni meoto ike*)

CAST OF CHARACTERS[1]

Shogunate

Lord Yoshiteru: the Ashikaga shogun, portrayed as the epitome of a bad ruler at the end of a dynasty, driven by lust and unable to distinguish between trustworthy ministers and villains.
Lady Yoshiteru: official wife of shogun.
Ōyodo: a courtesan who becomes the wife of the shogun, supplanting Lady Yoshiteru.
Hatsuyuki: in service to the shogun and Lady Yoshiteru.
Shiragiku: in service to the shogun and Lady Yoshiteru.
Umegae: in service to the shogun and Lady Yoshiteru.
Lord Yoshiaki: younger brother of Yoshiteru. He takes the name Sankaibō (and later Keigaku) when he takes the tonsure. He is a conscientious individual who tries to save the Ashikaga shogunate.

Ministers

Fujitaka (Asakawa Sakyō no Dayū Fujitaka): loyal senior minister of the shogun.
Chōkei (Miyoshi Nyūdō Chōkei [Nagayoshi]): scheming senior minister who tries to overthrow the shogun.
Kuninaga (Awaji no Kami Kuninaga): Chōkei's son, in the mold of his father.
Iwanari Chikara: in league with Chōkei. He is the foster father of Kiyotaki.

Matsunaga Danjō Hisahide: one of Chōkei's retainers.

Kanemori (Kaijō Tarō Kanemori): a low-ranking official whose mother nursed Yoshiaki and him at the same time; therefore he is a loyal Ashikaga supporter. A brash, loyal, and strong figure, found in most of Chikamatsu's history plays.

Reizei Family

Bunjibei (Reizei Nagafusa Bunjibei): foster father of Mikinoshin and natural father of Kiyotaki. He is the protagonist of act 3. He lives near Osaka Bay, retired from the world.

Wife: wife of Bunjibei, natural mother of Kiyotaki, and foster mother of Mikinoshin.

Mikinoshin (Reizei Mikinoshin): foster son of Bunjibei and his wife, in service to Fujitaka.

Kiyotaki: natural daughter of Bunjibei and his wife, in service to Lady Yoshiteru. Foster daughter of Iwanari Chikara.

Act 1

—Scene 1
Muromachi shogunal palace in Kyoto, early spring in the middle of second month, 1564

NARRATOR:

(*prelude*) Blossoms elicit smiles of delight, but soon wither and fall.
Painted eyes loved dearly vanish with the moon at dawn.
Birds rejoice in conjugal play;
A gentle ruler cherishes his wife;
His subjects are at peace, the realm stable.[2]

Under the reign of Emperor Ōgimachi, the Japanese islands are ruled by the thirteenth Ashikaga shogun, minister of the left of the first rank, the great shogun Minamoto no Ason, Lord Yoshiteru.[3] His ancestor is Lord Takauji, from whose line he inherited the title. He rules the nation, keeping it free of the four evils,[4] and makes his residence in Kyoto in the Second Ward at Muromachi. (*cadence*) There he maintains the five virtues.[5]

(*sung*) The wife of the shogun, Lady Yoshiteru, is the daughter of Ōmiya no Dainagon, Lord Akitada. She has been with child since the winter of last year and is now five months pregnant. On this day, in the middle of the second month, the ceremony of tying the maternal obi is to be held. All daimyo resident in the capital have arrived for the auspicious occasion. On the right sits the commander of the four Imperial Guard Regiments, Awaji no Kami Kuninaga, heir of Miyoshi Chōkei Nyūdō[6] and now retired to live as a lay priest; to the left sits first the shogunal councillor, Asakawa Sakyō no Dayū Fujitaka,[7] and then the officers Kyōgoku, Hatakeyama, Niki, Akamatsu, Kira, and Ōdachi. Farther back sit the daimyo lords, the long-standing traditional allies of the shogunate, and finally, those paying homage from distant provinces. All sit hushed and orderly before His Highness according to rank, (*cadence*) joined auspiciously together in celebration of birth and longevity.

(*sung*) The shogun sits on a raised platform behind the bamboo blinds. The blinds are raised a little, and he moves forward to propose the celebratory toast when a messenger announces:

MESSENGER: (*spoken*) The father-in-law of His Highness, Lord Ōmiya no Dainagon Akitada, has arrived (*sung*) on service from His Majesty.

NARRATOR: Miyoshi no Kuninaga addresses the shogun.

KUNINAGA: (*spoken*) What a strange moment for an imperial messenger! Impossible to guess what his mission is. Although Lord Ōmiya is a relative, he has arrived on official court business, and so it is proper for the shogun to step down from the dais.

NARRATOR: No reply from the shogun.

KUNINAGA: (*sung*) Should we not raise the blinds fully?

NARRATOR: But still no reply as the shogun seems to squirm in discomfort. Lord Ōmiya's arrival is announced. Kuninaga jumps up to raise the blinds and is shocked to see that in place of Shogun Yoshiteru sits his younger brother Yoshiaki.[8] Kuninaga, although dressed in full formal court dress, rises up like a general taking command.

KUNINAGA: (*spoken*) What is this deception? What devilry in this fake shogun!

NARRATOR: (*sung*) He grabs Yoshiaki and pulls him down, (*cadence*) and all, from Fujitaka downward, express shock and disbelief. (*sung*) Everyone moves aside to allow in the imperial envoy. Fujitaka steps forward to speak.

FUJITAKA: (*spoken*) His Highness Yoshiteru has been indisposed with a cold since last night, and because he is still ill, Yoshiaki was asked to represent the shogun to the imperial messenger.

NARRATOR: (*sung*) His reasonable explanation calms the gathering.

YOSHIAKI: (*spoken*) Could you then please announce the message, and I shall relay it to my elder brother, Yoshiteru.

NARRATOR: Lord Ōmiya straightens his kimono.

ŌMIYA: Recently a two-headed turtle was found in Lake Biwa by some fishermen who then presented it to the emperor. In ancient China when Emperor Fuxi took the throne, sacred white turtles and magical horses appeared,[9] and since then, such auspicious happenings have been common. In our court during the reigns of Genshō [715–24] and Shōmu [724–49], and in the Ōei [1394–1427] and Meiō [1492–1500] eras, there were reports of strange turtles appearing more than six times. Sometimes era names were changed to suit the occasion such as "Reiki" (turtle spirit) and "Shingi" (sacred turtle), (*sung*) but we have no previous reports of two-headed turtles either here or from other lands.[10] The learned houses of Sugawara, Kiyohara, Abe, and Urabe have all been consulted, but their reports to the court have been inconclusive. His Majesty has ordered that the shogun's officials must determine whether the omen is good or ill. You are therefore ordered to view the turtle and (*cadence*) judge for His Majesty.

NARRATOR: (*sung*) Fujitaka moves forward and opens the box, and there truly sits before them one body with two heads fighting each other for food. It looks like some mythical two-headed bird. Yoshiaki, Kuninaga, and Fujitaka all clap their hands in disbelief.

FUJITAKA: (*spoken*) If the courtier scholars were unable to determine its significance, then it is not possible for simple, untutored soldiers to judge (*sung*) whether it is fortuitous or bodes ill.

NARRATOR: They all seem at a loss, but Lord Ōmiya intervenes.

ŌMIYA: (*spoken*) The shogun Yoshiteru is ill disposed, and we cannot expect a response immediately. (*sung*) It would not be polite to press him to answer while he is recovering.

NARRATOR: He rises and (*scene cadence*) is escorted respectfully to the main gate.

NARRATOR: (*sung*) Yoshiaki moves to return behind the blinds but is held back by Kuninaga.

KUNINAGA: (*spoken*) Younger brother of His Highness, rice is a treasure that nourishes human life, but rice stalks are used to make sandals. Although rice and stalk come from the same root, it is heaven's natural way that the stalk does not ape the rice. No matter if you are his younger brother, to wear his formal robes and take the official shogun seat on the dais and brandish your power in front of all the daimyo is nothing other than an insurrection! The two-headed tortoise signals to all that brother against brother are struggling for the throne and an uprising will follow. (*sung*) It is undoubtedly an oracle from the Sun Goddess Amaterasu and Hachiman. That fact has hit home; you cannot deny it. This must not disturb the nation. During the investigation, I shall take over the responsibilities of the office. Move aside!

NARRATOR: Fujitaka leaps to restrain Kuninaga.

FUJITAKA: (*spoken*) This is an outrage! First we must consult your father,

His Holiness Chōkei, and then receive an official order from His Highness. Furthermore, we must at least allow Lord Yoshiaki to respond to these accusations before . . .

NARRATOR: But Kuninaga doesn't allow him to finish.

KUNINAGA: That is far too lenient! Would someone admit to planning an insurrection? Long ago, Yoshitsune pledged his loyalty seven times at Koshigoe, but Yoritomo didn't pardon him.[11] (*sung*) My simpleton of a father is too naive. It won't help to consult him. Now, will you withdraw voluntarily, or must you be bound?

NARRATOR: Just at they begin jostling each other, Kaijō Tarō Kanemori, whose mother nursed both him and Yoshiaki, bursts into the room, breaking down a door after listening to the scuffle, grabs Kuninaga by his hair, formal hat and all, and tosses him to the floor.

KANEMORI: (*spoken*) How dare you yell such accusations against my lord, branding him a traitor, a usurper, before all those assembled! Where is your evidence? On what authority are you going to tie him up? Is this all a ruse to make your father Chōkei appear loyal to the shogun by slandering Yoshiaki? You and your father are plotting something. Repeat what you said just now. I'm here, listening.

KUNINAGA: What? This concerns the highest matters of state. I don't have to consult someone as lowly as you. Get away!

KANEMORI: I'll twist that jaw of yours till you spit it out.

KUNINAGA: (*sung*) I will not speak to you.

NARRATOR: They argue loudly until Fujitaka intervenes.

FUJITAKA: Both of you, stop, be silent!

NARRATOR: But neither takes any notice. Yoshiaki stares angrily at Kanemori.

YOSHIAKI: That's enough, Kanemori! You are not to speak, Kaijō.

NARRATOR: He forces them to stop.

YOSHIAKI: (*spoken*) Everyone, all of you, listen well. Although I am untutored and simple, I tried as hard as I could to imitate the shogun's manner and sit boldly in his place. It is natural that a fool might think that I was trying to usurp the throne by tricking the assembled daimyo. Furthermore, as far as the appearance of the two-headed tortoise is concerned, and the suggestion that it was a disturbing omen signaling that brother against brother were fighting over the shogun's throne, I couldn't reply. Had I replied and explained the situation, it would have shamed my brother before all the lords. (*sung*) Then he and I would have never been able to see each other again. So I decided to remain silent.

NARRATOR: He quickly takes out his short sword and cuts off his topknot and throws it aside, effectively retiring from government. Kanemori and Fujitaka (*cadence*) are shocked, struck dumb.

(*sung*) Yoshiaki strikes the floor.

YOSHIAKI: (*spoken*) Ah, what shame! My brother Lord Yoshiteru, was he possessed by the demon of lust? He went off secretly to the pleasure quarter in Kujō[12] for a night of revelry, but he hasn't returned for two days. Because of the important ceremony to be held for Her Highness today, we sent messengers, but he is still in a drunken stupor. The lords began to assemble, but we all were flustered and at a loss. After consulting with Her Highness, I chose this strategy. Now, after causing such a scandal, I cannot stay at the palace a second longer. Having explained the situation, (*sung*) I ask Fujitaka to take charge. The government will run smoothly. As for myself, from now on I will be called the priest Sankaibō. (*spoken*) Kanemori, can I count on you to join me on this journey to seek enlightenment? If you hesitate, then you are released from my service. Follow Fujitaka and always serve him loyally.

NARRATOR: (*sung*) He quickly moves to the turtle and slashes off one of the heads.

YOSHIAKI: Now there is no one to usurp the throne. Heaven and earth are in harmony and peace will reign forever—that is my answer to the omen. Although I seek no more than "paper bedclothes, a hempen robe and a bowl of broth,"[13] I shall take this turtle (*spoken*) and release it into the pond as an offering to help me on the path to Buddhahood.

NARRATOR: (*sung*) He is almost out when from the office next door comes a voice, "Wait, young master," and Kuninaga's father, the lay priest Chōkei, emerges. He throws himself to the floor, and tears well up in his eyes.

CHŌKEI: (*spoken*) If I had come forward sooner, you would not have needed to cut your hair. Coldhearted Fujitaka and Kanemori! Even if you had to restrain him, why didn't you stop him? Because of my rude and treacherous son, all my more than sixty years of loyalty have come

FIGURE 28 (Center) Yoshiaki severs one head of a two-headed turtle; (right) Chōkei kills his own son, Kuninaga.(*Muromachi senjō-jiki* [*Tsu no kuni meoto-ike*], 1742, Keio University Library.)

to nothing. How can we show you a loyal heart? (*sung*) Come here, Kuninaga.

NARRATOR: Kuninaga answers and approaches his father with head bent in shame, and suddenly Chōkei lops off his head (*cadence*) in one swift blow.

CHŌKEI: (*spoken*) This has surely cleared us of any doubts about our loyalty.

NARRATOR: (*sung*) He grabs the hair and holds up the head. Yoshiaki glances back.

YOSHIAKI: (*spoken*) Hmm, Chōkei, you've got everything wrong. I wouldn't retire to become a monk because of scum like Kuninaga. I have a particular reason. Had I cut my hair simply as a strategy to get back at someone else, even one single hair of the head of the shogun's younger brother, Minamoto no Yoshiaki, would be greater than your and your son's heads put together. (*sung*) Pray for his soul.

NARRATOR: Without looking back, he sets off afresh on the path of Buddhist Law which, together with the Way of the Confucian Sages, is the true Way (*scene cadence*) to govern the people.

—Scene 2

On the road to the Shimo Kamo Shrine in north Kyoto, a few days later

NARRATOR: (*sung*)[14] At the Kamo Shrine, I cast my wish and pull the sacred rope. Will the bells chime for success, or will silence condemn me?[15] Such thoughts fill Her Highness as she imagines the wicket fence surrounding the shrine. There, ages ago, Princess Tamayori[16] gave birth to the deity Wakeikazura.[17] Her Highness goes to pray that her delivery also (*light cadence*) will be safe and easy.

(*sung*) It is a warm sunny day in spring, the middle of the second month. The shogun Yoshiteru's wife is on a pilgrimage accompanied by the shogun's women Umegae, Shiragiku, and Hatsuyuki. Each wears a scarf to cover her face and to hide any jealousies or enmities common among palace women. They keep to themselves, avoiding the eyes of passersby, trying to remain inconspicuous. An approaching storm stirs the branches of the willows, which give them courage as they saunter along. Her Highness is invigorated by the walk, and they all delight in the unfamiliar scenes on this rare trip outside the palace. (*nagaji melody*) They stop to pick early spring wildflowers along the path, although they do not know their names. They delight in the colors, wondering which is which among the seven spring wildflowers: cottonweed, chickweed, henbit (dead nettle), turnip, radish, dropwort (Japanese parsley), and shepherd's purse.[18] Leaves from the seven plants cooked with rice gruel on the seventh day of the New Year bring health and long life. (*cadence*) Now, long after that season, their leaves are tossed aside.

(*sung*) The fields are ablaze with the colors of thousands of wildflowers like an autumn scene, exciting the throb of the poet's heart from which seeds blossom into flowers of verse.[19] They spy flowers lying entangled, which look like passionate lovers who meet stealthily to pick evening primrose by moonlight. Come here, come here! We'll soon see our lover in a dream filled with cherry blossoms. We'll lie side by side on one kimono with grasses for our pillow; they'll be of the finest damask and brocade. Fancy Kinran gold-threaded gowns and Donsu Chinese robes will be our bedding, but we need nothing, nothing,[20] just each other to hold tight through the cold night. On the morrow, we'll cherish memories that will grow like wild chrysanthemums. Will he take me for his "wife-flower,"[21] (*highest pitch*) or disappear with the morning dew? Envy at seeing you all wet with love. Pluck me; this young flower will give all to her lover and bend like horsetails and reeds before the wind.[22] It is early yet for the glorious Kamo Shrine cherry blossoms, but wildflowers are jealous of the fragrant blooming plum. If wildflowers lend their shelter to hide lovers, then we'll wander tomorrow and the next day picking blossoms. Young hearts bent on finding husbands,[23] (*cadence*) the women meet no one and finally tiring, stop to rest a moment.

(*sung*) At a site with a pleasant view, they lay out a cover and set up screens for Her Highness. Her lady-in-waiting Kiyotaki has come to meet Her Highness and offers greetings.

KIYOTAKI: (*spoken*) Well, who would expect to find Her Highness out on the road (*sung*) when in the palace she doesn't walk on the ground even in the garden in her condition? Please rest for a moment behind the canvas screens.

NARRATOR: Her Highness is elated to see her.

LADY YOSHITERU: This is all a delight for me. The rest of you also must be excited. (*spoken*) We'll return to the palace later tonight. Let's go behind the screen.

NARRATOR: She leads them (*cadence*) inside the enclosure. (*sung*) After they have relaxed for a while, a young maid appears with a message.

MAID: (*spoken*) Lord Fujitaka has sent a young man named Reizei Mikinoshin as a messenger to Your Highness. (*sung*) He requests leave to convey the message.

NARRATOR: Her Highness replies, knowing that Kiyotaki likes Mikinoshin.

LADY YOSHITERU: (*spoken*) Thank you for the message. Fujitaka's messenger must be that young man we saw earlier on the pilgrimage. Kiyotaki, you go and listen to the message for me. (*sung*) You must have something else to talk to him about. The rest of you, turn your eyes away.

NARRATOR: At her words, all the other ladies become excited.

LADIES: Kiyotaki's reward for this outing is to meet her lovely beau. If we look away, we won't know what they might be up to. Why can't this happen to us? She always has the luck!

NARRATOR: (*cadence*) All the ladies whisper among themselves. (*sung*) Kiyotaki, too, is flustered.

KIYOTAKI: (*spoken*) Stop that kind of talk. Watch your manners! Her Highness agreed sometime ago that Mikinoshin and I could get married, but as yet we haven't been able to. So, I can't be the one to go meet him. (*sung*) No, that's not true. I do want to go. How couldn't I? You all must forgive me if we seem a bit intimate.

NARRATOR: So, undaunted, she goes out boldly. The others peek out between the canvas screens, (*cadence*) wondering what is going to happen.

(*sung*) Reizei Mikinoshin Fusahira cuts a fine figure in the fashion of his stylish master, Lord Fujitaka. The color of his coat contrasts with that of his formal *hakama* trousers. He carries a long sword with fancy fish designs on a wooden sheath; he is a young man, now over twenty, of impeccable breeding and destined for success. He kneels on the grass and bows politely with three fingers together touching the ground. Although Kiyotaki had calmed down, at the sight of him, her love presses on her even more strongly, and she feels a surge of blood to her heart. Words burst forth like rapids in a rushing stream.[24]

KIYOTAKI: (*spoken*) If you've come as a messenger to offer congratulations on Her Highness's pilgrimage, then you must do your duty properly, (*sung*) but while you are here, I want you to tell me what has kept you away.

NARRATOR: She grabs his arm, but he pulls away.

MIKINOSHIN: (*spoken*) I received an urgent command and galloped here on horseback. I'm soaked with sweat and have no time to dally about with you. My lord Fujitaka has an important message for Her Highness. Lord Yoshiteru's favorite courtesan, a woman called Ōyodo, is to be ransomed from the Kujō pleasure quarter by the priest Chōkei and, of all things, to become his adopted daughter. Then at the end of the year, she will be presented at court to His Highness. This is all Chōkei's plotting. Fujitaka realized that even the slaying of his own son, Kuninaga, was only a sycophantic ploy to win the favor of His Highness, but unless Chōkei commits an obvious crime, there is no way that Fujitaka can intervene. (*sung*) When he accused Chōkei of treachery, His Highness only grew angry and accused Fujitaka of slandering Chōkei out of malice and jealousy. (*spoken*) If the woman is allowed to enter the court, then it will be the end of the Ashikaga house. We cannot stop this without the help of Her Highness. (*sung*) She must return to the palace immediately. I have been ordered to accompany her. Be quick and tell this to Her Highness.

KIYOTAKI: (*spoken*) What? This is disastrous! (*sung*) We must not let this happen.

NARRATOR: But before she is able to finish, Her Highness comes forward.

LADY YOSHITERU: (*spoken*) Mikinoshin, I have heard all you've said. Although your message comes from the respected Fujitaka, it is the custom from ancient times that a ruler may have eight mistresses but only one official wife. If I refuse to allow that woman to enter the palace, (*sung*) then I shall be shamed as a woman fearful and jealous of a lowly courtesan. If it pleases His Highness, then I cannot object to Ōyodo's coming. Return and report what I have said, Mikinoshin.

NARRATOR: Her Highness seems completely undisturbed by the news. (*spoken*) Umegae comes out.

UMEGAE: Listen, please, Your Highness. All three of us here have served His Highness. If I were to say that it is wrong that you are not jealous of us, my words would probably be turned against me, but we feel a hundred times more affection for Your Ladyship than for His Highness. We serve Your Highness faithfully and never go against your wishes, but a high-class courtesan is a picture of pride itself.[25] A sure sign is that even at the celebration of the maternal obi, that woman kept him from returning to the palace. Lord Yoshiaki's retirement, too, is all due to that harlot's scheming. If things are this bad while she is still in the Kujō pleasure quarter, then what havoc will she wreak when she reaches the palace? She'll rule as if she were queen and treat His Highness as her own. (*sung*) She'll treat Your Highness with contempt, looking down her nose at you. Even if you keep from getting angry nine-tenths of the time, what will be your recourse? It will be too late to be bitter, too late for regrets; you won't be able to show jealousy. If you try to evict her, she won't budge. It will be the seeds of an ugly and spiteful conflict. Shiragiku, Hatsuyuki, Lady Kiyotaki, tell Her Highness of the danger.

NARRATOR: (*cadence*) Concern for His Highness is a concern for them all. (*sung*) Her words kindle the flames seething in Her Ladyship's heart; her face glows crimson; her eyes redden with tears.

FIGURE 29 (Right) Lady Yoshiteru and her women at the Kamo Shrine; (below) Mikinoshin and Kiyotaki; (top left) Kanemori fighting outside Muromachi Palace; (far left, top) Lady Yoshiteru escaping from the palace. (*Muromachi senjō-jiki* [*Tsu no kuni meoto-ike*], 1742, Keio University Library.)

LADY YOSHITERU: It's as you say. It will be a disaster if she enters court. Accompany me home Mikinoshin. Everyone, let us go.
NARRATOR: They all scurry about getting the carriage ready, their spirits as bubbling as the rushing spring that flows into the Kamo River. (*scene cadence*) They hurry off as if riding the currents home.

—Scene 3
Later that evening, at the gate of Muromachi Palace

NARRATOR: (*sung*) Kanemori, whose mother nursed both him and his master, Lord Yoshiaki, has decided not to accompany his lord, who has become a monk. He has halfheartedly joined the service of Chōkei but is bitter that he is now treated as an untrustworthy outsider. (*spoken*) Undaunted, like the guardian demon Niō, he strikes a defiant pose, his elbows out, but on his own he strikes little terror.[26] He has decided to set off (*sung*) to find the shogun Yoshiteru, but since his ancestors have for generations served the Ashikaga family, he wants at least to offer a final farewell at the palace gates. Walking along Konoe Avenue, he notices that the Muromachi palace gate is open and a platform lined with tall candles, glistening like rows of stars, has been put in place for a high-ranking visitor. He asks the guard.

KANEMORI: Is there a poetry gathering or a banquet tonight? What is the occasion?

GUARD: (*spoken*) Tonight is an auspicious occasion; the shogun welcomes a new official wife. Guards have been placed at all the crossroads, and inside, a banquet has been prepared to welcome her: lucky red beans and rice, decorative rice cakes, and pickled fish mixed with vegetables. Both the garden and the house have been swept clean; (*cadence*) everyone has been frantic.

KANEMORI: (*spoken*) Then, what princess is this new "Her Highness"?

GUARD: None other than the famous courtesan of Kujō, Lady Ōyodo. She has become the daughter of Miyoshi Chōkei. Look, over there, at the lanterns! Iwanari Chikara is leading the palace guards. Everyone, out of the way, (*sung*) step aside, or you'll feel the force of a guard's club!

NARRATOR: (*cadence*) With these words, he disappears into the palace grounds. (*sung*) Kanemori is known to be short tempered.

KANEMORI: (*spoken*) What a lot of fuss to welcome a courtesan who's been ransomed! A common prostitute! Ridiculous, impossible, that such a woman will become Lady Yoshiteru! She's the harlot who made my lord retire to become a monk. I can't bear the thought of her swaggering into the palace. I won't stand for it! (*sung*) As recompense for my lord's shaven head, I'll beat up that pretty painted face.

NARRATOR: He thrusts himself into the darkness; he gives his hair, tied high on his head, a wild shake and strikes a fierce pose. His huge Kongōbei sword is loosened, ready to be drawn. The sword at his side (*cadence*) is as firm as a railing on a bridge.

(*sung*) A moment later, the lanterns of the procession come into view, followed by a palanquin fit for the princess bride of a shogun and accompanied by the priest Chōkei, as the shogun's representative, with

Iwanari Chikara as his second. The leader of the archers, Mabuchi Danhachirō, and the foot soldiers and pages are all in fine formal robes for this grand occasion. (*cadence*) They clear away everything from each corner of every street.

(*sung*) Kanemori runs to the vanguard, kicking the soldiers aside, grabs the palanquin pole, and yells.

KANEMORI: (*spoken*) I've heard that the Muromachi Palace has become a brothel where courtesans are bought. What a grand courtesan's procession this is! I've had my eye on Ōyodo and thought about buying her. Tonight I'll make her mine, even though I don't have any money. But I do have the precious metal of this huge sword of tempered steel. I'll buy her guts with it, too. (*sung*) Out with you, woman, strut a bit for me. Show me your charms. Let's have you, then, hurry up!

NARRATOR: He charges forward, sword drawn, and the palanquin bearers (*cadence*) fall to the ground one on top of the other.

(*sung*) Iwanari and Mabuchi call out.

IWANARI: This fool has no care for his life.

NARRATOR: The soldiers advance from all sides, but he kicks them away. He jumps forward and kicks open the palanquin door and, to his horror, sees Lord Yoshiteru with Ōyodo clinging to his sleeves, terrified. Kanemori is aghast.

KANEMORI: I had no idea.

NARRATOR: (*emotional cadence*) He falls to the ground and buries his head in shame. (*sung*) The guards surround him and glare.

YOSHITERU: (*spoken*) Listen, young man, this time you've gone too far. You were brought up at the feet of Yoshiaki, so you were allowed freedoms and don't know your own limits. An attack on my palanquin cannot be forgiven, even if it were by imperial decree. Or was this an order from Yoshiaki?

NARRATOR: (*cadence*) His face colors with rage.

KANEMORI: (*spoken*) Forgive me, Your Highness. I had no idea you were in the palanquin. I have not gone mad. I serve my lord and would do nothing against his will. However, even in my wildest dreams, I could never have imagined that the ruler of the realm, the great shogun Lord Yoshiteru, would travel in a palanquin with a courtesan. Because of this whore, you have been in the Kujō quarter night and day, and (*sung*) as a result. your brother has retired to the priesthood and Her Highness is wretched. Order in the palace is a shambles. The lower ranks mock those above them, and if you are not careful, your authority will be tarnished, your power weakened. This would be a disaster for the nation. This is all happening right under your nose, but you keep at bay anyone who questions your actions. You're being tricked by Chōkei, that badger in monk's garb, and that fox Ōyodo. I've come to bag one of those beasts. I'll take revenge for my lord's enforced retirement. I'll pluck out every hair of that whore's head till it gleams bare.

NARRATOR: (*cadence*) He boldly lays bare all the facts so as to shock His Highness. (*emotional cadence*) Ōyodo dissolves into tears.

ŌYODO: (*spoken*) This is what I have been telling you along the way. How could any decent woman be happy to arrive like this, considering the feelings of Her Highness, not to mention the other women. All the rumors and scandal will bring you shame. I don't want to enter the palace. I won't. (*sung*) Take me back. I'll walk back myself. Farewell.

NARRATOR: She starts to leave but is restrained.

YOSHITERU: (*spoken*) Wait, wait! Kanemori, listen, you insolent little mutt. You are speaking to Yoshiteru, prime minister of the realm. Who are you to tell me how to rule the nation? This is useless drivel! (*sung*) Iwanari, Mabuchi, have him beaten.

NARRATOR: They obey the command and advance from both sides. With poles raised, they prepare to attack.

IWANARI: (*spoken*) What're you going to do now?

MABUCHI: (*sung*) Under the command of His Highness.

NARRATOR: With this cry, they beat his body dozens of times, striking his ribs, his back, his eyes, and nose. They beat him to a pulp.

YOSHITERU: (*spoken*) Ah, how irritating this is! Our journey has been ruined. Ōyodo, (*sung*) let's go inside for a celebratory drink.

NARRATOR: (*cadence*) Yoshiteru leads Ōyodo through the palace gates. (*sung*) Iwanari, Mabuchi, and all their underlings gloat.

IWANARI: (*spoken*) Ah, what a clever lad. Have fun making a racket out here all by yourself!

NARRATOR: (*sung*) The sound of the gate locks slamming shut mingles with the laughter. Inside, the banquet commences with auspicious songs, (*nō chanting*) "health and happiness forever, treasures galore."[27] (*spoken*) Kanemori raises his head and glares angrily at the gate.

KANEMORI: I'm completely in the right, and loyal. How humiliating to be beaten up by an army of maggots. I've never been afraid of anything, not even a bolt of lightning, (*sung*) but what could I do after the angry rebuke of His Highness? I couldn't even raise my head. How heavy is the power of the shogun's authority! Too great the gulf between the low and those on high.

NARRATOR: (*cadence*) Tears as big as fists run down his battered face. (*sung*) He notices a figure climbing up the large cherry tree from inside the walls and along the branches that overhang outside. It's a woman climbing (*high pitch*) like a spider, although she is in fear of falling. She clings to the branches, but her hem catches and her skirt tears. She looks down, wondering how to descend. He notices that she is wearing elegant robes with flowery designs. She crawls to the tip of a branch and, with a final swing, (*cadence*) flies to the ground below.

(*sung*) Kanemori immediately runs to her side (*spoken*), wondering who it is. "Who goes there?" he calls out roughly.

LADY YOSHITERU: Not so loud! Is that Kanemori? I am Lady Yoshiteru.

KANEMORI: What are you doing, climbing trees alone in the middle of the night in your condition? This is ridiculous.

LADY YOSHITERU: (*cadence*) You're right. It is ridiculous. (*sung*) Lately, because of Ōyodo, all His Highness's other mistresses have been upset, and I've had to keep them all calm. Seeing Ōyodo's reception at the palace tonight, I felt, was the last straw, and I couldn't stay any longer. (*spoken*) I thought of cutting my throat with a knife, but this child would suffer, too, and I couldn't go through with it. I didn't know what else to do, so I decided to escape to my father's house. (*sung*) But I don't even know the way home. How helpless and pitiful I feel, Kanemori.

NARRATOR: (*cadence*) She bursts into tears.

KANEMORI: (*sung*) You are right to escape. It is fortunate that we met. I'll accompany you wherever you wish to go. You don't need to worry anymore.

LADY YOSHITERU: (*spoken*) No, no. It mustn't appear that I have been encouraged by anyone. If there is a scandal, it would make things even worse.

NARRATOR: As she speaks, (*sung*) voices are heard from within the walls.

MAIDS: Her Highness is missing! Where is Lady Yoshiteru?

NARRATOR: The women's crying causes a panic.
GUARDS: Search outside the walls. Hurry!
LADY YOSHITERU: Oh, my god!
NARRATOR: (cadence) She runs to escape being discovered. (sung) An instant later, the gates open up and more than forty soldiers armed with poles rush out. They meet Kanemori.
GUARDS: (spoken) What are you doing here still, useless Kanemori? He must be an ally of Her Highness. You won't get away!
NARRATOR: They grab him, but he resists.
KANEMORI: Even if I knew where she was, do you think I would tell you? (sung) What clever fools you are.
NARRATOR: He kicks the soldiers aside and grabs the leader by his kimono.
KANEMORI: (spoken) You all were brave beating me up on His Highness's orders. Now I'll return the favor.
NARRATOR: (sung) He kicks him to the ground and pummels him.
KANEMORI: (spoken) Shall I let you lead me to your master Chōkei? Or shall I simply kick you to death? What'll it be?
GUARD: Please spare my life. I'll take you to my master Chōkei.
KANEMORI: You promise?
GUARD: I swear on my honor as a samurai.
KANEMORI: (sung) Well then, lead the way.
NARRATOR: He lets the guard go, but he runs off screaming.
GUARD: (spoken) If you want to meet Master Chōkei, it can't be this year. Not until there's a leap year in June or a thirty-first day of February or when New Year starts on the third. Only then can you meet him!
NARRATOR: With these parting words, (cadence) he disappears through the gates, which slam shut after him.
KANEMORI: (sung) You hairy, puny little mutt! Your time is up. But I'll just contribute an auspicious stone to the party.
NARRATOR: With a grunt, he lifts up a huge stone post used to tether horses, raises it above his head, and, with another grunt, throws it at the gate. (cadence) The earth trembles and the elm wood doors shatter as if they'd been hit by a catapult.
　(sung) The guards panic, and Mabuchi sticks his head through the broken door.
MABUCHI: (spoken) Have you no fear of the gods? For your own life? You've gone too far now, you thug. Out! Get away from here!

NARRATOR: Kanemori grabs Mabuchi's head and (*sung*) yanks him forcefully. (*kowari fight music*) Mabuchi tries to flee but is pulled back again. Both grunt in this tug of war until Mabuchi's neck snaps. (*sung*) Kanemori pulls and pulls until Mabuchi's head comes off.

KANEMORI: It's not much, I know, but consider it my offering for this auspicious night.

NARRATOR: He tosses the head at the gate.

KANEMORI: The night is late, and there's a falling star. (*high pitch*) The river flows south; I'll head north.

NARRATOR: The moon, too, (*highest pitch*) flees west as it sinks over the horizon. From the east comes a faint hint of dawn. Cocks crow here and there, and temple bells toll the morning hour, six times, waking the bustling voices of the city.[28] Kanemori lingers, (*high pitch*) pounding the door to see if he can gain entrance, but even in his dreams, he cannot penetrate the walls. Frustrated and still fuming, he gives up and runs off.

Act 2

—Scene 1
Along the Nanase River near the Toba Road, a few days later

NARRATOR: (*sung*) In the realm of our sovereign, the myriad grains ripen for the harvest, a bounty for all.[1]

NARRATOR: At a crossroads near the Nanase River on the Toba Road to the capital is a small village where Asakawa Fujitaka and Miyoshi Chōkei have properties on which they graze horses and nurture weakened ones back to health. Just at the boundary between their lands, the body of a woman has been discovered; her head is on Fujitaka's land and her legs on Chōkei's. Reports of the find have gone to both manors, and two groups of officials arrive at the scene. One speaks of the dilemma.

OFFICIAL: (*spoken*) If she were only a few feet to the east or a few to the west. It would be easy to take care of this if it were one or the other. (*sung*) Her spirit's troubled enough wandering between worlds;[2] even her body left behind can't find a resting place.

NARRATOR: (*cadence*) They whisper among themselves. (*sung*) "The inspectors have arrived!" announce the soldiers, (*cadence*) who quickly take up positions around the body.

(*sung*) Just after them comes Lord Fujitaka's representative, Reizei Mikinoshin, followed by the priest Chōkei's representative Matsunaga Danjō Hisahide, (*cadence*) each with their assistants. (*sung*) They set down their instrument boxes on either side of the body. The lower officials step back (*cadence*) to wait for a resolution of the dilemma of who is responsible.

HISAHIDE: (*spoken*) Well, Mikinoshin, shall we hear the local officials' reports?

MIKINOSHIN: If you are ready, let the investigation begin. We can dispense with the formalities.

HISAHIDE: (*sung*) Then let me call the witnesses. Will the senior officials of the Asakawa and Miyoshi estates come forward? (*spoken*) Well then, who was first to discover the body? Was anything unusual noticed at the time? Tell us everything you know. During the investigation, if we discover that anyone is lying, he will be punished.

FIGURE 30 Scene of the murder investigation; Mikinoshin is seated on the right. (*Muromachi senjō-jiki* [*Tsu no kuni meoto-ike*], 1742, Keio University Library.)

NARRATOR: One official steps forward.
OFFICIAL: The person who first found the body was a farmer of the Chōkei estate, Naruki Rokubei.
HISAHIDE: (*sung*) Explain exactly what you saw.
NARRATOR: Rokubei is pushed forward.
ROKUBEI: (*spoken*) I was on my way to let water into the fields early this morning when I discovered the body. It was still dark and eerie, so I ran off without looking closely. On the way home, I went to my master's office to report, and then I did a round of the village and had someone run to the Asakawa residence to let them know as well. I wanted the two estates to deal with the matter and (*sung*) only covered the body with rush matting. That's all I know about it.
NARRATOR: The assistants from each estate (*cadence*) record the facts of his statement. (*sung*) Mikinoshin and Hisahide prepare to investigate the

corpse. Both move up to the body to remove the matting. The figure seems to be that of someone of the upper class, but her facial skin has been stripped off, which makes it impossible to identify her. Her under-robes of are fine white silk; over them is a padded outer robe of simple design. On the body, there are only scratches as fine as rabbit's fur, no punctures, no cuts. The worst is that she wears a brocade maternity sash. She has died with her child still in her womb.

HISAHIDE: (*spoken*) Mikinoshin, as you can see, this woman was no ordinary townsman's or farmer's wife. She's surely the lady of a courtier, daimyo, or some governor. If it were robbers, you'd expect them to remove the clothes. The facial disfiguring, too, doesn't seem to be the work of thieves. Her hair, in the court style, is undisturbed. It's clear from the state of the body (*sung*) that she was killed and left here on purpose. This is not a random act. Don't you agree, Mikinoshin?

MIKINOSHIN: (*spoken*) Your judgment seems correct. (*sung*) The kimono fabric is that preferred by the shogun's family, popularly called the Muromachi pattern. It's not something a lower-class woman would be wearing.

NARRATOR: Before he can finish, Hisahide interrupts.

HISAHIDE: (*spoken*) Yes, that must be it, Mikinoshin. Mention of the shogun made me remember that last night, Her Highness fled the palace and is still at large. She, too, was with child, just as this woman is. Her hair style is no ordinary coiffure. (*sung*) It must be Her Highness!

NARRATOR: Mikinoshin, too, wonders, and they both take a closer look at the corpse's face to see any similarities, but the disfigured face offers no clues. (*cadence*) Both sigh and lower their heads in despair.

(*sung*) After a moment, Hisahide remembers something.

HISAHIDE: (*spoken*) On the maternity sash of an aristocratic family, I've heard that it's customary to note the date and name of a boy as a prayer for giving birth safely to a son. If there is such a note, then it'll be our best proof.

NARRATOR: He moves closer (*sung*) to untie the brocade sash and solve the case. He finds a "safe-birth" amulet with prayers to the Five Great Guardian Buddhas, the Six Merciful Kannon, and the Seven Yakushi Healing Buddhas, signed by the great shogun Minamoto no Ason Yoshiteru.

HISAHIDE: (*spoken*) Look, look! Proof it's Her Highness. This'll cause a national turmoil, mourning throughout the realm. Who could've done such a thing? (*sung*) What a pitiful tragedy for Her Highness.

NARRATOR: He sheds tears of anger and impatiently paces about, infecting the others. Mikinoshin is shocked, but the more he looks at the woman, the more something seems wrong. Her hands and feet seem too coarse and big. The amulet is strong proof, but although she is similar, the woman is not Her Highness. He keeps his thoughts to himself, knowing Hisahide would get angry if contradicted.

MIKINOSHIN: (*spoken*) Since we've determined the identity as Her Highness, then we cannot waste any more time here. This is clearly a problem for the Miyoshi estate. I'm sorry to withdraw like this, but the Asakawa estate has no responsibility here. (*sung*) We'll leave immediately to report to the capital. Men, let's be off.

NARRATOR: He starts to hurry off, but Hisahide runs after and holds him back.

HISAHIDE: (*spoken*) Wait just a minute! How can I let you leave, shifting the responsibility for an Asakawa scandal to the Miyoshi estate? We all can see clearly by the marker that the body is exactly across the border between the lands. Can't you see that? Farmers from each estate measure from the marker to the body to show exactly where it lies.

NARRATOR: (*sung*) A rope is pulled straight and taut from the marker. A ruler measures the body's length on either side.

FARMER: To the west in Asakawa land, (*spoken*) one foot, two feet and a half; to the east into Miyoshi land, one foot, just under two feet.

NARRATOR: The two local officials look carefully, close up.

OFFICIAL: (*sung*) The measurement is correct.

HISAHIDE: Did you hear that, Mikinoshin? (*spoken*) Half a foot more is on the Asakawa side, and furthermore, it's the half with the head. Just a little farther, and it wouldn't even be on Miyoshi land. Is there a law that says the greater should give way to the lesser? If you don't change your mind and take responsibility for this body and investigate the crime, it will cause a scandal for the Asakawa estate.

NARRATOR: (*sung*) Hisahide cleverly drapes over Mikinoshin the weighty robes of his master's reputation. The Asakawa farmers lament among themselves.

FARMERS: Well, it looks like our side lost this one. (*cadence*) It'll cost the village a bundle.

NARRATOR: (*sung*) Mikinoshin laughs loudly.

MIKINOSHIN: (*spoken*) It doesn't matter that she is two or three feet in our territory. If her feet are in the Miyoshi estate, then the matter won't be an Asakawa concern. If you still doubt what I say, farmers, keep her feet still and lift the body until it's standing. You'll see what I mean.

NARRATOR: (*sung*) Some Miyoshi farmers quickly grab hold of the woman's feet, and the Asakawa farmers pull her up so she is standing in Miyoshi land.

MIKINOSHIN: Now do you see, Hisahide? (*spoken*) This matter has absolutely nothing to do with us. I shall report that the care of the body and the investigation of the murder are the responsibility of the Miyoshi estate. You have no objections, I presume? (*sung*) Well, what do you say?

NARRATOR: Although pressed to answer, Hisahide has no response, felled by the logic of the argument. (*cadence*) He is a picture of silent despair. (*sung*) The Asakawa farmers are still holding up the body.

FARMERS: After all is said and done, you seem to have lost the game. Ah, what a troublesome dead body!

NARRATOR: The Asakawa farmers let go, and the body falls to the east for the Miyoshi farmers to pick up. The Asakawa in the west are free of the burden. In human society, loyalty and betrayal, good and evil, run on fine lines. Those who can distinguish between the two follow heaven's straight path. (*scene cadence*) The two parties part ways, each still glaring at the other as they walk away.

—Scene 2
In the Muromachi shogunal palace, a few days later

NARRATOR:

>   (*sung*) A golden dais,
>   a jeweled bed,
>   a brocade cushion,
>   all through the night,
>   (*popular song*) I slept with you

in my dream,
only to regret
waking.³
I think only of you
(*handayū* singing) as I strum the shamisen
and sing of dreams of love
far away.
I wake and lie again
in a palace that knows no
heat in summer
or cold in winter.
How splendid!
The magnificent shogunal suite
(*cadence*) of the Muromachi Palace.

(*sung*) The Hamamatsu song is a background to the endless frolics in the shogun's women's quarters. In the next room, the notes of the accompanying shamisen have grown languid, as everyone is weary from lack of sleep. Each takes turns playing and then singing various shamisen "Nagebushi" popular love songs.⁴ Their voices grow hoarse, fragile, as fleeting as morning frost on a wintry field. (*cadence*) They struggle to keep the entertainment lively for another day.

(*sung*) Suddenly the banquet falls silent. The shogun Yoshiteru shouts.

YOSHITERU: (*spoken*) Yesterday you were the courtesan Ōyodo; today you are the shogun's bride. What is it that doesn't please you? (*sung*) All of you, come closer and cheer her up.

NARRATOR: His voice is slurred, but it penetrates into the next room, startling Umegae and Hatsuyuki. They hold their breath and peek into the shogun's chamber but hear the sound of a door opening. Her Highness's messenger Kiyotaki comes rushing in.

UMEGAE: Kiyotaki, what is it? Why are you in such a hurry? Tell us what's the matter.

KIYOTAKI: (*spoken*) Umegae, Hatsuyuki, you both have the duty of humoring your new mistress, the courtesan Ōyodo. She's become bored again. She's been moody all morning. Now there'll be the usual judgments and punishments to humor her. My father, Iwanari Chikaranosuke, has ordered me to bring another woman for him to slay. (*sung*)

Is it my bad karma to have such a fate? Fate, too, that my father must be the executioner! Her Highness has been murdered, and the investigation is still in progress. And I've got to do this! I know that you don't want to sing or play the shamisen or entertain her, but you must be patient. Don't make her angry by showing your displeasure or sadness.

NARRATOR: (*cadence*) After telling them her tale, she hurries off. (*sung*) The two left behind shiver with fright.

HATSUYUKI: Umegae, every day there's some new, terrifying happening. Did you hear what she said? (*spoken*) Who'll be the one murdered today?

UMEGAE: Ah, Shiragiku has been missing since last night! (*sung*) But even if it is some lackey or footman who is the object of her displeasure, no matter who it is, it is an awful pity. Every life is precious. But we must keep up a calm appearance. Let's play a song again as we've been ordered.

NARRATOR: They pity the fate of others and fear for their own, tuning their instruments—one higher to create a lively tune, and the other lower to sing of their sad and frightened hearts—but the plectrums slip and slide under their anxious hands.

> (*ballad song*) Yesterday I thought of others, today myself,[5]
> tomorrow along the Asuka River,
> though innocent, I may sink into sin
> and drown in bubbling water.
> Well now, well; well now, well.

What was Shiragiku's crime that she should meet such a fate? An innocent girl caught in a web, (*cadence*) she is chased into the palace garden. (*sung*) Iwanari chases Shiragiku, following her with his cruel eyes, alert to everything around. When the two women see him chasing her, they drop their instruments and run into the garden after them.

UMEGAE: How heartless! I heard that another was to be slain tonight. Is it to be Shiragiku tonight? Until yesterday, all three of us were equally cherished by His Highness. No matter that he is fickle, it is too cruel to kill someone for the pleasure of another. (*spoken*) This is your farewell to this world, Shiragiku. Why don't you say something? (*sung*) Is that a gag on your mouth? That heartless, cruel demon, that devil, Ōyodo! She must have been the one who ordered Her Highness killed as well. From what we've seen and heard, next it will be our turn.

NARRATOR: Their pleas and cries affect Shiragiku (*highest pitch*) who seems anxious to speak but only breaks down in tears at this farewell. All three hug one another, collapsing in a flood of tears, (*cadence*) all too understandable.

(*sung*) Iwanari brushes the two aside.

IWANARI: (*spoken*) If you have so much time, then use it to humor Lady Ōyodo. If both of you jabber on and on, (*sung*) it won't be long before you get the monkey gag as well.

NARRATOR: He curses at them as he opens the inner door (*cadence*) and drags Shiragiku in.

UMEGAE: (*sung*) How horrible, Hatsuyuki. I always thought the terrors of fiery hell were for the next life, but Ōyodo is the demon general that guards the gate of deepest hell beyond that wall. Let's sneak a look and say a farewell prayer for our dearest Shiragiku.

NARRATOR: They creep toward the door left ajar to steal a look.

HATSUYUKI: Look, Umegae. (*spoken*) Shiragiku has been tied up over there. The rope has been loosened. Will she be let free? No, both of her arms are stretched out and tied to a pole. (*sung*) Iwanari is going around behind her. What is he going to do?

NARRATOR: While watching, they hear the tremendous thud of a sword striking.

UMEGAE: How terrible! Both her arms have been chopped off! I can't breathe. My chest feels heavy. I can't move! Namu Amida Butsu. Please save her, Amida Buddha.

NARRATOR: (*cadence*) Terrified, she shakes uncontrollably.

UMEGAE: (*sung*) Look, Hatsuyuki, that woman Ōyodo is laughing at the bloody scene. She's hugging His Highness.

NARRATOR: Just then another cracking sound.

HATSUYUKI: Umegae, what was that?

UMEGAE: Horrible, it was her head.

NARRATOR: (*intense emotional cadence*) Umegae collapses from grief. (*sung*) Struggling to breathe, she has an idea.

UMEGAE: (*spoken*) Listen, long ago in China, Emperor Zhou,[6] the last of the Yin emperors, had a beautiful empress, Daji,[7] who loved to watch people being killed. (*sung*) At flower parties in the morning, banquets under moonlight, time and again she had one after another cruelly killed. She had no concern for the suffering it caused the subjects. And in no time, the realm was overthrown, all lost. I thought it was just a tale, but we witness it before our eyes. Ōyodo is worse than Empress Daji, or at least as evil. In the end, we, too, will meet the same fate as Shiragiku. Let's not wait for the murderer to come; let's escape while we can.

HATSUYUKI: Let's flee now.

NARRATOR: They whisper to each other next to the royal bedroom. Suddenly they realize they have been overheard by Lord Yoshiteru and Ōyodo.

YOSHITERU: Is there anyone near? Isn't there anyone on duty?

NARRATOR: At this order to appear, the two women panic, unable to flee but too afraid to remain still. (*cadence*) They just want to vanish.

IWANARI: (*sung*) Iwanari is here.

NARRATOR: He runs to Yoshiteru.

YOSHITERU: (*spoken*) Catch those two women and prepare them for their punishment. Let's delight Ōyodo. Give her a real treat.

NARRATOR: (*sung*) He responds in a flash, draws his sword, and slashes Hatsuyuki's right shoulder. Umegae steps back and steadies herself.

UMEGAE: (*spoken*) Now, Your Highness, my torrent of words has been stemmed by just that one title of "Your Highness." Where can my anger be vented? Listen, you flesh-eating demon-woman, you serpent! Whether in rebirth or in dying again and again, for five hundred lives, I'll pursue you. You'll never ever have a moment of peace. (*sung*) Watch now to see if there truly is a soul and spirit in mankind.

NARRATOR: She grinds her teeth in rage; not one tear clouds her eyes. Her piercing glare is fixed.

UMEGAE: Well, come and kill me, Iwanari!

NARRATOR: When she sticks out her head, Iwanari moves forward timidly, as if afraid. He raises his sword and as it falls, (*cadence*) so, pitifully, falls Umegae's head.

YOSHITERU: (*spoken*) Ōyodo, did you see that? Wasn't it magnificent! It's a pity that someday I may be overthrown and you dragged away to face the executioner. I want your desires to be satisfied by having thousands slaughtered for your pleasure. (*sung*) We've had enough saké. Shall we go to bed? Iwanari, clear away the bodies and you're excused for the night.

NARRATOR: Just then a messenger arrives.
MESSENGER: (*spoken*) The murderer of Her Highness who died at Nanase River in Toba has been arrested by the priest Chōkei. He requests permission to question the man in front of Your Highness.
NARRATOR: Yoshiteru is delighted.
YOSHITERU: That is splendid, splendid! Her father Lord Akitada has been pestering me day in and day out to return his precious daughter to him. What a delight to be rid of that business. (*sung*) This is not an ordinary investigation. Reverend Chōkei and Lord Fujitaka together must pass judgment on this matter. I, too, want to listen to the questioning. Bring the suspect forward.
NARRATOR: The shogun's orders pass down the ranks. The two lords sit together alongside His Highness. Matsunaga brings the accused out onto the gravel area in the garden in front of the lords. He is about thirty, small, with an ordinary face, not particularly evil looking. (*spoken*) Chōkei glares at him.
CHŌKEI: You don't seem to have had a particular grudge against Her Highness. Who was it that paid you to do this? Why did you commit such a terrible act? Confess and tell us all. If you show the slightest resistance, we'll whip you with arrows and pound you with rifle butts. We'll torture you until you talk.
NARRATOR: Threatened with torture, the man seems unperturbed. He looks over to where the shogun is, far to the other side.
ACCUSED: Well now, it has been a long time, Your Highness. Long ago when Your Lordship needed some favor, I was always there to help. How heartless to ignore your old friend. I was always the fool who took care of your needs, willing to sell even my life, anything for a copper or two. Even if I'm cut into little pieces, I'll never speak. Don't worry about me, Your Lordship. (*sung*) I'll show you I'm a loyal fellow.
NARRATOR: Although he names no one, his gaze is fixed on His Highness, who colors with anger. The row of guards grows fearful, (*cadence*) their palms cold and sweaty.
  (*sung*) Chōkei intervenes.
CHŌKEI: We know what you're up to. You won't distract us with your foolish tactics. Matsunaga, drag him over there and cut off his head.
NARRATOR: Fujitaka, however, restrains him.
FUJITAKA: (*spoken*) No, wait a moment. How can you execute him before

we know why he felt such enmity or who paid him to do this? Cutting his head off now, before we know the facts, will only confuse our investigation, Chōkei.

CHŌKEI: Your reaction is understandable given your inexperience in these matters, Fujitaka. His words just now have made clear who employed him. I thought it best to stop him from confessing the name because it might inconvenience His Highness. Will you be able to cover up the affair and complete the investigation if a scandal is exposed?

FUJITAKA: Well, then, I will pronounce judgment on this case. Listen, prisoner, don't speak in confusing riddles; give us the plain facts. You have the privilege of an audience before His Highness. (*sung*) Raise your eyes and speak to Chōkei and Fujitaka, who head this investigation.

NARRATOR: The prisoner looks up at his judges.

ACCUSED: (*spoken*) If you say that I'm not to worry about the consequences, then I'll break my oath and confess all. I was paid by His Highness, sitting over there. I was promised that if Her Highness was killed and Ōyodo replaced her, I would be raised to a daimyo. Here are the fifty *ōban* gold coins[8] I received as proof of his promise.

NARRATOR: (*sung*) At this revelation of the facts, His Highness panics and loudly gnashes his teeth in rage. (*emotional cadence*) His body shakes visibly.

CHŌKEI: (*spoken*) Didn't I tell you so, Fujitaka? This is what I meant by exposing a scandal. (*sung*) There's no way around it now. We'll have to send an apology to her father, Lord Akitada. He'll be troubled and upset. Matsunaga, the criminal must be executed.

NARRATOR: Chōkei rushes things again, but Fujitaka intervenes once more.

FUJITAKA: Wait, I say. Wait! You vicious liar! There's another scoundrel behind this scandal. I will now submit evidence for the inquiry. Mikinoshin, come forward.

NARRATOR: He shouts, and Reizei Mikinoshin comes running out from the Records Office leading a carriage across the garden. He stops at the edge of the veranda.

MIKINOSHIN: I present to you the most important witness in this investigation.

NARRATOR: He opens the door of the carriage and, to the surprise of all the lords and the shock of His Highness, out steps a pregnant Lady

Yoshiteru. Chōkei frowns. Lady Yoshiteru looks upset, but she stays close to Lord Fujitaka, (*emotional cadence*) her head downcast. (*sung*) Matsunaga rushes forward to complete his order and with one stroke executes the prisoner. Fujitaka is furious.

FUJITAKA: You fool, was it Chōkei's order that you carry out the punishment before the investigation was complete?

NARRATOR: Despite being threatened, Chōkei doesn't blink an eye. (*spoken*) He turns to face His Highness with tears flowing down his cheeks.

CHŌKEI: Allow me to speak. It will seem that I am being slanderous or envious, but if I didn't speak out, it would be disloyal. Although it may seem I'm completely confused, remember that I killed my own son Kuninaga for the realm, to save our sovereign. You can't imagine that I would lie. It is a pity, but I had heard that a man had seduced Her Highness and taken her away to a secret place. As a plan to get her to reappear, I had a beggar girl sought out and killed. Look at the results! (*sung*) Just as I foresaw, Her Highness has immediately reappeared. Now instead of praise, scheming villains plan to smear me with the crime. After you hear the facts, if you decide that I am at fault, then without another word, I'll commit *seppuku* before Your Highness.

NARRATOR: He puts hand to sword but is stopped.

YOSHITERU: No, you mustn't be hasty, Chōkei. You're not the guilty one, not at fault. These eyes can see clearly who are the good and who are the bad.

NARRATOR: Yoshiteru draws his royal sword.

YOSHITERU: Adulterous woman, disloyal retainer, I'll cut you down like this.

NARRATOR: He slashes out at the tatami mats again and again in a fury.

YOSHITERU: Ah, it felt splendid to vent my anger, Chōkei. I won't let you go to bed yet. Let's drink a toast and clear the air. Come over here.

NARRATOR: Called to his master, Chōkei follows Yoshiteru back into the inner rooms. (*cadence*) Those left behind can only despair at the absurdity of it all.

(*sung*) Her Highness is distraught.

LADY YOSHITERU: This is too hateful! I am the daughter of Dainagon Lord Akitada. I'm too angry for words! How could I be accused of adultery? It's despicable! If it means my death, so be it, but I'm not going to die because of this monstrous slander.

NARRATOR: She runs to accost His Highness but is restrained by Lord Fujitaka.

FUJITAKA: Your anger is entirely understandable, (*spoken*) but when His Highness has had too much to drink, it's impossible to change his mind. The more you reason, the greater your fall from grace. Leave it all to me. Listen, Mikinoshin, I've heard that you and Kiyotaki are now married. (*sung*) If so, then there will be no taint of impropriety. Have Kiyotaki smuggle Her Highness into one of the women's rooms and make sure that you both protect her.

MIKINOSHIN: Yes, sir.

NARRATOR: (*cadence*) He slips swiftly out by the side door to the other building.

FUJITAKA: (*sung*) We'll wait now for that scheming priest to come out and see him punished, but perhaps it would be better not in front of His Highness. It's now or never!

NARRATOR: He paces swiftly up and down, uncertain what to do and full of anger when he catches sight of a woman's shadow.

FUJITAKA: It must be the courtesan Ōyodo.

ŌYODO: (*spoken*) Is that Lord Fujitaka?

FUJITAKA: (*sung*) It is Fujitaka.

NARRATOR: He moves to her and in one swift blow plunges the sword deep into her side. He pounces on top of her to muffle her cries and stop her struggles.

FUJITAKA: (*spoken*) Because of you, how many have died and suffered ignobly. (*sung*) This sword will take you to your judgment day. You're not an apparition, an evil demon, or a poisonous serpent. You couldn't really enjoy watching people be murdered. Chōkei has enlisted you to incite an insurrection. Spit out the truth!

NARRATOR: He presses down harder and harder.

ŌYODO: (*spoken*) Oh, Lord Fujitaka, I called out to you so that I could tell you all. All the samurai in the palace are allied with Chōkei. They're waiting for the moment to strike and assassinate His Highness. It is all terrifying, but His Highness is unaware of the threat. His life is flickering like a faint flame in the depths of night, about to face a strong wind. (*sung*) I knew of the danger (*cadence*) but didn't know what I could do.

(*sung*) I wanted to get word to you, but His Highness wouldn't allow me out of his sight, out of his room. I decided to become evil and perverted and have him lose interest and get rid of me. If I could find someone to trust, I was ready to tell him everything. I know I was a foolish woman, but it was all I could think of. When I had someone sacrificed at His Highness's order, I laughed aloud, but inside, my heart was tortured a hundred times worse than the one killed. (*cadence*) Only the gods can know my suffering.

(*sung*) Even then, no one accused me of my evil. No one admonished me. (*spoken*) Then I wondered whether someone outside the palace would hear about the awful cruelty, but when I had another killed, nothing came of it, no reaction at all. (*sung*) I feel pity even for the squashing of a mosquito or a fly; even that is a crime. How much more, a human being. How distressed I was that I'd become a murderer, and when I could no longer put on a happy face, His Highness had another killed to raise my spirits. Each and every time I felt their bitterness and anger (*highest pitch*) weighing down my evil karma, heavier and heavier. Even though I am still alive, I felt that I should have grown horns on my forehead like an animal, scales like a serpent.[9] It was surely a sign of Buddha's punishment that I remained in His Highness's favor until today—I knew that I was destined to suffer in hell. How sordid it all is! (*spoken*) A low, vile woman of my profession shared a pillow with the shogun. (*sung*) To be slain by Lord Fujitaka, known as a model of moral virtue and martial prowess, (*spoken*) how could I have any regrets for my life? (*sung*) In order to avenge the anger and hate of those who died on my behalf, make my end long and painful. It is my offering to Her Highness. Please forgive my vileness. Take care of His Highness; that is all I ask.

NARRATOR: (*high pitch*) With these words, (*cadence*) she reaches her sad end.

FUJITAKA: (*sung*) This was a woman of unexpected valor and spirit.

NARRATOR: He stands up straightening his kimono, but suddenly voices sound from all sides, a commotion throughout the palace.

SOLDIER: No one knows what it means, but four or five thousand soldiers bearing different banners have surrounded the palace.

NARRATOR: Even before he has finished, the advance group reaches the main gate; battle horns and bells sound the cry to arms, (*cadence*) shaking the foundations of heaven and earth.

156 Lovers Pond in Settsu Province

FIGURE 31 The insurrection against Shogun Yoshiteru and the destruction of the Muromachi Palace; (top center) Ōyodo's death; (left center) Fujitaka fighting; (top left) Yoshiteru's death; (lower right) Kiyotaki killing her stepfather, Iwanari. (*Muromachi senjō-jiki* [*Tsu no kuni meoto-ike*], 1742, Keio University Library.)

FUJITAKA: (*sung*) It's just as I imagined. This is all Chōkei's plan, hatched years ago. He humored and flattered His Highness. I regret that my negligence has been our downfall. First we must take care of Her Highness and then tackle that vile priest.

NARRATOR: He yells out in rage.

FUJITAKA: (*spoken*) All you men, if you're loyal to His Highness, then cut down not only those animal samurai who've joined the enemy but also their footmen and grooms. Fly at them and (*sung*) die with glory!

NARRATOR: Shouting orders, he dives into the fray. Mikinoshin has to leave the fate of His Highness to others as he leads Her Highness out. Kiyotaki draws her sword, showing them the way to the Kasuga side gate. They hurry through the garden in the shadow of trees. Kiyotaki's father, Iwanari, comes toward them with spear raised.

IWANARI: Come back here. You won't get away!

NARRATOR: He gives chase. Kiyotaki turns to face him.

KIYOTAKI: (spoken) The bonds of parent and child are private. Loyalty between lord and subject is public. You have shamed us forever. I shall be your foe. Are you ready?

IWANARI: What! Have you forgotten it was I that raised you? Have you no thanks? (sung) You ingrate! So be it, you vixen, I'll take you on.

NARRATOR: He thrusts at her, but she parries the blow, knocks the spear away, and strikes out. Though heavy as a rock, his head flies through the air.

KIYOTAKI: So now, I no longer have a father; I'm all alone. My life is only for my lord and husband, even to the depths of hell.

NARRATOR: (cadence) Strong words lead their charge. (sung) The battle cries grow louder, closing in. A hail of musket fire and flying arrows assaults the palace. Chōkei emerges from the wardrobe room and faces the royal bedroom. His voice bellows out, shaking the building itself.

CHŌKEI: (spoken) What a fool you've been, Lord Yoshiteru. I killed my only child to show a true heart, encouraged your lust, and gained control of your spirit. I've been planning this for five long years. All the Kyoto soldiers are under my command. The dream of splendor has ended for the Ashikaga reign of thirteen generations. The touch of a cold sword will wake you from your slumber. Take your own life nobly, commit *seppuku*. (sung) The great shogun is a bird trapped in a cage. Soldiers, advance from all fronts! Attack and destroy all in your path! Don't let even baby ants escape, crush them all, attack and take no prisoners!

NARRATOR: His orders rally the troops, who unsheathe a magnificent array of fine weapons, glistening and ready to be tested in battle. Swords and spears fill the air as more than six thousand horsemen advance, marching eyes front, chopping down everything in sight. Only a few remain loyal, the personal attendants of His Highness and a bodyguard of only fifty mounted men. Among them is one horseman, a match for a thousand, a fierce hawk, a crested eagle who routs the hordes of soldiers as if he were scattering pheasants. (battle-scene cadence) He charges into the fray, fighting furiously.

NARRATOR: (sung) The multitude of enemy troops divides into seven groups and advances, surrounding the few loyal soldiers who are soon annihilated. Among them, Fujitaka still fights on gallantly.

FUJITAKA: This is my last chance. Chōkei, come out and face me! I won't let you escape.

NARRATOR: He searches out his enemy, but just then Matsunaga emerges carrying the Ashikaga banner with its distinctive circle with two horizontal lines. He has Sunomata Gonbeita raise it high, and he himself holds up the head of the shogun on the tip of his sword. He gives a yell.

MATSUNAGA: (*spoken*) The great shogun Lord Minamoto no Yoshiteru has been killed by Matsunaga Danjō Hisahide! (*sung*) Raise the victory cry!

NARRATOR: Matsunaga enters the battle, grandly holding his prize. Fujitaka turns angrily, his face as fierce as a demon from hell. He makes a beeline for Matsunaga, cutting down everybody in his way.

MATSUNAGA: That's Asakawa! It's Fujitaka!

NARRATOR: Seeing their commander flee, the troops panic, trampling over one another to escape.

FUJITAKA: Come back here, Matsunaga. I'm right behind you, Danjō.

NARRATOR: He chases them everywhere, and they fall into confusion. Gonbeita loses his way. Fujitaka grabs his armor, throws him to the ground, and stamps on his chest. He wrests away the banner, holds it aloft, and calls out bravely.

FUJITAKA: You won't get away!

NARRATOR: He pursues them, calling out.

FUJITAKA: I know that you are all show and no mettle.

NARRATOR: He grabs everyone near him and throws them off like pebbles, like flying hailstones in a storm. They scatter like leaves blown off trees (*cadence*) until not one of the enemy is left. (*sung*) Emperor Liang threw the dragon, and Xiangyu[10] had the strength to lift a mountain. Fame and honor come to nothing.

FUJITAKA: His Highness Yoshiteru has been lost, his head taken, a terrible tragedy. I have no more strength; without my lord, no tree to lean on,[11] I'm lighter than the wings of a cicada. Though I regret living on, I'll keep going until I avenge his death.

NARRATOR: His will is firm as stone and iron, but he collapses with grief and tears flow like a shower of gems. Precious stones from China were polished into jewels (*high pitch*) and inlaid by the craftsmen of Japan to decorate the Ashikaga Palace now razed to the ground. Fujitaka makes his escape through the haze and smoke.

Act 3

—Scene 1
A few hours later, on the road to Fukushima in Settsu Province

"Journey in a Maternity Sash"

NARRATOR:

(*sung*)[1] How poignant the scattered blossoms at Muromachi Palace.[2]
Her Highness's flower, too, may fall before its time.
Her precious child is due to be born.
Kiyotaki carries sacred herbs to induce labor,
as well as sweet herbs for the newborn's soup
and five cleansing incenses for the first bath.
It's still four in the morning, before any sign of dawn.
Accompanied by Mikinoshin, they have escaped from the capital
but their legs are tired, sore and weary from the long journey.
They are disguised so as not to appear of the Ashikaga,
but Her Highness's fullness casts a moon-shaped shadow.[3]
Faces downcast, they've fallen far from the Palace in the Clouds.[4]
(*cadence*) A wretched sight.
(*sung*) Yesterday we cast our eyes across the capital from the palace lookout
to view the tall Tōji Pagoda through the spyglass.
We need not ask the name of the "autumn mountains"[5] in the southeast.
How brilliant in the moonlight!
Next we pass Koizuka, Princess Kesa's grave.[6]
And then Yotsuzuka.
Will we ever return this way past the Toba Road crossing?
We cross Koeda Bridge, next Yodo's Great Bridge
and with the morning sun cross Kobashi Bridge,
finally reaching the other shore.[7]
Waves glisten like precious jewels,
the water's surface a flowing brocade, most splendid.[8]
Hiding from other travelers, they seek the shade
of auspicious pines lining the river bank.
They pass below Chitose, recalling its meaning of "thousand years."

They await at any moment the royal birth.
No one knows when it will come,
when a woman must ford the river between life and death.
They cross Hato Peak near Iwashimizu Hachiman Shrine.[9]
From there they bask in the god's guiding light
(*highest pitch*) which graces all around
as sunbeams through gossamer on a summer tree.[10]
Boulders rise higher and higher, growing into mountains.
Through the valleys, tree branches intertwine.
They pray fervently to the god to protect their beloved.
Strong and steady is the Iwashimizu Hachiman Mountain Shrine,
may it restore the purity and strength of the Minamoto clan
now threatened in this sullied world.[11]
May it lead us back to the cherished "capital beyond the clouds,"
now so distant.[12]
Prayers so impassioned that jeweled tears flow forth.
Wandering on, they advance along the road near Hashimoto.
(*cadence*) The bells toll two in the afternoon.

NARRATOR: (*sung*) Still far to go, Her Highness is overcome with grief and begins to suffer pains and collapses in the grass, gasping for breath. Mikinoshin and Kiyotaki are alarmed and comfort her, knowing that in her condition, she must be exhausted. Her time has come, and before they realize it, she has easily given birth to a healthy baby whose voice cries out like the birds in paradise.[13] He shines, this jeweled prince. We may find joy amid suffering. (*cadence*) How true the saying is.

KIYOTAKI: (*sung*)[14] Ah, how wretched is the fate of the poor prince, to be born this way, far from the palace on the roadside under the sky, not even a cover for his body or a simple hovel for a home. We have only tears for his first bath, no means to build a fire. And this is the heir of the great shogun, commander in chief, minister of the left, Yoshiteru. (*highest pitch*) How pitiful that we have nothing with which to celebrate the birth of this prince!

NARRATOR: Kiyotaki weeps for the baby's misfortune, pity from a woman's soft heart. (*spoken*) Mikinoshin steps forward.

MIKINOSHIN: No, it's not true that he is unfortunate. There are good precedents from the past. From the time of Hachiman Bodhisattva in Tsukushi onward, we have many auspicious examples of births on top of rocks or under trees.[15] (*sung*) This site near Iwashimizu Shrine on Mount Otoko is especially auspicious, falling under the protective gaze of Hachiman. The god Kōra, Takeuchi no Sukune,[16] who lived to be almost three hundred, too, is worshiped at a shrine nearby. (*spoken*) The child is blessed by the karma of his ancestor Lord Takauji. (*sung*) His nursery is nature and the open sky; he will be a great shogun with the Sun Goddess's blessings. With such an auspicious birth, who if not he will live to become the master of the nation? Congratulations!

NARRATOR: He rejoices at the birth (both chanters) and takes Her Highness's hand to encourage her to travel on to Amano River, suggesting the constancy of the lovers of the Milky Way.[17] (*cadence*) But here they find no boat to board. (*sung*) Along the banks of the Shimeno River, they spy a boat tied to a willow tree whose branches blow in the wind, the wind that carries them past Hirakata along the Yodo River. Next they cross Sata farther downstream.

>(*popular song*) Walking away from the river,
>I look across and see peasant girls:
>what're they doing, what're they doing?
>They've tied up their skirts
>and wade barefoot in the water,
>soaking cloth, narrow cloth, at the "Bleaching Village,"[18]
>(*cadence*) which they now pass.

(*sung*) This morning we set out and have traveled for only a day, but how much suffering in that time! Now we have come to places known by name from poetry of the past, the Ōe Banks[19] of the great Yodo River, and next we pass the Watanabe Banks, (*scene cadence*) finally to reach Fukushima.[20]

—Scene 2
A little later, at Reizei Bunjibei's home in Fukushima village

NARRATOR:

>(*sung*) Even deep in the mountains,
>(*high pitch*) How poignant the cry of the deer.[21]

(*sung*) These are the thoughts of Mikinoshin's father Reizei no Bunjibei Nagafusa, now a poor hermit, hidden but still in the midst of world. Rather than bow to a lord for a meager stipend, he has retired to a site near Watanabe at Fukushima where the water is pure. The tools his wife uses to spin and weave cotton can be seen, along with different kinds of cotton cloth and padding. She sells her work to help them make a living. Although she has had no training in spinning, she has developed techniques to make the balls of cotton fluff up to look like Mount Fuji's snowy peak, (*cadence*) a mistress magnificently resourceful.

(*sung*) Mikinoshin approaches the house, leading Her Highness while Kiyotaki carries the newborn prince. He points out the house.

MIKINOSHIN: (*spoken*) This is my father Bunjibei's home. In order to make a living, he acts like a townsman, but his samurai spirit hasn't changed one bit. Both my father and mother are extremely upright and proper. If they find out that Kiyotaki and I are secretly married, then I'm sure to be disowned. (*sung*) Not a whisper of this to them!

NARRATOR: His voice is low as they walk down the narrow path. They hear someone singing. "No worries in the world, alone with my fishing rod. I wouldn't change it to be prime minister or shogun, this marvelous life in the mountains along the river."[22] Mikinoshin's father, carrying his fishing pole, walks past them without a glance and goes into his house. Mikinoshin calls him back.

MIKINOSHIN: (*spoken*) I beg your pardon, father, but it's me, your son Mikinoshin. What a delight to see you so spry and healthy!

BUNJIBEI: Hmm, is that you Mikinoshin? The disturbance at Kyoto has put everyone around here on edge. Even I thought of pulling down the old rusty spear and running into battle, but to seek fame on the battlefield when you aren't even asked is a waste of time just to get a stipend. So I've been down to the river enjoying myself by washing my ears of the dirt of this world.[23] (*sung*) I was thinking that with the death of His Highness, you must be busy with your duties. Why have you come here at such a time? (*spoken*) It looks like you've brought a couple of Kyoto beauties with you. The area around here is Miyoshi's territory. It's no place to come for a holiday. (*sung*) Quick, be on your way.

NARRATOR: He turns away and starts to go inside.

MIKINOSHIN: (*spoken*) Listen, wait a moment. I haven't come fleeing to

save myself. This is Her Highness, Lady Yoshiteru, and the young prince she gave birth to along the way.
NARRATOR: Bunjibei interrupts.
BUNJIBEI: Quiet! You're talking too loud. You've done well. What a feat! Hurry, come inside.
NARRATOR: (*sung*) He motions them inside and the mother, too, having heard Mikinoshin, comes to welcome them.
WIFE: With the world in chaos as it is at the moment, I suppose you've chosen not to use a royal carriage and have come to seek the services of an excellent retired warrior. Such an honor for our family.
NARRATOR: She bows with knees bent (*cadence*) and has Her Highness sit in the position of honor. (*sung*) Her Highness has tears in her eyes.
LADY YOSHITERU: What a shock to be betrayed by our trusted retainer Chōkei, like being suddenly attacked by a favorite pet dog, a terrible fate. Although I hate the idea of living on after His Highness, since I was with child, I was determined to avoid the assassin's sword. Mikinoshin has helped me this far, and now I beg his parents as well to assist us.
NARRATOR: How dreadful (*cadence*) that she has been driven to become so bitter. (*sung*) Bunjibei bows reverently.
BUNJIBEI: (*spoken*) Human fortune in this world is like the twists of a rope, the good and the bad come round and round.[24] Your troubles now are severe, but the birth of the young prince has brought hope of spring sunshine to your clan's fortunes. It's like waiting for the plum blossoms to peep through the snow. Although that villain Chōkei is throwing his destructive weight about everywhere in the nation, from heaven's vantage point, no more damage has been done than a sparrow's beak or a mouse's tooth might do,[25] nothing to worry about. (*sung*) Though still an infant, this child is heir to Lord Yoshiteru. If the call comes to raise the banner to avenge Chōkei's crimes, the powerful samurai of the five home provinces and from all the highways of the nation will put their honorable names forward to serve the Ashikaga house for generations to come. No one, not a single samurai, will refuse the call to be your ally. (*spoken*) In a corner of our property, I have built a small study under a thatched roof. You can rest safely there for the time being. Wife, show them where it is. Lower the lamp and make sure that no one sees you as you walk through the grounds.

NARRATOR: (*sung*) Strong words from such an upright man encourage them all. Led by the wife, (*scene cadence*) Her Highness and Kiyotaki withdraw.

(*sung*) Bunjibei moves closer to Mikinoshin.

BUNJIBEI: (*sung*) I'll look after Her Highness. You go and find Kanemori, and then go off to Awa to raise the Awaji troops. That'll be our first plan.

NARRATOR: But before he can finish, (*sung*) his wife comes rushing in, her face pale with shock.

WIFE: (*spoken*) Listen, I just heard that Kiyotaki's father is Iwanari Chikara, the right-hand officer of the villainous enemy himself, Miyoshi Chōkei.

NARRATOR: (*sung*) Bunjibei, too, colors with rage at the news.

MIKINOSHIN: (*spoken*) No, wait, there's nothing to worry about. From childhood, she has been in Her Highness's service. She is uncommonly loyal for a woman. She even fought against Iwanari and in the end killed him herself. She's a woman who knows duty and propriety.

NARRATOR: Bunjibei's expression is all the more suspicious after this spirited defense.

BUNJIBEI: A woman who knows her duty so well is not one to be unfilial. (*sung*) She's shown loyalty to her lord once, but I'm sure that next time she'll avenge her father's death in order to prove her filial love. Even if she doesn't plan a direct revenge, Iwanari's clan is widespread, and this area is Chōkei's territory. She'll get caught up in family connections and be tricked into leading the enemy to attack. It's easy to see how a woman could be deceived and become an unwitting spy. If her actions lead to the downfall of the Ashikaga, my negligence would be to blame. (*spoken*) The best strategy is to avoid danger. I know that it may seem heartless, but only when she is cut down will we be able to sleep in peace. (*sung*) Call her out and while we're chatting, Mikinoshin, you cut her down. Wife, use your skills to get her to come out with you.

NARRATOR: He adds oil to the lamp and sits down. His face glows excitedly in the flickering light.

MIKINOSHIN: (*spoken*) Then, you want me to do it here and now?

BUNJIBEI: The longer we wait, the more danger for Her Highness.

MIKINOSHIN: This is too cruel a task. We'll regret losing a trusted ally. I swear that she is not a traitor.

NARRATOR: (*sung*) He almost says too much but stops, realizing that he may alert his wily father to their relationship. (*cadence*) He chooses caution.

BUNJIBEI: (*spoken*) No, no, youth can never understand these matters. Remember the clever strategy that Sasaki adopted when he killed the fellow from Fujito Bay to hide the knowledge about the currents.[26] Since she was Iwanari's daughter, we cannot take a chance on such a woman. We're better off without an ally like that. One woman won't be missed. (*sung*) Wife, hurry up and call her here. Go on and speak to her. I'll sit here and watch for her arrival. When I give the signal, you strike. Is your sword sharp enough? Don't fail me here!

NARRATOR: Mikinoshin nods his readiness, but now faces the worst crisis of his life. His heart races, his nerves are taut.

MIKINOSHIN: (*spoken*) My sword is quite sharp enough, regularly honed and polished, but it has never been tested on a woman. If by chance Kiyotaki is an incarnation of Kannon Bodhisattva, then won't my sword shatter?

NARRATOR: (*sung*) His words are jumbled and his voice high pitched.

BUNJIBEI: Quiet, they're coming. Your mother has signaled.

NARRATOR: Mikinoshin looks out the back and sees his mother leading Kiyotaki.

MIKINOSHIN: Oh my god! She's being led to her death. If only Her Highness would call her now, then she could live even a little longer.

NARRATOR: (*cadence*) Desperation and despair. (*sung*) Bunjibei acts naturally.

BUNJIBEI: (*spoken*) Miss Kiyotaki, I understand that you're a daughter of Iwanari Chikara. We know you're loyal, you've proved it by your actions against your father, but you must retain some affection for your clan.

NARRATOR: (*sung*) He tries to draw out her true sentiments. Mikinoshin sits poised, waiting to attack at his father's signal, his eyes tearful and Buddha's prayer filling his heart. Kiyotaki has no inkling.

KIYOTAKI: (*spoken*) You've touched on an embarrassing point. In fact, I'm not Iwanari's natural child. I was abandoned at Yotsuzuka near Tōji temple by parents whom I never knew. I was supposedly found there and then raised by Iwanari. (*sung*) I had no love for him, only hate. He even tried to murder me, and in the end I killed him myself. (*emotional cadence*) Consider me a hapless woman without a single relative. I beg your blessing.

NARRATOR: She breaks down in tears.

BUNJIBEI: (*spoken*) No, Iwanari surely deceived you. He was plotting something from the time you were born. He presented you as a foundling without any proof of that fact.

NARRATOR: He pushes Kiyotaki to reveal the truth.

KIYOTAKI: Never. It's not a lie. I have proof; it's sewn into the lining. I've an amulet from the guardian Buddha Fudō, a small statue about an inch and a half long. (*sung*) The cloth it's wrapped in has the date, year, month, and day. I've never taken it off nor let it out of my sight, this reminder of my real parents. Here, look for yourself.

NARRATOR: Bunjibei and his wife are shocked and rush to open the cloth. The more they look, the more sure they are.

WIFE: I'm the mother who gave birth to you! This statue was a family treasure. The seal on the cloth, that was from your father here. What a joy to discover our daughter again! (*spoken*) Miki, this is your little sister. Kiyotaki, he's your elder brother. (*sung, highest pitch*) What suffering we've caused you, you poor dear!

NARRATOR: The parents pull her close, overcome with emotion, unable to believe it is not a dream. Mikinoshin is even more shocked.

KIYOTAKI: How could you abandon your own daughter! Why?

NARRATOR: She clings to them, her anger all too understandable.[27]

BUNJIBEI: (*spoken*) You're right to be angry. We didn't abandon you for any fault of yours. When you were born, Miki was three. (*sung*) We were struggling. I was a rōnin unable to support two babies. We just couldn't follow our hearts, or both of you would have starved to death. They say a girl is born with good karma that promises good fortune. So we abandoned the daughter to keep the son. How dear you were to us, how precious. (*cadence*) It was a terrible, stupid thing we did.

(*sung*) If you were Iwanari's real child, then Mikinoshin was ready to kill you at my signal. It was surely the gods' or Buddha's reins that kept us from killing you. (*spoken*) You've been plucked from the jaws of death. You've been given new life. (*sung*) Please don't hate us.

NARRATOR: He caresses her gently.

KIYOTAKI: (*spoken*) Then Mikinoshin is my real brother. (*sung*) Oh my god!

NARRATOR: Unable to say any more, she steals an embarrassed glance through tearful eyes. Her brother is still in shock, a cold sweat covering his body. Fated to be both siblings and lovers, (*high pitch*) neither regrets nor lament can sever the ties that bind them. They're like the mythical

FIGURE 32 (Right) Lady Yoshiteru and her newborn baby arriving at Bunjibei's house with Mikinoshin and Kiyotaki; (left) Bunjibei's wife; (below) cats playing while Mikinoshin and Kiyotaki stand aghast at the revelation that they are brother and sister. (*Muromachi senjō-jiki* [*Tsu no kuni meoto-ike*], 1742, Keio University Library.)

bird with two bodies linked as one,[28] now caught in a net, (*cadence*) their love pitifully entangled in a weir.

NARRATOR: (*sung*) Father and mother rejoice.

BUNJIBEI: (*spoken*) Everyone has been living an upright life and has remained loyal in adversity, (*sung*) and now we've been blessed by heaven with the reunion of parents and siblings. Her Highness, too, will be delighted at this news. Let's go and tell her.

NARRATOR: The parents take Kiyotaki's hands.

BUNJIBEI: (*spoken*) Mikinoshin, you stay here and keep a lookout for any sign of trouble. You'll find gunpowder and a musket in the cupboard. There are lots of greedy, beastly farmers on Miyoshi's lands, real animals. If they should come around, fire away.

NARRATOR: (*sung*) His words are aimed at the enemy outside, but they strike Mikinoshin's heart (*exit cadence*) like a bullet in the chest. Despair.[29]

NARRATOR: (*sung*) Left alone, Mikinoshin turns on himself.
MIKINOSHIN: (*spoken*) I was born human with hands and feet, all in perfect order. I'm the dutiful samurai, Reizei Mikinoshin Fusahira, favored by the great shogun Lord Minamoto no Yoshiteru himself. (*sung*) Married to my own sister! I've fallen to the realm of beasts.[30] No tail has sprouted, but I crawl on all fours. Ignorant fool! What a terrible fate! I hate myself.
NARRATOR: He grinds his teeth and clenches his fists so hard that his nails cut the skin. (*cadence*) Blood mixes with tears, an unraveling brocade.
MIKINOSHIN: (*sung*) Now that I have safely entrusted Her Highness to father, my mind is at rest. Rather than go on living with this shame and turn my family into a pack of mongrels or a flock of fowl, I'll become a beast myself and bring my life to an end. Then, the family's name will not be soiled. Farewell.
NARRATOR: He grabs his sword but hesitates.
MIKINOSHIN: (*spoken*) Ah, this used to be father's, a fine specimen made by Bizen Kiyomitsu. (*sung*) It wasn't given for killing beasts.
NARRATOR: He grasps his short sword.
MIKINOSHIN: (*spoken*) No, this, too, is from His Highness, a masterpiece made by Yukihira.[31] These form a set of armor made to lead the shogun's army's charge into battle, for routing the enemy, for cuts and thrusts, for capturing a famous foe, for taking an enemy's head—that's why I was presented with these. (*sung*) But none of that. It'll cut the belly of a beast, and both magnificent swords will forever fall out of samurai hands. They'll be wasted tools, lost to Japan. They've lost divine favor. Both hanging and swallowing one's tongue are human ways of killing oneself. I know of no model for a beast's suicide. How shall I do it? What an awful fate!
NARRATOR: He mumbles to himself, choked with tears. (*high pitch*) He claws at his body in anger and despair, (*cadence*) a pitiful sight as he collapses in grief.

(*sung*) Kiyotaki comes running in, no longer able to restrain her tears[32] but then becomes embarrassed, realizing she can no longer hug him in the same way. No more sweet moments of intimacy. If only it were a dream—suddenly to become brother and sister and have to keep a distance, reserved now before each other. (*highest pitch*) How agonizing not to be able to move closer. (*emotional cadence*) She bursts into tears.

(*sung*) Her brother looks up and their eyes meet. Their faces burn as signal fires at night, but the flame inside begins to smolder[33] under beads of sweat. Yesterday's warmth in bed is replaced by today's cold meeting, ignoring each other. (*cadence*) Nothing to do but cry.

(*sung*) Sitting quietly, they notice a cat in heat calling her mate from under the eaves. Its cries grow louder with rising passion, (*popular song*) enough to rouse any cat dozing in front of the camellias. The cats climb down the pillar and rush back up again in (*high pitch*) play, delighting in each other, (*cadence*) their feline passion unashamed before others' eyes.

(*sung*) Mikinoshin stares at the cats through tearful eyes.

MIKINOSHIN: (*spoken*) That pair of lovers have the same color coats; surely they're siblings, too. They say that unless you have wings, you can't know a bird's heart.[34] Humans cannot know the heart of a bird, but the animals seem to know that we are one of them. This is disastrous, horrible. (*sung*) I'm disgusted and can't watch them any longer.

NARRATOR: He douses the lamp, and then darkness.

KIYOTAKI: Then, those cats too are siblings. I'm jealous. They can vow love as brother and sister, and no one blames them, no one slanders their name. (*highest pitch*) I want to become a cat. I am a cat![35]

NARRATOR: While speaking, she moves slowly closer to Mikinoshin, pawing him with her foot, but her brother stealthily moves his feet away. The cats' playful mating antics in the rafters grow more passionate and wild; they topple over a bucket, and both fall down the old well in the garden. They hear a splash as the cats strike the water.

KIYOTAKI: (*highest pitch*) How dreadful! They'll drown. We must save them.

NARRATOR: She looks down the well, but the water is deep. The sound of their struggle persists for a while, (*cadence*) and then a final silence falls. (*sung*) The cats' death strikes deep.

MIKINOSHIN: No death by sword, or hanging, or swallowing one's tongue. We've been shown the model for an animal's suicide. I can't live on any longer. Tonight I'll meet my end in a river's depths or in a pond, whichever I find.

NARRATOR: His will is firm.

MIKINOSHIN: Sister, are you there?

KIYOTAKI: Mikinoshin, don't leave me, stay near.

NARRATOR: She searches him out following the voice, but he moves away. She stumbles around in the darkness, blind with love, determined to find him. She follows the sound of his footsteps, feels the draft of a passing skirt, the scent of hair oil. She grabs hold of him, but he pulls away and she tumbles down. She runs after him to the gate. "I'm coming with you," she cries, as she grasps him again. He casts her off again and again, but every time she comes back, struggling like a wild cormorant caught in a sluice[36] (*highest pitch*) in the fisherman's ropes all twisted up, (*highest pitch, scene cadence*) losing strength.

—Scene 3
A little later at Lovers Pond

NARRATOR: (*sung*) Along roads or on footpaths through fields, they run desperately on and on, in this direction and that, oblivious of the way. So many fields, so many groves to wander in, so many paths to choose. They stumble about among the grasses and roots, all twisted and entangled like ropes—suddenly, (*high pitch*) they collapse on the ground together, (*cadence*) panting for breath.

   (*sung*) Kiyotaki hasn't stopped crying.

KIYOTAKI: (*spoken*) Oh, you're too cruel Mikinoshin! Why have you suddenly become so cold and distant? (*sung*) I'm not to blame for our fall into the realm of beasts, and neither are you. We're fated by the karma of past lives. How can you want to die alone? The scandal of our bonds as lovers will not disappear with death. If the brother's reputation is soiled, how much more is his sister's. My life is in your hands. Let me die with you. Once we've been lovers, there's no turning back. (*sung*) Whether we're to be dogs or cats, we'll be married in our next life. At this moment of death need we be reserved before each other?

NARRATOR: (*emotional cadence*) She hugs him desperately.

MIKINOSHIN: (*spoken*) You're right. I'm sorry that I was foolish. If one dies alone or two together, it won't cleanse our sullied name. So let us die together. I wonder where we are now. (*sung*) I think I remember that village off in the dark over there. It's more than a mile to the Tenjin

Woods Barrier Post. (*spoken*) Look, look, stars are reflected in the grass! That means a pond. Just what we hoped for, we've found water so we can die like animals. Heaven's guidance! I'll test the depth.

NARRATOR: He takes up a stone and tosses it into the murky pond. Its sound resonates deeply.

MIKINOSHIN: You go into the pond here; I'll go over there.

NARRATOR: He starts to walk away, but Kiyotaki stops him.

KIYOTAKI: (*spoken*) You still say such hateful things. (*sung*) I want us to go hand in hand together into the pond to drink the same water.

NARRATOR: She pleads with tears.

MIKINOSHIN: I'm sorry I hurt you. You're right, of course. (*spoken*) I, too, wanted us to die together, but when we're completely dead, our bodies will float to the surface. If we're separate, then people will think we had felt the shame and at least died as samurai, even though we'd become lovers ignorant of our past. It would be an apology to father and mother, a gesture to the world. (*sung*) We can't write on the water,[37] but if we show our true hearts, the pond will be our testament. (*spoken*) My kimono has my family crest on it. Yours was given to you by Her Highness with her crest on it. Neither are suitable to robe the bodies of dead beasts, don't you agree?

KIYOTAKI: (*sung*) Yes, of course. Let's take them off.

NARRATOR: They loosen their outer sashes and remove their kimonos, and hug each other even more tightly. They recall the poem, "Together we cast ourselves into Lovers Pond,"[38] not the one far away in Kyoto but Lovers Pond here in Settsu Province. They hang their robes on a tree branch along the shore.

MIKINOSHIN: West is that way.

NARRATOR: He points to the fields across the way (*spoken*) and sees flickering lanterns, people running, and then hears his mother's voice.

MIKINOSHIN: Over there among the pines, isn't that Bunjibei?

NARRATOR: They hear cries calling out to them.

MIKINOSHIN: (*sung*) Oh my god! If we fail to die now, it'll add shame upon shame.

NARRATOR: They slip between some thick reeds to hide,[39] to await the chance to die. (*cadence*) Not much longer to wait.

(*sung*) A lantern in one hand and leading Her Highness with this other, Bunjibei brings all three of them to the site.

BUNJIBEI: (*spoken*) They've only been gone a little while, but if they're no longer in the area, we'll never find them now. Both of them, elder brother and younger sister, are of fine and upright character. They must've been devastated to learn that they had shamed themselves by unknowingly committing incest like beasts. They're surely overwhelmed with despair. Leaving home, they must be determined to live no longer. You take Her Highness and the young prince back home. What a shame that we've lost them.

NARRATOR: He weeps, but his wife retorts.

WIFE: (*sung*) Don't speak so despairingly. Don't give up so easily. (*spoken*) We'll check all the roads to the capital and not give up hope yet.

BUNJIBEI: Yes, you're right. Until we find a body, we won't despair. (*sung*) This way. Let's go.

NARRATOR: They walk on, but in the light they see a red kimono.

BUNJIBEI: Look here, in the light. (*sung*) A sign of the couple. Oh, no! Kiyotaki's robe is hanging on this tree!

WIFE: (*spoken*) On this tree hangs Mikinoshin's kimono.

BUNJIBEI: (*sung*) Then there's no doubt that the pair have thrown themselves into the pond. They must've felt that only in death could they find release. This is awful! I've made them die for no reason. (*highest pitch*) If only they would float to the surface, we could at least see their faces.

NARRATOR: Her Highness, too, is overcome with grief. They all search around the edges of the pond, finally collapsing in the grasses, wailing aloud.

MIKINOSHIN: What a pity that we cannot even fulfill our duty to our parents. How awful that it is the children instead who cause them such grief.

NARRATOR: Repenting their sin of neglect, they weep again. More ashamed than ever to go on living, they hide deeper in the reeds. (*cadence*) Tears as full as the rising tide.

   (*sung*) Bunjibei collapses in tears, beyond despair. He looks out over the pond and yells.

BUNJIBEI: (*spoken*) We're but an hour too late, how dreadful. Even if Mikinoshin weren't a samurai, he's an upright man and would commit suicide by *harakiri* or by a sword down his throat. Even a menial knows how to cut his own throat. (*sung*) How horrible! I can imagine what he felt at the end, choking on the murky water. (*spoken*) Since he fell unexpectedly into the realm of beasts, he must've been afraid of using his swords, afraid of soiling them. They were even afraid of shaming us and so left their robes behind because of the crests. So sensitive to our feelings, so caring! That's what makes you a true human, a true samurai. The parent is no match for his child. He nobly entrusted Her Highness and the young prince to my care before dying, thinking I was worthy of the task. What a waste! My negligence killed a true samurai. Wife, our daughter, too, had a pure heart. A flower in full bloom, she, too, felt such shame, (*highest pitch*) her body now among the weeds at the bottom of the pond.

NARRATOR: The parents hold each other and grieve aloud. Her Highness calls out.

LADY YOSHITERU: A samurai, one among a hundred, a thousand, and Kiyotaki even more loyal than a man. How pitiful that she is gone, how wretched for the young prince's future.

NARRATOR: The pair, hidden only by a thin screen of reeds, pity Her Highness in agony (*cadence*) and weep with their parents so near.
  (*sung*) Bunjibei controls his tears.

BUNJIBEI: A flower has its fragrance, the moon its glow.[40] A samurai has his lineage. Hear me out, you spirits under water. Your Highness, as well, listen carefully. (*spoken*) Mikinoshin and Kiyotaki are, in fact, born of different parents. Since they're entirely unrelated, nothing blocks their marriage, they've broken no taboo. He was not adopted, nor did we find him as a foundling. The karma that led us to become parent and child, it's a complex story I've hidden far too long. (*sung*) I let the hours pass, then the days, and forgot about my most important duty. My regrets must now face this tragedy. Drunk on the mud of the world of pleasure, I'm far beneath the four-legged beasts. (*spoken*) Like small fish starving in the shallow ruts where pools of rain collect,[41] I struggled for survival.

NARRATOR: (*emotional cadence*) He breaks down in a flood of tears. (*sung*) Mikinoshin is shocked again.

MIKINOSHIN: Then I owe him even more for his loving care.

NARRATOR: (*cadence*) He folds his hands, offering thanks as he listens.

BUNJIBEI: (*spoken*) Now they're gone, it's no use telling the tale. His real father was Komagata Ichikaku Kanetsuna, who was with me in service to Lord Ōuchi Yoshitaka,[42] governor of Suwō. His father was a samurai of some fame. His mother died only a week after his birth. Soon after that, Ichikaku married the woman who is now my wife who was only seventeen, saying that the child needed a mother's care. At the time when their marriage was announced, Ōuchi was at the height of his glory. (*sung*) Go, *shōgi* chess, tea ceremony, court-style football, *waka* poetry, and linked verse all were encouraged. Ichikaku was born with talent. He was a disciple of the Hananomoto school of linked verse. He was on the way home from a linked-verse gathering in Asakura at the Hachiman Shrine.[43] (*spoken*) The time was midsummer on a dark, rainy night, on his right was a row of trees, to his left a brook. His attendant's lantern went out in the rain. He couldn't see around him,[44] and some fellow who bore him a grudge cut him down from behind without a word. Ichikaku, though known as a skilled swordsman, must've been thinking of a verse. He was given no time to draw, was struck with one blow, and died instantly. Already twenty-two years have passed, (*sung*) as swiftly (*cadence*) as a colt in full flight.[45]

(*sung*) His poor wife, not even twenty yet, was in desperate straits, the baby boy in her arms. I felt that I couldn't ignore our friendship, and so asked if I could seek out the murderer and help the boy avenge his father when he reached fifteen. (*spoken*) Then, on a promise to seek revenge, we got married and left the estate, and I became a rōnin. (*sung*) Tied by this promise, we had Kiyotaki, but driven by duty to her elder brother, we cast the innocent child out to her fate in order to bring up Mikinoshin. Her mother was willing to give up her own child to fulfill her duty toward Ichikaku, whose vengeful spirit was suffering in the Ashura Realm of Never-Ending Battles. We kept our aim in our hearts day and night over the years (*spoken*) until Lord Fujitaka invited Mikinoshin into his service, a summons we could not refuse. He served well from his thirteenth year, enjoying special favor from His Lordship. He rose and rose through the ranks to become a trusted retainer. Watching from afar, we postponed revenge for a month, then a year, never forgetting the plan, but we were lost in the quest for samurai glory. We told ourselves that our revenge could be had any time. We would let him rise higher, realize his potential and become a lord in his own right. (*sung*) Now see what we've done. Pitiful. (*high pitch*) He's just the lord of a small, murky pond. I'm like the sly fox caught by the delicious smell of mouse bait.[46] I could only think of my son's success as a samurai. I've failed to fulfill my vow, my duty as a true samurai. This fox in human skin will see his end in this pond. (*spoken*) Wife, you're a true human being. Watch my demise and take heart that the enemy of your former husband has been avenged. (*sung*) Stay loyal to Her Highness and the prince. Entrust him to his uncle, Lord Yoshiaki, now a priest in Nara, and wait for his fortune to rise.

NARRATOR: He runs off toward the water, but his wife clings on to him.

WIFE: Have you gone mad? How dreadful!

NARRATOR: From the reeds a voice is heard.

MIKINOSHIN: (*spoken*) No, that would be a waste. Stop, wait!

NARRATOR: (*sung*) They come running out from the reeds.

BUNJIBEI: What, then you're still alive, magnificent! Truly a return from the nether world!

NARRATOR: Their mother and Her Highness, too, cling to them, (*cadence*) crying tears of joy.

(*sung*) Mikinoshin gets down on his knees, his head lowered, still weeping.

MIKINOSHIN: We were so ashamed at not carrying out the suicide. And then we caused you such grief by not coming forward. We feel terrible for the pain we've caused our dear parents, whom it is our duty to cherish. (*spoken*) I am blessed with four parents and still shocked at the revelations, but to you both I owe more gratitude and love than to my own ancestors, a debt greater than the mythical giant Mount Shumi in India. I shall fulfill my duty to you by taking upon myself your promise to avenge my father's death. (*sung*) It will not be difficult to carry this out without further delay. I'll be able to fulfill your plan and to offer a memorial at my father's grave. I'll set off right away. (*spoken*) Mother, even though the villain may have changed his name by now, tell me his real name or what he was called, where he lives, something to give me a lead. (*sung*) Even if it's just a rumor, tell me all you know.

NARRATOR: The fire of youth is ignited. His mother bursts into tears.

WIFE: You fool, you speak without thinking about what you're saying. If I knew the name of the culprit, would I now have a second husband and still not have done the deed? I'd have put a small sword into your little fingers, I wouldn't have needed to ask others to help. (*spoken*) It's because I had no clue at all that I have caused such trouble for Bunjibei. (*sung*) For more than twenty long years, (*cadence*) as he promised, (*sung*) he brought you up to manhood and at the same time kept on seeking

176 Lovers Pond in Settsu Province

FIGURE 33 (Right) The parents in pursuit of Mikinoshin and Kiyotaki, shown hiding above; (left) Bunjibei and his wife commit suicide. (*Muromachi senjō-jiki* [*Tsu no kuni meo-toike*], 1742, Keio University Library.)

out the criminal. We owe him so much. Now it is your turn to take the lead and avenge the crime and repay both your parents. (*highest pitch*) Those who have two fathers must serve them both. It makes me feel bad that you have to take on this hateful task.

NARRATOR: (*emotional cadence*) She bursts into tears again.

BUNJIBEI: (*spoken*) Wife, stop your tears, rejoice! I know who the murderer is, his name and his home.

WIFE: Then, who and where is he?

BUNJIBEI: The man who killed Komagata Ichikaku was a man of this area and this village, none other than Reizei Bunjibei Nagafusa.

WIFE: What . . . what?

NARRATOR: (*sung*) Is all she can utter as she straightens herself up. Her Highness seems about to faint. Mikinoshin is aghast. Kiyotaki alone speaks.

KIYOTAKI: No one is to strike father!
NARRATOR: She searches Mikinoshin's eyes to gauge his feeling. They all remain shocked, (*cadence*) each face altered, registering confusion. (*sung*) Bunjibei alone doesn't change.
BUNJIBEI: (*spoken*) At this point, my words may seem worthless, but let me speak. I didn't kill Ichikaku in a fight or out of hatred. The reason rests with my wife. She was talked about all around as being a graceful beauty, with elegance and charm. I was twenty-three and unmarried. I hoped for a goose to carry my message[47] but could only smolder with frustration, unable to get word to her. Fortunately, Ichikaku knew my wife. (*sung*) I decided to ask him to intervene and prepared a letter, carrying it in my pocket when I went to see him. But before I could speak, Ichikaku said, (*spoken*) "If I didn't have a wife already, I'd make that woman mine." Because his expression of love preceded mine (*sung*), I returned home devastated. How many times I wrote letters, only to discard them, thousands of messages. I became more and more desperate, my chest choked with emotion. (*spoken*) Then Ichikaku's wife died in childbirth. While still in mourning he proposed to her and made her his wife. I was angry and jealous. I couldn't bear it any longer and ruthlessly killed him, making the woman of my desires my wife. (*sung*) But reflecting on it now, we were a husband and wife who slept with a sword between us. She knew nothing of this and, trusting in me, came to love me. How pitiful! First passions grew (*high pitch*) into agony a hundred-fold stronger. My heart has held this in for twenty years, and the time has now come. I shall be killed by Mikinoshin, and the murky fog will clear. I've made you wait too long for this once-in-a-lifetime confession. (*spoken*) Well, Mikinoshin, strike me down! Kiyotaki, don't try to stop him or save me. If you raise a finger, you're not my daughter. Anticipating this moment, that was the reason you were abandoned as a baby. Well, won't you strike, Mikinoshin? (*sung*) Have you lost your nerve? Too weak kneed, too slow?
NARRATOR: Despite being pressed to act, (*cadence*) Mikinoshin can only sink lower and weep.
BUNJIBEI: (*spoken*) You must slay me or cease to stand as a samurai.
MIKINOSHIN: Both the murderer and his victim are my fathers. (*sung*) If a samurai must distinguish between the duties owed to each father, then I'm no longer a samurai.

NARRATOR: He hurriedly draws out his two swords and throws them as far as he can. His mother picks up his sword and unsheathes it.
WIFE: (*spoken*) Bunjibei, feel the wrath of my husband's vengeance!
NARRATOR: (*sung*) She flies at him and slices off his ear.
WIFE: (*spoken*) Now, the vendetta is complete. I knew Ichikaku for but half a year. I've been together with you for almost twenty-two years, but I was fated to be born a samurai's daughter. (*sung*) I've brought such hardship on you. Think of this woman (*high pitch*) as an ingrate, inhuman, as a dog, a beast!
NARRATOR: (*cadence*) She collapses in a flood of tears.
WIFE: (*sung*) Wretched fool that I am. In order to avenge his murder, I sullied my body time and again loving my enemy. Our pillows aligned, (*highest pitch*) we lay naked in each other's arms. All the time thinking myself dutiful to my former husband, have I lived immorally, hated by the gods, abandoned by the Buddha? On Judgment Day, what sort of deceptive reply can I make (*emotional cadence*) to escape Lord Enma's inquiry? Not even Puruna's wit can save me.

   (*sung*) Daughter, witness the end of this animal. Don't follow in my path!
NARRATOR: She thrusts the sword into her throat and dives into the pond. Everyone gasps in shock and runs to the water. Bunjibei, staggers to his feet.
BUNJIBEI: (*spoken*) I've killed a man to steal his wife. This bestial body has cruelly killed for its own pleasure.[48] (*sung*) Don't cremate it, don't bury it either. I'll be food for snapping turtles.
NARRATOR: He dives into Lovers Pond, but Mikinoshin grabs his left arm.
MIKINOSHIN: (*spoken*) If you must die, then commit *seppuku* and let me be your second.
NARRATOR: (*sung*) He pulls him from the water, but Bunjibei's glares angrily.
BUNJIBEI: (*spoken*) I don't need your offer of help. Your duty is to Her Highness and the prince, that is all that matters for Japan. (*sung*) Both of you, don't forget your loyalties.
NARRATOR: He pulls his sword from beneath the water and in one swoop severs his own arm; his body sinks to the bottom, a life wasted. Thinking to jump in after them, Mikinoshin panics and runs into the shallows, his kimono soaked, but the bodies are lost in the floating weeds.

MIKINOSHIN: Father, father, come back!

KIYOTAKI: Mother, mother, please . . . !

NARRATOR: Their screams mingle with the croaking of the frogs. They struggle to raise the parents' bodies from the murky water. Pulling and dragging, they bring them near to shore and warm them with their own bodies, but even though it is a warm spring night, (*cadence*) the bodies, lapped by the waves, remain stiff and cold.

(*sung*) Mikinoshin and Kiyotaki embrace their parents and then each other. Grief draws them to cross the Sanzu River of Death, pushing them to step into the shallow rapids, but they remember the call to loyal duty, the last testament of their samurai father, deeper than the murky marsh. Leaving their tears mingling with the muddy water, they set off for home. Enemies for a brief moment, the parents are now married in the next life. Siblings for a short while, the young pair are now free to be a couple in this life. Their story has lived on in the name "Lovers Pond."[49] The jeweled water weeds hallow the memory of the gemlike souls of the departed.[50] The reeds and grasses flourish along the shore, (*high pitch*) witnesses to this sad tale passed down to us.

Act 4

—Scene 1
About a half year later in late autumn, a retreat near Kōfukuji temple in Nara

NARRATOR:

(*sung*) Retreating from the world, one does not ride a cloud into oblivion.[1]
The heart is drawn back by friends and family, they say.[2]
For good or ill, Lord Yoshiaki has dragged himself far to Yamato,[3]
to the village of Nara, the old capital.
At a site near Kōfukuji temple[4] he has a small retreat
where he clears his mind through prayer and religious practice.
The gate is always shut, the fence covered with moss and ivy.[5]
The morning dew glistens radiantly on the bush clover,
like the gems of truth that all are equal before the Buddha's Law,
gems of learning that must be polished every day.
(*cadence*) The evening wind rustles through the reeds
and sweeps away the horrible dream of meeting hateful people.[6]
(*sung*) Hidden away, he gazes at the moon from his window[7]
and whistles a tune to himself;
Paradise (*highest pitch*) radiates here in the palm of my hand.
Time passes, summer is gone, leaves falling like rain.
Deep into autumn, no travelers come to this mountain village
where morning and eve the chanting of sutras resounds.
(*emotional cadence*) What a pity that he must live here,
(*sung*) Yoshiaki, younger brother of the late shogun Yoshiteru.
Now, the priest Keigaku,[8] he fled the world to this hermitage.
(*cadence*) Though praiseworthy, pity his plight.

(*sung*) Lord Fujitaka has managed to find Lady Yoshiteru and has given Kiyotaki and Mikinoshin the responsibility for taking care of the infant prince. Kaijō Tarō Kanemori leads them all to the hermitage. Fujitaka listens through the walls.

FUJITAKA: (*spoken*) Splendid! The sound of sutra chanting signals that His Lordship is at home. (*sung*) Let's offer our greetings.

NARRATOR: He is about to enter, but Kanemori says, "Wait," and stops him.

KANEMORI: (*spoken*) Not so long ago, I came here and spoke with Lord Yoshiaki. I begged him to give up the tonsure and return to active life, to help in the revival of the Ashikaga house by destroying Miyoshi Chōkei, thereby relieving his elder brother's tortured soul, languishing in the Shura realm of revenge. I spoke again and again of his duty to his ancestors, begging him to return. He said that he would consider the request and give an answer. He told me to come back a few days later. (*sung*) If he has decided to give up the religious life, we'll all rejoice. I'll go in alone first. If his answer is yes, then you all follow and offer thanks. If it's no, then we all shall plead again. That'll be our strategy. Wait here for a moment.

NARRATOR: He opens the wicker gate, enters the garden and, with head lowered, speaks.

KANEMORI: (*spoken*) Kaijō Tarō Kanemori is here to see Your Lordship.

NARRATOR: (*sung*) Keigaku continues to concentrate on the sutra, giving no answer. The expression of Keigaku's face, full of pious devotion, makes Kanemori lose patience.

KANEMORI: (*spoken*) Has Your Lordship decided whether to return or not? May we have your answer please?

NARRATOR: Kanemori speaks gruffly.

KEIGAKU: Hmm, so you've come about that matter again, have you? Since I've taken the tonsure, it is no shame for me not to kill my brother's slayer. No better duty to my ancestors than to offer memorial services. I've no need to ponder further over this matter. Don't bother me anymore. I won't hear of it again. (*sung*) Go away.

NARRATOR: Kanemori is shocked at this rebuff. He sees the distraught faces of the others outside the fence. Unable to restrain himself any longer, Kanemori rushes to Yoshiaki and grabs his legs.

KANEMORI: (*spoken*) You know that I am short tempered. For a man like me, your answer marks the border between life and death. It is that important. Are you sure of your answer, no mistake?

KEIGAKU: Yes, I assure you, that is my final answer. A samurai priest does not change his word.

KANEMORI: I never dreamed that was your true spirit. Even if I keep on pleading, it will be a waste, hot air, and only parch my throat. I can't bear this any longer. I resign from your service. If you're not my lord, (*sung*) then I have neither respect nor fear.

NARRATOR: He grabs the reading desk away.

KANEMORI: Thieving wastrel!

NARRATOR: Kanemori, overcome with anger, begins to beat Keigaku, his former lord.

KANEMORI: You amoral, selfish, ungrateful, bald-headed, horned-owl, useless monkfish!

NARRATOR: He punches and pounds away. Fujitaka and the others are shocked to hear the disturbance and come running in.

FUJITAKA: Kanemori, what's come over you? Have you lost your mind?

NARRATOR: They pull him back from Keigaku.

KANEMORI: (*spoken*) No, let go of me! If I let him live, it'll only make me insane with anger. All the way to the farthest bays, the most distant islands, everywhere, Miyoshi Chōkei's edicts travel; all I hear is slander about the generations of Ashikaga rulers, blamed for all ills, everything. With that priest Chōkei welcome in the imperial palace, all his lackeys, down to the footmen, are strutting about as if they owned the world. Every time I see one of them, I fume with rage. Every organ in my body twists and turns. The prince is still a baby. It is imperative that we persuade Keigaku to give up his tonsure, and immediately raise the Ashikaga banner with its distinctive noble circle and crossed parallel bars. (*sung*) Only then, when we've taken Chōkei's head, will my rage be calmed. We must pray to the moon and stars, the Buddha and the gods, with all our heart, to beg for His Lordship's return. My only wish in this world! (*spoken*) But this lily-livered, chicken-hearted coward of a monkfish makes up excuses for why he can't come. (*sung*) I want to trample him to death and die myself!

NARRATOR: (*emotional cadence*) He screams out his anger, collapsing in a wail of tears.

(*sung*) Fujitaka, still weeping, holds the young prince and sits him down in front of Keigaku.

FUJITAKA: (*spoken*) This is truly a treasure left behind by Lord Yoshiteru. Although we think of Japan as large, you have no other nephew besides him. (*sung*) Who can stand behind him as protector, regent, and see him to his rightful position? You spend day and night buried in sutras and classics; from morning till evening you consider questions of right and wrong, loyalty and filial service, impropriety, but you have no comment on this as a man of the world. Is it that you think the punishment for abandoning the priesthood is suffering in the fiery pits of deepest hell? Standing behind this young prince, avenging his father's death, restoring the Ashikaga line, and fulfilling all our dreams, isn't that an act of great merit? (*spoken*) Lady Yoshiteru, please beg him to relent.

NARRATOR: (*sung*) Aroused by Fujitaka's call, Her Highness lifts her head.

LADY YOSHITERU: Lost from my husband, I'm like a mandarin duck bereft of its mate, ashamed to go on living, suffering in this floating world, but I live on for the sake of my son. I beg you to return. Please, we all depend on you.

NARRATOR: (*cadence*) Her words drown in a stream of tears. (*sung*) Kiyotaki and Mikinoshin encourage the prince to go to his uncle.

KIYOTAKI: (*spoken*) Young man, don't be shy, go up to your uncle.

NARRATOR: (*sung*) The boy responds to their voices, and although he does not know his uncle's face, he looks up and smiles brightly at Keigaku. The child's features are a living reflection of the late shogun.

LADY YOSHITERU: Pity the child, rejected by his uncle at their first encounter.

NARRATOR: (*emotional cadence*) Unable to restrain his tears, (*sung*) Kanemori steps forward again.

KANEMORI: (*spoken*) A nephew is like your own child, an uncle like a father. Even more so when you are blood related. And yet you cruelly ignore the smiling face of your brother's child. Have you no pity, no compassion? Please, you must reconsider. (*sung*) You're too heartless!

NARRATOR: To his earnest pleading, (*spoken*) Keigaku finally nods his head.

KEIGAKU: (*sung*) Even if it were one of the worst of the eight offenses against the state, or violations of the Buddhist mortal sins,[9] how could I ignore the plight of the young prince and Her Highness, how could I remain unconcerned? I'll cast my fate to the wind. From now on, I will return to a secular life.

FUJITAKA: What, you'll give up the tonsure? We thank you for giving us hope.

NARRATOR: All lower their heads in gratitude; wilting flowers offered the blessings of dewdrops, (*cadence*) they take heart, revived in spirit, to face the coming challenges.

(*sung*) Keigaku continues.

KEIGAKU: (*spoken*) Well then, Fujitaka, as you well know, in the Ashikaga house from the time of Minamoto no Yoshi'ie,[10] who came of age at the Iwashimizu Hachiman Shrine, we have treasured his suit of armor and helmet, which is worn into battle by the commanding general of each generation. Have you brought it with you, or has it been entrusted to an ally? Who has it? Tell me.

NARRATOR: Fujitaka blushes at his lord's order.

FUJITAKA: The shogun's armor was lost in the battle when the shogun was killed. Chōkei burned the palace to the ground. The armor may have been burned to ashes and buried under the rubble, or Chōkei may have stolen it. We simply don't know what happened to it. But when our allies get word that you have returned and hear your call to arms, (*sung*) all the daimyo long loyal to the Ashikaga will immediately send orders throughout their domains to raise armies. It will be done. Be reassured.

NARRATOR: But Keigaku colors in anger.

KEIGAKU: (*spoken*) Even the trusted ally Chōkei has betrayed and murdered his own lord? In a world of usurpers, who can be trusted? Even if I return and give the call to raise an army, it will be dust against a storm. How are we to fight Chōkei? With what? It's absurd, foolish Fujitaka! (*sung*) You've won honors on the battlefield time and again, received the secret court teachings on *waka* poetry.[11] You're known as a master of both the brush and the sword, yet your plans are shallow! Such a stupid plan will destroy the Ashikaga house. We are finished if that is all we have. Abandoned by the gods and Buddha—but I can't blame them; I regret only the eclipse of the Ashikaga star.

NARRATOR: Tears well up in his angry eyes, and he goes into the inner room weeping. (*exit cadence*) All the others' joy wilts instantly, (*cadence*) a picture of despair.

NARRATOR: (*sung*) Kanemori panics and speaks forcefully.

KANEMORI: (*spoken*) All this talk and gentle persuasion will get us nowhere. (*sung*) I'll make sure that he comes!

NARRATOR: (*cadence*) He runs off after Keigaku. (*sung*) Fujitaka is impressed by Keigaku's resolve.

FUJITAKA: Splendid! Truly the younger brother of our former lord! His character always chastises carelessness, pleads caution. He bears the traits attributed to his ancestor Lord Takauji. We can hope that he will wear the mantle proudly as the inheritor of the Kamakura shoguns.

NARRATOR: Kanemori comes running back.

KANEMORI: (*spoken*) The priest has fled his hermitage. There's a break in the fence leading to the forest. He must have been possessed by the god of cowardice and run away.

NARRATOR: (*sung*) Everyone is shocked again; Fujitaka alone remains calm.

FUJITAKA: (*spoken*) No, don't worry. He's achieved the realm of enlightenment. He knows his own mind. How could he be a coward? He's fled to give us encouragement, I'm sure. (*sung*) He'll visit the various daimyo and when he sees the amount of support there, he'll cast off the tonsure and lead the army. Therefore, we'll entrust Her Highness and the prince to Kiyotaki, and the three of us will go our separate ways. (*spoken*) Kanemori, you head off to Kantō. In Mino I want you to visit Toki and Saitō.[12] Then, go on to Suruga and Sagami to call on Hōjō Ujiyasu[13] and Imagawa Yoshimoto.[14] In Kai, you'll find Takeda Shingen[15] and, in Ise, Kokushi Kitabatake.[16] In Owari we'll seek the support of Oda Nobunaga.[17] Once the armies are assembled, we'll have them attack from the Yamato area. (*sung*) Mikinoshin, you'll go farther north to Echigo and call on Nagao Kenshin.[18] In Aizu you'll find the Ashina[19] and Satake[20] daimyo. We'll have the Asakura[21] of Echizen join Sasaki of Ōmi[22] and attack from the Wakasa area across the mountains from Ōmi. I'll go to the southwest region and gather the Mōri, Kikkawa, Kobaikawa, Amako Haruhisa, and Sue Nyūdō.[23] In Tsukushi I'll call on the Shōni, Kikuchi, Ōtomo, and Ryūzōji.[24] They'll bring their forces and board ships in the ports of the Inland Sea. They'll then attack from the south, and the enemy will be trapped in the middle. The plan will go smoothly, you can be sure.

NARRATOR: (*high pitch*) His fame is as a poet, but now Fujitaka takes the reins of power and harnesses all the forces of the land to restore the Ashikaga. (*scene cadence*) He has to shoulder the responsibility of leading them to victory, and he moves quickly to the task.

—Scene 2
A short time later, at the ruins of the Ashikaga Palace

NARRATOR:

(*nō chanting*) Worldly cares, though discarded,
come around and around again,

> but the awakened one
> (*cadence*) sees with a distant heart.²⁵

(*sung*) His elder brother the shogun has fallen like a Yoshino cherry blossom, and Keigaku has heard that the once flourishing Ashikaga Palace is now but a desolate, charred wasteland. He sets out determined to see once again his beloved capital and to survey the ruins of the palace, to remind himself of times now past. Searching among the rubble, in his mind he sees it in its former glory, even though nothing now remains, a sad farewell. Walking along on a stormy night, he feels the awful force of the old Chinese tale of the destruction of the grand Qin Palace, Xian Yang Gong,²⁶ annihilated in a great fire that raged for three months. The wind blows back the grasses in front of him, and he sees a foundation stone, the only remnant of former glory. But who will notice? Who will preserve it? Roof tiles marked with the Ashikaga crest are now broken and burned, mixed with the soil from which they came, the colors of destruction, like the fallen leaves of autumn; fallen, too, the fate of the Ashikaga house. "It hurt when I listened to others tell the tale of devastation; now the pain strikes my eyes; no hope remains." Unable to speak of his woe, Keigaku buries it inside himself, (*cadence*) but it bursts out in a flood of tears, the drops glistening on his sleeve.

KEIGAKU: (*spoken*) I thought the day was longer; it's already long past sunset. Time passed swiftly during my grieving reverie, how stupid of me.²⁷ (*sung*) Where shall I go to find lodging for the night? I wonder whether someone who knows the area will come this way.

NARRATOR: Thinking only of finding a bed for the night, he catches sight of a youth of perhaps nearly twenty, with a pleasant, moonlike face. The youth approaches, (*cadence*) apparently on a mission of some sort.

KEIGAKU: (*sung*) Excuse me, young man.

NARRATOR: He calls out to him.²⁸

KEIGAKU: (*spoken*) Would you be able to give lodging for a night to a traveling priest?

YOUTH: As it happens, my family has an inn nearby, (*sung*) but Miyoshi Chōkei has strictly forbidden us to give lodgings to traveling priests, and so I shall have to refuse, although that makes things difficult for you. (*spoken*) If you go a little farther along this way, you will find the old palace of the Ashikaga shogun, Lord Yoshiteru. (*sung*) Since no one is there to stop you, why don't you stay there?

KEIGAKU: But that palace was razed to the ground by Miyoshi Chōkei. The only things that remain are these foundation stones here. I can't believe that anything else has survived. How strange!

NARRATOR: Keigaku is suspicious.

YOUTH: We have no proof of its existence or its destruction; you must see for yourself. I'll lead the way. Follow me, please. The evening mist is settling on the inn of creeping vines. It is only a pitiful hovel, but lay down your robe for a bed.[29] Please, come this way, reverend priest.

NARRATOR: (*scene cadence*) They walk on (*highest pitch*) toward the palace.

—Scene 3
At the Ashikaga Palace, continuing from the previous scene

NARRATOR: (*sung*) Guided by the youth, Keigaku approaches the palace gate. To his surprise, the roof tiles are just as they were long ago. Lord Yoshiteru's death, Chōkei's ravaging of the palace, was it all a lie? Who tricked me? The palace, his lodging for the night, (*cadence*) glistens, covered in evening dew.

(*sung*)[30] The outer gate, the inner Chinese-style gate, the side gate, the massive hundred-square-yard palace guards compound all are standing. He opens the sliding doors to the Great Room and sees the Fishing Pavilion in the center of the pond, the Records Office, and the covered passage leading to the Thousand-Mat Great Room, made of the finest Chinese timber. Its vast pillars and roof timbers made of rosewood, its rafters of Chinese quince, the alcove timbers of aloes wood, shelves of fragrant Canton aloes wood, (*cadence*) everything now covered with layers of dust.

(*sung*) Deeper inside, the inner rooms lead on (*spoken*) to the shogun's personal wing where his favorite women lived in room upon room. He has never been inside this wing even once, only heard of its glories. Umegae used to be in the Naruto Room, Hatsuyuki in the Autumn-Colors Room with its skylight to the heavens. Shiragiku had the South-Facing Room, and the others were farther on. (*sung*) All now felled by the cruel usurper's blade. They lay here with His Highness intertwined in lovemaking like vines, like the mythical birds joined at the wings. Their lover, too, is no more of this world. Although knowing it to be the way of this transient life, Keigaku cannot hold back the teardrops, which fall on to his rosary beads, (*cadence*) swelling their number.

(*sung*) He walks through the palace rooms, one after another, until he reaches the raised Shogun's Room.

KEIGAKU: (*spoken*) Ah, this is where His Highness spent his time! (*sung*) How I miss him and long for the old days.

NARRATOR: He thrusts open the sliding doors.

KEIGAKU: (*spoken*) What is this?

NARRATOR: (*sung*) There upon the raised dais sits the shogun's helmet and armor, together with his royal robe.

KEIGAKU: Yes, this is what I have been searching for. Then it didn't fall into the enemy's hands. Here it sits! Surely a sign that the Ashikaga house will rise again.

NARRATOR: He joyfully takes the armor into his hands, (*kowari threatening style*) but suddenly the building shakes and the sky is clouded by darkness. Even the trees and grasses tremble. "Aah!" he cries out and falls, (*sung*) stumbling up the stairs to the dais, rolling over and over. The time is early spring, and the fragrance of the plum blossoms[31] fills the palace, now at the peak of its luxuriant glory. Is it only a reflection, a mirage? (*scene cadence*) Is this a dream or reality?

The Thousand-Mat Great Room[32]

(*nō chanting*) Gold and silver lie like sand in the garden.[33]
Each sliding door, inlaid with jewels.
All who pass, attired in robes that gleam.
Is this the famous Jeweled Palace of Shakyamuni?
Were the pleasures in Indra's castle on Mount Shumi like this?
What a sight to behold!
(*Heike chanting*) To the west, gilded sliding doors for sixty yards,
background for a grand painting of "sunset over Naruto's whirling pools."
To the east, silver doors stretch as far again
decorated as an autumn color scene.
Such a palace, recalling
the splendor of Chinese pleasure pavilions long ago,

Lovers Pond in Settsu Province 189

FIGURE 34 (Bottom center) Keigaku (Yoshiaki) dreams the scene of the recreation of Muromachi Palace while (center) the spirits of the murdered three women attack the spirits of Yoshiteru and Ōyodo; the Ashikaga armor is seen at the top; (bottom left) the senior chanter, Takemoto Yamatodayū, accompanied by the shamisen player, Takezawa Yashichi. The text says that the grand stage special effects (*ōkarakuri*) were an unprecedented success. (*Tsu no kuni meoto-ike*, 1721? Tenri University Library.)

Emperor Xuanzong's "Long-Life" Pavilion never saw autumn end.[34]
Before the "Never-Grow-Old" Gate, the sun never sets.[35]
(*highest pitch*) Its roof higher that Mount Fuji.
(*The spirits of Yoshiteru and his various consorts appear. The scene is played as a fantastic dance sequence.*)
(*sung*) Over mountains of luscious color,
Through valleys of desire.[36]
Plum branches shelter bush warblers.[37]
(*two chanters*)[38] Dew settles on white chrysanthemums along the wicker fence.[39]
Woven into a design on a kimono, they appear as "first snow."[40]
(*tataki melody*)[41] Consorts called each night,

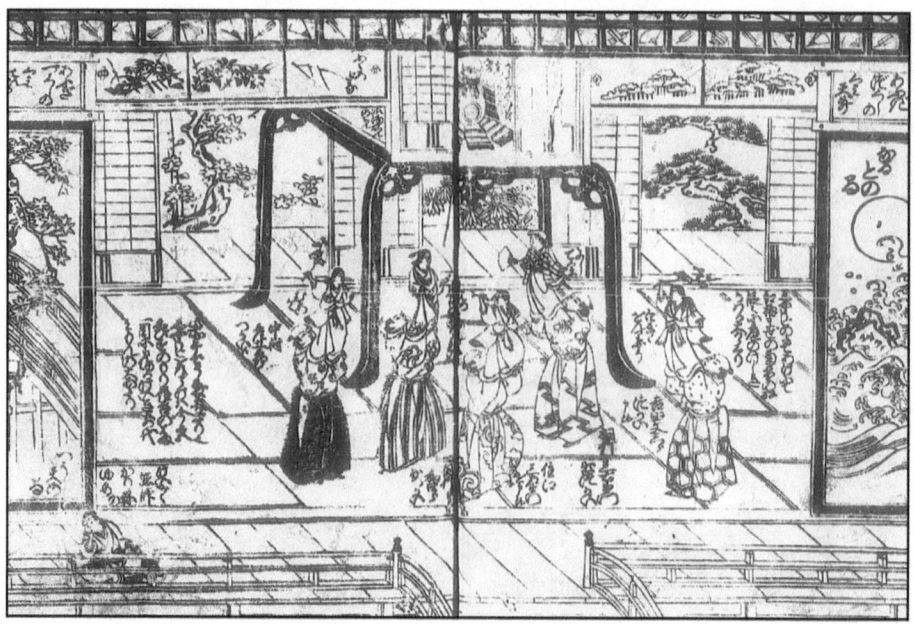

FIGURE 35 Same as the preceding figure, but with puppets. (*Muromachi senjō-jiki* [*Tsu no kuni meoto-ike*], 1742, Keio University Library.)

in the morning their hair disheveled on His Lordship's pillow.
The fragrance of their long black hair,
lost its allure
and, as a fan in autumn, *(cadence)* was cast aside.[42]
(sung) "No anger, no bitterness toward the world, toward people.
No, only hatred for one—Ōyodo, her name a 'great pool' of hate.
Like rapids on the Yodo River that turn the water mill,[43]
(reizei melody) the force of our vengeance is a rushing flood of tears.
The river may run dry but never our bitter tears.
(tsure) Look there! They're sleeping in the royal bed.
Let's step inside and give vent to our hatred."
(spoken) Umegae peeks inside the sliding door.
(sung, shite) The others, too, crowd around for a look,
eyes glistening green with the fires of jealous hate.
(two chanters) His Highness's cup is raised in toast after toast,

His face flushed deep with color.
Look there! He rests on her lap for a pillow.
(*cadence*) How I hate to see them together.
(*sung, shite*) Take that drum, beat it to make their pillow shudder.
Strike, strike it, make it loud, louder still!
We'll lose ourselves in its sound. We must hide away. (*exit*)
(*cadence*) Beat it again and again and again.
(*sung, tsure*) The doors open wide, and even the heavens (*exposing Yoshiteru and Ōyodo*)
are drunk on the pleasures of pink plum blossoms.[44]
The garden, too, is tipsy with the color and scent of flowers.
Saké is the jeweled broom to brush away our troubles.[45]
One precious moment on a spring eve is worth a thousand gold pieces.[46]
(*shite*) Flushed from the saké, Lord Yoshiteru takes up the drum.
He beats notes so real, yet dreamlike.
Is that the wind in the pines?
Or Yoshiteru's peaceful sleeping breath?
Or notes from a *koto* zither?
Ōyodo tickles his side, waking him up.
He sits up laughing with joy.
(*spoken*) I drifted off to sleep and saw such a marvelous dream.[47]
We lay down to sleep but were awakened.
(*tsure*) With whom? (*shite*) With me.
(*both, high pitch*) We broke off plum branches in full bloom.
The plum blossom fragrance (*cadence*) wafts this way from the garden[48]
(*shite, spoken*) like a nasty herb to wake our slumber,
like an enemy at our gate.
Dew drops, jewels beneath the chrysanthemum leaves[49]
rest on creeping vines pulling at your love.
My affection for this uprooted blossom from Kujō will never wither[50]
Such delightful flowers line the pleasure quarter,[51]
blushes of the finest hue.
(*sung*) At the main gate, the tall willow beckons all to enter.[52]
In the many "meeting houses" we hear the sounds of parties,
and see first-time guests daunted by the scene.
To the west is Tōin Street and then Naka no Dōji.
If they want to shop around and taunt the women, let them.

Along Kami and Shimo Streets, and Naka as well,
each house displays its pretty wares in show windows.
Even a man of experience may fall prey to vanity here
and throw away his fortune in pursuit of a prize flower,
here, where money is king.
A jester will intervene to settle a lovers' quarrel.
An older courtesan worries about getting customers for festival days.
A young apprentice girl fears the madam's wrath.
A courtesan's true joy, to meet her lover for a secret rendezvous,
to slip away for a moment for that special tryst in a quiet back room.
But we also find the rancor of the spurned courtesan,
left for a rival, her bitter spirit haunts the corridors each night.
(*cadence*) How terrifying its anger. (*Enter Umegae, Hatsuyuki, Shiragiku*)
(*sung, shite*) Bitterness may boil and seethe,
grow hotter than heated Nara saké,
but taste cold, cold as death.
(*kowari threatening melody, tsure*) Their ire grows more fierce with every day.
Shiragiku, Hatsuyuki, and Umegae, all fly to attack,
grasping and snatching at Ōyodo.
Yoshiteru grabs them.
(*spoken, shite*) What is this?
(*nō chanting, tsure*) What is this club you beat a poor woman with?
(*sung, shite*) It's a *kiseru* bamboo pipe.[53]
Lord Yoshiteru, have you fainted?
Hear the pounding drum, pounding waves that strike the shore.
Not one, not two, not three, but four women bend to your will.
Turn to one, and the other is bitter;
affection for one, and the other is jealous.[54]
His spirit, drunk on wine and women, is bruised and beaten,
(*cadence*) and he collapses into a stupor.

(*spoken, shite*) Remember times long past,
recalling the Tang emperor Xuangzong's pavilion
With its three thousand butterfly consorts.
There he reveled with the beauty Yang Guifei.[55]
Here butterflies play among the fragrant flowers
alighting on the sleeves of my love.

(*sung, tsure*) "Catch one, catch it in my hand.
Take the flowered branch."
(*both chanters*) Butterflies alight and fly off again,
disappearing into the mists.
"Are those fluttering wings, blossoms, or snowflakes?"
Beautiful butterflies, wings so delicate.
Dew drips on this morning,
"Young butterfly, rest in my hand.
Alight on this branch, now fly away.
(*cadence*) Such colorful butterflies!
(*sung*) Delightful butterflies resting on Ōyodo's sleeve.
Look, they're trying to sleep, that pair with joined wings."[56]
"Let us hold each other close and enter the royal bed."
(*Umegae*) "Look over there!
(*kowari threatening melody*) Hateful woman! Jealousy makes this bed a sea,
where you suffer the eight tortures, battered by the waves.
No, you won't lie with him, never again.
Never again.
Anger burns our bodies,
singes our souls.
Red as these plum blossoms,
are the fires of hell."
Suddenly, a burst of flames,
three clouds of smoke rise up,
(*scene cadence*) whisking the spirits away.[57]

(*popular song, shite*) "Oh, to give up being His Lordship
and prance about as dandy of the palace ladies,[58]
with garlands for their robes.
(*high pitch*) How delightful to strut with them beside you,
and others in front, (*spoken*) and some enticed to follow on behind.
(*tsure*) Come along, (*sung, shite*) you there, walk in front.
Seductive hips swivel under curving sashes.
(*spoken, tsure*) Ah, heaven's delight!
(*sung, both*) Summer robes float on the fragrance of chrysanthemums
covered in dew, (*cadence, tsure*) blossoming wildly along the bamboo fence."
(*nō, shite*) "We'll live forever, forever more,
drinking chrysanthemum saké, an elixir of eternal life."[59]

(*popular song*) "You and I are budding blossoms;
Hidden yet is the color and fragrance of our passion.
I'll wait and wait. We'll burn sesame stems
and mix them with chrysanthemum leaves.
How terrible! No water to douse the fires,
(*cadence*) The fires of vengeance!"
(*sung, tsure*) Even flowers have jealous rivals.
The spirits crush the fence draped with blossoms.
(*shita kowari threatening melody*) The earth trembles suddenly;
from the swirling smoke and raging fire a spirit rises.
It speaks no name, who can it be?
(*cadence*) Shiragiku returns to haunt from the other world.
(*spoken, shite*) (*Yoshiteru*) "Life in this world flashes past like a bolt of lightning.
How could we waste time in hating others?
(*sung*) Nor should we ever be sad.[60]
(*cadence*) When did you first come to hate me? Why such bitterness?"
(*sung*) Go back to the other world!" he cries.
(*Yoshiteru*) "Our spirit is tied to this world
like the thin strings of a mosquito net stretched taut,
which hides us from the terrors in summer.
Snap the cord, free me from this pain, and let my body go cold!"
(*Shiragiku*) "Who kept me from loving my lord for two lives?
Who is my enemy?
Torturing swords of hell cut me to the bone,
And severed links with my love.
Hate won't leave me, won't go away!
It clings and clings, wraps round and around,
Round and around, into the future, forever more!
(*spoken*) Know that you suffer for me!
In the heavens, I unleash storms;
from beneath the earth winds arise
and rage through the mountains,
rushing through the fields, tearing up the trees.
A stinging, searing wind, chases you
into the palace, into your bedroom,
a phantom attacks and tortures.

(*sung*) Darkness and delusion burn as black smoke
smothering, engulfing you in flames.
Your bed is now full of razor-sharp blades;
the shelves, too, now castle walls to entrap you.[61]
A great sword slices your body into five parts.
(*scene change*) Watch my wrath in its full glory."

(*sung, high pitch*) "The pain! Can't stand the pain any longer."
Her voice remains as an echo, wind in the pines.
Her phantom shape vanishes
with the passing autumn.
The days of winter pass as quickly
as the falling snow[62] that covers the garden branches
(*highest pitch*) creating a white blanket at dusk.
(*popular song, both*) His Highness and Ōyodo beneath one umbrella
their sleeves overlapping like large tobacco leaves,
as thick with passion as the rank grasses,
intertwined like swirling smoke.
Snowflakes fall gently on their scarves.
(*popular song*) "My lord, how cold you are!
Could I but warm you with a fire, (*high pitch*) adding coals.
Let me warm you, warm you.[63]
(*cadence*) If we must be in the snow,
(*sung, tsure*) let it snow, ever deeper, and turn to ice.
I'll never leave you, never let you go.
(*shite*) Though this is not Mount Wu,
our umbrella bears a heavy mantle of deep snow.[64]
Let's shake off the snow from this bent umbrella.
If only we could move it.
How heavy it grows and grows,
until it weighs as much as a huge stone,
breaking up into pieces, as heavy as hail stones.
Look, there, the fury and vengeance of Hatsuyuki,
there in the air, her spirit wandering between worlds."
Hatsuyuki stands defiantly before them.
"Hate piles higher and higher in the eight depths of frozen hell.
Buried beneath the blood red ice at the very bottom, trapped,

crushed, I suffer and suffer—for whom?"
Her cries fill the heavens, shaking the earth,
Her breath whirling, (*hatsumi melody*) violent gusts of snow.
(*cadence*) In a flash she disappears, carried off by the wind.

(*sung, shite*) "How terrifying it was just now!"
They start to flee but Hatsuyuki returns to haunt them,
(*kowari threatening style, waki*) her face bright crimson like the madder plant,
poised to lash out in fiery anger.
She draws them to join her at the bottom of hell.
(*sung, high pitch*) They try to run away, to flee the terror,
but lose their way, blocked by door after door,
entangled in prickly plum branches, attacked by red blossoms,
caught in the fires of Umegae's venom.
(*kowari threatening, both*) Go that way and meet Shiragiku's eyes
that glisten with rage and strike like lightning.
(*sung*) Chased by the three carriages of lust, drunkenness, and violence,
(*scene cadence*) round and around they run.

(*sung*) Yoshiteru cries out.

YOSHITERU: (*spoken*) Ōyodo dear, I was enticed by your erotic charms, and I have made you suffer so. (*sung*) When will we be free of this agony?"

NARRATOR: He screams his pain, but the harping spirits crack their torture whips. "Feel the fiery lust that ties you to this world! Feel our bitter hatred, our rage!" The spirit voices (*cadence*) shake heaven and earth.

(*sung, tsure*) Keigaku suddenly wakes up and wonders whether his vision was only a dream—the intensity of the images, the force of the women's wrath. "Trust in the sutras: 'If one should seek to know the Buddhas of the three worlds past, present, and future, look at the workings of your own heart and soul; all can be apprehended from the mind.'[65] Know that these precious words have the power to free us from the tortures of hell." He takes off his priest's robe and throws it at the spirits. The power of the Buddha is beyond measure, beyond understanding. The words of the Law soften the raging spirits; calm and merciful they now appear.[66] Seeing Buddha's Paradise before them, they rejoice. Wisps of blue, yellow, red, and white, the four female spirits fly off, (*exit cadence*) disappearing into the jeweled night sky.

NARRATOR: (*sung, shite*) "How wonderful to see Your Holiness! The lord of this manor is your brother Yoshiteru. You must return to the secular life, protect the young prince, and destroy Chōkei and defeat his forces. Please, I beg you to save me from the tortures of the Shura Hell of Never-Ending Battles. Here, I present you with the treasured Ashikaga suit of armor and helmet which have survived the smoke and fire." His voice trails off, and his figure (*cadence*) is transformed into a suit of scarlet armor.[67]

(*sung, tsure*) Keigaku is delighted and rises to receive the armor. (*shite*) He wears the suit over his gray priest's robe, (*cadence*) shedding a tear at leaving the religious life, (*sung*) but he turns to pray for Yoshiteru's salvation and accepts the armor's power to overcome Chōkei and clear away the shame of the Ashikaga. He stands alone in the grand Thousand-Mat Room, his proud spirit reaching to the heavens. He had thought it was still night, (*shite*) but the sun is already high. (*tsure*) The plums blossomed in spring, (*shite*) but chrysanthemums now bloom. (*tsure*) Is it autumn? (*shite*) Then the snows fell. (*cadence, both*) Four seasons in succession. (*sung*) The splendors of the palace, all its women, its magnificent rooms and buildings—now all gone, (*scene cadence, shite*) disappearing like the remnant of a dream.[68]

NARRATOR: (*sung*) Keigaku awakes from his dream on a stone pillow and rejoices to see the armor. Above him, the four female spirits fly as banners that lead the loyalists—Fujitaka, Kanemori, Mikinoshin, and Lady Yoshiteru. Each has been whisked here in the flash of a moment. (*cadence*) How marvelous the power of spirits!

(*sung, tsure*) Keigaku relates the marvels of his dream to the loyal allies from the different provinces. All rejoice as more and more banners arrive, signaling the swelling of the Ashikaga forces. (*both*) All the banners follow the flowing Ashikaga suit of scarlet armor. They dance the courtly *bugaku* "Great Peace" and "Return to the Palace," rejoicing that Keigaku has returned from his hermitage to lead them, not through the gate of salvation, but through the virtuous warriors' gate of learning and martial prowess.

Act 5

—Scene 1
The latter part of the fifth month, 1569, at the Miyoshi Chōkei residence, Kyoto

NARRATOR:

(*sung*) Suqin of Zhai[1] did not see
that loyalty may be his enemy's poison,
Heaven will punish negligence, as he discovered.

The sly lay-priest Miyoshi Chōkei decisively revealed his hand and, riding a wave of fortune, swept aside the Ashikaga shogunate. He has built a new residence at Asahigaoka at the northeast edge of the capital, fortifying it with a high stone wall and moat on the south side. Dozens of guards are on constant patrol, ever vigilant. To the north, a thick grove of pines forms a barrier onto Iwakura Mountain and Rōei Valley in northeast Kyoto, which even wild animals cannot breach. He spends day and night (*cadence*) in revelry at drunken banquets, free to force his will on the world.

(*sung*) The time is midsummer in 1569.[2] Intending to cleanse his family's intolerable shame by exacting revenge against the hated usurper Chōkei, Lord Ashikaga Yoshiaki leads Asakawa no Fujitaka, Kanemori, and Mikinoshin across Iwakura Mountain by night. They plan to slip into Chōkei's residence by stealth, using ladders to scale the walls, and they grow increasingly impatient as they anticipate their goal. An alliance of forces (*kowari threatening melody*) follows as the rearguard:[3] From Ōmi, Sasaki Rokkaku, Kyōgoku Takanari, and Asai Nagamasa; from Mino, Ōdachi and Numata no Heiji; from Ise, Aki'ie; from Iga, Kanamori and Isshiki Fujimaru; from Echigo, the Uesugi Nagao clan; from Echizen, Asakura, Kusakabe Yoshikage, Momonoi, Koyama, and Utsunomiya; from Kai, Takeda Shingen, Takasaka Danjō, Hara Hayato, and Yamamoto Kansuke; from Owari, Oda's most trusted general, Hashiba Echizen no Kami Hideyoshi; from Sagami, Negoshi, Igarashi, and Mutsura; from Suruga, Ujiyasu; from Shinano, the Genji descended from Emperor Seiwa; from Musashi, the seven Heike clans descended from Emperor Kanmu. Each general on horseback leads his men poised to attack; rows of banners, spears, and lanterns as far as the eye can see surround the walls; (*cadence*) the clamps of the trap close in.

(*sung*) Fujitaka, Kanemori, and Mikinoshin successfully scale the wall and stand on the roof. Fujitaka calls out in a loud voice.

FUJITAKA: (*spoken*) All our loyal allies, allow me to speak. With your support and goodwill, we have managed to get this far undetected. Many of you harbor a deep hatred for Chōkei; however, if one of you were to kill him, then we would lose this precious chance to avenge our beloved lord. I beg of you to allow us to strike first. Please keep your men poised and ready at the foot of the mountain. If we encounter difficulties, then I'll signal by blowing on this flute. That will be the sign for you to attack with all your forces. Lord Yoshiaki waits at the front gate. The armies of the western and central provinces have promised to support His Highness. (*sung*) Now is the time to move into position.

NARRATOR: All agree to his plan and (*cadence*) withdraw to the foot of the mountain.

(*sung*) Kanemori is impatient, however.

KANEMORI: (*spoken*) But things are different from what we expected. It's been so easy to sneak in. Let's just burst into his bedroom (*sung*) and off with his head!

NARRATOR: He jumps up, but Fujitaka holds him back.

FUJITAKA: (*spoken*) Don't be stupid, Kanemori! Chōkei is a clever villain. He's sure to have taken precautions. (*sung*) If he is alerted and goes into hiding, we'll never find him. (*spoken*) First, we'll quietly survey the grounds and buildings. Whether in attack or retreat, we three move as one. (*sung*) Don't rush anything, keep close.

NARRATOR: As he finishes, they hear the sound of the wooden clappers of the guard making his rounds.

FUJITAKA: (*spoken*) Heaven has thrown us a helping hand.

NARRATOR: He leaps down from the roof, killing the guard with one swift blow and deftly picks up the clappers without missing a stroke. "Take care, be vigilant!" He cries out rhythmically (*cadence*) as they stealthily slip into the residence.

(*sung*) All remains quiet for a moment.

MATSUNAGA: It's a night attack! (*spoken*) The front gate is secure. They must've come from the rear. To keep themselves concealed, the enemy carry no lanterns. Have all our soldiers fix a lantern to their waists. Lure them out to the pine grove. Let no one try to be a hero and attack alone. We'll keep together and kill them all.

NARRATOR: (*sung*) All of Chōkei's forces attach lanterns to their waists and make themselves easy targets for Fujitaka, Kanemori, and Mikinoshin, who stand in front of the pine trees with swords drawn. They valiantly yell out their names and fight with the might of lions and fury of tigers; they seem to fly through the air as they attack,[4] using every possible kind of technique. Cuts to the shoulder, neck, and body, but again and again they come, only to meet their deaths; fifty in all scattered in the field, gone like dew and frost on the grasses. (*battle cadence*) They cut and parry, thrust and slice, fighting valiantly.[5]

NARRATOR: (*sung*) Fujitaka and the others fasten lanterns to their sides (*cadence*) and continue to cut through the enemy ranks. (*sung*) They close in on Chōkei.

CHŌKEI: (*spoken*) This is dreadful! The front gate will soon be breached. We'll be overwhelmed. What can I do! Where can I hide?

NARRATOR: Talking to himself, he flees, hoping at least to save his own skin. (*sung*) His only prospect is the thousand-year-old pines. His old body struggles to climb up a huge tree, his hands and legs, his whole body shaking. He climbs out on a limb, slipping and sliding, holding on for his life, (*exit cadence*) praying to escape notice high in the branches.

NARRATOR: (*sung*) The three kill more than one hundred of the enemy but cannot find either Chōkei or Matsunaga. They search through the house and find Matsunaga running out of one of the rooms. He tries to escape, but Mikinoshin confronts him.

MIKINOSHIN: (*spoken*) Leave Matsunaga to me. You two search out Chōkei.

NARRATOR: (*sung*) They nod to Mikinoshin and throw themselves back into the fray, (*cadence*) fighting with renewed vigor.

(*sung*) Matsunaga, a skilled swordsman, attacks Mikinoshin with full force. Mikinoshin deftly parries his thrust aside but sustains a small cut to his shoulder. He replies with a blow that cuts halfway through Matsunaga's thigh. Matsunaga falters, and Mikinoshin strikes out for the kill, cutting off his head with one swift slice.

MIKINOSHIN: (*spoken*) Mikinoshin has taken the head of Matsunaga Danjō Hisahide!

NARRATOR: (*sung*) Lord Yoshiaki comes running in at his cry, followed by Fujitaka, Kanemori and the other allies. They raise a great lantern in victory. Lord Yoshiaki yells out angrily in a voice that reverberates throughout the pine grove.

YOSHIAKI: (*spoken*) Every inch of the residence has been combed, and nothing more is to be found. Chōkei must have grown wings and flown away into the sky. Where could he possibly be? If we fail to catch him today, we surely won't get a second chance. (*sung*) Have we been abandoned by heaven? Have we exhausted our samurai virtue? Horrible! Infuriating!

NARRATOR: Even a stern, dry-eyed Yoshiaki, sheds tears of anger. Fujitaka, too, seems lost. (*cadence*) All the others are driven to the edge of despair.

(*sung*) Kanemori's impatience increases as his anger grows.

KANEMORI: (*spoken*) I've an idea. That's it; I've got it! All these pine trees, we've forgotten to check them. He must be hiding on one of the branches. Let's uproot them all one by one and search him out. No, it'll take too long to pull them up. Let's set fire to the grove and burn him out.

NARRATOR: (*sung*) They all agree and call for fire and kindling. Chōkei realizes that he cannot remain in the tree and crawls from branch to branch, but suddenly his sword gets caught on a branch, and the blade falls out of its sheath, falling to the earth with a thud.

KANEMORI: (*spoken*) There, up there! Someone is on that branch. Bring lanterns!

NARRATOR: (*sung*) He takes a long spear into his hands and throws it. It strikes as deep as a skewer through potato or fish: heaven's punishment for killing one's own lord. The body flutters for a moment and then falls, landing at the feet of Yoshiaki, who quickly severs the head. The uprising is crushed, the shogun's death avenged. (*high pitch*) Rejoice in victory! The Ashikaga weather another turbulent storm, restored to rule over this land of many islands. Celebrate the long-lasting peace of the reign.[6]

(The postscript is almost exactly the same as the one at the end of *Twins at the Sumida River*.)

Battles at Kawa-nakajima
(Shinshū kawa-nakajima kassen)

attles at Kawa-nakajima[1] was first performed on the third day of the eighth month, 1721, only three weeks after *Woman-Killer and the Hell of Oil*,[2] the last of Chikamatsu's series of three murderer-hero plays. *Kawa-nakajima* marks a considerable shift in theme from Chikamatsu's dramas of the preceding two or three years, which had explored the psychology of crime and responsibility and were highly critical of corruption in government. He alters the fundamental nature of a period play: in contrast to *The Battles of Coxinga* and the first two plays in this volume, the opposing forces around which the play revolves are not depicted as one being good and the other evil. Rather, the two famous generals Takeda Shingen (1521–73) and Uesugi (Nagao) Kenshin (1530–78) and their sides are portrayed as noble samurai caught in a complex world affected by both private and public considerations.

Ōhashi Tadayoshi has provided an outline of the sources from which Chikamatsu created his tale depicting the ideals of a samurai leader.[3] Until Ōhashi's work appeared, *Kōyō gunkan*, a history of the wars of the Takeda, completed around 1600 and then published in the mid-seventeenth century, was considered the main source.[4] Ōhashi notes that this and other popular histories such as *Hokuetsu gunki* (1711)[5] and *Kawa-nakajima gokado kassen* (one of many surviving manuscripts from the Edo period)[6] kept the rivalry of the great generals Shingen and Kenshin fresh in the minds of Chikamatsu's audience. However, the text that Chikamatsu used as his source most directly is *Takeda sandai gunki*, particularly chapters 10 and 12, published in the first month of 1720.[7] This gives Yamamoto Kansuke an important role as Shingen's chief military strategist. The preceding works, all military tales, have few women figures, and none in important roles. Chikamatsu thus created all the major women characters in this play: Kansuke's widowed mother, his sister Karaginu, his wife Okatsu, and Lady Emon, daughter of Kenshin. Furthermore, Ōhashi has shown that the source for the central story of the mother of Kansuke, in acts 2 and 3, is the Japanese translation of the Chinese *San guo zhi yan yi* (*Romance of the Three Kingdoms*), called *Tsūzoku sangokushi*, first published in 1692.[8]

Chikamatsu created "mother" figures as tragic heroes in two early works, *Yōmei tennō shokunin kagami* (1705)[9] and *The Battles of Coxinga* (1715).[10] Both women sacrifice themselves for love of their children and, in the case of Coxinga, for a higher cause. In *Battles at Kawa-nakajima*, the mother has the leading role in act 3, the most important act in the play. Chikamatsu's use of the Chinese source and his creation of this mother figure as the heroine of the play indicates that his purpose was not simply to write another version of the tale of the battles between the two generals but, rather, to explore the nature of samurai honor.

The climactic scenes of both acts 2 and 3 are based on episodes in chapter 15 of *Tsūzoku sangokushi*. The first is when Liu Xuan De, king of Shu, humbles himself three times (on the final occasion, traveling through the snow) to persuade the military strategist Zhu Ge Kong Ming to serve him. The second incident, crucial background to the tragedy of act 3, is when Xuan De's rival Cao Cao, king of Wei, at the suggestion of Cheng Yu, asks the mother of Xu Shu (Dan Fu) to write a letter to her son to persuade him to leave Liu Xuan De and come to serve him. Although she refuses, they forge her handwriting. Xu Shu falls for the trick and goes to see his mother. Ōhashi suggests the following parallels between the characters in Kawa-nakajima and the figures in the Chinese source:

Act 2

Shingen
(King Liu Xuan De)

Gengorō
(Zhang Fei)

Kansuke; his mother
(Military strategist: Zhu Ge Kong Ming)

Act 3

Shingen
(King Liu Xuan De)

Kenshin
(King Cao Cao)

Kansuke	Naoe Sanetsuna; his wife Karaginu
(Xu Shu)	(Cheng Yu)
Kansuke's mother; Kansuke's wife Okatsu	
(Xu Shu's mother)	

The fundamental theme in both the Chinese story and *Kawa-nakajima* is the true nature of nobility and honor among warriors and, in particular, among rulers or generals. The mother of Xu Shu is presented as an upright, severe figure who scolds Xu Shu for being a fool after she discovers that he has been duped by a fake letter into coming to see her in the territory of Cao Cao. She then kills herself. Chikamatsu expands the role of the mother of the military strategist Kansuke by setting her in contrast to both the generals, Shingen and Kenshin. She is presented as the measure of true honor, which must include compassion and love. In particular, the confrontation with the short-tempered and less-experienced Kenshin in act 3 in which she humiliates him, first by refusing his gift of a precious robe and then by kicking the serving tray that he has personally set before her, is a lesson in the education of a samurai leader. Chikamatsu further complicates the story by having the mother's daughter be the wife of a man in service to Kenshin while her son Kansuke is in service to the rival Shingen. Her death at the hands of her daughter and daughter-in-law—as an offering to Kenshin, whom she had humiliated—strikes Kenshin deeply, revealing him, too, to be of noble character. As a gesture to the dying mother, Kenshin allows Kansuke to go free and offers to deliver salt to Shingen because his enemies have cut the supply of this vital commodity as a military strategy to starve out the landlocked Shingen. This "salt" incident is recounted in *Takeda sandai gunki*, in which Kenshin disparages the use of such cowardly tactics as being beneath the dignity of a true samurai.[11]

Act 4 focuses on Shingen and his son Katsuyori, the theme being again nobility and compassion, but this time Chikamatsu emphasizes the role of art in humanizing the heart of the warrior. Act 5 is the fifth battle of the two sides at Kawa-nakajima. Here Kansuke stands in for Shingen to confront Kenshin and is wounded and captured. He reveals his true identity and speaks of his strategy to end the enmity between the two houses. His mother had told him to avoid causing shame for either general, even if it meant sacrificing his own life. The first lines of the final act, "A hundred battles fought, / A hundred battles won, / Not the best strategy to win a war," allude to Sun Tzu's *The Art of War*. "To fight one hundred battles and win one hundred times is not the mark of a good general. A truly good general defeats his enemy without fighting."[12] This is the essence of Kansuke's strategy, which does end the war. The drama ends with the marriage of Katsuyori and Emon, bringing the two houses together as one.

Although the play is not true to history, such strategic marriages between both allies and enemies were common in samurai culture, and often family members were at odds because of divided loyalties. In fact, there was a marriage connection between these houses: one of Shingen's daughters, Kikuhime, was married to Kenshin's adopted son (Kenshin's nephew) and heir, Kagekatsu. Chikamatsu used a variety of sources to create a complex drama about the nature of honor and nobility. Central to this world is a respect for others, even one's enemies. The ideal strategy is to avoid confrontation, often the most difficult option for an individual, demanding both vision and personal sacrifice to maintain one's principles.

The first quarter of the eighteenth century was a fertile period for discussion about the nature of the samurai, initially stimulated by the 1702 "Forty-Seven Rōnin Incident" (often referred to as "Chūshingura" after the most famous play depicting that vendetta), in which a group of samurai plotted for more than a year to avenge the death of their lord and then surrendered to await judgment. Their seemingly unselfish and loyal sacrifice stirred the nation from the lowest to the highest, eventually leading to an array of treatises and popular works still being composed today. *Bushidō* works on the "way of the samurai," such as *Hagakure*,[13] date from the first two decades of the century, as do philosophical writings by Ogyū Sorai, Muro Kyūso, and Arai Hakuseki on the raison d'être of the samurai ruling class. Yoshimune's appointment as shogun in 1716— he immediately began the major government reforms that became the foundation of the modern Japanese state— was also a stimulus for Chikamatsu. Presented to the public as a "martial" leader, strong, stern, and self-disciplined but also fair and compassionate, Yoshimune's image was important in the popular mind as that of an ideal samurai leader. Chikamatsu's late plays can be read as contributions to this debate on the nature of the samurai and, by extension, on the nature of honor and nobility in general.[14]

Act 3 was revived on both the jōruri and kabuki stages in the mid-eighteenth century as a separate play, and it has remained alive on the kabuki stage since then. It was revived in bunraku in 1939 after a lapse of seventy-nine years and since 1962 has been performed regularly. A silent film based on act 3 was made in 1910.

Battles at Kawa-nakajima
(*Shinshū kawa-nakajima kassen*)

CAST OF CHARACTERS

Takeda Household

Shingen (Takeda Daizen no Tayū Harunobu Nyūdō Shingen): lord of Kai and known as a clever military strategist, a stern but wise and upright individual. "Shingen" is his lay-priest (*nyūdō*) name.

Katsuyori (Takeda Shirō Katsuyori): son and heir of Shingen. He falls in love with Emon.

Kōsaka (Kōsaka Danjō Masanobu): loyal Takeda retainer.

Gorō (Hara Gorō Masatoshi): loyal Takeda retainer.

Nagao (Uesugi) Household

Terutora, later Kenshin (Nagao Kagetora, later Terutora): lord of Echigo. His "lay-priest" name is Kenshin, which he assumes during the play. Known to be short tempered and a fierce but also noble general. Historically he is known today by the surname Uesugi, which he took in 1561.

Lady Emon (Emon no Hime): daughter of Kenshin, who falls in love with Katsuyori.

Sanetsuna (Naoe Yamashiro no Kami Sanetsuna): retainer of Kenshin and brother-in-law of Yamamoto Kansuke.

Karaginu: wife of Sanetsuna and sister of Yamamoto Kansuke.

Tokitsuna (Naoe Yamato no Suke Tokitsuna): younger brother of Sanetsuna.

Yamamoto Household

Kansuke (Yamamoto Kansuke Haruyoshi): an eccentric samurai strategist pursued by both Shingen and Kenshin, who want him to join their side.

Mother: Kansuke's mother, a widow aged seventy-two and a stern figure who becomes the protagonist in acts 2 and 3.

Okatsu: Kansuke's wife, who developed a stutter after the shock of a miscarriage.

Murakami Household

Murakami (Murakami Saemon Yoshikiyo): lord of Shinano. He wants Emon for his wife and accuses Katsuyori and Emon of an illicit affair, precipitating the crisis of the play.

Genba: a retainer of Murakami and a comic-villain type of character.

Act 1

—Scene 1
Suwa Myōjin Shrine, autumn 1559

NARRATOR:

>(*prelude*) He stands tall, self-disciplined,
>a thousand-foot pine, firm and taut,
>with many branches gnarled and twisted.
>Although useless as sawed timber,
>placed as the main pillar,
>a great house will flourish, strong and stable.[1]
>A brave general sees men.
>A wise general knows men.

Such an example is the lay-priest Takeda Shingen, the respected lord of Kai Province,[2] the nineteenth-generation descendant of Minamoto Yoshimitsu,[3] who has taken orders as a priest but remains active in the world. His fourth son and heir is young Katsuyori,[4] (*cadence*) the bud of a magnificent orchid ready to blossom into a leader.[5]

(*sung*) Katsuyori has set off to the Suwa Myōjin Shrine,[6] its deity known as a god of warriors, in the neighboring province of Shinshū,[7] to offer prayers for the fortune of the Takeda house and for the success of his father Shingen's journey to the capital to request a court rank. The votive offering has been embellished with precious gems. The drawing, of a spirited horse led by a foot soldier, is by a Kano painter. Katsuyori offers it to the deity for display in the shrine. The priests recite prayers and conduct the rituals. They hang Katsuyori's paper offerings around the sacred room where female shrine dancers, dressed in bright kimono, (*cadence*) perform dances for the god, a sublime sight.

(*sung*) Katsuyori offers his own prayers from the garden and then prepares to ascend to the shrine building, but suddenly Kōsaka Danjō,[8] his father's trusted senior officer, tugs at his sleeve.

KŌSAKA: (*spoken*) Look, over there! It looks as though a carpet has been laid for a ceremony. Your Reverence, is that carpet for us or for another party?

PRIEST: That is for the lord of Echigo,[9] Nagao Kagetora.[10] His daughter Lady Emon[11] has brought an *ema* votive picture (*sung*) which is displayed in the shade of that pine tree. It shows an image of a horse in a spring field. Now we shall prepare for your ceremony. Please rest in my residence.

KATSUYORI: I've heard much about Lady Emon. This is a welcome chance to meet her.

NARRATOR: Kōsaka's expression shows his concern that it would not seem fitting to have a rendezvous with a woman on a pilgrimage. While he is wondering what to do, one of Nagao's retainers, Naoe Tokitsuna, quietly approaches them.

TOKITSUNA: (*spoken*) Please forgive my intrusion. My lord Kagetora has gone to the capital with a petition, and we have come to offer prayers for his success. It seems that Lord Shingen has also gone to the capital. Then we both must have come to offer prayers. The carpet has been laid for the occasion. Please, Kōsaka, don't concern yourself with formalities, please have your party proceed first.

KŌSAKA: You are too polite. Thank you for your kindness, (*sung*) but please have Lady Emon go first.

TOKITSUNA: No, by all means, you should precede us.

KŌSAKA: No, we could never do that. Please.

NARRATOR: Emon interrupts their negotiations and steps demurely forward.

EMON: Propriety must certainly be observed by a gentleman. In this case, your parent and mine are as close as a fish to water. Although I am a young woman, if the man is of such a family, then I will be a fish swimming near the surface looking for a place to rest. I'll follow in your current. Let's approach the altar together.

NARRATOR: She takes his hand in her soft fingers, soft as the Echigo summer silk, softer than even the hand of a beauty from the capital. Katsuyori is delighted at this unexpected invitation to enter the sanctuary as a pair entwined like the rope on which they now pull to ring the bells and summon the god. Blind to others, passion blossoms (*high pitch*) as they pray to the god, their vows of love whispered between prayers for their fathers' success. "What will be, will be." This is their thought as they hurry through the gates of the inner sanctum, (*cadence*) oblivious to the eyes of others.

(*sung*) At that moment, a priest approaches hurriedly along the corridor.

PRIEST: (*spoken*) The lord of this domain, Murakami Saemon Yoshikiyo,[12] has asked to meet both of you and will be here immediately.

KATSUYORI: (*sung*) It will be awkward for him to meet us together. I'll sneak away.

NARRATOR: But as he speaks, they hear the neighing of Murakami's horse.

TOKITSUNA: Fortunately, Lady Emon will be able to go to the head priest's quarters. Let's go.

NARRATOR: Tokitsuna points the way, but Katsuyori and Emon look confused and uncertain. The god of Suwa Shrine has been their go-between, (*cadence*) and their ties are now deeper than Suwa Lake. (*Katsuyori and Emon exit.*)

NARRATOR: (*sung*) Murakami Yoshikiyo arrives and sets down his traveling things near the shrine, (*spoken*) his expression sullen.

MURAKAMI: Now, Tokitsuna, Kōsaka, you both are senior councillors of different domains and surely know the rules of etiquette among samurai. Even if you are just passing through someone's territory on the way to the territory of another, it is the rule to send a messenger ahead to announce your arrival. Although this shrine is in my territory, you have nevertheless entered without any advance notice, an unforgivable breach of protocol. (*sung*) The *ema* votive pictures show horses as deities. Look at the two presented by you. Shingen's horse's coat is the black color of Kai horses from his own domain. The horse in the picture is shown as so strong that it cannot be restrained. This must certainly mean a plan to have the horse enter my territory. It symbolizes the desire to steal my Shinano domain. Further, I have requested the hand of Lady Emon from her father, Kagetora, and she is as good as betrothed to me. Tokitsuna and your brother are Katsuyori's retainers—don't you know the rules of propriety between a lord and subject?

NARRATOR: The young Tokitsuna cannot restrain his anger.

TOKITSUNA: (*spoken*) What are you talking about? Are you referring to me and my elder brother Naoe Sanetsuna? We are not under the rule of Lord Kagetora; we bow to no master anywhere. Nor do we receive any stipend from you. How dare you insult me by calling me your subject!

Say it again, go on! (*sung*) I'll lop off that long tongue of yours at the root.

NARRATOR: He jumps forward, but Kōsaka restrains him.

KŌSAKA: Wait, hold back! You have the care of a precious personage, and I am accompanying the young heir. This is not the time or place to argue. Calm down. (*spoken*) You are right to be angry that we entered your territory without notice, but if we had sent messengers ahead, then you would have had to have the roads cleaned and so forth, and to ready horses and make other preparations for our arrival. We wanted to spare you from such concerns. That is the only reason. There is no need to think something sinister is afoot. We are sorry to have unexpectedly caused a problem. Please relax. There is no reason to be angry.

NARRATOR: He bows with hands to the floor in supplication. Yoshikiyo is pleased with his attitude of submission and presses his point even more arrogantly.

MURAKAMI: No, don't try to get out of this with clever words. Katsuyori and Emon are secretly having an affair. They've come to my domain for a rendezvous, to use it for a tryst. (*sung*) I'm not a fool wrapped around his lover's little finger. Until we get a judgment on the impropriety of this pair's behavior, I'll take them under my control. They're not to leave my territory. Both of you, be off immediately! My soldiers will surround the head priest's residence. We must take all precautions to keep these two under our care. Take down the votive pictures and destroy them.

NARRATOR: As the soldiers start to push the two about, Emon's maids cry out.

MAIDS: This is terrible! The lady and Katsuyori have fled before we realized. We found a letter in the room.

NARRATOR: Kōsaka quickly grabs the letter. He and Tokitsuna are at their wits' end. Murakami seizes the advantage.

MURAKAMI: (*spoken*) Well now, well now. We have proof of their affair before the god. He has given us this sign. (*sung*) A soldier who has lost his lord is no longer a samurai. We'll shave your head, give you a begging bowl, and you'll make a fine mendicant monk.

NARRATOR: Tokitsuna cannot restrain his anger at these insults and moves to attack, but Kōsaka stops him.

KŌSAKA: (*spoken*) We haven't been in the least shamed as samurai. (*sung*) Let me take care of this.

NARRATOR: He raises the hems of his traveling outfit, poised defiantly before Murakami.

KŌSAKA: (*spoken*) Listen, Murakami, you said that you've taken charge of the lady and Katsuyori. The vow of a daimyo of a province is not forgotten. Why, then, have you let the pair escape? Well, what do you have to say?

NARRATOR: (*sung*) Clever logic traps Murakami, who is at a loss for a reply. Tokitsuna is emboldened to push the advantage.

TOKITSUNA: If you conceal their whereabouts, you'll be an accomplice. The responsible party must remain a hostage until they both are found. I'll take you to our castle. Come with me now!

NARRATOR: He presses the point as far as he can go. Murakami's expression shows his dismay at this turn of events, but he is unable to speak.

KŌSAKA: Since he's an important criminal suspect, shouldn't we tie him up?

TOKITSUNA: Yes, of course.

NARRATOR: Both are heroic spirits, alert to what is happening.

MURAKAMI: (*spoken*) Yes, it's natural that you should be angry at the way things have gone. But it is, of course, the head priest who harbored them who is at fault. To vent your anger, cut him down together with all the priests or take them all into custody. If that's not enough, smash the Suwa Shrine to pieces. (*sung*) Whatever you do is all right with me.

NARRATOR: (*cadence*) Having given these orders, he runs off. (*sung*) Kōsaka and Tokitsuna watch him depart and nod to each other. They read the note left by Katsuyori.

KŌSAKA: (*spoken*) "We send this letter via others, as in the old tales. Because we dread the possible shame of Murakami's discovering our vows of love, we have decided to disappear for a while."

NARRATOR: (*sung*) Both are shocked.

KŌSAKA: (*spoken*) Tokitsuna, both Lady Emon and Katsuyori have authority over two provinces; their households are vast; and their subjects many. They could even find refuge among the farmers if need be. They'll surely find a safe retreat. (*sung*) If we pursue them into other territories, it'll cause havoc and only bring shame on our lords. Let's first leave here and discuss a general strategy with everyone from both sides. I'll make sure that the women who accompanied the lady return in proper order to keep any rumors from starting. You, too, retreat with your soldiers, keeping in tight formation.

NARRATOR: He gives the orders for departure and leads the party out in a dignified manner, truly in the style of his lord Shingen, a fine example of an honorable and discerning samurai. As tall as a fragrant chinaberry tree, shimmering like a precious stone from the mythical Mount Kunlun in the far west of China; the everlasting light of the gems of the many generations of the Takeda house (*scene cadence*) is unrivaled.[13]

—Scene 2
The same time as before, at the port of Ōtsu on Lake Biwa

NARRATOR: (*sung*) Long ago famed in verse as the imperial capital,[14] Ōtsu, in the province Ōmi on the shore of Lake Biwa, is a busy port for travelers and goods from the north to the capital. The shipping agent Maruya flourishes there, with piles of stock mountains high. Along the shore, hundreds of loads marked with banners wait for a boat. Holding the red banner with the paulownia crest of Nagao Terutora, a group of foot soldiers come running up.

SOLDIERS: (*spoken*) We got here early from Nyoigatake in the capital. The advance party's over there; the goods're here. Why ain't it loaded?

NARRATOR: (*sung*) Northern accents and distinctive haircuts signal that the daimyo of Echigo, Lord Nagao Terutora, (*cadence*) is on his way home overland from the capital through Ōmi.

(*sung*) From the other side of Ōtsu come the foot soldiers of Takeda Shingen, a contingent of fifty under the command of Yokota Heisuke. He stops in front of the Toimaruya warehouse, catching his breath.

HEISUKE: (*spoken*) This is where we order our boats. I want to speak to the man in charge.

NARRATOR: The manager emerges.

HEISUKE: As you must have heard, Lord Shingen of Kai is on his way home from the capital and will travel by boat from here as far as Maiwara. Because he made a pilgrimage to Shinra Myōjin, his party stopped for a rest at Miidera temple[15] and will be here shortly. We trust that you will be able to provide twenty large boats and sixty small craft. Hurry, we will need to board at once.

NARRATOR: But the manager is in a bind.

MANAGER: Lord Terutora of Echigo has already ordered ships to be prepared for his entourage. As you can see, everything is ready. I've brought in all the boats available for miles around. Unless you use fishing craft, there are no boats at all. (*sung*) Although it is an inconvenience for such a personage, could I suggest that you travel around the lake to Seta and order boats from there?

NARRATOR: He bows prostrate, his head to the ground.

HEISUKE: (*spoken*) My lord is the direct descendant of Lord Shinra Saburō Yoshimitsu in the Seiwa Genji line. He was able to call on His Imperial Highness, who has bestowed on him the title of Great Teacher, "Daisōshō," the highest rank of the priesthood.[16] Furthermore, he is cherished by the Ashikaga shogunate. The lord of Echigo, too, went to the capital. He has been given the Chinese character "teru" from the shogun Ashikaga Yoshiteru and has arrogantly changed his name from Kagetora to Terutora, flaunting his shogunal favor, even though he traces his ancestry to the house of Kamakura Gongorō Kagemasa,[17] retainers of the Genji. How can you say that you have prepared all the boats in this harbor for such a fellow and left none to be hired? Pull down the Nagao banners and replace them with ours!

NARRATOR: (*sung*) While he is yelling these orders, one of Terutora's footmen, Shindō Kohei, saunters out from the shop.

KOHEI: (*spoken*) I don't want to hear any more of this drivel! So what if this weak-kneed, lily-livered Takeda Shingen is now a high priest; he's still a bowlegged lout of a cleric. How dare you demand that the boats be given to Shingen and say that my lord is just a servant to him! If you're ready to lose your head, then go ahead on, (*sung*) rip down our banners.

NARRATOR: He draws his sword and attacks, but Heisuke parries his blow and draws his own weapon. They fight desperately, pushing each other back and forth, without fear for their lives. They fall on the sand along the shore and wrestle, each unwilling to cede an inch. (*cadence*) Fiercely they fight.[18]

(*sung*) The advance parties of both lords arrive at the same time. They finally manage to pull Heisuke and Kohei apart.

SOLDIERS: (*spoken*) Yokoda Heisuke of the Takeda and Shindō Kohei of the Nagao, both of you, stop this fight at once! Step back this instant! Hold back the horses.

NARRATOR: (*sung*) Shingen, calm and collected, and Terutora, short tempered, arrive on horseback, both in full ceremonial armor, their retainers all standing in line, bowing formally (*emotional cadence*) as they wait for them to dismount.

TERUTORA: (*spoken*) Bring them both here.

NARRATOR: (*sung*) The pair are brought before Shingen and Terutora, who dismount from their horses. Terutora bellows angrily.

TERUTORA: (*spoken*) You know that it is explicitly forbidden throughout the country for anyone to fight while accompanying his lord. Was the cause of this some grievance, or did it start from a disagreement? Depending on the circumstances, this could lead to serious trouble between the two houses. Explain exactly what happened.

NARRATOR: Shindō Kohei bows respectfully.

KOHEI: The root cause was a dispute over the boats. I was unable to ignore the insult that the Nagao house (*sung*) is descended from Gongorō Kagemasa and are servants of the Genji. It led to this fight.

NARRATOR: Heisuke interrupts before he can finish.

HEISUKE: (*spoken*) He called Lord Shingen a weak-kneed, lily-livered cleric. I could not let such an insult go undefended. I speak the truth without fear of punishment.

NARRATOR: Both speak honestly, appealing to their masters. Terutora laughs aloud.

TERUTORA: Did you hear that, Shingen? Sometimes the servant earns praise above his lord. Martial prowess does not depend on one's lineage. I don't feel any insult at all over this. How do you feel about this?

SHINGEN: Just as you say. How priceless to be called a "weak-kneed, lily-livered cleric"! Even if he were called a blind begging-priest, it wouldn't bother a true samurai. I'm not in the least worried by this fracas. In fact, this pair of foot soldiers have shown extraordinary valor, (*sung*) real martial spirit. In order to settle this dispute and leave no bitterness, may I ask that this fellow Shindō Kohei join the personal service of my inexperienced son Katsuyori?

TERUTORA: (*spoken*) Yes, certainly, and then, may I take this foot soldier Yokota Heisuke as my point man, wielding the long spear, to lead my troops?

SHINGEN: Then it's all settled. I entrust him to your service.

TERUTORA: Perfect, perfect. In turn, I present Kohei to you. Shindō Kohei, from today you are in service to the Takeda house.

SHINGEN: Yokota Heisuke, you are now a retainer of Lord Terutora.

NARRATOR: (*sung*) Both acknowledge the commands and exchange places. Each bows before his new master, following protocol. The dispute is settled fairly and with honor; everyone relaxes.

TERUTORA: (*spoken*) Lord Shingen, the number of boats is too few for all our troops, a cause of great concern to the shipping agents. It will be somewhat cramped, but the journey is not too far; may I welcome you to accompany me in the same craft?

SHINGEN: Even before you spoke, I had hoped that you would ask. I shall be delighted to accept.

NARRATOR: (*sung*) The stormy dispute over the boats disappears on calm waters. (*emotional cadence*) The snows on Mount Hira melt in spring, a harbinger of the warmth between these stern generals. Geese come to rest along Katada shore.[19] Shingen and Terutora, too, settle down on the dais set up for them on the boat, (*cadence*) just as the famous Zhang Liang and Huang Shi Gong met on an embankment long ago.[20]

(*sung*) Just then a cry is heard.

MESSENGER: I am a messenger from Lord Murakami of Shinano.

NARRATOR: A formal place is prepared before Terutora to receive him. He is an older man with flecks of gray hair; he announces himself as Kasuo Genba. He has his men present three different barrels of gifts—fishes, gold, and rolls of silk.

TERUTORA: (*spoken*) Please come forward to deliver your message.

NARRATOR: Invited forward, Genba advances respectfully.

GENBA: Lord Murakami wishes to congratulate you on receiving a new name from the shogun Lord Yoshiteru. This surely reflects your valiant service to the realm over the years, and it gives inestimable prestige to the Nagao house. Lord Murakami is concerned that although he has several times requested the hand of your daughter Lady Emon, you have not yet responded. A daughter whose marriage is delayed too long will surely give rise to gossip, and this will make suitors suspicious. She'll not only end up an old maid but will bring shame on her family. If this happens, it will bring harm to the Nagao house. Your accepting the proposal of Lord Murakami will put an end to any malicious rumors and protect Lord Terutora. My master has therefore sent me to greet you with these betrothal gifts on the way, even before you enter his land. (*sung*) He respectfully requests Lord Terutora to accept these gifts as acknowledgment of your agreement to their betrothal.

NARRATOR: Even before he finishes, the fiery-tempered Terutora scowls.

TERUTORA: (*spoken*) I am a samurai general of northern Japan, and who in the whole realm does not know of Nagao Terutora?! Although my daughter's hand has been requested, I haven't given an answer. We haven't announced the wedding plans! How dare you be so presumptuous! This is the height of rudeness! Is this pressure Murakami's arrogance, implying that Terutora's castle is smaller than one of his stables? Is this an insult, an affront? Your concern that a daughter whose marriage is delayed will cause gossip about impropriety and bring shame on her family is unwarranted meddling. If my daughter has committed an indiscretion, the other party will be discovered and punished, too. But Lord Terutora of Echigo has not hired you to cleanse his shame. Since I am on a journey, I shall let you leave unharmed, but take your gifts and leave at once. (*sung*) Someone, see this impudent messenger off!

NARRATOR: His voice is deafening, and his whole body trembles with anger, but Genba's face shows no gloom.

GENBA: (*spoken*) Amazing that even a great general from a powerful land doesn't know his etiquette. There are many worthy samurai in Shinano and among them is Murakami's trusted adviser Kasuo Genba. If these gifts don't find favor, then send your own men to return them. (*sung*) I won't take them back with me.

NARRATOR: He starts to rise.

TERUTORA: (*spoken*) You vindictive old man! (*sung*) Load the gifts onto this fool!

NARRATOR: His young attendants strip away Genba's swords, pin his arms, tie all the barrels together, and load them on to his back.

SOLDIERS: Now off with you. When you get home, be sure to get your porterage fee from Murakami!

NARRATOR: They lift him up and push him off.

GENBA: (*spoken*) Because of my master's rudeness, I've been humiliated beyond belief.

NARRATOR: (*sung*) Complaining of his master's faults, he sets off, stumbling on his way, For although he is a senior adviser, he is unable to offer advice or to see his own errors, even when facing Mount Kagami (Mirror).[21] (*exit cadence*) They wipe his face, and he sets off, fleeing for his life.

NARRATOR: (*sung*) Those high and low from both houses burst out laughing. Even Terutora smiles broadly.

TERUTORA: (*spoken*) What about that, Lord Takeda! Murakami rules over territory trapped between our lands of Kai and Echigo, but have you ever seen such manners in either of our houses? What remarkable insolence, the height of vulgarity! Such impudence will surely see the demise of that house.

NARRATOR: (*sung*) As he finishes, a messenger from his senior minister, Amakazu, left in charge in Echigo, comes running from the direction of Ōmi. Panting for breath after running, he bows before Terutora.

MESSENGER: (*spoken*) This past twenty-second, Lady Emon made a pilgrimage to Suwa Myōjin Shrine where she had a tryst with Takeda Katsuyori. They have fled outside our domain and are still at large. Naoe Tokitsuna, who was with her, set off immediately in pursuit but has not been heard of since.

NARRATOR: (*sung*) He hands over the urgent letter. Just then another messenger arrives, this time from Itagaki, who was left in charge of Takeda's castle. He bows before Takeda, trying to catch his breath.

MESSENGER: (*spoken*) This past twenty-second, young Lord Katsuyori made a pilgrimage to Suwa Myōjin Shrine, where he had a rendezvous with Lady Emon of Echigo. They have fled, their destination unknown. Kōsaka, who was with him, has set off in pursuit. (*sung*) The details are here in this letter.

NARRATOR: Both take up the letters from their respective houses and break the seal at the same time. Both generals gasp, and the other samurai fear the worst as they try to read the faces of each, (*cadence*) now frozen stiff.

(*sung*) A bold and resolute Terutora grinds his teeth.

TERUTORA: (*spoken*) Did Murakami know about all this when he said that a daughter whose marriage is delayed would surely gain notoriety? Or was it a coincidence? His words have struck home, yet I did not respond. *(sung)* I'll never cease to regret the humiliation of being reproached by that scum Murakami, far beneath any samurai of the Nagao house.

NARRATOR: His face flames crimson.

TERUTORA: How can I cleanse this shame?

NARRATOR: His fierce glare shakes the Shinano Road, and steam seems to rise from his head, *(cadence)* suggesting to all the force of the Mount Asama, a smoldering volcano.

(spoken) Shingen remains calm.

SHINGEN: My son Katsuyori and your daughter are still young. *(sung)* Any glory or shame will fall on the parents alone. Murakami may be the arbitrator in our battle; that is perfectly acceptable. Therefore, the two of us will lead our forces to fight at Shinano. The victor will be decided there, and it goes without saying that this will determine whether I take Echigo or whether Kai is taken by you. There, too, any shame will be cleansed. *(sung)* Victory must be determined by our military skill and prowess.

NARRATOR: *(cadence)* He calmly throws down the gauntlet.

TERUTORA: *(spoken)* I have long wanted to test my skills against Lord Shingen. *(sung)* From now on we face each other with swords drawn for battle. *(spoken)* Yokota Heisuke, my newest recruit, come here.

NARRATOR: *(sung)* As he answers this command, Shingen calls out to his new retainer.

SHINGEN: Shindō Kohei, come here. *(spoken)* You were one of Terutora's men before. Be the first to take a battle prize.

TERUTORA: Heisuke, you, too, were one of Shingen's soldiers before. *(sung)* Be the first to offer blood to the god of war.

NARRATOR: Tested by their new masters to fight against their former lords, both immediately draw swords and begin to fight, but the two generals intervene.

SHINGEN: *(spoken)* That will be enough for the moment. You will have your chance again on the battlefield. *(sung)* As a sign that we shall have no more contact, I offer a toast.

TERUTORA: A toast to our enemy!

NARRATOR: Each bows to the other in a show of boldness. Lapping waves echo the swish of arrows, *(scene cadence)* signaling the call to battle.

—Scene 3
Sequel to scene 1, at the remote Kikyō-ga-hara

NARRATOR: (*sung*) The famous road of Shinano cuts deep through mountains, winding between boulders, overgrown with moss. Travelers walk among the clouds as they cross mountain peaks, occasionally hearing the sound of crashing timber[22] (*cadence*) and the ripple of shallow brooks.

(*sung*) Here lives a rōnin from Ushikubo in Mikawa Province, Yamamoto Kansuke Haruyoshi.[23] Having lost his father at a tender age, he was brought up lovingly by his mother. Although not learned, he mastered the strategies of battle laid down in treatises by Huang Shi Gong, Sun Wu, and Wu Qi. His skills are famous throughout the land, and many generals from near and far seek his services, but waiting to choose the right lord, he bides his time, a sleeping dragon in the manner of Zhu Ge Liang.[24] Here he has withdrawn as a hermit mountain-man, passing life quietly, carting firewood and cutting grasses, (*cadence*) his tools at his waist.

(*sung*) "A rustic fellow wearing rough Kiso hemp," as in the old verse,[25] sleeves too short, he walks along narrow grassy paths, (*cadence*) returning to Kikyō-ga-hara. (*sung*) Kansuke's brow is furrowed, perplexed.

KANSUKE: (*spoken*) This land of Shinano is deep in the mountains and the clouds are always billowing, but today there is something strange in the atmosphere. (*sung*) To the south, the horizon continues to Shiojiri Peak. To the north, there is Mount Torii. From the peaks, the clouds advance toward each other. (*highest pitch*) The clash of white clouds and the chaos that follows are (*cadence*) like a battle scene.[26] (*sung*) This surely means that Kai and Echigo are at loggerheads. Shingen is the wise general; Terutora, the brave general. This cloud battle is fascinating. No matter which wins or loses, it's all the same to me, free and beholden to no one.

NARRATOR: He gazes at the sky, which is already growing faint on this short late-autumn day. He takes out his pipe and strikes his flint on a stone. The smoke rises from his pipe. He compares its shape with the smoke from Mount Asama, (*cadence*) absorbed in the sight.[27]

(*sung*) Takeda Katsuyori and Lady Emon, accused by Murakami of having an affair, have fled from Suwa Myōjin Shrine to seek refuge, and they find themselves lost in the mountains. Their feet are cut and sore from the long walk, their sandals stained red as they struggle over thorny fields. Even the wind haunts them, sounding like pursuers about to pounce. Despite being worried about what lies ahead, they must still keep an eye to what lies behind them. Lady Emon stumbles against Kansuke.

EMON: Oh, please excuse me.

NARRATOR: (*emotional cadence*) She and Katsuyori are stunned, astonished. (*spoken*) Kansuke stares at them with suspicion.

KANSUKE: A young lady and a lad, traveling alone . . . hmm. . . . Ah, I see. You didn't like whoever your parents wanted you to marry, and each of you decided the other was the only one. You couldn't bear the idea of another splitting this precious sweet cake open.[28] Love has no reason, they say, (*sung*) and over hill and dale, passion leads the way. You may have to struggle as a woodcutter and not be able to nibble her cake, but you should be able to savor her luscious cups of tea.

NARRATOR: (*cadence*) Kansuke gets up to be on his way. (*sung*) Katsuyori grabs Kansuke's sleeve.

KATSUYORI: (*spoken*) Your assessment is correct. We are a couple together without our parents' approval and must keep hidden from the world, but we have done nothing wrong, not committed adultery. Neither of us has a spouse. (*sung*) Someone else has tried to steal her away, someone she has no interest in. We're fleeing from this enemy. I know that this is an unreasonable request, but could you possibly hide us for a while? If I am successful as a samurai, I promise that I shall repay the favor.

NARRATOR: His manner shows his breeding as a daimyo's son. Kansuke laughs loudly.

KANSUKE: (*spoken*) I was not born a woodcutter, but I bear this burden for the sake of my mother, now alone in the world. If I sought service in a daimyo's house, I could most likely command a stipend of land worth a hundred or two hundred *kan*[29] of silver. However, if I join his service, then I'll have to die in battle to repay the wages. That'd be following the path of loyalty. (*sung*) To serve my mother, I'd have to preserve this body. That would be disloyal, like stealing a stipend from a lord. If I fulfill filial duty, then I lack loyalty; if I'm loyal, I'm unfilial. Pressed by this problem, I decided to put my sword aside and live as a mountain monkey, a hermit more or less, but seeing my mother's lively expression in the morning—(*cadence*) could even the wealth of a million *kan* of silver compare with this?

(*sung*) It is because of my filial duty that I must refuse your request. Although you may feel you have no one to depend on in this floating, uncertain world, don't be angry or despair. (*spoken*) This area is where in ancient times Yamato Takeru, when he was fighting the Emishi and pushing the court's power farther northwest, was able to foretell the future from a single leaf. Therefore, Kikyō-ga-hara is known for its auspicious omens. (*sung*) The fact that your flight has led you here bodes well for your fate. (*spoken*) If you follow this reed field to the left, you'll find Echigo Road. (*sung*) This bit of information will be my parting gift to you. Ah, the changing fortunes of life in this floating world!

NARRATOR: He picks up his burden and sets off, this samurai, loyal and filial, compassionate and just, an unpolished gem like Bian He in Zhou-dynasty China.[30] (*cadence*) What a pity that his shining virtue is hidden from the world.

KATSUYORI: (*sung*) What a magnificently noble samurai! Even among a constellation of brave officers, one always seeks out a warrior compassionate and just. I regret not having asked his name, but nevertheless let's take his advice on finding the road.

NARRATOR: They walk farther, making their way through the reeds and tall grasses, but he has an idea.

KATSUYORI: Lady Emon, (*spoken*) Musashibō Benkei once wore his sandals backward when walking through the snow to ward off pursuers and protect Yoshitsune.[31] We're sure to be followed through this high grass. (*sung*) We'll trick them by hiding behind some bushes until they pass and then flee.

NARRATOR: They push their way through the thick growth of mugwort and creepers, when suddenly they catch sight of an old and grizzly wild boar crouched under some bush clover. Emon shrieks with fright and (*emotional cadence*) clings to Katsuyori.

KATSUYORI: (*spoken*) Don't be alarmed; it won't hurt us. Boars really are ferocious wild predators, but they don't attack humans. A wounded boar may have the strength of a thousand men, but otherwise it is known to fear men. (*sung*) You can see here how this one has learned to hide from hunters by lying low. Let's make this our hiding place, too.

NARRATOR: They lie down in the wild boar's autumn bush-clover lair.[32] They hide in the tall grasses to escape detection from prying eyes; (*cadence*) such is often the fate of passionate lovers.

FIGURE 36 Kansuke killing the boar and saving Katsuyori and Emon (*Shinshū kawa-nakajima kassen*, 1726 [fiction version], Daitōkyū bunko).

(*sung*) Some of Murakami's men, led by Tōta carrying a musket, come running after them.

TŌTA: I just spotted them from that ridge just now. Where could they have got to?

NARRATOR: All the foot soldiers search through the undergrowth.

SOLDIER: Look, here there are tracks. I'll get a reward for this.

NARRATOR: He runs after them, but Tōta stops him.

TŌTA: Don't rush, anyone! Something smells fishy here. I'll test things out by firing a shot.

NARRATOR: He loads and fires a few shots. (*spoken*) They hear a reaction to the volley.

TŌTA: I've surely hit Katsuyori. (*sung*) Now to get his head.

NARRATOR: They move forward and hear a rustling in the grasses. A wild boar the size of a small mountain, wounded and with back arched, bursts out in front of them.

TŌTA: May the god Hachiman forgive me. I made a mistake, I'm sorry, please forgive me.

NARRATOR: They all flee. Katsuyori, too, rises and unsheathes his sword to protect Emon. The boar has the fury of a lion, eyes alight with fire, fangs bared, ready to attack anyone, friend or foe. He chases after them all with the strength to smash boulders and bore through iron gates. Everyone flees desperately, some stumbling over the cliff, others behind boulders, others into the valley. (*scene cadence*) Chaos as they flee in all directions.

NARRATOR: (*dōguya melody*) The sun descends early over the mountain ridge as Kansuke collects firewood, carrying the load of ten men. He follows a familiar road home but notices that the grasses along the path have been roughly trampled. From over the hill he hears the echo of cries of distress.

KANSUKE: (*sung*) Hmm, I wonder if that young couple are fighting their enemies. I hope they're safe.

NARRATOR: As he worries about them, a wild boar suddenly attacks his left thigh. The force of the blow (*cadence*) knocks him flying for more than three yards. (*spoken*) Kansuke recovers his footing.

KANSUKE: You vile beast, I'll skin you and use the hide for a rug. (*sung*) Get back here! Come back.

NARRATOR: Spurred by his call, the boar returns to the attack. (*kowari threatening melody*) It runs past him and then turns again. Kansuke parries its attacks and finally jumps on its back. He grabs its tail with his left hand and with the sickle in his right, he attacks its ribs. The blood of boar and man color the boar's coat scarlet like that of an orangutan. (*low threatening melody*) The boar tries to throw Kansuke and brushes him against an old tree. (*sung*) He hits a boulder, and Kansuke falls off. They struggle, first one on top, then the other, (*fight-scene cadence*) battling for an hour.

(*sung*) Kansuke is gored in many places, and his right eye has been gouged. The gushing blood clouds his vision. He wavers for a moment, and the boar attacks with its tusks. On the edge of a cliff, he fears falling into the valley. He reaches out and barely manages to grab the branch of a pine tree, perhaps a blessing for his filial service. (*cadence*) With the speed and agility of a monkey, he quickly scurries up the tree to safety.

(*sung*) The raging boar attacks the base of the tree, digging at the roots with tusks and snout, tearing up rocks and sand, (*cadence*) ferociously churning up the soil like a plowshare. (*sung*) The boar gradually digs away the roots of the young pine tree, which begins to sway back and forth. Before the tree crashes to the ground, Kansuke uses all the strength he can muster to pound at the boar's head. The boar staggers under the blows, and Kansuke jumps on it, trying to break its neck. Just then Katsuyori sees them and runs up to stab again and again at the boar's vital parts, finally killing the beast. Kansuke collapses, totally exhausted.

KATSUYORI: (*spoken*) Ha, what valor! You were kind earlier, and now you've saved us from this terror. We are even more beholden to you. I am Katsuyori, the only son of Takeda Shingen.

EMON: (*sung*) I am Emon, the daughter of Nagao Terutora. Harassed by

Murakami Yoshikiyo, we have had to elope and become desperate fugitives. We owe our lives to you, even more than to our parents.

NARRATOR: Kansuke opens his one good eye.

KANSUKE: (*spoken*) Then you must be the heirs of both estates. I am Yamamoto Kansuke Haruyoshi. My sister is the wife of Terutora's retainer, Naoe Yamashiro Sanetsuna. (*sung*) That means that we are no strangers. It's wonderful that we have escaped. (*spoken*) This is Murakami's territory. You cannot remain here for a moment longer. (*sung*) Let's be off.

NARRATOR: But just as he speaks, Tōta comes racing up with his men.

TŌTA: Don't let them get away!

KATSUYORI: If that party has found us, then we can't try to hide in the bushes anymore. A bunch of dirty maggot samurai, not worthy of a sword. I'll exterminate the lot!

NARRATOR: He grabs a branch of pine and, with one leap, attacks, killing all in his path. Thrown into confusion by his ferocity, they scatter in confusion.[33] Tōta leaps at him defiantly.

TŌTA: Katsuyori, you won't get away from me!

NARRATOR: Katsuyori turns to face him.

KATSUYORI: Now its your turn, you green maggot.

NARRATOR: He strikes with a cross blow and cuts Tōta in two; (*cadence*) killing him instantly.

KANSUKE: (*sung*) At last the roots of your enemy are severed. I would like to go with you to the border, but my leg is badly hurt and I'm worried about my mother. We'll meet again perhaps. I pray for your safe return.

KATSUYORI: I pray that your wounds will heal.

NARRATOR: They each bid farewell. (*kowari threatening melody*) Kansuke's compassion is like that of Xuan De,[34] his wisdom, like Kong Ming, his valor, like Guan Yu.[35] His fame, known in the three lands of India, China, and Japan—high as Mount Fuji—and, as in the hunting party of Yoritomo long ago, like Nitan Tadatsuna,[36] he has bested the wild boar, riding it to submission. But he is not unscathed; his whole body aches from the encounter, his leg gashed and eye gouged. He walks away, limping like a cripple, his face disfigured. The fame of brave Kansuke, (*high pitch*) "vanquisher of wild boars," lives on in legend.

Act 2

—Scene 1
Kansuke's home in the Kiso Mountains, later, the same day

NARRATOR:

(*sung*) To rule the realm seek out the best counsel,
Even if you must be three times supplicant.[1]

Takeda Shingen has his guards stay at the foot of the mountain and takes only Hara Gorō Masatoshi with him as he enters the Kiso Mountains. Snow continues to fall steadily. The path is treacherous under deep layers of snow, the mountain slippery and sharp as crystal.[2] The forest is veiled in white gold; no one sees their arrival at the gate of the hermitage of Yamamoto Kansuke, (*cadence*) hidden far from the eyes of the world.

(*sung*) Gorō bows before his lord in the snow.

GORŌ: (*spoken*) I couldn't imagine where we were going in this blizzard. With this freezing wind and driving snow, we couldn't even ride a horse or hold an umbrella. Have we traveled this far only to find ourselves at the hermitage of that crusty old rōnin? If you have business with him, there's no need to come all this way. I could have come and brought him to you.[3] (*sung*) It is most improper for me to say this, but it seems odd that the famous General Shingen, lord of Kai, is traipsing through the forest in this snowstorm. This hardly reflects well on you. Let's go back.

NARRATOR: He tugs at Shingen's sleeve but is shaken off.

SHINGEN: (*spoken*) What would a callow youth know about this rōnin? Kansuke is blind in one eye, crippled, and looks like a peasant brought up in the mountains, but he has the spirit of the famous general Kusunoki Masashige.[4] He's a strategist who can stand alongside China's renowned Kong Ming, Sun Wu, or Wu Qi. He's courted far and wide but has not been impressed by any of the lords. I want Kansuke and no one else to be my right-hand man. I know of no one in all Japan who is superior in tactics. (*sung*) Last month I came twice to his hut, but he was out and I couldn't speak to him. I am determined to meet him today and have brought my horse to the foot of the mountain. I have brought it for Kansuke, not for me. Seeking a master is like seeking the blessing of the gods. (*spoken*) Be on your best behavior. If it is too cold for you here, then go back and get someone else to come in your place.[5] (*sung*) What a sniveling, foolish fellow!

NARRATOR: So chastised, Gorō follows his master, muttering to himself as he steps into the deep snow.

GORŌ: What can be so important in this snow? If a deep snowfall is supposed to mean a bumper crop and a warm hearth, this snow should keep me warm.

NARRATOR: He tries to cheer himself up, but his lips turn purple (*cadence*) and his teeth chatter in the freezing cold.

(*sung*) Inside the house a snow-haired old woman sits in the master's seat, tending the hearth. (*nō chanting*) Smoke rises, floating out into the night. (*sung*) Her face (*cadence*) is as strong as the brewing tea, stiff and stern.[6]

SHINGEN:

(*sung*) What a delight to find someone at home! Today finally I shall succeed.[7]

NARRATOR: He approaches the door.

SHINGEN: (*spoken*) Please forgive my unannounced appearance, but I have come drawn by the fame of Lord Yamamoto Kansuke. Last month I came twice, but he was away. I have come through this blizzard to speak directly with him. I am Takeda Shingen. Could you convey my greetings to him?

NARRATOR: His manner is humble and polite.

MOTHER: Hmm, Takeda Shingen, I've heard of him. My feet get cold away from the fire. (*sung*) If you have something to say, then come in and speak.

NARRATOR: She replies reclining, (*cadence*) leaning on her elbow.

SHINGEN: (*sung*) Please forgive this intrusion.

NARRATOR: He opens the door and enters, but the old woman shows no sign of getting up. Gorō is incensed at the affront.[8]

GORŌ: (*spoken*) It is usual to greet a visitor, but you haven't even risen from your pillow. Are you ill? Has this cold weather brought on a stomachache? (*sung*) Let me take on the bug and kill it.

NARRATOR: He starts to get up threateningly, but Shingen scowls at him.

SHINGEN: (*spoken*) We have not been invited to this house. It was impertinent of us to approach unannounced. (*sung*) Move back next to the door.

NARRATOR: He rebukes him sternly.

SHINGEN: (*spoken*) You most likely have heard that because of a dispute between us, Nagao Terutora, lord of Echigo, and I are at war. It is likely that a battle will be fought soon here in Shinshū.[9] I feel that it is a pity that Kansuke, famed for his rare military genius, is left to wither away deep in the mountains. (*sung*) I would like to invite him to become my chief strategist and to lead my three divisions. It is easy to find ten thousand soldiers but difficult to find one general. I have come three times to show my sincerity. May I humbly beg the support of his revered mother?

NARRATOR: He bows deeply, head to the floor, observing in every detail the etiquette of a disciple to his master. (*emotional cadence*) His manner shows his utmost respect.

(*sung*) The old mother continues to recline and opens her toothless mouth wide and laughs loudly.

MOTHER: (*spoken*) Ah, Lord Shingen has strange tastes. My son has grown up in the mountains from childhood, and although he has held the reins of wild oxen, he has never ridden in a saddle. He regularly cuts down trees for firewood but hasn't ever cut even the finger of a man. (*sung*) Furthermore, he's crippled and can't travel far, and because he's blind in one eye, his lack of vision is a handicap. He's short and has trouble even reaching things down from shelves. (*spoken*) Knowing all that about Yamamoto Kansuke, you want to make him a general? What a joke! Ha, ha. Various lords have sought him out, but he has always refused them. If you've come with some such request, then you'd best be off home again. (*sung*) My, oh my, how cold it is today!

NARRATOR: She turns away defiantly to warm her legs near the fire. Gorō (*spoken*) loses his temper.

GORŌ: Lord Shingen, have you no response to this? This rustic rōnin of yours, if he's the son of this old crone who's ignorant of the world and its ways, then we can have some idea of his measure. (*sung*) Let's get out of here.

NARRATOR: He starts to get up, but Shingen scowls fiercely again.

SHINGEN: *(spoken)* Hmm, I had heard that he wanted to choose his master. Although I do not have the kind of admirable character that would attract his favor, I am determined to succeed. *(sung)* I shall await the moment when we vow to be master and disciple, lord and subject, even if the day turns to night, today turns into tomorrow, and then to the day after. My body will become a corpse on this mountain.

NARRATOR: He sits firmly, a model of the virtuous general *(cadence)* who seeks a wise man.

(sung) The old mother sits up.

MOTHER: My, my, you are a persistent, obstinate fellow who won't listen to reason. If you want him so much, then I just might consider having him enter your service. *(spoken)* It's said that a crane will not favor a nest in a rotting tree; a great fish will not live in a small pond. If you want to take Kansuke into service, then he must choose a worthy lord. Well then, Lord Shingen, how do you deploy your soldiers? What is the basis of your military strategy?

NARRATOR: She challenges him to respond.

SHINGEN: *(sung)* Yes, madam.

NARRATOR: He rises and goes to the hearth. He removes the burned-out embers from beneath the cauldron and breaks up some firewood into little pieces and stokes the fire. The fire glows red hot as the flames rise, causing the large kettle to whistle as the steam hisses out, *(cadence)* almost as loud as waves striking the shore.

SHINGEN: *(sung)* First, I would use my soldiers in this way.

NARRATOR: He points to the fire and cauldron. The old mother claps her hands in appreciation.

MOTHER: Magnificent, surely a first-class general! *(spoken)* You've mastered Huang Shi Gong's ideas from San Lue: by putting small, separate pieces together, the soft can be made to overcome the firm; the weak can conquer the strong.[10] Yes, you are a worthy leader. Of the two tactics, "reactive" and "active," this one is the active, where one follows a plan. What about using the resourcefulness of your mind?

NARRATOR: She challenges him again.

SHINGEN: *(sung)* Yes, madam.

NARRATOR: He goes outside and captures a sparrow that was foraging for food in the snow and returns *(cadence)* holding it in his hand.

SHINGEN: *(spoken)* Well, madam, I hold a sparrow in my hand. Answer me, is it alive or dead?[11]

MOTHER: What a clever and rare strategy! If I say that it is alive, then you'll kill it in your hand before showing it to me. If I say it's dead, you'll let it free to fly away. This is the tactic of reacting to the actions of your enemy from the *San Lue*.[12] Either way he moves, you win. You've offered the best answer. A great general, indeed! My son Kansuke should certainly ask Lord Shingen to take him into service.

NARRATOR: She sits up and bows respectfully.

MOTHER: *(sung)* I shall bring him to you.

FIGURE 37 Shingen visiting Kansuke's house and speaking with his mother (*Shinshū kawa-nakajima kassen*, 1726 [fiction version], Dai-tōkyū bunko).

NARRATOR: She gets up and goes into the next room. Shingen is delighted to have gained a jewel to brighten the night.[13] Gorō, too, is surprised at the turn of events.

GORŌ: What an impressive old woman!

NARRATOR: *(cadence)* He cannot help praising her.

(sung) Almost immediately a voice is heard from the next room, "Yamamoto Kansuke will now offer greetings to his lord. Who will acknowledge his greeting?" An imposing figure emerges in full formal armor, a black helmet covering his face, chain mail, all bearing the emblems of the family crest; he sways as he walks because of his limp after the battle with the boar, *(cadence)* which makes his armor look crooked.

KANSUKE: *(sung)* Yamamoto Kansuke Haruhisa presents himself to his lord.

NARRATOR: He bows formally.

GORŌ: *(spoken)* I am Hara Gorō Masatoshi. Allow me to approach.

NARRATOR: He quickly moves forward.

GORŌ: For a man of your fame, we must have some show of your prowess. Shall it be swords or spears. Or bare hands? (*sung*) Kansuke, I am ready to be your opponent.

NARRATOR: He grabs at him, but Kansuke loses his balance under the weight of the armor and collapses on the floor, unable to get up.

GORŌ: Are you made such a coward, just by putting on armor? Then you'll faint when you hear battle cries. Instead of riding on a horse, Kansuke, you'd be better off riding in a coffin.

NARRATOR: (*cadence*) He laughs loudly.

MOTHER: (*sung*) Your laughter is understandable. (*spoken*) Recently, Kansuke was hurt badly in an encounter with a wild boar. He has gone with a young couple to a hot spring in Hakone to recover. So he is not at home. I was fearful of committing him to a promise to join your service. (*sung*) This armor is the samurai soul of my son. If his spirit presents itself to offer loyalty, then it will be the same as Kansuke himself. Think of this armor-clad soldier as Kansuke. Take it as proof of a mother's unshakable promise.

NARRATOR: She bows before Shingen. Gorō is flabbergasted, lost for words. General Shingen is delighted (*cadence*) and more impressed than ever.

SHINGEN: (*spoken*) With a provision of land worth 300 *kan*[14] of silver, we tie the bonds of lord and retainer for three lifetimes,[15] (*sung*) providing samurai glory for your descendants. I request your guidance.

NARRATOR: She bows deeply, acknowledging his offer.

MOTHER: For a severely disabled Kansuke to find a master to serve is as rare (*cadence*) as a one-eyed turtle finding a floating log.[16] (*sung*) A warrior must be prepared to move into battle in full military dress. I present his swords and armor for inspection.

NARRATOR: She pulls out a battered wicker chest. Inside, neatly folded by a loving mother's hand, lie layers of battle kimono and accoutrements, never worn but preserved carefully by his mother for this day. In Kansuke's place, she accepts the offer to serve Shingen. (*cadence*) A parent will always be the child's parent; a child, too, will always be a child of the parent.

(*sung*) Gorō bows.

GORŌ: (*spoken*) The snow is getting deeper, and the day is late. We should be off.

NARRATOR: He turns to set off for the foot of the mountain.
GORŌ: Let me accompany you back.
NARRATOR: (*sung*) He takes the roles of footman and guard, carrying the sword and spear, (*cadence*) and he leads his master's horse through the snow.
MOTHER: (*sung*) I would like Kansuke to accompany you as well.
NARRATOR: She removes the garland and helmet and offers it to him as a sign of cementing the new relationship. He respectfully receives it.
SHINGEN: Just like Tai Gong Wang,[17] who was hidden from the world, idly fishing along the Wei riverbank,[18] and found by the Zhou emperor Wen, (*spoken*) who returned with him in the imperial carriage, Kansuke, too, rides together with his lord.
NARRATOR: He gratefully takes Kansuke's helmet and places it on the saddle, tying it firmly, symbolizing the bonds between this mountain hut and the castle for which they now set off. Kansuke's armor sits high in the saddle, and General Shingen's spirit rises to the sky, (*sung*) confident as a dragon. (*scene cadence*) They depart for Kōfu.[19]

—Scene 2

The journey of Lady Emon and Katsuyori[20] from Kikyō-gahara to a shrine at the foot of Mount Kurokami, winter of 1558

NARRATOR:

(*nō chanting*)[21] "Steps through the snow,
seem to crush the flowers of youth."[22]
The path is treacherous along steep mountain cliffs
and from the shadows below in the valleys
rises the roar of rushing streams.
Fierce winds of a mountain storm
scatter leaves that chase after the lovers,
who imagine hunters' cries in pursuit.
(*intense*) Glancing back with each step,
they hurry deeper and deeper into the mountains,
(*cadence*) with no hope of finding help.
Only a light traveling coat for protection,
now worn thin with long wear,

they wander here and there seeking shelter.
Lady Emon, raised as a delicate flower,
(*cadence*) is frightened on this dark and narrow path.
(*nagaji melody*) Her spirit is lifted,
seeing Katsuyori's shadow beside her own, a party of four.
Pain and suffering at fleeing the world
lead them to Kikyō-ga-hara.
Nothing is familiar about the grasses and trees,
but she grieves at parting with every scattered leaf.
"Look, over there, Lord Katsuyori,
(*song*) a pair of geese have lost their way home in spring,
but she is contentedly flying close beside her mate.
How hateful her complacent cries, the envy of lonely widows.
(*cadence*) No regrets about following the mate one loves."
(*sung*) Their cries noisily fill the sky
echoing across the mountain tops.
Emon looks up and sees the vast Suwa Lake
with its waves that reach the clouds.
"How deep was the passion
of Lord Narihira, such a fine man,
(*nō chanting*) who journeyed for love,
like we who now travel
across Shinano (*sung*) near the peak of Mount Asama.[23]
The smoke rising from its summit,
cannot compare with the heights of my love,
(*cadence*) nor even the peak of Mount Fuji."
(*sung*) Her skin fair as the snow on its peaks,
Her face a blossom,
(*high pitch*) Her sash a dappled pattern of speckled snow.
Her shoulders adorned with zigzagging gold thread,
embroidered on her skirts—
a steed rushes across a field under a full moon,
chased by autumn winds that rustle pine branches.
(*song*) "Don't be prickly and nervous like the pine needles,
(*high pitch*) be bold like the broad *bashō* leaves.
How hateful! Restore the leaves, torn so easily.
Was the bold life (*cadence*) only a fragile dream, now past.[24]

(*sung*) Yesterday now a dream,

today now passing,

tomorrow no one to depend on,

(*cadence*) no longer a home in Kai or Echigo.

(*sung*) Lost souls we float through this world,

our hearts riven like melons on this mountain slope,

(*Edo song*) treacherous with narrow cliffs leading to peak after peak,

deep in the mountains now harsh in the dead of winter."

(*sung*) "We first met during the blossoms of spring.

You often rushed to see me in summer.

In autumn we basked in the cool evening breeze.

Reeds, bush clover, and eulalia ears rustled in the breeze.

Pine crickets, 'Bell-ring' crickets, giant crickets, all sang in chorus,

crisp echoes mixed with the cold of frost.

Colorful leaves, our only souvenir from autumn long gone.

Ice now grows thick on our threadbare sleeves,

ragged like this weather-beaten Usui Pass,

as the weak rays of the sun sink behind the hills.

In the nearby village crows caw,

but we dare not ask the village name.

We cannot speak or unravel the strands of

(*cadence*) Mount Kurokami[25] to find our way in the dark night,

(*sung*) fighting the torrent of rain without a coat,

no inn for refuge.

There in the field, a simple shelter, a roof with no walls,

(*high pitch*) to us a jeweled palace."

(*scene cadence*) They stop to rest.

—Scene 3

At a small shrine in the foothills of Mount Kurokami, later that night

NARRATOR: (*sung*) Naoe Tokitsuna, realizing that Lady Emon has fled, cannot return to face Lord Terutora's anger or the shame that his actions have caused. He sets off to find the princess, traveling to Mikawa and

Tōtōmi,[26] but no trace can be found throughout Kai Province. And now the moon is hidden by rain clouds. Arming himself with a Kagase "scarecrow" straw rain hat, he hurries through the darkness toward the unknown Mount Kurokami (*cadence*) on the way to Kōzuke Province.[27]

TOKITSUNA: (*sung*) I'm at the end of my tether. No sign of an inn. Oh, for a sturdy tree to shelter me from the wind and cold.

NARRATOR: He struggles on searching here, there, and everywhere, and spies something ahead.

TOKITSUNA: (*spoken*) What's this! It's a simple shrine. Splendid! A fine inn for free.

NARRATOR: (*sung*) He moves closer and sees a samurai traveler dressed as he is, with a large rain hat, lying across the entrance, fast asleep and snoring.

TOKITSUNA: (*spoken*) Well, well, what a wide world this is! A wretched traveler like myself, I'm sure you'll allow me to share this inn.

NARRATOR: He moves the fellow's legs aside and sits down.

TOKITSUNA: Ha, what a relief! While I was walking, I was so determined that neither rain nor wind could affect me, but now as I relax, I feel totally exhausted. This shelter doesn't block out the cold wind, and there are no blankets. (*sung*) This saké, kept for a special occasion, the gourd cast aside by the hermit sage Xu You,[28] are my only bedfellows.

NARRATOR: He pours from the gourd into a cup and gulps down the saké.

TOKITSUNA: (*spoken*) It's just as Confucius described the pleasures of Yan Hui:[29] "cherishing a small box for rice and a cup for soup."

NARRATOR: (*sung*) While he is savoring each sip of saké, the other samurai lifts his head and frowns severely.

KŌSAKA: (*spoken*) What a rude fellow! I'll teach him a lesson for sharing my room without asking and then stirring my envy with saké to boot. (*sung*) I'll just borrow that saké for a while!

NARRATOR: He boldly grabs the gourd and downs the remains in one long gulp and then sets it back in front of its owner. He spreads himself out to sleep, (*cadence*) a sight both comic and impudent.

(*sung*) Tokitsuna drains his cup.

TOKITSUNA: (*spoken*) Ah, this is wonderful! Just one more to help me relax.

NARRATOR: (*sung*) He picks up the gourd and finds it strangely light but still tries to pour some into his cup. Not even a drop comes out.

TOKITSUNA: (*spoken*) What's this? Did it spill? Is it leaking? I'll suck it out.

NARRATOR: He caresses the gourd but (*sung*) then notices the smell of saké on the other's breath.

TOKITSUNA: Then it was this fellow.

NARRATOR: He grabs his kimono and pins him down.

TOKITSUNA: (*spoken*) A bell thief gets caught because of the sound; a saké thief, by the smell. You can't hide your crime. Give back the saké from this gourd. If you refuse, your head'll fly. What'll it be?

NARRATOR: Hand on sword, Tokitsuna threatens the other, but the man is unruffled.

KŌSAKA: What's all the racket? Ordering me to return saké already drunk, you're a fairly naive samurai. "Saké once given is never returned." (*sung*) If you must, then cut me in two.

NARRATOR: His words show him ready to die. Tokitsuna recognizes his voice.

TOKITSUNA: (*spoken*) Isn't that the voice of Lord Takeda's man Kōsaka?

KŌSAKA: Who is it that knows my name?

TOKITSUNA: I am Naoe Tokitsuna in service to Lord Nagao.

KŌSAKA: Tokitsuna?

TOKITSUNA: Kōsaka, (*sung*) it's good to meet you again.

NARRATOR: They grasp each other's hands.

KŌSAKA: It's dangerous to be about in the dark. I'm delighted you're safe. (*spoken*) Well then, do you know where Lord Katsuyori is?

TOKITSUNA: That's my problem. I've searched in four or five provinces along the Eastern Mountain Road but to no avail. Even if the pair are tied together with irons, I'm determined to have them sever their ties immediately and each return home. If not, then even my suicide will not be enough to make amends. I fear that Katsuyori might harm himself in a fit of anger. (*sung*) I suffer even more at the thought of his dying before me.

NARRATOR: They confess their woes to each other, (*emotional cadence*) their tears all too understandable.

   (*sung*) Katsuyori and Emon, who also are taking refuge in the shelter, overhear them.

KATSUYORI: Both Kōsaka and Tokitsuna have suffered because of us. If they catch us, they'll force us apart.

NARRATOR: His words strike terror in the lovers, who hold their breath, (*sung*) fearing detection.

(*spoken*) Tokitsuna thinks aloud.

TOKITSUNA: Today before dusk when I crossed the border at Kai, there was panic among the farmers, and they told me that the armies of Kai and Echigo were massing for battle. They said, too, that the origin of the rumors about the love affair between the two houses came from Murakami Yoshikiyo. Some say that Takeda and Terutora plan first to join forces to attack Murakami. Whether they are fighting each other or Yoshikiyo, the news is serious. I've decided that I must first go back home. Do you know the real facts?

KŌSAKA: I don't know what's true either. As soon as it's dawn, I'm going home. If our lords decide on war, then you and I will be either allies or enemies. Tonight is perhaps our last time to talk. What time is it?

TOKITSUNA: It's after three in the morning. The rain has stopped. (*sung*) Look, over there, to the south, there is a faint glimmer of red, but that's not the direction of the sunrise. How odd!

NARRATOR: As they watch, the flames of war rise, engulfing the clouds, and the sound of drums can be heard. Carried on the wind, (*cadence*) battle cries pierce their ears.

(*spoken*) Tokitsuna jumps up.

TOKITSUNA: Those sounds surely signal a battle between our two sides. This is no time to seek refuge. I've no idea where my lord is, and I cannot return home empty-handed. Since our lords are now at war, (*sung*) this will be our battlefield. Rise to face me. The victor will take home his prize. There is no other choice. Come. To the victor the spoils.

KŌSAKA: (*spoken*) Wait, don't be hasty, Tokitsuna. It would be strange for the Takeda and Nagao to fight each other and ignore Murakami. Those fires are on the road to Murakami's castle at Komuro. It must be a night attack to catch the enemy off guard. Better than one of our heads, let's get Murakami as our prize.

TOKITSUNA: (*sung*) You're right. The main road takes the long route. If we take a shortcut, it is only a few miles away. The battle is still to be won, let's go!

KŌSAKA: Quite right. What are you waiting for, Tokitsuna?

TOKITSUNA: Follow me. Be careful, it's dark and the mountain path is steep.

KŌSAKA: I'm right behind.

TOKITSUNA: Well, then hurry up, quickly!

NARRATOR: Each jumps forward, two fierce guardian demons, (*cadence*) seeming to fly through the air.

NARRATOR: (*sung*) The couple left behind weep with despair, blaming themselves for the events.

KATSUYORI: (*spoken*) They say illness begins with only a trifle, that duty to parents withers when lured away by beauty.[30] The words ring all too true. Love for us has driven our parents into the Buddhist Shura Realm of Never-Ending Battle. We've committed the worst of crimes, causing grief to our parents. Look over there, the battle fires glow from our parents' angry hearts, all because of us. Because of my carnal desires, thousands of ordinary people will suffer. I cannot ignore their fate. (*sung*) My father cannot see me here, but the sun and moon are his eyes. While father fights father, heaven cannot sanction their children's affair. (*spoken*) To see one's duty and ignore it is cowardice.[31] From this point on, we are no longer a couple. If we can wash away all our many crimes, then we'll serve our parents, and be dutiful. (*sung*) Our hearts will stay unchanged, but you are the daughter of Lord Terutora. There's no use going over this again and again.

NARRATOR: He speaks coldly, but tears fill his eyes. Lady Emon breaks down into a flood of tears.

EMON: To cast aside precious love for duty, (*cadence*) brave words that ring true. (*sung*) And yet is the battle between our parents or with Murakami? Who can tell us? How can we know what's happening? If the battle is against my father, (*spoken*) then I can agree to sever our ties, but after Murakami is defeated and the anger dissipates, it is not impossible that our case can be resolved. Whether we're to stay together or separate, we'll know the answer by dawn. (*sung*) Until then, let us remain husband and wife. If we have betrayed our parents, then an hour or two longer matters not. Let's hold each other tightly until we tire and face the consequences bravely.

KATSUYORI: (*spoken*) No, the time for that is gone. Such clinging is disgraceful!

NARRATOR: He pushes her away, but she grabs hold even tighter. (*sung*) Each time he turns away, she woos him back, her heart entangled in his sleeves; she clings to him, her regrets driven by the dark depths of passion. Dawn will throw its light on their future; (*scene cadence*) the small temple becomes the couple's lotus calyx in paradise.[32]

—Scene 4
A little later, along a mountain road near the small shrine

NARRATOR: (*sung*) The first bell of dawn strikes[33] as Murakami Yoshikiyo comes rushing past, driven by the combined forces of the Takeda and the Nagao, his army defeated and scattered. He has lost both his long sword and his helmet and has only one soldier who bears his banner. He stumbles and falls again and again, covered in mud, fleeing for his life. He stops for breath.

MURAKAMI: (*spoken*) It's all gone wrong, a disaster. I thought by stirring enmity between Shingen and Terutora, I'd catch them out, as in the old story of the snipe with his beak caught in the grip of a mussel, and defeat them both.[34] But my plan has failed. Instead they've joined together for a surprise night attack. My men have been decimated and my castle is under siege. I must somehow save myself and avenge this shame. I have an idea. Listen to my plan. Shingen's territory is landlocked, and merchants have always done well transporting salt from Enshū. We've been close to Imagawa Ujinao,[35] lord of Enshū, for a long time. I'll get him to join me to stop the flow of salt. (*sung*) Without salt, they won't be able to fight, and Takeda will be destroyed.[36] With that old monk Shingen out of the way, it will be easy to dispose of Terutora. With all three provinces under my command, I can then hunt out my rival Katsuyori and cut him down (*spoken*) and look forward to a warm bed with Emon for my pleasure alone. (*sung*) How's that for a grand plan!

NARRATOR: As he gloats over his great scheme, a voice is heard.

KATSUYORI: Your rival Katsuyori is right here!

NARRATOR: He emerges ready to attack.

MURAKAMI: This is terrible, another sneak attack! I must get out of here!

NARRATOR: Twice shamed by Katsuyori, he flees again for his life, faster than it takes for his bannerman to fall to (*cadence*) Katsuyori's sword.

(*sung*) Emon grabs hold of Katsuyori's sleeve to keep him from abandoning her.

EMON: (*spoken*) What a coward Murakami is! He will be easy to dispose of. Let him go for now. More important, are you unhurt? Didn't I tell you before that tonight's battles were to oust Murakami? (*sung*) What a relief! Now we can relax. My heart was pounding, now the pain inside has gone.

NARRATOR: But even as she speaks, the sound of battle drums is heard again, and the sky lights up with fires ready to fuel thousands of muskets. Katsuyori feels as if he has been struck a heavy blow to his chest and throws his sword aside.

KATSUYORI: (*spoken*) This time the battle will surely be between our fathers. We must separate, no longer husband and wife.

NARRATOR: (*sung*) Emon is shocked by his words and panics in despair.

EMON: What are you saying? No, never!

NARRATOR: (*cadence*) She clings even more desperately.

(*sung*) The flickering fires among the mountains reveal an array of banners, but the light is not bright enough to identify their colors. Katsuyori stretches up and leaps trying to see, his heart in turmoil, dark with uncertainty as he looks down from Mount Kurokami. Every time her husband leaps up, Emon also jumps to her feet. The fires are below them, but up above all is bleak, pitch black. The light is still too faint to recognize a crest or color.

KATSUYORI: Why won't the sun rise? Hurry up!

NARRATOR: He pants for the dawn to come, but Emon cherishes the night.

EMON: (*spoken*) Even for a man, you are too cold. With the light of dawn, we'll see the banners' crests, and if our houses are at war, then we shall separate. (*sung*) How cruel that you beg the dawn to hurry. (*highest pitch*) This evening, may one night last a million years. May the sun pity us and stay hidden, may night never end.

NARRATOR: She breaks down in tears, collapsing on the ground, but a (*high pitch*) harsh light suddenly brightens the sky. (*kowari threatening melody*) From the eastern seas thousands of miles offshore, a ball of fire rises and illuminates clouds of white banners, each with a diamond crest.

KATSUYORI: (*sung*) Look, that is my father's, the Takeda crest.

EMON: Oh no! Over there on the opposite side, the fiery red banners with the paulownia crest signal that we must separate. I curse the Nagao banner that tears us apart!

NARRATOR: The battle is far below, but the pain is felt in their hearts.

Emon weeps, her face as red as the rising sun. (*kowari threatening melody*) The sky is dyed an (*cadence*) array of colors.

    (*sung*) Clouds billow, rising like waves on the shore, glistening in the sun's bright rays racing across the sky at a thousand miles a step, and each step tears the couple farther and farther apart. (*high pitch*) Pity this pair, their night bed now empty, separated by the cold light of day.

Act 3

—Scene 1
Later, at Uesugi Castle

NARRATOR: (*sung*) The Chinese artist She Gong[1] liked dragons and depicted them in paintings and stone, but when he saw a real heavenly dragon, he fainted. This is a case not of one who likes dragons but of liking only the image, not the real thing. A general desires clever officers but seeks those who only seem to be clever but aren't. How few are the brilliant soldiers.[2]

Nagao Terutora has lost his first battle with Shingen and retreated to his home castle. He calls together a council of his senior officers, including his right-hand general, Naoe Sanetsuna, as well as Amakazu, Kakizaki, and Usami, and the other company officers.[3]

TERUTORA: (*spoken*) At the last battle, our forces of some thirty thousand men were crushed by Takeda's mere twelve thousand, (*sung*) a devastating defeat that cut us to the marrow. Until now, Shingen has never been a daring strategist, but this time he used the morning mist to cross the wide river and ambushed us at a narrow point in the road, driving back our main force. It was a magnificent tactic that cut right through our center. That plan did not come from Shingen. Who could he have as such a clever strategist? Have any of you heard who it is?

NARRATOR: His brow is furrowed, his eyes intensely angry, (*cadence*) his fury even greater than they feared.

NARRATOR: (*sung*) Amakazu and Kakizaki both speak at once.

AMAKAZU: (*spoken*) We, too, came to the same conclusion and have sent a spy to find out. Shingen has recruited a fellow called Yamamoto Kansuke Haruhisa. Everything, from the particular arms and equipment to the deployment of troops, is said to be entirely under his direction.

NARRATOR: Terutora interrupts.

TERUTORA: Yes, I've heard of him. Isn't he in fact the elder brother of Sanetsuna's wife? Sanetsuna, you're related to him. Why didn't you persuade him to come to our side? Such negligence in letting him be stolen by the enemy! If Shingen is giving him a stipend of a thousand *koku*,[4] double it. If he's getting three thousand, then make it six. (*sung*) Even if he's been offered five thousand, I'm willing to double it. Does he think the Nagao are not good enough? Or am I unworthy to be his lord? If you know something about this, speak up.

NARRATOR: (*cadence*) His expression is angry, his impatience obvious. (*sung*) Sanetsuna remains calm.

SANETSUNA: (*spoken*) Even before you asked, I was ready to speak. His sister is indeed my wife, but in fact I have never met him. (*sung*) He was a hermit, far away in the hills, and he tilled his land with his own hands, composing songs in the autumn moonlight. He gathered his own firewood and made wildflowers his companions. He showed no ambition to rise in the world or to seek service as a samurai. He enjoyed his life under the heavens and is known as a highly principled samurai. Were you to give him even half of Echigo, he is not a man to come for more money just because his brother-in-law asks him to. (*spoken*) Forgive my forthright manner; my lord is known for being short tempered and proud, unwilling to humble himself before anyone. You are naive to think that the world will always follow your will. If you think you can get anyone, even Fan Kuai[5] or Zhang Liang,[6] to come just by the enticement of riches, you are terribly wrong. This time I am sure that Shingen used a clever stratagem, all his wiles, to woo Kansuke to serve the Takeda. I regret that we didn't get him for our side and have been racking my brains for a plan. (*sung*) Calm your temper and cool your anger. If you agree, then I will tell you my idea in secret.

NARRATOR: Sanetsuna speaks without a trace of fear. Terutora is impressed at his words and bows to reason, agreeing to see him alone. He raises his eyes to look at the council members (*cadence*) and all his generals leave the room.

(*sung*) Terutora's expression softens.

TERUTORA: (*spoken*) Sanetsuna, it has long been the custom to respect a brilliant strategist like a parent or a teacher. If Kansuke comes to serve me, I swear by Hachiman, god of warriors, that I'll be patient and submit even to the humiliation of being kicked. What is your plan? Let me hear the details.

SANETSUNA: Very well, this is my idea. Kansuke lost his father when still a young child. He is devoted to his mother, now more than seventy years old.[7] He could be ranked alongside the twenty-four famous Chinese paragons of filial piety. First, in order to entice his mother here, (*sung*) I have sent my wife to bring her to our house.

NARRATOR: As he speaks, he points to his wife Karaginu at the door.

KARAGINU: (*spoken*) Sanetsuna, Mother has already arrived, accompanied by Kansuke's wife. (*sung*) As you suggested, I immediately let their carriage into the castle and directed them to the reception room to relax.

NARRATOR: Terutora is delighted.

TERUTORA: An excellent move! Come closer to speak.

SANETSUNA: Come forward, Karaginu.

TERUTORA: (*spoken*) Hmm, your mother is quite elderly, isn't she? Is she of gentle temperament?

KARAGINU: She has had a long life as a poor rōnin's mother. It has not been easy; her back is bent and her hair white as snow. (*sung*) She looks ten years older than she is, but she is stiffly formal and proper, as she was in her youth. I met Kansuke's wife Okatsu for the first time; she seems an excellent woman, well mannered and a good daughter-in-law. (*spoken*) Her one fault is that she stutters and is shy about speaking. She always responds through her writing brush. She also is accomplished on the *koto*, and when there is no time to write an answer, she replies by singing to the *koto*'s tune.[8] Mother says that she can speak quickly without stuttering when she sings. (*sung*) Her calligraphy is magnificent; the ink flows with grace. Her talent is not inferior to our professional calligraphers. I would like to cure her stutter and propose her for service.

SANETSUNA: That sounds perfect. Entertain your mother and invite them to stay as long as they wish. At her age, she will surely grow tired soon. Invite her into this room to rest and attend to her every need. Lord Terutora and I will be in the next room, and when the time seems right we shall approach to speak to her.

NARRATOR: (*cadence*) Terutora and Sanetsuna leave.

(*sung*) Karaginu prepares the Japanese zither and a table with brush, ink, and paper. She goes into the corridor and bows.

KARAGINU: (*spoken*) Madam Yamamoto Kansuke and mother of Kansuke, please come this way. (*sung*) Madam Yamamoto, Mother, please.

MOTHER: Karaginu, your voice is far too loud. I'm an old crane who has left her nest.[9] I've flown to see my child, but if anyone asks, I'm just a nameless bird. Karaginu, keep quiet. (*spoken*) This territory of Echigo is enemy to Kansuke's lord Shingen. Your husband is a senior councillor of the enemy. I wasn't obligated to come here *(sung)* but was drawn by your wish conveyed in this letter to see me before I die. *(spoken)* I, too, longed to see my daughter again and have come discreetly accompanied *(sung)* only by Okatsu, who has a speech impediment. Don't yell "Mother, Madam Yamamoto!" like that. Ah, let me sit down.

NARRATOR: She starts to sit down, but Karaginu takes her hand and leads her into the other room. Her daughter-in-law Okatsu follows, gripping her sword tightly, cautious and wary, as they go into the formal reception room. Led to sit on the woven dais, *(cadence)* Okatsu feels even more intimidated.

   (sung) Karaginu comes closer.

KARAGINU: *(spoken)* Let me thank you, Okatsu. You have taken over all my duties as daughter, helping Mother morning and night. *(sung)* On this journey, too, you've suffered the wind and rain, traveling over mountain and river. You must be exhausted. I can never express my gratitude in words.

NARRATOR: The more Karaginu speaks, the more tongue-tied Okatsu becomes, and she is able only to say, "Yes, yes," and smile politely. She draws the inkstone nearer, her face flushed as bright as the color of wet autumn leaves. Her hand moves gracefully, smooth as an autumn shower, her brush flowing in the Sesonji style,[10] *(cadence)* elegant but also easy to read.

   (sung) Karaginu accepts the letter.

KARAGINU: Oh, thank you so much. Just as you write here, although we are sisters-in-law, let us be as intimate as real sisters. *(spoken)* Although I am not familiar with the art of calligraphy, the elegance of your brush strokes is truly wonderful. *(sung)* I wish I could write half as well.

NARRATOR: She rolls up the letter and puts it in her kimono sleeve. From behind, Sanetsuna emerges, now in formal attire and carrying a folded kimono with an array of mixed patterns, and bows respectfully.

SANETSUNA: *(spoken)* I am Naoe Sanetsuna. I should have visited you at your home to offer greetings. Forgive me for sending my wife to bring you here. We are most grateful that you were able to make the long journey safely. We are grateful to Kansuke's wife for accompanying you. We want you to relax and enjoy your time here and therefore have not prepared anything formal for you. This kimono was worn by Lord Terutora. It has the Ashikaga crest of two gold *ryō* bars. Lord Terutora wishes to present this to you. It has been worn only once or twice. It gets quite cold here. Terutora would be delighted if you were to use this as a cover for your sleep.

NARRATOR: He presents it to the mother, who sits up and smiles with delight.

MOTHER: Well, well, has rumor reached even Lord Terutora of the arrival of this old woman of no account? I thought this was your residence, but then it is in fact the master's residence. My goodness, what an honor to be offered this kimono of your master's. It certainly is a splendid robe with a delightful mixture of patterns, certainly worthy of a shogun. However, since Lord Terutora has worn it once or twice, it is simply an old hand-me-down of his. To this day, this old woman has never worn a hand-me-down from anyone. (*sung*) Just thinking about it makes me feel disgusted, dirty.

NARRATOR: Her harsh words ruffle the gentle silk robe, (*cadence*) which seems to lose its color.

SANETSUNA: (*spoken*) No, no. It was only a formality to suggest that you wear this robe. The design is, of course, for a man. It was intended as a souvenir for Kansuke.

MOTHER: No, that is not possible. Kansuke is well provided for by his lord Takeda Shingen. As for a souvenir of this journey, we can get some of the salted salmon famous in Echigo or, along the way home, pick up some sun-dried sweetfish at the Kiso River. Or some pickled plums from Shinano would be nice.[11] Kansuke will be happy enough to see this wrinkled face safely at home. (*sung*) I've had enough of this troublesome talk. Leave us alone to rest, please.

NARRATOR: She stretches out her legs and leans on her elbow for a pillow. Sanetsuna is flustered and starts to get up but doesn't want to leave. He claps for the servants in the kitchen.

SANETSUNA: Have someone come at once. Hurry! It's time to serve the meal. What's holding things up? Tell the cook to hurry up.

NARRATOR: He hopes the meal will suit his mother-in-law, (*exit cadence*) that the salt and spices will put her in a better mood. (*cadence*) He leaves the room.

NARRATOR: (*sung*) A moment later, a samurai in formal dress, complete with courtier cap, emerges with a tray full of a delightful assortment of fish, fowl, and exotic vegetable dishes, exquisitely presented. He crosses the room, sliding his feet across the tatami mats in formal style.

SAMURAI: Allow me to serve you.

NARRATOR: He kneels, holding the tray up and offering it to the mother. (*cadence*) He places it before her and steps back.

(*sung*) Karaginu is shocked to see that it is in fact Lord Terutora but manages to hide her embarrassment, sensing the importance of this act.

KARAGINU: Mother, your food has been served.

NARRATOR: At this, she gets up and sits in front of the tray. She has noticed that the sliding walk and arrangement of the tray are in the Kamakura court style.[12] Terutora bows before her.

TERUTORA: (*spoken*) You are a neighbor. Please accept this meal as an offering from our hearts.

NARRATOR: The old mother acknowledges the offer.

MOTHER: Well now, this banquet is rather awkward for me. In particular, to be served with such grand style as if I were a deity, by someone dressed in full court attire. Is this for a trusted retainer or for a distant emissary? As an old woman, I'm usually served by women, without all this fuss. I have hardly any teeth, and my mouth is always dry. I don't feel comfortable eating in such a formal setting, having to use my best manners. I'll just go to the kitchen and relax there. Karaginu, you take my place here.

TERUTORA: No, please don't leave. That would be most unfortunate. Your son Yamamoto Kansuke's martial talents in both bravery and intellect surpass even those of Kusunoki Masashige,[13] should he return to life. How regrettable that Kansuke has gone to serve Takeda Shingen; it's like throwing a jewel into mud,[14] like leashing a powerful Kirin dragon[15] as if it were a dog. You are the proud mother of this hero. (*sung*) It is fate that you have come here, drawn by your link to the Naoe family. We are fortunate to see the rare udumbara[16] blossom here in our lifetime. (*spoken*) As a pledge that I consider you my own mother, myself your child, let me offer you this toast. Let me, Nagao Danjō Shōshitsu Terutora, offer this tray of food (*sung*) as my first duty to my mother.

NARRATOR: He bows deeply, the top of his courtier's cap touching the tatami mat. Okatsu and Karaginu are shocked at this show of humility (*emotional cadence*) and bow to the floor.

(*sung*) Kansuke's mother straightens her kimono and laughs aloud.

MOTHER: (*spoken*) It's certainly true that you witness unusual things if you live long enough. Along the Kamakura shore, one supposedly catches bonito with animal horns. At the mouth of the Yodo River, they say you can land carp with just a few grains of barley, but here in Echigo, what a wonder that you want to use this old withered woman to lure Yamamoto Kansuke; it's too ridiculous! The great general must reflect on the will of heaven.[17] Do not cast aside the tenets of nature; know heaven's time, and it will lead to success on earth.[18] Keep to principles and you will reap just reward. In general, there's a need for a sense of proportion in human affairs. For an old woman like myself, it is most suitable to be served by a serving woman or a young girl. (*sung*) As Confucius told us long ago, "To kill a chicken one does not use an ox-cleaver."[19] Your deception is obvious from your inappropriate manner. You won't ever lure Kansuke with a hook bent by a crooked heart. If I accept this meal, then I'll be in your debt. I am the mother of Kansuke, your enemy. If I receive a favor from an enemy, it will weaken my son's resolve. How could I ever accept this meal offered under deception, from a man not brave enough to speak his mind directly?!

NARRATOR: She stands up and kicks the small tray table, spilling it all over Terutora; the miso soup covers his kimono; the fish lands in his lap. Okatsu and Karaginu gasp in shock, (*cadence*) their livers chilled in terror.

(*sung*) The short-tempered Terutora immediately jumps up.

TERUTORA: I should've killed you earlier, you spiteful woman! (*spoken*) When I gave you a fine robe, you cursed it as a hand-me-down. Terutora bows to no one, not even the shogun or the emperor. Although I served you respectfully, (*sung*) you rudely kicked it back in my face. Though I take you to be a madwoman, I won't stand this any longer. Off with your wrinkled head!

NARRATOR: Terutora grabs his great sword, "Azuki Nagamitsu,"[20] handed down for generations, but Naoe Sanetsuna rushes in and stays his arm. Karaginu holds her mother-in-law, begging her to apologize, trying to calm her down.

MOTHER: Why should I apologize?! I will neither fight my son-in-law's lord nor apologize to him. Well then, on with it, cut off my head!

NARRATOR: She stands defiantly ready to face the sword.

TERUTORA: Let me silence that woman; let go, Sanetsuna.

FIGURE 38 Kansuke's mother kicking over the tray served by Kenshin (Terutora) (*Shinshū kawa-nakajima kassen*, 1726 [fiction version], Daitōkyū bunko).

SANETSUNA: Now, now, calm down. Have you forgotten your vow to bear any insult, even being kicked? Now is the moment for propriety.

NARRATOR: (*emotional cadence*) Although chastised, Terutora's body still shakes with fury, his eyes full of angry tears.

(*sung*) Okatsu, Kansuke's wife, is flustered, her agitation making her stuttering even worse. She scurries about trying to calm everyone down. Tears and frustration lead her to take up her *koto*. She sets the bridges for the standard pitch.

OKATSU: (*song*)[21] Please forgive my old mother; (*ai no yama melody*) her strength is too weak for travel. My husband entrusted me to take care of her, but I am afflicted with a terrible stutter. (*spoken*) She is my mother-in-law, (*song, high pitch*) her life more fragile than the dew on the cut grasses. How awful if I should fail to protect her and see her (*high pitch*) wither like a fragile broom tree, her body fade like fleeting smoke. (*high pitch*) How could I return alone, (*ai no yama melody*) carrying only her ashes? What could I say to my husband? (*sung*)[22] Take my life instead, and let her go free. (*highest pitch*) Please, I beg your mercy and compassion.

NARRATOR: She bursts into tears and (*cadence*)[23] collapses onto the *koto*.

(*sung*) Even Terutora, fierce as a demon, is moved by her appeal, and his heart seems to soften. Sanetsuna sees his chance to intervene.

SANETSUNA: Let me apologize for this inconvenience. Karaginu, Okatsu, take Mother to my residence immediately.

NARRATOR: Okatsu is delighted and wants to express her gratitude but can only bow her head again and again. Her legs move as quickly as a dancer's. (*song*) "How compassionate are the flowers, the cherry blossoms at the palace, the branches tall and firm. *Ei, ei, etchiri na*,"[24] (*sung*)

FIGURE 39 Triptych by Shunkōsai Hokuei, from a kabuki production of *Battles at Kawa-nakajima* at the Osaka Naka-za theater in the third month, 1833. (Right) Arashi Rikan II as Terutora (Kenshin); (center) Nakamura Karoku as Kansuke's wife Okatsu; (left) Jitsukawa Gakujūrō as Kansuke's mother Koshiji. *(Japan Ukiyo Museum.)*

goes the chant; let us celebrate the prosperity of Echigo (*scene cadence*) and face the future bravely.

—Scene 2
A few days later, at Naoe Sanetsuna's residence

NARRATOR: (*sung*) Geese always know when it's time to return north to their true home. How much more does this old woman wish to return—today, tomorrow, hoping against hope; pity the despairing heart of Kansuke's old mother. Ordered by her husband to entertain her mother and keep her in the residence, Karaginu has all the servants treat her mother as an honored guest, constantly bringing gifts and new flowers each day, beautiful painted screens, books and poetry, delightful stories, caged songbirds, all possible diversions for the mother's pleasure. The small servants' room along the corridor is filled with things ready to offer her mother. Takada no Tsubone is in charge of the other women, directing them to keep up a steady stream of distractions for the mother and Okatsu. She is busy (*cadence*) just keeping a record of all the items presented.

FIGURE 40 From a kabuki production of *Battles at Kawa-nakajima* at the Tokyo Kabuki-za theater in 1970. (Right) Kataoka Nizaemon XIII as Terutora (Kenshin); (center) Nakamura Utaemon VI as Okatsu; (left) Nakamura Ganjirō II as Kansuke's mother, Koshiji. *(Courtesy of Nakamura Ganjirō III.)*

(*sung*) Just then a messenger from the Shinano border rushes in.

MESSENGER: (*spoken*) Today, just before dawn, a samurai arrived at the border station. He is blind in his right eye and his left leg is crippled. He wanted passage, and so we asked his name and where he came from and his destination. He replied that he was Yamamoto Kansuke from Kōshū and was on his way to see the wife of Naoe Sanetsuna. He left his attendants and horses at the border and should be here soon. (*sung*) I took a shortcut to announce his arrival.

NARRATOR: (*cadence*) The messenger leaves. (*sung*) Takada no Tsubone is delighted and claps her hands.

TAKADA: This is magnificent news. Yamamoto Kansuke is the son and heir of our honored guest and is therefore the elder brother of Madam Karaginu. She will be delighted to hear this news. Before he arrives, clean the formal reception room.

FIGURE 41 Bunraku puppets of Okatsu trying to calm Terutora.

NARRATOR: (*cadence*) Leaving her orders, she sets off to find Karaginu. (*sung*) The servant girls flit about with feather dusters, brooms, and wet cloths, making the room spick-and-span.

SERVANT: (*spoken*) Hey, Odai, did you know that Kansuke is Okatsu's husband? And that he's the famous military strategist? And yet he's supposed to be blind in one eye and lame to boot? On top of that, his wife is a stutterer. Doesn't that make you wonder about how inconvenient all that must be for making love.

ODAI: No, it shouldn't matter that much, even if she can't talk. (*sung*) At the crucial moment, all she has to do is pant and squeal. As for him, even if he were blind in both eyes, in the dark he must be excellent at the night raid, quick with his hands and first to strike home; it's no problem for him, I'm sure!

NARRATOR: (*cadence*) They laugh loudly. (*sung*) Takada's voice can be heard in the kitchen.

TAKADA: Madam Karaginu is at the castle. Quick, send a carriage for her. Someone, go to bring her home.

NARRATOR: The house is a flurry of activity. At the sound of the rear gate opening, Takada no Tsubone emerges.

TAKADA: (spoken) Everyone listen! Lord Sanetsuna has been at the castle since morning, and Madam Karaginu, too, has gone for some reason. The orders are that until the couple return, we mustn't let the mother or Okatsu know of Kansuke's arrival. (sung) Serve him tea and sweets in this room and keep him entertained.

NARRATOR: Just then the arrival of Yamamoto Kansuke is announced. A young woman attendant leads him in. He is still in his rough traveling clothes, all filthy and torn, and with his lame left leg and blind right eye, he looks like a gnarled pine tree, its branches bent with snow, above which shines a lone star. A strange, fierce-looking man indeed. (cadence) He enters the reception room.

(sung) All the women try to suppress their laughter with nervous coughs; from the next room, peals of laughter are heard. A young page brings tea with trembling hands, (cadence) spilling the contents. (sung) Kansuke is not one to worry about formal greetings[25] or about mocking laughter.

KANSUKE: (spoken) Are you, Madam Tsubone, in charge here? Please tell Lord Sanetsuna's wife Karaginu that I have arrived.

TAKADA: Ah, both are at the castle on duty and haven't returned yet. (sung) Please wait here a while and relax with some tobacco and sweets.

KANSUKE: (spoken) Hmm, if they are on duty, then you don't know when they're likely to return. My business is not with Naoe or his wife. I was shocked to receive a letter saying that Mother wasn't well and rushed straight here through the night. (sung) Please lead me to Mother. I want to see her immediately. Let me through to see her.

NARRATOR: He starts to stand up but is stopped.

TAKADA: (spoken) No, wait. Your mother is quite well, better than ever. Since her arrival here, she hasn't as much as sneezed. (sung) The whole household has been entertaining her daily with flowers, songbirds, and all sorts of diversions.

NARRATOR: The more she says, (spoken) the more worried he grows.

KANSUKE: Then could you take me to see my wife Okatsu?

TAKADA: No, no. Lady Okatsu, too, is well and constantly at your mother's side. Lord and Lady Naoe will return very soon. (*sung*) Why not have a nice relaxing bath and then take a rest? The bed is all prepared for you. Oh, I forgot. I'll have some saké brought for you.

NARRATOR: (*exit cadence*) All the ladies leave the room.

NARRATOR: (*sung*) Kansuke is left alone in the reception room. His irritation grows.

KANSUKE: (*spoken*) Everything is strange in this house. (*sung*) My wife's message said that Mother was on her deathbed, critically ill and wouldn't survive long, so I rushed here thinking of nothing else, but there's no sign of anyone being ill, and I've been told Mother's never been better. It's strange, too, that I can't meet my wife, and what does it mean that both Sanetsuna and Karaginu have been called to the castle? A general

FIGURE 42 The character Yamamoto Kansuke, from a kabuki production of *Battles at Kawa-nakajima* at the Osaka Naka-za theater in 1833. The actor is Arashi Rikan II, and the artist is Shunkōsai Hokuei. (*Victoria and Albert Museum.*)

of Terutora's experience would not consult a woman on military strategy. This is the most peculiar of all. (*spoken*) Hmm, now I see! Mother's been used as bait to lure me to become an ally. It's all as clear as a reflection in a mirror. Although my sister is my flesh and blood, she is dutiful in supporting her husband and lord. That is only to be expected. The fool has been my stammering wife. (*sung*) It was Terutora's plan to have Mother feted and treated as an honored guest in order to be tricked by Sanetsuna into writing a letter to me saying that my healthy mother was on her deathbed. It was all a strategy to draw me into the heart of the enemy camp. How could I be so stupid! I should have been expecting such a ruse, but the desire to see Mother's living face once more drove out all other thoughts. I ran and stumbled, the only time I've slipped in all my life. I'll be laughed at for generations to come. But there's no time to dawdle. I must free Mother and escape before they realize what's up.

NARRATOR: He jumps up and looks about, but there are too many rooms and he doesn't know the way.

KANSUKE: It would be better to go out the gate and scale the back wall. Now is the crucial moment of my life. Like Yoshitsune at the battle of Ichinotani, I must be decisive and bold and charge down the steep cliffs of Tekkai Mountain to rout the enemy.[26]

NARRATOR: (*high pitch*) Kansuke is at a loss and can only pace (*cadence*) like a lame horse. (*sung*) Just at that moment, his wife Okatsu, alerted to his arrival, comes running in. But "H- he- here" is all she can utter as she tries to grab Kansuke; he ignores her and pushes her aside. She grabs him again.

OKATSU: (*spoken*) Wha- wha- wha- what're you do- do- doing here? W- w- were you af- afr- afraid that your wi- wi- wife, couldn't ma- ma- manage? I was ju- ju- just ready to fl- fl- flee with M- Mo- Mother. (*sung*) Just r- r- ready to escape.

NARRATOR: Her heart has the will, but the words just won't come; (*emotional cadence*) tears flow before words.

KANSUKE: (*sung*) What do you mean accusing me of being foolish to come here, you stammering woman? (*spoken*) Is it strange that I was driven to come by your letter saying that dearest Mother was dying? Who asked you to write such a letter to trick your husband? (*sung*) Who was it, tell me!

NARRATOR: She is hurt even more by his false accusations and can only say, "It's a, l- l- lie!" before collapsing in tears.

KANSUKE: (*spoken*) Oh, then, let me prove it true or false. The letter is here in my pocket. (*sung*) Look it's your handwriting.

NARRATOR: She looks at the calligraphy and is shocked to see that it seems to be her own.

OKATSU: (*spoken*) Thi- thi- this is ter- ter- terrible. May this hand r- r- rot. Although I d- d- didn't wri- write this, it's in my h- h- hand.

NARRATOR: (*sung*) She reads it through carefully, again and again.

OKATSU: (*spoken*) No, no, no, it's not mine. It's a f- f- fake. I must f- find out the villain. (*sung*) We must investigate.

NARRATOR: She starts to go back inside, but Kansuke stops her.

KANSUKE: Wait, you're being foolish. (*spoken*) Whom are we going to investigate? It was partly your fault to let your hand be imitated. They would've needed a model to copy from. When entering enemy territory, one must always be on guard, even taking care with every single word uttered. It is a samurai's duty, man or woman, never to be negligent. Although I've heard many times the Chinese story of Dan Fu from Shu who was tricked for love of his mother,[27] I was fooled by the word *mother*. Investigating the culprit will only bring further shame on me. (*sung*) Disgraced! I've never before been duped by an enemy's strategy. My mind was blinded by the word *mother*, and I ventured into enemy land. It was your handwriting that led to my downfall. Can you still consider yourself wife of Yamamoto Kansuke?

NARRATOR: He roughly kicks her aside, his sole eye glistening with bitterness, bright as the sun, moon, and stars together. Releasing the force of his ire, (*emotional cadence*) he collapses in grief.

OKATSU: (*sung*) Ha- ha- hateful affliction! N- never before today, ev- ev- even in my dreams, h- h- have I let my g- g- guard down when away from h- h- home, but one rainy night among wom- wom- women only, wh- when we drank tea and t- talked, I didn't play the *koto*. Instead, I sp- sp- spoke through my brush. I di- didn't think that someone w- w- would collect my cast-off notes to use as a m- m- model for deceit. Seven years ago, when I lost our child in a miscarriage at four months, the sh- sh- shock affected my tongue, and s- sud- suddenly I was afflicted with this st- st- stutter and h- had to use a brush for my tongue. It h- has become my enemy. If only it could be cured! I w- w- want to c- cut my j- jaw open, r- rip out my tongue at its root, and at least d- die chanting pr- prop- properly, (*highest pitch*) "Praise to Amida B- B- Buddha."

NARRATOR: Grief and regrets burst forth, but her tongue will not follow her heart. (*cadence*)[28] Only her tears flow freely.

(*sung*) Her bitterness at her affliction rings true to Kansuke, a man fearless even of evil demons. (*cadence*) Tears of sympathy.

KANSUKE: (*sung*) Your stuttering came at the shock of the miscarriage years ago. No one can blame anyone; it was heaven's fate. (*spoken*) I too, after the encounter with the wild boar, have been a cripple, but I cannot blame the animal. I still have the same spirit as before. Your stammer has not affected your heart. Control yourself and if you are truly Kansuke's wife, (*sung*) then since you know the way, go to the inner room and sneak Mother out. I will circle around to the back wall and climb over. We'll then escape. Are you willing?

OKATSU: (*spoken*) Th- th- then, am I s- still y- y- your wife?

KANSUKE: Of course, you're my wife through the next seven lives![29]

OKATSU: Th- th- thank you. (*sung*) I'm r- r- ready.

NARRATOR: She hurries to the other room, (*cadence*) a model of resolve.

KANSUKE: (*sung*) At least I'm ready for travel, no need to change clothes.

NARRATOR: He moves to go out, but a voice is heard from a space in the fence.

VOICE: (*spoken*) Don't let Kansuke escape. If he forces his way out, then kill him.

NARRATOR: The glitter of sword-tipped spears lights the area.

KANSUKE: (*sung*) I have no fear of a bee sting or two.

NARRATOR: He jumps down into the garden and follows the stone path, with just a clog on his short, crippled left leg. So fitted, he stands up straight. His good eye surveys all eight directions. From behind comes a soldier with sickle-tipped spear; in front appears a soldier with a straight-tipped spear. They attack at once, but Kansuke cleverly jumps back and (*spoken*) the spears clash. Kansuke loses no time in pulling down one, knocking another away, until one spear strikes low and is pinned under his clog. (*sung*) The other spear is thrust high, but Kansuke grabs it below the blade with his right hand. He grabs the other with his left hand and pulls them together with great force. The soldiers' heads clash with a thud. Beaten, they abandon their spears and flee. (*spoken*) Others try to tackle him, but he is too strong. One flies at him but he holds him in a headlock; another grabs his thigh but is beaten off. Others fly at his waist, his knees, and his elbows. (*sung*) Suddenly he is surrounded by seven or eight. He holds one up in his left hand and throws him with his right. He lifts one with his right hand and tosses him with his left. Again and again, he skillfully parries their blows, throwing them in all directions, using both arms. Bodies fly all over the place, covering the ground. (*cadence*) All at once they scatter and flee.

KANSUKE: (*spoken*) This is all a waste of time. I fight under the banner of Lord Shingen and will die rather than serve two masters. Kansuke will never take a salary from any other. (*sung*) Enticement, then entrapment, what's planned next?

NARRATOR: (*cadence*) He runs after them, hobbling on one clog.
  (*sung*) Sanetsuna hurries back from the castle.
SANETSUNA: Damnation! Kansuke, it's a bit thoughtless of you to be leaving already! (*spoken*) It was Lord Terutora's strong wish that you stay here. The sun and moon don't shine on Kai alone. Stop being so stubborn. (*sung*) If you must go back, then take my head as a trophy.
NARRATOR: He calls after Kansuke and follows him. From the inner room comes the clash of swords between daughter and daughter-in-law.
KARAGINU: (*spoken*) Hateful Okatsu! In order to send a letter imitating your handwriting, I carefully collected your discarded notes and had my ladies practice your style. I did all I could to help my husband. (*sung*) Although my brother Kansuke is a well-regarded samurai, it was my duty as a wife to try to soften him through family ties. After finally getting Mother here, do you think I'm going to let you steal her away? She's not just my brother's mother, she's mine, too. You'll have to take my head first. You can take her over my dead body!
OKATSU: (*spoken*) I c- c- can't believe you, K- K- Karaginu. To m- make a f- fool of a st- stutterer and fake her h- h- handwriting. H- h- hateful woman! M- my eyes are f- filled with tears. H- how could I leave b- b- behind M- Mother, entrusted to my care? (*sung*) I will take her home or die trying.
NARRATOR: She parries Karaginu's blows and counterattacks. Back and forth they battle fiercely, unconcerned for their own lives, whether they turn to ashes or dust. Their swords clash again and again, the sound reverberating throughout the house. Suddenly the sliding door opens, and they see the old mother's face.
KARAGINU: (*spoken*) Mother, don't try to stop us!
MOTHER: Stop you? Magnificent, don't stop. Don't pull back your swords. Don't move!
NARRATOR: (*sung*) Before they can react, she grabs both swords and drives them into her sides. The swords turn crimson (*cadence*) as they pierce deeply into her spine.
  (*sung*) "What is this!" is all the two daughters can utter as they collapse into tears. The house descends into chaos, and both Kansuke and Sanetsuna rush back in. Terutora, hearing the news, gallops bareback from the castle.

TERUTORA: (*spoken*) It is terrible for an important guest from an enemy land to die in our custody. Others will hear of this. (*sung*) It will be a disaster for us.

NARRATOR: In the midst of the confusion, Kansuke speaks in a tearful voice.

KANSUKE: (*spoken*) Your son was Yamamoto Kansuke, retainer of Takeda Shingen; did you have a grudge against me, were you disappointed? Or was this aimed in anger at another? Oh, how coldhearted.

NARRATOR: (*emotional cadence*) He tries to give strength to his wounded mother. (*sung*) She lifts her head.

MOTHER: My child, do not speak things that are untrue. (*spoken*) If I wanted revenge against another, I would fight them to the death. I'm not one to kill myself out of hatred.[30] My life's end was already determined. I was fated to fall to Lord Terutora's sword. I kicked the tray of food served reverently by the great lord of Echigo. The anger in his eyes I remember well. I was impressed at his restraint. (*sung*) Since food is offered from heaven,[31] even if served by servants, one must show respect and gratitude. This insolent old woman flouted the law. He was bitter enough to see me torn apart on the rack or pulled in half by oxen. He won't forget my crime (*cadence*) for many lives to come.

(*sung*) After having his offer spurned by Kansuke, Lord Terutora would surely have sent a party to capture him along the road. If I had heard that he'd tortured and killed Kansuke out of spite for his mother, then I would have forever regretted not dying here and now. (*spoken*) If one hates a priest, one comes to hate the sight of any black robe.[32] As this proverb implies, (*sung*) I feared that he would come to despise even Karaginu and that she would suffer a terrible fate. These thoughts tore at my heart. Such grief has led to this end. (*highest pitch*) Look at my fate! I've been executed, crucified, and stabbed by the humble swords of my daughter and daughter-in-law. I've been cut down by the long spear of Terutora's judgment. His enmity ends with my death. Sanetsuna, I beg you to plead for Kansuke's freedom (*cadence*) to return safely.

(*sung*) Yes, yes, no matter how often we say this world is transitory, uncertain, is there anything more fleeting than my life? I was born in Owari, grew up in Suruga, was married in Mikawa, lived as a recluse in Shinano, came to serve under the lord of Kai; now here my body will (*highest pitch*) rest as the dew. I never dreamed I would become part of the dust of Echigo. (*high pitch*) Such a tumultuous, uncertain world as this; how can we trust in the vision of Amida's Paradise?

NARRATOR: Tears pure as rain fall; (*cadence*) daughter and daughter-in-law cry out their grief. (*sung*) Kansuke's eyes cloud; even the lionlike Lord Terutora is unable to hold back tears; (*cadence*) he rubs his eyes.

(*sung*) Unable to keep it in any longer, Terutora cries out.

TERUTORA: (*spoken*) This is terrible, a disaster! (*sung*) For all of us, on the surface, being a samurai seems splendid, but nothing is more fleeting, more fragile. (*spoken*) This old woman has given her life for duty. (*sung*) She has offered herself to save our samurai honor. How pitiful! The osprey is known to catch fish. (*spoken*) A woodland hawk's chick, born to an osprey mother, will follow its mother's ways, and catch carp deep in the river.[33] (*sung*) A samurai is the same. Few are born from both a seed and a womb that are outstanding. What a gem was this mother of Kansuke! How tragic that I caused her untimely death. All your grief is my fault.

NARRATOR: Even this fierce, mercenary general (*emotional cadence*) wrings his sleeves.

TERUTORA: (*sung*) No, there is something I can do as an offering.

NARRATOR: He takes out his short sword, and with his left hand he grabs his topknot and cuts the tie.

TERUTORA: (*spoken*) Although I shall not give up my samurai status, my appearance will show my awakening. From today I shall change my name to Terutora Nyūdō Kenshin.[34] I do not offer my shaved hair to Buddha or keep it for myself. Kansuke, take this to symbolize your slaying of Kenshin. (*sung*) Let this be offered at her funeral. Let it give heart

FIGURE 43 The death of Kansuke's mother *Shinshū kawa-nakajima kassen*, 1726 [fiction version], (Daitōkyū bunko.)

to her final moments. It is not so unusual to find a soldier brave on the battlefield, but I am overwhelmed by the depth of your love and duty to your mother.

NARRATOR: (*cadence*) He offers the hair with tearful eyes.

KANSUKE: (*sung*) Thank you, thank you, for such compassion.

NARRATOR: He bows deeply on the veranda. Grief engulfs his whole body, but he manages to speak.

KANSUKE: (*spoken*) Furthermore, I am grateful that you have set aside your anger at my refusal to serve you. I could never express my thanks or repay my debt to you for your kindness. (*sung*) In appearance and heart I serve Shingen, but although I should face you in battle and shoot my poor, rusty arrow, I shall at least join you on the journey to Buddha by cutting my hair.

NARRATOR: He takes his short sword and in the same manner cuts off his topknot.

KANSUKE: After today, my name shall be Yamamoto Kansuke Nyūdō Dōki. The first character, "Dō," means the "Way," so I can lead my mother on the path to Buddhahood. The second character, "ki," means "demon," so I can drive off any demons along the way. This is my offering for Mother's final journey.

NARRATOR: He takes both clumps of hair (*high pitch*) and places them on her blood-stained lap. He bows to the floor, trying to hide his tears. His mother, in great pain, (*cadence*) opens her eyes.

MOTHER: (*sung*) From birth until now I have lived in six different lands, with no fixed home. Now in my seventy-second year, I shall find a permanent home in the Western Paradise. (*highest pitch*) These two tufts of hair will serve as the holy ornaments to decorate my home and give me pleasure. (*spoken*) I am ashamed to say farewell to Lord Kenshin. (*sung*) Daughter-in-law, daughter, son-in-law, son, good-bye, farewell. Namu Amida Butsu.

NARRATOR: Grasping a sword in each hand, she draws them out and begins her journey along the road to death. Although she rides no sleigh through the icy Echigo winter, (*cadence*) her passage is quick, like melting snow in spring.

(*sung*) Everyone gasps once again and gathers around the body. Karaginu and Okatsu weep loudly, devastated at her death. Although overwrought with grief, they restrain themselves in order to honor the mother in a samurai funeral service. Their sorrow knows no bounds, but words are exhausted, and they can only bow to the deceased and to each other. Sanetsuna and his wife are left with the body to grieve over; Kansuke and his wife must go their way alone. Seeing Kansuke's bereft figure, Kenshin feels even more anguish.

KENSHIN: (*spoken*) Wait, wait just a moment longer. Let me make an offering to your mother. Let me offer a parting gift. I've heard that Murakami, lord of Shinano, has cut off all deliveries of salt to Kai as a strategy to make the people suffer and surrender. That is a despicable, cowardly tactic. I do not want to defeat Shingen by denying him salt. That is no way to win a battle. (*sung*) My territory of Echigo borders on the sea, and so we have plenty of salt. I shall send horse carriages to deliver enough for Kai.[35] (*spoken*) Tell Shingen to get his forces ready for battle with mine.

KANSUKE: (*sung*) I am even more impressed by your generosity and compassion. It warms my grieving heart. My eyes swell with tears of gratitude.[36] Farewell.

NARRATOR: A true samurai has compassion for humanity; his enemy is his enemy; his heart distinguishes the two. Although Kai's weakness in being surrounded by mountains[37] will not be exploited, its chief strategist has lost his mother to the battle, left behind to lie in the shadows of the oak trees of Echigo. He is held back also by his wife's slow walk and her slow tongue, stuttering and stammering her farewells. She weeps, unable to express her words with a brush or to voice her feelings in song. She cries out and tries to leave but returns again and again. Kansuke pulls her forward but is pulled back; both leave their hearts behind as they depart.

Act 4

—Scene 1
Mount Tenmoku in Kai Province, autumn 1561

NARRATOR:

(*song*)[1] Autumn mountains laid with a quilt of colored leaves,
a stag lies sleeping, so gentle.
(*high pitch*) A brocade in cross design, laced with dew and frost,
how magnificent the autumn scene.
Floating leaves paint the river bright;
ford the stream and tear the brocade.
Oh, dear, if a fawn should cross,
(*cadence*) it will be lost.[2]

(*Edo jōruri*) The Shirane Mountain Range[3] is at its most glorious in autumn when rows of maple trees along the foothills glisten with crimson foliage in full brilliance. Hunters' hearty voices can be heard as they prepare their arrows, making ready for the descent of the deer, (*cadence*) here in the shade of the forest on Mount Tenmoku.[4]

(*sung*) Kōsaka Danjō and Hara Gorō, officers of Shingen, walk up, both carrying sharpened arrows ready for the hunt. Shingen opens the bamboo blind of his lookout post in the camp and glares down at the two.

SHINGEN: (*spoken*) Despicable! You know it's forbidden to kill; you're being irresponsible. I have built this lookout site as a part of my battle strategy. Although we have dared to scale this mountain, everyone is terrified of the curse of its gods, the scourge of its *tengu* demons, and the mischief of its foxes and badgers. Mount Tenmoku is known to be haunted and is feared in all the lands around here. (*sung*) I have prayed to the mountain gods and vowed that no killing shall take place. I've composed one thousand *waka* poems as an offering, and we can see clearly the power of verse, its ability to move mountains. Its force has been felt by the gods and demons; their ire has disappeared, and the fury of the other spirits has been calmed.[5] (*spoken*) At this lookout, all the warriors are to mature in spirit, to cleanse their hearts by contemplating the beauty of blossoms of a spring morning and maple leaves in autumn.⁶ *(sung)* Concentrate your mind, never waver from thinking about strategy. What are you doing then, with bow and arrow *(spoken)* ready to hunt deer? Are you disobeying my orders? Don't you fear the wrath of the mountain gods? Furthermore, think of the fawn, the mate left behind, the cry of the deer as it wanders through the fallen maple leaves in search of its slain mate.⁷ *(sung)* Don't you feel *(cadence)* any pity in your heart? *(sung)* A samurai knows compassion. From now on, you must take more care.

NARRATOR: The fierce warrior Shingen's face shows a softened heart, *(cadence)* all due to the merits of *waka* poetry.

   (sung) Kōsaka and Gorō move closer to speak to Shingen.

KŌSAKA: *(spoken)* Yes, we understand, sir. We defied your ban on hunting, setting off to slay a young deer, even against our own feelings. We did it to incur your anger and punishment. It was a strategy to expose the severity of your banishment of Lord Katsuyori. You have shown compassion and sorrow for the deer that worries about its child. *(sung)* You have steeped yourself in the art of verse. Poetry is also said to soften the hearts of men and women toward each other.⁸ How harsh it seems to banish young Katsuyori, known to all for his integrity; it has been two years. How hurt he must be. The Nagao and Takeda have been like the moon and sun to each other, always close. *(spoken)* I have heard discreetly through my sources that Lord Katsuyori grieves and regrets his indiscretion that has brought our two lands to battle. We know youth falters at least once. This does not mean that he is evil. Everyone in our house grieves for him. If he is pardoned and Lady Emon welcomed, both sides will rejoice. Please pardon him out of consideration for your retainers.

NARRATOR: They bow to the ground, begging Shingen to forgive his son, but his expression remains stern and he offers no reply. He continues just to gaze intently at the tips of the maple branches, *(cadence)* ignoring their pleas. *(sung)* Gorō and Kōsaka move closer.

GORŌ: *(spoken)* The origin of this problem was the parents' anger at the revelation of the secret love affair, but look no further than your own ancestor Shinra Saburō Yoshimitsu for precedent. His affair with the daughter of Taira Gon no Heita Kagenari was common knowledge.⁹ If you are going to punish Katsuyori's affair, then can you yourself, as a descendant of such a union, show your face in public? *(sung)* We refuse to move from this spot until you grant a pardon.

NARRATOR: They cry out their demands for all to hear. Shingen's face colors.

SHINGEN: (*spoken*) Oh, when it suits you, you hold up Shinra Yoshimitsu as an example. No matter if it's ancestors or not, it is hardly proper to hold up their foibles as an excuse to pardon Katsuyori. Gorō, get away this instant!

NARRATOR: Shingen, now furious, gets down from his lookout. The chastised pair can only stare at the ground (*cadence*) and depart with no further comment.

SHINGEN: (*sung*) It seems they have not heard the saying that an unfilial son receives his own deserts; a loving father cannot care for him.[10] I've come and purified this site in order to pray to the mountain spirits. I won't listen to any more sordid tales. I've soiled my ears. I must wash them clean.[11]

NARRATOR: He goes to the (*scene cadence*) waterfall just below.

—Scene 2
Mount Tenmoku in Kai Province, autumn 1561

NARRATOR:

> (*song*)[12] If you're to scoop up water, (*Lady Emon enters*)
> well then, well then,
> dip your ladle in the gentle brook.
> Step along the stones,
> careful not to slip,
> careful not to fall, look there!
> (*sung*) The wind has scattered leaves in the stream, and trapped, they've collected to form a weir (*cadence*) where fish swim under the brocade of color.

(*sung*) Along this shore comes a rustic-looking young woman, her sleeves tied back with a pretty cord, carrying a tub on her shoulder. She ladles water and then washes her towel.

> (*song*) At Sumiyoshi, at Sumiyoshi from long ago,
> the ancient pines were washed by salt breezes

from rising waves striking the shore.
How delightful the spray.
Girls' robes are clean and white,
faces tanned by the sun.
Let's wash our robes in the maple-leaf brocade:
delightful autumn colors!
(*ainote*) Plum-scented lavender sleeves flow with the current,
rushing, twisting about,
entangled like long, wild grasses in passionate embrace.

"Even if I could hang out this robe, no time to dry, no time to dry my tears, no time to forget him. (*emotional cadence*) No, I float through days and nights in misery." (*cadence*) She breaks down in tears and rests on the riverbank.

(*sung tsure*)[13] Weighed down by similar thoughts, a rustic-looking Katsuyori, face hidden by a scarf, carries a basket full of cut grass and leads an ox. He is attracted by the beckoning reeds in the fields, which remind him of his love[14] burning inside, but he must keep it hidden from the woodsmen who pass. They spy each other from each shore.[15]

EMON: (*shite*) Oh my dear Katsuyori, how thin you've grown! (*cadence*) It hurts to see your gaunt face.

KATSUYORI: (*spoken*) How wonderful to see you dearest Emon, but your face has changed. (*sung*) How it hurts to see you suffering!

NARRATOR: Sleeves hide their tears which overflow, (*cadence*) rushing into the depths of the stream.

EMON: (*spoken*) Kōsaka and Gorō have advised me to hide here in this area. How rare our encounters. These last few days (*sung*) I've been miserable and have mountains of things to tell you. Couldn't you at least cross this bridge so that we can talk? Please, come over here.

KATSUYORI: (*spoken*) Don't be foolish! The other side of this bridge is my father's territory. I would be courting the wrath of heaven if I crossed without permission. It would be reckless and tempt fate.

EMON: (*sung*) This land, its soil and trees, belongs to no one but you. I feel terrible that because of me, you have been thrown out on to the highway, having to hide like an outcast. I feel your suffering. Let me come to you.

NARRATOR: She starts to cross the bridge.

KATSUYORI: Wait, wait! You can easily cross this bridge, but we've vowed to the gods not to meet. We'll tempt their curse.

EMON: Then I cannot cross either. I've heard stories of a bridge between earth and heaven, but that bridge we cannot see. (*honbushi melody*) Our hearts suffer from the ties of our vows, our duty to parents, bound by winding vines. Though we try to bridge our love, like the stone bridge built by the god Hitokoto-nushi for the ascetic En no Gyōja in the mountains of Katsuragi, it collapses in the middle.[16] We cannot even cross in the night; (*cadence*) must we be a couple that see each other's face only in daylight?

KATSUYORI: (*spoken*) I feel the same as you. (*sung*) There is the famous story of Youzi and Boyang, the Oxherd Boy and Weaver Girl, who vowed their love to the moon and became stars, united forever as a couple.[17] Today we celebrate their love at the Tanabata Festival of the seventh day of the seventh month; we vow forever to be intimate. Don't despair. Wait until we can be together again.

EMON: In fact, just now when I saw you drawing the ox, I thought you were the Oxherd Boy of the legend.

KATSUYORI: You are the Weaver Girl and this is the Magpie Bridge that brings us together.

NARRATOR: (*sekkyō melody*) The fierce autumn winds have blown down the maple leaves from the mountains to form a bridge across the river.

EMON: Where will the currents lead us?

KATSUYORI: Although the story says the lovers (*highest pitch*) cross the milky River of Heaven to meet and confirm their eternal love, we are not so fortunate. Last year has gone, this year as well, and we have not slept the night together or spoken to each other. (*high pitch*) What will the new year bring?

EMON: We must have faith that my father will soon forgive my transgression.

NARRATOR: (*high pitch*) Both collapse along the shore; (*cadence*) tears overwhelm their voices.

(*sung*) At that moment, there is the sound of birds taking flight from just above the nearby waterfall. Katsuyori looks back and sees someone sitting beneath the falls purifying himself.

KATSUYORI: That's surely my father Shingen.

NARRATOR: His heart flies to his dear father, but fear pulls him back. He takes down the two swords resting on the ox's back and fastens them to his waist. He then drives the ox across the bridge alone.

KATSUYORI: (*spoken*) You can lead this ox as if you were grazing it and approach my father. (*sung*) Even if he does not forgive us, you will at least be able to express your feelings. It wouldn't be good for me to be seen with you.

NARRATOR: Reluctantly he hides behind some hedges out of sight, but his feelings reach out to his father. He finds a simple hut (*cadence*) in which to hide and watch.

NARRATOR: (*sung shite*) Shingen surveys the area around the falls.

SHINGEN: What a delight this waterfall is! (*spoken*) Many come here to escape the heat of summer, but it is rare in autumn to see anyone this deep in the mountains. (*sung*) How marvelous it is here in this valley with its rock walls dyed in brocades of maple leaves. This is a mountain site where I'd love to live; it makes even a humble man feel noble and proud. But something now blocks my view.

NARRATOR: Lady Emon leads her husband's ox and approaches.

EMON: (*spoken*) Pardon me please, sir. Hermits are known to make fallen trees their pillows and moss their robes and to clean their mouths in mountain streams. They have left the burning house[18] of desire and delusion entering the holy realm, but you, sir, a proper samurai, why do you wash your ears in this waterfall? How strange!

SHINGEN: Such clear reasoning from a gentle young girl. One does not wash one's mouth in the stream only to become a priest. I have come to clear my ears of the soiled words of my foolish and naive officers who beg me to forgive my son's indiscretion. Is it so strange for me to come to wash in this waterfall?

EMON: (*sung*) If you are using this water to wash your ears, then my ox must not soil it.

NARRATOR: She pulls the rope leading the ox away from the stream and begins to leave.

SHINGEN: Wait a moment, young woman. (*spoken*) Your words make me wonder, too. (*sung*) To leave saying that you must not let the ox sully the water, you are surely not one of the hermits, Xu You and Chao Fu.[19] Who are you who know of this old Chinese tale? How strange.

EMON: (*highest pitch*) I am embarrassed to tell you. I am Emon, daughter of

Nagao Kenshin. It is because of my illicit affair with Lord Katsuyori that our fathers are at war. To avoid further scandal, we have separated and been apart these two years. Until today, I haven't seen the face of my poor dear Katsuyori. *(spoken)* He is concerned that his father has hidden himself away alone deep in the mountains. What if some spies were to sneak up and attack? He worries that you might be hurt and wants to rush to your side to drive any enemy away. *(sung)* He has traveled secretly through these mountains, but because your land lies south of this river, he cannot cross, disowned by your order. It hurts to know he suffers as he listens to us talk across the river. Before, he walked proudly, wearing fine maple-leaf colored robes, and now he wallows in the dirt and grime of the floating world. His downfall is all my fault. Take pity on him as a farewell gesture to me, have compassion. If you can forgive and pardon him from the mercy of your father's heart, then I will not regret the loss of my life. Isn't a deer fearless of hunters in following the cries of its mate; *(highest pitch)* won't an insect fly into the fire for love of its spouse?[20]

NARRATOR: Tears flow as precious jewels into the rushing waterfall.[21]

SHINGEN: *(spoken)* So you are the daughter of Kenshin. To risk your life to plead for Katsuyori's pardon *(sung)* is most kind and tender, but if I had not disowned him, there would be no need to pardon him now. *(spoken)* Further, I've yet to see him do anything to warrant a pardon. Katsuyori is another matter, but I cannot ignore your plight. Murakami Yoshikiyo stopped the flow of salt to Kai as a strategy to weaken my army, but although he is my enemy, Kenshin showed compassionate generosity, and as a gesture of praise to Yamamoto Kansuke, he shipped several hundred oxen loads of salt. Such a heart shows a true samurai, the most exalted ever known. I do not know how I can repay this debt of kindness. The least I can do is plead on your behalf to your father. *(sung)* For the time being, please stay here. You are no burden for me.

NARRATOR: His kind words strike Emon deeply.

EMON: This is a good omen that I, too, will be pardoned.

NARRATOR: She feels as if she's found an impossible dream, a full moon on New Year's Eve. *(emotional cadence)* All she can say is, "What a noble man!"

(sung, both chanters) Dusk falls early in late autumn; already the setting sun has dipped beneath the mountain horizon. *(hatsumi melody)* Not

waiting for the rising moon's light, (*cadence*) the soldiers have lit a string of lamps from the branches, (*cadence*) which seem to brighten the twilight sky.

SHINGEN: (*sung*) Look, over there! The tips of the branches across the mountains blow free, and leaves scatter. Maple leaves tossed about by mountain storms are the colorful thread woven into a brocade by the mountain goddess. The freshly scattered leaves are like flowers to decorate her hair. Old and young alike can forget their cares in the glory of this evening sight. Just gazing on it offers such solace. Let us go inside.

NARRATOR: (*cadence*)[22] They go inside the camp.

NARRATOR: (*nō chanting*) Just then, as the night deepens, a lantern on someone's head can be seen rising from the valley below. (*spoken*) The figure is disguised in a hempen cloak covered with long grass. He advances stealthily, moving fallen branches from his path. His appearance is threatening. (*sung*) Katsuyori watches him carefully as he moves closer, hidden by the shadows. He glares fiercely at this demonlike figure and then makes his move, (*kowari threatening melody*) rushing noisily through the sand and grasses and crushing all in his wake as he climbs up on the lookout.

KATSUYORI: (*sung*) You won't get any farther!

NARRATOR: He challenges, but the demonlike man ignores him, shaking him off, and he then grabs Katsuyori's head, trying to climb higher up the hill.

KATSUYORI: Do you think I'll fall so easily?

NARRATOR: His head still in a grip, Katsuyori punches the other's body to get free. Thrown on his side, Katsuyori fights back with all his strength. He growls fiercely and attacks, using his bow as a stick to beat the demon into the ground. Katsuyori is thrown into the air but flies back and grabs his enemy. The demon yells out, shaking the mountains with his cry.

DEMON: (*spoken*) I have lived on Mount Tenmoku from time immemorial when Sarudahiko led the heavenly gods to these islands.[23] (*sung*) If you attack me, you'll suffer my curse. Get off, away with you!

NARRATOR: Katsuyori laughs at such bravado.

KATSUYORI: It matters not if you're god or monkey. I've got hold of a fake. Now then, are you going to use your supernatural powers and disappear, or die a mortal's death at my hand? Let me show you the skill of a man!

NARRATOR: Katsuyori clings to the demon as he tries to crawl away. He lifts him up on his shoulders, throws him to the ground, and pounds him with his fists. The lantern on his head and the robe of leaves and grass fall off, leaving Murakami Yoshikiyo exposed. He yells out.

MURAKAMI: (*spoken*) Everyone knows that demons roam on Mount Tenmoku, so I dressed as a fierce mountain guardian demon as a plan to kill Shingen. Regrettably, I may have failed in that attack, (*sung*) but I'll make sure that you go to hell before your father!

NARRATOR: He attacks boldly, and Katsuyori parries his advance. Their swords clash loudly as each refuses to give an inch. Lady Emon hears the fight.

EMON: Look, down below, Katsuyori and Murakami are fighting. He's in danger. Help him!

NARRATOR: At her cries, Kōsaka and Gorō come running out, but Shingen stops them.

SHINGEN: Leave them alone, keep back. If you go, you are no longer in my service.

NARRATOR: Ordered to stay away, they can only gnash their teeth and (*cadence*) glare down at the pair.

(*sung*) Katsuyori strikes deftly and cuts Murakami across his shoulder and chest but is wounded in the thigh by Murakami's return blow. Both wounded, their bodies are covered in blood as dark (*battle cadence*) as the deep autumn colors in which they stumble about.

(*sung*) Unable to sit still any longer, Emon descends to where they are fighting. Thinking that reinforcements have come, Murakami panics and loses his sense of direction. He runs up the hill toward the lookout and then climbs up farther, slipping on the gravel and twisting his ankle. He crawls along the grasses, clinging to tree roots. Katsuyori gives chase, the moonlight illuminating the path.

KATSUYORI: You won't get away from me. No escape!

NARRATOR: (*battle cadence*) He climbs bravely after Murakami.

(*sung*) Below, Lady Emon is terrified as she watches the pair gripped in battle, first one on top, then the other, stumbling and standing up again. They roll about fighting fiercely until Murakami breaks away for a moment and jumps down the hill from the lookout, rolling head over heels down to the foot of the mountain. He starts to run to the bridge to escape but is so exhausted that he can only crawl. He gets halfway across the log bridge when Emon and Katsuyori between them lift up and overturn the log, (*cadence*) spilling Murakami into the river.

(*sung*) Katsuyori dives in after him (*battle cadence*) riding the current in pursuit of his prey. (*sung*) Murakami swims for his life and somehow manages to reach the other bank, but just as he tries to climb out, Katsuyori raises his sword and, with a swift blow, severs his head.

KATSUYORI: (*spoken*) Takeda Katsuyori has slain his enemy, Murakami Zaemon no Jō Yoshikiyo.

NARRATOR: At this cry (*sung*), his father Shingen suddenly stands up.

SHINGEN: Magnificent! Well done! Now I can pardon my son's indiscretion.

NARRATOR: Everyone collapses onto the ground and weeps tears of joy. Shingen, the fierce warrior, has braved the feared curse of the mountain spirits and, like the mountain peak Tenmoku that sits atop the Shirane Range in Kai Province, he stands tall and firm. Just as Ki no Tsurayuki wrote long ago,[24] the power of verse never ceases to amaze! Shingen's one thousand poems have softened the invisible demon spirits as well as a fierce warrior's heart. A colorful brocade of maple leaves now embraces parent and child together once again. Poetry is the song of lovers in delight. It teaches us to cherish and to love and to know compassion. We feel its power forever.

Act 5

—Scene 1
Battle at Kawa-nakajima, tenth day of the ninth month, 1561

NARRATOR:

(*sung*) A hundred battles fought,
a hundred battles won—
Not the best strategy to win a war.[1]

The armies of Takeda Shingen and Nagao Kenshin have locked horns four times without a decisive victory for either side. It is now the tenth day of the ninth month of the fourth year of Eiroku (1561). This fifth battle is the fiercest, with the clash of spear and sword shaking the heavens, the stamping feet of men and horses shattering the firmament. The battle reaches a critical moment as the armies meet on Kawa-nakajima Island between the Chikuma and Sai Rivers. Kenshin's camp is at Saijōsan, and Shingen is at Amenomiya.[2] (*cadence*) Shingen's men have created a platform for their general.[3]

(*sung*) The bannerman to the left is Kōsaka Danjō Masanobu; to the right is Hara Gorō Masatoshi. Poised like hawks, they survey the ebb and flow of the battle. (*spoken*) Shingen's scout Someta Saburō comes running in, gasping for breath, his armor pierced by an arrow.

SOMETA: Kenshin's forces were cut to pieces by the company led by Sakagaki and were forced to retreat, company by company. (*sung*) If we now surround them with our rearguard, we'll be able to strike a decisive blow and defeat them. We must advance at once.

NARRATOR: After delivering his report, (*cadence*) he returns to his camp. (*sung*) Shingen makes no move to give the orders.

SHINGEN: (*spoken*) No, no. A fiercely brave general like Kenshin would never retreat so easily. This is one of Kenshin's tactics to move his flank farther and farther to the right, as if in retreat, and then to challenge the enemy's bannerman. (*sung*) Don't move until we have another report from the scouts.

NARRATOR: Just then one of the lookouts comes running up, out of breath.

LOOKOUT: (*spoken*) The enemy has crossed Chikuma River in the night. They have crossed the road leading to Kaizu Castle and taken position on Mount Akasaka. (*sung*) Sakagaki and Anayama Shuzen were killed in a surprise attack.

SHINGEN: (*spoken*) Just as I suspected. Have our allies in Kaizu Castle come out to attack them from the rear? Can you see the banners?

NARRATOR: (*sung*) At that moment, a soldier from Kaizu comes running up.

SOLDIER: (*spoken*) Hara Haito no Suke Masakuni has surrounded Kenshin from the rear and killed Shida Genshirō and Ōkawa Suruga. He had planned with Sakagaki to get Kenshin in a pincer movement from the front and rear. But Kenshin has crossed the Sai River and disappeared. Our forces have won the day.

NARRATOR: (*sung*) Shingen waves his battle fan.

SHINGEN: We must not lose momentum now. Don't waste another minute, Kōsaka and Gorō. Hurry, hurry!

NARRATOR: With a few men, Kōsaka and Gorō mount (*exit cadence*) and ride their horses furiously into the fray.

NARRATOR: (*sung*) Suddenly from out of nowhere comes a voice behind a hill.

KENSHIN: Nagao Kenshin stands here before you. Face your enemy. Yaa!

NARRATOR: With a fierce yell, he dives like a skylark in full flight, on his fleet-footed, dappled, black-maned steed.[4] He rides straight as an arrow for Shingen, sword raised to strike, but Shingen uses his large battle fan to deflect the blade. Although engaging in the battle, Shingen doesn't leave his platform. He withdraws a little, drawing his enemy closer in order to strike a decisive blow. Kenshin's sword strikes again and again; each using techniques for offense and defense, to jab and parry. Kenshin uses all his skills learned from Wu Tzu; Shingen exploits all the craft of Sun Tzu. Locked in battle, they struggle on the edge of death, (*cadence*) a sight spectacular but terrifying.

(*sung*) In blocking Kenshin's sword, Shingen takes a blow to his shoulder, a gash three inches long. Blood gushes like a waterfall, but Shingen still doesn't draw his sword. He stares defiantly, daring Kenshin to cut him down. Kenshin dismounts.

FIGURE 44 Two "Shingens" confronting Kenshin on the battlefield; Kansuke is the one below (*Shinshū kawa-nakajima kassen*, 1726 [fiction version], Daitōkyū bunko.)

KENSHIN: (*spoken*) Have you given up, Shingen? If you're finished and know you cannot beat me, then remove your helmet and surrender. (*sung*) Surrender now!

NARRATOR: In response to the demand, a voice is heard rising from the shadows of the nearby valley.

SHINGEN: Takeda Shingen is here.

NARRATOR: He runs over, and suddenly there are two Shingens dressed exactly the same. Kenshin is shocked (*cadence*) and can only gasp in astonishment.

KENSHIN: (*sung*) Then one of these two is an imposter. Let the true Shingen step forward, and let us decide this battle.

NARRATOR: The wounded Shingen steps down from the platform and removes his helmet with its white-haired trappings, revealing Yamamoto Kansuke Nyūdō Dōki. Tears well up in both men.

KANSUKE: (*spoken*) When I entered service, my old mother gave me strong advice. She said, "It is fortunate you are under Shingen. Naoe Yamashiro Sanetsuna, in service to Kenshin, is your brother-in-law. Work hard to bring together Emon and Katsuyori, who are so much in love. When the two famous generals go to battle over their honor, (*sung*) the best strategy is for neither house to be shamed. If need be, you must give your own life to restore relations. Never forget these words!" She urged me again and again to remember these words, (*cadence*) her final testament.

(*sung*) Therefore, in battle after battle, my strategy was always to end with no clear victor. (*spoken*) But I had lost all means to end the enmity and unite Emon and Katsuyori. I despaired that I would not be able to follow mother's wishes. It was impertinent to pretend to be Shingen and yet not attack when provoked. (*sung*) The wounding of "Shingen" has left him unscathed; Kenshin has vented his anger and we pray that he now is mollified. Now I ask your compassion. Take the head of Yamamoto Dōki and end the war between your houses. This will fulfill Mother's wish and give her joy in the next world. It will save my honor in this world and after my death.

NARRATOR: *(emotional cadence)* He breaks down with emotion. *(sung)* Kenshin is greatly moved.

KENSHIN: Such a gentle and trustworthy man! A true model of samurai. To have Dōki's sacrifice wasted goes against the warrior's principle. No matter what Shingen decides, Kenshin's forces will fight no more. Further, I pardon my daughter's indiscretion.

SHINGEN: *(spoken)* I, too, agree and hold no grudges, no anger.

NARRATOR: *(sung)* Warriors equal in valor, equal in skill, agree to split Shinano in half, gaining honor and glory. *(cadence)* The battle has ended. *(sung)* Kansuke is delighted and calls out in a loud voice.

KANSUKE: *(spoken)* The Takeda and Nagao houses are at peace again. Bring in Master Katsuyori and Princess Emon.

NARRATOR: At this cry *(sung)* Naoe Yamashiro, Kōsaka, and Gorō enter with the young couple. Everyone raises a cheer of joy; *(cadence)* voices ring through the air celebrating the union. *(sung)* Shingen takes up the battle fan.

SHINGEN: From today on, you are no longer a stranger but fall within the spread of this encompassing fan.[5]

NARRATOR: He jests lightly and hands her the fan.

KENSHIN: To celebrate the joyful occasion, let me offer this strong sword, "Azuki Nagamitsu," to Lord Katsuyori as a sign of our firm bonds as father and son-in-law.

NARRATOR: Kai, Echigo, and now Shinano, three together as one. Parent and child forever. A gentle breeze across this land now at peace.[6] The earth is held firmly, bolstered by the ironlike strength of a young leader ready to rule the great land Japan. From the fertile earth arises food aplenty. For thousands, millions of years, may everyone prosper and grow.

(The postscript is almost exactly the same as the one at the end of *Twins at the Sumida River*.)

Love Suicides on the Eve of the Kōshin Festival

(*Shinjū yoigoshin*)

First performed on the twenty-second day of the fourth month in 1722, *Kōshin Festival*[1] is Chikamatsu's final contemporary-life play. Like most of the other twenty-three, it was based on an actual incident in Osaka, in this case, only two weeks earlier on the sixth day of the same month. A married couple—the wife pregnant—committed suicide. The event seems to have caused a great stir, spurring both Chikamatsu and his rival, Ki no Kaion (1663–1742) at the nearby Toyotake-za theater, to dramatize it. Kaion's *Shinjū futatsu hara-obi* (*Love Suicides and a Double Maternal-Sash*)[2] is thought to have been performed first and to have influenced Chikamatsu's version. Kaion's play was the more popular of the two, at least during the first run.

Two different graves have been found with information on the incident, one in Kyoto Prefecture at the Raigōji temple from where the wife's family came, and one in Osaka in the Tennōji Ward at the Ginzanji temple.[3] Although in both plays Ochiyo (the wife) is presented as pregnant, both gravestones include a reference to a baby boy, probably because prayers were offered separately for each of the three to enable their souls to achieve salvation.

A later version of the facts of this incident, by the kabuki playwright and writer Nishizawa Ippō (1801–52), states that Ochiyo was divorced because of her father-in-law's attempts to seduce her.[4] In both plays, however, her mother-in-law is portrayed as the villain, although Chikamatsu emphasizes that she is not intentionally evil.

Both *Double Maternal-Sash* and *Kōshin Festival* were adapted for kabuki and rewritten for the jōruri stage, the later versions usually taking elements from both dramas. Chikamatsu's original was revived in 1775 and performed until the late nineteenth century and again in 1932, and since 1962, acts 2 and 3 have been part of the bunraku repertoire.[5] Versions were performed in kabuki since the late eighteenth century, and it has been regularly performed since the 1870s.[6] *Kōshin Festival* was made into an award-winning television drama in 1983.

Hanbei, the protagonist of both plays, was born a samurai in the castle town of Hamamatsu near Nagoya but was sent away to be adopted by a greengrocer in Osaka. In act 1 of both Kaion's and Chikamatsu's plays, Hanbei returns to his original home, where he is challenged to show his mettle as a samurai, even though he has been a townsman for many years. The following comparison with Kaion's play shows Chikamatsu's method. First is an outline of Kaion's *Double Maternal-Sash*.

Act 1 begins in Hamamatsu, a castle town; Bokusai, the archery master, sets the theme with a short lecture on what it means to be a true master of the martial arts—spiritual training as well as physical training. We learn that in his youth, Hanbei was a promising star of the martial arts, particularly archery. While in Hamamatsu, he is willing to challenge his old cronies even after fifteen years of merchant life. In the end, he defeats his old rival in a judo match, causing a crisis that almost leads to a fight to the death.

The first act focuses on the samurai's obsessive need to uphold his honor in the face of an insult. We learn that after a fortune-teller predicted that Hanbei would die by the sword, he was sent away by his compassionate lord to be adopted by a merchant's family. Hanbei therefore feels indebted to his lord, his natural father, and his foster parents. Act 1 presents him as still a samurai in spirit. Act 2 begins along the Yodo River in Osaka where Ochiyo (Hanbei's wife) is mistaken for a fugitive courtesan because of her manners and rich clothes. She has been divorced from him while Hanbei was away. The narrator introduces her as an alluring beauty wearing seductive dress. Indeed, constant comments describe her as beautiful and coquettish, with the airs of a high-class courtesan. This is also the mother-in-law's view in act 3, when she states her reasons for demanding that Ochiyo be divorced, accusing her of extravagance enough to bankrupt them all.[7] We are left with the clear impression that the mother-in-law is jealous of Ochiyo.

Kaion has Ochiyo coming from a poor family, of which only her mother is still alive (whereas Chikamatsu has her coming from a rich family with only her father still alive). Kahei, the nephew of Hanbei's foster father

Niemon, tries to stop Hanbei and Ochiyo from committing suicide. The town elders, too, try to change the mother-in-law's mind, but to no avail. The mother-in-law says that either she or Ochiyo must go, forcing Hanbei and Ochiyo to flee.

In Kaion's version, Hanbei shows his spirit in a judo bout, proving that he is physically, as well as mentally, still a samurai. Chikamatsu, in contrast, focuses on the demands on a samurai to keep his promise even in the face of death. Kaion's Hanbei is brash, ready, and willing to challenge his old cronies to an archery or judo match, whereas Chikamatsu's Hanbei is reserved and circumspect, showing a wisdom far above that of the samurai. Kaion stresses the importance of a samurai's standing up for his honor, willing even to die over an insult, whereas Chikamatsu shows the ideal samurai as one who is principled but able to analyze situations and avoid conflict if possible and who has love and compassion for others.

Chikamatsu also uses the setting at a samurai residence in Hamamatsu to comment critically on the reforms and actions of the shogun Yoshimune and his government. According to Suwa Haruo, Chikamatsu's references to the lord's attitude toward modesty and frugality in matters of food and clothing, as well as the samurai passion for falconry, are based on specific edicts or stories about Yoshimune recorded in the *Tokugawa jikki*.[8] Chikamatsu is extremely precise in his references to incidents and places throughout, a technique of the contemporary-life genre, producing a powerful realism for his audience and readership.

Hanbei and Ochiyo, however, differ considerably from the heroes of Chikamatsu's earlier love-suicide plays in which the man is almost always portrayed as weak and indecisive (until the moment of the decision to die) and the woman is strong and resolved. Hanbei compares well with the other strong male protagonists in *Battles at Kawa-nakajima* (1721) and *Tethered Steed and the Eight Provinces of Kantō* (1724). In these three works, Chikamatsu probes the nature of an ideal person, a virtuous man, one with both principles and compassion. Hei'eimon, Ochiyo's father and the main character of act 2, is in the mold of the stern but compassionate father figures such as Magoemon in *Courier for Hell* (1711) and Jōkan in *The Uprooted Pine* (1718).[9] Chikamatsu describes in considerable detail the wealth and personality of this strong-willed but now ill old man. Many commentators have remarked on Chikamatsu's brilliant depiction of Hei'eimon, now weakened and desperately worried about his daughter, unhappy in her third marriage, who will be left behind when he dies. One cannot help but see something of Chikamatsu himself in this figure: Chikamatsu fell ill after this play's run ended and did not produce his last work until more than a year and a half later.

In contrast to the other four period plays translated in this volume, the references in *Kōshin Festival* are mostly to specific contemporary matters, with few allusions to classical tradition. In one of the scenes of act 2, Ochiyo reads a literary passage aloud to entertain her bedridden father. This quotation, from *The Tale of the Heike*, has special significance. Its theme, the abandonment of the dancer Giō by Taira no Kiyomori for another mistress, is thrown at Hanbei as an example of the fickleness of a man's heart. *Love Suicides at Amijima*,[10] Chikamatsu's own work, is also mentioned as a possible reading choice, the story of an Osaka merchant who abandons his wife for another woman.

Hanbei, shown in act 1 as a man demanding the highest standard of integrity from others as well as himself, in act 2 is made to confront his own principles. A term that appears frequently in Chikamatsu's late plays is *keiyaku*, meaning "promise" or "vow." In the first act, it is used to describe the bonds of homosexual love between Hanbei's younger brother and another man, and in act 2, it is used to describe Hanbei's promise never to abandon Ochiyo.

Buddhism, particularly that of the popular Pure Land sects, often figures prominently in the final journey-to-death (*michiyuki*) scenes of Chikamatsu's love-suicide plays. The imagery suggests that the journey is taken by two spirits already separated from their bodies, traveling through one or other of the lower realms of existence, a path of reflection and suffering that will lead them to salvation in the next life. The pair finds solace in Buddha's mercy and the vision of a better life together in paradise. In this play, since the couple and their unborn child were based on real people, the ending would have been seen as an offering for their salvation and for release from the violence of their suicide.

Buddhism also figures prominently in the daily life of Hanbei's parents and the neighborhood in general. Here, however, it seems to be used for entirely different purposes. The mother, openly cruel to her daughter-in-law and nephew, is nevertheless a "believer" and active in parish activities. It is impossible not to see the hypocrisy of the contrast. Cynicism colors the view of Buddhism presented in act 3. Chikamatsu seems to lead the audience to view religion antagonistically as they watch the mother set off for her parish meeting, singing happily while sending the pair to their death. Often in his late plays, Chikamatsu presents a complex view of the human condition by criticizing the pretences of characters who express high morals for selfish ends. He contrasts two views of Buddhism. The first is cynical and coldly realistic, which is answered in the denouement by the power of a vision of romantic idealism in the face of death.

Since the audience was most likely aware of the rumors that the father-in-law's attentions to Ochiyo had spurred the mother-in-law to evict her, they would have read the mother-in-law's words in both plays as stemming from jealousy, whether or not presented as conscious. Izaemon's remark in *Kōshin Festival* that all men are ruled by the ark shellfish (*akagai*, a type of mussel and slang for the female sex organ) points to the psychology underlying the attitudes of the father, mother, and Hanbei toward Ochiyo. The "Kōshin" festival itself has a sexual theme, in that couples were told not to have sexual intercourse during the night before the festival, because children conceived on that night were thought to be sickly or to become criminals.[11] Indeed, one was not supposed to sleep at all during the night before the festival. Both writers, however, only hint at the reasons for the older woman's animosity toward her daughter-in-law. Chikamatsu creates Ochiyo as an attractive woman, well meaning but not skillful as a housewife or at working in the shop and without an obviously seductive manner, as she has in Kaion's play. Although the theme of sexual attraction and jealousy is not overt in Chikamatsu's play, it does suggest the existence of sexual tension and jealousy in the household. The NHK television movie of this play, directed by Wada Ben, makes explicit the desire of the mother for Hanbei and her jealousy of Ochiyo. Hanbei, a serious and principled man, is caught in a net of conflicting responsibilities: his high ideals of honor and commitment, his vow to Ochiyo's father, his love for Ochiyo (and their unborn child), and his duty to his foster parents. The play is a complex tale about the tragic demands placed on those of high principle.

Love Suicides on the Eve of the Koshin Festival
(*Shinju yoigoshin*)

CAST OF CHARACTERS

Osaka Greengrocery

Hanbei (Yaoya Hanbei): thirty-seven years old, a former samurai adopted by a family that owns a greengrocery in Osaka.

Ochiyo: Hanbei's wife, four months pregnant with their child. She is from a wealthy farming family, and this is her third marriage. She is twenty-seven years old.

Iemon (Yaoya Iemon): the owner of the greengrocery, foster father of Hanbei, and retired. A weak character who spends his time with the local temple parish group of retired folk.

Wife: Iemon's wife and the foster mother of Hanbei. She dislikes Ochiyo, is still active in running the shop, and is a harsh person.

Tahei: nephew of Iemon's wife, who works in the grocery.

Hamamatsu

Gōzaemon (Sakabe Gōzaemon): an older samurai, Hanbei's former master.

Koshichirō (Yamawaki Koshichirō): younger half brother of Hanbei, still a samurai.

Koichibei: a footman and servant, who proves himself to be equal or better than other higher-ranking samurai.

Ueda Village

Hei'emon (Shimada Hei'emon): a wealthy farmer, now old and ill, father of Ochiyo.
Okaru: elder sister of Ochiyo.

Act 1

Hamamatsu in the spring, second month, 1722

NARRATOR:

(*sung*) Cherry-blossomed Edo lies sixty leagues to the east,
plum-blossomed Naniwa,[1] sixty leagues to the west;
in between, far from the capital Kyoto is Tōtōmi.
Here Lord Asayama of Hamamatsu Castle[2]
presides over his territory.
Shops and homes bustle with activity,
for there is no relaxing in the marketplace.
Samurai train rigorously at archery and horsemanship,
every other day going out on falconry expeditions.[3]
Spurred by the ceaseless diligence of Lord Asayama,
(*cadence*) even sleeping dogs must not be left to lie
but always poised and ready for the hunt.

(*sung*) The fief's archery master, Sakabe Gōzaemon, though now a wrinkled sixty-year-old, stays busy all day and all night. As the chief attendant on hunting trips, he is always at his master's side, and so he is in attendance on today's expedition. The watchman at the castle gate cries out, "The falconry party is returning!" Cooks and lower-rank soldiers, young samurai, and even townsmen all rush around preparing the house, changing the tatami mats, arranging the scroll in the alcove, dusting and wiping the tables for the tea ceremony. The garden is hurriedly raked and weeds removed. Tea leaves are carefully ground in mortars, where they say truth is forgotten.[4] (*cadence*) Pages brush the sand to form pointed cones.

(*sung*) In the kitchen, cutting boards and tables are piled deep with vegetables, and mountains of both fowl and fish are piled high. The menu calls for three soups and nine dishes of vegetables, fresh fowl, and fish. Each is carefully inspected by an official. "This will bring good fortune," he says as they prepare fillets of felicitous red snapper. The greengrocer, a specialist in the culinary arts, is delegated to prepare the *wasabi* horseradish and a mélange of flavors to suit the lord's palate. Chinaware from Nanjing and colorful lacquer dishes together (*cadence*) create a magnificent table, set for a lord.

(*sung*) A group of young bloods from the archery division, their hair knotted dandy fashion and wearing their kimonos loose, arrogantly rule over the kitchen while their lord and elders are away. Kaneda Jinzō, Oka Gun'emon, and Ōhashi Ippei are in good form.

JINZŌ: (*spoken*) Everyone! Fine job! A job well done! It's been announced that the hunting party will be coming here to rest. We must have everything ready and in order at once.

GUN'EMON: Is the food ready? Get things moving!

IPPEI: Since we're off duty today, feel free to call on us if you need help.

NARRATOR: Each offers his two bits of advice. (*sung*) The handsome page[5] Yamawaki Koshichirō, his dangling forelocks glistening with "Blossom Dew" pomade, descends gracefully into the kitchen to throw out the flowers left over after arranging the floral display.

KOSHICHIRŌ: (*spoken*) Now look who's here! The cozy little band has got together for today's affair. The master Gōzaemon should be pleased with the preparations. Unlike his father, the present lord is impulsive and straightforward; he rides his horse hard and recklessly over fences.[6] And the decision to have dinner here was made on the spur of the moment. The master is away on the excursion, and we're all anxious about the preparations. We have hurriedly cleaned everything from the garden and the formal entrance room to the alcove. I've done the flower arrangement myself. My attempts are no doubt clumsy, but it is my duty to try to make things presentable. (*sung*) Please look them over and put them right.

NARRATOR: His speech and manners are soft and restrained. The three dandies are entranced by the charms of this favorite dish of the household, (*cadence*) caught amid the wafting aromas of the brewing feast. (*spoken*) All three plead their case at once.

JINZŌ, GUN'EMON, and IPPEI: How could there be a flaw in your work! Your only flaw is to be cold and aloof once you have captured a man's heart.

NARRATOR: (*sung*) Even during the frantic bustle, their eyes grow misty and they are dizzy with affection. Each frowns at the other as he vies for this young beauty's favor by tugging at his sleeves and giving him love pinches. Only in the rustic countryside do you still see such crude, (*cadence*) old-fashioned approaches.

(*sung*) Sakabe Gōzaemon likes to keep his wardrobe fashionable, but even though there is no punishment for such extravagance, he now follows the example of his lord and wears only cotton robes and dark blue undergarments.[7] Ahead of the returning hawking party, he hurries home, a commanding figure.

GŌZAEMON: Everyone, has the house been cleaned throughout? Thank you all for such careful preparations. Never, never wish to grow old. At the gate of Gansuiji temple in Iwamatsu village, I excused myself from the party just to get home in a few quick steps, but my legs refused to obey me. However, there is no need to rush because the lord won't be coming until they bag one more bird. (*sung*) First, let's have a look at the menu.

NARRATOR: The list is long, and after glancing only at about half, he remarks in great surprise.

GŌZAEMON: What is this?! (*spoken*) Although I explicitly ordered the dinner to consist of only one soup and three vegetable dishes,[8] this is an extravagant feast of three soups and nine dishes of all kinds of vegetables, fish, and fowl! Are you trying to mince me and my estate right here on the chopping board? (*sung*) Whose idea was this?

NARRATOR: (*cadence*) He scowls furiously. (*sung*) Koshichirō answers gracefully.

KOSHICHIRŌ: (*spoken*) Please forgive us for this mistake. The menu was not the work of a samurai. The chef is Yaoya Hanbei of Utsubo Aburakake-machi in Osaka, who has been staying in the samurai quarter for a few days. Originally he was born here in Tōtōmi Province and is my elder brother by a different mother. When he was only five, for certain reasons, he was sent into service in an Osaka merchant's house, and later he became their adopted heir. His adopted father is Yaoya Iemon. Our real father, Yamawaki Sanzaemon, died the year I was born. Since this year is the seventeenth anniversary of his death, my brother has come to offer prayers. I have not seen him for years, and because I hoped to show gratitude for my master's kindness, I took the opportunity of this visit to enlist his services in preparing the meal. His business is vegetables, and he is an excellent cook. I take full responsibility for this mistake. (*sung*) Please, since this is an occasion for celebration, calm yourself and speak to my brother.

NARRATOR: At this polite apology, the master's expression softens.

GŌZAEMON: Oh! Hanbei, your debut's come at an excellent moment. Please come out here, and change the menu. Quick, hurry!

NARRATOR: He calls out loudly. Although the elder brother Hanbei has the spirit of a samurai, after more than thirty years, he is a merchant in both actions and appearance, through and through. In a borrowed and stained chef's apron, he stumbles and slips from nervousness as he emerges from the kitchen of his former master. He bows with his hands to the floor.

HANBEI: (spoken) Forgive me for my error. I am unaware of the culinary customs in this part of the country. Although I had received the orders for a meal of one soup and three dishes, I was rash and thought that the messenger had made a mistake. In Osaka, where I used to serve at daimyo functions, even an extremely light meal consisted of two soups and five dishes. When I was asked to prepare a feast for a visiting Korean embassy at the Great Hall of Nishi-Honganji temple in Osaka, I learned how to prepare dinners of thirteen or fifteen courses in the style of the Heian courtier Chūnagon Fujiwara no Yamakage.[9] Please forgive my imprudent and excessive extravagance. I will prepare your desired meal of one soup and three dishes with my own hands. (sung) I will quickly slice the food, prepare the seasonings, and cook it to suit your palate. You shall have *matsutake* mushrooms and pickled bamboo shoots prepared in a secret way that makes them taste better than if they were fresh.

NARRATOR: His mellifluous tongue (cadence) and enticing spices delight the master.

(sung) Gōzaemon laughs aloud.

GŌZAEMON: (spoken) Well, if you're a son of Yamawaki Sanzaemon, then you're a member of my household. It is quite admirable, impressive of you to have come to make offerings at your father's grave. You grew up from a tender age in another area, so it is only natural that you don't know our present customs. Certainly in culinary matters and with clothes and accessories, the lord deplores any extravagance. In Kyoto or Osaka, haven't there been any rumors? Last year in the tenth month at the hunting grounds of Mount Takeshi, a friend of mine, Sano Buntaza, was attending the lord for the first time. He wore a fancy crepe silk coat, and the lord frowned with great displeasure and said: "Crepe silk blows too easily in the wind and gets in the way. Don't ever wear it again! Here, take this." Buntaza was handed a simple cotton cloak and turned crimson.[10] Later after thinking about the incident again, I realized that while in attendance, Buntaza would not normally wear crepe silk. The lord had planned the incident beforehand with Buntaza. By making an example of Buntaza in front of all the retainers, he managed, without making a formal decree, to show that he wanted to put a stop to waste and extravagance. But some of the young retainers who didn't understand this gesture still wear such fashionable robes that would even catch the eye of Edo kabuki actors at the theaters in Kobikichō or Sakaichō. They have no regard for the dignity of a samurai. All they do is complain and slander the daimyo: "How stingy, what a miserly lord." A daimyo in damask robes is certainly a daimyo, but one in cotton is still a daimyo, too. The warrior Saitō Bettō Sanemori wore brocade in his final battle, but his style of loyalty, betraying the Genji to fight for the enemy Heike, showed his heart to be a soiled rag.[11] Another warrior, Sasaki Genzō, who served only one lord, covered himself with rags and patiently waited for Yoritomo's triumph with a brocade heart.[12] These days those who prefer extravagance are Sanemori. Praise for Sasaki Genzō encourages a more frugal government in order to make the populace more comfortable by reducing demand and prices. Samurai, of course, but you townsmen, too, must never forget this benevolence. Breakfast and dinner must consist of only one soup and three vegetable dishes. Saké must be limited to three small cups per person. Tonight's feast, too, must be humble. Don't write out the menu. Old and discolored rice must be cooked until it hardens, then crushed into powder and added to the miso soup. The side dish should be grated radish and pickled sardines. The cooked dish should be mackerel boiled with salt and a little vinegar, two pieces per serving. Next comes pickled eggplant. Finally, as the centerpiece, let's see. . . . Ah yes! Perfect! Bring in the giant mountain yam that was brought back from the outing. (*sung*) Over here, over here!

NARRATOR: He calls out, and a five-foot mountain yam wrapped in rush mats is carried in by two attendants (*cadence*) who place it on the chopping board.

(*sung*) When Hanbei removes the covering, he strikes his hands together and exclaims.

HANBEI: Incredible! Is this area famous for potatoes? I've never before seen anything like this. (*spoken*) If I displayed it in Osaka, I could collect a fortune. This is a great omen for the house: since the daimyo comes here today, this foreshadows the master's success. (*sung*) Soon the yam will turn into an eel![13]

NARRATOR: Hanbei flatters with a honeyed tongue, slipperier than an oily eel.

GŌZAEMON: (*spoken*) Be that as it may, today's fortune is due to a farmer in my domain who, after hearing of the daimyo's visit, waited along the road for my return and offered the yam for the dinner. Tonight's pièce de resistance will be this prize yam. I'm counting on your culinary prowess. (*sung*) Please prepare a masterpiece.

NARRATOR: Just as he finishes speaking, the sound of the gate opening is heard. "The daimyo has arrived," and the house buzzes with activity. Gōzaemon hurries into the next room to slip into his more formal clothes. He is followed by Yamawaki Koshichirō, with Oka, Ōhashi, and Kaneda (*cadence*) all scurrying behind him.

(*sung*) Hanbei puts his whole heart into the preparations, as though frantically dancing and playing accompaniment too. His skilled hand slices the five-foot yam into three-inch portions and peels each slice cleanly. He adds spices to the arrowroot powder and soy sauce stock, bringing it to a boil. Hoping to observe the daimyo's face, Hanbei peaks into the main room where he sees the lord of the castle relaxing on the dais in his informal clothes. In the next room, the attendants, the falconry master, dog trainers, hunting attendants, and foot soldiers pack the house and overflow into the garden in front of the entrance. They mill about in front of the kitchen, filling the whole house as if it were an inn. In the kitchen, preparations proceed at a feverish pitch. Hanbei brings in Lord Gōzaemon's tray, (*kowari threatening melody*) holding it at the proper height, just below his eyes, and sets it down with due formality. (*spoken*) Each helping of soup is accompanied by a portion of rice. The first fish dish is one slice of octopus. By the second cup of saké, the lord is in good spirits and exchanges his small saké cup for a dish cover. A specially prepared sea vegetable from Kada Bay in Wakayama is served next on a small tray. At the stipulated third cup, the lord Asayama draws the line. The last soup is made with small river clams. An unusually humble feast, but one that greatly pleases the daimyo. (*sung*) The final cup of saké is poured to the brim for Gōzaemon himself, (*cadence*) bringing the feast to an end with a grand flourish as the trays are gracefully removed.

(*sung*) Gōzaemon bursts into the kitchen and glares at Hanbei in an angry pose.

GŌZAEMON: (*spoken*) Today's dinner was to have the giant yam as the centerpiece. It was to delight by its spectacular size. No matter how expertly you slice it, a five-foot yam diced into small pieces is ridiculous. Though you're an experienced chef, you're a foreigner here. Since the daimyo is now in residence, (*sung*) I cannot allow you to remain in this house. Leave at once!

NARRATOR: He chokes with anger, (*cadence*) his words few but fierce. (*spoken*) Hanbei doesn't flinch.

HANBEI: I do not pretend that this was the master's order. I prepared today's meal carefully, feeling proud that I had achieved a success by my conscientious efforts. Yet instead of appreciation or thanks, I receive only an unwarranted rebuke. Generally, when serving nobles or lords, it is customary, without exception, never to exhibit such an unusual specimen. Daimyo and nobles are phlegmatic by temperament, and when they see something, be it even just once, they assume it must be plentiful. They boast to other daimyo of the marvelous mountain yams in their domains, and suddenly requests flow in from all around. Unable to refuse such requests, they have the land scoured, but none is found. The lord is then shamed for appearing to lie. With such consequences in mind, I thought that I would best serve the lord if I prepared the gigantic yam in the usual way. (*sung*) It is my misfortune that my efforts have displeased you. Do with me as you wish.

NARRATOR: Hanbei's words, clear and thoughtful, show traces of a strict samurai spirit. Gōzaemon is flustered.

GŌZAEMON: (*spoken*) Hmm. . . . You're right of course! Your reasoning is flawless. I withdraw my orders. I was wrong. (*sung*) Your words served to the lord will be another feast! Well, it seems I stumbled over small potatoes.

NARRATOR: (*cadence*) He gives out a hearty laugh. (*sung*) "The lord is about to depart," calls out the attendant, and the house bustles again. The feathered lances, umbrellas, decorative sheaths, palanquins, and horses are all prepared. Gōzaemon joins the procession to accompany the party's return to the castle. "I'll return by dusk" are his parting words (*scene cadence*) as he hurriedly follows the setting sun.

NARRATOR: (*sung*) The cleaning of the house is left to the samurai; care of the garden is the duty of the underlings and pages. Each sets out to do his assigned task. Hanbei, now alone in the kitchen, quickly washes the carving knives, cooking utensils, and chopping boards, putting all in order. Then, like the Chinese wizard Tie Guai,[14] he pauses to smoke his long pipe, (*cadence*) calming his mind with each puff.

(*sung*) The young samurai, one by one, gather around Hanbei.

GUN'EMON: (*spoken*) We all are in the archery unit under Gōzaemon. They say that you are Yamawaki Koshichirō's elder brother. I have a desperate request. Although it may seem ridiculous to ask you for the hand of your brother, I swear to god that I love that fluffy-forelocked lad from the tips of his toenails to the top of his head. Day in and day out, I swear my love in eternal vows cast in tender missives that come from my heart. The cost of such fancy paper alone is around 500 *monme*.[15] Even when I offer him all my possessions, Koshichirō remains unreceptive. Please, as his older brother, could you kindly convey my offer? I, Gun'emon, prostrate myself before you with head bowed to the floor. Please, I pray, grant my request.

NARRATOR: (*sung*) He continues to babble on, but Jinzō and Ippei interrupt.

JINZŌ: (*spoken*) Listen Hanbei! This affair cannot be decided in a word. Others, too, have fallen for him. The price of fancy paper is a pittance! I spent 1 *kan*,[16] 500 *monme*, just for mouth freshener to win me a taste of love. I vow on my honor as a samurai to the warrior god Hachiman, please allow me to have him!

IPPEI: (*sung*) Wait just a minute! I must get a chance to present my case!

NARRATOR: Each vies for favor as their voices rise to a deafening roar. A mist of steamy foul air clouds their eyes, (*cadence*) each lost to the power of lust.[17]

(*sung*) Hanbei, calmly with pipe in hand, continues to sit relaxed in a cross-legged position.

HANBEI: (*spoken*) In all castles, it is the rule that sexual relations between men are forbidden. So, if I say yes to one of your proposals, my brother will lose his head.

IPPEI: That's no problem. At this castle, only illicit relations with females are forbidden, right down to the lowest class. There's no ban on relations between men. Choose one from among the three of us. (*sung*) Take your time to make a careful decision.

NARRATOR: (*cadence*) From behind the commotion, (*sung*) Koshichirō approaches, holding in one bundle all the love letters he has received, and places them in front of Hanbei.

KOSHICHIRŌ: (*spoken*) Although I am embarrassed to speak of this before my brother, (*sung*) I can no longer keep it concealed after this exposure. All this affection for someone as worthless as I am has warmed my heart and given my youthful years a memory to be cherished forever. For this I am most grateful. I have received letters from many quarters, but I have replied to none. Thinking it insensitive simply to return them, I have kept them all. Since I have not broken even one seal, I have been fair to everyone. I have given my heart to no one. (*spoken*) Hanbei, you are an impartial observer. Take these letters, seals unbroken, and return them. Please, everyone, let us forget this matter.

NARRATOR: With words soft and tender, (*cadence*) he maintains the highest principles of homosexual love.

JINZŌ: (*sung*) It's just that gentle style that makes us adore him even more.

NARRATOR: Each falls into a glassy-eyed stupor, dazed by love. (*spoken*) Hanbei finally intervenes.

HANBEI: Well, it is clear that each of you desires him, but we need a means of choosing among you. I appear to be a merchant, but my heart is samurai. I will judge the one who truly loves my brother, and to that one he will be given. (*sung*) Here, Koshichirō, change into these robes.

NARRATOR: With his eyes, Hanbei shows his heart's intent. Koshichirō nods to show that he understands (*exit cadence*) and goes into the other room.

NARRATOR: (*sung*) Hanbei then reads the names of the senders on the many letters.

HANBEI: (*spoken*) The letters of each of you three are here, but who is this Koichibei? Do you know him?

NARRATOR: To this question, all three respond in unison.

THREE: That little runt is a lackey in this house. It's incredible that such worthless scum would be up (*sung*) to something like this.

NARRATOR: They burst into scornful laughter.

HANBEI: *(spoken)* No, you're wrong to dismiss him. In the ways of love, there is no high or low class. Call Koichibei, too, and have him join the group. We must have all present to make a fair decision.

THREE: No! No! We can't allow that slovenly lout to be in the same room with us. *(sung)* In any case, he's not at home now, and we haven't seen him about. Don't worry about him.

NARRATOR: Just as they say this, Yamawaki Koshichirō, dressed in a pure white robe with a pale yellow formal coat, *(cadence)* enters the room and takes his seat. His face shows calm resignation to his harsh fate.

(sung) Hanbei immediately takes the small formal offering table, sets two unsheathed swords on it, and places it in front of Koshichirō.

HANBEI: *(spoken)* Four profess their love for only one, my brother. No matter who is chosen, three will remain bitter. I live far from my brother and am concerned for his future. I take your requests seriously. I am a poor commoner before you distinguished samurai and cannot ignore your pleas, so I have persuaded my brother to wear death robes. The one who truly loves Koshichirō will remain true to him into the next world. No others will block their true love in the next world. I am now ready to entrust my brother to another. *(sung)* Who will vow[18] to become his eternal brother and join him in death?

NARRATOR: Hanbei glares sternly at the three. The samurai jump back in shock at this unexpected challenge. They are terrified to see swords and a death robe instead of the auspicious saké cup. "Ahem. Ahem." They cough and stutter trying to conceal their fear. *(cadence)* They squirm in consternation, trying to make themselves small,[19] silenced by this proposal.

(doguya melody) From the soldiers barracks next to the main gate, Koichibei, a young fellow wearing a plain, solid dark blue kimono with tight sleeves, *(rough melody)* the hem tied up in the sash at his waist, comes striding into the room. Beckoned by the call of love, he swaggers in front of the other suitors *(low pitch)* and flaunts his backside under their noses *(cadence)* as he sits down.

KOICHIBEI: *(spoken)* Although in front of Koshichirō's elder brother, Master Hanbei, I am terribly embarrassed, I must profess my love for Master Koshichirō, who has captured my heart. It's as if this lowly lackey's rice bowl had filled to the brim and suddenly the rice stuck in my throat, choking me and making life unbearable. But today my savior has showed such kindness, offering a lowly lout like me a chance in a future life to be Koshichirō's lover. My heart is bursting with joy! Oh, the pain in my soul! Oh, what feelings. . . . Five or six chili peppers couldn't make my tears as hot as they are now. Never, never!

NARRATOR: (*sung*) He quickly takes the bared sword and slides up next to Koshichirō, who moves closer in readiness. In a flash, Hanbei puts himself between their shining swords.

HANBEI: What's this! Have you gone mad, Koichibei?

NARRATOR: Hanbei forces them apart.

KOICHIBEI: Master Hanbei from Osaka, you have given me all the miso soup a servant could desire, this young man's beauty. If I do not die now, how can I prove that my feelings are true? (*sung*) You must let me die.

NARRATOR: He stands ready to act but is pulled down again.

HANBEI: (*spoken*) We have seen your true colors. You alone are Koshichirō's true lover. If more than one wished to compete to die with Koshichirō, (*sung*) then I was ready to have my precious brother killed. But no challengers stepped forward. I, Yamawaki Hanbei, will stand as your go-between. Henceforth, as the older partner, I ask that you accept the responsibility of taking care of my brother.

NARRATOR: "Yes, I do," exclaims the joyful Koichibei.

KOICHIBEI: (*sung*) A lowly footman like me is not fit to sit among you great samurai, but I have spirit no less than the best warrior. How grateful I am to be given the chance to be the lover of such a fine young fellow! This is more than I deserve. It's too much for me even to hold his hand. Forgive me for being too forward, Master Hanbei.

NARRATOR: He lovingly embraces Koshichirō. Deep solid blue against immaculate white—(*cadence*) a brotherhood of unblemished purity.

(*sung*) Oka Gun'emon coughs violently in (*spoken*) a fit of unreasonable jealousy.

GUN'EMON: What do you think you're doing, you worthless runt? (*sung*) I can't bear it. Stop it!

NARRATOR: He grabs Koichibei's shoulders and pulls him away.

KOICHIBEI: (*spoken*) Hey, what are you doing? Oh, I get it. Was the saké at the daimyo's feast too much for you? Hmm, I understand now. It's just like a samurai with his two swords to expect special treatment. So you want to have some judo practice, do you? I know this is unprecedented, (*sung*) but allow me the honor.

NARRATOR: Koichibei playfully dances about as he approaches the other. With one deft move, he lifts him in the air and throws him over.

KOICHIBEI: (*spoken*) Ha, ha. That was too easy. Much too simple! Beginner's luck.

NARRATOR: (*cadence*) Koichibei feigns ignorance of the art. (*sung*) Unable to bear the insults, Jinzō and Ippei jump up and grab the collar of his kimono.

JINZŌ: You insolent servant boy, how dare you throw our brother? We'll teach you a lesson. We'll make you eat dirt!

NARRATOR: They threaten and grab at him.

KOICHIBEI: (*spoken*) Such noble intentions, so kind of you to offer me judo lessons! Who's first? (*sung*) Let's begin.

NARRATOR: They pace round and round. Koichibei gauges the breathing of his two opponents and suddenly lashes out with a couple of kicks that send them both onto their backs on the wooden floor.

KOICHIBEI: (*spoken*) Ha, ha! Much too easy! (*sung*) Please forgive my rudeness.

NARRATOR: While he apologizes, (*spoken*) the threesome crawl slowly to their feet.

THREE: What are we hanging about here for? We offer saké and our goodwill and get our backsides kicked.[20]

NARRATOR: (*sung*) Grumbling and moaning, they grudgingly withdraw, (*cadence*) nursing sore hips and battered pride.

(*sung*) Hanbei, now in high spirits, speaks approvingly.

HANBEI: Well, Koichibei, you certainly are adept. I live far away, so I must ask you to look after my brother, who has no one else to depend on. (*spoken*) As payment for my services at today's feast, I'll ask the master to approve your relationship. (*sung*) I stand as go-between in your love. May you always remain close.

NARRATOR: (*song*) Hanbei sanctions their vows of unity and fidelity, (*scene cadence*) offering prayers to the myriad gods for eternal protection.

Act 2

Hei'emon residence, Yamashiro, Ueda village,[1] third month, late spring 1722

NARRATOR:

    (*song*) Torrential rains of early summer
    steeped us in fervent love,
    but now it is weary autumn
    when the fields are drained dry.[2]
    Precious droplets[3] of rain drip
    from the eaves, plop, plop, plop.
    Come in, you're welcome any time.
    Come again and again
    until rumors are rife. . . .[4]

    (*sung*) Near Tamamizu in Yamashiro lies the village of Ueda where a prosperous home sits next to the headman's house, both with well-kept thatched roofs. Inside this warm house sit the servant girls all in a row, (*cadence*) busily spinning yarn.

    (*sung*) Here the wheel of fortune looks bright. How many piles of grain fill the stores? Five layers of bags, piled high as the Mountain of the Chinese Immortals, reflect the prosperity of the Shimada clan. The patriarch is Hei'emon, a powerful landowner. His wife died with last year's autumn mist, but he has two daughters. The eldest, Okaru, has married a man from Torikai who was adopted into the Shimada house. The younger, Ochiyo, has married a respectable gentleman in Osaka. With this security in the harvest time of his life, Hei'emon has given up the supervision of his fertile fields. Now retired after a lifetime of work, he has suddenly fallen ill. Okaru is always at his side, attending to his needs. The servant girls in the kitchen talk loudly.

GIRLS: (*spoken*) Don't you think we got a lot done this morning? (*sung*) Let's take a break. Otake, Onabe!

NARRATOR: (*cadence*) They follow one another quietly, tiptoeing past the sickroom. (*sung*) Okaru sees that her father is sleeping peacefully and gets up quickly to take advantage of the opportunity.

OKARU: (*spoken*) What! Not a soul in the kitchen! Heiroku, that husband of mine, has gone to petition for land reclamation along the Yodo River.[5] He's gone to Kyoto and abandoned our precious patient. All the workers are in the fields! Those lazy girls, they work diligently while I'm watching, but as soon as I turn my back, they scamper off. They haven't even thought of warming father's medicine. (*sung*) What sort of help are they! Someone, make up a fire in the hearth! Jirō, Jirō!

NARRATOR: As she calls out for the rest of the household, a palanquin arrives at the front gate, unnoticed by anyone in the house.

BEARERS: (*spoken*) Hello, is anyone home? We've come from Iemon, the greengrocer in Shin'utsubo, Osaka.

NARRATOR: (*sung*) When the palanquin door is opened, (*song*) a delicate young woman emerges. Her eyes are weary from weeping, (*cadence*) her fancy crepe silk obi soaked with tears. (*sung*) Her eyes filled with tears, she gets out, and the bearers prepare to leave.

BEARERS: We've delivered the goods.

NARRATOR: With these cold and curt parting words, (*cadence*) they quickly take off for home.

(*sung*) Even at her parents' house, a married daughter finds it difficult to cross the threshold.[6] Finally Okaru notices Ochiyo lingering near the doorstep.

OKARU: (*spoken*) Oh! Is that you Ochiyo? Thank you for coming all this way to visit father. He's feeling better but is still not well. Why didn't you keep the palanquin bearers? Call them back for a drink. You should at least send them off with a cup of saké. You act as if you're a stranger in this house. (*sung*) Call them back.

NARRATOR: Ochiyo responds only by sadly lowering her head. (*emotional cadence*) At this show of concern, Okaru, too, is saddened.

OKARU: (*spoken*) You're right, certainly right. I meant to send word earlier, but since there is no immediate danger from this illness and since your in-laws are so difficult and Hanbei so busy, I thought that even if I told you, you wouldn't be free to come. Since it would only make everyone worry, father ordered me not to inform anyone. Not wanting to irritate him, I haven't told a soul, (*sung*) not even our aunt in Kōraibashi or the relatives in Tokiwamachi.[7] (*spoken*) Please don't worry! Since we've employed the imperial household's physician, the medicine has been showing some effect. This morning he ate three full bowls of rice gruel. The doctor said that the illness is under control and that his condition is improving. So, he's almost well again. (*sung*) Seeing your face will complete his recovery. My, my! How good it is to see you. Let's go to see father.

OCHIYO: (*spoken*) What? Father's sick? I didn't know anything about it. When did he fall ill?

OKARU: What! You didn't know he was sick! Then why did you come? What are you crying about?

OCHIYO: (*sung*) I'm so ashamed. I've been divorced again.

NARRATOR: (*emotional cadence*) She hides her face as she chokes back tears. (*sung*) Okaru flushes in surprise.

OKARU: (*spoken*) Listen, Ochiyo, we hear about people remarrying three or even five times, but one must never imitate such bad examples. You can say again and again how ashamed you are, but can you say you really understand shame? (*sung*) This is your third marriage! To be sure, the first husband, Tahei of the Fushimiya in Dōshumachi, Osaka, couldn't settle down and managed to squander all his assets and ruin the business. With no place to live, you were forced to part against each other's will. The next fellow left you a widow. Even though neither case was your fault, you still are criticized. (*spoken*) People say, "It's because she's not determined enough that she's lost two husbands. And look, in no time at all she's been kicked out again." The villagers who have daughters gossip over tea, spreading rumors: "Don't be negligent, don't let your daughter follow the path of Shimada Hei'emon's child." (*sung*) You know all too well that to be divorced even once makes it difficult for the parents and family. This time when you got married, we told you over and again, "No matter if you have to pass through a raging fire or have your bones smashed, under no circumstances are you to return." Yet you've managed to come home in fine style and in good time! Father will be furious. We'll see father later. We'd better keep our voices down. (*spoken*) So did Hanbei give you a letter of divorce and send you back?

OCHIYO: No. Last month, while Hanbei was visiting his birthplace in Hamamatsu to offer a memorial service for his father who died seventeen years ago, my things were gathered together and I was told, "A letter of divorce will follow, but now just leave this house." My mother-in-law forced me (*sung*) and this child only four months in my womb out of the house and into a palanquin and sent me away—without offering any reasons! How cruel and hard she is!

NARRATOR: (*emotional cadence*) Okaru is pained, seeing her sister's suffering.

OKARU: (*sung*) What a foul, low trick for a mother-in-law to evict a pregnant daughter-in-law while the husband is away. She must have some trick up her sleeve. (*spoken*) Although he is the husband of our aunt, Kawasakiya Gengobei of Kōraibashi is your guardian. It is spiteful of her to ignore him and send you directly to us. Be that as it may, we'll wait until my husband returns from Kyoto and then decide what we must do. Normally one cannot be divorced in such a manner. (*sung*) Who is she to separate a legally married couple and cause such grief? How hard on you!

NARRATOR: Ochiyo bursts into tears.

OKARU: Oh, not so loud! Don't make such a noise! Father's in the next room sleeping. Stop crying.

NARRATOR: But the tears flow in an endless stream. (*cadence*) Only close family can feel the pain of one's troubles.

KINZŌ: (*sung*) How's Master Hei'emon feeling today?

NARRATOR: With this greeting, Kinzō from the village abruptly lets himself in. Ochiyo quickly steps back into Okaru's shadow, hoping not to be noticed.

KINZŌ: (*spoken*) Hey, don't try to hide! You can't hide from me. Just now at the tea house on the river bank, I heard about your visit from the palanquin bearers who were on their way back to Osaka. Congratulations Ochiyo! It seems that you've been divorced and sent home.

NARRATOR: (*sung*) His unbridled tongue rattles on, unconcerned at the consequences. Okaru jumps up in alarm, afraid that his loud voice will reach their father.

OKARU: (*spoken*) Mr. Kinzō, lower your voice. We're not deaf. We can hear you well enough even if you speak more softly. Ochiyo has not been divorced. She has come to pay a visit to our sick father, (*sung*) who is in the other room peacefully sleeping. We mustn't wake him, so please be quiet! Better still, you should be on your way.

NARRATOR: But Kinzō ignores her and becomes even more boisterous.

KINZŌ: (*spoken*) So, your father's sleeping, is he? That's interesting. No matter how you struggle to conceal it, he will eventually hear the truth. Ochiyo, go on and get divorced as many times as you like. Even if the fields have been plowed and trampled by a herd of grooms, it won't matter when you become a farmer's wife. (*sung*) Under my reins, you'd never know a lonely night. Don't let your spirits be low because you've been divorced. Don't lose those feminine charms of yours. (*spoken*) Last spring when you got married, it should've been to me. Since I'm the one who loves you the most, you'll never be settled anywhere else. You've been married and divorced over and over again! It means we're fated for each other. I'll make the proposal to your father, and after today you'll be mine. (*sung*) Okaru, I'll take precious care of her.

NARRATOR: His yelling deaden the spirits of the sisters; their hearts tremble. From the other room comes the clap of frail hands.

HEI'EMON: Karu, Karu!

OKARU: Yes, yes, I'm coming.

KINZŌ: (*spoken*) Holy saints! The old man is awake! Tell him Kinzō dropped by to see how he was (*sung*) and that I'll come again tomorrow.

NARRATOR: He quickly leaves, but Okaru goes after him angrily.

OKARU: (*spoken*) Where are you off to? Then you're not going to take Ochiyo!

KINZŌ: (*sung*) No, not now. A marriage proposal is an important matter. I'll choose an auspicious day to seek her hand.

NARRATOR: (*cadence*) Babbling away, he scurries out the door.

OKARU: (*sung*) Father, are you awake?

NARRATOR: She opens the sliding door. From behind it, Ochiyo peeks hesitantly into the room. Their father struggles to rise from under the heavy quilt—(*emotional cadence*) a tired and tortured old man climbing up the mountain of age. (*sung*) Although stalked by no hunters, his limbs have fallen limp, his face is rough and wrinkled like a felled beast's. (*cadence*) The eyes of parent and child meet. (*sung*) Ochiyo cannot bear the agony.

OCHIYO: Father, you must take your medicine and get well again.

NARRATOR: Before she knows it, she collapses in tears. Tears cloud her father's eyes too.

HEI'EMON: Don't worry. Just come here, come closer.

NARRATOR: She moves close to his bed.

HEI'EMON: (*spoken*) So you've been divorced and sent home again. A parent's heart will journey even a thousand or ten thousand miles for his child.[8] How much more will he love her if she's in the same house. I would have heard your voice even if I had been asleep, but I couldn't go to sleep even if I had wanted to. (*sung*) Do you think that it would change things between us? Once in his fifties, a man can no longer do everything as he used to do, even though his spirit is the same as when young. Then I was strong willed and righteous, (*spoken*) and if you were divorced again and sent home, I was determined not to see your face or speak to you. But when a man reaches his sixties, it is not just the years that pass by quickly, he feels older with each month and day (*sung*) and falls deeper into the depths of sickness. My only worry equal to, no, greater than that for this decaying body is anxiety for my child's welfare. Three times it's happened . . . , yet even if you were divorced a hundred or a thousand times, resign yourself to such a fate, karma from a former life. Who can be bitter, who can be angry? (*highest pitch*) Let them laugh if they will; let them slander if they wish, or point at you. Nothing will change my love for you or the pain I feel.

NARRATOR: He repeats himself, as the old are wont to do; his breath grows short.

HEI'EMON: (*spoken*) That good-for-nothing Hanbei took off for Hamamatsu, did he! Away for a while, he knew very well what would happen. If that fellow should happen to visit, don't let him in, don't say a word to him, don't even look at him! We'll marry you into a family that has one hundred times his wealth. Don't worry about this. (*sung*) Now, Karu, the workers are in the fields, aren't they? Make some tea and give Chiyo some lunch.

NARRATOR: Okaru rejoices to see her father's face free of anger or grief.

OKARU: (*spoken*) Look, Ochiyo, father's feeling better than anyone in Japan.[9] Stay at his side and nurse him well. (*sung*) Oh, how happy I am! What a load off my mind.

NARRATOR: (*exit cadence*) She quickly closes the door and goes into the kitchen.

NARRATOR: A greeting is heard from the gate, "Hello, is anyone home?"

OKARU: Who is it?

NARRATOR: Okaru quickly realizes that it is Ochiyo's husband Hanbei. She wonders if he has come to finalize the divorce.

OKARU: Mr. Divorce Papers, you are most welcome.

NARRATOR: Hanbei doesn't notice her remark and removes his traveling hat and loosens the strings of his straw sandals, shedding the weariness of the journey.

HANBEI: *(spoken)* Well, Okaru, I trust that everyone is fine. I went to visit my birthplace in the country and was busy, and left there in a rush. Forgive me for not letting you know that I was coming. My parents aren't the type to consider such things and probably haven't sent word that I've been away. The trip to Hamamatsu was without mishap. It is certainly nice to be here again.

OKARU: Is that so! What a tiring journey you must have had.

NARRATOR: *(sung)* She turns her face away, lifting her nose defiantly.

OKARU: Servants! Maids! Isn't anyone going to serve some tea?

NARRATOR: She calls out to an empty house, which only angers her more. Hanbei notices her mood but, unsure what the matter is, remains still. Unknown to each, only a single door separates the couple. . . . Suddenly the door slides open, and Ochiyo emerges.

FIGURE 45 Hanbei on the road, returning from Hamamatsu. From a kabuki production (*Sewa-ryōri yaoya no kondate*, a rewrite of the *Kōshin* play) at the Osaka Kado-za theater in the ninth month of 1849. Hanbei is played by Jitsukawa Enzaburō, and the artist is Hasegawa Sadanobu. *(Courtesy of Matsudaira Susumu.)*

OCHIYO: *(spoken)* Okaru, please warm the medicine.

HANBEI: Huh! Ochiyo! *(sung)* What are you doing here?

NARRATOR: Ochiyo turns and flees to the inner room, closing the door tightly shut. *(cadence)* Hanbei is both surprised and angry.

HANBEI: *(spoken)* Okaru, my wife—when did she come here? *(sung)* Why didn't she speak to me?

OKARU: *(spoken)* Search your own heart for the reason she ignored you. Who are you trying to fool with that innocent act? Ha, ha, ha! How ridiculous all this is!

NARRATOR: *(sung)* Hanbei is bewildered by her strained laughter but only sighs to himself and lowers his head, *(cadence)* now heavy with anxiety.

(sung) From the next room, the father's hoarse voice is heard, broken by incessant coughing.

HEI'EMON: (spoken) Short nights and long days are generally best for old folks, but that is only for those healthy enough to move about and keep busy. Long days wasted sick in bed leave one bored. Chiyo, take a book from the shelf and read something to me. Where is Karu? (sung) Someone come and keep me company.

NARRATOR: Father is impatient and short tempered, but Okaru feels she cannot leave Hanbei.

OKARU: Yes, yes, I'll listen here in the next room while I'm working.

NARRATOR: She moves closer to the door.

HANBEI: What! Is your father sick?

NARRATOR: "Let me see him," he wants to say, but holds back because he senses animosity. He remains silent to wait for the right moment (cadence) and meanwhile moves closer to listen. (sung) Ochiyo takes a few books from the shelf.

OCHIYO: *The Tales of Ise*, *The Jinkōki*,[10] (spoken) this doesn't seem suitable. There's also *Love Suicides at Amijima*, as well as *Essays in Idleness* and *The Tale of the Heike*. Well, father, which would you prefer?

HEI'EMON: Let's listen to the part where Okaru left off, book 1, the "Giō" chapter of *The Tale of the Heike*. Read from there.

NARRATOR: Ochiyo opens the book.

OCHIYO: Yes, there's a bookmark at that point:

> Toji, her mother, tearfully comforts her again. Since we live in a land dominated by his [Kiyomori's] mighty power, we cannot refuse his command. Some profess their love for one thousand, a myriad years, yet part soon after. Others think only of the fleeting moment and then remain true till death. Transience and uncertainty are the way of love in this world.

That's certainly true.

NARRATOR: (highest pitch) Pierced by the force of words that strike home, she stops reading, (cadence) her eyes cloud with tears. (sung) Her father, too, brushes away tears of pity.

HEI'EMON: In the distant past as now, the heart of man remains forever fickle. (spoken) Karu, you too, listen well. If we were to compare *The Tale of the Heike* with Chiyo's condition, then Kiyomori would be Yaoya

Hanbei and Giō would be Chiyo, a woman who is discarded by an inconstant Kiyomori. What a despicable figure Kiyomori is! Last year when he came here to offer greetings after the marriage ceremony, I told him, "I have given you an incompetent daughter, if she does something of which you disapprove, then beat her, even bind her limbs to make her mend her ways. But never, never cast her away, I beg of you always to keep her with you. This is her third marriage. This village is small, so if she is sent back again, then I will not be able to show my face. Even if you hate her, take pity on me and take care of her. You must never divorce her, no matter what. Don't let go of her, ever! Don't ever send her away." At that time, he replied, "When you pass from the world, the front pallbearer will be Heiroku, and I, Hanbei, will bear the rear. Consider us to be your true sons. Now I am a townsman, Hanbei the grocer, but originally I was the son of the samurai Yamawaki Sanzaemon of Hamamatsu. You have my vows as both a samurai and as a merchant. I will never divorce Chiyo, so please rest your mind." I said, "Oh, how happy that makes me! I have never in my life lowered my head to a government official or landowner, or anyone, but now I bow to the floor with supplicant hands in gratitude for this pledge." (*sung*) Although I am an absentminded old man, that moment of joy sank deep into my bones, and I've never forgotten it. Rather, is it the young who forget? As proof that you have forgotten, (*spoken*) you used the trip to Hamamatsu to offer a memorial service for your father as an excuse to avoid responsibility. You set off after arranging to have Chiyo evicted by your mother. Only an ungrateful, unfilial person would smear his foster parent with his own crime. Don't you know the meaning of moral responsibility? Of the law? (*sung*) What kind of samurai scum are you? I can hear her mother's anger from the grave, "You threw away our precious daughter by marrying her to a beast! Didn't you check his background, his character!" (*high pitch*) How I regret this mistake!

NARRATOR: Hei'emon, reserved and prudent by nature, is overcome with emotion and lets his bitter feelings emerge. His daughters break down in tears.

HEI'EMON: I wonder whether you were fated never to hold a man's affection.

NARRATOR: (*emotional cadence*) He weeps loudly.

HANBEI: (*sung*) Then my wife's been divorced and sent home?

NARRATOR: Hanbei is shocked at the realization and feels as if he had been crushed by a heavy boulder. He is dumbfounded, dazed, and cannot speak for some time.

HANBEI: (*spoken*) Ochiyo is too coldhearted. Even when strangers exchange only a word or spend but a night in each other's company, one may understand the other's heart. (*sung*) Then how much more for us who have spent two intimate years and have created a child. Doesn't Ochiyo yet know her husband's heart? Why have you not spoken to me, explained? I can understand the reasons for your father's anger, (*spoken*) but I could not imagine even in a dream that I could be accused of filial ingratitude for smearing my foster parents with the blame for my crime. The more I repeat that I have not divorced her, the more I tarnish my parents. I shall show you a samurai spirit that never violates a vow. (*sung*) Watch and remove your doubts!

NARRATOR: Hanbei deftly unsheathes his sword, but Okaru quickly grabs hold of him, and Ochiyo, too, jumps up in surprise and opens the door to run to him.

OCHIYO: This only hurts me more! I have no anger for you.

NARRATOR: The two women are unable to stay his strong arm.

OKARU: Father, please help.

NARRATOR: They cry out desperately, but Hei'emon remains calm.

HEI'EMON: (*spoken*) Knowing you were here, I directed my remarks at you. Is this suicide provoked by unpleasant accusations? What a splendid notion! After you have killed yourself, consider the fine consequences. The Iemon couple will be shamed because it will seem that because they hated their daughter-in-law and divorced her, their own son had to commit suicide. What fantastic rumors will spread of your great feat, of your glorious fame! (*sung*) Daughters, don't restrain him, let him have his wish to kill himself. We shall sit back and be his audience.

NARRATOR: Hanbei's deeply filial heart is shaken by these words.

HANBEI: You are right. I am sorry. I apologize.

NARRATOR: (*emotional cadence*) He bows to the floor, hating himself.

HANBEI: (*spoken*) Chiyo, then let's go home together.

OCHIYO: Then, you will have me as your wife?

HANBEI: Yes, even if you die, I shall not return your bones. We will be husband and wife until the end of time.

Love Suicides on the Eve of the Kōshin Festival 307

FIGURE 46 From a 1920 kabuki production at the Osaka Naka-za theater. (Left) Nakamura Kasha as Okaru; (center) Nakamura Ganjirō I as Hanbei; (right) Nakamura Baigyoku III as Ochiyo. (Shōchiku Ōtani Library.)

OCHIYO: How grateful and happy I am! (*sung*) Father and sister, rejoice with me.

NARRATOR: Ochiyo rearranges her obi and moves close to Hanbei. Hei'emon chokes with tears.

HEI'EMON: (*spoken*) Hanbei, look at this wretched, sick old man. I'm so happy that you two will go home together that I'll try to forget my ills (*sung*) and show a happy father's face to (*high pitch*) his precious daughter as she sets off for home. (*high pitch*) I am so grateful to you. She is incompetent and doesn't please your parents, so I must depend solely on your heart's mercy. I am a weary, sick old man who trusts not in tomorrow. Even from the very depths of hell, I shall worry about Chiyo. Even if my eyes should close forever tomorrow, you will not have to fear poverty. I have arranged for ten or twenty gold *ryō* to be given to you. Work hard and expand your business. (*cadence*) Take good care of Chiyo. (*sung*) Let's toast to your renewed vows. Some saké, Okaru, bring some saké. What! We're out of saké? We're all one family. We need not stand on formalities. If we consider something to be saké, then saké it is. Bring some water in a pot.

NARRATOR: Love for his child makes even an old man impatient. He drains the cup in one gulp.

HEI'EMON: (spoken) Hanbei, I offer this toast of water for parent and child, for husband and wife.

NARRATOR: (sung) The cup goes back and forth, round and round. Although they pour and pour, it never drains; although they drink on and on, they never get drunk on toasts of water. Yet the father's face flushes with the grief (cadence) he cannot conceal in his heart.

HEI'EMON: (sung) Should we live, let us meet again. If death takes its toll, then this will be the final toast. In the life to come, the water fills the Pond of Eight Virtues in Paradise. I have no more concerns to tie me to this life. Return home as a married couple. Farewell!

NARRATOR: Fearing that he will embarrass himself if he speaks another word, (nagaji melody) he rearranges his nightclothes and gives detailed instructions to Okaru and returns to bed. However, he soon sits up again.

HEI'EMON: (spoken) Wait a moment! Okaru, to ensure that they never return, light a congratulatory fire at the gate.[11]

NARRATOR: (sung) Although she fears it will be a bad omen, she follows her father's wish and builds a small fire at the gate.

HEI'EMON: Congratulations! May this fire consecrate your union.

NARRATOR: The heart of the fire catches alight (high pitch) while in the hearts of this couple smolders the smoke of evanescence.

HEI'EMON: Even as ashes, you must never return!

NARRATOR: With these words, they part for the last time. For those left behind, for those who must depart, (highest pitch, scene cadence) it is the long farewell.

Act 3

Iemon greengrocery in Osaka, fifth day of fourth month, 1722

NARRATOR: (*sung*) Summer has come for the greengrocers, who lower bamboo shades to protect their wares from the parching sun. Shaded, too, is the life of Ochiyo, kept in the dark away from this shop in nearby Aburakakemachi, Shin'utsubo. Iemon, the master, is a devout follower of Pure Land Buddhism and, until the priest's recent death, regularly attended the sermons of the priest Ryōkai.[1] Iemon is a member of the volunteer parish group that works at the temple and assists at religious services. He has handed over the responsibilities of the shop to Hanbei and become a devout pilgrim, traveling to every one of the temples in Osaka. His wife, who attends to both house and shop, is all of five years his senior. She is in a bad temper from morning to night.

MOTHER: (*spoken*) What's Hanbei doing fooling around in the storehouse! All the vegetables are going to shrivel and wither away. Hey! Where's that Matsu? Hurry up and splash some water on the vegetables. And San! The starched clothes are dry. Take them in, fold them up, and pound them smooth on the clothes board. Ah, the clunk of your pounding reminds me that we must slice the turnips and greens for dinner. Hurry up, Matsu, today is the fifth, the eve of the Kōshin Festival;[2] the Kinoe-ne offering is due soon.[3] Put out our forked daikon radish as an offering to Daikokuten. (*sung*) Watch out, there, San! The fire under the kettle is too high.

NARRATOR: An endless barrage of commands fills every chink in the array of groceries. Her fiery tongue lashes about at such a frantic pace— (*cadence*) one would think that she had been born on busy New Year's Eve.[4] Tahei, her nephew, who is nothing like the aunt, returns from the market carrying freshly picked, first-of-the-season bamboo shoots on one end of his pole; on the other are various roots, ginger, chilies, and two melons.

TAHEI: (*song*) "Fresh and early for the season,". . . Oh dear, oh dear, I'm late.

MOTHER: (*spoken*) You lazy scoundrel! You left at six this morning. What time do you think it is? It's midday, I'll have you know. What woman had you by the nose? At this time of year, even if you carefully cover the goods with an awning, they'll still go bad. How could you expose this expensive merchandise to the sun all day! (*sung*) I'll take that pole and beat some sense into you.!

NARRATOR: She picks up the pole with a flourish, but Hanbei quickly comes running out.

HANBEI: Mother is certainly right. (*spoken*) Where have you been fooling around all this time? From the Sasaya shop in Okubimachi, a messenger came urgently demanding the bamboo shoots. The Tambaya shop people from Awazabori also came, wanting immediate delivery of the chestnuts. And the Asakuraya shop came for their order of chilies, but since we were out of them, I didn't know what to say. Even though it'll mean some extra work, go and deliver the orders immediately to make mother feel better.

TAHEI: Why? I've done nothing wrong. I was called over to the Yamashiroya shop nearby and just chatted for a few minutes. I've done nothing more than that! Someone said they want to meet you. They told me to tell you that they'd be waiting for you this afternoon. (*sung*) I'll deliver these things. You go on and take care of that business.

NARRATOR: Tahei gathers up the orders, (*cadence*) arranges the packages, and leaves.

(*sung*) When Hanbei hears "Yamashiroya," he thinks "Ochiyo's come," but he acts casually to keep his mother from becoming suspicious.

HANBEI: I wonder what the Yamashiroya people could want. I'll just run over to find out.

NARRATOR: He tries to run out but is grabbed by his mother.

MOTHER: (*spoken*) Now, son, where do you think you're going?

HANBEI: Someone wants to see me at Yamashiroya's.

MOTHER: Oh, now I see why you want to go there. That won't do. What's that nonchalant expression on your face? Do you think we don't know anything? That wife we hate and sent home—you visited her there on your return from Hamamatsu and brought her back on a leash. I know you're keeping her at your cousin's place in Tokiwamachi. You make every appearance of working hard, but every little chance you get, you go running off to your sweetheart. Do you think that I wouldn't notice? You've surely slandered my name about town. I've taken care of you for fifteen years, and yet you show no gratitude and ignore us while being magnificently dutiful to that woman we despise. (*sung*) You don't know the meaning of gratitude.

NARRATOR: Amid the violent taunts and tantrums of the mother, the priest Sainen, wearing a modest blue robe, enters the house without a greeting.

SAINEN: (*spoken*) As promised by Mr. Gon'emon of the Kumanoya, at the unveiling ceremony of the new temple bell made by Sōmi, there will be a light meal. We would like to have all the faithful, especially the local congregation, together for the service. Please bring your spouse. (*sung*) We shall begin immediately.

NARRATOR: Having tossed off this message, he quickly takes his leave. (*cadence*) Only a fool would depend on this blundering priest for the salvation of his soul.

MOTHER: (*spoken*) Hey, Father! They've come from the Kumanoya to call you to the ceremony. Hurry up and go with them. I'm not going. (*sung*) Hurry! Be on your way.

NARRATOR: Her voice and manner are snappish. Iemon, a lay devotee of the religious life, has given up all to seek happiness in the next world.

IEMON: (*spoken*) What! Mother, what are you yelling about? You keep Hanbei waiting and waiting, treating him as if he were an enemy. It's hardly unusual for young folk to be called out to meet someone. Don't worry about such trivial matters.

MOTHER: Listen, too much kindness, and the child will make a fool of his parents. I renounced my real nephew, Tahei, to will this house and business to a complete stranger—this lazy fellow. What is wicked about that?

IEMON: Now, Mother, everyone is perfectly aware of that. There's no use digging up that business again. The best medicine for anger is prayers to the Buddha. In any case, you who burn with a fiery, choleric humor have been called by the hand of Amida to lead you to Amida himself. Let's go together to join him in the Western Paradise (*sung*) and forget your worries.

MOTHER: (*spoken*) Never! If we both leave, then he'll bring that woman Ochiyo into this house. I won't have any frolicking in my house while I'm away. You go by yourself. Even if my head gets dizzy and I faint or suddenly die, just go on doing as you please.

IEMON: Now, Mother, just this minute Reverend Sainen came to invite us. Are you going to make a liar out of me? There's a commandment against telling lies. Recently at a certain temple, I heard a sermon that discussed in detail the five commandments.[5] Even though there may be three hundred or five hundred commandments, the sermon said that after all, it all comes down to that juicy red mussel . . . you know . . . the one between a woman's legs. Your scolding of Hanbei is due to its powers; (*sung*) my counsel to you is spurred by the power of its muscles. Let us be reborn together on the same lotus bed.

NARRATOR: Iemon jokes hoping to humor her, (*cadence*) but with no effect.

MOTHER: (*spoken*) Well then. . . . You just go on ahead. If I try to chant sutras, angry as I am, (*sung*) the words will all stick in my throat. As soon as I calm down a bit, I'll follow you. In any case, that lot of incompetent parishioners should realize that it's best to postpone the service at times like this. They haven't got a bone of sensitivity in them. In that prayer group, not a single soul has a brain in his head.

NARRATOR: Harsh words from this fearless and utterly selfish woman.

IEMON: Well, then, I'll go first. You come later. (*spoken*) They say, "to hear rain on a thatched roof or the Buddha's teaching you must go outside." Today, if you go out for the day, you can witness another marvel. At the Ikudama Daihōji temple, they have on special display a man-made mountain decorating the garden that is said to be the stage prop from the fourth act of Chikugo's play *Battles at Kawa-nakajima*.[6] You can't learn about such wonderful things without going outside. (*sung*) Yes, yes, it's all thanks and praise to the marvelous Amida Buddha.

NARRATOR: Fingering his rosary beads, (*cadence*) he mumbles prayers and takes his leave. (*sung*) Hanbei, silenced by his mother's barrage of complaints, (*emotional cadence*) finally raises his head to speak, his eyes clouded with tears.

HANBEI: (*spoken*) Listen to me, mother, even though I may sound insincere at this point. I was raised around the hearth of a samurai family, but since the age of twenty-two, you have taken care of me and have even renounced your only nephew to give me both the house and the business. I am grateful to you from the depths of my soul and never neglect your wishes. I owe you so much, and if you hate my wife, then I should divorce her to fulfill my filial and social duty. But since Ochiyo was evicted while I was away in Hamamatsu, rumors have spread that Hanbei's mother has divorced Ochiyo because she hates her. Even if the problem is entirely Chiyo's fault, it looks bad for a mother-in-law to divorce her son's wife.[7] The world is sympathetic to unfortunate heroes like Yoshitsune,[8] and only you have been blamed. How will you be able to deal with young people if your name is sullied? Father, too, will be shamed. Listen to my plea. For just a little while, bury your animosity, be gracious, and allow Chiyo to return. After that I will formally write out a bill of divorce and dismiss her. I can do that as her husband. Even if the wife is a princess or an aristocrat, when the man divorces her, no one will say anything. Chiyo will not be bitter toward you; rather, she will consider you merciful. This is my first request in all my sixteen years here. (*sung*) Death does not always take the old before the young. Should I, for instance, die first, your one word of agreement will be worth more than a million prayers offered for my salvation. Your assent will be (*highest pitch*) as precious as the prayers of sages or famous priests.

NARRATOR: Caught between duty and love toward his wife and her family and his own parents, (*high pitch*) Hanbei's emotions are a tangled web[9] from which tears stream forth. (*sung*) His mother's face radiates joy.

MOTHER: (*spoken*) Hmm, although it hardly seems possible, since you two have always been so loving and close. But tears don't lie. Are you really going to divorce her?

HANBEI: If I were trying to trick you, do you think that I would make this formal request?

MOTHER: Oh, how happy this makes me! I don't want to be a demon. Are you positive you'll get rid of her? If you're playing for time and plan to deceive me—look! I'll slice my throat with this butcher's knife! Will you kill your mother or divorce your wife? The choice is yours. Ah, I feel as if my soul's been liberated from all the suffering of this dark world. I've become a living incarnation of the Buddha. I must hurry to be in time for the meal at the temple. (*sung*) Although my husband will never desert my bed, I'm sure he's waiting for me in a temper. (*spoken*) Namu Amida Butsu. All Hail to Amida Buddha. San! As you're dressed, come with me. Ah, Namu Amida Butsu. Matsu! Don't you dare steal any of the dried fruits. Namu Amida.

NARRATOR: (*sung*) Mixing prayers with commands, (*exit cadence*) she mutters her way out of the house.

(*sung*) Ochiyo bears the weight of a five-month pregnancy, but her feet scurry lightly along, (*cadence*) skirts raised in her hand.

OCHIYO: (*sung*) Ah, what a long while it's been since I've seen the inside of the house! Oh Hanbei dear, what a fine day to walk proudly through the neighborhood to come home. What a joy it is!

NARRATOR: (*cadence*) She hugs Hanbei tightly, (*sung*) but he remains cold and stiff.

HANBEI: (*spoken*) Why did you return? Mother left just now. Didn't you meet her?

OCHIYO: Yes, I did. She stopped by the Yamashiroya and looked in with a smiling face that I'd never seen before and said, "How sad, how wretched it was for you. I was wrong to cause you so much grief. From now on, I'll never tell you to leave or mention the word. I swear with all my heart. I don't have a daughter of my own, and you're the only daughter-in-law I have in this world. I have only you to offer prayers and memorials for me in the next life. Only you will take care of the funeral and care for my grave. You must be faithful and serve my needs. I've grown fond of you, too. I'm just on my way to the prayer service—you run along and hurry home. I'll see you later on, hurry now, hurry on." Her kind words seemed to flow from her heart like water from an upturned bucket. All this I owe to you. My gratitude to you knows no bounds. And Matsu, it's been quite a while since I've seen you. Already there are mosquitoes all over the place. Without a mistress in the house, even the hooks for the mosquito nets never get put up. Is San off taking a nap? The winter clothes will never be washed. Look at the dust on these shelves. The floor heater, too, hasn't been covered over yet. I'd better take a look at the daikon pickles. (*sung*) Where shall I begin? I'm just too excited. Let's start with something familiar.

NARRATOR: She sits down before the kettle, but even though she boils the water, it stays cold. (*cadence*) Pity this happy woman unaware of her fate. (*sung*) Hanbei ignores her.

HANBEI: (*spoken*) Matsu! Don't just sit there dreaming, go to the storehouse (*sung*) and choose some good mushrooms.

NARRATOR: He tries to avoid the eyes of others by staring at Ochiyo's face until tears cloud his eyes.

HANBEI: (*spoken*) How pitiful. You appear clever, but your woman's heart is naive. Did you really believe mother? Every word was a lie! But as she always says, she follows bits of Buddha's Law and even understands the meaning of mercy. She put aside her own nephew and took a stranger like me for her heir. Isn't that proof she isn't wicked to the core? Fate determines relationships. Even natural parents and children don't always get along. Yet a brief encounter on a riverboat may lead one to think fondly of a stranger. This is the way of the world. However awful our plight, it won't help us as a couple in the next life to cause others to view mother as a heartless and cruel woman because of her treatment of you. She is not intentionally evil. I shall summon her back, win back her favor, and divorce you with my own hands.

OCHIYO: What! Then after all, I am to be divorced?

HANBEI: How can you be surprised? We're both prepared for the end. We shall die with nobility and leave no coward's name behind. My foster parents will not be shamed, nor will your father bear any grudge. We shall die bravely. I tried every persuasion possible on mother. I've written a last will and prepared my death shroud—even the sword is packed in this blanket. I don't have a grain of regret for this world, but I don't want any rumors to start that we died because of money problems. (*sung*) That alone worries me.

NARRATOR: Hanbei breaks down in tears.

OCHIYO: If you have fulfilled your duty to your parents, (*highest pitch*) then I have no regrets.

NARRATOR: They embrace, clinging to each other tightly and (*cadence*)[10] collapse onto the floor.

(*sung*) The mother is more worried about the young couple than the Buddhist service and suddenly finds herself back home just as the neighborhood shops are closing up.

MOTHER: (*spoken*) Oh, Ochiyo, have you returned? As I told you earlier, I was wrong and apologize for causing you such grief. How hard it must have been for you. Consider me a living Buddha. We are not long in this sad world. How can we stand by and see others suffering. It's awful. Oh, Hanbei, I've sharpened the kitchen knife, sharp as a sword. Namu Amida Butsu. (*sung*) All Hail the Buddha Amida.

NARRATOR: Her words send a signal to Hanbei. She thinks that Ochiyo is ignorant, (*cadence*) but only Mother is the Buddha left in the dark.[11] (*sung*) The couple rejoice to see her happy face and can leave with no regrets, but death falls as rain. (*cadence*) How pitiful they are as they struggle to hold back tears.

MOTHER: (*sung*) Hanbei, haven't you forgotten something? On long summer days, we're all likely to be absentminded. Can't you remember?

Ochiyo, don't cry, come over here. Are you still afraid of me? (*sung*) Come here, closer to me.

NARRATOR: She summons Ochiyo as if she were coaxing a cat.

OCHIYO: Yes, yes, I'm coming.

NARRATOR: But when she gets up to approach his mother, Hanbei jumps between them and drags Ochiyo aside.

HANBEI: (*spoken*) Only the wife is beyond the control of the in-laws. It is I who despise you. I divorce you this instant! Leave at once! Listen everyone, San, you too, all you clerks, listen well. Hanbei has divorced his wife! No one is to spread rumors against Mother anywhere. (*sung*) Don't just stand about, Chiyo, leave at once!

NARRATOR: (*emotional cadence*) He glares bitterly, but tears glisten in his eyes.

MOTHER: (*spoken*) Listen, daughter, I'm not the one divorcing you. Parents can never run the affairs of their son and daughter-in-law. (*sung*) Don't hold a grudge against me.

NARRATOR: Ochiyo silently weeps.

MOTHER: (*spoken*) Hmm. . . . Tears mean you still hate me. If you do, then speak up. I'll listen.

OCHIYO: No, I have nothing against you who are so kind. (*sung*) I've no . . .

NARRATOR: (*high pitch*) She collapses in tears, unable to continue.

HANBEI: (*spoken*) There's no need for you to say anything. She has no bitterness for you. (*sung*) You are too slow to leave, hurry up!

NARRATOR: Hanbei grabs her arm and thrusts her out the door. While signaling with his eyes, he whispers.

HANBEI: I'll follow soon—right after you.

NARRATOR: (*high pitch*) Both are in tears (*low threatening*) and feel regret at this (*cadence*) final parting from home.[12] (*sung*) Hanbei quickly slams shut the door to hide the weakness in his heart and immediately closes up the shop. The temple bell sounds dusk at six, or is it the bell of evening darkness at eight? Time is confused and their hearts unsettled (*cadence*) as their spirits race toward the dark hour of death.

(*sung*) Even at the forced separation of a married couple still in love, the mother offers no farewells. She simply turns away and goes into the inner room to chant sutras to the steady beat of the sin-absolving bell. The maid nods off into darkness, blind to the light that illuminates the distinctions between good and evil. Had she greater vision, she would spy the sixteen-inch blade hidden in Hanbei's bundle. "This will guide us through hell" are his thoughts as he picks up the will sealed with his spirit in a box. "Will we fall into hell or rise to paradise?" Although uncertain of the outcome, he is sure of his death shroud, pure white. (*low threatening*) He wraps his bundle in the crimson cloth, which seems to glisten with drops of blood. His determination grows stronger. "We mustn't fail now!" Yet from the other side of the screen, the sharp sound of the bell and (*threatening*) piercing voice of his mother's chants strike terror in his heart, and his whole body quivers. He tiptoes on unsure feet, releases the latch with shaking hands, (*cadence*) and finally slips through the door. At the gate he calls out.

HANBEI: (*spoken*) Ochiyo, are you there?

OCHIYO: Yes, I'm here.

HANBEI: We've finally escaped the crocodile's jaws. (*sung*) Let's go.

NARRATOR: He takes her hand, but she holds back.

OCHIYO: (*spoken*) Please wait just a moment. This will not do. I returned but once, only to be divorced and rejected by you. This will worry me through the next life. Here at the gate, please say just the words—we are not divorced.

HANBEI: How can you have such a trivial complaint! Tonight is the fifth, the eve of Kōshin.[13] Isn't it enough to believe that as man and wife, we're freeing ourselves from this house forever?

OCHIYO: You're right. Let us, hand in hand, depart from this world. Freed from the cycle of rebirth, released from delusion.

NARRATOR: (*sung*) Tonight is the final journey of these lambs[14] (*scene cadence*) led to the slaughter by fleeing legs.

The Farewell Journey of Hanbei and Ochiyo

NARRATOR:[15]

> (*sung*) No regrets for summer past, a light cotton gown cast aside.
> Bush warblers fondly nurture eggs as their own,
> only to watch them become alien cuckoo birds.[16]
> For sixteen years I, too, was nurtured by foster parents,
> and though their own, was not their true child.
> This body, no longer human, abandons them to follow

FIGURE 47 Bunraku puppets showing Ochiyo and Hanbei leaving their house, intent on suicide. *(Waseda Theater Museum.)*

(*cadence*) the nightingale's song that leads to death[17]
(*sung*) Are we of the same flock, man and wife,
who bear upon our backs this scarlet cloth—
stained from the nightingale's blood?[18]
Legs weary of life guide us through the darkness
on this foggy summer night,
the fifth day of the fourth month, the eve of Kōshin.
Our vow to be one in death
will be realized on this holy night.
They mingle stealthily among the many pilgrims.
Hanbei, a greengrocer with many products under one roof,[19]
Is not like the "Han" ["half"] of his name.
His roots are firm and his character serious,
but plucked by circumstance, his flowering heart

Love Suicides on the Eve of the Kōshin Festival   319

FIGURE 48 Bunraku puppets showing Hanbei and Ochiyo on the road to death.

is ashamed that certain vows are unfulfilled.
The wise do not waver, nor do the brave know fear.[20]
Such is the natural seed of Hanbei, (*cadence*) samurai born.

(*sung*) And for Ochiyo too, her third marriage bud withers before it blossoms.
She strove to perform her duties well, to be a flower of perfection,
and listened gingerly to her parents' orders.
She held her husband's parents dear as a precious meadow pea
and served them faithfully day and night.
Never refusing to obey, she served them like royalty.
"Mother, (*highest pitch*) by nature impossible to please—
bitter as dropwort, prickly as nettles—
Pressed, harassed, and tormented me to the edge of despair.
I wanted to throw myself into the depths of a river valley,
to tumble like a pear, a gourd, and be crushed,

to become a nun or fisher girl, floating like laver in the sea.
My spirit strives for heights but will never know clear cool skies,
only the pain of peppered mustard,
till we reach the pure lotus on the mountaintop.
What shall become of our bodies, once gone never to return?
How sad that the world will snigger,
blaming that horrible mother-in-law for driving us to death."
Hanbei sheds tears of gratitude for Ochiyo's concern.
"If you hold such noble sentiments, then what of me?
I will die without repaying any of their many years of love and care.
How awful that Heaven's retribution awaits this ungrateful son."
Ochiyo sees his tears of blood fall like cherries and runs to him.
"I too should care for my sick father;
instead I shall cause grief to him.
But we are a couple joined as a single pine tree."
She clings tightly to him.
From the tips of the pine branches dewdrops fall
and seem to spring up like mushrooms out of the earth.
"Listen to the loud voices of the crowd.
They are singing a rowdy song returning from the shrine.
We mustn't be seen!"
They hide in the shadows.

(*song*) (*Crowd*) "My life of love is a shamisen without strings.[21]
I wait till dawn, but no sound of love.
The way of the world, the way of love.
Look there, see the gloomy clouds
as they wrap the mountain in darkness.
A toast, a drink!
Don't say no, just one sip.
If you say no,
then, enough for me.
Have it your way.
That's how it'll be.
Now a fine young woman
in her fullest bloom
sways her willowy hips as a young wife will.

Strutting, strutting, with supple hips,
floating down the lane.
These lovers will float on the River of Fame.[22]
Yes, surely they'll reach the River of Fame.
That's how it will be."

The revelers pass on, and (*cadence*) the pair come out into the open again.

HANBEI: (*sung*) That bit from a popular song just now: "They'll reach the River of Fame. That's how it will be." The words of the song must refer to us. It is a good omen. Let's hurry on.

NARRATOR: (*high pitch*) Brave words from a determined heart. "Such joy!" are his words that carry them along together. Ochiyo is touched by his passion, and with racing hearts they rush on toward death. (*cadence*) The crowd disperses into silence.

(*sung*) They find a moment's respite from their journey to death in an area of temples and shrines, now completely quiet. Near the stable on the edge of Ikudama Shrine,[23] they stop at a donation office for Nara's Tōdaiji temple, which is known to save all, even those most desperately enmeshed in the desires of this world. They pause to pray at the gate of "Release from Delusion" (*emotional cadence*) and trust in the power of the Buddha.

HANBEI: (*sung*) Ochiyo, the sutra's words, "the soul, constantly transformed, travels endless worlds,"[24] show us that our spirits float in constant reincarnation, depending on our karma. (*spoken*) Chiyo, your posthumous name will be "Fūgaku-ryōkun-shin'nyo,"[25] "A Modest Laywoman, a Beautiful Fragrance Borne by the Wind." Hanbei the Grocer will become "Roshū-zen-jōmon,"[26] "A Gentle Layman, Autumn Dew Seeking Salvation." (*sung*) While still breathing, because we're already among the dead, I had hoped to let our bodies rest in peace in this temple garden, far from the mundane world, but we don't have the strength to open the locked gate. This is the office that accepts donations for repair of the Great Buddha Hall of Tōdaiji in Nara. (*spoken*) Over the last few years, the priest Ryōkai preached here on the doctrine that all souls will be saved by the merciful Buddha. Here at this very spot, even now after the holy man's death, (*sung*) my parents continue to come as devout followers of his teachings. Since we have a connection to this place, let us leave our last thoughts here, unless you wish to die elsewhere.

OCHIYO: I am ready to die and desire nothing. Be it in water, or fire, I only want to die with you holding me as your wife.

HANBEI: (*spoken*) How happy your words make me. As I have written in this last testament, ever since I was adopted sixteen years ago, I have tried to please our customers near and far, rich or poor. When business was slow, I traveled the streets peddling our wares. The shop was just a small vegetable stand when I came. Now we have profits enough to be a modest moneylender. (*sung*) Yet we must accept our fate of never knowing even an hour's true peace of mind. I thought of dying, five times all told. I was still bitter even when we became engaged. After we were married, my hope that all my suffering would clear away came true. Yet soon we were forced to part and now are together again, only to leap into the jaws of death. You have been drawn down by my ill fate. My chest aches and my stomach burns when I think of the pain we shall cause your father and sister. Ah! Could I but change this fate!

NARRATOR: His fists tighten in anger. (*highest pitch*) He presses his hands on his knees, as his body shakes and (*cadence*) tears flow, mingling with the morning dew.

OCHIYO: (*sung*) Now you are the one to have foolish regrets. You need not worry about them. My father and sister will bear this tragedy better than you. They sent us off with a toast of plain water and even burned a farewell fire at the gate, leaving us with the strong words, "Don't ever return here alive!" No more time for such worries, quick, kill me. Listen! Listen over there, over there, from all directions the alarm bells are ringing. Hurry, before someone comes, before they find us.

NARRATOR: She hastens the final moment (*cadence*) and like a clinging vine, holds her husband tightly and weeps.

HANBEI: (*spoken*) You are right. Those were useless regrets. From this moment on, no more words or thoughts for parents or siblings. No matter what happens, not a word about them. (*sung*) Come over here.

NARRATOR: He opens the blanket and places it on the ground.

HANBEI: (*spoken*) Ochiyo, this blanket is not simply a covering. It is the flower of Buddha's Law, (*sung*) a crimson lotus flower that will carry us to paradise—our last wish for rebirth on the same lotus. This last testament for parents, brother, and sister in this envelope will reach them tomorrow. Prepare your heart and mind. Your final prayers. Now is the end.

NARRATOR: He pulls his sword from its sheath and thinks sadly that this short sword, handed down from generation to generation, was never intended to pierce its heir. The end of hapless Hanbei. He thinks of long ago, and his hand shakes (*cadence*) and tears flow.

NARRATOR: (*sung*) Ochiyo turns toward the Western Paradise, hands folded in prayer.

OCHIYO: The bright light of the Buddha of Everlasting Life illuminates the ten realms of existence. None who seek mercy will be abandoned. All will be saved. Namu Amida Buddha, Hail to Amida Buddha.[27]

NARRATOR: Before she can complete her prayer, Hanbei pulls her to his side and aims the blade at her throat.

OCHIYO: Wait! Please wait a moment! Wait.

NARRATOR: She desperately tears herself away from him, but Hanbei glares in anger.

HANBEI: (*spoken*) To hesitate at this point means that you are not ready. Does this blade scare you? Are you afraid to die? You coward!

OCHIYO: No, no, never. I am ready. I am not a coward. (*sung*) My prayers just now were for myself. (*highest pitch*) How pitiful this child within my womb, a boy or girl, not yet five months old. Let me offer prayers for its innocent soul. What a joy it would be to give birth to a healthy child! All my preparations and plans for motherhood were wasted. How it hurts to think that we will kill it before it sees the light of day!

NARRATOR: (*emotional cadence*) She collapses in tears. (*sung*) Hanbei, too, weeps.

HANBEI: How could I forget the baby? (*spoken*) I was afraid to mention it for fear of hurting you, (*sung*) so I kept silent.

NARRATOR: (*highest pitch*) They weep together, (*cadence*) sharing their deepest grief. (*sung*) They align themselves as birds, feather to feather, but just then a rooster gives its dawn crow, hastening their final moments.

HANBEI: No time before the dawn. Tomorrow we shall be united in the next world. Our parting is only a short farewell for this life.

NARRATOR: They invoke the final precious ten prayers to Buddha, and while praying the last, he stabs her throat with all his strength. She writhes in pain struggling to breathe as the sword seeks the cord that connects her to life. Her limbs writhe in anguish as her body passes through the four, (*high pitch*, cadence) the eight sufferings of this life.[28]

NARRATOR: (*sung*) On this sixth day of the fourth month, the morning dew settles on the grass. (*cadence*) The crimson blanket hosts her everlasting fame.

(*sung*) Her age is twenty-seven. The checkered pattern of her kimono is now dyed red with her blood. Hanbei arranges her body and clothes before cutting her long obi into two. He bares his chest and ties the obi firmly above his waist. He holds the sword blade toward himself with one hand and reads two farewell poems.

> (*spoken*) Cast aside the past;
> think no more of duty.
> My body will wither;
> my soiled name will remain,
> (*cadence*) my only regret.

> (*sung*) Blown from afar by
> the winds of Hamamatsu,
> a sad cry echoes
> through the pines
> along the seashore.[29]

We now die and become Buddhas.

He thrusts the blade into his left side and in one motion pulls it around to the right and then slashes his throat. Ties to this world are severed and his breath sucked away. In the light of dawn, the guard at Tōdaiji temple's donation office catches sight of the pair and cries out, "Suicide, a lovers' suicide, suicide!" His voice carried by the Hamamatsu winds (*high pitch*) echoes throughout this peaceful land, where not a branch is disturbed.[30] The sight of this extraordinary suicide tells a story at which one can only wonder.

(The postscript is almost exactly the same as the one at the end of *Twins at the Sumida River*.)

Tethered Steed and the Eight Provinces of Kantō
(Kanhasshū tsunagi-uma)

First performed on the fifteenth day of the first month 1724, a year and eight months after *Love Suicides at the Kōshin Festival*, this final play was meant to be an auspicious opening to the New Year.[1] Chikamatsu had been quite ill for much of this long break, and he perhaps sensed that this was to be his swan song: it is his longest drama. He died on the twenty-second day of the eleventh month of the same year.

Judging by the commentary in the illustrated books of this play published during its first run, its reception was favorable, especially act 4; however, during the third month a fire destroyed much of Osaka, including the Takemoto-za theater itself. It was rumored that the burning in act 4 of a bonfire on a mountainside in the shape of the character [大] *dai*, meaning "great" or "large," in imitation of the Kyoto *obon* festival to see ancestral spirits back to the nether world, was a bad omen for Osaka, the first character of which is the same *dai*, read as "ō." Perhaps for that reason, the play was not performed again until the Meiji period in 1890.[2] It nevertheless remained in print over the centuries, and today is considered one of Chikamatsu's most important works. (Nakamura Ganjirō III's "Chikamatsu-za" troupe is preparing a kabuki revival.)

The collection of stories surrounding Minamoto no Yorimitsu (Raikō, 948–1021) and his "Four Guardian" (Shitennō) warriors was a popular subject in theater from the mid-seventeenth century onward, beginning with a long string of "Kinpira" (son of Kintoki, one of the "Four Guardians") plays particularly popular in Edo. This focus on what Chikamatsu terms the first Genji shogun, Yorimitsu, was not entirely a matter of chance.[3] The ruling Tokugawa house claimed descent from the same Genji lineage, and so the plays were as much about "Tokugawa" as about Heian Japan. Chikamatsu himself wrote several variations based on these legends in his mature period, clearly using them as a context in which to discuss current Tokugawa government matters, sometimes praising and sometimes criticizing government policy and actions.

Recently, *Tethered Steed* has been the focus of work by several scholars who have, from different angles, shown the play to be a complex portrayal of the samurai ideal and its heroic demands on the individual.[4] The theme of honoring one's promise (*keiyaku*), which came to be important in Chikamatsu's late works, takes center stage here. Like Hanbei in *Kōshin Festival*, Minamoto no Yorihira cherishes keeping a pledge as an ideal to be defended even with one's life. He chooses to honor his pledge to join the enemy Yoshikado, even though it means death. The protagonist Yorihira, a historical figure about whom almost nothing is known, is portrayed at the same time as flawed and noble, as well as intelligent, compassionate, and resolute. Decisions he makes at three points in the play prove crucial to his fate. The first is in act 1, during the ceremony to choose a successor to the shogun Yorimitsu from between his two younger brothers, Yorinobu and Yorihira. The Genji clan leaders have to choose an arrow in the dark: a majority of white arrows and the older brother, Yorinobu, will be the shogun; red arrows mean it will be Yorihira. Yorinobu is eventually chosen, but while the lights are still out, the young Tomozuna, who is a little tipsy, makes a pass at Kochō, a pretty woman in service to Lady Yorimitsu. Kochō, hoping to show herself loyal to Yorinobu with whom she in love, immediately cuts off the string of Tomozuna's court cap and raises an alarm. She asks for the candles to be lit in order to expose Tomozuna's act. Yorihira quickly intervenes and has everyone cut off their cap strings before the lights are lit, thereby saving Tomozuna from shame and possible suicide for his frivolousness at such an important formal gathering. This "cap-string cutting" incident is based on a well-known Chinese story originally from the *Shuo Yuan*, which demonstrates a ruler's quick-thinking compassion for his retainers. The incident shows Yorihira to be a natural leader, one eligible to succeed Yorimitsu, ahead even of his older brother.

The second crucial decision comes in act 2. Kochō encourages Yorihira to meet secretly with Lady Eika, who is betrothed to Yorinobu, because Kochō wants Yorinobu for herself. Yorihira, who intimates that he harbors a fancy for Eika, agrees to the plan and is led to Eika's bedroom. After their tryst in the dark, Eika is shocked to find that her lover is Yorihira and not Yorinobu as she expected, but she has no regrets and the pair flee.

Yorihira goes on to honor the consequences of his affair with Eika. Along the way, they are accosted by a gang of robbers commanded by Yoshikado, son of Taira no Masakado (d. 940) who led an unsuccessful insurrection against the Heian court in the mid-tenth century. Eika is captured in the fight, and Yorihira makes a third decision, choosing to pledge his loyalty to Yoshikado and join the rebellion against his own brothers in order to save Eika. This action brings on the crisis of the play.

As with *Battles at Kawa-nakajima* a few years earlier, Chikamatsu does not present the "villain" character Yoshikado as evil but as a noble opponent of high lineage. The climax of act 3 is the self-sacrifice of Tomozuna to save the life of Yorihira and persuade him to relent and give up his pledge to Yoshikado. Only when Tomozuna is dying does Yorihira learn that it was Tomozuna whom he saved by having everyone cut his court-cap strings. Just as in the Chinese tale, the one thus saved from humiliation is happy to fight fearlessly and die bravely for his lord.

Although Chikamatsu presents Tomozuna's actions as heroic and noble, the final focus of the climactic act 3 is on the aria-like song (*kudoki*) of Tomozuna's mother (Aunt Mita) who sings her grief:

AUNT MITA: (*spoken*) Who is it you call "mother"? A woman with a child
is a mother. (*sung*) From today, I am childless, an old woman all alone.
(*highest pitch*) Don't speak (*cadence*) foolish words!

Aunt Mita represents another theme of the play, that of the conflict between the private sphere of family, in which love and compassion are predominant, and the public sphere of duty, which often demands the cold suppression of private emotions. Aunt Mita's dialogue with the shogun Yorimitsu in act 3 is a fascinating discourse on the importance of compassion and mercy in rulers. Here again, the focus is on the "promise" that Yorimitsu once made to Aunt Mita. Tomozuna's action in secretly serving his lord Yorihira by his death reflects an ideal presented in the *bushidō* treatise *Hagakure*, thought to have been completed around 1716, in which such service is termed *shinobu-koi* (hidden love of a retainer for his lord) or *hikage-bōkō* (service from the shadows).

Chikamatsu, however, has a far more complex sense of samurai honor and duty than that depicted in *Hagakure*. Chikamatsu's works were an important element in the popular discourse on creating the image of heroic nobility and honor. His contribution is a humanistic one: the samurai must know compassion (*nasake*) and be sensitive (*aware*) to human psychology, particularly its emotional, "weak" side.[5] This idea had, of course, been a current in the discourse on the samurai, as in battle narratives such as *Kōyō gunkan*, which were so influential in the Tokugawa era.[6]

The opening lines of the play suggest a theme of cause and effect in the affairs of man and how one seemingly minor choice, action, or happening can have major consequences. The passions of Yorihira and Tomozuna lead them to commit indiscretions that affect a broad canvas. Both of these "fallen" figures choose the path of honor, offering their lives to clear their names or to aid those to whom they are indebted. Yorihira uses the metaphor of snow as a cleansing agent at the end of act 2 when he throws it at the feet of his brother and again in act 3 when he finally explains himself, defiantly refusing to renege on his pledge to join the enemy Yoshikado. The view of responsibility for one's actions presented here is severe. Honor is not bought cheaply, and Chikamatsu's play depicts the consequences of such an ethic.

Acts 4 and 5 shift the focus to the theme of the power of legitimate government as represented by the supernatural powers invested in particular swords received or blessed by the gods who protect the imperial center, a major theme of traditional battle literature from earliest times.[7] The nō play *Tsuchigumo* (*Earth Spider*),[8] the source of the action in acts 4 and 5, is a fantastic dance piece, but it is also about protecting the center from threatening forces at the periphery, in this case a supernatural spider. Chikamatsu merges three elements: the Masakado-Yoshikado rebellion, the vengeful spirit of jealousy represented by Kochō (Yoshikado's sister) who becomes the earth spider, and the traditional "earth spider" story, with its focus on the might of the "spider killing" (*kumo-kirimaru*, or *hizamaru*) sword, representing the power of the "legitimate" forces who protect the imperial center.

Tethered Steed, like the other period plays, alludes to various Japanese and Chinese classics that support Chikamatsu's themes. Taken together, the references in *Tethered Steed* to Chinese works suggest an underlying complexity in the affairs of men at both the public and private level. The opening lines are from a famous passage originally in the *Han shu* (*History of the Former Han Dynasty*); it is also in the collection *Wen xuan* (*Selections of Refined Literature*), popular in Japan. The scholar-official Mei Cheng tries to dissuade the Wu king from starting a rebellion against the Han. His rhetorical method is to use parables and metaphors to show how we must perceive the effects of each action as it occurs: small, seemingly insignificant matters may grow to have a tremendous, unforeseen impact. These opening lines suggest that in the spirit of Mei Cheng, Chikamatsu was offering his play to the samurai rulers at the top as well as to his fellow Osakan townsmen. In the same opening, he quotes a line from the *Analects* in which Confucius describes the wise ruler as one who can perceive the truth behind slander or false accusations and who is able to maintain his position without wavering.

Later in the same act, Chikamatsu quotes from the *Shiji* (*The Book of History*) on the implementation of new laws and how those at the top must adhere to them if the populace at large is going to submit to the rule of law, which is an implicit criticism of the Tokugawa government. Next comes a witty reference to a passage in the Daoist treatise *Lao tzu*, which likens ruling a large country to cooking a dish of small fish. This begins Watanabe Tsuna's lecture delivered during a comic scene. Tsuna's incisive criticism of an overbearing government that invades the private lives of individuals is a direct comment on the Tokugawa sumptuary legislation being implemented at the time of the play.

In act 3, Chikamatsu then uses the opening section of the Daoist treatise *Chuang tzu* as the foundation stone for a fascinating exchange between Aunt Mita and the shogun Yorimitsu on the nature of government and particularly on the importance of the rights and needs of the private sphere of the individual or family in relation to the public sphere of government. The *Chuang tzu* passage presents a case for the need for an awareness of relativity in individual perceptions, which are necessarily limited by personal experience and consequently for the importance of understanding perspectives outside one's own. Allusions to both the rationalist Confucian and the mystical Daoist streams of Chinese thought support Chikamatsu's discourse on the complex nature of both individual psychology, with its desires and passions, and individual perceptions and their importance in the context of effective, enlightened government.

The "Yorimitsu" world, with the famous "Four Guardian Demons," led by Watanabe Tsuna and Sakata Kintoki, was a popular subject throughout the Tokugawa period and is still part of children's reading. In the mid-seventeenth century, "Kinpira" plays dominated Edo jōruri theater for decades, and Chikamatsu himself wrote several plays based on these legends. The *Zen-taiheiki*,[9] published in the 1690s, is a popular history covering the period between 907 and 1113 and was a major source for this play. The notes to the translation make it clear that Chikamatsu also was alluding to many other writings on famous warriors to construct a complex portrait of the samurai. One can see this play as Chikamatsu's final contribution to the lively debate in the first quarter of the eighteenth century on the nature of both the samurai as individuals and samurai government. His humanistic view remained an important undercurrent in Japanese culture until the modern era.

Tethered Steed and the Eight Provinces of Kantō
(*Kanhasshū tsunagi-uma*)

CAST OF CHARACTERS

Minamoto House (Genji)

Yorimitsu (Raikō) (Minamoto no Yorimitsu): shogun, elder brother of Yorinobu and Yorihira.
Lady Yorimitsu: wife of Yorimitsu.
Yorinobu (Minamoto no Yorinobu; Kawachi no Kami): younger brother of Yorimitsu, chosen to become the next shogun after Yorimitsu's retirement.
Iyo no Naishi: wife of Yorinobu.
Yorihira (Minamoto no Yorihira; Dewa no Kanja): younger brother of Yorimitsu and Yorinobu. He steals Yorinobu's betrothed, Lady Eika, and joins forces with the enemy Yoshikado.

Minamoto Retainers

Tsuna (Watanabe no Tsuna): one of Yorimitsu's "Four Guardian Demon" generals.
Kintoki (Sakata no Kintoki): one of Yorimitsu's "Four Guardian Demon" generals.
Suetake (Urabe no Suetake): one of Yorimitsu's "Four Guardian Demon" generals.
Sadamitsu (Usui no Sadamitsu): one of Yorimitsu's "Four Guardian Demon" generals.
Hōshō (Hirai no Hōshō): retainer in the Minamoto house.

Iwafuji: wife of Tsuna.
Oshiyana no Mae: wife of Kintoki.
Rangiku: wife of Suetake.
Kohata: wife of Sadamitsu.

Taira no Masakado House

Yoshikado (Shōgun Tarō Yoshikado): heir of Taira no Masakado, who led a rebellion against the Heian court but was defeated. He is raising an army to avenge his father's death and defeat by the emperor's forces.

Kochō: younger sister of Yoshikado, in service to Lady Yorimitsu as Yoshikado's spy. Falls in love with Yorinobu and acts as a go-between so that Yorihira can secretly meet Lady Eika.

Ebumi House

Ebumi (Ebumi no Saishō Tamenari): courtier and prime minister in the Heian court, foster father of Lady Eika.

Hagi no Tai: wife of Ebumi.

Lady Eika: daughter of Hagi no Tai, foster daughter of Tamenari. Is betrothed to Yorinobu, but Yorihira meets her secretly at night and they elope.

Mita House

Tomozuna (Mita no Jirō Tomozuna): grew up as a baby with Yorihira, both nursed by Tomozuna's mother. In service to Yorihira.

Aunt Mita: mother of Tomozuna, who was also Yorihira's nurse. She is the aunt of Watanabe no Tsuna and offered Tsuna into Yorimitsu's service. She is a strong-willed old woman who is a major figure in act 3, in which she dresses up as a samurai under the name Sasame no Shōni.

Act 1

—Scene 1
The imperial palace, Kyoto, middle of the second month, 988

NARRATOR:

(*prelude*) Water is not a stone drill
but its drops falling from Mount Tai
bore through rocks.
Rope is not a wood saw
but the rope that draws water from a well
cuts through fences.
Originally one is
neither thoroughly bad
nor entirely virtuous.[1]
Slander may stain the accused
and accusations hurt the innocent,
but not in the reign of a wise ruler.[2]

Emperor Ichijō is the sixty-sixth in a long line of benevolent rulers, and although he is only seven years old, we rejoice that he is reigning wisely (*cadence*) over the many islands of Japan.
    (*sung*) Lord Higashi Sanjō Kane'ie is the emperor's regent in royal affairs, and Lord Ebumi no Tamenari is his prime minister. Minamoto no Yorimitsu, a descendant of Rokusonō Minamoto no Tsunemoto, serves as shogun, protector of the imperial borders, in the line of his forebears.[3] By royal decree, he keeps the frontiers safe, and with his officers, he subdues internal uprisings and polices the realm. The people flourish—no need to steal what others happen to drop.[4] The farmers clap their hands in rhythm and sing in celebration of the rich harvest. Everyone around the capital rejoices (*cadence*) and feels content in this peaceful age.
    (*sung*) It is early spring, in the middle of the second month of the second year of Yōen (988). Shogun Yorimitsu has been called to the palace. He arrives accompanied by two of his generals: Watanabe no Tsuna, who carries the shogun's famous Raijōdō bow, and Sakata no Kintoki,

who holds the quiver. Both wear sleeveless kimonos, wide sashes at their waists, and formal court hats and bear great swords with black-lacquered handles and sheaths. They walk at his side (*cadence*), and all sit down facing His Highness, who is separated from them by a screen.

(*sung*) The regent Lord Kane'ie moves to the front of the royal dais.

KANE'IE: (*spoken*) Everyone knows why we have all been summoned. Recently an apparition has been sighted inside the palace. It takes the form of a black steed and always appears at noon, the hour of the horse. No one knows where it comes from, but it suddenly appears at the fence of the imperial quarters. It prances about wildly between the cherry and mandarin orange trees in the garden and even tries to get inside the royal quarters, neighing fiercely all the while. The men from the royal stables try to stop it and rein it in, but although they see it right before their eyes, they can never catch hold of it. (*sung*) All manner of exorcists and high priests have tried their prayers and secret incantations, as yet to no avail. His Highness is still just an innocent child, surely guilty of no offense. This demon has come, it seems, to attack me. It is the duty of his subjects to chastise evil and to right wrongs. (*cadence*) I report all this to His Highness as true to the best of my knowledge.

NARRATOR: (*sung*) Yorimitsu bows low.

YORIMITSU: When faced with an apparition, if one confronts it calmly and without fear, it usually disappears, or so it is said.[5] (*spoken*) Long ago in the reign of Emperor Uda, Kose no Kaneoka painted the sliding doors in the palace. Every night, the horse would jump out of the painting and graze on the bush clover at Bush Clover Gate.[6] In China, there is the tale of Wu Dao Zi's[7] painting in a temple from which a donkey sprang out and caused havoc for the monks. We have countless examples of famous artists instilling spirits into their paintings and sculptures. (*sung*) I have heard about my own ancestor Minamoto no Tsunemoto Son'ō's valor in shooting a deer running wild inside the palace.[8] If such an animal really does appear, then I shall accept the order on His Highness's authority to shoot a special arrow that makes a loud and terrifying sound, like a thunderclap, on contact. This should surely frighten off this fiendish spirit. Whether it is a god or a demon, it shows itself as a beast. I shall dispatch my two best officers at once to carry out this task.

NARRATOR: The courtiers are delighted by his strong and confident answer.

They feel reassured seeing his generals, Tsuna and Kintoki, who sit perched like eagles about to fly, their strength a match for any demon or serpent. They thrive on fierce enemies; the stranger the foe, the more delight they take in the battle. The courtiers who live in the palace "above the clouds" rejoice in the comfort of such strong guardians, and everyone, down to the footmen, carriage drivers, and charcoal burners, no longer live in fear. (*cadence*) All take heart from these brave-looking warriors so well suited to their task.

(*sung*) The time approaches noon, the hour of the horse. Before they can say that it was about this time yesterday, the steed emerges from behind the music room, neighing loudly. Its mane is as high as the mythical Mount Sumeru[9] and so long that it covers its hooves. Its ears are as large as conch shells, its eyes the size of bronze mirrors. The breath from its nose is strong enough to blow rocks a thousand miles across the sea. Its legs stamp with strength enough to drive off a herd of stampeding elephants. The steed appears more powerful (*cadence*) than even the ancient strong man Wulai.[10]

(*sung*) Kintoki boldly strides forward and grabs the horse around the neck, trying to pull it down. Then with a leap Tsuna tries to grab hold of the saddle straps, but the horse breaks free. They both run after the steed yelling; it rears defiantly with a loud neigh; they struggle to rope (*battle cadence*) and master this (*highest pitch*) wild stallion in an open field.

(*sung*) Yorimitsu calmly takes up his bow and arrow and yells.

YORIMITSU: (*spoken*) I am Minamoto no Yorimitsu, shogun, protector of the imperial borders, and governor of Settsu, heir to Tada no Shinbochi Manjū, and fourth-generation descendant of Emperor Seiwa.[11]

NARRATOR: (*sung*) He announces himself three times and shoots the arrow, which resonates like a terrible thunderclap. His aim is faultless, the arrow striking the steed right between the eyes. It falters and seems to collapse, but suddenly a gale blows up and in a flash of lightning and a roll of thunder, it disappears. The courtiers cry out with joy, praising Yorimitsu's prowess. All acclaim him as Japan's own Yang You, master marksman, (*cadence*) cheering him in gratitude.[12]

(*sung*) The regent Kane'ie steps forward.

KANE'IE: (*spoken*) Yorimitsu's valor has once again shown itself. (*sung*) The bravery of Tsuna and Kintoki, too, shall be rewarded. However, first we must consult the diviner to find our where this creature has fled.

336 Tethered Steed and the Eight Provinces of Kantō

FIGURE 49 (Center) The phantom horse appears in the imperial palace; (center right) Kintoki; (center left) Tsuna; (top left) Yorimitsu. (*Kanhasshū tsunagi-uma*, 1724, National Diet Library.)

NARRATOR: The diviner Ban no Bettō[13] is summoned (*entrance cadence*) and brought before those assembled.
   (*sung*) Prime Minister Ebumi steps forward to question him.
EBUMI: (*spoken*) The phantom has just been struck down by Yorimitsu's arrow. Can you divine its true form and the source of its curse? There must be some precedent.
NARRATOR: (*sung*) Bettō immediately pulls out *The Book of Secret Divination* from his kimono and opens it. He consults various sections and ponders for a while.
BETTŌ: (*spoken*) Hmm. The line here symbolizes thunder. The sign for lightning is above it. This signifies the pattern for the way the mouth chews. Therefore, my reading is the following: When there's something hard in our mouth, we chew it and swallow it.[14] This leads to the following interpretation: in the realm, something hard in the mouth means evil. When this evil, undigested, penetrates the bowels of the realm, it

causes great problems. The direction points toward the southeast, and there it lies. (*sung*) Please investigate immediately.

NARRATOR: (*cadence*) His divination is clear and precise. (*sung*) Following his suggestion, the courtiers have the storehouse of the Treasury opened and searched. They find a Chinese-style cabinet deeply pierced by Yorimitsu's arrow. The courtiers look inside and find a banner bearing a date: Tengyō 3 (940), third month. No one can fathom its significance. (*cadence*) Everyone is more baffled than ever.

(*sung*) Yorimitsu examines it closely.

YORIMITSU: This date falls in the reign of Emperor Shujaku-in, (*spoken*) exactly when the rebel Taira Shinnō Masakado was killed. I have heard that near his stables, a falling star was seen to turn into a dragon-like steed.[15] He considered it a sign intended for himself, as it was related to the Sōma house.[16] He worshiped the Sōma family deity, the martial Batō Daimyōjin, to ensure success in battle.[17] (*sung*) He then took the Sōma family crest, a tethered steed, as his own. (*spoken*) In the Shōhei era in the 930s, he spread his power throughout the eastern Kantō region.[18] Just when it seemed he might actually usurp the throne, an army led by Taira no Sadamori, Tawara Tōta, and Fujiwara no Hidesato destroyed him. As a symbol of this victory, (*sung*) Masakado's banner was presented to the court and preserved in this cabinet. This is undoubtedly the source of the apparition. (*spoken*) Masakado's youngest son has now reached maturity and has secretly taken the name Shōgun Tarō Yoshikado.[19] In town, he breaks into houses, stealing everything. Outside the city, he has a mountain gang that is ambushing travelers and robbing them of their treasures. (*sung*) My spies report that all this is part of his strategy for an attack on the capital. It is strange, but both father and son seem to be obsessed with overthrowing the court. The appearance of the tethered steed is an incarnation of Masakado's rebellious spirit. It is surely a sign that an attack is imminent. With the court's permission, I shall today dispatch patrols to make night rounds in order to crush this disturbance. We shall defeat the impetuous and violent spirit in Shōgun Tarō. After that, the realm and four seas will be at peace again, and your subjects will be even more fervent in their loyalty and duties.

NARRATOR: His insight is perceptive; his words flow pure and clear (*cadence*) as if reflected on a surface of shimmering water. (*sung*) From the regent down through all the levels of government, everyone is moved by his display of valor and prescience, *(cadence)* truly the rightful heir of the Seiwa Genji.

KANE'IE: *(sung)* Let us open the cabinet and see the proof.

NARRATOR: The lid is removed, revealing, just as Yorimitsu had said, a huge, five-foot banner with the "tethered steed" crest. All are shocked to realize *(cadence)* that it is the sign of the heir of the Sōma clan.

(sung) His Highness raises a toast to Yorimitsu.

KANE'IE: The banner will be entrusted to the care of Prime Minister Lord Ebumi, who will guard it in his residence. *(spoken)* Yorimitsu is the heir of an eminent family that has long served the court, and we have been pleased to confide to his care the responsibility of government in all matters, from the least significant to the most important.[20] However, as yet, he has chosen no heir. We request that he choose from among his two younger brothers, Kawachi no Kami Yorinobu and Dewa no Kanja Yorihira,[21] *(sung)* and report to the palace.

NARRATOR: Yorimitsu is overwhelmed by the emperor's unprecedented praise for both his clan and himself, and all the courtiers wave their sleeves in approval. The banner displays the Sōma crest, but the power of the Genji clan embraces the whole land and tames all wild stallions, its influence reaching to the end of the continent. *(scene cadence)* All flourish under its rule.

—Scene 2

Yorimitsu residence, Kyoto, an evening during the eleventh month, 988

NARRATOR: *(sung)* General Yorimitsu, triumphant after conquering the phantom of Masakado's angry spirit, grows more powerful day by day. Ordered by imperial decree to choose one of his younger brothers as his heir, he has set aside this evening for the occasion. An inner room has been made ready, with an offering to the Genji family god Hachiman in the large alcove. Thirty-three white- and thirty-three red-feathered arrows, representing the sixty-six provinces of the realm under the shogun's hegemony, have been prepared. A shrine *shimenawa* rope marks off the sacred space *(cadence)* where Hachiman's power and beneficence shine over the Genji clan, guiding the decision.

(*sung*) Lady Yorimitsu enters the room and sits down. Hirai no Hōshō steps forward.

HŌSHŌ: (*spoken*) As ordered, we have summoned here all the heads of the main families, beginning with Suetake and Sadamitsu. Everyone is assembled in the large parlor. Only Tsuna and Kintoki, who are on night patrol in the capital, are absent.

NARRATOR: Lady Yorimitsu is delighted at this report.

LADY YORIMITSU: (*sung*) Yorimitsu's younger brothers are equal in both quality and character, and so he finds it impossible to choose between them. (*spoken*) The shogun's heart and actions must be in accord with Heaven, and the heir cannot be appointed unless he has the virtue to command the respect of both soldiers and the populace at large. Therefore, Yorimitsu has decided to ask the support of the god Hachiman (*sung*) and to assemble all the heads of the main families allied with the Genji. The lights will be extinguished in the room, and each will choose one arrow from the quiver. The will of Hachiman will determine the choice: (*spoken*) a majority of white-feathered arrows will signal Yorinobu, and red-feathered arrows will mean Yorihira. This will be done in complete darkness. In this way, there can be no obvious personal favor or prejudice. Their fate is in the hands of the god. This sacred drawing of a lot will be as an oracle from heaven. By right, it should be you, Hōshō, representing the "Four Guardians" of the realm, who bears the arrows, but it is thought that a man could be influenced by his personal wish to tamper with the arrows, and so some might complain or dispute the result. Therefore, tonight's ceremony will be conducted solely by my attendant Kochō[22] here. I have told Yorinobu and Yorihira that they should first offer a prayer to Hachiman; (*sung*) the rest of the details of the procedure I have explained to Kochō. I beg you to cooperate to produce a satisfactory result.

NARRATOR: Lady Yorimitsu gets up and leaves the room. (*exit cadence*) Hōshō goes to the brothers' room to summon them.

NARRATOR: (*sung*) Kochō, left behind alone, smiles to herself.

KOCHŌ: We never know what makes another happy. I've loved Yorinobu for many years but have had to keep my passionate tears hidden, like the rain-filled streams that move beneath the sand. Fearful of being scolded because of my lowly position, I've kept my passion secret, never betraying a sign, (*spoken*) but he will come to pray to Hachiman before the ceremony. Tonight will be my chance for the flower of love to blossom. Oh, to be plucked by Lord Yorinobu, to receive his favor, his vows of love, to be his wife, such a delight; nothing could make me happier. (*sung*) Where is this man who will make me happy?

NARRATOR: She trembles with excitement. Just then, Lord Yorinobu appears in full formal court attire to offer his prayer at the image of Hachiman. She hears him clap before praying.

YORINOBU: The gods command the heavens . . .

KOCHŌ: (*spoken*) He looks so handsome in his courtier outfit, and his reverent voice thrills me. I can't bear to wait any more. How I long to fly into his arms to be held close, to feel the warmth of his cheek! This is driving me mad! Why won't he look this way? (*sung*) Please caress this hand of mine. Oh, that fragrance wafting from his robe, (*spoken*) I remember it from other times. A delightful perfume, so, so enticing. Oh such torture! I can't keep down my impatience. I can't even see his face.

NARRATOR: (*sung*) She becomes more and more excited, wanting to flee but wanting to touch him. She feels like that writhing fox tempted by the smell of a young mouse (*cadence*) in a baited trap.[23]

(*sung*) Her heart distracted, she slips and conveniently stumbles against Yorinobu, grabbing his sleeve for support. Yorinobu is surprised and turns around, their faces close together. (*emotional cadence*) He remains calm and says nothing.

KOCHŌ: (*spoken*) Forgive me, I am sorry for my clumsiness. I just slipped and grabbed hold of you for support. I know this isn't proper, but I've fallen in love with you. (*sung*) Forgive me.

NARRATOR: She falls silent (*cadence*) and can only stare at the floor. (*sung*) She calms herself and whispers.

KOCHŌ: (*spoken*) All I have thought about is when I could get a chance to speak to you secretly, (*sung*) but now when I see your face, I have lost my nerve. I still can't speak.

NARRATOR: Yorinobu nods to her.

YORINOBU: (*spoken*) Say no more. I understand. You say you have something to say to me; that is also how I feel. You have probably heard that I have been often to the residence of Lord Ebumi. No one knows yet, but Lady Eika and I have exchanged letters and fallen in love, (*sung*) but my position as the shogun's brother makes it impossible for me to visit her secretly. She must have been impatient and asked you to speak to me. That's it, isn't it? (*spoken*) Tell her that I have spoken to the four commanders and have mentioned the plan to Lord and Lady Yorimitsu. (*sung*) Tonight, after the ceremony of choosing the heir, I shall come to ask her to be my wife. Urge her most strongly not to worry, to be patient.

NARRATOR: Fearing that others will overhear, he is unable to plead any harder.

YORINOBU: I entrust everything to you, Kochō. Please tell her.

NARRATOR: (*cadence*) With that remark, he gets up and goes into the other room. (*sung*) Kochō is devastated.

KOCHŌ: (*spoken*) What is this? How could I have so misunderstood things? (*sung*) My heart has been on fire from the time I first fell in love with him. How I suffered every time I entered the shogun's residence where he might be; I returned to the women's quarters with my heart in shreds every time. I never once slept peacefully through the night. I gave my every thought to him; it was all for him alone. I lived on the hope that some day, some day. . . . I never once regretted working as a servant. I strove to be more diligent than the others, praying to the gods to grant my wish, then I bowed to the buddhas. I cast a million strings of prayers to all the gods and buddhas at the Tanabata Festival, but tonight all ties were severed at one stroke. (*spoken*) Oh, hateful Lady Eika! You always seemed so transparent, so open and kind to others. This alone you've kept hidden; clever woman to pull matters off so well! (*sung*) But envy knows neither rank nor status. Wait, I'll put a block in the way of this love; I'll get my revenge! (*highest pitch*) I hate that woman!

NARRATOR: Her heart is inflamed with rage; it shakes her whole body, but just then (*emotional cadence*) an unsuspecting Yorihira walks through the half-moon–shaped door. (*sung, high pitch*) Yorihira straightens the folds of his kimono as he sits on his knees in front of the Hachiman shrine, his courtier hat tipping as he bows in prayer.

KOCHŌ: (*spoken*) Although this is probably not the best time, I've been asked a favor by someone I couldn't refuse. So I shall take this chance to speak to you. Lord Ebumi's daughter Lady Eika has somehow taken a fancy to you and appeals to me every time I see her to help relieve her suffering. She called me to her room and begged me to be the boat that

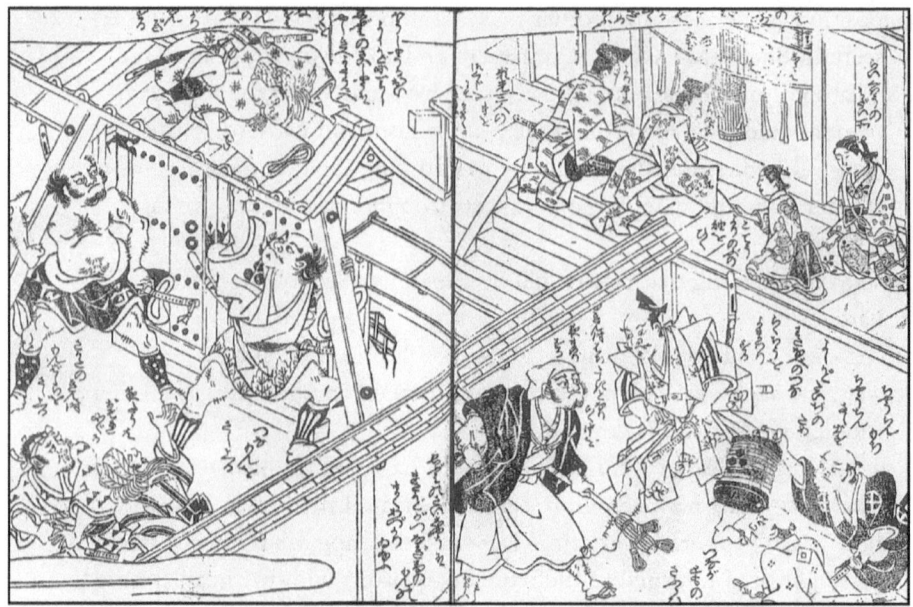

FIGURE 50 (Top right) Yorihira and Yorinobu praying to Hachiman as Kochō and Lady Yorimitsu watch; Kochō tugging Yorinobu's sleeve; (bottom right) Kintoki and Tsuna search the capital for Yoshikado and his men; (left) Yoshikado's men attempting to steal the Yoshikado banner from the Ebumi residence but thwarted by Kintoki and Tsuna. (*Kanhasshū tsunagi-uma*, 1724, National Diet Library.)

carried you across the Milky Way to meet your bride.[24] (*sung*) She said that it was asking too much to hope to meet you once a year, like in the "Weaver-Girl and Oxherd-Boy Milky Way" story; but "at least once in my lifetime, please bring us together for just one night." She begged me to speak to you. (*spoken*) Such depth of passion! (*sung*) If you have any feelings for her, how happy it would make me as well.

NARRATOR: But Yorihira interrupts.

YORIHIRA: (*spoken*) Wait, wait. I did see Lady Eika in the garden at the emperor's Hakuba banquet on January seventh, and she did strike my fancy, (*sung*) but I've heard that she has exchanged intimacies with my brother Yorinobu. Isn't that true?

NARRATOR: He blushes.

KOCHŌ: (*spoken*) No, no, you needn't be timid. It is true that Lord Yorinobu has sent a few notes to her, but she has not yet fallen in love with him. She hasn't decided yet that he is to be the one. That was just a passing fancy. If they were to be married, then I would have failed in my duty as a go-between. (*sung*) I will do nothing to harm your interests.

NARRATOR: Her earnest manner makes her words ring true to Yorihira.

YORIHIRA: (*sung*) If it is not improper and will lead to no scandal, then I am ready to accept this chance to board the boat that takes me to my love. (*sung*) I leave it to you, Kochō, to take care of everything.

NARRATOR: His reply is a relief to Kochō. Her rival now cast aside, (*scene cadence*) she suddenly feels faint at the sound of the tolling of the evening bell.

—Scene 3
Follows the previous scene

NARRATOR: (*sung*) The time has come for the ceremony to commence. Hirai no Hōshō, Suetake, and Sadamitsu lead the heads of the allied families of the Genji clan into the room, (*nō chanting*) all clad in formal matching *hakama* trousers and kimono, with courtier caps. (*cadence*) They follow each to their places. (*sung*) On the dais sits Lady Yorimitsu, flanked by Yorinobu and Yorihira. Kochō speaks for Her Ladyship.

KOCHŌ: (*spoken*) As each of you passes the quiver of arrows, as instructed, you are to concentrate on the matter at hand and carefully choose one. (*sung*) The lights will now be put out.

NARRATOR: With one swift movement of her elegant fan, the lingering firefly sparkles give way to winter's cold wind. The candles stand lifeless on their silver holders; (*cadence*) the screen paintings vanish into darkness.[25]

(*sung*) Everyone is silent and serious, not even nodding to one another (*entrance cadence*) as they approach, blindly casting their choices to the gods. Watanabe no Tsuna's cousin Mita no Jirō Tomozuna comes back after his turn to choose an arrow. He walks past Kochō, and a waft of her delightful perfume captivates him. He is a bit tipsy after a few cups of saké at the banquet earlier and, without thinking, slides up next to her, but she pushes him away. He moves closer again and hugs her. To show her fidelity to Lord Yorinobu, she grabs the string of his courtier cap with her left hand and pulls it taut. With her small knife she cuts it off. She steps back and cries out.

KOCHŌ: (*spoken*) At this most important official ceremony to choose the shogun's heir before the god Hachiman, one of this illustrious gathering proved to be a lecherous samurai, accosting me in the dark. I have no idea who it is that has tried to hug Kochō under cover of darkness. To expose the culprit, I have cut the string off his cap. (*sung*) I shall now reveal who he is. Girls, quick, bring a candle.

NARRATOR: Everyone is shocked and dismayed by this outburst. Tomozuna instantly sobers up.

TOMOZUNA: My god, this will be my ruin! I'll have to kill myself.

NARRATOR: He puts hand to sword.

TOMOZUNA: Hateful witch! I'll kill her too. I won't die alone for this.

NARRATOR: He writhes in torment, but no one notices because every one is checking his own cap and suspecting the rest. "Safe only until the lights come on," he panics, not knowing what to do, his brave heart lost in the depths of darkness. Just then Lord Yorihira, pitying the plight of the accused, acts as Tomozuna's guardian god Hachiman.

YORIHIRA: (*spoken*) This is Yorihira, and I have an idea. Don't light the candles yet. Let everyone, immediately cut the string off his hat! When all have done so, call out together. Only then, light the candles.

NARRATOR: (*sung*) His angry voice stays any objections. Each takes out his short sword and cuts off the string.

ALL: (*spoken*) Everyone has cut his cap strings.

NARRATOR: (*sung*) Tomozuna joins in this cry, and one after another candles are brought in, brightening the room as if the Sun Goddess had emerged from the cave, but no samurai is shamed. (*cadence*) How sure and sound is the heart of this general.[26]

(*sung*) Lady Yorimitsu, always composed and elegant, makes no mention of the "cap string incident."

LADY YORIMITSU: Bring all the drawn arrows to me.

NARRATOR: At this command, all move forward, placing the arrows together: twenty-eight individuals present and twenty-eight white-feathered arrows. Everyone is surprised (*cadence*) that no one has chosen a colored arrow.

NARRATOR: (*sung*) Lady Yorimitsu surveys the heap of arrows presented to her.

LADY YORIMITSU: Among all these, (*spoken*) not a single red arrow, a sign that Lord Yorinobu is the chosen heir. He is the next brother in age, and therefore this follows the accepted custom. The will of Hachiman is manifest in the honest minds of all present today; there can be no doubt about this result. (*sung*) Lord Yorihira will be Lord Yorinobu's assistant in the service of the realm. I shall, as the woman presiding over this ceremony, humbly report this to His Highness, and an auspicious day will be chosen for an imperial proclamation. But first, let us celebrate tonight's result. (*spoken*) Hōshō, Suetake, Sadamitsu, (*sung*) have the drinks prepared and let the banquet begin.

NARRATOR: Yorinobu and Yorihira together lead the group behind the curtains to the banquet room, the realm now in firm hands for future generations.[27] One can never know the distant future, but Hachiman has blessed the ceremony with white-feathered arrows, (*scene cadence*) promising prosperity for the Genji clan.

—Scene 4

Outside the gate of the Ebumi residence, at night, a day or two later

KINTOKI: (*hachi-tataki*)[28] May we trust in the shining light; trust in Buddha's light that fills the world.[29] Buy one of these tea whisks, clickety-click, to clear away your troubles, on your way to the temple. Oh, the well near the pond, how cold, cold. Just keep tapping, tapping the beat. Make your home the whole wide world; flow through it. Round and round I go, tapping my begging bowl. Oh, Gorō, Saburō, if you're off to the country and have gone cool on your little pumpkin,[30] then leave her behind for me; leave the little dear for me. A woman, that would make it easy. I tap this begging bowl, tappity-tap, as I travel the land, but how lonely without my pumpkin, such a pity. On the way to heaven, we must cross the river of tears and pain, but even the deepest pools become shallow fords, thanks to the blessings of heaven and earth, the beneficence of our sovereign. In this world of illusions, are we awake or asleep?[31] Let's have faith in the promise of rebirth in paradise. Namu Amida Butsu, All faith in Amida Buddha. Trust in Amida's vow to save all those who pray to him. Even though we can't see the stars on a rainy night, even if the clouds never clear, *(return to gidayū music, cadence)* he'll lead us to the Western Paradise.³²

NARRATOR: *(sung)* From the west of the capital to the east and from the north, bordered by Ichijō Avenue, to the south as far as Kujō Avenue, there are all together 98,000 residences. Sakata Kintoki relies on his strong legs to patrol throughout the night. In order to capture the roving gangs that have been terrorizing the capital, he has disguised himself as a mendicant monk and covered his face with a scarf. He has hidden his identity under the cloak of an itinerant peddler of tea whisks from the Kūya Temple. The rough warrior Kintoki chants Buddhist prayers for the first time in his life. "Namu Amida Butsu, All Hail to Amida Buddha." He taps out the beat on his begging gourd, *(cadence)* resolutely trying to flush out the robbers.

(sung) Even the muffled sound of thumps on a pumpkin ring clear and sharp on this cold night as the moon sets; Kintoki approaches the formidable earthen wall that surrounds the residence of Lord Ebumi, the father of Lady Eika, in West Sanjō. He is surprised to notice a thin rope hanging over the eaves, to which is tied a single narcissus bulb.

KINTOKI: What's this? *(spoken)* Hmm, maybe a talisman to ward off a plague? Perhaps something to fend off the robber gang? If it's to ward off illness, then the usual thing is to hang out some bamboo and garlic. Ah, I see. Courtiers are always delicate and must be offended by anything that smells strong. Instead of garlic, they've used narcissus because it looks like scallions. I should've been ready for such poetic sensibilities, for such a clever variation. *(sung)* In any case, I think I'll take this home as a gift for the wife.

NARRATOR: He grabs hold and tugs at the bulb, and a woman's voice calls out. Thinking it odd, he tugs again. "Yes, yes, I'm here" is the cry. The voice gets closer and closer until the small trap door opens. Out comes a servant woman who looks Kintoki over.

SERVANT: How fashionable to come in disguise! The lady of your dreams awaits you. Please come in.

NARRATOR: Invited in, Kintoki has no idea what's going on.

KINTOKI: *(spoken)* Disguised for a love tryst? What's this all about? I'm a lowly beggar depending on this one gourd. If you want one of these tea whisks, it'll cost you six bits. These're beautiful bamboo whisks that'll whisk the powder up into a fine cup of tea with a delicate froth. I'll accompany you, (*sung*) tapping a beat on this gourd.

NARRATOR: He begins to beat the gourd.

SERVANT: (*spoken*) You men are so witty! If we stay here too long, someone may notice. You'll offend the one you love if you make a joke of coming here. (*sung*) Please, may I ask you to come inside?

NARRATOR: She grabs his hand, but he pulls it away.

KINTOKI: (*hachi-tataki*) No, no, I'm never going to understand this. Never seen a pot that's been shorn smooth or a stone with a beard, never ever seen this lady, who must be elegant and quite a darling. I'm no stone or tree, I've got feelings, but at home I've left behind a mountain goddess who is as quick to get angry and jealous as a whisk goes through tea. Careful not to stir her up, on, no! Her rage is something to fear, oh, terrifying! Cold, cold is the night as I make my way tapping the beat. Soon she'll be coming to fetch me. Before I get a bruising, (*cadence*) I'd better say my good-byes.

NARRATOR: He starts to flee, (*sung*) but she runs after and grabs him.

SERVANT: You've come here secretly and pulled the cord as the signal, but then you run off. Is this just a trick to have me chase after you? Your games go too far.

NARRATOR: She pulls him closer and steals a glance at his face—bright scarlet, like a lacquered tray, eyes huge as bowls. Shocked at the sight, she panics.

SERVANT: Are you a demon, a goblin? How awful!

NARRATOR: (*cadence*) She lets him run and bolts the door shut.[33]

(*sung*) At the intersection of Nishi Sanjō and Bōmon, a fellow approaches carrying a lantern displaying the three-starred crest of Watanabe no Tsuna. Dressed in traveling clothes, he marches along holding two poles with bells on top, which ring with his every step.

KINTOKI: (*spoken*) That must be Watanabe no Tsuna on night patrol, looking quite impressive. (*sung*) Let's have a little fun with him.

NARRATOR: He covers his face with his scarf and beats the gourd loudly.

KINTOKI: (*hachi-tataki*) The Great Teacher Buddha, like the autumn moon, is hidden behind the clouds of Nirvana,[34] it seems. But tonight's moon beams bright, no need for a host of lanterns. If you're afraid to walk in the dark alone, then just recite the chant Namu Amida Buddha,

Namudda, and trust in Amida's protection. Trust in Kintoki; he'll save you.

NARRATOR: (*sung*) He takes the gourd and shoves it in front of Tsuna's nose.

KINTOKI: (*spoken*) Listen, Watanabe, have you seen anything like this? Isn't this a great disguise for carrying out the orders of His Majesty? You're always berating me for being slow; when needed, I can use my wit quite well. Taira no Masakado's heir Shōgun Tarō Yoshikado leads a gang of thieves who terrorize the capital, and at the same time the two of us turn up. You with your curvy pointed moustache and me with my bald head the color of cooked prawns, both trademarks known throughout Japan. So I've disguised myself as a chanting mendicant priest. Even if the thieves see me, they won't get the slightest hint that it's Kintoki, and they'll leave me alone. Compared with me, you are prancing about with a bright lantern and two noisy bell poles, making a racket. (*sung*) If you want to impress your soldiers, then why not just make a parade of it? Get the portable shrine from the Gion Shrine Festival or the Hōshōe Festival of Iwashimizu Shrine. How about it, Watanabe?

NARRATOR: (*cadence*) He roars with laughter. (*sung*) Tsuna remains unflustered.

TSUNA: (*spoken*) Ha, ha, ha! It's said that a little bit of knowledge can sometimes hinder one from following the right way.[35] Governing a great country is like cooking small fish.[36] For with any fish or small carp, if you let them boil too long and constantly fiddle with them and move them about in the pot, the scales and fins will crumble and the fish will lose its shape. The principles of public government are the same. The sentiments of those officials who sit in important government posts—to take an example close at hand—it's as if they were cleaning square lacquer food-boxes with wooden pestles. If we take the realm to be a set of lacquer boxes set one on top of the other, the government is the wooden pestle. When they clean the boxes with a pestle, if they clean only what they can reach easily and don't try to get into every corner, then the boxes will be saved and the country preserved. This is sage-like government. A stupid government is fastidious about cleaning each and every corner; it destroys the boxes and endangers the stability of the realm. As the saying has it, in houses we find mice; throughout the country we find thieves. Even if we get rid of a few hundred, they won't all disappear, they'll soon spring up again. If there is love and compassion inside and we keep a careful guard on the outside, then we have no need to use the sword, and people will follow the way of virtue and govern themselves. Did you follow all that, Kintoki? All your chatter about clever disguises to sneak about ferreting out thieves (*sung*) seems a bit silly now, doesn't it?

NARRATOR: Kintoki is chastised by his words. His face puffs up with indignation, but he is unable to offer a retort to Tsuna's logic.

KINTOKI: All that fancy talk and big words I don't follow at all. Lacquer food-boxes and wooden pestles and gourds and tea whisks, they're always needed, but the man of action will win the glory. I've got plenty of tea whisks here to sweep away your troubles. Listen to my song as I beat the bowl. We'll see who does the job.

NARRATOR: He chatters on and on, undeterred by what went before. (*exit cadence*) The pair part ways as if they were following the forks of a stream.

—Scene 4
Outside the gate of the Ebumi residence, later that night

NARRATOR:

> (*sung*) Hopeless to write on a flowing stream,
> even more vain to long for a lover
> who thinks not of you.[37]

Like the lover who crosses the Milky Way on the wings of magpies, Yorihira, now obsessed with desire for Lady Eika, depends on Kochō, "the little butterfly," to lead him through the dark across the bridge to meet the woman long the object of his dreams. His hair is messy, his courtier cap long cast off, no care for his appearance.[38] He covers himself with a white silk robe so as not to look like a man. (*cadence*) He and Kochō stop outside the earthen wall at the Ebumi residence.

YORIHIRA: (*spoken*) Kochō, I am indebted for your efforts to spirit me into the house to meet Eika. (*sung*) I could never express my gratitude in full. I beg you to lead me the last steps of the way.

KOCHŌ: (*spoken*) No need to be so grateful to me. For a long time, my every care has been for Lord Yorinobu, for whose love I would give my life. Unless I break the tie between Lady Eika and Lord Yorinobu, my love will never be fulfilled. As things turn out, it is lucky that Lady Eika has fallen for Yorinobu without yet seeing his face. At this point, when she seems to be losing interest in Yorinobu, I am giving you your chance to plead your love. Nevertheless, because this is the first time that you may sleep together, don't make a point of telling her you are Yorihira. (*sung*) Leave it unclear whether it is "Nobu" or "Hira." I'll refer to you as Lord "Yori" as you enter her bed chamber. Once you've had your fun and games, then it won't matter who you are. Even if your disguise is revealed, your tail exposed, she'll be all yours. Here, pull this narcissus bulb to show you've fallen for the flower on the other side of the wall. It's the signal.

NARRATOR: As he tugs, he feels his heartstrings pulled with desire. His heart pounds with excitement ready to set sail at high tide. A servant appears and cautiously beckons him inside. His will, like blossoming reeds, bends to the winds of passion. Enticed by the flower's scent (*cadence*) and lured by the "Little Butterfly," he sets off on the rising tide, entering the gate and disappearing inside.

(*sung*) After a while, the younger brother of Hirai no Hōshō, Ukyōnosuke, and the father and son pair Fujiwara no Yasusuke and Uhyōenojō Tokiakira appear,[39] villains through and through. Rejected by Yorimitsu, they have turned against their own families. Cut off from everyone, they have joined to form a gang to plunder the capital. Attacking and killing at random, for no apparent reason, they have now joined the forces under Shōgun Tarō with the grand purpose of overthrowing the emperor. Leading a group of twenty-four other liked-minded, swaggering sorts, they move about stealthily, their faces hidden by robber scarves, looking like a row of lumpy trees. Yasusuke and Tokiakira come close to the wall.

YASUSUKE: (*spoken*) This is the Ebumi residence. Our Lord Yoshikado's family banner with the "tethered steed" crest is being kept here. It would be easy enough to break down this one gate and steal it, but it wouldn't be wise to underestimate even a lily-livered aristocrat. Let's use some information I overheard on the street to trick our way in. Be careful! Keep your guard up.

NARRATOR: He knocks loudly on the gate.

YASUSUKE: I am a messenger from Lord Yorimitsu with urgent business. Open the gate.

NARRATOR: His deception stirs the house. (*sung*) The sleeping guards wonder what it can be. They are disturbed by the continuous pounding on the gate.

GUARD: (*spoken*) Lord Ebumi is on duty at the palace and so is not here. Any business can wait until tomorrow.

NARRATOR: They refuse to go away.

YASUSUKE: Don't worry, our message is auspicious. Lord Yorinobu, governor of Kawachi, has been chosen as heir to Lord Yorimitsu. Further, Lord Yorinobu wishes to ask Lady Eika to be his bride. Good tidings demand speed. Even though it is the middle of the night, please open the door. Watanabe no Tsuna has arrived with the nuptial gifts. (*sung*) Be quick and open up.

NARRATOR: The foolish guards, all inexperienced samurai, fall for the trick and open the main gate, (*cadence*) making it easy for Yasusuke and his gang to enter.

(*sung*) News of messengers from Yorimitsu shocks Yorihira. He jumps up, still disheveled from his lovemaking, and attempts to leave. Lady Eika grabs his sleeve.

EIKA: Wait, Lord Yorinobu, were all those letters you sent just lies? How could you leave now so coldheartedly? (*spoken*) We've just now heard that Lord Yorimitsu has sent someone named Tsuna as a messenger to announce our marriage. (*sung*) What a delight to have your brother's blessing on our union. Now we are acknowledged as husband and wife by all of society. I'm not going to let you leave, even if the cock crows or the sun rises.

NARRATOR: Drawn back to bed, Yorihira decides to confess.

YORIHIRA: The messenger's auspicious words stick in my throat. (*spoken*) I can't pretend any longer. I'm not Yorinobu but Dewa no Kanja Yorihira. (*sung*) Although I knew you favored my brother, I wasn't the only one to suffer the pangs of a secret passion. Kochō, too, pined for Yorinobu and so plotted this ruse to get me into your bed, but I knew nothing about your formal betrothal. (*spoken*) If your parents have agreed to the marriage, then I've cuckolded my own brother. Mencius says that propriety demands that a man should not grab the hand of his brother's wife even if she's drowning,[40] but I've trampled on a brother's trust, destroyed all respect. I can accept the blame for my own actions, but I regret that I have led you astray from the path of virtue.

NARRATOR: (*emotional cadence*) He collapses in a flood of tears. (*sung*) Lady Eika is aghast and speechless for a while.

EIKA: (*spoken*) What can be done? Now that we've slept together, regrets will change nothing. No turning back. Now that my body is stained, I have no wish to be with Lord Yorinobu. Before the messenger can return with an acceptance of the marriage offer, let's flee. Take me away from here. (*sung*) I'll be spared the shame of adultery. Even if I'm now with a man other than the one I expected, a woman's duty is to cleave to one husband. After this one night together (*highest pitch*) you are my whole family, all I can depend on. Don't abandon me now, Lord Yorihira.

NARRATOR: She clutches him in her arms. They embrace, a couple now inseparable.

KOCHŌ: Splendid, magnificent, Lady Eika. Leave it to me to take care of explaining matters to both families. Don't worry about anything here. The two of you be off, hurry up and flee before the dawn.

NARRATOR: She leads them out. No destination in mind, Lord Yorihira covers Lady Eika with a hooded cloak. How great the pain of fleeing, (*cadence*) how much more they have still to suffer.

(*sung*) Suddenly there is a disturbance inside the gates, the sound of a struggle and inner doors being ripped out, the cries of women, "Thieves!" "Burglars!" But no help comes as the servants, both men and women, face the robbers' swords. Everyone runs for their lives, covered in blood. Lord Ebumi's wife Hagi no Tai comes running out, bravely clutching the tethered steed banner and wielding her sword with her right hand, locked in battle with Yasusuke. She parries the blows of his huge sword and tries to escape through the front gate, slashing at all in her path as she runs.

HAGI: (*spoken*) These are no ordinary thieves. They haven't even looked at the gold or valuables. You brigands only want to get this banner, entrusted to us by His Highness. As long as I live, I'll never hand it over. I dare you to despise a courtier's wife. (*sung*) If you come any closer, you'll pay with your life.

NARRATOR: Brave words hide her anxiety about what has happened to Eika. Unable to concentrate, (*cadence*) she stays to fight rather than flee.

YASUSUKE: (*sung*) Hey, woman, had enough of this life, have you? Hand over that banner like a good girl.

NARRATOR: He attacks again, but she parries his blow once more. Tokiakira sneaks up behind her and knocks down her sword, pinning her to the ground. Yasusuke grabs the banner and is delighted with his trophy.

YASUSUKE: Splendid! We've got what we were after. Cut her to bits.

NARRATOR: With this order, he heads back inside the gate. Tokiakira grabs Lady Hagi by her hair and raises his sword for the kill, when suddenly from each side Tsuna and Kintoki swoop in like a pair of fierce guardian gods riding down on clouds. Kintoki immediately knocks over Tokiakira and pins him down. Tsuna helps up Lady Hagi and carefully brushes off the dirt, *(cadence)* making sure that she is not hurt. *(sung)* Kintoki lifts up the chin of the fellow he holds down.

KINTOKI: *(spoken)* Now, isn't this Tokiakira, the nephew of Hōshō? No matter how many times Hōshō scolded you, you have remained dishonest. You must have a thief's virus in your blood. I'm a specialist at healing by massaging the pressure points on the fourteen meridians. *(sung)* This may hurt a bit, but just bear up and be patient.

NARRATOR: He grabs his head and gives it a sharp twist, ripping it off. Tsuna shouts.

TSUNA: *(spoken)* You all are guilty of crimes against the rightful sovereign. Change your evil ways now. If you surrender immediately, your lives will be spared. *(sung)* If you persist with force, this is what you can expect.

NARRATOR: He throws Tokiakira's body inside and strikes a fierce pose glaring at the villains. *(cadence)* The force of his stare even penetrates the thick earthen wall.

(sung) Yasusuke stands tall on the roof of the gate.

YASUSUKE: *(spoken)* Listen, you. With the unfurling of this banner Lord Shōgun Tarō will ascend the throne, and I myself will be his prime minister. You're a bit of a loud mouth to demand that I surrender to you. *(sung)* What an insolent, impertinent brute! Watch your tongue when speaking to one far above you. Impudent fool!

NARRATOR: His stream of abuse rolls on and on.

TSUNA: *(spoken)* Oh, that sounds splendid, a prime minister! If you have ambitions for such august heights, then leave it to us.

NARRATOR: *(sung)* Tsuna and Kintoki close the gate and seal the lock. Each then grabs one of the side pillars and lifts them up with a grunt. The tall, tightly packed and cemented earthen wall crumbles, and the whole gate is lifted cleanly off the ground. When they raise it up above their shoulders, Yasusuke almost falls all the way to the ground below but manages to hang on to the roof tiles. He cries out.

YASUSUKE: (*spoken*) Please, Sir Tsuna, these heights are too exalted for me. I'm getting dizzy. (*sung*) Here, I'll hand over the banner. Please, Sir Kintoki, save me. I beg you, spare me, please.⁴¹

NARRATOR: He breaks into cowardly sobs, (*cadence*) his tears flowing like rain rushing off a thatched roof, a wretched sight.

(*sung*) Tsuna and Kintoki roar with laughter.

TSUNA: Yasusuke, you're not much of a roof tiler. Next time you'd better build one that doesn't leak!

NARRATOR: They pull the gate one way and then another, increasing Yasusuke's suffering even more. When they pull the pillars apart, (*kowari fight melody*) the beams, girders, and joists all come loose. The mortar holding the tiles breaks apart, and the tiles come crashing down. (*sung*) Yasusuke falls from the roof, and his backbone is crushed by the two pillars that crash together on top of him. He dies among the heap of broken tiles. The rest of the villainous gang come doggedly out to fight. Tsuna and Kintoki grab them one by one and twist off his head. The pair are better than the finest Nanbō tweezers or nail pincers from Nagoya. No one escapes; (*cadence*) all their heads are plucked off as easily as picking cherries.⁴²

(*sung*) Kintoki hangs the heads on the pillars which he hoists on to his shoulders as if they were light poles. He sets off chanting his tune.

KINTOKI: (*hachi-tataki*) Last night I beat on a gourd; this morning I beat on heads. How about that, Tsuna!

NARRATOR: (*cadence*) Taking up his tune, (*sung*) Tsuna joins him to become a wandering mendicant to follow the Way.

TSUNA: (*hachi-tataki*) Although we are blessed with the great teachings of Shakyamuni, he has passed on into the Nirvana clouds. All hateful villains, all enemies of the realm, not one of them will remain free. Amida, Namu Amida Butsu. (*sung*) Trust in the power.⁴³

KINTOKI: To the wisdom and virtue of our sovereign is added the martial virtue of the Genji, protectors of the realm. Even if the traitor Shōgun Tarō were to grow scales and swim or wings and fly, we would chase him into water, find him in the clouds. As proof, we'll defeat him. Here, look at this banner.

NARRATOR: They rein in the tethered steed, now their ally. *(high pitch)* Tsuna and Kintoki, their valor and strength legendary, stand at the head of the "Four Guardians" of the realm. Their fame and exploits will thrill generations to come.

Act 2

—Scene 1
Yorimitsu residence, near the Kamo River, several days later

NARRATOR: (*sung*) Kyoto's own "Mount Fuji," the formidable Mount Hiei, guardian of the capital's northeast face, rises tall, firm as the backdrop to the magnificent garden in the shogunal residence. In the far distance, even shabby village huts, seen amid the garden trees, contribute to the idyllic scene, a veritable Chinese landscape painting, created with great style in this splendid garden that was designed with such aesthetic charm. The stepping-stones were cut in Shirakawa, and the water basin is filled through bamboo pipes that draw directly from the nearby Kamo River. In the northwest corner of the compound are Lord Yorinobu's quarters, where until tonight he has slept alone. The announcement of the arrival of a guest that evening (*cadence*) has the servant girls frantically rushing about to clean the rooms in time.

    (*sung*) The formal room with its raised dais, the study, and the tea room are being cleaned, and Nezame puts fresh flowers in the vase then wipes the wooden frames and lintels; Sarashina and Sugino dust the *shōji* sliding doors, chattering away all the while.[1]

SARASHINA: (*spoken*) Who is this guest tonight, anyway? Unless we know what's being celebrated, we have nothing to rejoice about. Nezame, dear, have you heard anything?

NEZAME: Ha, haven't you heard the news? The guest tonight is to be the bride of this house. This is what I've heard rumored. Lord Yorinobu was for a long time infatuated with Lady Eika. So much in love, and it seemed all was going well, but then his younger brother Lord Yorihira stole her away. Kyoto is all stirred up at the scandal, everyone saying that the lovers have eloped and are nowhere to be found. His Majesty, hearing of this, (*sung*) has presented Iyo no Naishi, a beauty unsurpassed by Lady Eika, as a bride for Lord Yorihira. She is to arrive soon by palanquin. This auspicious event is all due to Lord Yorimitsu's eminence and the excellent service of Lord Yorinobu. (*spoken*) Tomorrow they'll pound rice cakes as part of the marriage ceremony. Tonight, though, the two of them will be pounding other things in bed. (*sung*) I envy Iyo no Naishi, her pumpkin'll be full and content. They'll pound plenty of rice cakes tonight!

NARRATOR: (*cadence*) She laughs aloud.

(*sung*) Sarashina's eyes have a mischievous glint.

SARASHINA: (*spoken*) Those precious aristocratic personages are so refined; even with one pestle's pounding, they're soon producing little baby rice cakes,[2] but the likes of us are not so delicate. Our mortars[3] are used most often to grind out miso bean paste from soybeans, so we never produce little rice cakes.

NARRATOR: (*sung*) They laugh coquettishly, these pretty wildflowers (*cadence*) chattering away.

SUGINO: (*spoken*) Be that as it may; I wonder where that Kochō's been. The sly wench hasn't shown her face since this morning. (*sung*) Kochō, Kochō!

NARRATOR: Kochō hears her name called, but this butterfly is in a pitiful state, her makeup smudged by her tears, her face haggard. She feels oppressed at the thought of Yorinobu's marriage and is despondent, unable even to answer. (*cadence*) Still weeping, she plods in.

SUGINO: (*spoken*) You've kept well hidden. Today is a grand wedding day for this house, and we've been desperately short of hands, ready even to put the cats to work. What does that teary face mean? Aren't you feeling well? (*sung*) Her Ladyship's secretary, Tsubone, has ordered us to take special care to clean every speck in the bride's room. You've left all the work to us, finding some hole to hide in, you clever thing. Look, the sun is setting on the western hills. Her palanquin will be arriving at any moment. (*spoken*) We've almost finished tidying the rooms. Your job is to sweep the leaves in the garden and clear away the cobwebs and spiders. Then spray some water around. After you've done that, you can be as lazy as you want.

NARRATOR: (*cadence*) Service at court demands the suppression of any private cares.

(*sung*) Unable to follow the wishes of her heart, Kochō sullenly takes up the bamboo pole and steps down into the garden. As she gazes at the spider webs, her thoughts become twisted, thinking about Lord Yorinobu. She is determined with all her heart and body to prevent him from being with another woman. Anger winds a tight net around her chest, like a spider spinning its web among the branches to snare its prey. Just then, Nezame notices something.

NEZAME: (*spoken*) Look, over there, Kochō. Look at that one! Oh, it's a huge green spider. How terrifying! It's poisonous and can kill an adult instantly with its venom. It's too close to the bride's room and could get in among the food before it's served. Quick, get rid of it!

NARRATOR: (*sung*) Kochō has an idea.

KOCHŌ: (*spoken*) Yes, even a slight brush of the lips with the venom is deadly. Yet the spider's gentle appearance belies its danger.

NARRATOR: (*sung*) Her words express her fear, but in her heart she decides to plant the spider for Iyo no Naishi and so get rid of her rival in love. Her jealous obsession (*cadence*) grows far more lethal than any spider's venom.

(*sung*) From the inner room, Tsubone's voice is heard.

TSUBONE: (*spoken*) Listen, listen! A messenger has just arrived announcing Iyo no Naishi's imminent arrival. Make sure that all the candles and lanterns are ready; it's most important for the ceremony. (*sung*) All of you, put on your formal cloaks and let your hair down in the courtly style. Hurry, everyone to the front gate!

NARRATOR: They all acknowledge her orders (*cadence*) and bustle about excitedly.

(*sung*) Left behind, Kochō sees her chance. She gets up on tiptoe to reach as far as possible and knocks down the web. The spider falls neatly into a waiting kerchief. She folds it up tightly, thanking heaven for her luck, and intones a curse against Iyo no Naishi.

KOCHŌ: (*spoken*) You, little spider, are a spirit like the gods, with powers beyond the human. I've heard that long ago in China, there was some poem entitled "Yematai"[4] which was put to Kibi no Makibi[5] as a test. A spider spun a web to show him the way toward unraveling the mysteries of the verse. This brought Japan great praise. It's also said that seeing a spider is a good omen: a lover will visit in the night.[6] (*sung*) But you also have the power to kill, far quicker than the venom of the Chinese Zhen bird or any other insect. My spirit has a strange force, beyond good and evil. Your tiny body will be filled with my full spirit.[7] (*kowari threatening melody*) During the night you will poison Iyo no Naishi, and your threads will tie my dearest Lord Yorinobu tightly to me, just as in Princess Soto-ori's poem.[8] I pray that the gods above grant my wish!

NARRATOR: She hides the spider in her sleeve, lifts up her skirts, and sets off, on the surface as demure as an elegant bodhisattva statue while underneath she seethes like a vengeful demon. Just a thin layer of skin conceals her fury. (*sung*) She opens the sliding door to the other room, (*cadence*) which is buzzing with excitement.

(*sung*) The bride has arrived, and everyone shares in the nuptial toasts. The formal *shimadai* table is decorated auspiciously with bamboo and pine, symbolizing longevity. Everyone sings out, (*nō chanting*) "A thousand autumns, (*scene cadence*) ten thousand years of health and prosperity, endless treasures."[9]

—Scene 2
Scene 1 continued, outside the Yorimitsu residence near the Kamo River

NARRATOR: (*sung*) Well known in the world is the tale of Taira no Masakado, also known as Sōma Jirō. A generation ago, he took up arms against the sovereign and met his end at Sarumata Castle in Sagami Province.[10] Forgotten, however, was his heir Shōgun Tarō Yoshikado,[11] strong of body, fierce in spirit like his father. Picking up the threads of his fearless father's insurrection, he plots to overturn the kingdom. He has planted his younger sister in service to Lady Yorimitsu, hiding her origins and changing her name to Kochō. They use the narrow bamboo pipes that bring water into the garden from the Kamo River to convey information on the household to each other. A decorative bamboo horse's head conceals the channel of their secret whisperings. Yoshikado moves some distance upstream along the banks of the Kamo River where the pipe meets the stream and takes out his flute to signal to her with a high-pitched note (*highest pitch, scene cadence*) that pierces the night air.

(*sung*) Inside the garden walls, Kochō recognizes the flute as her brother's signal. She slips away from the banquet and goes to the bamboo pipe at the far side of the garden where no one can see her. She puts her mouth to the opening and calls out.

KOCHŌ: (*spoken*) Is that my brother Yoshikado?

NARRATOR: (*sung*) Yoshikado blows his flute upstream and hears her voice travel through the water pipe. Although their mouths and ears are far apart, (*cadence*) the pipe is a bridge that carries their whispers. (*sung*) Yoshikado speaks into the bamboo pipe.

FIGURE 51 (Right) Kochō preparing to place a poisonous spider in Iyo no Naishi's food; (bottom right) Lady Yorimitsu coming upon Kochō talking to an outsider through a bamboo water pipe; (left) Yoshikado, Kochō's brother, listening to Kochō. (*Kanhasshū tsunagiuma*, 1724, National Diet Library.)

YOSHIKADO: (*spoken*) Kochō, although Yorimitsu's "Four Guardians" are like fierce demons, he himself is a general with only simple strategies, unable to understand the subtleties and complexities of battle. He has no idea that I am right under his nose; his men are far away searching blindly, and I've heard that not even one samurai of note is on duty. The chance to fulfill my dream has come. Furthermore, it's perfect that tonight is Yorinobu's wedding. All the soldiers will be drunk and off guard. (*sung*) This will give me the opening I need to slip in and take care of Yorimitsu and Yorinobu easily, capture the emperor, and usurp the throne. This is the chance to fulfill our father's long-held desire. Be careful to lead me in undetected.

NARRATOR: His words strike Kochō's heart. This pact between brother and sister has become love's enemy. Held back by her growing affections, Kochō is no longer capable of watching while Lord Yorinobu is cut down. Pain holds back her response. (*emotional cadence*) She wavers, lost in the dark depths of passion.

(*sung*) The sky is dark, black as the lacquered beams in the large study. Under the wide veranda, a figure stoops low, creeping along the shadows. Lady Yorimitsu, noticing Kochō's strange behavior, has followed her to the bamboo pipe to spy on the unsuspecting woman.

KOCHŌ: (*spoken*) Brother, the house hasn't yet settled for the night. If we move too quickly, it could be disastrous. It doesn't have to be done tonight. (*sung*) We mustn't rush this!

NARRATOR: She tries to stall for time.

YOSHIKADO: (*spoken*) Don't be cowardly. Are you having second thoughts? We dare not lose this chance tonight. Pull yourself together and be firm, sister.

NARRATOR: (*sung*) Overhearing this plot, Lady Yorimitsu immediately unsheathes her short sword and flies at Kochō, cutting her across the shoulder. Kochō screams and pulls away.

KOCHŌ: (*spoken*) Who's attacked me? Why? What for? Someone help! Save my precious life.

NARRATOR: She tries to flee, but Lady Yorimitsu grabs her hair knot and pulls her to the ground, delivering another blow. (*sung*) She screams once more. Hearing the cries, Hirai no Hōshō comes running out, candle in hand. He is shocked to see Kochō's deep wound. Outside Yoshikado waits with his ear to the pipe, unaware of Kochō's plight. He waits and waits patiently for her response, steadfast and resolute. Lady Yorimitsu shows her true colors as a general's wife. Calmly, she roughly throws Kochō aside.

LADY YORIMITSU: (*spoken*) Hateful girl! Look at her, Hōshō. Tonight a spider was found in the bride's food. It was a plan to poison her. Kochō was in charge of arranging the banquet. I followed her here, suspecting something was up. She was speaking through the water pipe to an ally outside. No question but that she's part of a robber gang. No excuses will save you now. (*sung*) Confess, tell us everything.

NARRATOR: Pressed to speak, Kochō painfully opens her eyes.

KOCHŌ: (*spoken*) Too cruel, Your Ladyship, to brand me a robber's pawn. No form of torture could have made me confess, but because it brings shame to my ancestors, I can't allow myself to be called a robber. I shall die with the name I and my brother bear on my lips. I am the daughter of Taira Shinō no Masakado, younger sister of Shōgun Tarō Yoshikado! I entered court service as a plan to avenge my father's enemy. Long months and years have I served for that cause, (*sung*) but a woman's heart is fragile. I was entranced by Yorinobu's charms. I lost track of my goal and thought only of love. Not wanting him to be with any other woman, I plotted to bring Lady Eika and Yorihira together and had them flee the capital. (*spoken*) Just as I was delighting at being rid of Eika, Iyo no Naishi was chosen by His Majesty to be Yorinobu's bride. Fearing another rival, I planted the poison and hoped to satisfy my jealousy. Yet now she is safe, and I am to perish. For love I forgot about revenge and betrayed my family. I'll be hated by both father and brother. Strike me if you will; kill me if you wish. I'll be reborn again and again. My vengeance is carved in iron and stone. I will keep Yorinobu and Iyo no Naishi apart forever, building layer upon layer between them. (*kowari threatening melody*) They will never be free to be together.

NARRATOR: Her angry eyes grow bright, lighting the night sky like fiery stars. Her face turns crimson, her hair stands on end. (*sung*) Her body rises up to fling itself on the woman inside, but Hōshō quickly attacks and skillfully fells her with one blow, her head lopped off, a pitiful sight. Even women cannot escape the fate of enemies of the realm: (*cadence*) heaven's wrath before our eyes.

(*sung*) Lady Yorimitsu is visibly shaken.

LADY YORIMITSU: (*spoken*) This evil woman was a spy in our midst, but her confession before dying is a clear sign that the fate of the Genji house is favored by the gods. Long will we prosper. The real enemy is Yoshikado. Let's use his own stratagem to lure him in. (*sung*) Hōshō, get together some men to overpower and capture him.

NARRATOR: She speaks into the bamboo pipe.

LADY YORIMITSU: (*spoken*) Brother, listen, the house is now quiet, everyone is asleep. They've all passed out from drink. I'll open the small door at the back of the garden. The time is ripe. (*sung*) Hurry now!

NARRATOR: Yoshikado thinks the voice is his sister's.

YOSHIKADO: Magnificent work! I'll be there in a second.

NARRATOR: At this response, Lady Yorimitsu and Hōshō nod to each other (*cadence*) and open the bolt to let him in, and then return to the house.

(*sung*) Yoshikado runs to the back gate. He listens carefully and then nudges the door, which opens easily. He smiles to himself, pleased at his success, and steps into the garden. Not knowing its design, he imagines trees to be men and stealthily makes his way through the dark, aiming for the light coming from the main building. He passes alongside bubbling springs and rolling hills, (*entrance cadence*)[12] through dangerous parts, finally approaching the bedroom.

(*sung*) Hōshō, wearing a woman's robe as a disguise, nods to his men and steps out to face Yoshikado, who approaches and then whispers.

YOSHIKADO: (*spoken*) Is that Kochō? You've done splendidly. Neither father nor I could expect any greater loyalty from a daughter or sister. Is this Yorinobu's bedroom? Where is Yorimitsu? (*sung*) Lead the way.

NARRATOR: As he steps forward, Hōshō throws off the robe, grabs Yoshikado around the waist, and holds on to him tightly.[13]

YOSHIKADO: (*spoken*) Ho, ho. Ridiculous, beyond belief! Such an unusual foe that must use petty deception to defeat Shōgun Tarō, unrivaled throughout Japan in martial prowess. Such daring! Since the "Four Guardians" are away, it must be Hirai no Hōshō, the "toy soldier." Don't hold it against me (*sung*) when I twist your arm up and you pass out.

NARRATOR: He draws his sword.

HŌSHŌ: Listen boy! You certainly talk big enough. (*spoken*) You're right. I am Hirai no Hōshō, but you've reached the end of your luck meeting me. If you think you can get free, (*sung*) then try it.

NARRATOR: He holds even tighter, determined not to let him escape. No matter how strongly Yoshikado tries to throw him off, he hangs on firmly, undaunted. Both powerful fighters, they tumble to the ground, rolling over, (*cadence*) one on top of the other.

(*sung*) Hōshō trips over an old pine root and twists his left ankle. Unable to stand, he struggles to get up, and Yoshikado is able to break free. He starts to run but is surrounded by soldiers holding lanterns. With no escape route, he fights madly for his life, grabbing five or six soldiers and throwing them as if he were scattering seed.[14] The others, fearing for their lives, step back, (*cadence*) no one brave enough to attack.

(*sung*) Thinking he can do no more tonight, he decides to escape the way he came. Hōshō waits in ambush behind a boulder. He lets him pass and then strikes out with all his might, slashing Yoshikado's side. Stunned by the blow, Yoshikado falters. Hōshō drops his sword and pounces, pinning both his arms back.

HŌSHŌ: (*spoken*) I've taken the daring enemy alive! Help me tie him up.

NARRATOR: (*kowari threatening melody*) But just then Kochō's corpse eerily begins to stir. They watch as her obsessive, lingering spirit pulls the severed head closer to the body. Then as if they were coming alive again, the head and body reunite. She suddenly springs up, grabs the front of Hōshō's kimono, and drags him aside. (*sung*) Her vindictive, angry spirit wields supernatural power. Although his body is writhing in pain, Yoshikado crawls to his escape, having stepped on the tiger's tail (*cadence*) and aroused the nest of poisonous spiders.[15]

HŌSHŌ: (*spoken*) This is disastrous! We've let the most important enemy escape. Who was his ally?

NARRATOR: He turns around to see the corpse of Kochō holding on to him and shudders. One by one, he peels off each of her fingers from his kimono, and suddenly like a stupa stone, the head severs itself from the body and rolls along the ground, its sound resonating with the power of a woman's passion (*cadence*)—terrifying, the vengeful spirit of a jealous woman.

NARRATOR: (*sung*) Fearful that left as it is, it might rise again, he chops the body to pieces.

HŌSHŌ: (*spoken*) He can't have got far. Everyone, after Yoshikado. We must kill him this time. (*sung*) Hurry!

NARRATOR: He rouses their courage, and they set off in pursuit, waving lanterns before them, (*scene cadence*) so many that it dims the starlight in the night sky.

—Scene 3
"Lady Eika's Journey": North Kyoto, along the road to Kurama and Ichiharano[16]

NARRATOR:

(*sung*) His warrior's bow and quiver cast aside,[17]
Yorihira bears only the heavy weight of love.
Lady Eika does not regret being carried by Yorihira,
though he was not the man of her innocent dreams.
(*dōguya style*) Thinking of another, her heart was stolen in the night.
Stolen away, fiery passion leads them now

through the cold snow, chilling, chilling.
"Don't cool toward me, don't ever change.
You're ever mine, we'll float always together,
(*cadence*) only each other to hold."
(*sung*) The sky is white with snow,
but with darkened hearts, we enter Kurama-guchi,
known for its demons who swallow men in one bite.
Here is Mount Kamo where the god of thunder reigns.
(*nagaji melody*) Listen, listen to it roar,
just as long ago, when Narihira felt the pounding rain[18]
along the River Akuta,
we fear not rain or snow from above,
though our bodies are fragile like the dew on the grasses.
Are we but jeweled drops of dew?
Refuse to answer, and we will perish as in Narihira's tale.
He looks up at her face,
she at his, together in love,
(*cadence*) but he regrets making her suffer.

(*sung*) He lets her down to walk along the rocky path, realizing that precious Eika has never ventured out before, never far from her jeweled comb box and her maids. Now she depends only on him, the two of them together but alone. Their hands in each other's sleeves, (*song*) like the legendary birds with joined wings, two lovers' shadows coupled as one, never will their bonds be broken. Seeing their reflections in the murky Mizoro Pond, they shudder at their gaunt faces, wasted by anxiety, (*cadence*) although they've journeyed but a few days.

(*sung*) (Eika) Look, over there on the mountain peak! Willow branches bend and blow unfettered in the wind, washed by the snow, just like my untended, flowing hair. Will it ever be arranged for a wedding night? That would be as hard as it is for me to get past the huge boulders on the way to Iwakura. (*reizei elegant style*) Even on those nights when we steal an embrace,[19] our robes intertwined, dawn will come and cleave our love asunder. Just thinking of such painful partings, my sleeves become a sea of tears; better the time before our love blossomed. Even after many nights of waiting, waiting, (*high pitch*) will this body just burn with bitter regrets? At least for one night, let us share a bed. (*sung*) Will he come?[20] (*cadence*) Still no inn where we can rest.

(*sung*) In the end, who will pine for me here at Matsugasaki? How I suffer not knowing if we'll be together or I'll be left alone. (*cadence*) A pitiful fate.

(*sung*) (*Yorihira*) Although you worry so, even if we should meet no more, as in the old poem, "both from Naniwa, our names are tied together" as we pass Hatadae.[21] Grieve no more. I have risked life to ford the rapids of love. Only once have we been submerged in passion, but its colors are dyed deep. Here at Yashio Hill, winter is harsh; the trees are bare. Even the evergreen pine (*high pitch*) is looking thinner,[22] faint as the tints of dawn, already signaled by the temple bell. The early-rising crows abandon their nests, three, then four, and then two more.[23] There's three, five, six snowflakes, pretty as flower petals. In the cherry blossom season, will we ever again visit Mibu in the capital with its many trees in bloom and (*san-sagari song*) watch the kyōgen plays at the Mibu Temple's festival? (*ainote melody*) But just as flowers reach their peak and fall, humans too, in the space of one night's dream, may be torn asunder by a sudden storm, struck down and down. (*sung*) Only for you will I strive to rise again in this world. (*cadence*) We are coming to Hokoeda village.

(*sung*) We've crossed the River of Three Fords into the netherworld and now pass Two Fords village near the Fudaraku Temple. Long ago, at this Ono Memorial in Ichiharano, Captain Fukakusa's angry spirit arose to avenge haughty Ono no Komachi for one hundred nights unfulfilled.[24] Now only bamboo grasses bend in the wind as memories of this tale.[25] (*cadence*) They stop to rest at Ichiharano.[26]

NARRATOR: (*sung*) A despondent Yorihira raises his head.
YORIHIRA: (*spoken*) Listen, Eika, my lady. You had never looked beyond the elegant walls of your palace, but for love you have braved snow and frostbite, walking for days without complaint. Such spirit, such beauty, no wonder my brother was so entranced with you. Without Kochō's intervention, you would now be Yorinobu's wife. Yet unexpectedly you found yourself his younger brother's bride. My love's arrow hit the target, and you were the lucky prize.
NARRATOR: (*sung*) He reflects (*cadence*) on the path of his impetuous love. (*sung*) Lady Eika, too, ponders their fate.

EIKA: Although they say the way of the world is strange, surely no love is stranger than ours. Yet the gods who united us as a couple surely made no error. It was our karma from previous lives. It's a woman's virtue to follow her man into fire, to the depths of the sea, until they part as dust. I was ready to suffer and face hardship. (*spoken*) Don't worry about me. You are Minamoto no Yorihira, known to all. Face the world with pride and dignity. (*sung*) Don't stain your name by worrying over a woman.

NARRATOR: (*emotional cadence*) She breaks down in tears.

YORIHIRA: (*spoken*) Yes, I do have ambitions, but no hope in sight. We'll ask the steward-priest of Mount Kurama Temple to offer prayers for us. He is a friend of mine. Planning to press him to help us, I've dragged you this far, but the snow is heavier in the mountains. It's impossible to go on, so we'll have to rest here and hope the storm passes. This is a disaster, all my fault! (*sung*) There's a scarecrow left behind (*cadence*) in that barren winter field. (*sung*) Here, cover yourself with this cloak; (*high pitch*) think of it as a painted screen.

NARRATOR: He puts it on her shoulders and breaks down in tears.

EIKA: No, you more than I must be protected.

NARRATOR: She covers him with the robe, their sleeves overlap, and eyes meet. (*high pitch*) Tears fall, (*cadence*) freezing on their cheeks, (*sung*) mixing with the hail falling (*cadence*) on the bamboo grass in the open field.

  (*sung*) The sun's rays grow distant on a winter afternoon. Along a narrow path from Yase, a group of large men, six or seven, appear, carrying bundles and packs and leading an ox loaded with strong-boxes full of booty and packs of swords and spears of all sizes. They approach, shuffling through the snow, looking like the entourage of a corrupt official doing his rounds (*cadence*) or like a traveling theater troupe.

  (*sung*) The suspicious-looking characters stop when they see the couple, nod and whisper to one another, and set down their loads. They approach in a threatening manner.

FIRST BANDIT: (*spoken*) Well, just look at this darling! She's quite something.

NARRATOR: (*sung*) He grabs at her sash, but she slaps his hand away.

EIKA: How could you be so insolent! Disgusting.

NARRATOR: She nestles closer to Yorihira.

FIRST BANDIT: (*spoken*) A bit cheeky aren't we, my innocent. No need to

FIGURE 52 (Top center) Yorihira carrying Eika through the snow on the road to Ichiharano and Kurama; (right) Yoshikado capturing Eika and confronting Yorihira; (left) Yorinobu, on horseback, shooting Kidōmaru, who is hiding inside a dead cow; (bottom left) Tsuna capturing Yorihira. (*Kanhasshū tsunagi-uma*, 1724, National Diet Library.)

tell me; I know I'm a fast one. We couldn't give a flea's fart for a pretty face. It's your magnificent kimono that I've fallen for. How you answer my request doesn't matter, I'll strip it off anyway. And as for you, pretty boy, you have a fine sword I want. Don't think of resisting; I'd be sad to see those childish forelocks fall like blossoms. We like both men's and women's things. The slightest rip from a sword means the robes are no good to us. Just be a good boy and girl and strip off those robes nicely. Whether I threaten you with tough words or caress you with gentle smiles, the result will the same in the end. Those kimonos are coming off. The choice is yours, but it's certainly in your interest not to get hurt. That's right, isn't it fellows? (*sung*) Ah, all praise to Amida Buddha.

NARRATOR: He makes these rough jokes, (*cadence*) unaware that he is insulting the shogun's younger brother, Yorihira.

(*sung*) Lady Eika ignores the mountain bandits, not caring who they are. She fears how Yorihira will react.

EIKA: (*spoken*) Listen, you must protect yourself. (*sung*) No matter what, you mustn't lose your temper and do something foolish.

NARRATOR: (*emotional cadence*) Her voice trembles, her expression desperate.

YORIHIRA: (*spoken*) I'm not going to lose my temper over these ruffians. If they want my swords, then I'll be happy to hand them over. (*sung*) Well then, come on and take them.

NARRATOR: In a flash, he unsheathes his sword and strikes at the bearded giant nearest to him, who parries his thrust.

FIRST BANDIT: Well it seems I underestimated our foe, and he got in the first blow. I'll see you cut to shreds, beaten to death!

NARRATOR: (*battle cadence*) The others yell out, draw swords, and attack. (*sung*) Yorihira, young and brave, fights fiercely with the strength of Wu Huo[27] and the cunning of Sun Wu and Wu Qi,[28] cutting down bandits with both hands. Although they don't fear death, the brigands grow tired and weary, (*cadence*) and just as it seems they'll retreat,

(*sung*) A huge man with the air of a leader, slips out of the shadows and grabs Lady Eika.

YOSHIKADO: (*spoken*) Listen, listen, you, young fellow. If you fight back, you'll see this woman cut down with one blow.

YORIHIRA: Wait! Don't do anything rash. My wife is of noble birth, worth giving up one's land for. Don't do anything foolish; don't be careless! (*sung*) I won't resist.

NARRATOR: He throws his swords down but remains defiant in spirit, unwilling to surrender. Knowing the moment is crucial, his heart floats between attack and retreat, his forehead steams from the fires burning within. (*cadence*) Beads of sweat show the tension in his body. (*spoken*) The leader nods his head slowly.

YOSHIKADO: Your prowess with the sword just now, it wasn't just from training in technique. You're that rare thing, a natural swordsman. Your eyes and complexion prove you're no ordinary foot soldier. (*sung*) We, too, are not just brigands stealing for a living. We're out searching for fine warriors like yourself to join our cause. (*spoken*) I am Shōgun Tarō Yoshikado, heir of Taira no Masakado. I am plotting to avenge my father by overthrowing the court, and I planted my younger sister Kochō as a spy in Yorimitsu's house, but she was discovered and struck down. Her death has made me all the more determined. Won't you join us? This woman's life *(sung)* hangs on your answer.

NARRATOR: Threats to his hostage give force to his words. *(cadence)* Yorihira's face pales.

YORIHIRA: *(spoken)* Then Kochō was your younger sister, and you are the famous Yoshikado, heir of Taira no Masakado and leader of the rebellion against the court. Well, that woman, too, is no common mistress or harlot. She is Lady Eika, daughter and heir of Lord Ebumi no Saishō Tamenari. My relation with her began because of Kochō's intervention. I, myself, am Dewa no Kanja Yorihira, third son of Tada no Manjū. Although I knew of my elder brother Yorinobu's interest in Lady Eika, I stole her for myself. We have eloped and fled in disguise, *(sung)* but I had hoped to meet a rebel like yourself and take his head. I could bring this to my brothers Yorimitsu and Yorinobu to restore my honor and soften their anger. Just as I was dreaming of returning home in triumph.... *(highest pitch)* I'm like a whale prepared to devour a ship, but trapped instead in a wire fishnet. Curse this fate!

NARRATOR: He kicks at the ground, *(cadence)* scattering a mound of ice into thousands of tiny icicles.

EIKA: *(spoken)* What, Lord Yorihira, are you mad? Demented? How could you expect to serve yourself or your clan by joining up with a treacherous rebel bent on overthrowing the court! When I begged you never to shame yourself in defense of one insignificant woman, this is what I meant. *(sung)* Brace yourself to know that our love was fated to be short lived, and let me die. Take the head of Yoshikado and recover your honor. *(spoken)* If you were to join him, *(sung, highest pitch)* you'd forever regret your cowardice.

NARRATOR: Her body wilts; *(high pitch)* only her spirit cries out to him, *(cadence)* but he remains unmoved.

YOSHIKADO: *(spoken)* What'll it be, Yorihira? Will you join us or see the woman killed? It's cowardly to delay. Your choice!

NARRATOR: Pressed to respond, Yorihira speaks.

YORIHIRA: *(cadence)* Ah, I have no choice. *(sung)* Even if I, Minamoto no Yorihira, became an enemy of the state and gave up my life, it would be a far greater shame to stand by and allow a woman under my care to be killed. Not only myself alone, (*spoken*) but all my clan, back to its founding patriarch Rokusonō Tsunemoto, would be disgraced. Well then, from today onward, I cast aside forever my ties to family and friends (*sung*) and become your steadfast ally.

NARRATOR: Eika tries (*highest pitch*) desperately to prevent his pledge.

EIKA: Have you been possessed? Has the devil seized your soul, Lord Yorihira?

NARRATOR: Her pleas fall on deaf ears.

YOSHIKADO: Speak no more.

NARRATOR: He forces her sleeve into her mouth and, delighted, turns to Yorihira.

YOSHIKADO: (*spoken*) Spoken like a true Minamoto warrior! What a decisive pledge! You are welcome as an ally. My late father Masakado surely rejoices from his grave. My Lady, (*sung*) you must be uncomfortable.

NARRATOR: He releases her, (*emotional cadence*) but she loses her balance and collapses.

YOSHIKADO: (*spoken*) Yes, Yorihira, you are a direct descendant of the Seiwa Genji who trace their origins to Imperial Prince Momozono. I am a Taira, direct descendant of Emperor Kanmu through Prince Katsurabara, only a few generations from direct imperial lineage. I'm no upstart. It's not unreasonable for me to seek the throne. (*sung*) Cast your fate to the winds and join me in raising an army. Let's raise a toast to our pledge.

NARRATOR: He draws the ox closer and takes out his sword. He cuts off its ear and (*cadence*) squeezes the blood into a bowl.

YOSHIKADO: (*spoken*) We'll follow the Chinese example from the Spring and Autumn Age.[29] Drinking the blood of an ox's ear, we pledge an iron vow, equal to drinking sacred water before the gods. (*sung*) As the older of the two, I shall drink first.

NARRATOR: Yoshikado downs the cup in one gulp and places it refilled in front of Yorihira. He raises the cup, accepting the toast, and then drains it.

YORIHIRA: (*spoken*) Sharing a toast of blood links our spirits for eternity. Whether you seek a thousand or ten thousand mounted warriors, (*sung*) hurry then, and hoist your banner, and let me join you in raising an army.

NARRATOR: His vow is youthful and brash, all bridges burned. Lady Eika is devastated.

EIKA: *(spoken)* Listen, think what you're saying. A general's word carries heavy weight; *(sung)* once given, it determines fate, for good or ill.

NARRATOR: She tries to stop him, to hold him back, but he ignores her pleas. As the philosopher Mo Tzu lamented, a white thread once dyed cannot be made pure again.[30] *(cadence)* Fear for the fate of this young man who is now entangled in a mesh.

(sung) Yoshikado's scout Kidōmaru[31] comes rushing back, panting for breath.

KIDŌMARU: *(spoken)* Minamoto Yorinobu is making his regular pilgrimage to Kurama Temple. He'll pass along this road on his return.

NARRATOR: He stops to catch his breath. Yoshikado dances with joy.

YOSHIKADO: I'll avenge my sister's death. After killing him off, we'll offer his blood to the god of war. Yorihira, are you with me on this?

YORIHIRA: After our pledge, you need not question my loyalty. I accept my first command, to attack my brother Yorinobu.

YOSHIKADO: Magnificent! I've complete faith in you. Kidōmaru, cut out the guts of this ox and hide inside it. *(sung)* We'll make it look like a dead wild ox to fool Yorinobu. When he approaches you jump out and cut him down.

NARRATOR: Yoshikado explains the plan in detail and then leads Yorihira and the others out of sight into the shadows of a cliff *(exit cadence)* hidden by the veil of snow.

NARRATOR: *(nō chanting)*[32] Suspecting nothing, Lord Minamoto no Yorinobu makes his way along the snowy road, accompanied by only a few soldiers, led by Watanabe no Tsuna, who alone is worth a thousand men. *(spoken)* Under his formal coat, Yorinobu wears a light mail vest. Attached to his horse is a bow wrapped at the ends with rattan, and arrows tipped with tempered steel. *(sung)* Astride his horse, he cuts a fine figure, both calm and firm. *(bun'ya style)* He shakes off *(high pitch)* the snow from *(low pitch)* his sleeves.

YORINOBU: Magnificent, this view![33] "A sure sign of a blessed harvest throughout the realm, fields and mountains *(high pitch)* blanketed in glistening snow."[34]

NARRATOR: Recalling an old verse, he is touched by the scene. He reins his horse back, reluctant to let its hooves *(high pitch)* disturb the beauty of this first, deep snow, (*sung*) as stunning as a field of flowers in full bloom.[35]

YORINOBU: (*spoken*) Look, over there, Watanabe! There's a dead ox in that field. But I can't understand why its belly keeps moving still. (*sung*) A dead animal doesn't go on moving. There's something suspicious about that.[36]

TSUNA: (*spoken*) What shall we do about it? (*sung*) If it's suspicious, we can't ignore it.

NARRATOR: He adjusts his bow and draws an arrow. It strikes its target, sinking into the ox as far as the feathers. He rushes up, but before he can remove the arrow, out pops a wounded Kidōmaru.

KIDŌMARU: Blast, I've been discovered!

NARRATOR: He runs toward Yorinobu, but Watanabe grabs him and pins him to the ground.

TSUNA: (*spoken*) What a clumsy, cloven-footed, cud-chewing clod of a thief! And a stupid, yellow-bellied, bovine trick to boot. Where's the rest of your herd? One little calf on its own isn't going to be a match for the shogun; his horns reach to the heavens and his eyes see everywhere. (*sung*) You'll feel the kick of this bull's rage; off to the slaughterhouse with you.

NARRATOR: (*cadence*) Tsuna cuts off his head and throws it aside.

(*sung*) From the edge of the mountain, a voice echoes out at the head of the ambush. Yorinobu and the others are completely surrounded.

YOSHIKADO: (*spoken*) Well now, Yorinobu, I'll take my revenge for my sister Kochō's death. You won't evade the vengeful sword of Yoshikado. Act like an honorable man and take your own life. Go on, now, do it as it should be done!

NARRATOR: Watanabe laughs heartily at his taunts.

TSUNA: You want us to stab ourselves in the belly? What a laugh! The thought makes my sides split. Not one, but now two generations of Taira rebels from the east. It's my job as general to see you're taken care of as your father was. The guardian god Tamonten of Kurama Temple protects the court from enemies to the north. Your head will be my Kurama trophy to take home.

NARRATOR: (*sung*) He draws his sword and attacks, leading some thirty soldiers, without armor, against an enemy ten times in number, fully armored. They clash, yelling with each charge, fighting blindly in the swirling snow, stirring the winds down from the mountain, tempting an avalanche. Are young blossoms to be strewn over the battlefield, (*cadence*) or are these falling snowflakes?

(*sung*) Robes fly this way and that among the carnage. The field, once pure white under a blanket of snow, is dyed crimson with the blood of fallen warriors, their bodies buried under a foot of snow. They fight valiantly in close combat, but the odds of this battle are against them. (*battle cadence*) Desperation sets in.

(*sung*) The battle is fierce, and before long, most of Yoshikado's men are dead. He fights on fearlessly, with only one brave follower at his side. With no chance of victory, Yoshikado runs off in retreat with his few survivors. Yorinobu calls out after him.

YORINOBU: (*spoken*) You won't get away!

NARRATOR: (*sung*) He runs after the rebels, but Watanabe no Tsuna stops him.

TSUNA: (*spoken*) They're only a band of criminals, not worthy of a general. I'll take care of them.

NARRATOR: He sets off in pursuit. (*sung*) From the shadows of a snow-covered pine, Yorihira emerges in his path.

YORIHIRA: (*spoken*) Have you forgotten Yorihira? I'm now in league with Yoshikado.

NARRATOR: He immediately draws his sword and attacks. (*sung*) Watanabe is taken aback and uneasy about fighting his lord. He parries his blow and strikes back cleverly, knocking away Yorihira's sword. He tackles Yorihira, pins him to the ground, and ties his hands firmly behind his back with a bowstring.

TSUNA: (*spoken*) What has the rage of heaven done? How could you join forces with an enemy of the court and be captured by one of your own soldiers? (*sung*) You've dishonored the Genji name. Have you nothing left of the spirit of a warrior in you?

NARRATOR: Tsuna stands over him, (*spoken*) stunned and appalled. (*sung*) Lady Eika rushes forward stumbling through the snow.

EIKA: How shameful! (*highest pitch*) Have you been tied up? Now, no matter what defense you might offer, it is too late. A samurai knows compassion.[37] Tie me up instead, with a thousand ropes. Vent your anger on me; cut and slash me into little shreds, but I beg you to let Lord Yorihira go.

NARRATOR: She pleads passionately, but Tsuna ignores her. Yorihira shows no sign of fear.

YORIHIRA: (*spoken*) When I joined the enemy, do you think I didn't realize it meant a shameful execution? I'm hardly surprised to be tied up. I am Yorihira, son of the Genji patriarch. Just because I face a dilemma, it doesn't mean I am lily livered; I'm not one to change my colors so easily and be reviled for generations to come. Never! Whether I'm killed or saved depends on what is decided today. Until then, I'm deaf and dumb. (*sung*) Not another word.

NARRATOR: He spits out his words through clenched teeth; (*cadence*) his eyes speak his determination.

EIKA: (*sung*) Since you are so determined, I shall be the same. Until our fate to die or live is decided, no word or sound will come from me. Together we stand silent.

NARRATOR: Her lips are tight shut as their eyes meet. No words are spoken, but silent tears gush from their hearts, (*cadence*) a silent waterfall that melts the snow.[38]

(*sung*) Just then Mita no Jirō Tomozuna, whose mother nursed both him and Yorihira as babies, arrives in search of his liege lord Yorihira. Seeing Yorihira bound, he rushes forward and glares angrily at Watanabe.

TOMOZUNA: (*spoken*) What is this insolence? What has my lord done to deserve to be tied up? It is true that Lord Yorihira has fallen in love with Lady Eika, but she was not married and so it is in no sense adultery. With the passion of youth, he ignored deference toward his brother and secretly courted Lady Eika, (*sung*) but one is not bound by a rope for such a crime.

NARRATOR: He starts to untie the rope, but Tsuna pushes him aside.

TSUNA: (*spoken*) Your mother is in fact my aunt and we're cousins, but don't depend on our private relations in this matter.[39] Do you think that I would shackle Lord Yorihira for no good reason? His crime is grave beyond belief. He joined forces with Yoshikado and ambushed his brother returning from Kurama Temple. We have just now driven off the traitors in a fierce battle. If you raise a finger in his defense, you too will be an enemy, and even your innocent mother, my aunt, will be guilty. Go away, you fool!

NARRATOR: He holds the rope even tighter.

TOMOZUNA: What! Have you joined Yoshikado? How could you do such a thing! (*sung*) A shameful, wretched deed!

NARRATOR: Shocked, he clings to Yorihira and weeps. General Yorinobu gives up his pursuit of Yoshikado and, gnashing his teeth, turns on Tomozuna.

YORINOBU: (*spoken*) Listen, Tomozuna, if you defend Yorihira, a vile enemy of the realm, you too are a traitor.

NARRATOR: Tomozuna flushes with anger.

TOMOZUNA: Only a blind fool would call me a traitor. Lord Yorihira and I nursed together at my mother's breast. In his wisdom, Shogun Yorimitsu asked me personally to serve and protect Yorihira. Entrusted thus, should Lord Yorihira die, I shall follow at his side. I had no idea that he had eloped and fled, no inkling that he had joined Yoshikado and was captured. This is a grave crime. He will be shamed forever as a samurai, reviled by the world, the butt of laughter. (*sung*) It will bring shame to the Genji clan, too. I beg Your Lordship's compassion as a general. Until the truth of these accusations is determined, hand him over to me for custody. If you refuse, I'll take this sword and kill myself here and now. Farewell to this world.

NARRATOR: His demand is brash. Yorihira rushes forward and kicks Tomozuna aside and then turns to Yorinobu. Without a word, he thrusts his neck forward signaling execution. He turns to Tomozuna and sticks his neck out, then again to Yorinobu, taunting them, fearless of death. Yorinobu ignores him and turns away.

YORINOBU: (*spoken*) Tomozuna, you've spoken as a true samurai, your words to the point. Although Yorihira has been found guilty of treason and should be executed, I would be sorry if it were said that Yorinobu, governor of Kawachi, cruelly killed his brother in anger over losing a woman. In particular, your mother is Tsuna's aunt who raised him as well; you can be trusted. (*sung*) I am moved by your loyal heart and entrust Yorihira and his wife to your care. This is not a personal request; consider it the official command of Yorimitsu himself. You are to await further orders.

NARRATOR: Tomozuna bows happily in thanks, his forehead to the snow. Feeling as if he is returning from the dead, (*cadence*) he unties Yorihira's ropes.

TOMOZUNA: (*sung*) Well then, let us be off, Lord Yorihira.

NARRATOR: He grabs Yorihira's arm, but Yorihira shakes him off and (*kowari threatening melody*) begins to pile up the snow into a huge ball. He lifts it with both hands.

YORIHIRA: (*lively, sung*) Since I went against my duty as son and brother and joined the enemies of the Crown, I have no wish for my life to be spared. The snow falling now is my spirit. I mean that the Chinese character for "snow" [雪] can also be read in Japanese as both *susugu* "to cleanse" and *kiyomeru* "to purify." My swords have been wrenched from my side. I'm a prisoner stripped of his sword, buried under snow, shamed. Although my name may be buried, watch carefully. I "cleanse" this shame by bearing further shame; I "purify" my sullied name by maintaining my villainy. Watch me to the very end. See if my words ring true or prove false.[40]

NARRATOR: He throws the snowball at the feet of Yorinobu. It breaks apart, (*intense, sung*) splitting into six blossom-like clumps.[41] Near and far, all is a blanket of snow or clouds. The eight cold winds of hell pierce the skin to the bone. Yorihira walks off, his teeth clenched. (*high pitch*) Only a fierce enemy is worth taking on as an ally. Right and wrong are the same; good and evil are not different.[42] Sometimes firm and at other times gentle; this is the basis of the way of the warrior, resolute and courageous, as transmitted from old.

Act 3

—Scene 1
Yorimitsu official shogun residence, the day before Yorihira's execution, twenty-seventh day of the twelfth month, 988

NARRATOR:

(*sung*) A clever fox hidden in his small lair
will deceive a tiger
who rules a thousand leagues.[1]
One sharp retort will quell a flood of foolish chatter.[2]

General Minamoto no Yorimitsu has completed the transfer of shogunal power to his brother Yorinobu, who has routed the enemy at the battle of Ichiharano. The capital is at peace, but because the rebel General Yoshikado has fled, leaving no trace, all five home provinces near the capital and the seven major roads, as well as every corner of the remote mountains and forests, are being searched by government soldiers. Officials anxiously await word of his capture at General Yorimitsu's residence, which is serving as the (*cadence*) government's judicial court.

(*sung*) Lord Ebumi no Tamenari (father of Lady Eika) and his wife Hagi no Tai arrive escorted by armed guards to be judged and sentenced because of their close relationship to Yorihira, who has been declared (*spoken*) "an enemy of the court." They have been held under strict house arrest awaiting trial, and (*sung*) today General Yorimitsu has been ordered by the emperor to decide their sentence. Torabe no Suetake and Usui no Sadamitsu take charge of the pair, and (*cadence*) the official escorts depart. (*sung*) Suetake and Sadamitsu lead the couple to the judicial bench and bow:

SUETAKE: (*spoken*) Yorihira, lord of Dewa, defected and joined forces with the enemy Yoshikado. Yorinobu has captured him and has placed him before the court for judgment. His Royal Highness has declared that his offense is most grave and that family concerns for him as a brother are private and outside consideration. (*sung*) Insurrection toward the court by one of its officers must meet with a death sentence or exile—according to legal precedent. General Yorimitsu has been ordered to determine the judgment. (*spoken*) Yorihira has consequently been sentenced to execution. You both have long served the court, but as of today, in accordance with samurai law, it has been decided that you are to be stripped of your position and title, demoted to commoner status, and banished from the capital. We have orders from His Majesty to deliver this verdict to you in person. Therefore, from today you both are declared commoners. You are in our custody, and our soldiers will escort you to the Toba Highway and exile. (*sung*) Now, you shall remove your court robes and put on commoners' clothes.

NARRATOR: Both look around in shock, only able to mutter, "What is this?" Hagi no Tai moves forward to speak.

HAGI: Please, wait a moment! Although I do not dispute the crime itself, Lord Tamenari is entirely blameless in this matter. (*spoken*) If his punishment rests on the fact that Lady Eika, wife of the traitor Yorihira, is his daughter, then let me submit evidence to the contrary. Eika is in fact not the child of Lord Tamenari. She is my daughter by another man. (*sung*) Eika was already five years old when I married Lord Tamenari. We presented her publicly as our child and have brought her up as such to this day. Although she was not his own daughter, he raised her as his true child, as is well known to all. She, however, has shown little gratitude; rather, because of her he is to lose both his estate and his status. He is too noble to show his anger and regret, but his heart is (*cadence*) deeply grieved and hurt.

(*sung*) A woman, whether high born or lowly, should be a strength for her husband and should clear away any shame if she can. Because of me, however, he is being destroyed. I have no words to express the pain and agony this brings. I alone am Eika's parent. I am ready to face any punishment, even execution, but please, I beg you both to (*highest pitch*) present my pleas for Lord Tamenari's pardon to those above.

NARRATOR: (*emotional cadence*) She breaks down in tears, regardless of others' eyes.

TAMENARI: (*sung*) Wife, your concerns are unnecessary. Although she is not my natural daughter, all these years we have truly lived as father and child. (*spoken*) If this disaster had not occurred and she had married Yorinobu and been raised to be one of the highest ladies in the land, would I have then not continued to claim her as my daughter? (*sung*) I certainly would not have protested that I was not her real father. We sympathize even with a stranger who falls on hard times. How could I now abandon my own child Eika, who has been such a loving daughter?

NARRATOR: Even though he tries to stem his wife's protests, she refuses to listen.

HAGI: Eika has no father. I am both her father and mother. Please present my petition!

NARRATOR: (*highest pitch*) She pleads to everyone—high officials, ladies of the palace, and the samurai—she bows to them all in supplication, her hair in disarray. She writhes on the tatami floor, (*cadence*) weeping shamelessly, a pitiful sight.

NARRATOR: (*sung*) Suetake and Sadamitsu are sympathetic but reply roughly.

SUETAKE: (*spoken*) What groveling cowardice! An adopted child, one who you consider your own, is bound to you by custom. Even if the natural mother or father is another, once proclaimed openly, the bond of parent and child cannot be broken. Today's ruling follows a careful investigation by the highest council at court. The sentence of demotion and exile comes directly from His Royal Highness. Even Lord Yorimitsu cannot alter this. Any leniency will cause Lord Tamenari to commit a further offense against the Crown. (*sung*) You must immediately leave the capital and offer your sincere apologies. As I've said before, we are messengers of the imperial will. Please do not think ill of us.

NARRATOR: With that, they quickly take off Lord Tamenari's official court hat, flinging it to the floor. His official robes, too, are roughly stripped off.

SUETAKE: (*spoken*) Lord Tamenari of Ebumi and his wife, you are banished from the capital. (*sung*) Have them led away.

NARRATOR: Foot soldiers come forward with spears and poles and roughly prod the pair along. Suetake and Sadamitsu follow after. The couple are pitiful, like reluctant birds driven out of the forest into the (*exit cadence*) hunting ground before their time.[3]

—Scene 2
The Yorimitsu residence

NARRATOR: (*sung*) An old man arrives at the gate. His hair is silver, and his appearance is old-fashioned, upright, strict, and stubborn, with an air of having borne the weight of a hundred years of frost and snow. He wears an elaborate, amber-colored, antique sword-sheath, and his worn face has as many wrinkles as his ancient *hakama* skirt.

OLD MAN: (*spoken*) The old fool before you is Sasame no Shōni. I've come to see General Yorimitsu to present a petition. (*sung*) Allow me to pass.

NARRATOR: He barges into the residence, but the guards of the inner room flush with anger.

GUARDS: You ignorant fool, leave at once, this minute!

NARRATOR: But he remains unflustered (*cadence*) in the commotion, stubbornly defiant.

(*sung*) Ōya no Tadamasa comes forward.

TADAMASA: (*spoken*) Is this a private appeal, or are you a messenger? If you have come to plead for Yorimitsu's younger brother Yorihira, then it's no use. I cannot even speak to General Yorimitsu for you. (*sung*) Have a cup of tea, and be on your way.

NARRATOR: With this, Tadamasa turns to go back inside but the old man laughs loudly.

OLD MAN: (*spoken*) If I were content to have a message relayed, I'd have stayed at home and had my daughter or grandchild come. I'd have composed a letter at my leisure while lying in bed. I've got something to put directly into Yorimitsu's ear from my own lips. It is of great concern to the realm. Shall I just yell it out from the entrance? I'd be happy to crawl to the inner chambers to meet the great general, who seems to fear people, (*sung*) but that would be rude and improper. Let me meet Lady Yorimitsu. Someone, maids! Lead me to the inner rooms!

NARRATOR: His husky, harsh voice resounds throughout the residence. Tadamasa rises in anger.

TADAMASA: (*spoken*) What unspeakable bad manners! Are you a rōnin or in service to someone? You don't look like a lackey or laborer. You should know what the rules are for entering an official residence, especially since this is a general's house. (*sung*) You are being outrageous. Are you drunk? Demented? Guards, have this man removed!

NARRATOR: The guards respond quickly, brandishing their spears threateningly as they surround him. They taunt him, but his old eyes gleam like polished silver, keeping them at bay on all sides. He laughs aloud.

OLD MAN: (*spoken*) What a frightening bunch you are! I'm quaking with fear! If you make this much fuss over a shriveled old locust like me, what would you do if I were a strong young enemy? What an uproar there'd be! Do you think that I'm afraid of a jab in the side or a thrust at my leg! No guards' threats are going to keep me from speaking. (*sung*) Come on, have a go at me. Come on!

NARRATOR: He remains stubbornly firm.

TADAMASA: You must be an ally of Yoshikado, playing the fool to get at Lord Yorimitsu. This is all a plan. Guards, kill him!

NARRATOR: Just as the fight begins, a soft voice calls out from within.

YORIMITSU: (*spoken*) Listen, listen to me! Don't be rough with that man. Allow him to see Lord Yorimitsu.

NARRATOR: (*sung*) At this order, all turn quiet and put their weapons aside. Lord Yorimitsu calmly enters and takes his place of honor. Even the rude and rough old man withdraws for the first time and bows (*cadence*) deeply with respect. (*sung*) After a moment Yorimitsu speaks:

YORIMITSU: (*spoken*) This Sasame no Shōni is an old samurai it seems, but it's not a name I'm familiar with or a face I've seen before. Government is like traveling a distant road across difficult mountains and along rough shores. Between the ruler at the top and the myriads below, there are many layers of authority. You must have been frustrated that an important point was not being conveyed from below, and so you rudely forced your way, forgetting the propriety of this official place. Is your petition private, or do you have a complaint that Yorimitsu's government is at fault? Calm yourself and take your time to present your case.

NARRATOR: During this speech, the old man keeps his head bowed to the floor. He slowly raises his tearful, weathered face.

OLD MAN: Thank you for this kindness in not condemning my rudeness and in granting me a chance to speak frankly. (*sung*) How different are those on high from those below! The small blackbird that flits about among the willow branches laughs at the great phoenix who travels thousands of leagues across the sky.[4] Truly, one's station affects one's perceptions; that is certainly so for this old man.

(*cadence*) However, (*sung*) from those at the pinnacle, emperors and ministers, to the lowliest woodcutters and fishermen, all have in common their love and compassion for family—parent and child, child and siblings. (*spoken*) How, therefore, can Lord Yorimitsu loathe and (*sung*) hate his own brother?

NARRATOR: But before he can finish, Yorimitsu's expression alters and his face colors with anger. He rises to go into the inner chambers. The old man runs after and clings to the skirts of his official robes. Yorimitsu's voice shows his anger.

YORIMITSU: (*spoken*) I wondered what you might say but didn't expect you to speak about my family relations. That is forbidden. Are you an envoy from Yorihira? No matter who asked you to come—how could you know the heart of Yorimitsu, the mirror of the realm, never!

NARRATOR: But even at this stern rebuke, the old man remains firm.

OLD MAN: No, anyone who hates his younger brother cannot be called a "mirror of the realm." Among siblings, some are born before others; your brother, too, is of your parent's blood. The hearts of an older and younger brother are not different, but the fiery blood of youth can be volatile, and youth often goes against the will of parents or older brothers. If one casts off blood relations at each rebellion, how can Japan maintain an ethical society? Such actions are hardly a mirror of virtue. In particular, Yorihira is the youngest and the favorite of his mother. If you kill him, you will be unfilial to your mother. Is being unfilial a "mirror of the realm"? Furthermore, you promised[5] to grant me one petition in my lifetime, no matter what it was. Does a great general and a "mirror of the realm" betray his word? The eyes of this old fool see a shattered mirror. A clouded mirror becomes bright with polish, but no matter how skillful the polisher, he cannot save a broken mirror. This bronze mirror no longer brightly reflects heaven's virtue. (*sung*) Donate it to some rustic temple as scrap to be melted down and cast as a new bell.

NARRATOR: (*cadence*) He laughs aloud showing a toothless grin.

(*sung*) Yorimitsu returns to his seat.

YORIMITSU: (*spoken*) You are wrong to say that I hate my brother. He is not the only one to be punished. His wife Eika's parents have just now been banished by imperial order. How could Yorihira himself then be pardoned? Further, what is this promise to grant a petition of a lifetime? Is it some sly blackmail trick! I only once made such a promise, to Yorihira's nurse, Watanabe no Tsuna's Aunt Mita. When Tsuna was still young, she brought him to me as an orphan of good parentage and upbringing.[6] As a reward for offering such a fine lad to my service, instead of land or wealth she asked me to promise to have one wish granted, no matter what, once in her life. Only Aunt Mita has such a pledge from me. I haven't made a promise to any Sasame no Shōni. Get on your way!

AUNT MITA: Well, then, you admit to a pledge to Aunt Mita. She stands before you. Since you remember who I am, you must accept a letter from me. My only son Tomozuna has come to your residence time after time but has been turned away at the gate, unable to present his letter. *(sung)* So I came myself several times, to the front and back and service entrances, but *(spoken)* was refused each time. Since I had no one else to go in my place, I dressed up as this old warrior. It is like taking dirty snow and trying to make it look pretty or trying to straighten a broken, withered bamboo. My old bent back won't straighten, and I've never worn swords. *(sung)* With no one else to depend on, I had to present myself in this ridiculous costume. I've come to put my one and only request to you. Will you honor your pledge?

NARRATOR: Her plea puts pressure on Yorimitsu.

YORIMITSU: *(spoken)* But I made my promise to a woman. Aren't you Sasame no Shōni? Get on your way!

NARRATOR: *(sung)* His reply is cold.

AUNT MITA: Far too small-minded for a great general. I'll show you that I'm a woman.

NARRATOR: She stands up and loosens the belt of her *hakama* and then her Hitachi obi, finally removing all her formal robes, to reveal a frail old woman of one year less than a hundred in age, an ancient cherry tree,[7] withered nakedness, her breasts dry melons. Her thin undergarment reveals skin the color of fallen autumn leaves. Her flesh sags under skin wrinkled like waves. Her thin legs bent even further in humility, she shivers on the tatami in the large windswept room, teeth chattering. Finally she grits her teeth to control her shivers and speaks in a loud voice.

AUNT MITA: *(spoken)* Lord Yorimitsu, known for his ability to see into the affairs of far-off lands, surely has not forgotten this woman who served him, offering her breasts as nurse to his younger brother Yorihira. *(sung)* Although I called myself Sasame no Shōni, you should be able to distinguish between a man and a woman. How cruel of my Lord Yorimitsu to force *(high pitch)* this stubborn old woman to such extreme humiliation!

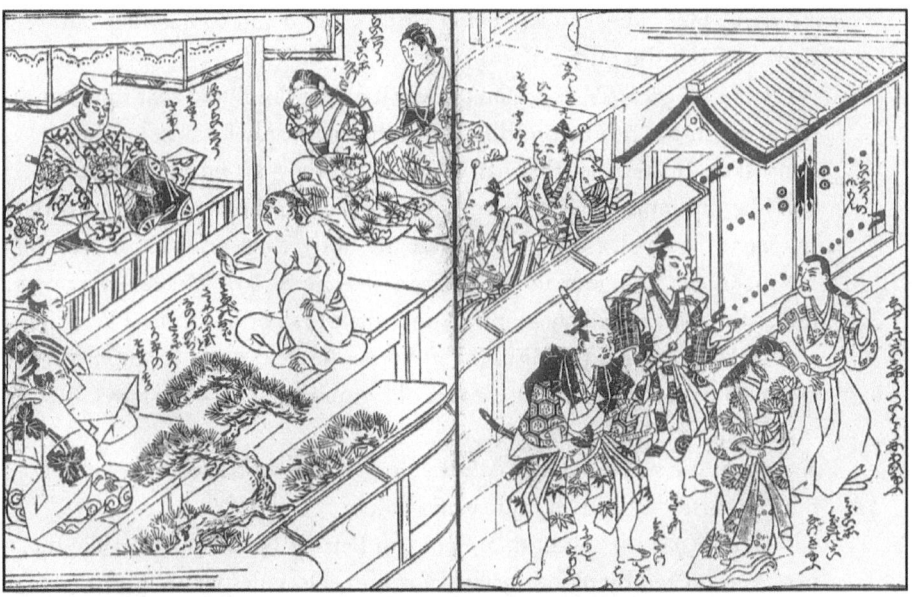

FIGURE 53 (Right) In front of the gate to Yorimitsu's residence, Lord Ebumi and his wife Lady Hagi are being banished from the capital by Sadamitsu and Suetake; (left) Aunt Mita, half naked, after discarding her disguise as the samurai Sasame while Yorimitsu and Lady Yorimitsu look on. (*Kanhasshū tsunagi-uma*, 1724, National Diet Library.)

NARRATOR: (*high pitch*) She collapses in grief, her appearance like those depicted in paintings of hell, showing poor women digging up bamboo roots.[8] Ashamed of her actions, (*cadence*) she weeps uncontrollably, a wretched sight. (*sung*) All those who witness this scene hide their eyes with their sleeves, whispering to one another. (*spoken*) "What a fierce, upright old woman, what a show of will! (*sung*) It's as if the Rashōmon demon has become Watanabe's aunt in order to get back his arm cut off in that famous fight.[9] (*cadence*) She's a fierce demon!"

(*sung*) From the inner room, Lady Yorimitsu has overheard all and comes forward.

LADY YORIMITSU: Is that really Aunt Mita? It has been such a long time. How good it is to see you again. Had I known it was you, I would have invited you immediately to my quarters. You must be cross with us. You, who were known for your propriety even in youth, must, even at one hundred, regret showing your body. You must be embarrassed; quick, someone cover her with a robe.

NARRATOR: Her ladies quickly bring clothes and begin to help her put them on, but she pushes them away.

AUNT MITA: (*high pitch*) No, don't cover me yet. I've heard that the skinny monkeys in the mountains differ from humans only because of their hairy skin. If they lose that hairy hide, then they are no longer beasts. I'm like the monkey. I've shaved my forehead in the samurai style with my hair whitened. (*spoken*) If I cover my body, then Lord Yorimitsu will see me as the strange male monkey Sasame no Shōni. Naked, he knows me as the aunt of Watanabe no Tsuna, the nurse of his brother Yorihira, and the one owed a promise. (*sung*) Someone help me. I have (*highest pitch*) no branch to cling to; I'm an old monkey fallen from a tree. Let me die here!

NARRATOR: She shivers and shakes, her anger and frustration revealed in her contorted mouth and quivering voice.

AUNT MITA: (*spoken*) You both are cold and cruel! Even someone like me, not even related by blood, grieves for him. How desperate must Lady Eika's agony be. My son Tomozuna has come every day and night to offer his petition. (*sung*) Compared with their suffering, it is nothing for this old (*cadence*) woman to strip naked. (*sung*) To wear fine, many-layered clothes in this life and fail to save my lord whom I raised, such a crime would haunt me at the Three Rivers of Hell where I would be harshly stripped by the old hag Datsue.[10] Why should I wear clothes now?

NARRATOR: She pushes the robes away and cries out in grief. Tears rush forth as if wrung from (*highest pitch*) her withered, shriveled frame, only to freeze in the icy cold. Lady Yorimitsu and her women (*cadence*) weep in sympathy. (*sung*)

Unable to stand aside any longer, Lady Yorimitsu moves forward and begins to dress the aunt herself. The other women follow, and they all manage to get her into the kimono, straighten the folds, and fit the obi. When the aunt tries to loosen the obi, Lady Yorimitsu gently takes her hand and puts it on her own lap.

LADY YORIMITSU: (*spoken*) You who nursed him have such love that you are willing to humiliate yourself like this; how must his late mother suffer from her grave! Lord Mitsunaka (Manjū) left only three sons. For all, high and low, the youngest child is most cherished. On her deathbed, his mother took my hand and said, "After I die, don't think of Yorihira just as a brother-in-law. Think of him as a son you've given birth to. (*sung*) Have love and compassion for him." These were her final words, and they still echo in my mind. I can see her face now. The wife of Lord Tsunenori served the Minamoto family well during its rise to power and fortune, seeing our position rise (*cadence*) to become unrivaled.

(*sung*) When she (Lord Tsunenori's wife) died, Mitsunaka's wife took care of all the memorial services without fail, so I had little duty as a new wife to Yorimitsu. I must at least serve her by intervening to save Yorihira's life. It won't be enough to erect a memorial tablet after his death. I don't want to regret later being branded as one who let him die. But there is no hope. No matter how much I plead, (*spoken*) Yorimitsu remains intractable. He is angry that his own brother has joined the enemy Yoshikado and is now a prisoner of the court. He refuses to be persuaded by family[11] concerns, even his mother's own will, because it would bring chaos to the nation's government.[12] (*sung*) After that, even I have had to give up. Please, you must try somehow to forget Yorihira.

NARRATOR: Her words resonate with the coldness of those (*highest pitch*) in power, but her heart tries desperately to convey its agony. Under her flowing sleeves, she folds her hands, and hidden from Yorimitsu, her actions entreat Aunt Mita both to forgive her and (*high pitch*) to beg her to plead further with Yorimitsu. Tears speak when words cannot, (*cadence*) a pitiful sight.

(*sung*) But General Yorimitsu refuses to look their way and remains stubbornly silent. Aunt Mita moves close to Yorimitsu and puts her plea forcefully.

AUNT MITA: (*spoken*) What a strong-willed leader! But strength alone does not make a warrior. Doesn't Confucius caution hotheaded leaders that soldiers will not follow a general who does not fear a wild tiger or a rushing river?[13] We who are connected to Yorimitsu all are guilty of conspiring with the enemy Yoshikado. Well then, this old woman is your prisoner. (*sung, high pitch*) Put my head high, high on the blocks. Show the world your samurai heart, show them that government has no place for private concerns!

NARRATOR: She raises herself ready for sacrifice, (*cadence*) forcing Yorimitsu into a corner.

(*sung*) Yorimitsu is moved by her appeal. He measures his words carefully and speaks with judicious authority.

YORIMITSU: There is no shame in being the aunt of Watanabe no Tsuna. (*spoken*) From the first, I recognized you in your disguise as an old loyal retainer but wondered what your plan was and so feigned ignorance. Yorihira has been found guilty and has been sentenced to be executed tomorrow. It would be difficult to save him at this stage, but I cannot ignore my promise to you. Today, the twenty-seventh, is the memorial of Lord Mitsunaka. I grant Yorihira seven days until the fourth of next month. I give him this reprieve for your sake. During that time, after being shown his error, if he reveals a heart clean of betrayal, his father-in-law Lord Ebumi will be pardoned, and Yorihira will be free to live a full life. If, however, there is no change, then at dawn of the fourth, at the eighth crow of the cock, his head will fly. (*sung*) If it comes to that, don't hold a grudge against me.

NARRATOR: With that he rises and goes into the inner chamber. Aunt Mita bows in gratitude, weeping again, this time in joy. Lady Yorimitsu, (*cadence*) too, bows in thanks.

LADY YORIMITSU: (*sung*) Aunt Mita has saved the life of the child she once nursed, becoming the natural mother who gave him birth.

NARRATOR: Yet amid this joy, concerns arise.

AUNT MITA: But seven days will pass as quickly as a brief daydream.

NARRATOR: Her matronly heart is already anxious at the thought of facing tragedy again.

AUNT MITA: (*spoken*) No need to worry. (*sung*) What can overcome evil will work on good as well. The worst of sinners is known to change suddenly and become a saint. Good and evil are like pools: they join the stream of a leader. Our young Yorihira is one of the best among men, and this old woman will be able to pull him around to sense again. (*spoken*) Tomozuna and Lady Eika will be waiting for me. I mustn't stay any longer.

NARRATOR: (*sung*) She groans as she tries to get up but is too stiff to move. The ladies gather around to help. They straighten her kimono and help her up. The old woman who nursed three boys lets the women take care of her. Her face and clothes show an old woman, but her hair is that of an old man. Her appearance startles everyone. Though there may be no true teetotalers, (*cadence*) there certainly are ghosts.[14]

LADY YORIMITSU: (*sung*) Now here, here. It's cold and stormy outside, your head will get cold.

NARRATOR: She kindly covers her head with a cotton scarf. Aunt Mita thanks her gratefully for this parting gift. She takes up her walking stick. They try to get her into a carriage, but she refuses.

AUNT MITA: (*spoken*) That's too grand for me. If I ride in that I'll become senile even sooner. With my stick I can still walk twenty or thirty miles. I'm not a helpless old woman yet. My old back does hurt from keeping it straight for so long. (*sung*) At least now I can stand as I please.

NARRATOR: Her bent figure walks off, skirts tucked up and leaning on her stick. As it hits the ground briskly, everyone is struck again by her appearance. The demon-child of Ibaraki[15] turned into an old woman. This old nurse was turned into a man by her own hand. To save the life of Yorihira, she became the old nurse once again. Hiding her shaven forehead with the scarf, (*scene cadence*) she heads off for home.

—Scene 3

Seven days later at the residence of Mita no Jirō Tomozuna in Watanabe, Settsu Province,[16] evening of the third day of the first month

NARRATOR: (*sung*) All those beneath heaven are our sovereign's subjects. Here, on a misty night at the home of Mita no Jirō Tomozuna near Tamino Island in Naniwa Bay, seven days have passed since Aunt Mita gained a week's reprieve for Yorihira's life. Like a morning glory, his enemy is the cock's crow—(*high pitch*) tomorrow's dawn will be his last. He stands as alone as an island (*cadence*) while all around him grieve.

(*sung*) Her hopes uncertain as this floating world, Lady Eika kneels in front of her mirror, a gift from her mother. Tonight, she thinks, will be my farewell to this as well. (*Edo jōruri*) Who will tell her parents? Hair ornaments and oils mix (*high pitch*) with tears spilling into the powder. Like the dew that awaits the dawn, she prepares her evening toilet for the last time. Suddenly reflected in the mirror, she (*cadence*) imagines her mother's face.

EIKA: (*spoken*) Dear mother! I trust you are keeping well. How delightful to see your smiling face. (*sung*) You mustn't worry about my plight. Take care of yourself and live a full life.

NARRATOR: Her voice mingles with the cries of the crows and night sparrows who seek their nests. (*cadence*) How she longs to see her mother.

(*sung*) Tomozuna returns home after being gone since morning trying to pick up any news or rumors. He loosens the scarf covering his face. His expression is creased like the scarf. He disguises his voice.

TOMOZUNA: (*spoken*) How impressive, how magnificent![17] At the fall of dusk, to paint your face like the Yūgao Moonflower! A *waka* poem has thirty-one syllables, but Eika's artifice surpasses it with thirty-two different charming faces. The pinnacle of beauty in all the more than four hundred provinces of Tang China was Yang Guei-fei;[18] the beautiful consort of the Chu emperor Xiang Yu, Yu Shi-jun; the beauty of Yue, Xi Shi; Li Fu-ren, the consort of the founder of the Later Han; Wang Zhao-jun of the Early Han—none of these compare! In Japan with more than sixty provinces, all the blooming brides of the gods or the flowery Sakuya Princess, or the Shining Princess found by the bamboo cutter at the foot of Mount Fuji—none compares. Even Soto-ori, the Weaving Princess, would be cast away without her robes. Princess Shitateru, who shines from the heavens, or Princess Otohime, who emerged from the palace beneath the sea, or the celestial Saho Princess, or Orihime.[19] All are but wildflowers in an open field. No blossoms in this world compare with Eika's charm. No autumn colors are as pretty; her hair shines like dark jade; her eyes are as beautiful as the new moon, (*sung*) curved like a fishhook to catch a great fish. Her trophy was Lord Yorihira, a man among men. (*spoken*) You're famous as the cruel thief who stole his life and carelessly saw him into his grave. What a woman! What a beauty![20]

NARRATOR: (*cadence*) At these words of praise, (*sung*) Eika is startled and starts to run away but then sees that it is in fact Tomozuna.

EIKA: (*spoken*) Is that Tomozuna? Are you serious? Lord Yorihira's life will end at dawn's first light. From your old mother down to the lowest servant, everyone is ill with anxiety; no one has had a moment of peace. Even though this is such a crucial day, you have been out since morning and only just returned. What is the meaning of your outburst, you who are like a brother to Yorihira and would be the first to reprove such behavior? I have no desire to be praised as an angel or a Yang Guei-fei. (*sung*) Is all your show of loyalty just a lie? It's painful even to talk to you.

Tethered Steed and the Eight Provinces of Kantō   391

FIGURE 54 (Top center) Tomozuna (with a scarf around his face) spying on Eika, who is in front of her mirror; (bottom right) Tomozuna shocked to see Aunt Mita strike Yorihira with the bow of Yorihira's father Manjū; (left) Eika speaking to her mother, Lady Hagi, as she climbs over the wall. (*Kanhasshū tsunagi-uma*, 1724, National Diet Library.)

NARRATOR: She starts to leave, but Tomozuna grabs her robe. He removes the scarf from his face.

TOMOZUNA: (*spoken*) How clever that you could see through my disguise and call my words false. But I don't think that you see the meaning of my words. You don't need to tell me that Lord Yorihira's life will end at dawn. I've known that for seven days now. Hoping to hear rumors that Yorimitsu or his brother had decided to extend the deadline by a day or two, I left early this morning to spy about for news from the capital and (*sung*) went as far as Hashiramoto and Yodo on the way to Kyoto. But a general's orders are as firm as an imperial decree; they cannot be rescinded. I learned that Lord Yorihira's guard will be that rough and crude Sakata no Kintoki. He is to be sent to deliver Yorihira to his execution. His boat will have an official banner, and along the river, all traffic is banned. Tonight is the last chance to save Lord Yorihira. After hearing all this and rushing home, (*spoken*) what a shock to see you at your toilet preparing yourself like a courtesan for her evening's patron, all your makeup, the pride of your pretty face, beautiful eyes, red lips, and white-powdered face. My words of praise just now had an edge of irony; they made you frown, but did they strike into your heart? How pitiful that Lord Yorihira has to be confined, unable to play his great role in the world. (*sung*) His life, which should have been full and long, will be cut short tonight. The source of this tragedy is your beautiful face! General Yorimitsu and his brothers, the whole clan, it is you alone they all hate. Furthermore, your father has, by decree, lost his status and title and been banished—all because of this lipstick and powder! (*spoken*) A proper woman would take this final opportunity before the guards arrived to plead with Yorihira to relent. A good wife would try to save her husband's life. Your face is beautiful, but your heart is ugly. How terrible that Yorihira has no idea that (*sung*) he has been trapped by such a cold heart. How awful a fate! You're a woman like no other.

NARRATOR: His anger shows in his clenched teeth and fierce eyes. Eika, however, is not shocked at his outburst.

EIKA: (*spoken*) Have you gone mad? How could anyone be surprised to hear that tonight is Yorihira's last! I agree that I was the cause of the trouble and am the object of the clan's anger and hate, but my family, too, blames Lord Yorihira for the demise of our clan. That is the way of the world. Highborn or not, a woman follows her husband. If pleadings fail, there is nothing more to do. (*sung*) If my husband is good, then I am too; if bad, then so am I. If he dies before me, I'm prepared to die immediately after him. (*spoken*) Listen, samurai, you prepare for battle by donning armor and weapons and facing death bravely, don't you? (*sung*) Likewise, the wife of Minamoto no Yorihira, Lady Eika, doesn't want the shame of dying with her hair untidy and her face unprepared, an ugly sight. My preparations are for my death visage. I want an unsullied name. I want the wife of Lord Yorihira to have died bravely, with dignity and elegance. What a pity that your vision is so poor. Tomozuna, how dare you accuse me of being a courtesan preparing coquettishly for a patron. (*highest pitch*) What a shame your eyes are so clouded.

NARRATOR: (*emotional cadence*) Her voice grows loud, her words full of passion.

(*sung*) Lord Yorihira, having overheard this exchange, roughly slides open the door, his expression angry.

YORIHIRA: (*spoken*) Tomozuna, I can understand if your old mother continues to badger me with advice, but it is unbecoming to hear complaints from a young samurai. For better or worse, once a word has left my lips, it cannot be taken back. My will is as firm as stone, harder than Buddha's bones. Do you think that I would listen to a woman's advice? (*sung*) Eika, come with me.

NARRATOR: As they are leaving, the old aunt, dressed now as a nun, takes up the famous Murashigetō bow and strikes the floor.

AUNT MITA: No farewell! No compassion. How sad!

NARRATOR: She clings to Eika but is knocked aside by Yorihira.

AUNT MITA: (*spoken*) Yes it's true; your considered words and vows are firmer than stone, but is the promise this old woman got from Yorimitsu worth nothing, just dirt or sand? I should have already shaved my head to serve Buddha, but I fear for my nephew and you whom I nursed as a child, all fine samurai. I decided to go to Sujiemon the barber and had him shave my few white hairs in the samurai style. My efforts bore fruit. Lord Yorimitsu was not allowing any petitions, and previously I hadn't been able to speak with even a palace guard. But after I furrowed my brow into a fierce and angry expression and called myself Sasame no Shōni, I got Yorimitsu to agree to a seven-day stay of execution. (*sung*) This was my last wish in the world. But even having my head shaved has been to no avail. I only regret that my action has inflamed your wrath and made you even more determined not to change. I who nursed you know you are stubborn, that once you've spoken, whether right or wrong, good or evil, you never recant. You also remember that I have a habit of countering you with even stronger words. (*spoken*) Even if you don't want to listen or watch, you have ears to hear me and eyes to see me. This bow was used by your father, Lord Manjū, in defense against the enemies of the court. (*sung*) He would be shocked and saddened to hear that Aunt Mita is using it to strike a wayward son. (*spoken*) How pitiful that because of his daughter's marriage, Lord Ebumi has lost his position and been banished. You know that but turn a blind eye! Is it bitterness against Yorimitsu for not naming you his heir? Is it jealousy of your brother Yorinobu that makes you an enemy of the court? (*sung*)

This old woman's frail arm will strike the stubborn words from your stony heart.

NARRATOR: She raises her arm to strike, but Yorihira grasps her gently and signals to her to hold back. He speaks with tears in his eyes.

YORIHIRA: *(spoken)* Boyu[21] of the famous twenty-four Chinese filial tales grieved for his father's weakened arm when he was struck—that was true love for his parent. But to be struck by Manjū's bow is truly to be whipped as an errant son. Although I know my principles are confused, my sense of good and evil perverted, *(sung)* a parched seed cannot blossom; a fallen petal cannot return to the branch. Even though I could save my own life, I cannot escape the fact that I stole Eika for myself, knowing she was to be my brother's wife. How could I sit proudly among my brothers and officers again, feeling their fingers pointed at my back? Is there a reason to go on living? *(spoken)* Further, my actions have shamed the entire clan. Yoshikado is a direct descendant of Emperor Kanmu. I am of the line of Emperor Seiwa. As equals, we openly swore a blood oath to be allies. *(sung)* If it is seen that my vow was all a trick and that I betrayed my own side to save Eika when she was captured, that I gave up my sword and acted as if I had joined Yoshikado to escape the danger, that it was the only way to save my wife, I'd be laughed at forever as a coward, too weak to fight. I'd truly shame the Genji clan—I'd be one of its highest officers branded as a coward who betrayed his side for a woman and then lives on in shame. If this blot remains, will it serve my brother's interest? *(spoken)* Rather, if I keep to my pledge to Yoshikado, I'll be praised as a brave Genji warrior who sticks to his word and upholds his honor, one who bravely faces his enemy to die for honor, duty, and compassion. Wouldn't that be the true way to serve Yorimitsu? *(sung)* Of course, I know that all the advice from family and friends is right and proper, but sometimes a samurai must go against the Way in order to be true to it. *(spoken)* For example, gold is certainly the most valuable treasure, but if one is far up a mountain side, tired and thirsty, a thousand or ten thousand gold pieces are worth less than a cup of water. *(sung)* Silk brocade is truly the finest cloth, but at the height of summer, isn't it true that beautifully colored silk robes cannot compare with one thin layer of roughly woven hemp? Therefore, we should understand that all things depend on the fortune of the moment. The saying "For summer, a small hemp robe surpasses silk brocade" fits the condition of a warrior. (*spoken*) At the battle of Ichiharano, I understood the meaning of snow.[22] A further act of shame can cover shame; deeper infamy can cleanse a sullied name. I shall cast snow at my brother Yorinobu to cleanse my shame. If I refuse the offer of mercy, my brothers will be even more angry and ready to fight. This is no time to wail in despair. Try to understand my position and feelings. Don't think of it as just my stubbornness. (*sung*) I don't know who will be sent to summon me, but if he is polite and respectful, I shall submit gracefully by committing *seppuku*, expunging my bitterness.[23] If someone like that arrogant Kintoki,[24] who thinks he's as fierce as a wild boar, confronts me with the intention of taking my head and calls me an enemy of the court who has to be executed, (*spoken*) then I shall call myself Lord Dewa Yorihira, second in command to Shōgun Tarō Yoshikado, and fight with my sword to the very last ounce of strength, killing anyone in my path. I'll leave this world with the name of a brave and fierce warrior (*sung*) who cut down his enemies and then took his own life. Now, you who nursed and nurtured me as a child and made me into a man, you are the same as my true mother. I'm not a heartless tree or stone that knows no gratitude or one who squanders all your efforts. Don't bear me a grudge.

NARRATOR: He clings to the skirts of her robe and (*emotional cadence*) weeps aloud without shame, (*cadence*) a pitiful sight.

(*sung*) The aunt, unable to restrain herself, speaks.

AUNT MITA: You never once before revealed your true feelings. Such a noble general. Not knowing your intentions, I was rash, I could only see as far as the end of my nose. I should be punished by you, by heaven. (*highest pitch*) My harsh tongue should be slashed, this withered arm that struck you should rot away. Please forgive me. My child, please pardon my actions.

NARRATOR: She throws the bow aside and hugs him to her bosom, her caresses offering comfort. The tears and pleading of the old woman are eloquent and long, and nearby, Eika and Tomozuna are unable to speak. (*cadence*) They can only weep in sympathy. Tears fall as thick as rain.

AUNT MITA: (*spoken*) We mustn't weep. At the cock's crow tomorrow, I shall gladly join the first battle of Lord Yorihira, whom I raised. (*sung*) It will be a glorious moment for this old woman warrior, who will lead from the front. If the official who comes for you is rough and insulting, we shall attack at once and fight to the death, till no one remains. (*spoken*) Tomozuna, bolt the gate. (*sung*) Stop the tears and let us have a grand banquet to prepare us for battle. (*spoken*) I'll perform a dance to accompany the first course. It will be as if I'm seventeen or eighteen again, (*sung*) with makeup powder, rouge, teeth darkened. Since I'm a beautiful and passionate lover, all the men cling to my willowy hips. But now I'm slippery, I wiggle like a prawn. How's that for a start?!

NARRATOR: She rises, her eyes clouded with tears, her voice choking.

AUNT MITA: (*popular song*) The little seven-year-old girl sings touchingly that she wants a husband,[25] but for me instead of a husband or flowers, (*sung*) I want to protect the precious life of this man I nurtured.

NARRATOR: (*emotional cadence*) Her words dissolve into tears, but she quickly recovers her voice and proclaims loudly.

AUNT MITA: (*popular song*) In my youth, gashes or cuts were nothing to me. Even now, I can take on several at a time. Do you think Benkei would flinch? Bring on Fan Kuai or Zhang Liang.[26] (*sung*) I'll handle them easily.

NARRATOR: She brandishes words as fiercely as sword cuts (*exit cadence*) as she retreats into the inner chambers.

NARRATOR: (*nō chanting*) The banquet to bid farewell to the brave soldiers (*cadence*) before battle begins.[27] Autumn rain batters against the windows, mingling its sound with the many voices. (*sung*) A quiet tapping at the front gate by a secretive visitor is heard by Eika, who feels an ominous pang in her heart. She slips away without being noticed and hurries to the gate.

EIKA: (*spoken*) Who is it, this late at night?

HAGI: That voice, it's surely my daughter. Isn't that Lady Eika?

EIKA: Then, is that mother?

HAGI: Wonderful that you recognize my voice! Yes, it is your mother, wife of Lord Ebumi. (*sung*) How good to hear your voice. It's been so long. I want so much to see your face again.

NARRATOR: She speaks through the crack in the gate, but the door is bolted tight and the wall high. She peeks through a break in the fence where crickets have found a way through, (*high pitch*) but in the starlight after the storm, all she can see is a weather-beaten wicker rain hat.

HAGI: Well, open the door, open it up!

NARRATOR: She whispers, but the words strike Eika's sad heart (*emotional cadence*) harder than thunder.

EIKA: (*spoken*) Of course I'd like to open the door to see you, even before you ask, but not even a draft of air can pass this bolted gate. Why did you come tonight? You could have come earlier. (*sung*) Lord Yorihira's life will end with the crows of dawn. I, too, must face the end. (*spoken*) When I heard about what happened, I was saddened. Because of me, the Ebumi house has fallen, banished by imperial decree. (*sung*) They say one disaster is followed by a second. Accept it all as our karma. It won't be long now before the soldiers arrive. Please go home now. I am sorry.

NARRATOR: (*emotional cadence*) Her words turn into sobs as she clutches at the door. (*cadence*) She collapses in tears.

HAGI: (*spoken*) It is generally known that Lord Yorihira will be executed at dawn. That is precisely why I'm here. Lord Ebumi's imperial banishment is due to our connection to you, who are implicated with Yorihira. I am your real mother and accept this verdict, but Lord Ebumi is a total stranger, not related by blood. This disaster is caused by a child his seed did not spawn, but as a true nobleman, his heart is pure and he shows no anger or regret. (*sung*) But think of my position. I am so ashamed and sad that I can't face him. I am unable to speak and only lower my head in tears. (*spoken*) I have heard that tonight Yorihira will be executed. Lord Yorimitsu must carry out the imperial decree to kill an enemy of the court, whether the man be a stranger or his own brother. There's nothing unusual or heroic in that. But if the gentle nobleman Ebumi takes the head of Yorihira and presents it to the court, it will be proof of his loyalty. He'll be pardoned by the emperor and restored to his position. The Ebumi house will recover its proud place again. (*sung*) I've spoken secretly to the Prosecutor's Office through a connection. Daughter, I've come deliberately before the official party in order to take Yorihira's head. You are willing to sacrifice yourself for your husband. Your mother is the same. I know it is hard for you. Don't think me cold and cruel. If we strike down Yorihira, you will have been filial and saved your father. (*spoken*) Well, can you join me in this deed? We must be prepared to die in the attack. (*sung*) If you refuse, then your mother will kill herself and leave her body outside the gate. I won't return home if you refuse me. Time is short, be quick with your answer, hurry!

NARRATOR: She bangs her sword on the door; its echo resounds deep in Eika's heart. Already desperate with worry over her husband's dilemma, she must face her mother's resolve. Each impossible to ignore, she wavers, her answer stuck in her throat, but her mother impatiently presses her.

HAGI: (*spoken*) Well, what is your answer? Will you help me or watch your mother die? One hour tonight is greater than a whole day. (*sung*) This is your mother's only request of a lifetime. No time now to ponder the options.

NARRATOR: The more she is pressed, the more flustered Eika becomes. She thinks, "No matter if mother must die, it is against a woman's instinct to let her kill Yorihira—all my duty to him will be wasted, but if I refuse her, I'm an ungrateful child. But I have an idea." She alters the pitch of her voice and laughs.

EIKA: (*spoken*) Mother, if that is your wish, you've come at a perfect moment. Fortunately, Lord Yorihira has been drinking at his farewell banquet. He's passed out in the next room, insensibly drunk. It'll be the same as killing a corpse. However, Tomozuna and his mother are quick to notice anything. When I put the light out, that's the signal for you to sneak in. In the dark, you'll be able to tell Yorihira by his hair style. It is long and carefully arranged with the forelock unshaven. Strike after you make sure that his hair in front is bushy and long like a mountain ascetic's, and you won't fail. (*sung*) No matter what, you must not rush the deed!

NARRATOR: Lady Hagi is delighted.

HAGI: (*spoken*) This is marvelous, how happy you've made me! What obedience to your parents, even above that to your husband. I'll be forever grateful. (*sung*) Spurred by such devotion, I'll have the strength to scale this wall. I'll climb this pine to do what I must. Don't worry, I'll creep in somehow.

EIKA: (*spoken*) No, no, don't be rash! If anything goes wrong before cock crow, then the blame will fall on the Mita house. Wait for the first cock crow.

NARRATOR: (*sung*) Her words, calm and reassuring on the surface, conceal a heart overflowing with tears, sparkling tears like the jeweled hairpins she now loosens and scatters, determined to cut both her hair and her ties to those in this world. No regret for the sharp razor now, as she cuts and shaves her beautiful ebony hair. Both the flowing tresses and the forelock are cut away, cast aside like pampas grass in the fields. She goes into the bedroom and waits like the (*high pitch, exit cadence*) dew, to perish with the dawn. (*cadence*) A pitiful sight.[28]

NARRATOR: (*sung*) Outside the gate, Lady Hagi also waits, relying on her daughter's promise. The minutes pass like hours. Will the cock crow now? She waits and waits for the rosy herald of dawn.[29] She looks to the east to catch a glimpse of the dawn sky but panics when she sees what looks like (*spoken*) the official imperial party, holding up lanterns that shine like stars in the sky. (*sung*) The clatter of fifty horsemen! Afraid she will be seen and her plan foiled, she removes her wicker hat and nimbly grabs the tree branch, hurls her light body upward and climbs onto the wall. She then stealthily curls up her body and holds her breath—(*cadence*) a dangerous position.

(*sung*) A moment later, at the head of the soldiers in full battle armor and carrying spears, Kintoki rides up on horseback. (*kowari threatening melody*) The foot soldiers carry banners and a large Chinese chest. Their helmets and shields glitter in the light of the flickering lanterns. Among them, only Kintoki wears the formal robes and hat of the courtier over his armor. He is calm and measured in his movements as he approaches the gate and gently taps on the door.

KINTOKI: (*spoken*) Mita no Jirō Tomozuna and his mother Zenni! Dewa no Kanja Lord Yorihira has joined forces with the enemy Shōgun Tarō Yoshikado. At dawn this morning I, Sakata no Kintoki, have been sent either to encourage him to commit *seppuku* or to execute him—unless he shows a change of heart. In case I meet with resistance and have to use force, I have taken the precaution of bringing this company of soldiers. However, this is only to present a proper and official party on an imperial mission. I have arrived early to offer you the chance to show that you have changed your allegiance and returned to your brothers' fold. That is all I have come to ask at this moment before the cock crows. My intention is to persuade you, no matter what it takes, to return with me to the palace, restored to your position.

NARRATOR: His words are reasoned and calm, (*sung*) but from within, someone yells out.

VOICE: That's Kintoki! Don't drop your guard. It's not like him to be so polite. (*spoken*) Don't be fooled by a monkey in court hat or a wolf in fancy clothes.[30] (*sung*) If you try anything, I'll have that red-faced head of yours!

NARRATOR: Kintoki ignores the abuse and insults and has a bench prepared. He sits down calmly (*cadence*) to await an answer. (*sung*) On top of the wall, Lady Hagi lies low, trying to decide what to do.

HAGI: This is terrible! Everyone is now on guard. At this rate, I'll have no chance to take Yorihira's head. Are all the cocks too fast asleep? Won't at least one of them crow? If I fail, so be it.

NARRATOR: She climbs off the wall on to a pine branch and hides. Then she draws the biggest breath she can and crows like a rooster, *kakeikou, kakeikou*. Her fake cries resound in all directions[31] and invite the real cocks to begin their (*highest pitch*) chorus, which (*scene cadence*) fills the dark sky.

NARRATOR: (*sung*) Inside and outside the gate, everyone is surprised to hear cocks crowing in the darkness. In the confusion, Lady Hagi climbs down into the small garden.

HAGI: The bedroom light is out—my signal from Eika.

NARRATOR: She stealthily slides open the door and approaches the unsuspecting sleeping figure. She strikes and blood splatters the white *shōji* door.

HAGI: (*spoken*) Minamoto no Yorihira, the sole ally of the court's enemy Shōgun Tarō Yoshikado, has been slain by a retainer of Ebumi no Tamenari!

NARRATOR: (*sung*) Her loud cry echoes throughout the house bringing everyone to the room. Outside, a furious Kintoki pounds at the gate and bellows.

KINTOKI: (*spoken*) Mita no Jirō Tomozuna has broken the law. A courtier must not be allowed to strike the first blow at Yorihira. Aunt Mita is a tricky old badger who has deceived the court. Do you think that you'll send me away red-faced and empty-handed back to the palace? I won't ask you again to open the gate. I'll do it myself. My fist is the key!

NARRATOR: (*sung*) The force of his arms rattles the hinges, and with one strong kick, he cracks the inside bolt, (*cadence*) the door flies open. (*sung*) Kintoki enters the garden and the lanterns light up the grounds. Aunt Mita is shocked and runs out to open the sliding door. (*spoken*) She is even more shocked (*sung*) to see Tomozuna with a deep wound in his right side, holding down both a shaven-headed Eika and Lady Hagi, who clings tightly to the bloody sword still buried in Tomozuna's side.

HAGI: Ah, how terrible to have failed!

NARRATOR: Lady Hagi can only writhe in regret. Aunt Mita, even more amazed and shaken, (*cadence*) is unable to speak.

(*sung*) Tomozuna sits down on the edge of the veranda.

TOMOZUNA: (*spoken*) Mother and Kintoki, no wonder that you're struck dumb. Lady Ebumi bravely planned to take Yorihira's head as a way of showing the court that her house had severed ties with the enemy. She pleaded desperately with her daughter Eika for help. Poor Eika was caught between filial duty and love for her husband. She determined to sacrifice herself and cut her hair in a man's style, (*sung*) but I overheard this plot between mother and daughter and secretly intervened to take Yorihira's place. Although this wound from her sword is not Yorihira's, (*spoken*) it is nevertheless proof of her loyalty and will bring an imperial reprieve. Further, Lady Eika, take care of Yorihira from now on. Let Lady Hagi be cared for by my mother and Kintoki.

NARRATOR: (*sung*) He releases mother and daughter and instead of removing the sword, pulls it across to his left side.

TOMOZUNA: (*spoken*) Kintoki! I offer you Dewa no Kanja Minamoto no Yorihira's life. (*sung*) It's time; cut off the head, Kintoki.

NARRATOR: But even the mighty Kintoki is puzzled and at a loss. Tomozuna's mother realizes his intentions and (*spoken*) claps her hands, (*sung*) but just then Yorihira runs to Tomozuna's side.

YORIHIRA: (*spoken*) You crazy fool! Did you think that I would stand back and delay confronting Kintoki? I was waiting to see what Kintoki's manner would be. Your sacrifice is wasted. If I were intent on saving my own life and escaping, even if Kintoki had the help of supernatural demons, I would use my sword and easily make my escape. You don't owe me your life. I never asked you to sacrifice yourself for me. (*sung*) How cruel that you should die!

NARRATOR: (*emotional cadence*) His anger is bitter, his harsh words said through clenched teeth.

(*sung*) Tomozuna bursts into tears.

TOMOZUNA: How shortsighted, cold, and heartless! This small wound will enhance the jewel that lights the night sky. (*high pitch*) You're blind to

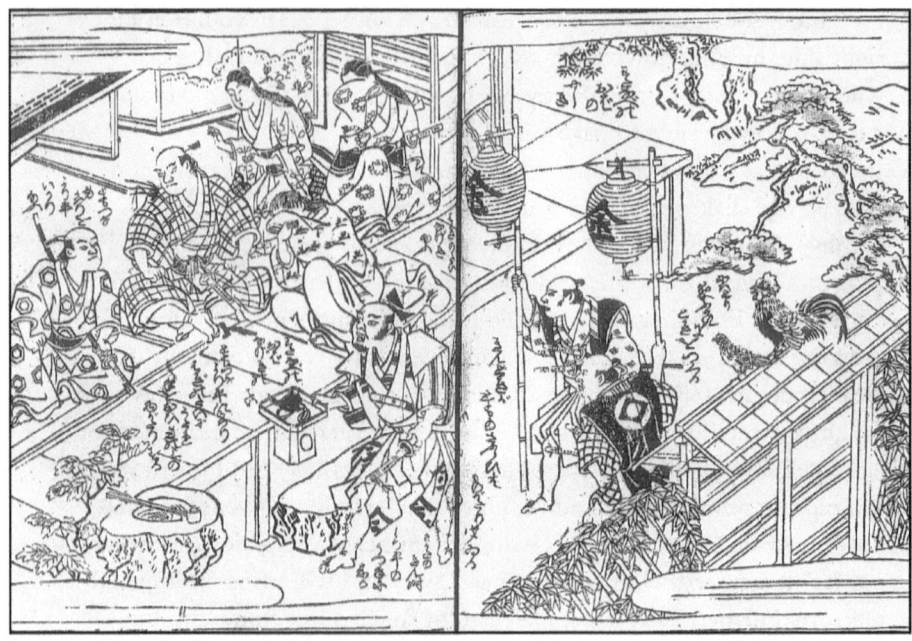

FIGURE 55 (Right) The cocks' crows signal dawn; (bottom left) Kintoki and his soldiers arrive; (left) Tomozuna stabbing himself, surrounded by an angry Yorihira and a grieving Eika, Aunt Mita, and Lady Hagi. (*Kanhasshū tsunagi-uma*, 1724, National Diet Library.)

think that Tomozuna dies to save Lord Yorihira. (*spoken*) It is only children at court who tell such tales of sacrifice for one's lord. There are examples of those who give their lives for a princess. How could I sacrifice myself for Yorihira who wants to die himself and stops others from helping him? I proclaim myself Minamoto no Yorihira as a sacrifice for the country. (*sung*) It must sound foolish and arrogant for a nobody like Tomozuna to make such a claim. But there is a story behind this. Lord Yorihira, mother, Kintoki and everyone else, (*cadence*) please listen quietly to my tale. (*spoken*) It all began with this.

NARRATOR: (*sung*) From a small brocade bag, he takes out a tall court hat and a severed cap string.[32]

TOMOZUNA: (*spoken*) This is it. Last year, late in winter, when Shogun Yorimitsu called us together in order to settle his succession, I wore this hat. That night all the leaders of the Minamoto clan were present, including the four generals and all the officers in the capital. It was a most impressive gathering. The lamps were extinguished in the formal room, and we were to choose between white and colored arrows to determine the heir. Because Lady Yorimitsu was on the high platform, the attendants were all women. Among them was one in particular, Kochō, who was by far the most attractive and alluring. Young and brash as I was, I had had one cup too many. Since it was dark, everything seemed unreal, and I grabbed her sleeve and playfully pulled her close to me. But she took a small knife from her kimono and cut off the string of my hat, and this is it here, this little string. Immediately, she cried out, saying that at this most important official meeting, someone had accosted her in the dark, a samurai had broken the rules. As proof of the crime, she cut off the hat string. She cried, "Maids, light the lamps! Check to see who has the severed string." In the midst of this commotion, I thought that my life was finished; I was ready to put hand to sword. "No, no," I thought, "if I die, who will clear my name?" But I felt that I had no choice but to die. I was terrified, soaked in sweat and in a desperate state. Just then, however, Lord Yorihira intervened and ordered that no candles be lit for the moment. He gave an order for all in attendance, young and old, high and low, without exception, to cut their cap strings and when it was done, to call out in unison, and only then was the room to be lit up. Everyone obeyed, cutting their hat strings. Each, including myself, made a cutting sound. When all had finished, the lights were lit and night turned to day. Since all had cut their strings, no one could be accused of accosting Kochō, and so no samurai was shamed or (*cadence*) lost his reputation.

(*sung*) I was so grateful for his compassion, for his benevolence and kindness that saved my life. Even if I were strong enough to carry the Xumi Mountain[33] in one arm and fly over the great seas, (*emotional cadence*) how could I ever repay such a debt?

(*sung*) But to my horror, my lord became an enemy of the court to be hunted down. Although I had waited for my chance to lead his troops into battle, it was all in vain. How could I contemplate the task of hunting him down like an enemy? Imagine how much I grieved to learn that he was a traitor. No one has known of this debt buried in my heart. I alone in this world have carried it, and even my mother learns of it only today.

NARRATOR: He looks (*highest pitch*) at his mother who meets his eye.

AUNT MITA: Such noble bravery.

NARRATOR: She sheds tears of grief and joy. Lady Eika and her mother and Lord Yorihira himself all weep. Even Kintoki, known for his cold heart, tries (*cadence*) to hide his tears by turning the lamp away.

(*sung*) Tomozuna's voice falters with the pain.

TOMOZUNA: (*spoken*) Kintoki, although I know that no one will regret my giving my life for the state, no more value than cow's piss or ground mold or a ripped drum, (*sung*) I do have one last request to ask of you and mother. After I am gone, (*spoken*) keep up the pressure on Lord Yorihira to break his vow with the enemies of the court. (*sung*) If he agrees, then it will be the shield that protects me from the arrows of the Shura Realm of Never-Ending Battles. It will keep me from suffering in the next life.

NARRATOR: His mother cries out at this plea.

AUNT MITA: (*spoken*) Dearest Lord Yorihira, you are too stubborn, too rigid. While he still breathes, change your mind, break your vow to Yoshikado. (*sung*) Let him hear the words that restore you to your brothers' camp. This request will link with the hat string and (*high pitch*) become the string that fastens his Buddha's hat as he takes his place in the Western Paradise. Give him the chance of salvation in the next life.

NARRATOR: (*emotional cadence*) She collapses under the strain.

(*sung*) Yorihira, his head bowed with tears, raises his eyes to speak.

YORIHIRA: (*spoken*) I was obstinate and refused to listen to any advice. The consequence is that I shall forever regret that I killed a good samurai. These words are worthless, too late. I renounce my pact with General Yoshikado. From now I am again an ally of my brothers. (*sung*) Our family's deity, Shō Hachiman, bears witness to my pledge. These words shall remain firm. Let all the anger and bitterness be cleared away.

NARRATOR: At his words, mother and son weep again, this time for joy. Tomozuna's face brightens.

TOMOZUNA: (*spoken*) No regrets, no bitterness. I shall die a happy man. Kintoki, it's time to finish the task. Take up your sword. Are you afraid of presenting to your commanders the head of such a lowly samurai? Let them see this courtier's cap, and tell them the story behind it. Kintoki, are you afraid to take my head? (*sung*) Are you too weak kneed to kill me?! Kintoki, I hate you!

NARRATOR: Kintoki reacts to this barrage of abuse only by sitting down on the gravel in the garden.

KINTOKI: (*spoken*) I don't know how to kill a samurai who has proved to be a true mirror of benevolence, duty, loyalty, and piety. Auntie, please complete the task.

NARRATOR: (*sung*) The lionlike Kintoki is (*cadence*) at a loss and dissolves into tears.

(*sung*) Tomozuna's blood oozes out and, with it, his life spirit, but he braces himself to speak again.

TOMOZUNA: (*spoken*) I have no time or need for this world anymore. Won't you cut off my head? Well then, I won't ask for your help.

NARRATOR: (*sung*) He pulls out the sword from his stomach and holds it to his neck. He recites a prayer to Buddha, and with both hands cuts off his own head. His lips open holding his last prayer, and his unblinking eyes mirror his mother's face. At the sight of this fallen but still lifelike head, all cry out to heaven and the depths of the earth. (*high pitch*) Oblivious of the rest, his mother takes up her son's head in her arms.

AUNT MITA: I haven't held your head like this since you were four, when you were weaned from my breast.

NARRATOR: (*emotional cadence*) She weeps, holding him tightly.

(*sung*) Kintoki, unable to restrain himself, cries out.

KINTOKI: He was a true samurai in both word and deed. What a terrible loss. If he had lived, (*highest pitch*) we would have added him to the group of four Yorimitsu guards Sadamitsu, Suetake, Tsuna, and Kintoki. With Tomozuna, we would have been the "Five Guardians." What a pity that he perished so young! How great he could have been!

NARRATOR: Kintoki's body sags as he weeps unashamedly. Yorihira, his wife, and her mother, everyone, even the insensitive young soldiers, (*cadence*) none can raise their heads. All silently weep.

(*sung*) Inside the house, it is still the deepest night, but outside a glint of dawn appears between the clouds. After a moment, a still tearful Yorihira takes up the court hat.

YORIHIRA: (*spoken*) This sat on the head of the finest Japanese warrior. Today, the compassionate tale that lies behind this string has thrown me a line of hope, giving me the means to change my path. Kintoki, take this, too, to be displayed prominently at court when you seek my pardon. *(sung)* At such time, request also, on my behalf, a pardon for Lord and Lady Ebumi.

NARRATOR: He hands over the hat, and Kintoki prepares the head for presentation. He carefully dresses it and places it on the ceremonial stand, and carries it with utmost reverence.

KINTOKI: Farewell Mother Zenni.

NARRATOR: His words arouse a sad voice.

AUNT MITA: *(spoken)* Who is it you call "mother"? A woman with a child is a mother. *(sung)* After today, I am childless, an old woman all alone. *(highest pitch)* Don't speak *(cadence)* foolish words!

NARRATOR: *(sung)* Her head droops to her chest. Eika and her mother comfort her and weep as they pray for the fate of this mother and son.

HAGI AND EIKA: The salvation of the Ebumi clan is all due to this woman. We are forever grateful.

NARRATOR: These words are followed by silent farewells as the soldiers leave along the garden steps.[34] Even that fierce hawk Kintoki, his wings withered by grief, is unsure of his way in the faint light of dawn. Sleeves drip with mist; the dew settles on the fragrant herbs and orchids; those who enter such gardens cannot help but carry the scent in their sleeves.[35] Great families inspire all to greatness. Among the stones of Mount Kunlun,[36] some shine without being polished. Fiercely loyal retainers emerge because of the merits of the great Genji shogun's martial and scholarly policies; such thoughts solace the grief of those who depart.[37]

Act 4

—Scene 1
The Yorimitsu residence, later the same day

NARRATOR: (*sung*) Long ago, the seven Chinese sages enjoyed themselves in a bamboo grove, reveling in the pleasures of a realm long at peace.[1] Sakata no Kintoki places his long sword and courtier cap on the table and, on his knees, bows before Lord Yorimitsu.

KINTOKI: (*spoken*) I was ordered to take the head of Lord Yorihira; I offer you this head which represents two figures. One is Lord Yorihira, a foundation stone of the realm, a pillar and girder of the nation. The other is Yorihira the traitor. (*sung*) As proof that this is a traitor, the courtier cap has its strings severed. The blood on this sword is proof that Lord Ebumi has cut his ties with the traitor. It would take too long for me to explain in detail, all of it is written in my report. (*spoken*) Ever since my youth, when I was known as Kaidōmaru, I hated study, and my writing still suffers. Even if you cannot read it all, you will be able to get my meaning.

NARRATOR: He hands over his report. (*sung*) Lord Yorimitsu reads it carefully several times.

YORIMITSU: (*spoken*) Even among his brothers, Yorihira stood out and was thought to have a character well suited for service to the court. All the more reason for our shock at his grave crime. How I grieved over his fate, but he has proved himself to be magnificent. (*sung*) Even the famous poems of Hitomaro and Akahito[2] would be lost if no one listened to them. Bo Ya's once renowned zither, too, only those who lived in China during his time knew its true excellence, now forgotten.[3] Mita Jirō Tomozuna knew Yorihira's virtue and, with deep gratitude, sacrificed his life for the realm. We regret losing such a man.

NARRATOR: He bows reverently, (*emotional cadence*) choking back tears.

VOICE: (*sung*) Following their summons, Lord and Lady Tamenari have arrived.

NARRATOR: At this announcement, Kintoki is delighted and goes to meet them. He leads them to sit before Yorimitsu, who greets them.

YORIMITSU: (*spoken*) Although you wear the robes of courtiers, you have proved yourselves equal to samurai in your bravery. I have appealed to His Royal Highness on your behalf, explaining the details of your loyal actions in severing ties with the rebels. (*sung*) Rejoice in your return to your position in the capital.

NARRATOR: At these words, the couple, with hushed breath, fold their hands in gratitude. "May it bring good fortune" (*cadence*) is all they can utter as they collapse in tears of relief.

　(*sung*) From the guardhouse, a loud cry is heard.

VOICE: (*spoken*) Suetake and Sadamitsu have captured Shōgun Tarō Yoshikado!

NARRATOR: (*sung*) This announcement arouses everyone. They watch as Yoshikado is led into the garden and seated on the gravel. Lord Yorimitsu is delighted.

YORIMITSU: (*spoken*) Word has it that you are a reckless upstart. Your father Masakado spread his power throughout the eight provinces of Kantō and declared himself to be Heishinnō, "Royal Prince," ruler of the hundred court ranks and ministries. But his treachery was destroyed by the armies of the divine emperor. And yet you have learned nothing, following your father to become an even greater menace to the court. You will not escape this time. Take him away for execution.

NARRATOR: Just as he issues this order, (*sung*) Yorihira and his wife rush forward, their hair still in disarray.

YORIHIRA: Having been pardoned and given leave to return, allow me to speak. This fellow is no ordinary, uncouth, uncultured rebel. Responsibility for his execution lies in the palm of my hand. (*spoken*) If you will accept my idea, then entrust his life to me.

NARRATOR: Yorihira approaches Yoshikado even closer.

YORIHIRA: At Ichiharano, you spared the life of Lady Eika. As proof that my pledge to join you has not changed, I shall spare your life for now. Henceforth we meet as enemies. I shall sharpen my spear for battle. Your life is mine until I take your head in battle. Now, be off!

NARRATOR: Yorihira unties the ropes, and Yoshikado leaps up.

YOSHIKADO: Well spoken. Magnificent! (*sung*) A great Genji general reveals a noble heart by honoring his pledge. Farewell until we meet again on the battlefield.

NARRATOR: He starts to leave, but Yorimitsu stops him.

YORIMITSU: *(spoken)* You're no brute and can distinguish good from evil. Your rebellion against the court to clear your father's shame shows a gentle and warm character. Let me offer you a gift. Here is your father Masakado's banner with the "tethered steed" crest. The Genji have no need of this; it is only a burden to us. Take it as your protecting charm.

NARRATOR: *(sung)* He throws it into the garden, and Yoshikado gratefully accepts it.

YOSHIKADO: *(spoken)* Your deeds match your reputation as the greatest general. I accept this family treasure and will repay your generosity with fierce bravery on the battlefield. *(sung)* I shall withdraw to Mount Kazuragi and raise this banner to lead my army.[4] Even if I face an enemy of tens of thousands, my sole aim will be Yorihira alone. His body may have returned to the Genji fold, but his head shall remain forever with me as an ally.

YORIHIRA: Such grand words and bravado are best saved for after the fight. You have only a little time left. Remember that your head is mine. Don't lose it to another.

YOSHIKADO: You as well. Your life is mine.

YORIHIRA: How you babble on! Enough talk! My answer lies in these eyes.

NARRATOR: He glares fiercely at his foe, silent. His eyebrows rise high and eyes open wide; *(scene cadence)* he scowls defiantly.

—Scene 2

The Minamoto residence in Tada,[5] Settsu Province, sixteenth day, seventh month, 989

NARRATOR:

(san-sagari song) How long it's been!
Does he remember me?
Partings in this world,
like the blossoms of spring,
may the winds carry their fragrance
forever to ride the clouds.[6]
Yet though his scent fills my robes,
longing is all it brings.

Tears fall freely from my sleeves,
like sleet off bamboo grass.
The geese, too, cry as they head for home.
No thought for them before,
now, envy for their wings.
(*sung*)[7] How my heart (*cadence*) longs to return!

(*sung*) The ladies-in-waiting sing their song to entertain Lady Iyo no Naishi, Yorinobu's wife, here at the impressive Minamoto residence in Tada. Poor Lady Iyo fell strangely ill some time ago, the cause a mystery. To comfort her, Watanabe no Tsuna's wife Iwafuji has brought the other three wives of the leading officers, Kohata, Rangiku, and Oshiyana no Mae—the spouses of the famous Minamoto "Four Guardian Gods." Their husbands are warriors; they are mistresses of charm and elegance, knowing in the gentle ways of love. Each wears a long gown that trails along the corridor (*cadence*) as they approach Her Ladyship's bedroom. (*sung*) Shōnagon, Her Ladyship's attendant, emerges from an inner room to greet them.

SHŌNAGON: (*spoken*) I trust that you are all well, and I am delighted that you have come to visit Her Ladyship. The doctors have not been able to diagnose her illness. Whenever she drifts off to sleep, day or night, she is soon taken with fever, seems terrified of something, and then faints, babbling nonsense. Could it possibly be possession by a jealous spirit? Although we ask her if she has had a nightmare, she is unable to answer and soon grows weary. It is terrible to witness her agony. We have tried all kinds of tricks and diversions to get her to explain her pains. The doctors have suggested that to restore her mind to normal, it might help to devise some entertaining amusements. If she relaxes, then maybe the medicine will have an effect. We were afraid that our clumsy songs and shamisen playing might make her worse and bring on a headache. Would you be able to devise some lively entertainment? You have famous husbands, and you all must have great experience in the ways of the world. Please think of something new and exciting.

(*sung*) In the face of this pressing plea, the four women can only sigh and lower their heads. Each looks at the other, hoping that a good idea will come up. (*cadence*) They discuss the matter among themselves.

(*sung*) Kintoki's wife Oshiyana no Mae steps boldly forward.

OSHIYANA: (*spoken*) As you've just said, her condition remains a mystery to Lord and Lady Yorimitsu, as well as to Lord Yorinobu, all of whom are desperate with worry. Our husbands are famous as fierce warriors able to quell demons, but they're hopeless when it comes to handling illness. Our women's diagnosis is that her affliction is most certainly caused by an accumulation of jealousy. Men follow their noses. Those self-disciplined like us have to restrain our anger. In the lower orders, however, when jealous rage erupts, the woman will scratch and bite. (*sung*) And after breaking a few household things, she feels much better, with a load off her chest. But those in higher society must maintain a serene surface, and so the anger seethes and smolders in her heart; she needs somehow to give vent to her spleen. (*spoken*) I know! Let me explain. Sumo wrestling excites the audience so that they forget themselves. First, in the big room we'll pile pillows at each of the four pillars and prepare a wrestling space. The four of us will then strip off our clothes and face each other in pairs like the East and West top-rank Ōzeki challengers. From the ladies-in-waiting, we'll choose the lower Sekiwake and Komusubi ranks; the rest will fill the lowest slots. We'll use fancy-colored Chinese damasks and satins for the *mawashi* belt. That's fine so far, but what happens when the lower part is grabbed? It'll most likely come apart and be embarrassing. But even if that happens, shall we just accept it as part of the show? Madam Suetake and Madam Sadamitsu, (*sung*) any thoughts on what we should do?

NARRATOR: Rangiku and Kohata's reply is to blush crimson.

RANGIKU: Oh, that would be most unseemly! It might have been considered innocent and charming of us when we were little girls, but with our old and freckled skin, if our *mawashi* belts were to come undone, it would be like a raven showing off an open sore. (*cadence*) Dreadful!

NARRATOR: (*sung*) Kohata, the clever one, speaks up.

KOHATA: (*spoken*) There are always ways of distracting a sick person in the daytime. It is after dark that we need to think of an entertainment to console her. Every year on the sixteenth day of the seventh month, Kyoto is host to its distinctive *obon* bonfire festival, held to send the souls of ancestors back to the other world, in which long rows of fires form the character "great" [大] on Mount Higashi. (*sung*) We'll do the same here on this big mound in the garden. We'll create a grand scene, signaling the advent of autumn.[8] At this sight, Her Ladyship is surely to be delighted.

IWAFUJI: *(spoken)* Both your ideas are extremely interesting, but I have another plan. It's said that long ago on Mount Kinugasa in north Kyoto they placed white cloth on the trees to create a summer snow scene for His Majesty. Let's drape the tree branches in the garden with kimonos. The many flowered designs will conjure up a magnificent scene depicting the four seasons: chrysanthemums, yellow wildflowers, plum, and cherry blossoms. Such an array of flowers will surely raise her spirits. What do you think, Shōnagon?

SHŌNAGON: *(sung)* Oh, every one of your ideas are splendid. I'll write them all down and ask Her Ladyship to choose.

NARRATOR: They all go into the room next to Her Ladyship's bedroom. *(exit cadence)* Shōnagon opens the sliding door and pulls the screen aside.

NARRATOR: *(sung)* Lady Iyo's cries out eerily, in terror, as if she were between dreaming and waking. She wails and groans, her body writhing around in the bed. Everyone rushes to wake her up. She sits up but has no strength, a delicate low-drooping willow.[9] Even her hairpins weigh heavily on her as she gasps for breath. The women, too, all wilt *(cadence)* at this pitiful sight.

(spoken) Iwafuji admonishes Her Ladyship.

IWAFUJI: You are always careful about every detail. It was only a bad dream. You mustn't take it seriously. Only dreams about gods or buddhas have a meaning; others are just illusions. Even the Chinese sage Chuang Tzu *(sung)* was said to have become a butterfly (*kochō*)[10] in his dreams.

NARRATOR: But before she finishes, Iyo pales.

LADY IYO: How could a butterfly enter my dreams? *(highest pitch)* Don't speak such foolishness. It's embarrassing.

NARRATOR: *(high pitch)* Her face becomes tearful.

IWAFUJI: *(spoken)* Now you are being silly. "The dream of a butterfly" is a common allusion in Chinese and Japanese verse. Why should you be afraid of such things? You must tell us about whatever is troubling you; don't hide anything. *(sung)* Getting things off your chest is the best medicine possible. To lift your spirits, we've all devised some entertaining diversions for your pleasure. You choose the one that suits your fancy.

FIGURE 56 (Right) Rangiku, Kohata, and Oshiyana decorating the garden with kimonos of flower design. The text notes that this scene was a great success; (top left) Iyo no Naishi watching; (bottom left) the other women enjoying the scene. (*Kanhasshū tsunagi-uma*, 1724, National Diet Library.)

NARRATOR: She shows the list of amusements. Lady Iyo reads them over and again.
LADY IYO: You have all gone to much trouble for me. (*cadence*) Each idea has its charm. (*sung*) Well then, among these, (*spoken*) let us create Mount Kinugasa blossoming with flowers of the four seasons, a brilliant display of colorful kimonos in the branches. (*sung*) Quickly, get it ready.
NARRATOR: At this order, the women rush to gather an array of kimonos and drape them among the branches in the garden.[11]
IWAFUJI: (*song*)[12] First, as harbingers of a bright spring sky, (*cadence*) grace these branches with color, (*bun'ya-style song*) plums and camellias delight our eyes. Over there! Quick, quick, hang wisteria on that pine: watch its blossoms bend with the wind like billowing waves.[13] Next are yellow mountain-rose patterns. (*high pitch*) Look, the design of a willow entwined with dark bamboo, on which a swallow alights. Thistles and

dandelions, (*hatsumi melody*) wildflowers and grasses, how delightful; and Yoshino cherry blossoms are lined up with the blossoms of the wild mountain-cherry tree. There, look, some Mikawa irises. (*highest pitch*) Peonies embroidered in threads of five colors,[14] with a lion playing with a ball. Over there, clusters of azaleas as well. Dappled red on white crepe, is that a sunflower? The pines, cypress, cedars, and nettle bushes all make (*low pitch*) a dark-colored background for the red plum patterns, turmeric golds, and deep violets. (*low threatening pitch*) Blown about, the reverse displays cherry blossoms of pale blue and soft yellow, others faint pink, some thickly petaled, Shiogama blossoms, pure white, and the famous "Waterfall" Yoshino blossoms. Some are single-petaled, others are small clusters of faint pink. Such delights! Look, the Uba blossoms on bare branches.

NARRATOR: Enchanting voices and exquisite beauties accompany this display of kimono designs to paint a landscape of spring flowers in the mountains alongside a field in autumn splendor. (*cadence*) All in all, a rapturous scene.

(*sung*) Lady Iyo laughs aloud, her expression brighter than usual.

LADY IYO: (*spoken*) From here the flowers seem absolutely real. Such a delightful diversion has cheered my spirits. Your lively descriptions (*sung*) and playfulness especially have been a pleasure to enjoy. My heart feels light again.

NARRATOR: They lead her by the hand among the draped kimonos on the hill.

LADY IYO: Each and every one of them, a marvelous design!

NARRATOR: She runs her fingers over the bush clover and bellflowers. She spies an embroidery of chrysanthemums with butterflies (*kochō*)[15] fluttering about.

LADY IYO: Oh, terrifying! Are there butterflies here, too?

NARRATOR: She screams, and suddenly her arms and legs go weak; her face pales. (*emotional cadence*) She collapses, falling to the ground. (*exit cadence*) The women quickly carry her back to her bedroom.

NARRATOR: (*sung*) The four women are aghast at Lady Iyo's relapse and gasp for breath. (*spoken*) Iwafuji nods to herself.

IWAFUJI: I understand. I see the reason now. Earlier, when we talked about the "Butterfly's Dream," her face turned pale. Now again when she saw an embroidery of butterflies, that was no ordinary dizziness. (*sung*) Her illness is related to seeing "butterflies." Do you see the significance now?

NARRATOR: "That's it!" they all exclaim.

IWAFUJI: That awful woman Kochō is venting her angry spirit. Let me see you, show yourself!

NARRATOR: They all get up and look around but find nothing. They assemble again to try to think of a plan. Kohata instantly has an idea.

KOHATA: (*spoken*) Listen, listen! I've got a perfect plan. Fortunately, today is the *obon* festival to send ancestral spirits back to the other world, the day when the Daimonji fires are lit on Mount Higashi in Kyoto. The fires mark the path of return to the nether world. If the fires are not lit, the souls will remain to wander about lost in this world. At dusk on the sixteenth, all of the capital assembles along the Kamo River offering farewells to their ancestral spirits, "Follow the sacred fires! Farewell and safe return." We'll do the same for Kochō's vengeful spirit, now wandering lost and seeking revenge. By offering a memorial service for her, we will clear away the bitterness that clouds her soul, and she'll be able to go to the next world in peace. Lady Iyo will then recover. I'm sure that will do it. What do you think?

NARRATOR: They clap their hands in unison, impressed by this splendid plan.

IWAFUJI: A wonderful idea, perfect! (*sung*) It's the right hour. Quick, prepare the fires!

KOHATA: Kindling.

RANGIKU: Some sticks.

OSHIYANA: Torches.

NARRATOR: They all rush to gather wood for the fire as the sun sets. A distant temple bell tolls dusk, (*scene cadence*) its echo lightening their hearts.

—Scene 3

The garden of the Minamoto residence in Tada, Settsu Province,[16] sixteenth day, seventh month, 989, at dusk

(*song*) Spirits! Follow the sacred fires! Farewell and safe return.[17]

Follow the sacred fires! Farewell and safe return.

Autumn is near; autumn is upon us.
Twilight brings sad thoughts,
(*sung*) but look, over there on the mountain
the flickering lights. Are they fireflies?
Bright stars on the horizon?
The light of three, no four torches.
Carried by the four women
(*cadence*) as they bravely climb up the steep mountain,
(*threatening melody*) east and west, above and below.
From the foot to the highest peak,
through valleys and hills,
rise the row of bonfires,
(*sung*) creating the character "Great" [大] on the mountain side.[18]
Long ago the great teacher Kūkai vowed
that these fires would bring us out of the darkness of delusion.
What a magnificent picture, six hundred feet square!
Give thanks for this sight, an image of the Pure Land.

Here the women have recreated the "Pure Land Temple" village of Kyoto where Amida Buddha descends to accompany souls to Paradise.

WOMEN: We pray for the salvation of all lost souls. Namu Amida Butsu.

NARRATOR: After offering their prayers, (*cadence*) they withdraw to the guardhouse for the night.

(*sung*) The Milky Way shines brightly in the cloudless heavens as the evening grows late. (*threatening melody*) The bonfires flicker faintly. Suddenly a terrifying flame leaps high into the sky (*sung*) and then seems to flash down to earth. (*cadence*) The figure of Kochō appears.

(*nō chanting*)[19] Floating clouds drift on and on, (*low pitch*) following the whims of the cold wind, (*song*) which carries the snow down, chilling the innocent heart of a sick woman. Should this snow melt away, the rushing waves will tumble over the rocks, (*high pitch*) roaring like rapids down the valley, (*cadence*) into the dark well of passion.

(*sung*) Each night she comes creeping through the bamboo and over the mountain in the garden, driven by the flames of unrequited love. "No one knows the fury of my jealousy." (*cadence*) Menacingly, she approaches Lady Iyo's bedroom door. Lady Iyo[20] awakes from her dream, her chest pounding.

LADY IYO: Strange, who's there?

KOCHŌ: (*spoken*) I am an attendant serving at the retired emperor's palace. Having heard of your unusual malady, His Highness has sent me with the best medicines from both the continent and Japan. (*sung*) You must drink this medicine (*cadence*) obediently.

NARRATOR: (*sung*) Lady Iyo, thinking it extremely strange for a visit this time of night, gets up. She opens the door and is petrified to see (*emotional cadence*) Kochō, the terrifying figure of her dreams. (*sung*) Iyo panics and rushes inside. Kochō runs after her, yelling angrily.

KOCHŌ: (*high pitch*) Foolish woman! You cannot escape.[21] You suffer because tonight you await my love. Crab-like, this spider spins a web of pain. Ignorant woman, all your suffering is due to me. My sticky strings wind around and around you, in thousands upon thousands.

NARRATOR: Lady Iyo's whole body writhes in pain. She struggles to get up and flee, but her weakened legs falter as the web entangles her, (*cadence*) like creeping vines.[22]

(*sung*) (*Kochō*) I struggle to control my rage, but like even well-kept secrets, it leaks out. My heart is twisted like this bent bamboo. My bitter regrets make you suffer a thousand, eight thousand times. (*Iyo*) Time and again, a hundred, a hundred thousand times I weep. (*Both chanters*) (*cadence*) Your suffering makes others weep; I suffer and weep for you.

LADY IYO: (*sung*) How terrifying! You're a frenzied stag driven by lust, a jealousy-crazed man. Obsession blackens your soul as it wallows in the depths of the murky pond.[23] Follow the fireflies, their torches will lead you to the next world.

KOCHŌ: No matter how you plead, my hate is too strong; it's a rusty arrow-tip poised to strike. Bitterness gives the bowstring the power to fire the venomous arrow. Like entwined branches cut from a tree, your love will crash to the ground!

NARRATOR: (*Both chanters*) She wields a mallet, giving vent to her wrath. Again and again she attacks, wreaking her revenge. The blows crack fiercely, and trees and branches fall in her path.[24] Her rage is terrifying.

KOCHŌ: You'll sink into the depths of the hell of demons, (*threatening melody*) never to arise again in this world. You'll serve forever as the slave of spiders!

NARRATOR: She claws again at Iyo, (*sung*) who is now almost dead, (*cadence*) and drags her round and round, a pitiful sight.

KOCHŌ: (*sung*) You came as a beautiful, blushing bride while I was led to the gates of hell. Now your dowry will be your curse. The cold steel of the Genji sword torments you like the terrible Sword Mountain of Hell. The damasks and brocades, the bedclothes, all now envelope you in a fiery heat. Feel the flames char your flesh.[25] The saké of the wedding ceremony has become the River of Fire consuming your soul. (*low threatening melody*) Waves of fire rise, swirl higher and higher!

NARRATOR: (*high pitch*) The garden trees all shudder; the water in the pond froths under the force of her power. The earth seems to rise; the heavens collapse as the flames roar into the sky. Thunder and lightning flash, (*cadence*) the gods vent their rage.

(*sung*) (*Second*) Hearing the disturbance, the four wives, swords in hand, fly to Lady Iyo, only to find her writhing in agony. Their eyes search the darkness for an assailant. (*First*) Suddenly behind Iyo, (*cadence*) the figure of Kochō appears, (*sung*) a human transformed into a fiendish creature with six arms and two legs.

KOCHŌ: (*threatening*) You don't recognize this figure? Once before, long ago, I lived in the world, harboring grudges, passing many years on Mount Kazuragi, waiting a chance for revenge. I am the spirit of the Earth Spider.[26] My brother Shōgun Tarō Masakado plotted to take over all Japan and make it the devil's empire. As his younger sister, I joined in his plan but lost my way for love, was murdered and left to rot in the earth. My spirit has taken form in the five elements. Know the power of my rage!

NARRATOR: Her glare is fierce, but the four women remain firm, unafraid of the phantom.

IWAFUJI (*Second*): (*spoken*) What foolish babble! Attacking the imperial realm draws the wrath of both heaven and hell.[27] Didn't you learn your folly when you were destroyed by Yorimitsu? (*sung*) Your deeds condemn you to suffer endless death and rebirth as an evil, poisonous spider. We'll sever your ties to this world.

NARRATOR: The four attack, swords in hand, pushing their skirts aside. (*First*) The spider flies up. (*Second*) They attack from the right. (*First*) She parries from the left. (*Second*) They attack from behind. (*First*) She whirls to face them. They try all sorts of stratagems to assail the monster.

WOMEN: (*second*) You won't get away. There's no escape! (*battle cadence*) No way out!

FIGURE 57 (Right) An image of the character for "great" [大] burning on the hill and Iwafuji attacking Kochō's angry spirit with a spear; (top) an earth spider attacks, breathing fire. The text says that the grand special effects (ōkarakuri) were a great success; (bottom) the spirit of Kochō attacked by Kohata and Rangiku; (left) Oshiyana protecting Iyo no Naishi. (*Kanhasshū tsunagi-uma*, 1724, National Diet Library.)

NARRATOR: (*sung*) The four cry out together as they surround the fiend.
(*Both*) The specter suddenly vanishes, and a fire roars up. (*cadence*) The flames explode into a raging inferno.
KOHATA: (*sung*) Curse it! We've lost her.
NARRATOR: (*emotional cadence*) In despair, they are left helpless in the garden.
(*sung*) (*First*) Amid the charred trees and singed kimonos, a hearty laugh is heard.[28] Kochō flutters about lightly as if walking on mist and carried by the fragrance of plum blossoms, (*Second*) yet heavy is the karma that weighs down the branches under her feet. (*Both*) (*cadence*) She seems neither to walk nor to fly.
(*sung*) (*Second*) Over there, no here, she disappears again, her movement too quick for the eye to follow. (*Both*) Over there on the garden

stairs she stands beckoning. When the four women race toward the phantom, suddenly a veil of snow and hail blocks the view, like clouds hiding the moon. They rush off again in all four directions around the garden, up the mountain, into every corner, catching sight of the figure only to lose it again: a sorcerer's power to bewitch. (*Second*) The women toss their useless swords aside and rush to tackle her with bare hands. (*First*) The monster, too, spreads its legs and arms to fend them off like a mad dog turning on its pursuers, its eyes bright fiery stars. She turns toward the bedroom, (*cadence*) breathing a rainbow of fire.[29] (*sung*) The women leap down the veranda in pursuit, then to the second floor, but she vanishes again. They spot her on the mountain and surround to attack.

WOMEN: (*Both*) (*threatening melody*) The mountain is a castle of iron; the water a shining sword. Come now, come to the Shura Realm of Never-Ending Battle![30]

NARRATOR: All four pull together. (*low, threatening*) When tossed to one side, they keep their hold; when shaken off, they hang on even harder. Tighter and tighter, they cling, harnessing the power of the monster, like crushing a mountain. (*sung*) As if they were dragging a boat on land, the four cry out "Harder, harder!" gasping for breath. Suddenly a fierce wind rises,[31] blowing sand in its path; smoke billows up, obscuring the phantom. (*exit cadence*) In a flash, it vanishes.

(*Second*) (*sung*) The four women, exhausted, collapse in despair, (*First*) but just then Lord Yorinobu and Hirai no Hōshō arrive. Yorinobu wields the famous Hizamaru sword, handed down from Prince Momozono as a Genji treasure.[32] He places it at Lady Iyo's bedside to protect her and yells to the sky.

YORINOBU: (*spoken*) Know that demons cannot defeat virtue.[33] No matter what kind of phantom you are, turning into rain or wind, into myriad forms, no matter what curses you send down, the authority of the Heavenly descended imperial throne, supported by the might of the Genji, extends over the four seas. Without bloodying this sword or raising a hand, we shall banish you to the nether regions of hell!

NARRATOR: He glares fiercely at the dark clouds. His voice stirs the mountains and rivers, grasses and trees. Suddenly the clouds seem to rain down bamboo poles, (*battle-scene cadence*) a shower of spider web blankets the earth.

(*Second*) (*sung*) Everyone scurries about to escape the onslaught. Suddenly the bedroom shudders, and a thunderous roar is heard. Everyone rushes over to see what has happened. (*Both*) (*threatening melody*) Hizamaru unsheathes itself,[34] and with a fiery lightning flash, the sword strikes at the heart of the phantom. The spider's blood gushes forth like a rushing waterfall. It looks terrified and ready to flee.

KOCHŌ: (*First*) I leave never to return.[35]

NARRATOR: Then suddenly (*Second*) Lady Iyo's color brightens, her spirit returns to itself. Everyone rejoices. The sword can be seen like a gleaming flash (*Both*) as it pursues the fleeing phantom through the sky, chasing it from cloud to cloud. The fame of this magical flying sword lives on today, when it is known as the "Spider-Slaying Sword."[36] It fights with a power feared by all. Smeared with the blood of the enemy, it cuts off the fiend's roots and slashes off its branches. It protects the realm, maintaining the peace and security of all subjects. With a massive weight of silver hanging from their belts, everyone rides the eternal crane that ferries us to the pleasures of the capital of Yangzhou.[37] All such pleasures are the benefits of (*high pitch*) being born in this wonderful age.

FIGURE 58 A kabuki production in 1970 at the Tokyo Kabuki-za theater. (Right) Nakamura Ganjirō II as Yorinobu; (center) Nakamura Utaemon VI as Kochō; (left) Nakamura Shikan VI as Iyo no Naishi. (Shōchiku Ōtani Library).

Act 5

—Scene 1
A few days later at the base of Mount Kazuragi

NARRATOR: (*nō chanting*) Our sovereign's realm covers earth and trees alike.[1] The demon has hidden, (*sung*) driven away by the powerful Hizamaru sword, but a trail of earth-spider blood leads to Mount Kazuragi. Hirai no Hōshō, given the command to kill the demon, rides ahead, leaving a division of several hundred soldiers to wait behind him. The troops surround the foot of the mountain, (*cadence*) hidden by the thick morning mist.

(*sung*) Impetuous Kintoki, always impatient, speaks out.

KINTOKI: Although this fiend has appeared countless times as a spider, it is, after all, nothing more than an insect. Do we really need swords or spears? Let's just squash this bit of vermin.

NARRATOR: He gathers some brush and bamboo and makes it into a broom, ready to sweep the bug aside—(*cadence*) a sight at once fearless and insolent.

(*sung*) Hōshō comes up alone, still able to hear behind him the sound of the horses champing at their bits. He wears a helmet and armor of light yellow and carries a matching bow and quiver. He rides a Torikai chestnut mare. He catches sight of Kintoki off in the distance, whips his horse to race toward Kintoki and gives a yell.

HŌSHŌ: (*spoken*) Is that the phantom that crosses this imperial warrior's path? Taste the might of His Majesty's arrow.

NARRATOR: He draws his arrow.

KINTOKI: Hōshō, don't be hasty! I'm no phantom, nor am I a spider. Look, it's me! Can't you recognize me in this morning mist? It's your good old, red-faced Kintoki. Don't do anything foolish.

NARRATOR: (*sung*) Hōshō lets him plead, knowing all along who it is. He decides to teach him a lesson and curb his habit of ignoring orders and rushing on ahead. Hōshō shakes his head.

HŌSHŌ: (*spoken*) No, I won't be tricked! A demon has the power to appear in all kinds of shapes. You're a fool to change yourself into Kintoki and hope to get close enough to slay me. Even if you are the real Kintoki, it would not be wrong to shoot a soldier who deliberately ignores his general's orders (*sung*) and advances before he is given the signal.

NARRATOR: He draws the bowstring taut.

KINTOKI: (*spoken*) It was cruel of you to taunt me, knowing it was me all along. I promise never to jump ahead without orders, never to be stubborn, or to stick my neck out ahead of the rest. I promise to follow everything you say. (*sung*) Now, will you forgive me?

NARRATOR: Kintoki, normally a match for the devil himself, is cowed into obedience by Hōshō: he looks like a boy caught at some mischief, unable to tough it out anymore. To each his own medicine. (*cadence*) They say a centipede hates spit,[2] and a snapping turtle, nettle.

(*sung*) Hōshō relaxes the bowstring.

HŌSHŌ: (*spoken*) That was a close call, my friend Kintoki!

NARRATOR: (*sung*) They have a good laugh. Sadamitsu, Suetake, and Tsuna rush up.

SADAMITSU: (*spoken*) Look, both of you, over there on top of Mount Kazuragi! The "tethered steed" banner is unfurled. Yoshikado has set up his fortress on the peak. Yorinobu and Yorihira have moved to attack from the rear. We'll take on the demon and the enemy at one go, one day's work. The time's right. We'll attack from the front.

NARRATOR: The conch-shell horn sounds the battle cry, and the drums pound the beat, (*scene cadence*) leading the troops to battle.

—Scene 2
Some time later at the peak of Mount Kazuragi

NARRATOR: (*sung*) This tall mountain, famous as a retreat of strict ascetics, is steep and full of crags and dangerous to climb. Hanging on to the vines that wind around the rocks, the soldiers advance deeper into the spider's lair. They gradually realize that the tendrils covering the tall trees and fallen logs are the threads of a vast web, so dense that neither sunlight nor moonlight can penetrate its pitch black depths. From between the trees, (*threatening melody*) a terrifying sight—a huge spider's eye, a bright shining mirror from which eight furry legs extend, each hair as sharp as a nail. Each breath a fiery torch, the spider creeps forward. (*sung*) The soldiers shudder and retreat, but some get caught in the sticky web, unable to escape. Pulled in by the eight legs, their bodies are crushed, and their blood is sucked out. Some die; others writhe in agony, helplessly entangled. (*cadence*) Truly a strange and horrible creature.

   (*sung*) Sakata no Kintoki rushes forward.

KINTOKI: (*spoken*) What, is the spirit of Kochō still so obsessed with jealousy? Do you think that you can defend your brother Yoshikado's fortress? (*sung*) I'll slice through the spider web and crush the defenses. Yoshikado's head is mine!

NARRATOR: He wields his broom to brush aside the cobwebs, but they reappear again and again. The spider spits poison; Kintoki notices that its belly is pregnant.

KINTOKI: (*spoken*) You evil black widow, trying to terrorize the land. I'll crush you in this bit of tissue paper and put you in my pocket. (*sung*) I'm waiting, where have you been hiding?

NARRATOR: He teases the creature, and then leaps in to attack, but it disappears, (*cadence*) leaving only a large pouch behind. (*sung*) Kintoki peers closely at it.

KINTOKI: (*spoken*) It does looks like a spider's egg sac, but is this what you get when you twist its belly button? It's huge! It looks like a mole on the Great Buddha.

NARRATOR: He gives it a kick, splitting it open. Millions of tiny, greenish spiders rush out. They gather in distinct hordes and then disperse in different directions. At first they seem to crawl, but then they stand upright as the tiny spiders change into armies of small demons. They surround Kintoki and fly at his arms and legs. He tosses them off, but they attack again. He kicks them and crushes many, but others climb the tree branches and fly down to attack. Each spider falls like a streak of lightning, giving off a glow, and then disappears; lights flicker in the darkness, (*battle cadence*) just like the fire executions over a volcano so loved by the Yin emperor Zhou's consort Daji.[3]

   (*sung*) Even the obstinate Kintoki is exasperated.

KINTOKI: (*spoken*) Unless the wind howls for three days straight, all Japan will be covered in cobwebs. It'll surely happen! There're simply too many of these little brutes. (*sung*) It's impossible to kill them one by one.

NARRATOR: He takes up the bamboo broom and strikes a threatening pose before beginning to sweep furiously in every crag and crevice. All one hears is the crack of bamboo hitting on spider legs.

Tethered Steed and the Eight Provinces of Kantō   425

FIGURE 59 (Right) Several spiders attacking while small spiders emerge to attack Kintoki; (center) Hoshō on horseback; (top center) Yorinobu on horseback; (bottom left) Yoshikado captured by Tsuna; (top left) Kochō's spirit (spider) is killed by the "Kumo-kirimaru" sword. (*Kanhasshū tsunagi-uma*, 1724, National Diet Library.)

KINTOKI: Now this is more like it. Good fun!
NARRATOR: Buoyed by the winds rushing through the pines,[4] his broom clears the mountain, (*cadence*) scattering the tiny spiders down the steep cliffs.
   (*sung*) While Kintoki is sweeping the mountain clean, Watanabe no Tsuna, Sadamitsu, and Suetake are advancing from the valley behind.
TSUNA: We must kill both the traitors and the scum that have joined them. Most important of all, we can't let Yoshikado escape.
NARRATOR: They chase after Yoshikado, who has been driven from his fortress. Ahead of him, Kintoki lies in wait, and just when he seems trapped, (*threatening melody*) Kochō mysteriously appears as a shadow in human shape. (*sung*) She rushes to Yoshikado. His sister's magical powers blind the four warriors. Her body is as strong as steel.

FIGURE 60 A kabuki production in 1970 at the Tokyo Kabuki-za theater; (right) Nakamura Utaemon VI as Kochō (spider); (left) Jitsukawa Enjaku III as Yoshikado. (Shōchiku Ōtani Library.)

YOSHIKADO: (*spoken*) Kintoki and Tsuna, I know you're there; Suetake and Sadamitsu, I'm ready for you.

NARRATOR: He taunts them; they blink furiously and spring to attack (*sung*) but are thrown back to the right and kicked to the left. Infused with Kochō's power, Yoshikado glares fiercely at them all, (*cadence*) seemingly invincible. Hōshō rushes into their midst, and the voices of Yorihira and Yorinobu are heard from afar.

YORINOBU: (*spoken*) That man is not human. He's possessed by the power of Kochō's spirit and the earth spider's venom. (*sung*) The extraordinary might of this sword is well known. It will sweep all from its path.

NARRATOR: He unsheathes it and raises it to the heavens.

YORINOBU: (*spoken*) The god Hachiman, guardian of the Genji, fills this sword with his strength, love, and compassion.

NARRATOR: He aims at Yoshikado and throws the sword. (*sung*) Suddenly the apparition of Kochō disappears, and Yoshikado appears as himself again (*cadence*) The mysterious power of the sword comes from the providence of the gods.

TSUNA: (*sung*) Now we've got him!

NARRATOR: Tsuna and Sadamitsu seize Yoshikado while Kintoki and Suetake pin down the spider. Yorihira and Yorinobu come rushing up. The traitors are crushed, the evil spider vanquished. The vengeful enemy has been defeated and bitter jealousy calmed. The brothers Yorimitsu, Yorinobu, Yorihira are reunited, all Genji pillars strong. Their house flourishes, and, with it, the (*high pitch*) realm prospers as never before. We praise this Genji era and pray that it may endure forevermore.

(The postscript is almost exactly the same as the one for *Twins at the Sumida River*.)

Notes

Notes to Chikamatsu: Five Late Plays, introduction

1. *Chikamatsu zenshū* (CZ), 17 vols. (Tokyo: Iwanami shoten, 1985–94).
2. Translated in Donald Keene, trans., *Major Plays of Chikamatsu* (New York: Columbia University Press, 1961).
3. This was told to the writer Ōta Nanpo (1749–1823) by Sorai's disciple Usami Keisuke (Shinsui, 1710–76) and recorded in Nanpo's 1788 essay "Zokuji kosui," in Nihon zuihitsu taisei no. 3, vol. 4 (Tokyo: Yoshikawa kōbunkan, 1977), p. 146. In the same work, Nanpo comments on the beauty of particular lines from several of Chikamatsu's other plays. I am grateful to Professor Hino Tatsuo for his clarification of the authenticity of Sorai's comment.
4. We also have a translation of Chikamatsu's short, one-act period play *Goban Taiheiki* (1710), translated by Jacqueline Mueller in the *Harvard Journal of Asiatic Studies* 46, no. 1 (1986), which is an early version of the "Chūshingura" story. *Semimaru* (1693) is translated in Susan Matisoff, *The Legends of Semimaru: Blind Musician of Japan* (New York: Columbia University Press, 1978). A translation of *Love Suicides at Amijima* (1720) is in Donald Shively, *The Love Suicides at Amijima: A Study of a Japanese Domestic Tragedy by Chikamatsu Monzaemon* (Cambridge, Mass.: Harvard University Press, 1953). There are some older prewar translations as well. *Soga kaikeizan* (1718) is translated in Frank Lombard, *An Outline History of the Japanese Drama* (London: Allen & Unwin, 1928). Six works are also translated in Asataro Miyamori, *Masterpieces of Chikamatsu: The Japanese Shakespeare* (London: Kegan Paul, 1926); three of those not translated in Keene, trans., *Major Plays of Chikamatsu* are *The Almanac of Love* (*Koi hakke hashiragoyomi*, a later version of *Daikyōshi mukashi-goyomi*, 1715); *Fair Ladies at a Game of Poem-Cards* (*Kaoyo uta karuta*, 1714); and a highly abridged version of

The Tethered Steed (*Kanhasshū tsunagi-uma*, 1724). We have a translation of the kabuki version of Chikamatsu's *Shunkan* (*Kikaigashima*) performed as a distinct play, but it was originally the second scene of act 2 of *Heike nyogo no shima* (1719), in Samuel Leiter, *The Art of Kabuki: Famous Plays in Performance* (Berkeley and Los Angeles: University of California Press, 1979).

5. See C. Andrew Gerstle, "Hero as Murderer in Chikamatsu," *Monumenta Nipponica* 51, no. 3 (1996): 317–56; Gerstle, "Heroic Honor: Chikamatsu and the Samurai Ideal," *Harvard Journal of Asiatic Studies* 57, no. 2 (1997): 307–81; and Gerstle, "Gidayū botsugo no Chikamatsu," in Torigoe Bunzō et al., eds., *Chikamatsu no jidai*, Iwanami kōza: Kabuki, bunraku series (IKKB), vol. 8 (Tokyo: Iwanami shoten, 1998).

6. This distinction is discussed in some detail in C. Andrew Gerstle, *Circles of Fantasy: Convention in the Plays of Chikamatsu* (Cambridge, Mass.: Harvard University Press, 1986), chs. 4 and 5.

7. Translated in Keene, trans., *Major Plays of Chikamatsu*.

8. *Imamukashi ayatsuri nendaiki* (1727), in *Nihon shomin bunka shiryō shūsei* (NSBSS), vol. 7 (Tokyo: San'ichi shobō, 1977), p. 12, is the first to use the term "god of writers" (*sakusha no ujigami*), which is often repeated in some form or other throughout the Edo period in writings on jōruri or kabuki theater.

9. *Naniwa miyage*, in *Shingunsho ruijū*, vol. 5 (Tokyo: Daiichi shobō, 1906). This passage is discussed by Yoshinaga Takao, ed., *Jōruri sakuhin yōsetsu* (3): Chikamatsu Hanji-hen (Tokyo: Kokuritsu gekijo, 1984), p. 8. Ikan was the father of Chikamatsu Hanji (1725–83), another famous jōruri playwright, who took the name Chikamatsu.

10. *Naniwa miyage*, in *Shingunsho ruiju*, vol. 5, pp. 322–23.

11. About fifty are listed in the record of the *Gidayū-bon kōso ikken* (1833), along with hundreds of other plays, under copyright of the guild of *shōhon* (jōruri book) publishers in the three cities of Kyoto, Osaka, and Edo. See *Gidayū-bon kōso ikken*, in NSBSS, vol. 7, pp. 99–105. See also Yamane Tameo, "Fushizuke to hanpon" in Torigoe et al., eds., *Chikamatsu no jidai*, IKKB, vol. 8; and Nagatomo Chiyoji, "Jōruribon: sono juyō to kyōkyū" in Torigoe et al., eds., *Ōgon jidai no jōruri to sono go*, IKKB, vol. 9, for recent research on the history of jōruri books.

12. For some detail on the popularity of chanting, see C. Andrew Gerstle, "Amateurs and the Theater: The So-Called Demented Art of *Gidayū*," *Senri Ethnological Studies* 46 (1995): 37–57.

13. Andrew Markus, *The Willow in Autumn: Ryūtei Tanehiko 1783–1842* (Cambridge, Mass.: Harvard University Press, 1992), p. 109. This number was his current collection as of the fifth month, 1818.

14. Quoted in Markus, *The Willow in Autumn*, pp. 92–93. Tanehiko refers to a

kabuki text, but it is clear that jōruri, with the chanter's notation in the text, was read in a similar manner.

15. V. M. Golownin, *Memoirs of a Captivity in Japan During the Years 1811, 1812, and 1813* (London: Henry Colburn, 1973), vol. 1, p. 303. Although this could possibly be a description of nō drama chanting, it seems clear from the description of the content that it refers to jōruri narratives. Research done for a paper I have presented at conferences but not yet published shows that from the late eighteenth century, the chanting of jōruri plays as an amateur hobby became widespread among both commoners and samurai throughout Japan. Takadaya Kahei (1769–1827), the ship captain who helped negotiate Golovnin's release after he was captured by the Russians, is known to have carried jōruri books with him on all his journeys. The point is that individuals commonly learned to "perform" dramatic texts as the process of learning to read them.

16. Andrew Markus discusses the extent of Ryūtei Tanehiko's use of Chikamatsu and other playwrights' works in his *Willow in Autumn*, pp. 72–95. He notes (p. 95) that nearly a third of Tanehiko's titles "derive their subject matter entirely or primarily from the corpus of Chikamatsu's works." (I have seen in various libraries numerous Chikamatsu texts with Tanehiko's notes written in them.)

17. Nakayama Mikio wrote a short "handout" for an exhibition in 1995 at the National Bunraku Theater in Osaka on the film and television dramatization of Chikamatsu which includes a list of the films to date. I received a copy of this from a friend, but it also should be available at the theater's library.

18. CZ, vol. 17, p. 29. There is some variation between two extant versions; the longer of the two, which is written on his portrait, is translated here. The other is considered to be a draft for the portrait.

19. The following outline of Chikamatsu's early life was gleaned from the introductions to various editions of Chikamatsu's plays, in particular Mori Shū et al., eds., *Chikamatsu Monzaemonshū*, vol. 1, NKBZ no. 43 (Tokyo: Shōgakkan, 1972). Mori did the most extensive recent work on Chikamatsu's biography, collected in his posthumously published *Chikamatsu to jōruri* (Tokyo: Hanawa shobō, 1990). His earlier *Chikamatsu Monzaemon* (Tokyo: San'ichi shobō, 1959) also has information on Chikamatsu's life. CZ, vol. 17, contains the existing records concerning Chikamatsu.

20. A *koku* is a measure of rice, about 180 liters. It was the measure of samurai stipends and therefore rank and wealth.

21. The important records have been printed in CZ, vol. 17. Chikamatsu's grandfather had been a rōnin without a samurai position for a time and had lived in Kyoto. His maternal grandfather's family were "Kamo samurai" originally from Kyoto. It is clear that the family had various connections to important families in Kyoto, which is not far from Fukui.

22. Mori Shū, *Chikamatsu to jōruri*, pp. 53–54.
23. Doi Jun'ichi, "Okamoto Ippōshi nenpu," *Nihon ishigaku zasshi* 23 (October 1997): 467–80.
24. CZ, vol. 17, pp. 91–92.
25. Recent research has documented the extent of the cultural activity of Go-Mizunō's circle, as well as that of his son Emperor Reigen (1654–1732, r. 1663–87). See Suzuki Ken'ichi, *Kinsei dōjō kadan no kenkyū* (Tokyo: Kyūko shoin, 1994).
26. CZ, vol. 17, pp. 91–92.
27. In *Nihon zuihitsu taisei* no. 3, vol. 20 (Tokyo: Yoshikawa kōbunkan, 1978), p. 289.
28. Yasuda Fukiko documented the extent of the practice of giving court titles (*juryō*) to jōruri chanters such as Kaganojō, who were known to perform for the imperial family. See Yasuda Fukiko, *Kojōruri: tayū no juryō to sono jidai* (Tokyo: Yagi shoten, 1998).
29. CZ, vol. 17, pp. 91–92. The works at Kōsaiji temple in Amagasaki are by Ano Sanefuji and Emperor Gosai. There is also a record there saying that Chikamatsu had presented works by Machigami Kanechika and others by Emperor Gosai, which are no longer extant. Chikamatsu presented them to the temple as a memorial offering for his mother.
30. CZ, vol. 17, p. 80. Chikamatsu's poem is translated in Keene, trans., *Major Plays of Chikamatsu*, p. 3.
31. CZ, vol. 17, pp. 82–86; Mori, *Chikamatsu Monzaemon*, pp. 50–51, names only two sons.
32. CZ, vol. 17, pp. 82–86.
33. See *Kabuki hyōbanki shūsei*, vol. 1 (Tokyo: Iwanami shoten, 1972), p. 244.
34. It is interesting that Chikamatsu uses the same verb, *kuchi* (wither, decay), in the last line of his final testament (just quoted) as is used here to describe Chikamatsu's determination to give his whole life to the theater.
35. *Kabuki hyōbanki shūsei*, vol. 1, p. 244.
36. There is also a temple of the same name in Shiga Prefecture near Ōtsu.
37. See *Minoharagusa* (1691) and other kabuki critiques in *Kabuki hyōbanki shūsei*, vol. 1, pp. 283–98, where the actor Chikamatsu Kannosuke is mentioned.
38. This preface is translated in full in Gerstle, *Circles of Fantasy*, pp. 183–88. Kaganojō's ideas are discussed there on pp. 24–29, and the Japanese text is in NSBSS, vol. 7, pp. 125–27.
39. *Imamukashi ayatsuri nendaiki*, in NSBSS, vol. 7, p. 9. Tsunoda Ichirō gave a thorough account of Gidayū and Kaganojō during the 1680s in Torigoe et al., eds., "Jōkyō ninen no dōtonbori," in *Chikamatsu no jidai*, IKKB, vol. 8.
40. *Kyōto machibure shūsei, bekkan*, vol. 2 (Tokyo: Iwanami shoten, 1989), p. 288. In

Edo, the ban lasted only three days. See *Edo machibure shūsei*, vol. 2 (Tokyo: Hanawa shobō, 1994), p. 99. Ōhashi Tadayoshi discusses the circumstances surrounding this incident in "Jōrurishi ni okeru jōkyō ninen," in Chikamatsu kenkyūjo jūsshūnenkinen ronbunshū henshū iinkai, ed., *Chikamatsu no sanbyakunen* (Osaka: Izumi shoin, 1999).

41. NSBSS, vol. 7, p. 130.
42. Translated in full in Gerstle, *Circles of Fantasy*, pp. 189–96; Gidayū's ideas are discussed on pp. 29–34. The original is in NSBSS, vol. 7, pp. 130–34.
43. For more detail on Gidayū's writings, see C. Andrew Gerstle, "Takemoto Gidayū and the Individualistic Spirit of Osaka Theater," in James McClain and Osamu Wakita, eds., *Osaka: The Merchants' Capital of Early Modern Japan* (Ithaca, N.Y.: Cornell University Press, 1999).
44. Gerstle, *Circles of Fantasy*, p. 129; NSBSS, vol. 7, p. 130.
45. Gerstle, *Circles of Fantasy*, pp. 190–91; NSBSS, vol. 7, p. 131.
46. Gerstle, *Circles of Fantasy*, pp. 32–33.
47. I discuss this in some detail in *Circles of Fantasy*, pp. 39–62.
48. Translated in Matisoff, *The Legends of Semimaru*.
49. Charles Dunn and Torigoe Bunzō, trans., *The Actors Analects (Yakusha rongo)* (New York: Columbia University Press, 1969).
50. Printed as "Genroku jūichinen nikki," in Torigoe Bunzō, ed., *Kabuki to kyōgen: Gengo hyōgen no tsuikyū* (Tokyo: Yagi shoten, 1992), pp. 401–61. Tsuchida Mamoru has commented on some discoveries about kabuki playwriting emanating from this text; see *Kōshō genroku kabuki: yōshiki to tenkai* (Tokyo: Yagi shoten, 1996), pp. 346–54.
51. Translated in Keene, trans., *Major Plays of Chikamatsu*.
52. Hirata Sumiko gives a detailed survey of this period of Chikamatsu's career: "Takeda Izumo to Chikugonojō," in Torigoe et al., eds., IKKB, vol. 8. Takeda Izumo II (1691–1756), the famous coauthor of *Chūshingura* and other works in the 1740s, was the son of Takeda Izumo I, who himself wrote plays from the early 1720s.
53. NSBSS, vol. 7, p. 12.
54. Uchiyama Mikiko, *Jōruri no jūhasseki* (Tokyo: Benseisha, 1989), pp. 51–154. See also Gerstle, "Heroic Honor."
55. *Ongyoku kudensho* (1771), reprinted in Nishiyama Matsunosuke et al., eds., *Kinsei geidōron*, Nihon shisō taikei no. 61 (Tokyo: Iwanami shoten, 1972), pp. 435–36.
56. See Donald Shively, "Tokugawa Plays on Forbidden Topics," in James Brandon, ed., *Chūshingura: Studies in Kabuki and the Puppet Theater* (Honolulu: University of Hawaii Press, 1982); Uchiyama, *Jōruri no jūhasseki*, pp. 51-154; Gerstle, "Heroic Honor."

57. An annotated version of this passage is in Shuzui Kenji et al., eds., *Chikamatsu jōrurishū* vol. 2, NKBT no. 50 (Tokyo: Iwanami shoten, 1959), pp. 355–59. For a complete translation, see Donald Keene, trans., *The Battle of Coxinga: Chikamatsu's Puppet Play, Its Background and Importance* (Cambridge: Cambridge University Press, 1951), pp. 93–96; a slightly abridged translation by Keene is published in Ryusaku Tsunoda et al., eds., *Sources of Japanese Tradition*, vol. 1 (New York: Columbia University Press, 1964), pp. 437–40. The quotations here are from Keene's translation.
58. These musical paragraphs, termed "primary units," are discussed in some detail in Gerstle, *Circles of Fantasy*, ch. 3.
59. Translated in Donald Keene, ed., *Twenty Plays of the Nō Theater* (New York: Columbia University Press, 1970).
60. Translated in Royall Tyler, trans., *Japanese Nō Dramas* (London: Penguin Classics, 1992).
61. Grammatically, these paragraphs can usually be considered as one syntactic unit, that is, one long sentence concluding with a *shūshikei* inflection signaling the end of a sentence. Chanters did not, however, always follow these grammatical markers when inserting cadences. The only punctuation in the texts is a triangle-shaped mark, thought to be from the Japanese character *ku*, for line. This was inserted by the chanter to mark breath stops. More detail on the notation can be found in Gerstle, *Circles of Fantasy*; and C. Andrew Gerstle, Kiyoshi Inobe, and William P. Malm, *Theater as Music: The Bunraku Play, "Mt. Imo and Mt. Se: An Exemplary Tale of Womanly Virtue"* (Ann Arbor: University of Michigan Press, 1990).
62. Kamiya Katsuhiro has written several articles examining the possible sources for Chinese references used by writers such as Chikamatsu, Saikaku, and Ki no Kaion. Two that focus on Chikamatsu are "Chikamatsu to tsūzoku gundan," *Nagoya daigaku: Kokugo kokubungaku*, no. 82 (July 1998): 31–42; and "Chikamatsu to *Yūgu zuihitsu*," *Kinsei bungei*, no. 67 (January 1998): 24–32. See also Takahashi Hiroshi, "Chikamatsu to *Enki kappō*," *Sugino joshi daigaku*, no. 17 (December 1980): 114–77; and "Chikamatsu to *Kinshūdan*," *Sugino joshi daigaku*, no. 18 (December 1981): 31–48.
63. See note 4. The translation was rewritten by Peter Oswald for this production.

Notes to *Twins at the Sumida River*, introduction

1. The text used for this translation is in Matsuzaki Hitoshi et al., eds., *Chikamatsu jōrurishū* (CJS), vol. 2, SNKBT no. 92 (Tokyo: Iwanami shoten, 1995). I am greatly in debt to Hara Michio for annotating the text for the first time.

2. Shirakata Masaru, *Chikamatsu jōruri no kenkyū* (Tokyo: Kazama shobō, 1993), pp. 276–309; the article on *Futago Sumidagawa* was originally published in *Niihama kōgyō kōtō senmon gakkō kiyō* 3 (1966). Hirata Sumiko, "Futago Sumidagawa ni tsuite—Edo to Chikamatsu," *Bunkyō daigaku kokubun* 13 (1984): 35–36. Hara Michio, "*Futago Sumidagawa* shikiron: Oiesōdōgeki to shite no seimitsuka," *Kokugo to kokubungaku* 898 (October 1998): 1–14. See also "*Umewaka engi* no kenkyū to shiryō," in *Kokubungaku ronsō shinshū*, vol. 8 (Tokyo: Ōfūsha, 1988), for other articles on the development of this legend. Kaewrithidej Ladda recently published a study of this play: "Chikamatsu jōruri ni okeru 'kyōran' no igi: *Futago Sumidagawa* o rei ni," *Kyōto Daigaku: Kokubungaku ronsō* 1, 1998, pp. 16–41, in which she compares Chikamatsu's play with the earlier versions, particularly focusing on the question of the portrayal of "madness."

3. Koyama Hiroshi et al., eds., *Yōkyokushū*, vol. 1, NKBZ no. 33 (Tokyo: Shōgakkan, 1973); translated in Royall Tyler, trans., *Japanese Nō Dramas* (London: Penguin Classics, 1992).

4. Koyama Hiroshi et al., eds., *Yōkyokushū*, vol. 2, NKBZ no. 34 (Tokyo: Shōgakkan, 1975); translated in Tyler, trans., *Japanese Nō Dramas*.

5. Sanshō Dayū was the name of a legendary cruel provincial magistrate in Tango (Kyoto Prefecture on the Japan Sea side) who kidnapped children. The basic story told over the centuries in many forms is that the son and daughter of an aristocratic couple are stolen and mistreated. The mother, too, is sent to the exile island of Sado. The elder daughter dies helping her brother escape, and the son eventually is restored to his rightful position and, at the end, has Sanshō Dayū executed.

6. Yokoyama Shigeru, "Sekkyō shōhon ni junzuru shōhon," in *Chūsei bungaku: Kenkyū to shiryō* (*Kokubungaku ronsō*, vol. 2) (Tokyo: Shibundō, 1958), pp. 119–20. See also Yokoyama Shigeru, ed., *Sekkyō shōhonshū*, vol. 3 (Tokyo: Kadokawa shoten, 1968); this volume contains *Sumidagawa*, *Sumidagawa monogatari*, and *Hanako koi monogurui*. The Yamato Tosanojō *ko-jōruri* play *Sumidagawa* is in *Shingunsho ruiju*, vol. 5 (1906; reprint, Tokyo: Daiichi shobō, 1976). The Kaganojō *ko-jōruri* play *Sumidagawa* (1690), also issued by Takemoto Gidayū, is in Ko-jōrurishū kankōkai, ed., *Ko-jōruri shōhonshū: Kaganojōhen*, vol. 4 (Tokyo: Daigaku shoten, 1993).

7. Shirakata, *Chikamatsu jōruri no kenkyū*, pp. 286–89.

8. Ibid., pp. 290–96, 297.

9. Conrad Totman described the extent of the problem of deforestation during the second half of the seventeenth century, which parallels Chikamatsu's lifetime. This topic was a real concern among both ordinary people and government officials. See Totman, *The Green Archipelago: Forestry in Preindustrial Japan* (Berkeley and Los Angeles: University of California Press, 1989).

10. See C. Andrew Gerstle, "Hero as Murderer in Chikamatsu," *Monumenta Nipponica* 51, no. 3 (1996): 317–56.
11. "Ongyoku kudensho," in Nishiyama Matsunosuke et al., eds., *Kinsei geidōron*, Nihon shisō taikei no. 61 (Tokyo: Iwanami shoten, 1972), p. 428.
12. Ibid., p. 435.
13. In NSBSS, vol. 7 (Tokyo: San'ichi shobō, 1975), p. 102.

Notes to *Twins at the Sumida River*, act 1

1. Emperor Xuan Wang (ca. 370 B.C.). This story is originally from *Zhan Guo Ce: Chu*. This was translated by James Crump as *Chan-kuo ts'e*, from *Annals of the Warring States* (Ann Arbor: Center for Chinese Studies, University of Michigan Press, 1996), book of Chu, sec. 4, pp. 226–27. The fox (i.e., a clever and devious minister or lord) borrows the majesty of the tiger (Emperor Xuan Wang) and makes all other beasts bow to the fox, thereby deceiving the tiger. That is, rulers must be able to judge where the real power lies and to be able to distinguish between loyal and disloyal retainers. See Matsuzaki Hitoshi et al., eds., *Chikamatsu jōrurishū* (CJS), vol. 2, SNKBT no. 92 (Tokyo: Iwanami shoten, 1995), p. 3, nn. 1 and 3.
2. This phrase is found in the important guide to composing haiku, *Kefukigusa* (1645), reprinted in Takeuchi Waka, ed., Iwanami bunko yellow series no. 200-1 (1943; reprint, Tokyo: Iwanami shoten, 1988), p. 94. Many of Chikamatsu's phrases and sayings appear in this popular guide, showing his style of word association to be influenced by *haikai* linked verse. Commentators have noted other phrases, sayings, and associated words in Chikamatsu's plays found in haiku guides such as *Sewa-yakigusa* (1658) and *Ruisenshū* (1676).
3. These are the tall gates at the entrances to Shinto shrines.
4. Pronounced "Hiyoshi" today. The original god of this ancient shrine on Mount Hie (Piye) is mentioned in the *Kojiki*. See Donald Phillipi, trans., *Kojiki* (Princeton, N.J.: Princeton University Press, 1969), p. 118. It became an imperial shrine under Emperor Tenji in the seventh century when he had his palace at Ōtsu on Lake Biwa. Emperor Tenji invited the god of Miwa Shrine to join the local deity at the shrine. Hie Shrine became extremely important with the founding of the capital at Kyoto in the late eighth century as the guardian gate (*kimon*, "demon gate at the northeast direction") of the Enryakuji temple complex on Mount Hiei, which is the guardian (*kimon*) of Kyoto itself and therefore, by extension, of all Japan. The "demon gate" keeps out demons or evil spirits. The monkey is an important symbol of this shrine because of its role as the messenger of the god Sannō Gongen. Today there is a caged monkey on

the shrine grounds. Such monkeys are known as "masaru" ([神猿], god-monkeys), which is also written with the characters to mean "demons depart" (*masaru* [魔去る]). In the northeast corner of the Kyoto Imperial Palace is an image of the *masaru* monkey who keeps demons at bay, known as "Sarugatsuji." The monkey statue is outside this corner, under the eve of the wall. Monkeys still live in the wild on Mount Hiei. Chikamatsu's choice of this site for the opening introduces two of the important images of the play: demons and monkeys. Furthermore, Sakamoto, the site of the Hiyoshi Shrine, has associations with the "Sumidagawa" legend because earlier versions of this tale noted this as the place where young Umewaka was captured by slave traders. Finally, it is Sarushima no Sōta ("Monkey Island," Sōta) who both kills one twin son and, by turning himself into a *tengu* goblin, saves the other in acts 3 and 4.

5. The illustration, figure 13, shows this to be a carpenter's tool, like an adze.
6. Ibuki is in Shiga Prefecture; Makimoku is in Nara Prefecture; Kiso is in Nagano Prefecture; and Shigaraki is in Shiga Prefecture.
7. Chikamatsu invented this figure of a relative who tries to usurp the Yoshida house. Chikamatsu made Yoshida the elegant courtier, in contrast to Momotsura, the samurai usurper. He is presented not as an evil man but as one driven by ambition to take over the Yoshida house where his sister is the official wife but also where Yoshida has Hanjo as his preferred mistress.
8. A quotation from the nō play *Kanawa*. See Yokomichi Mario and Omote Akira, eds., *Yōkyokushū*, vol. 2, NKBT no. 41 (Tokyo: Iwanami shoten, 1960), p. 351; Donald Keene, ed., *Twenty Plays of the Nō Theater* (New York: Columbia University Press, 1970). This is the first of twenty-five references to different nō (three kyōgen are also quoted) over the five acts of this play, each contributing to the overall themes and imagery. The quotation here sounds auspicious and suitable to the setting of harmony between yin and yang, man and woman, but the rest of the nō play is a portrayal of hatred. *Kanawa* is, in the entire nō repertoire, one of the most powerful depictions of the vengeful anger of an abandoned woman, The woman is mad with jealous rage and goes to pray at the Kibune Shrine in Kyoto to raise all the demons (*mōryō kishin*, spirits of mountains and streams, plants and animals) to make her former husband and his new wife suffer, which suggests an underlying irony in the auspicious opening scene and an omen of the crisis to come.
9. Male and female deities who gave birth to the sun, moon, and earth, particularly the Japanese islands.
10. Shinto thought has a theory that the right pillar was yin and the left, yang.
11. In Shiga Prefecture on the western side of Lake Biwa, northeast of Mount Hiei, famous for being one of several mountains across Japan inhabited by *tengu* goblins, and therefore important as a religious site for *yamabushi* ascetic rituals. The

nō play *Kagetsu,* quoted in act 4, lists Mount Hira among such famous mountains. *Hirasan kojin reitaku* (ca. 1239) describes an encounter and discussion between the priest Kesei and the Great Tengu of Mount Hira (*Hirayama no daitengu*). The spirit of the *tengu* had possessed a young woman in court service. See Koizumi Hiroshi, ed., *Hōbutsushū, kankyo no tomo, Hirasan kojin reitaku,* SNKBT no. 40 (Tokyo: Iwanami shoten, 1993), pp. 455–82. The *tengu* theme, the destruction of nature out of personal greed and its consequences, is one of the unifying elements of the play. The Hie (Hiyoshi) Shrine's role is to protect the capital from threatening demons to the northeast; therefore, to cut down *tengu* goblin trees from Mount Hira to build *torii* at the Hie Shrine is to invite disaster.

12. The linking of Hanjo's lover "Yoshida" (from the nō play *Hanjo*) with the "Yoshida" of the nō play *Sumida River* predates Chikamatsu's play.
13. A similar name, Awazu no Rokurō Toshikanu, was already part of the tale from the time of *Sumidagawa monogatari.*
14. "Madness" (*kurui*) is a major theme of the play.
15. Hara Michio remarks that this kind of fallen samurai figure is common in many of Chikamatsu's mature-period plays. See CJS 2, p. 9.
16. This was an entertainment center from Heian times. The author of the *Sarashina nikki* (mid-eleventh century) refers to being entertained by women singers (*yūjo*) in Nogami. See Ivan Morris, *As I Crossed a Bridge of Dreams* (London, Penguin Books, 1975), p. 43, but Morris's translation does not mention that the entertainers were women.
17. Matsuwaka's hair was already cut short, implying that he has no desire to be Yoshida's heir.
18. A reference to Zeami's nō play *Shunnei,* which is about the love between two brothers. The younger has been captured and condemned to death after a battle. The elder, wounded in the same battle, seeks him out and asks that he die in his place or that they die together. A reprieve comes at the last moment before the execution, and the final lines are a celebration of love between parent and child and between siblings. The important image here is strands of hair as a symbol of blood ties. This metaphor reappears in acts 3 and 4. See Yokomichi Mario and Omote Akira, eds., *Yōkyokushū,* vol. 1, NKBT no. 40 (Tokyo: Iwanami shoten, 1960), p. 378; Mae Smethurst, *Dramatic Representations of Filial Piety* (Ithaca, N.Y.: Cornell University Press, 1998).
19. Chikamatsu was the first to make the brothers twins. Before this, they were most often portrayed as half brothers by different mothers.
20. Hara Michio notes the source *Hyakushō-bukuro* (1721), by Nishikawa Jōken, which explains this belief. See CJS 2, p. 16, n. 5.

21. A quotation from the demon nō play *Nue*. A *nue* is another name for a *toratsugumi*, a golden mountain thrush, but is also the name of a fantastic creature: head of a monkey, body of a badger, tail like a snake, arms and legs of a tiger, and a voice like a golden mountain thrush. It appears in stories from the time of *The Tale of the Heike*. Here Chikamatsu uses imagery from *Nue* to conjure up a threatening supernatural force. The nō play is about the suffering of the spirit of the *nue* demon that was killed by Minamoto no Yoshimasa, which suggests that demons are not just evil but have feelings and are part of nature. The *nue* seeks enlightenment and in the end disappears down the river into the sea. The predominant image is the river, and the spirit appears first as a boatman. See Koyama Hiroshi et al., eds., *Yōkyokushū*, vol. 2, NKBZ no. 34 (Tokyo: Shōgakkan, 1975), p. 397; Kenneth Yasuda, *Masterworks of the Nō Theater* (Bloomington: Indiana University Press, 1989).
22. A quotation from *Nue*. See Koyama et al., eds., *Yōkyokushū*, vol. 2, p. 399.
23. The reference is to the gambling term *tengu tanomoshi*, which refers to a game in which a player holding a pick stabs one wooden tablet from a group of them numbered one to fifteen. See CJS 2, p. 17, n. 19.
24. This theatrical device of spirits creating doubles was fairly common in kabuki and the puppet theater.
25. In earlier versions of the "Sumidagawa" legend, Matsuwaka is stolen by *tengu*, but Chikamatsu innovates here by making this the consequence of the curse for cutting down sacred trees on Mount Hira.
26. A reference to *Kokinshū* poem no. 42 by Ki no Tsurayuki. The poem's theme is that we don't know if the heart of friends will change, but we can trust in the fragrance of village flowers. It is a subtle comment on human relations and the preciousness of friendship. Tsurayuki is buried on Mount Hiei, above the Hiyoshi Shrine, near where he lived in the final years of his life. See Laurel Rodd, with Mary Henkensius, trans., *Kokinshū: A Collection of Poems Ancient and Modern* (Princeton, N.J.: Princeton University Press, 1984); Helen McCullough, trans., *Kokin Wakashū: The First Imperial Anthology of Japanese Poetry* (Stanford, Calif.: Stanford University Press, 1985).
27. A reference to the nō play *Hotoke no hara*. Hotoke-gozen, a dancer, gained the favor of Taira no Kiyomori, displacing Giō, who left with her mother to become a nun. Hotoke-gozen then followed Giō and became a nun. The theme is relations between women in competition for a powerful man and their sisterly feelings for each other. There is an irony here: Hotoke-gozen had gained the favor of the most powerful man of the time but gave it up in sympathy for the woman she displaced. Furthermore, the particular quotation is about the acceptance of the brevity of one's moment of glory, the fragility of a

cherry blossom. See Sanari Kentarō, ed., *Yōkyoku taikan* (YTK), vol. 4 (Tokyo: Meiji shoin, 1927), p. 2793; Helen McCullough, trans., *The Tale of the Heike* (Stanford, Calif.: Stanford University Press, 1988), pp. 30–37.
28. A common Edo-period euphemism for sex.

Notes to Twins at the Sumida River, act 2

1. Chikamatsu has added this element to the "Sumidagawa" tale.
2. The image of paradise suggests the nō play *Kantan*, hinting that this is not real and will be but a short-lived dream. See Koyama Hiroshi et al., eds., *Yōkyokushū*, vol. 2, NKBZ no. 34 (Tokyo: Shōgakkan, 1973), pp. 131–32; Royall Tyler, trans., *Japanese Nō Dramas* (London: Penguin Classics, 1992). Furthermore, the idea of all four seasons blossoming at once and constantly recalls the opening of Chikamatsu's *Battles of Coxinga* (1715), which is followed by an uprising and chaos. See Donald Keene, trans., *Major Plays of Chikamatsu* (New York: Columbia University Press, 1961).
3. An allusion to a phrase from the nō play *Hanjo* about being abandoned by a lover, like a fan cast aside in autumn. "Hanjo," "bedroom," and "fan" are related words in linked verse. See Koyama et al., eds., *Yōkyokushū*, vol. 2, p. 54; Tyler, trans., *Japanese Nō Dramas*.
4. An allusion to *Kokinshū* poem no. 864, expressing regret at leaving friends after an enjoyable party. See Laurel Rodd, with Mary Henkenius, trans., *Kokinshū: A Collection of Poems Ancient and Modern* (Princeton, N.J.: Princeton University Press, 1984); Helen McCullough, trans., *Kokin Wakashū: The First Imperial Anthology of Japanese Poetry* (Stanford, Calif.: Stanford University Press, 1985).
5. This story was well known, but we don't know from where Chikamatsu took the tale of the emperor's painting the carp without eyes. Hara notes that a story of keeping an animal on the canvas by not painting the eyes is in *Kokon chomonjū* (1245), in Matsuzaki Hitoshi et al., eds., *Chikamatsu jōrurishū* (CJS), SNKBT no. 92 (Tokyo: Iwanami shoten, 1995), p. 116, n. 9. While working on this play in Kyoto, I visited the Shūgakuin Imperial Detached Palace (built for Emperor Go-Mizunō) and was intrigued by a painting on a wooden door of a carp by Sumiyoshi Gukei (1631–1705). Legend has it that every night the carp would fly off the door and frolic in the large pond. Chikamatsu, who had connections with Emperor Go-Mizuno's immediate family—his son Emperor Gosai—could have visited Shūgakuin in their company or at least heard about this painting. Later in the century, Maruyama Okyō painted a net over the carp. I was encouraged in this supposition when I later read that in his introduction to this play, Kitani Hōgin had also wondered about Chikamatsu and

this painting. See vol. 12 of *Dai Chikamatsu zenshū* (16 vols.) (Tokyo: Dai Chikamatsu zenshū kankōkai, 1923).

6. The image of Yang Guifei bathing is from Bai Juyi's (772–846) most famous poem *Cheng Wen Ge* ("Song of Everlasting Sorrow"); translated as "Song of Lasting Pain" by Stephen Owen, ed. and trans., *An Anthology of Chinese Literature* (New York: Norton, 1996), pp. 442–47. The comparison of a woman's beauty to lotus blossoms is from the nō play *Yōkihi*. The reference to Yang Guifei suggests that overindulgence in the pleasures of beautiful women lead to chaos and the destruction of the house. Act 3 also opens with a reference to Bai Juyi's poem. See Sanari Kentarō, ed., *Yōkyoku taikan* (YTK), vol. 6 (Tokyo: Meiji shoin, 1927), p. 3119; Donald Keene, ed., *Twenty Plays of the Nō Theater* (New York: Columbia University Press, 1970).

7. The word *iro* for her beauty evokes highly erotic imagery for this section.

8. Chikamatsu paints Yoshida as a selfish, arrogant, and highly sophisticated aristocrat. Yoshida's use of "woman" (*onna*) here for Lady Yoshida sounds extremely heartless.

9. From the *Kokinshū* poem 294, by Narihira, an autumn poem describing the exquisite beauty of a brocade of autumn leaves falling on a river. The setting in *Tales of Ise* is an elegant party of aristocrats on a riverbank. See Rodd, trans., *Kokinshū*; McCullough, trans., *Kokin Wakashū*; also Helen McCullough, trans., *Tales of Ise* (Stanford, Calif.: Stanford University Press, 1968), sec. 106.

10. The following is a lyrical song (*fushigoto*), a mosaic of images drawn from nō plays and poetry. The imagery suggests Buddha's Paradise.

11. A quotation from the nō play *Obasute*, which is about the continuing obsession of the spirit of an old woman left to die by her son on "Abandoned Old Woman" Mountain (*obasuteyama*). She cannot be freed from her passion for life (*shūshin no yami; mōshū no kokoro*), which keeps her from salvation. The quotation is in praise of the midautumn harvest moon, considered the most pristine of the year cycle. The old woman takes solace in her lone companion, the moon, its light the symbol of Amida's saving grace that touches all beings. Her imagination paints a serene Western Paradise, a magnificent garden, but in the end she cannot, or will not, give up her obsession for life, now long past. Paradise remains a figment of her imagination. See Koyama Hiroshi et al., eds., *Yōkyokushū*, vol. 1, NKBZ no. 33 (Tokyo: Shōgakkan, 1973), p. 420; Keene, ed., *Twenty Plays of the Nō Theater*.

12. Wind in the pines is a common metaphor for intense loneliness in late autumn and for waiting for a lover who doesn't come.

13. From the nō play *Kinuta*, the story of a wife who goes mad waiting for her husband's return. She beats the *kinuta* (fulling block). As Royall Tyler remarks in his introduction to this play in his *Japanese Nō Dramas*, this is the closest work in

the nō repertoire to *Hanjo*; both describe the obsession of a lover who feels abandoned. In *Kinuta*, the woman's passion turns to anger and hate, driving her into hell. In the end, her husband's love and prayers allow her to be released from this hatred, and she attains salvation. The particular quotations describe, first, her desire for her passionate feelings to be carried by the winds on the sound of the crack of the fulling block and enter her husband's dream and, second, her growing anger at the shallowness of his vow of conjugal love. See Koyama et al., eds., *Yōkyokushū*, vol. 2, p. 216; Tyler, trans., *Japanese Nō Dramas*.

14. A reference to *Kokinshū* poem no. 165, a lighthearted verse playing with the traditional Buddhistic image of the lotus flower remaining pure in the midst of the murky pond. The poem asks the lotus flower, if you are so pure, why do you fool us by making the dew on your petals look like jewels? See Rodd, trans., *Kokinshū*; McCullough, trans., *Kokin Wakashū*.

15. Chikamatsu alludes to the nō play *Tokusa*, which is similar to *Kagetsu* in that it is the tale of the love of a father and son. Matsuwaka, the son of a Kyushu man, was stolen years before. Hoping to see his father again, the son visits his birthplace with a priest from the capital. They encounter an old man who cuts *tokusa* (scouring rush) for a living. He is "mad" with love for his lost Matsuwaka. The climax is his dancing, mad from drink (*suikyō*) and expressing love for his son, an obsessive love that has engulfed his life for all the years since the boy disappeared. The play ends happily with their reunion, and together they build a temple at their home. Chikamatsu is again hinting at the troubles to come and, in referring to Yang Guifei, *Obasute, Kinuta*, and *Tokusa*, gives a dark undercurrent to this portrait of Yoshida's paradise. A sense of irony also emerges: Yoshida himself shows little concern for his son Matsuwaka, stolen by the *tengu*, or for his murdered wife, dead not yet one hundred days. See Sanari, ed., YKT, vol. 4, p. 2207.

16. From the nō play *Taema*. Chūjōhime, a legendary figure from the Nara period (mid-eighth century), was treated cruelly by her stepmother who had her abandoned in the mountains. She took refuge in Taima (Taema) Temple and became a nun, praying that Amida would come to her while she was still alive. She achieved enlightenment and, from the strands of a lotus, wove a mandala depicting Amida's Paradise. In the legend, her father came upon her when hunting near the temple. He invited her to return home, but she chose to stay and pray to Amida. Her mandala was woven to help others achieve salvation. Chikamatsu thus continues the theme of lost children. See Sanari, ed., YKT, vol. 3, p. 1843; Kenneth Yasuda, trans., *Masterworks of the Nō Theater* (Bloomington: Indiana University Press, 1989).

17. The cuckoo's (*hototogisu*) call is thought to start with *hozon*, which means a Buddha statue or image.

18. Huiyuan (334–416) was the founder of the Chinese Pure Land Sect of Buddhism, the Pure (White) Lotus Society, in which the focus is on constant prayer to Amida. Huiyuan is also mentioned in the nō play *Tokusa*, cited earlier. Huiyuan was well known for his abstinence from wine, but he broke this when the poet Tao Yuanming (365–427), famous for his love of wine and chrysanthemums, visited him at his mountain temple.
19. This is a dance scene in which performers mime the fish and turtles. Takemoto Gidayū said that these song pieces within an act are like deep pools in the flow of the drama. The allusions here suggest a pattern, as noted in the introduction. First we are given an image of Buddha's Western Paradise as seen by a woman abandoned to die, for whom it is unattainable because she cannot shed her obsession with life; then the *Kinuta* reference moves us on to the world of erotic passion, transformed into an obsessive desire leading to hell; third is the obsessive love of a father for a lost son; and fourth is the abandoned Chūjōhime, who rejects her father and finds relief in Buddhism, which leads us to Huiyuan and the lotus image, the saving grace of Amida. This brings us back to an image of paradise and a vision of the harmony of nature, the familiar world transformed by the experience of art. Thus from being a metaphor for erotic beauty, the lotus image becomes a symbol of a pure heart untouched by the concerns of the mundane world.
20. This scene is intended to have a variety of stage tricks. *Takemoto Fudan Sakura* (1759), a work that ranks plays and makes brief comments on famous scenes, refers to the success of this "carp" scene. See *Nihon shomin bunka shiryō shūsei* (NSBSS), vol. 7 (Tokyo: San'ichi shobō, 1977), p. 474.
21. This finale (*dangiri*) section is a dancelike flourish in which the action and music are more forceful than the language. Sometimes these sections have catalogues (*mono-zukushi*) of things that are woven into the text through wordplay, which in itself is a tour de force. Here the theme is cuisine. In his *Sixteen Eighty-Seven Gidayū Collection of Jōruri Scenes*, Takemoto Gidayū states that the second act should be martial (*shura*) and vigorous, especially in its finale. Translated in C. Andrew Gerstle, *Circles of Fantasy: Convention in the Plays of Chikamatsu* (Cambridge, Mass.: Council on East Asian Studies, Harvard University Press, 1986), p. 193.

Notes to *Twins at the Sumida River*, act 3

1. The Shu mountains are in the remote Sichuan area of western China and evoke Bai Juyi's (722–846) most famous poem *Cheng Wen Ge*, "Song of Everlasting Sorrow." This is translated as "Song of Lasting Pain" in Stephen Owen, ed. and

trans., *An Anthology of Chinese Literature* (New York: Norton, 1996), pp. 442–47). The Tang emperor Xuanzong fled the An Lushan rebellion to the distant Shu Province. It is said that on the way he was forced to execute his favorite concubine Yang Guifei. The nō play *Yōkihi* has a phrase about searching the heavens and beneath the earth for Yang Guifei's spirit, and the image of longing for someone lost is a major theme of the play. These mountains are known to be almost always enveloped in fog and mist. See Sanari Kentarō, ed., *Yōkyoku taikan* (YTK), vol. 5 (Tokyo: Meiji shoin, 1927), p. 3116, also p. 3121; Donald Keene, ed., *Twenty Plays of the Nō Theater* (New York: Columbia University Press, 1970). Li Bai's (701–62) poem "Shu Dao Nan" also refers to them as always shrouded in clouds. Monkeys (gibbons) are said to cry because they can't get across them. The twin Matsuwaka is lost in the mountains, captured by *tengu* goblins. See Kamata Tadashi and Yoneyama Toratarō, eds., *Kanshi meiku jiten* (Tokyo: Taishūkan, 1980), pp. 143–44.

2. The significance of the reference to Baling (J: Haryō) is more difficult to determine. In poetry, Baling is most often associated with Lake Dongting in Hunan; however, the image presented is of a calm lake rather than a rushing river. Baling is also the name of a mountain in Hubei. If Chikamatsu meant Baxia (J: Hakyō, with the same first character "ha"), the river valley in Hubei known for its rapids, then the significance is obvious.

Five *Wakan rōeishū* poems associate this river with the sad cries of monkeys (gibbons). See nos. 454, 455, 456, 457, and 500 in Kawaguchi Hisao and Shida Nobuyoshi, eds., *Wakan rōeshū, Ryōjin hishō*, NKBT no. 73 (Tokyo: Iwanami shoten, 1965). Chikamatsu quotes no. 454 in his earlier *Komochi yamanba* (1712). Also see J. Thomas Rimer and Jonathan Chaves, eds. and trans., *Japanese and Chinese Poems to Sing: The Wakan rōeishū* (New York: Columbia University Press, 1997). A Six Dynasties collection of stories, *Shi Shuo Xin Yu*, recounts how a mother monkey runs along a riverbank following a boat carrying her captured baby. She finally catches up with the boat but dies, overwrought by emotion; this is the background to the *yuefu* poem "Nü Er Zi." See Kamata and Yoneyama, eds., *Kanshi meiku jiten*, pp. 387–88. Another possible source is the Cen Shen poem "Ba Nan Zhou Zhong." See Matsuura Tomohisa, ed., *Tōshi kaishaku jiten* (Tokyo: Taishūkan, 1987, pp. 311–12. It is a comment on the human condition that even a monkey loves her child so much that she is willing to die for it.

These first few lines thus reinforce the recurring motifs and themes of the first two acts: longing for a lost loved one, the difficulty of travel, passion leading to downfall, a mother's love for a child, and finally the deep emotion felt even by beasts for a loved one. Monkey images are dominant throughout this act: for example, "Monkey Island," Sōta, has already been mentioned (and see

n. 25); the "monkey harness" (a gag) used on children; *mashi*, a pun meaning both "more than" and "monkey" (n. 30); and the "story of monkeys drowning trying to grasp the moon's reflection" (n. 38). See also the reference to the kyōgen *Utsubozaru* (n. 20) on the love of a master for the monkey he has trained. Also echoed here are the sacred monkeys of the Hie Shrine from the beginning of the play. And of course, being lost along a river suggests the fate of the second twin, Umewaka.

3. One of Buddha's sixteen disciples, known for his rhetorical skill.
4. A reference to the proverb "God lives in the heads of the honest." Listed in the haiku guidebook *Sewa-yakigusa* (1658); see Matsuzaki Hitoshi et al., eds., *Chikamatsu jōrurishū* (CJS), vol. 2, SNKBT no. 92 (Tokyo: Iwanami shoten, 1995), p. 36, n. 14.
5. A reference to a poem from *The Book of Odes*, no. 16 (no. 138 in Arthur Waley's *The Book of Songs*). The duke of Shao was said to have sat beneath a favorite apple tree and listened to the petitions of the people. Since he was thought always to be fair and just, after his death the apple tree was well tended and never cut down. The role of the bakufu courts and fair justice for all is an important theme in several of Chikamatsu's late history plays. This is perhaps a positive comment on the Kyōhō Reforms being implemented at this time.
6. This name would more commonly be read Toshikane, but the text consistently has the *furigana* reading *kanu*. A Yoshida retainer with the name "Toshikanu" appears in earlier versions of the Sumida tale.
7. A measure of gold. One *ryō* equals four *bu* or, in silver, sixty *monme* (3.75 grams). In the Tokugawa period, it was the name of a gold coin of this weight.
8. A history of Japan compiled in A.D. 720. See W. G. Aston, trans., *Nihongi: Chronicles of Japan from Earliest Times to A.D. 697* (Tokyo: Tuttle, 1972).
9. Chikamatsu creates a realistic portrayal of Hanjo's fall into madness after losing her husband and two sons in succession and then being subjected to trial before the emperor and his highest officials. Portrayed consistently as being highly strung, she finally tips over the edge and loses her sanity.
10. A similar phrase can be found in Chikamatsu's earlier *Komachi yamamba*, act 2. One major theme of that work is the desire of a disgraced samurai to restore his honor through force of will. He kills himself and his spirit enters his wife's mouth, and she becomes a *yamamba* who gives birth to the hero figure, Kintoki. Children born of *yamamba* were supposed to leave big footprints in the snow. This quotation is taken from a scene in which two courtesans fight fiercely over a man, Genshichi, in the pleasure quarter. This incident leads to his being disinherited. His father is later murdered, and Genshichi divorces his wife Yaegiri to seek revenge but fails, his younger sister carrying out the vendetta without him. He commits suicide after this, and his spirit enters his

11. These are common references to *The Tale of Genji* and may have been part of a popular song of the time. Kashiwagi caught a glimpse of the Third Princess when the courtiers were playing football (*kemari*) at the Rokujō Palace. This section of Hanjo's madness is performed as song and dance. Images go from the capital to the sea and then to the mountains. These three, and the associated water and clouds, are predominant images in this act.
12. From the nō play *Yamamba*. *Yamamba* ("mountain crones") were known to be the wives of *tengu*; they, like the *tengu*, have complex characters, known both for eating or abducting children and for helping the unfortunate. Zeami's nō play creates a figure who is seeking release from "wrongful clinging." The quotation here is about the help the mountain crone gives to woodmen to lighten their loads. See Koyama et al., eds., *Yōkyokushū*, vol. 2, pp. 518–19; Royall Tyler, trans., *Japanese Nō Dramas* (London: Penguin Classics, 1992).
13. Commoners are used to seeing only Shinto priests wearing tall, formal hats, and so she takes the courtiers to be priests.
14. *Monbi* were festival days in the pleasure quarters when regular customers were expected to give gifts to or have kimonos made for their favorite courtesans. The courtesans therefore had to be at their very best to earn such gifts and show off their success.
15. A similar phrase is in the kyōgen play *Hanago*, a direct parody of the nō play *Hanjo*, in which the tale is brought down from the lofty heights of aristocratic pleasure seeking and aesthetics to the everyday world of domestic realism. This quotation is only in the Toraaki version. The man on a trip through Nogami in Minō becomes entranced by a courtesan, Hanago, and promises to come again, but his overbearing wife (termed "mountain god" for her ferocity) won't let him out of her sight. When he begs to go on a two-year religious pilgrimage, she laughs and calls him "mad" (*bukkyō* or *kyōkotsu*, depending on the kyōgen school). After being allowed to meditate for one night without his wife bothering him, he gets his servant Tarōkaja to take his place and sets off to see Hanago. He comes home singing and talks to what he supposes to be the hooded Tarōkaja about his wonderful time with Hanago, but the wife has interposed herself and sits hooded and brooding darkly, steaming with anger as he talks, until she springs out and chases after him. In the Toraaki version, the man describes to Tarōkaja (really his wife) how he told Hanago about his ferocious wife; the angry wife responds that if he doesn't swear by striking the bell that he will never look at another woman, she will crush him. See Ikeda Hiroshi et al., eds., *Okura, Toraaki-bon: Kyōgenshū no kenkyū* (Tokyo: Shūgensha, 1973), p. 213.

16. In a kyōgen song entitled "Hanago," there is a phrase expressing the anger of the courtesan for the men who strike the temples bells at dawn. See Kobayashi Yoshinori et al., eds., *Ryōjin hishō, Kanginshū, kyōgen kayō*, SNKBT no. 56 (Tokyo: Iwanami shoten, 1993), p. 339.
17. A reference to a passage from *Narihira Odoriuta*, no. 10, in Takano Tatsuyuki, ed., *Nihon kayō shūsei*, vol. 6 (1927; reprint, Tokyo: Tokyo shuppan, 1961), p. 61. These are early-seventeenth-century kabuki dance songs originating in the period of women's kabuki. The content is erotic banter from a woman who provocatively drops her colorful, rather gaudy sash (*date na kyasha na kyafu*), with designs of plums and pines among other things, and invites a samurai to pick it up.
18. References to plum (*ume*) and pine (*matsu*) suggest Umewaka and Matsuwaka.
19. A quotation from the nō play *Miidera*. This is another story of a crazed mother's search for her stolen child. The central image of this nō play is the bell of Miidera temple in Ōtsu, where the woman has gone in search of her son Senmitsu. She worships at Kiyomizu Temple in Kyoto and has a dream in which Kannon tells her to go to Miidera. At Miidera, in her madness she strikes the bell again and again, finally attracting the attention of Senmitsu, now a novice there. See Koyama Hiroshi et al., eds., *Yōkyokushū*, vol. 1, NKBZ no. 33 (Tokyo: Shōgakkan, 1973), p. 492; Karen Brazell, ed., *Traditional Japanese Theater* (New York: Columbia University Press, 1998).
20. A quotation from the kyōgen play *Utsubozaru*. This is a "serious" kyōgen in the sense that it borders on tragedy. A man and his performing monkey encounter a daimyo lord who wants the monkey skin for his quiver. The man thinks he is joking and laughs. The lord threatens him with his sword, but in the end the man cannot kill the little monkey he has trained and come to love. The lord is finally moved by the man's compassion and relents. The man sings and the monkey performs an auspicious dance in which the preceding quotation appears. The conclusion is an ode on the preciousness of life. Predominant images in this kyōgen are boats and rivers. The line following the quotation has the phrase *azuma-kudari* (to go east), a reference to the Sumida River. See Koyama Hiroshi et al., eds., *Kyōgenshū*, vol. 2, NKBT no. 42 (Tokyo: Iwanami shoten, 1960), p. 180; Richard McKinnon, trans., *Selected Kyōgen Plays* (Tokyo: Uniprint, 1968).
21. The children are young flowers scattered before their time; the mother lives on, a withered reed in winter.
22. The opening lines suggest the nō play *Sumida River*.
23. The wife was formerly a courtesan; the "floating (suffering) world" (*ukiyo*) is a term for the pleasure quarter.
24. A reference to the preface of the *Kokinshū*. "Bun'ya Yasuhide uses words clev-

erly, but the style does not suit him. It is as if a merchant wore courtly robes." See Laurel Rodd, with Mary Henkensius, trans., *Kokinshū: A Collection of Poems Ancient and Modern* (Princeton, N.J.: Princeton University Press, 1984); Helen McCullough, trans., *Kokin Wakashū: The First Imperial Anthology of Japanese Poetry* (Stanford, Calif.: Stanford University Press, 1985).

25. Sarushima, "Monkey Island," is a place-name in Ibaraki Prefecture; today the same characters are read "Mashima." Chikamatsu has invented this name for the slave-trader character.
26. "Sanshō" also means "pepper," and Sōta's nickname "Tōgarashi" means "red pepper."
27. In present-day Chiba Prefecture.
28. Sōta stole 10,000 *ryō* of gold in pursuit of his wife, who was then a courtesan.
29. *Haigashira* (Lord of the Flies) is the name for a kind of artificial fly-fishing lure, said to get good catches. The English "Lord of the Flies," with its biblical reference to the Lord of Evil as well as to the world of children and cruelty, would seem to fit with the meaning here.
30. The sentence contains a wordplay on *mashi*, which means both "more than" and "monkey." The implication is that Sōta is a monkey worse than a demon.
31. One *kan* is 3.5 grams.
32. Hachijō Island is abut 400 kilometers from Tokyo and was a place of exile. Located on the other side of the Kuroshio Current, it was considered extremely remote.
33. In present-day Tochigi Prefecture.
34. This section is based on the nō play *Sumida River*.
35. From a phrase in the *Gikeiki*: true breeding will always show itself. See Helen McCullough, trans., *Yoshitsune: A Fifteenth-Century Japanese Chronicle* (Tokyo: University of Tokyo Press, 1966), p. 82.
36. Edo kabuki versions of the "Sumidagawa" legend had established, before Chikamatsu's play, the pattern of a former retainer unknowingly killing his master.
37. During the Edo era, killing one's master was the worst crime possible, with the most severe form of execution as punishment. This method was used on Sanshō Dayū, the legendary medieval child slave trader.
38. A famous story, originally from the Chinese Buddhist text *Fang San Seng Zhi Lü*. Some monkeys climbed out on a branch over a well, trying to grasp the moon reflected in the water. The branch broke and all were drowned. The story is found in the Edo-period guide to quotations, *Kango Yamato koji* (1691, copy in Kyoto University, Faculty of Letters Library), which has not been reprinted in modern times.
39. Similar to a phrase in *Tsurezuregusa*, sec. 128; Donald Keene, trans., *Essays in*

Idleness (New York: Columbia University Press, 1967). There is also a reference to it in *Lovers Pond in Settsu Province*, act 3.

40. This would be a scene for elaborate stage effects (*karakuri*). Gidayū's disciple, Takemoto Harima no Shōjō (Masatayū, 1691–1744), who performed the third act, offered advice for its success: "While being careful to portray distinctly Umewaka's aristocratic bearing, Takekuni's anger, and Sōta's regrets and repentance, a performer must have the resolve and bravery in his heart somehow to become a *tengu* demon." See "Ongyoku kudensho," in Nishiyama Matsunosuke et al., eds., *Kinsei geidōron*. Nihon shisō taikei no. 61 (Tokyo: Iwanami shoten, 1972), p. 428.
41. The three torments faced by dragons and serpents are the burning of flesh and bones, a fierce wind blowing away house and clothes, and having one's children stolen and eaten by a golden-winged bird. A deity goes through these torments in order to help humankind, and so Sōta chooses suffering as a penance to help Matsuwaka.
42. One of the major themes in the plays of Chikamatsu's mature period is the power of the human spirit and will to overcome even death for a purpose.
43. The word *konpaku* [魂魄] (spirit) has two characters for spirit together in one word. *Kon* is *tamashii* which travels to the next world (yang), and *haku* (*tamashii*) stays in this world (yin).

Notes to *Twins at the Sumida River*, act 4

1. A *yakko* beard is a kind of handlebar moustache, sweeping to either side of the face like the curved blade of a sickle. The illustration (figure 22) shows him with long sideburns.
2. This refers to the legend of a badger taking the form of a large tea kettle. When it is discovered, the kettle sprouts hair. Gunsuke is a straightforward type of man, strong, honest, and loyal—no nonsense. The *yakko* character played here is a street performer, quick of wit and tongue, and appears in earlier versions of the "Sumidagawa" tale.
3. Konpira is known for its connection to *tengu* goblins because the images of the god Konpira Daigongen have long noses. It was a custom to pray to these *tengu* and to offer *ema* votive tablets with a *tengu* image.
4. Long-handled spear (*nagae no yari*), long-handled sword (*naginata*), long-handled parasol (*daigasa*), parasol for a rider (*tategasa*), daimyo's banner (*umajirushi*), portable chests (*hasami-bako*), and feathered banner (*ōtorige*).
5. The word *furu* (shake, dance, move, wave, swing, wag, wiggle) is used in its variety of meanings in the preceding and following sections.
6. These refer to traditional interpretive techniques for *The Tale of Genji*. This sec-

tion is a barrage of wordplay (*tsukushi*) on "kinds of sandals." See Matsuzaki Hitoshi et al., eds., 1995. *Chikamatsu jōrurishū* (CJS), vol. 2, SNKBT no. 92 (Tokyo: Iwanami shoten, 1995), p. 58, n. 26.

7. A reference to a spring poem from the imperial anthology *Shikashū*, poem no. 29. Nara is known for multipetaled (*yae*) cherry blossoms and also for multi-stringed (*yae*) sandals. See Kawamura Teruo, ed., *Kinyō wakashū; Shikashū*, SNKBT no. 9 (Tokyo: Iwanami shoten, 1989).

8. Kantan journeyed to the city to make his fortune but stopped along the way to eat and fell asleep on a pillow. He dreams of a life of luxury and then disaster and so decides to return to his home. This was originally a Chinese tale but became popular in Japan from medieval times.

9. A reference to a love poem from the imperial anthology *Gosenshū*, poem no. 776. The predominant metaphor is water rushing down from Mount Tsukuba to Mina River which leads to deep pools (of love). See Katagiri Yōichi, ed., *Gosenwakashū*, SNKBT, no. 6 (Tokyo: Iwanami shoten, 1990).

10. This suggests the nō play *Hagoromo*: there is no deceit among heavenly beings, only among humans. See Koyama Hiroshi et al., eds., *Yōkyokushū*, vol. 1, NKBZ no. 33 (Tokyo: Shōgakkan, 1973), p. 353; Royall Tyler, trans., *Japanese Nō Dramas* (London: Penguin Classics, 1992).

11. This element, a *tengu* assisting a Yoshida retainer's search for Matsuwaka, was established in pre-Chikamatsu versions of "Sumidagawa."

12. This scene is performed by two chanters, one for Hanjo and one for Hōkaibō, and is presented as song and dance by puppets or actors.

13. Azuma means east of the capital Kyoto and came to refer to the area of present-day Kantō, or greater Tokyo.

14. Enma stands guard at the gates of the other world to pass judgment on the lives of the dead souls.

15. An eighth-century ascetic priest who is considered to be the founder of the *yamabushi* mountain-priest tradition.

16. One of the seven gods of good fortune.

17. Chikamatsu weaves many words and phrases from the nō play *Sumida River* into the next three scenes. See Tyler, trans., *Japanese Nō Dramas*.

18. This suggests a line from the nō play *Tōsen*, the story of a Chinese man and his four sons, two in China, and two in Japan. His boat was captured in a battle, and for thirteen years, he was forced to raise cattle in Japan. He had left two sons in China, who travel to Kyushu with treasures to buy their father's release. The father is allowed to leave, but without his Japanese sons. Because he cannot choose among his children, he tries to kill himself. The Japanese official is moved by his love for his children and allows all five to depart together. The theme of father-son love again supports Chikamatsu's play. The quotation is

about the love of even birds for their children: "How each parent worries—the pheasant in the burning field, the crane in the dark of night, the swallow in the crossbeam." These images further suggest earlier works such as *Taiheiki*, a *Shikashū* poem, and *Konjaku monogatari*. See Sanari Kentarō, ed., *Yōkyoku taikan* (YTK), vol. 3 (Tokyo: Meiji shoin, 1927), p. 1819, headnote.

19. This suggests a line from the nō play *Hōkasō*, the story of two brothers who dress up as mendicant performers (*hōkasō*) in order to avenge their father's murder. The particular quotation, about flowers and willow branches being buffeted by wind and water, comes just before the pair strike down their father's murderer at the end of the play. See Yokomichi Mario and Omote Akira, eds., *Y'ōkyokushū*, vol. 2, NKBT no. 41 (Tokyo: Iwanami shoten, 1960), p. 406; Arthur Waley, trans., *The Nō Plays of Japan* (London: Allen & Unwin, 1921).

20. This passage by Hōkaibō is chanted together by the two chanters.

21. This section is based on the nō play *Kagetsu*, which is the name of a boy who was captured by *tengu*. All the mountains listed are famous for goblins and religious pilgrimage and ascetic practice. Kagetsu is known as a "mad" (*kurui*) young boy who performs wildly and speaks in parables. His father becomes a priest to search for his son and sees him performing in the capital. When Kagetsu tells his tale of being stolen by *tengu* at the age of seven, the father realizes it is his son. The passage quoted is from the end of the nō play when Kagetsu relates his sad tale of being taken to all the mountains inhabited by *tengu*. He sees his father as a priest who will lead him out of his madness on to Buddha's path. See Yokomichi and Akira, eds., *Yōkyokushū*, vol. 1, pp. 301–2.

22. The nō play *Kurumazō* also mentions Tarōbō of Mount Atago. A *tengu* takes the form of a *yamabushi* mountain priest and has an argument (dialogue) about Buddhism with the priest Kurumazō. He is, however, unable to best the priest. In the second half, he comes out as a fierce *tengu* but is still unable to oust the priest, who has mastered the Way. The *tengu* finally bows to his power and disappears. See Sanari, ed., YKT, vol. 3, p. 967.

23. A reference to the kyōgen play *Kaki yamabushi*. The play makes fun of the *yamabushi* figure who is supposed to be so powerful after his rituals deep in the mountains. He is caught stealing persimmons from an orchard, and the farmer gets the better of him. See Hashimoto Asao, ed., *Kyōgenki*, SNKBT no. 58 (Tokyo: Iwanami shoten, 1996), p. 98; a different version is translated in Carolyn Morley, *Transformation, Miracles and Mischief: The Mountain Priest Plays of Kyōgen* (Ithaca, N.Y.: Cornell University Press, 1993).

24. The following section is performed as a song and dance pantomime in which Hanjo's journey from Kyoto to the east is related. It is sung by both chanters. Chikamatsu weaves into the text place-names with double meanings, word associations, or suggestions throughout. The audience would enjoy the melody

and dance and suggestive place-names. Initially, he quotes several lines from the nō play *Kamo monogurui*, another "madwoman" play. In the play, the woman's husband travels to Azuma in the east and does not return for three years. Mad with love, she searches for him, traveling twice to Azuma, but without success. She goes to the Kamo Shrine festival, where her husband sees her but waits until after she performs her "crazed" song and dance to reveal who he is. The quotation is from the woman's song, describing her fruitless journey to Azuma in search of him. Sanari Kentarō notes that in a Genroku-period (late-seventeenth-century) version of this play, the man has been gone for ten years and the woman goes to the shrine to pray to forget him and be freed from her obsession. The man is portrayed as extremely cold and embarrassed to acknowledge his wife in front of others at the festival. They leave later separately like strangers, to meet at home. See Sanari, ed., YKT, vol. 2, pp. 755, 748.

25. This suggests lines from act 1 of Chikamatsu's own play, *Yosaku from Tamba* (*Tamba Yosaku machiyo no komurobushi*, 1707). The quotation is from the section describing the game *sugoroku* in which the players on the board travel from Kyoto to Edo. The play has an abandoned son as a major figure. In a climactic scene, his mother must deny that she is his mother and reject him, out of duty to her master. See Mori Shū et al., eds., *Chikamatsu Monzaemonshū*, vol. 1, NKBZ no. 43 (Tokyo: Shōgakkan, 1972), p. 445; translated in Donald Keene, trans., *Major Plays of Chikamatsu* (New York: Columbia University Press, 1961).

26. This echoes the opening lines of act 3.

27. This alludes to a passage in the nō play *Miidera*. Driven mad for love of a child, a parent knows no shame nor cares for the public eye. Chikamatsu here, however, uses the word *koishii*, usually used for a lover. Hanjo's madness has elements of longing for both child and husband. The nō play *Sumida River* has a line that says that feeling (*omoi*) for a spouse or child is the same path (*koiji*). See Koyama et al., eds., *Yōkyokushū*, vol. 1, p. 500; Karen Brazell, ed., *Traditional Japanese Theater* (New York: Columbia University Press, 1998), n. 19 in act 3.

28. *Kudoki* usually means a highly lyrical musical section in which the character bares his or her deepest feelings. Here Hanjo speaks of her experience.

29. This section is a clever enumeration of Chinese character radicals within a song and is not easily translated. The mad woman sees language as made up of its components, an intense, heightened consciousness in which one sees all the parts but cannot grasp the whole.

30. This suggests a line from the nō play *Yūgyō-yanagi*, which is about the spirit of an old, withered willow tree that is seeking enlightenment with the help of a priest's prayers; this is based on the idea that plants can achieve Buddhahood. See Yokomichi and Akira, eds., *Yōkyokushū*, vol. 2, p. 125; Donald Keene, ed.,

Twenty Plays of the Nō Theater (New York: Columbia University Press, 1970). This quotation is originally from a Saigyō poem in the *Shinkokinshū*, no. 262, about stopping along a stream in the shade of a willow and staying longer than intended under its cool cover. The willow is the symbol of life for Umewaka in this play: he asks that his baby hair be planted under a willow, and his grave is placed under a willow tree. See Minemura Fumito, ed., *Shinkokinwakashū*, NKBZ no. 26 (Tokyo: Shōgakkan, 1974).

31. In the next two scenes, Chikamatsu weaves in many lines from the nō play *Sumida River*, essentially writing a new jōruri version of the nō. Hanjo is the *shite*, and Karaito is the *tsure*. This is performed by two chanters. See Tyler, trans., *Japanese Nō Dramas*.

32. This is the first time in the play that Hanjo is referred to as "mother" (*hahagozen*). The two figures, Hanjo, the courtesan lover of Yoshida from the nō of the same name, and the mother of Umewaka from the nō *Sumida River* were already fused into one character in versions of the story before Chikamatsu's.

33. Too much grief for a child can block the child's salvation by not allowing him or her to be free of the attachment to parents left in this world.

34. There is a saying that it is as difficult as a blind turtle finding a log; the udumbara (J: *udonge*) supposedly blooms only once every three thousand years. See Matsuzaki et al., eds., CJS 2, p. 74, nn. 8 and 9.

35. These are lines from the nō play *Zekai*, in which the powerful *tengu* Zekai from China comes to Japan to destroy the power of Buddhism, as he has successfully done throughout China. He goes to Mount Atago, northwest of Kyoto, to discuss his plans with Tarōbō, the resident *tengu*, who says that in Japan, the gods of Buddhism and Shinto are strong. In the second half, Zekai engages the abbot of Enryakuji in battle on Mount Hiei. The power of Fudō Myōō, Sannō Gongen (deity at the site of the *torii* scene that opens the play, and protector of Mount Hiei), and the other deities pin down his wings and overwhelm him. He is allowed to fly off only after promising never again to attack Japan. This quotation is from the priest's words: to the enlightened, the devil and the Buddha are no different.

36. This final song section is a celebratory flourish with the display of fireworks on boats and along the shore, and complex wordplay built on punning, allusion, and association. Because the Japanese word for fireworks is *hanabi*, which literally means "blossoms of fire," they are associated with flowers.

37. A poem in the nō play *Ōmu Komachi*: the theme of longing for times past in an elegant court setting. Komachi is referred to as a "mad woman" (*monogurui*), a hundred-year-old woman who still clings to life. Emperor Yōzei sends her a poem with the following meaning: "'The Palace above the Clouds' remains as long ago; how one longs to live again within its 'jeweled screens.'" She replies

by "parroting" (ōmu) the poem, changing only one syllable to make it more poignant. See Sanari, ed., YKT, vol. 1, pp. 19–20; Roy Teele, Nicholas Teele, and Rebecca H. Teele, *Ono no Komachi, Poems, Stories, Noh Plays* (New York: Garland Press, 1993).

38. Captain Fukakusa was told by the beauty Komachi to come to her house for one hundred nights and that then she would meet him. He failed because on the final night he died (or in another version, his father died). His angry spirit seeks revenge in the nō plays *Kayoi Komachi* and *Sotoba Komachi*. See Keene, ed., *Twenty Plays of the Nō Theater*; Waley, trans., *The Nō Plays of Japan*.

39. This alludes to a passage in the kyōgen *Utsubozaru*. See Koyama et al., eds., *Kyōgenshū*, vol. 1, NKBT no. p. 179; Richard N. McKinnon, trans., *Selected Kyōgen Plays* (Tokyo: Uniprint, 1968). Also see. n. 20 in the preceding act 3.

40. A passage taken from the nō play *Aoi no Ue*. This is a reference to Lady Rokujō from the *Tale of Genji*, whose jealousy is thought to have destroyed several of Genji's lovers. The famous battle of carriage wheels between her and Genji's wife, Aoi no Ue, is a cause of Lady Rokujō's humiliation and anger. This quotation describes the cycle of anger and revenge. The various references at the end of this act to Komachi, Fukakusa, and Rokujō suggest an ironic undercurrent to the auspicious ending. See Koyama et al., eds., *Yōkyokushū*, vol. 2, p. 225; Waley, trans., *The Nō Plays of Japan*.

41. Matsuzaki et al., eds., CJS 2, p. 77, n. 20.

42. The references shift to the Osaka summer festival of Tenmangu Shrine, in which groups prepare boats as decorative floats and fireworks are a grand finale.

43. The name Matsuwaka suggests "young pine."

44. Chikugonojō was the honorary title of Takemoto Gidayū. He had died by the time of this play, but his name appears as representing the Takemoto theater. The Yamamoto publisher, with branches in Kyoto and Osaka, was the official publisher of Takemoto-za plays.

Notes to *Lovers Pond in Settsu Province*, introduction

1. The text used for the translation is in Matsuzaki Hitoshi et al., eds., CJS 2, SNKBT no. 92 (Tokyo: Iwanami shoten, 1995). I am greatly indebted to Professor Ōhashi Tadayoshi's pioneering work in annotating the play in detail for the first time.

2. Translated in Donald Keene, trans., *Major Plays of Chikamatsu* (New York: Columbia University Press, 1961).

3. *Go-Taiheiki*, Teikoku bunko series, vol. 65 (Tokyo: Hakubunkan, 1900).

4. Ibid., p. 802.

5. Helen McCullough, trans., *The Taiheiki: A Chronicle of Medieval Japan* (New York: Columbia University Press, 1959), pp. 107–250.
6. Ibid., p. 107.
7. Yoshida Kenkō and Mizusawa Toshitada, eds., *Shiki*, SKT no. 38 (Tokyo: Meiji shoin, 1973), pp. 132–42.
8. Kamakura Keiko, "Chikamatsu jidai jōruri: sandanmekō: *Tsu no kuni meoto ike o chūshin ni*," *Chikamatsu ronshū* 8 (June 1986): 22–31.
9. Translated in Donald Keene, trans., *Major Plays of Chikamatsu* (New York: Columbia University Press, 1961).
10. These three plays are discussed in C. Andrew Gerstle, "Hero as Murderer in Chikamatsu," *Monumenta Nipponica* 51, no. 3 (1996): 317–56.

Notes to Lovers Pond in Settsu Province, act 1

1. The full title is "Go-Taiheiki: Yonjūhachikanme: Tsu no kuni meoto-ike" ("Go-Taiheiki: Chapter Forty-eight: Lovers Pond in the Province of Settsu").
2. Commentators have not been able to find the source of the first two lines, which imply the fragility and transience of erotic beauty. The second line suggests that the charm of a beautifully painted face will not last for long. Chapter 4, section 7, of the *Taiheiki*, referred to later in this play, has a vivid description of the power of a woman's charm to bewitch a ruler. Some of the imagery is similar: "Now Hu Shih was the most beautiful woman of the realm, one with a hundred delights, though she smiled but once, for the flowers of the earth were nothing before her. When she gazed in silence, by a thousand graceful poses she would melt a man's heart, causing the moon to pale suddenly as though hidden by a cloud." Helen McCullough, trans., *The Tale of the Heike* (Stanford, Calif.: Stanford University Press, 1988), p. 121. The third and fourth lines are from the Chinese poem "Guan Ju," the first poem in *The Book of Odes*. See Arthur Waley, trans., *The Book of Songs* (New York: Garland Press, 1993), no. 87; quoted in the *Analects*. For this, see Yoshida Kenkō, ed., *Rongo*, SKT no. 1 (Tokyo: Meiji shoin, 1960), par. 60; Arthur Waley, trans., *The Analects of Confucius* (London: Allen & Unwin, 1938), book 3, no. 20, p. 99; and thereafter as an example of the importance of conjugal love for rulers and their subjects. In the same chapter, par. 48, Confucius refers to another poem, originally from *The Book of Odes* but now lost, which speaks of laughter making a woman's eyes even more beautiful. He relates this to the arrangement of a painting and to the importance of propriety and loyalty. In the opening to Chikamatsu's play, a contrast between the first two lines and the following is suggested: surface beauty entices but is transient, ephemeral, whereas carnal love in a well-ordered household leads to stability.

3. His dates are 1536–65 (shogun from 1546 to 1565). He committed suicide during a siege of his residence. Although he is thought to have been talented, he is portrayed in this play as a profligate womanizer who precipitates a crisis in the shogunate.
4. These are from *The Analects*: ordering cruel punishments to be inflicted on one's subjects without teaching them ethics; demanding results suddenly without admonishing them first; warning them that the time is up for completing a task, without giving explicit orders beforehand; being chary of rewarding properly executed duties. See Yoshida, ed., *Rongo*, par. 498; Waley, trans., *The Analects*, book 20, no. 2.
5. From *The Analects*, par. 498: (1) not wasting the wealth of the people; (2) not overworking the people and inspiring their hatred; (3) not being greedy or taking what is not his (the ruler's); (4) not being arrogant; and (5) maintaining order without recourse to violent means.
6. Chikamatsu follows the *Go-Taiheiki* in having Chōkei be the murderer of Yoshiteru. Miyoshi Nagayoshi (Chōkei, 1522–64) did lead an attack on Yoshiteru but died before him. Instead, it was Matsunaga Hisahide (1510–77) whose attack led to Yoshiteru's death.
7. Fujitaka is another name for Hosokawa Yūsai (1534–1610), the cultured daimyo so influential throughout this period.
8. His dates are 1537–97. He was supported by Oda Nobunaga and restored the Muromachi bakufu for a time after his elder brother Yoshiteru committed suicide.
9. This is taken from the *Go-Taiheiki*, ch. 41, sec. 2, pp. 792–94.
10. Ōhashi Tadayoshi notes that a two-headed turtle was presented to the shogun in 1677 which Chikamatsu may be recalling. See Matsuzaki Hitoshi et al., CJS, vol. 2, SKNBT no. 92 (Tokyo: Iwanami shoten, 1995), p. 83, n. 21.
11. The irony of this is that Yoshitsune was thought to have been innocent and slandered by his enemies. From the *Gikeiki*, ch. 4, sec. 3, which contains Yoshitsune's letter to his brother Yoritomo pleading his loyalty. See Kajiwara Masaaki, ed., *Gikeiki*, NKBZ no. 31 (Tokyo: Shōgakkan, 1971), pp. 198–201; Helen McCullough, trans., *Yoshitsune: A Fifteenth-Century Japanese Chronicle* (Tokyo: University of Tokyo Press, 1966), p. 137–38.
12. This was Kyoto's first licensed pleasure quarter, established under the rule of the shogun Yoshimitsu (1358–1408).
13. A saying describing the simple needs of someone who serves the Buddha found in *Tsurezuregusa*. See Donald Keene, trans., *Essays in Idleness* (New York: Columbia University Press, 1967), sec. 58. Later in the same section, Yoshida Kenkō says that those who do not seek the Way and try to free themselves of desires are no different from beasts (*chikurui*).

14. This is a *michiyuki*-like section, a pilgrimage to the Shimo Kamo Shrine. It would be performed as a song and dance piece by at least two chanters.
15. Poem no. 1022 in the Saigyō collection *Sankashū*. The bells are thought to ring only for those whose wish will be granted. See Kazamaki Keijirō, ed., *Sankashū, Kinyōwakashū*, NKBT no. 29 (Tokyo: Iwanami shoten, 1961).
16. The deity enshrined at the Shimo Kamo Shrine.
17. An allusion to *The Tale of Genji*, "Fuji no uraba" chapter, referring to the "Miare" festival that celebrates the birth of Wakeikazura enshrined at the Kami Kamo Shrine. Lady Murasaki visits the Kamo Shrine to see the festival. It is just at the time that Genji's daughter by Lady Akashi is preparing to move into the crown prince's palace. Murasaki, who had become the foster mother of the child, kindly suggests that Lady Akashi accompany her daughter to live in the palace. Genji recalls that it was at the Kamo Festival that the carriage battle occurred between the rivals Lady Rokujō and Lady Aoi no Ue, resulting in the public humiliation of Rokujō and her anger at Aoi no Ue. The reference introduces two themes: destructive jealousy and rivalry among the women of a powerful man and the grace and dignity of Lady Yoshiteru, the shogun's official wife. See Edward Seidensticker, trans., *The Tale of Genji* (New York: Knopf, 1977), p. 530.
18. This section is a *kusa-zukushi*, a catalogue of wildflowers woven into a poetic tapestry for the elegant journey.
19. Suggests the preface to the *Kokinshū*. See Laurel Rodd, with Mary Henkenius, trans., *Kokinshū: A Collection of Poems Ancient and Modern* (Princeton, N.J.: Princeton University Press, 1984), p. 35; Helen McCullough, trans., *Kokin Wakashū: The First Imperial Anthology of Japanese Poetry* (Stanford, Calif.: Stanford University Press, 1985), p. 3.
20. A phrase that suggests popular songs in the collections *Matsu no ha* (1703), sec. 3, "Shioya," and *Matsu no ochiba* (1710), sec. 4, "Ogurayama-odori." See Niima Shin'ichi, ed., *Chūsei kinsei kayōshū*, NKBT no. 44 (Tokyo: Iwanami shoten, 1959), p. 446; and Takano Tatsuyuki, ed., *Nihon kayō shūsei*, vol. 7 (Tokyo: Tokyo Shuppan, 1961), p. 172.
21. *Yomena* is an aster or starwort and literally means "wife-flower."
22. From here the text indicates that two chanters alternated the parts.
23. An allusion to *Kinyōshū* poem no. 432. A woman complains that her lover's affection is shallow and has grown distant. The word *tsumu* can mean both "to pluck a blossom" and "to pinch." She wants to pinch him hard. See Kazamaki, *Sankashū, Kinyōwakashū*.
24. This suggests the preface to the *Kokinshū*. See Rodd, trans., *Kokinshū*, p. 44; McCullough, trans., *Kokin Wakashū*, p. 7.
25. Ōyodo is called a *tayū*, the highest-ranking courtesan in the official pleasure quarters.

26. Buddhist temples usually have a pair of Niō guardians at the gate. Alone, Kanemori is not as effective or fearsome.
27. From the nō play *Naniwa*, a first-category auspicious play about the spirit of a plum tree (*ume*). It celebrates the capital at Naniwa under the reign of Emperor Nintoku, a time of peace under a benevolent ruler. The quotation is part of a section that paints a picture of an ideal government. References to "Tsu no kuni" and "Settsu," the setting of act 3 and included in the title of Chikamatsu's play, are numerous. *Ume* suggests the character Umegae, who utters a curse when she is killed in act 2. See Sanari Kentarō, ed., YKT, vol. 4 (Tokyo: Meiji shoin, 1927), p. 2333.
28. These lines from "The river flows. . ." are from the nō play *Tenko*, based on the Chinese story about the young man Tenko (Chin. Tiangu) who received a hand drum from heaven. An emperor of the Han dynasty ordered him to hand over the drum, but he refused and drowned himself. The drum is brought to court and played, but no sound emerges. Tenko's father is summoned to play the drum. The father thinks that the emperor wants to torture him as well by having him strike his dead son's drum. At the father's touch, the drum emits a beautiful sound, expressing the love of parent and child. The emperor is moved and has prayers said to calm Tenko's angry spirit. The story is a criticism of a ruler cruelly abusing his power out of greed, a major theme of Chikamatsu's play. The quotation is from the words of the spirit of Tenko at the end of the play. He performs *gagaku* music through the night. His spirit is relieved of its suffering during his dance, and then dawn breaks and the spirit is again at the crossroads of the Six Realms of reincarnation. See Sanari, ed., YKT, vol. 4, p. 2145; Chifumi Shimazaki, *Restless Spirits from Japanese Noh Plays of the Fourth Group* (Ithaca, N.Y.: Cornell University Press, 1995).

Notes to Lovers Pond in Settsu Province, act 2

1. An allusion to the auspicious *Shūishū* poem no. 615, which speaks of a cane made at Yoshida in Ōmi; the meaning rests on the multiple meanings of the word *tsuku* (strike, exhaust). No matter how many times the cane strikes the ground, it is never exhausted, like the reign of the sovereign. Chikamatsu here also picks up another meaning of *tsuku*, "to husk grain." See Komachiya Teruhiko, ed., *Shūiwakashū*, SNKBT no. 7 (Tokyo: Iwanami shoten, 1990).
2. It was commonly thought that the soul wandered lost for forty-nine days before being reborn in one of the Six Realms of the reincarnation cycle.
3. An allusion to *Nurehotoke* (1671), a critique on courtesans focused on the famous courtesan Yoshino in the form of a dialogue on philosophy and religion

but really a guide to the pleasure quarters. The quotation is from a poem associated with the courtesan Tonomo. The theme is her feelings of bitterness at her lonely bed on waking from a dream in which she is with her lover, only to find her bed empty. See Takano Tatsuyuki, ed., *Nihon kayō shūsei,* vol. 6 (1927; reprint, Tokyo: Tokyo Shuppan, 1961), pp. 120–21.

4. During this scene, Chikamatsu weaves in an array of popular songs and melodies from the seventeenth century.
5. From *Nagauta kokinshū* (1682), "Seigen shichinen no bōkon," a ballad (*utazaimon*) about the spirit of the priest Seigen, who returns from hell to vent his anger. Chikamatsu earlier wrote a kabuki play, *Isshin niga byakudō* (1698), on the theme of Seigen's unrequited passion for Sakurahime. See *Chikamatsu zenshū* (CZ), vol. 15 (Tokyo: Iwanami shoten, 1985); Takano, ed., *Nihon kayō shūsei,* vol. 6, p. 180.
6. This story is in the *Shiji* (*The Book of History*), book 3, "Annals of Yin." The latter part of the description of the Yin dynasty depicts the carnal desires and dissipation of particular rulers, blaming them for the downfall of the government. Emperor Zhou, the last of the dynasty, could be a model for Yoshiteru. See Yoshida Kenkō and Mizusawa Toshitada, eds., *Shiki,* vol. 1, SKT no. 38 (Tokyo: Meiji shoin, 1973), pp. 134–42. The *Taiheiki,* ch. 4, sec. 7, also refers to this tale, emphasizing how lust for women destroys a ruler's ability to be effective and leads to chaos. See Helen McCullough, trans., *The Tale of the Heike* (Stanford, Calif.: Stanford University Press, 1988), pp. 108–25.
7. She is known to have laughed when watching executions, as recorded in the *Lie Nü Zhuan,* sec. 7, a book on famous Chinese women, both good and bad, printed many times in the Edo period under the title *Koretsu joden* (copy in Kyoto University, Faculty of Letters Library). The executions described are gruesome, for example, being burned in oil and death by other forms of torture.
8. These were large gold coins used from the sixteenth century, worth eight to ten gold *ryō,* and used more as gifts than as currency.
9. These signal a fall into the Buddhist Realm of Beasts.
10. Chu warrior (232–202 B.C.), whose exploits are recorded in the *Shiji* (*The Book of History*), "Xiang Yu Benji." He was a brave and valiant warrior but committed suicide after a defeat. See Burton Watson, trans., *Records of the Grand Historian of China, Translated from the "Shih chi" of Ssu-ma Ch'ien* (New York: Columbia University Press, 1961), vol. 1, "Basic Annals of Hsiang Yü," pp. 37–74. Chikamatsu refers to his strength also in his earlier *Soga gonin kyōdai* (1699), act 3. See CZ, vol. 3; Matsuzaki Hitoshi et al., eds., *Chikamatsu jōrurishū* (CJS), vol. 2, SKNBT no. 92 (Tokyo: Iwanami shoten, 1995) p. 117, n. 6.
11. His name, "Fuji," means wisteria, which hangs on trees.

Notes to *Lovers Pond in Settsu Province*, act 3

1. This is a song and dance scene. Many place-names are woven into the text, often for their double meanings. The journey is south from Kyoto to where the Yodo River is formed by three tributary rivers and then southwest toward where Osaka is today. It was chanted by two performers.
2. The deaths of the shogun's consorts.
3. Literally "the face of the moon," a phrase that suggests the nō play *Matsukaze*. In this quotation, Matsukaze describes their lonely life along the shore of Suma. Her lines include images of geese flying across the sky and of plovers along the shore, alluding to *The Tale of Genji* and Genji's exile at Suma. See Koyama Hiroshi et al., eds., *Yōkyokushū*, vol. 1, NKBZS no. 33 (Tokyo: Shōgakkan, 1973), p. 165; Royall Tyler, trans., *Japanese Nō Dramas* (London: Penguin Classics, 1992).
4. An allusion to the *Kokinshū* poem no. 367, about a man setting off on a journey and exclaiming that the woman left behind will always remain in his heart. In the poem, clouds are an image for far-off places. The "Palace in the Clouds" is a metaphor for the imperial palace. See Laurel Rodd, with Mary Henkensius, trans., *Kokinshū: A Collection of Poems Ancient and Modern* (Princeton, N.J.: Princeton University Press, 1984); Helen McCullough, trans., *Kokin Wakashū: The First Imperial Anthology of Japanese Poetry* (Stanford, Calif.: Stanford University Press, 1985).
5. Okayama hills in the Fushimi area of Kyoto.
6. Princess Kesa was mistakenly killed by Mongaku before he became a priest; he later built a memorial for her.
7. This is the area where the Katsura, Uji, and Kizu Rivers come together to form the Yodo.
8. An allusion to the nō play *Yūgyō yanagi*. The quotation refers to the story of an old willow tree turning into the bodhisattva Kannon at the site where Kiyomizu Temple was later built. See Yokomichi Mario and Omote Akira, eds., *Yōkyokushū*, vol. 2, NKBT no. 41 (Tokyo: Iwanami shoten, 1960, p. 127; Donald Keene, ed., *Twenty Plays of the Nō Theater* (New York: Columbia University Press, 1970).
9. This is one of the three most famous Hachiman shrines, important to samurai in general and this one, in particular, to the Seiwa Genji lineage, from which the Ashikaga claimed descent. The dove (*hato*) is the messenger of the god Hachiman.
10. Several phrases suggest lines from the nō play *Ominameshi*, which refers to this region between Kyoto and present-day Osaka, focusing on the origin of Iwashimizu Hachiman Shrine and the legends of Onna-zuka and Otoko-zuka

(Woman and Man memorial mounds). A woman was betrayed by a man who lived on Mount Otoko (the site of Iwashimizu Shrine). She then drowned herself in a nearby river, her spirit becoming an *ominaeshi* flower, which seemed to express her anger at the man. The man then followed her in death after feeling the force of her anger. The play concludes with an image of the man being tortured in hell by the demons of lust. See Sanari Kentarō, ed., *Yōkyoku taikan* (YTK), vol. 5 (Tokyo: Meiji shoin, 1927), p. 3494.

11. *Minamoto* means a source of water as well as being the name of the Genji clan.
12. An allusion to the nō play *Oshio*, the story of the spirit of Narihira, portraying him as a sensitive poet and lover who delights in the beauty of flowers, which comfort us in our sorrows. The latter half of the play is a celebration of poetry and love. See Sanari, ed., YKT, vol. 5, p. 3460.
13. An allusion to the nō play *Mochizuki*, a revenge play in which a former retainer (now running an inn) helps a widow and son avenge the death of their lord. The quotation, by the widow, is from the beginning of the song, at the end of which they kill the murderer. The legendary bird has the head of a man. The quotation here hints at the later uprising against the murderers of the child's father, Yoshiteru. See Sanari, ed., YKT, vol. 5, p. 3051.
14. The text indicates that this section was performed by two chanters *shite* (Kiyotaki) and *waki* (Mikinoshin).
15. The main god of Iwashimizu Hachiman Shrine is Emperor Ōjin (Hondawake no Mikoto), who was supposedly born under a tree in Tsukushi in Kyushu. This also refers to Buddha's enlightenment under the bodhi tree.
16. A legendary figure who served five emperors (from 71 to 310), living for almost three hundred years. He is the deity in the Kami Kōra Shrine in the Iwashimizu Hachiman Shrine complex.
17. Amanogawa is the name of a river that flows into the Yodo River in modern-day Osaka Prefecture but is also the "Milky Way" in Japanese and conjures up the "Tanabata" story of the "Weaver Girl and Oxherd Boy" love story.
18. A village named Kunijima at this site was known for the bleaching of cotton in the Yodo River.
19. This is where the Yodo River becomes its widest in what is now Osaka City.
20. Present-day Fukushima Ward of Osaka City.
21. From the *Senzaishū* poem no. 1151: "No path to flee the world / Alone with my thoughts / Even deep in the mountains / I hear the deer cry." The sense is that Bunjibei has fled the world to get away from things but that he cannot escape thinking about the past. See Katano Tatsurō, ed., *Senzaiwakashū*, SNKBT no. 10 (Tokyo: Iwanami shoten, 1993).
22. This is a poem by the Song poet Dai Fugu, found in the Japanese collection of Chinese poetry *Kinshūdan*, published in the early Edo period. A 1685 edition,

Shinkan kinshūdan yōkai (Kyoto University, Faculty of Letters Library), with a detailed Japanese commentary would have been available to Chikamatsu. The first two lines just quoted describe the ideal Daoist view of the recluse who wants to live away from the city and who has no ambitions for power or fame. The two lines that follow, which are not quoted, describe the famous name that a certain Zi Ling had gained simply because he had been a childhood friend of Guang Wu, who reigned from 25 to 57 as an emperor of the Han dynasty. Emperor Guang Wu's attention brought Zi Ling fame he didn't deserve. These lines also fit Bunjibei, a recluse with a good name because he has supposedly given his life to avenging the murder of his wife's first husband, but he, like Zi Ling, doesn't warrant such a reputation.

23. From a story, originally in Chinese, found in *The Tale of the Soga Brothers*, ch. 5, "Sōfu, Kyoyū no koto" (Xuyou and Chaofu). Xuyou is offered the throne by Emperor Yao, but to show that he has no such ambitions and to cleanse himself of the corruption that he has seen and heard, he washes his ears in the river. Chaofu is passing by and, on hearing the reason for the ear washing, leads his cow farther upstream because the water is dirty. The original Chinese version implies that Chaofu is not impressed with Xuyou because he is not really a hermit but still lives close enough to be called into service. His action of moving his cow upstream is a criticism implying that Xuyou has dirtied the water. See Kamata Tadashi and Yoneyama Toratarō, eds., *Kanbun meigen jiten* (Tokyo: Taishūkan shoten, 1995), pp. 281–82). The version in *The Tale of the Soga Brothers* emphasizes Xuyou as a noble figure who serves only one lord. See Ichiko Teiji, ed., *Soga monogatari*, NKBT no. 88 (Tokyo: Iwanami shoten, 1966, pp. 220–21; Thomas Cogan, trans., *The Tale of the Soga Brothers* (Tokyo: University of Tokyo Press, 1987), p. 132.

24. A similar phrase, originally from China, is found in the *Taiheiki*, ch. 29, "The flight of the shogun and his child." See Yamashita Hiroaki, ed., *Taiheiki*, vol. 4, Shinchō Nihon koten shūsei no. 72 (Tokyo: Shinchōsha, 1985), p. 334.

25. These are metaphors originally from *The Book of Odes*, no. 17, section of songs from Zhao Nan, "Hang Lu," about a wife who refuses to return to her husband's poor house where sparrows and mice have taken over. See Ishikawa Tadahisa, ed., *Shikyō*, vol. 1, SKT no. 110 (Tokyo: Meiji shoin, 1997), p. 51; Arthur Waley, trans., *The Book of Songs* (1937; reprint, New York: Garland Press, 1993), no. 68.

26. A story from *The Tale of the Heike*, book 10, "Fujito." Sasaki Moritsuna learned about the currents in the bay so that he could lead a cavalry charge on to the other shore, but then he killed the man who told him the way so that no one else could learn of it. This is somewhat ironic in the present context because Moritsuna achieved fame by murdering an innocent man who had helped him.

The point is that one may go to great lengths to deceive an enemy. See Helen McCullough, trans., *The Tale of the Heike* (Stanford, Calif.: Stanford University Press, 1988), pp. 355–56. Chikamatsu presents this story in the first act of his *Sasaki senjin* (1686). See *Chikamatsu zenshū* (CZ), vol. 1 (Tokyo: Iwanami shoten, 1985).

27. No *fushi* (cadence) mark is in text at a point where one might expect it, both grammatically (*koso dōri nare*) and in terms of the buildup of emotion. Perhaps the chanter's intention was to prolong the emotional impact, because the cadence marker *fushi* comes a few lines farther on in the middle of a soliloquy, or it may be a typographical error.

28. A metaphor from Bai Juyi's *Cheng Wen Ge* for the pledge of love between Emperor Xuanzong and Yang Guifei. See "Song of Lasting Pain," in Stephen Owen, ed., *An Anthology of Chinese Literature* (New York: Norton, 1996), pp. 442–47.

29. Chikamatsu gives Bunjibei's words an ironic edge. First, he says that they all are "upright and loyal" (*hito rashuu oitachi chūsetsu tsukusu*), which will return to haunt them after his confession. Then he says that the farmers are "greedy, inhuman, beasts" (*yoku fukeru hitodenashi no chikushō*) which suggests to Mikinoshin his bestial crime of incest but which also hints at Bunjibei's act of murder long ago.

30. This is one of the Buddhist Six Realms through which the soul transmigrates. It is below the Human Realm.

31. Both swordsmiths are historical figures. Chikamatsu seems to make a point of giving the lineage of swords in this play.

32. Chikamatsu uses a phrase from poem no. 1163 in the *Goshūishū*, which speaks of waterfalls (*taki*), troubled feelings, and tears but says that one must not despair and die, even if spurned by a lover. In the *Goshūishū*, it is said that this poem is the god of Kibune Shrine's reply to Izumi Shikibu's despairing poem (no. 1162) about her spirit about to fly away as the fireflies she watches, after she was abandoned by a lover. See Kubota Jun, ed., *Goshūiwakashū*, SNKBT no. 8 (Tokyo: Iwanami shoten, 1994).

33. An allusion to the *Shikashū* poem no. 225, a passionate verse that uses the analogy of the bonfires lit at night to guard the palace, which burn out during the day: feelings flame up in the night only to turn to despair in the light of day. See Kawamura Teruo, ed., *Kinyō wakashū, Shika wakashū*, SNKBT no. 9 (Tokyo: Iwanami shoten, 1989).

34. An allusion to a saying in the *Chuang Tzu* at the end of section 17. Chuang Tzu says that the fish seems to be enjoying itself. His companion Hui Tzu says that since he is not a fish, he cannot know what a fish feels. In the end, Chuang Tzu says that he can understand because at that moment his heart was at one with

the fish. See Ichikawa Yasushi and Endō Tetsuo, eds., *Sōshi*, vol. 2, SKT no. 8 (Tokyo: Meiji shoin, 1967), p. 586; Burton Watson, trans., *The Complete Works of Chuang Tzu* (New York: Columbia University Press, 1968), pp. 188–89. Chikamatsu uses another Chuang Tzu "fish" reference later in the act; cf. n. 41.

35. A similar scene of watching cats at erotic play is found in act 2 of Chikamatsu's kabuki play *Ima Genji rokujūjō* (1695) (CZ, vol. 15). In that play, the woman goes mad after discovering that her lover is in fact her brother.

36. An allusion to *Shinsenzaishū* poem no. 622. The poem's image is of a cluster of fallen maple leaves, now colorless in the dead of winter, caught in a sluice in a river. See Matsuzaki Hitoshi et al., eds., *Chikamatsu jōrurishū* (CJS), vol. 2, SNKBT no. 92 (Tokyo: Iwanami shoten, 1995), p. 130, n. 4.

37. The phrase "to write on water" is described in *Kango yamato kōji* (1691) (Kyoto University, Faculty of Letters Library), vol. 5, as meaning that one does not take in the teachings heard or read.

38. *Gosenshū* poem no. 855: "Together / let us cast ourselves into Lovers Pond (Narabi no Ike) / so that all may know." The headnote to the poem says that it is from a man to a woman. He said that he will die if he cannot see her. She replied, "Then be quick and die." His poem is a further plea. See Katagiri Yōichi, ed., *Gosenwakashū*, SNKBT no. 6 (Tokyo: Iwanami shoten, 1990).

39. An allusion to the *Shinkokinshū* poem no. 1049, which refers to reeds in Naniwa Bay and laments the brevity of life. See Minemura Fumito, ed., *Shinkokinwakashū*, NKBZ no. 26 (Tokyo: Shōgakkan, 1974).

40. From the poem *Chun Ye* ("A Spring Night"), also quoted in act 4. The flower has its fragrance which suddenly bursts forth in spring; the moon hidden behind a veil of clouds. The essence will show itself at the right moment, and such moments are more precious than any amount of gold can buy. See Kamata Tadashi and Yoneyama Toratarō, eds., *Kanbun meigen jiten* (Tokyo: Taishūkan shoten, 1995), pp. 18–19, by the Song poet Su Shi (1036–1101). This is also mentioned in the nō play *Tamura*; see act 4, nn. 44 and 46.

41. A reference to the *Chuang Tzu*, sec. 26. A man goes to ask a neighbor for some food. The neighbor replies that he is soon to get a large payment and that then he can lend him 300 gold pieces. The man grows angry and says, "Yesterday a little fish called out to me from a puddle left in the tracks of a cart. The fish asked me for a little water to stay alive. I answered that I'm off now to the south to see the kings of Wu and Yue. I'll ask them to have the river diverted to meet you." The fish got angry and said, "I need a little water now to survive. A lot later on will not help after I am hung up as dried fish in a shop." See Ichikawa and Endō, eds., *Sōshi*, vol. 2, pp. 689–91; Watson, trans., *The Complete Works of Chuang Tzu*, p. 295. Chikamatsu referred to Chuang Tzu's rapport with fish earlier in this act; cf. n. 34.

42. Ōuchi (1507–51) was lord of an area that is now a part of Yamaguchi Prefecture. He was known for developing trade with Korea and Ming China and for his cultural patronage.
43. In Yamaguchi City.
44. A line from *Taiheiki*, ch. 3, sec. 2. This refers to a sneak attack at night on the Kasagi Castle where Emperor Go-Daigo had fled. The small group of men succeeded in entering the castle and causing havoc, but in the end they are criticized in the text because most of them fled ignominiously to save their own lives. See Yamashita, *Taiheiki*, vol. 3, p. 127; McCullough, trans., *Taiheiki*, p. 77.
45. A reference to *Chuang Tzu*, sec. 22, "Man's life between heaven and earth is like the passing of a white colt glimpsed through a crack in the wall." This is in a philosophical passage on the importance of quiet meditation to understand birth and death, evoking Bunjibei's more than twenty years of contemplating his own death. See Ichikawa and Endō, eds., *Sōshi*, vol. 2, p. 584; Watson, trans., *The Complete Works of Chuang Tzu*, p. 240.
46. A reference to the kyōgen *Tsurigitsune*. The fox couldn't resist the bait, even knowing the danger of the trap. See Koyama Hiroshi, ed., *Kyōgenshū*, vol. 2, NKBT no. 43 (Tokyo: Iwanami shoten, 1961, p. 457; Richard McKinnon, trans., *Selected Plays of Kyōgen* (Tokyo: Uniprint, 1968).
47. Originally a saying of So Wu (143–60 B.C.) of the Han dynasty, mentioned in *The Tale of Heike*, ch. 2. The theme is a man's dream of returning to his home and lord after he is captured by an enemy or in exile; specifically, the difficulty of getting word to a loved one, and using geese to send a note. The *Heike* story links this Chinese tale to Yasuyori who is exiled on Kikaigashima. See McCullough, trans., *The Tale of the Heike*, pp. 94–95.
48. An allusion to *Tsurezuregusa*, sec. 128. In this section, Yoshida Kenkō makes a strong, moral stand against cruelty to any living thing, especially for pleasure. "Those who don't have pity or compassion for living things are not human." See Donald Keene, trans., *Essays in Idleness* (New York: Columbia University Press, 1967).
49. Ōhashi refers to a pond called "Meoto" (or Myōto) in Osaka near the Tenma Tenjin Shrine. There was a legend that a wife ran away and drowned herself there and later the husband followed her to his death. See Matsuzaki et al., eds., CJS 2, 1995, p. 141, n. 27.
50. *Tamamo* (water weeds or seaweed) and *tama* (soul), also suggest *tama* (gem).

Notes to Lovers Pond in Settsu Province, act 4

1. A quotation from section 102 of *Ise monogatari*. Although one may retire from the world and live as a monk, one cannot help being concerned about matters

left behind. A young man, although not well versed in poetry, was sensitive in matters of the heart. A woman of high rank, whom he loved, became a nun. He grew weary of life and withdrew to a mountain village. From there he wrote the woman a poem with the meaning: "Though we turn away from this life, we are not like the sages who ride the clouds. We simply ignore the pain left behind in the world." The reference to "sages and flying in the clouds" suggests the *Chuang Tzu*. See Helen McCullough, trans., *The Tales of Ise* (Stanford, Calif.: Stanford University Press, 1968).

2. An allusion to the nō play *Tamakazura*, about the woman Tamakazura in *The Tale of Genji*, who was sent to Kyushu after her mother Yūgao died in Genji's arms. She was miserable in Kyushu. The quotation refers to the power of her connection to this world, her obsessive attachment to court life even after death. She had been embarrassed when Genji released a bunch of fireflies to show her off to a prospective suitor. She regrets the rumors of scandal that arose as a result. Genji, too, desired her. She traveled to the Hase Shrine in Yamato near Nara where Keigaku has his hermitage. At the shrine she met her former nurse and was saved from the attentions of an unattractive suitor in Kyushu. The place-name Miwa is mentioned in the text, suggesting the next reference. See Sanari Kentarō, ed., *Yōkyoku taikan* (YTK) (Tokyo: Meiji shoin, 1927), vol. 3, p. 1964; Janet Goff, *Noh Drama and "The Tale of Genji"* (Princeton, N.J.: Princeton University Press, 1991).

3. An allusion to the nō play *Yamamba (Mountain Crone)*; the quotation "Yoshiashibiki" has several echoes. First *yoshiashi* (reeds along the shore) is an associated word (*engo*) for Naniwa, the setting of the previous act. *Yoshiashi* also means "good and evil" and refers to the mountain crone's search for Buddhist salvation as she wanders the mountains as if floundering in the Six Realms. Since she eats humans, the "beast" image resonates with a central metaphor of Chikamatsu's play. *Ashibiki* is an archaic pillow word for *yama* ("mountain"), as in *yamamba* ("mountain crone"). See Koyama Hiroshi et al., eds., *Yōkyokushū*, vol. 2, NKBZ no. 34 (Tokyo: Shōgakkan, 1973), p. 517; translated in Royall Tyler, trans., *Japanese Nō Dramas* (London: Penguin Classics, 1992).

The nō play *Miwa* is also quoted with an association to Yamato, the area around Nara, the old capital. This quotation comes at the beginning of the play and relates the tale of how a deity took the form of a human, with all the associated bad traits and desires, and each night slept with a woman but then always left before dawn. One night the woman tied the end of a ball of string to the deity's robe and followed it until she found it tied to the branch of a huge cedar. (Other variations of this legend have the god living in a hole and having the shape of a serpent.) In the nō play, *ashibiki* is part of a line about the god's carnal desire for the woman. See Koyama Hiroshi et al., eds.,

Yōkyokushū, vol. 1, NKBZ no. 33 (Tokyo: Shōgakkan, 1973), p. 470; Karen Brazell, *Twelve Plays of the Noh and Kyōgen Theaters* (Ithaca, N.Y.: Cornell University Press, 1988).

In the first few lines, Chikamatsu has suggested two central themes: our inability to flee responsibility and the power of our obsessive animal desires. Further, the allusions cluster around the Nara area.

4. Kōfukuji has a strong connection to the Ashikaga shoguns. Yoshimitsu had it rebuilt in 1399, and Yoshiaki became a monk under the name Kakukei there when he fled the capital. From *Go-Taiheiki*, Teikoku bunko series, vol. 65 (Tokyo: Hakubunkan, 1900), ch. 37, pp. 711–16, "Yoshiaki's Retreat to Nara."

5. An allusion to a poem by Tao Yuan Ming (365–427), entitled *Gui Qu Lai Ci*, about building a gate and always keeping it shut, found in the collection of Chinese prose and poetry, known in Japan as the *Kobun shinbō goshū*, popular in Japan from the Muromachi period and printed during the Edo period. The poem is about retreating from the world and leaving the city for home in the country where the poet wants to tend his neglected fields. It is a plea to himself to forget the world he has left behind, but the implication is that he cannot. There is a tension between the Confucian ideal of service to society and the Daoist dream of living simply and at one with nature. See Hoshikawa Kiyotaka, ed., *Kobun shinbō goshū*, vol. 1, SKT no. 16 (Tokyo: Meiji shoin, 1963), p. 18.

6. This is one of the eight sufferings that humankind faces in this world.

7. From the *Taiheiki*, ch. 37, sec. 7, which has three stories about different ascetic priests famous for their vigorous self-control and freedom from desire. Each, however, succumbs to a passion; the first to anger; the second and third to the erotic charms of a woman. The particular quotation is about a priest at a temple in Shiga, who glimpses an aristocratic woman on an outing and loses his ability to concentrate. He finally goes to her residence and stands outside as a beggar monk. She takes pity and speaks to him. The theme is the difficulty even for ascetics of remaining aloof from the temptations of this world. See Yamashita Hiroaki, ed., *Taiheiki*, vol. 5, Shinchō Nihon koten shūsei no. 78 (Tokyo: Shinchōsha, 1988), p. 325.

8. Chikamatsu has reversed the order of the characters of Yoshiaki's historical Buddhist name.

9. The eight are crimes set out in the Ritsuryō legal code; the ten sins are Buddhist commandments.

10. The Ashikaga claim lineage to the Minamoto. Yoshi'ie's dates are 1039–1106; he was known as Hachiman Tarō from his connection to the Iwashimizu Hachiman Shrine.

11. This refers to the model for Fujitaka, Hosokawa Yūsai (1534–1610), who

received the secret teachings from Sanjōnishi Sane'eda. See Matsuzaki Hitoshi et al., eds., *Chikamatsu jōrurishū* (CJS), vol. 2, SKNBT no. 92 (Tokyo: Iwanami shoten, 1995), p. 146, n. 18.
12. Gifu Prefecture area, where the Toki and Saitō families ruled different domains at this time.
13. 1515–71. Kanagawa Prefecture area.
14. 1519–60. Shizuoka Prefecture area.
15. 1521–73. Yamanashi Prefecture area.
16. Mie Prefecture area, where the Kitabatake family ruled at this time.
17. 1534–82. Nobunaga initially supported the Ashikaga but later destroyed them.
18. 1530–78. He later took the Uesugi name. Kenshin (his name after becoming a priest) was close to the Ashikaga and received the *teru* character for his name "Terutora" from Ashikaga Yoshiteru. The territory is in the Niigata Prefecture area.
19. Fukushima Prefecture area where the Ashina family ruled.
20. Daimyo of Hitachi, now Ibaragi Prefecture.
21. Asakura domain in Fukui Prefecture. Ashikaga Yoshiaki took refuge with Asakura Yoshikage (1533–73) for a short period.
22. Shiga Prefecture.
23. All these are daimyo houses of domains in southwest Honshu.
24. Daimyo in Kyushu.
25. Keigaku has become a hermit monk but is called back to the world and must face his former life again. The idea is that someone who has been enlightened sees with a different, more perceptive eye the world he left and now returns to. The quotation is from the first line of the nō play *Umegae*, spoken by the *waki*, a traveling priest. The play is about a woman whose spirit is still angry that her husband, the musician Fuji, was killed in an argument at court; the same tale is also the focus of the nō *Fuji-tenkō*, which concentrates more on the desire for revenge. See Sanari, ed., YKT, vol. 1, p. 436.
26. An allusion to a poem *A Fang Gong Fu* by Du Mu (803–852). "A Fang Gong" was a fabulous palace with huge grounds built by the first Qin emperor in 212 B.C. The poem describes the palace's magnificence and the emperor's vast entourage of attendants, especially female, as well as the extravagance of the treasures squandered on the pleasures of those in the palace. The latter part is a tale of how such extravagance causes rancor among the populace that leads to uprisings. Finally, the Chu king Xiang Yu (232–202 B.C.) burns the palace to the ground with a single torch. The moral is that governments bring on their own destruction. See Hoshikawa, *Kobun shinbō goshū*, vol. 1, p. 40.
27. An allusion to the nō play *Aridōshi*. Ki no Tsurayuki, the famous poet and editor of the *Kokinshū*, is traveling to Sumiyoshi and Tamatsushima (Soto-ori-

hime, "Weaver-Girl Star") Shrines, both famous for deities associated with poetry. The quotation is from the beginning of the play as the day suddenly turns to night and, lost, they must search for lodgings in total darkness. The play celebrates the power of a poem to calm an angry god. A similar phrase is also in the nō play *Umegae*; see n. 25. See Koyama Hiroshi et al., eds., *Yōkyokushū*, vol. 2, NKBZ no. 34 (Tokyo: Shōgakkan, 1973), p. 85.

28. As in a nō play, the traveling priest seeks lodgings from a local person, who is in fact the spirit of the protagonist, in this case the shogun Yoshiteru. The following scene is played as a jōruri variation of a nō play.

29. This passage alludes to the nō play *Umegae*; see n. 25. See Sanari, ed., YKT, vol. 1, p. 438.

30. This a fantastical, dreamlike section, and the music would have helped convey the opulence of the palace.

31. Plum blossoms suggest Umegae, one of the women cruelly killed on Yoshiteru's orders for the pleasure of Ōyodo. Her angry spirit comes seeking revenge.

32. This was performed as a dream sequence with various kinds of chanting styles: *nō, heike, reizei*, the last an elegant singing style. The illustrated version of this act presents it as a showpiece for elaborate stage and puppet tricks (see figures 34 and 35).

33. The opening lines up to the reference to Mount Fuji are from the nō play *Kantan*, creating an image of a perfect paradise, heaven on earth, which, however, is but a passing dream. See Koyama et al., eds., eds., *Yōkyokushū*, vol. 2, pp. 127–28; Arthur Waley, trans., *The Nō Plays of Japan* (London: Allen & Unwin, 1921).

34. The Tang emperor whose consort was Yang Guifei. The Zangsheng Pavilion was their private retreat.

35. Bulao Gate of the ancient capital Loyang.

36. This suggests Yoshiteru's lust.

37. Umegae (Plum Branch) is again a reference to the consort killed for pleasure.

38. Two chanters performed this section, termed *shite* and *tsure* in the text.

39. Shiragiku (White Chrysanthemum) was another of Yoshiteru's consorts killed for the pleasure of Yoshiteru and Ōyodo.

40. Hatsuyuki (First Snow) was a Yoshiteru consort also killed. The illustrations indicate that this scene was one of stage tricks in which doors would open leading inward, and the angry spirits of the murdered consorts appeared (see figures 34 and 35).

41. *Tataki* was a popular song genre, originating with wandering beggars but later becoming a style of singing in jōruri.

42. Image of an abandoned lover associated with Hanjo, originally from a Chinese poem in the collection *Wen Xuan*, by Banjieyu (Hanjo), who laments being

discarded by the Han emperor Cheng Di; used also by Chikamatsu in *Twins at the Sumida River*, translated in this volume. See Kanaoka Shōkō, ed., *Chūgoku koji seigo jiten* (Tokyo: Sanseidō, 1991), pp. 330–31.

43. An allusion to *Okuni kabuki-uta* (also known as *Kabuki sōshi* and *Okuni kabuki ekotoba*), a collection of songs, usually seductive, from the era of "women's kabuki" in the early seventeenth century. See Takano Tatsuyuki, *Nihon kayō shūsei*, vol. 6 (1927; reprint, Tokyo: Tokyo shuppan, 1961), p. 50.
44. These are lines from the nō play *Tamura*. Sakanoue no Tamuramaro (or "Tamuramaru") (758–811) was the general in the early Heian period who conquered the Ezo in eastern Japan, bringing large parts of territory under Kyoto's control. He also founded Kiyomizu Temple, claiming that it had been both the bodhisattva Kannon and the god Jishū Gongen who had ensured his success. The nō is a celebration of Kiyomizu's cherry blossoms and the power and saving grace of the deities. The line quoted is originally from a Chinese poem by Sugawara Michizane in the *Wakan rōeishū*. This and the other phrase quoted in the following lines create an image from Chinese poetry of a perfect garden at the height of spring. In the second half, Tamura comes out and explains that it was the power of Buddha that won him his victories in the east in which he quelled evil demons and brought peace to the realm. The final lines praise the defeat of all enemies due to Kannon's power. "Umegae" is mentioned just after the quotations. See Koyama et al., eds., *Yōkyokushū*, vol. 1, p. 135.
45. A popular phrase for saké, originally from the Chinese poem *Dong Ting Chun Se* by Su Dongpo (1036–1101).
46. A line from the Chinese poem *Chun Ye* by Su Dongpo, quoted in the nō play *Tamura*. See Koyama et al., eds., *Yōkyokushū*, vol. 1, p. 134. Also see nn. 44 and 41 in act 3.
47. This section is complex and seems to be a dream within a dream. Chikamatsu exploits the convention in nō drama in which a priest's prayers draw out spirits who appear to him in a dream.
48. Umegae's (Plum) angry spirit.
49. Shiragiku's (Chrysanthemum) angry spirit.
50. Ōyodo was ransomed (*nebiki*, "uprooted") from the Kujō pleasure quarter.
51. This and following few lines are from the nō play *Hōkazō*, a revenge play in which two brothers avenge their father's murder. The quotation is followed by a reference to Kiyomizu and its famous cherry blossoms which, as they fall, become the symbol of the death of their enemy. This section is also quoted in *Twins at the Sumida River*. See Yokomichi Mario and Omote Akira, eds., *Yōkyokushū*, vol. 2, NKBT no. 41 (Tokyo: Iwanami shoten, 1960), pp. 406–7; Waley, trans., *The Nō Plays of Japan*.
52. This refers to the willow at the gate of Kyoto's Shimabara pleasure quarter.

53. Here the text has the singing of sounds without meaning. This would be presented as a dramatic dance sequence with a lively musical accompaniment.
54. The two chanters trade lines back and forth, building up the intensity of the scene.
55. An allusion to Bai Juyi's famous poem *Chang Wen Ge* ("Song of Lasting Sorrow") about the love of Emperor Xuanzong and Yang Guifei. See Stephen Owen, ed. and trans., *An Anthology of Chinese Literature* (New York: Norton, 1996), pp. 442–47.
56. Ibid.
57. The illustrations suggest that the three spirits were burned up on the stage in some trick theatrics (see figure 34).
58. An allusion to the popular song "Hanami" in *Matsu no ha* (1703), sec. 2, which describes a gaudily dressed dandy. Chikamatsu weaves into this section phrases from popular songs of his day. See Niima Shin'ichi, ed., *Chūsei kinsei kayōshū*, NKBT no. 44 (Tokyo: Iwanami shoten, 1959), p. 418.
59. A quotation from the auspicious nō play *Shōjō*. A *shōjō* is a type of ape-like creature, but is also a word for a drunk. At the foot of Mount Jin near the mouth of the Yanzi River, a good man named Kōfū (Gao Feng) has a dream in which he is told that if he makes rice wine and sells it along the river he will grow rich. He does this and is successful. A young man comes and buys his saké, drinks it, but his face never gets flushed, nor does he ever get drunk. He then disappears into the sea, carrying a keg of saké. Kōfū takes some kegs of saké, adds chrysanthemum petals, and sits on the shore waiting for the creature to come again. The quotation is the first line of *Shōjō*, when he is anticipating drinking with Kōfū again. The word *shiragiku* ("white chrysanthemum") appears in the next line. The *shōjō* leaves Kōfū with a magical keg of saké that is never empty no matter how much one drinks from it. See Koyama et al., eds., *Yōkyokushū*, vol. 2, p. 531.
60. A quotation from the nō play *Aoi no Ue*, whose theme is destructive jealousy. The lines express the rational thoughts of the obsessively jealous spirit, Lady Rokujō, in which she acknowledges that life is too short to be bitter toward others or to let sadness engulf one. But then she asks, "When did my anger grow so violent, driving me to kill Aoi no Ue?" Shiragiku comes on stage, seeking vengeance against Ōyodo. See Koyama et al., eds., *Yōkyokushū*, vol. 2, p. 226; Waley, trans., *The Nō Plays of Japan*.
61. An allusion to the nō *Kiyotsune*. The wife of Kiyotsune hears that he has taken his own life by drowning, thereby abandoning her. He comes to her in her dream. She is bitter and accuses him of leaving her alone. He then relates his battle tale to calm her anger. Kiyotsune goes to the Usa Hachiman Shrine in Kyushu to offer prayers for the Heike success, but the negative oracle that is

472 Notes

handed down upsets them all. The quotation is from the end of the nō play: the depiction of the Shura hell where those killed in battle must fight forever in cycles of revenge. In the end, Kiyotsune seems to achieve release from this Shura realm and attain Buddhahood. See Koyama et al., eds., *Yōkyokushū*, vol. 1, p. 208; Chifumi Shimazaki, trans., *The Noh*; vol. 2: *Battle Noh* (Tokyo: Hinoki shoten, 1987).

62. Snow conjures up the spirit of Hatsuyuki ("First Snow").
63. Lines from a song in *Ochibashū* (1708), vol. 4, "Yanosuke-odori." "Yanosuke, you seem cold. Let me bring you a fire stoked with coals." Takano, ed., *Nihon kayō shūsei,* vol. 6, p. 464.
64. Lines from the nō play *Take no yuki*, the story of a man who coldly divorces his wife for no particular reason and sends her away with their daughter while keeping their son Tsukiwaka with him. He remarries, and the stepmother has the son go out naked to shake the snow off the bamboo until he finally dies of exposure in a bamboo grove.. The daughter and mother come back, and the daughter expresses her hatred of her father's cruelty. The quotation is the song of despair of the mother and sister for the boy. *Take no yuki* ends happily when the spirits of the seven sages of the bamboo grove bring him back to life. See Sanari, ed., YKT, vol. 4, p. 1884.
65. From the Kegon Sutra. See Matsuzaki et al., eds., CJS 2, p. 157, n. 22.
66. From the nō play *Aoi no Ue*. The quotation is from the end when Lady Rokujō's violent spirit, which has been trying to kill Aoi no Ue, is broken by prayers and seeks release and becomes a bodhisattva. See Koyama et al., eds., *Yōkyokushū*, vol. 2, p. 233; Waley, trans., *The Nō Plays of Japan*).
67. The illustrations show that this was achieved by a stage trick (see figure 34).
68. The preceding section is similar to a passage describing the end of a dream of splendor in the nō play *Kantan*, which leads to the character Rōsei's enlightenment. See Koyama et al., eds., *Yōkyokushū*, vol. 2, pp. 131–32; Waley, trans., *The Nō Plays of Japan*; and n. 33 for this act. The illustrations imply that a rapid scene change occurred here when Keigaku awakes to reality (see figures 34 and 35).

Notes to Lovers Pond in Settsu Province, act 5

1. An adviser to various rulers (d. 317 B.C.). He worked to get six smaller kingdoms to unite against the Qin but was assassinated. Miyoshi Chōkei, the Ashikaga shogun's trusted minister, presented himself as a paragon of loyalty as a ploy to usurp the realm. The Chinese characters [忠毒], meaning "poisonous loyalty," have been suggested as a possible reading for the *hiragana* "*chūdoku.*"

Chikamatsu also used this phrase in his earlier *Nihon seiōbo* (1701), act 5. See *Chikamatsu zenshū* (CZ), vol. 3 (Tokyo: Iwanami shoten, 1985).
2. This is taken from the *Go-Taiheiki*, ch. 38, "Yoshiaki's Return to the Capital": *Go-Taiheiki*, Teikoku bunko series, vol. 65 (Tokyo: Hakubunkan, 1900), pp. 731–33).
3. Chikamatsu lists many of the famous daimyo houses of this era.
4. A quotation from nō play *Kumasaka*. Kumasaka Chōhan was a legendary thief and gang leader who was supposedly killed by the young Minamoto no Yoshitsune (Ushiwakamaru) when they attacked a rich merchant. The quotation is Kumasaka's description of Yoshitsune's wielding of his sword and defeat of his gang. See Koyama Hiroshi et al., eds., *Yōkyokushū*, vol. 2, NKBZ no. 34 (Tokyo: Shōgakkan, 1975), p. 376; Arthur Waley, trans., *The Nō Plays of Japan* (London: Allen & Unwin, 1921).
5. Chikamatsu here weaves in a catalogue of terms for sword techniques.
6. Kitani Hōgin points out in his introduction to this play that this scene would have reminded the audience of the Akō forty-seven rōnin vendetta. See Kitani Hōgin, ed., *Dai Chikamatsu zenshū*, vol. 8 (Tokyo: Dai Chikamatsu zenshū kankōkai, 1925). Ōhashi notes that the revenge against Chōkei has a "private" flavor rather than just being "public" duty to avenge the shogun's death. See Matsuzaki Hitoshi et al., eds., *Chikamatsu jōrurishū* (CJS), vol. 2, SKNBT no. 92 (Tokyo: Iwanami shoten, 1995), p. 163.

Notes to Battle at Kawa-jima, introduction

1. The text used for the translation is in Matsuzaki Hitoshi et al., eds., *Chikamatsu jōrurishū* (CJS), vol. 2, SNKBT no. 92 (Tokyo: Iwanami shoten, 1995). I am indebted to Professor Ōhashi Tadayoshi for his pioneering work in annotating the play in detail for the first time.
2. Donald Keene, trans., *Major Plays of Chikamatsu* (New York: Columbia University Press, 1961).
3. In Matsuzaki et al., eds., CJS 2, pp. 515–33.
4. As in the entry for this play in *Nihon koten bungaku daijiten*, vol. 3 (Tokyo: Iwanami shoten, 1984), p. 474. *Kōyō gunkan* has been reprinted in various modern editions, the most recent being Sakai Kenji, ed., *Kōyō gunkan taisei*, 4 vols. (Tokyo: Kyūko shoin, 1995). This is a scholarly edition with an index volume and a volume of essays on the text.
5. Printed in *Essa sōsho*, vol. 5 (Tokyo: Essa Sōsho Kankōkai, 1933), completed in about 1625; it was later published in 1711.
6. Printed in *Zoku gunsho ruijū*, vol. 21, no. 2 (Tokyo: Zoku gunsho ruijū kan-

seikai, 1923). The three-volume *Echigoshishū* (Tokyo: Kokushi kenkyūkai, 1916) contains several variations of the tales of the battles between the Uesugi and Takeda.

7. Kurokawa Shindō, ed., *Takeda sandai gunki*, 3 vols., Kokushi sōsho no. 22 (Tokyo: Kokushi kankōkai, 1916). Other military tales of Takeda Katsuyori and Kenshin appear in other volumes in this series.

8. Ōhashi Shintarō, ed., *Tsūzoku sangokushi* (TS), Teikoku bunko no. 11 (2 vols.) (Tokyo: Hakubunkan, 1893). In this edition, the relevant chapters are in vol. 1, pp. 638–72, and vol. 2, pp. 502–10. Earlier, Chikamatsu had used other episodes from this work in his *Honchō sangokushi* (1719). See *Chikamatsu zenshū* (CZ), vol. 11 (Tokyo: Iwanami shoten, 1985). Two English translations of the Chinese tale are by C. H. Brewitt-Taylor, *San Kuo, or the Romance of the Three Kingdoms* (1925; reprint, Tokyo: Tuttle, 1959); and M. Roberts, *Three Kingdoms: A Historical Novel* (Beijing: Foreign Languages Press, and Berkeley and Los Angeles, University of California Press, 1991).

9. Shuzui Kenji et al., eds., *Chikamatsu jōrurishū*, vol. 2, NKBT no. 50 (Tokyo: Iwanami shoten, 1959).

10. Donald Keene, trans., *Major Plays of Chikamatsu* (New York: Columbia University Press, 1961).

11. Kurokawa, *Takeda sandai gunki*, vol. 1, p. 390.

12. Amano Shizuo, ed., *Sonshi*, SKT no. 36 (Tokyo: Meiji shoin, 1972), p. 64; Roger Ames, trans., *Sun-tzu: The Art of Warfare: A New Translation Incorporating the Recently Discovered Yin-ch'üeh-shan Texts* (New York: Ballantine Books, 1993); Ralph D. Sawyer and Mei-chuen Sawyer, trans., *The Seven Military Classics of Ancient China* (Boulder, Colo.: Westview Press, 1993).

13. Saiki Kazuma, ed., *Mikawa monogatari, Hagakure*, Nihon shisō taikei no. 26 (Tokyo: Iwanami shoten, 1974).

14. This is discussed in C. Andrew Gerstle, "Heroic Honor: Chikamatsu and the Samurai Ideal," *Harvard Journal of Asiatic Studies* 57, no. 2 (1997): 307–81.

Notes to Battle at Kawa-jima, act 1

1. A description of He Jiao, originally in the Chinese dynastic history *Jin Shu*, ch. 45, "Hu Jiao." Chikamatsu would have had ready access to the version in the collection of Chinese writings *Meng Qiu* (J: *Mōgyū*), "Hu Jiao Zhuan Che," which was published in Japan in the seventeenth century. The description is of a strong, rough-looking figure who is presented as an ideal pillar on which a government can rest firmly. He Jiao was known to be self-disciplined and stern

as a minister. The image also suggests the shogun Yoshimune. See Hayakawa Kōzaburō, ed., *Mōgyū*, vol. 2, SKT no. 58 (Tokyo: Meiji shoin, 1973), p. 254.
2. Yamanashi Prefecture.
3. 1045–1127. The Minamoto (Genji) lineage places the Takeda in the same line as the Tokugawa.
4. 1546–82. He became head of the Takeda family after Shingen died but lost in a battle with Oda Nobunaga and committed suicide.
5. A metaphor for a ruler, from *Kong Zi Jia Yu*, "Zai E," published in Japan during Chikamatsu's time. Confucius is held back on his way to enter service at the court of a powerful king by neighboring lords, who feel threatened by the prospect of Confucius's becoming adviser to the king. Confucius remains patient in the face of adversity, but his disciples grow angry that Confucius (and, by extension, the virtuous and intelligent man) is not respected by others. Fate is not always just. The metaphor is that of an orchid deep in the forest that still casts a magnificent fragrance even if no one is nearby to appreciate it. That is, the virtuous man must persevere. See Uno Seiichi, ed., *Kōshi kego*, SKT no. 53 (Tokyo: Meiji shoin, 1996), p. 276; Robert Kramers, trans., *K'ung tzu chia yü*, the School Sayings of Confucius (Leiden: Brill, 1950).
6. Suwa Shrine was supported directly by Shingen, who presented a scroll outlining how it was to be managed. Shingen also had it restored after it had been damaged during the wars of the sixteenth century.
7. Also known as Shinano, Nagano Prefecture.
8. 1527–78.
9. Niigata Prefecture.
10. 1530–78.
11. Chikamatsu created this figure; it is not found in the sources. Kenshin did not have children and adopted his nephew as his heir.
12. d. 1573. After losing to Shingen, he sought an alliance with Kenshin. In this play, Chikamatsu portrays him as a scheming, villainous character.
13. Chikamatsu completes this first scene with a return to the tree metaphor for the ideal samurai mentioned in the opening lines, adding the image of a precious stone. The emphasis here is on intelligence and quick thinking as much as on martial vigor.
14. In the time of Emperor Tenji's reign (667–72).
15. The Takeda ancestor Yoshimitsu had his coming-of-age ceremony at this shrine, which is the guardian of Miidera temple and is known as Shinra Saburō; therefore, Miidera temple and Shinra Shrine have a special connection with the Takeda house.
16. Chikamatsu takes this from ch. 12 of Kurokawa, *Takeda sandai gunki*, vol. 1, pp. 379.

17. See ch. 10 of Kurokawa, *Takeda sandai gunki*, vol. 1, p. 307. The Nagao (Uesugi) are in the Taira (Heike) line, tracing their lineage to Emperor Kanmu.
18. This quarrel scene between Takeda and Nagao retainers is taken from ch. 10 of Kurokawa, *Takeda sandai gunki*, vol. 1, pp. 306–8.
19. These both are scenes from the eight famous sights of Ōmi.
20. From the *Shiji* (*The Book of History*), ch. 55, "Liu Hou Shi Jia," in Yoshida Kenkō and Mizusawa Toshitada, eds., *Shiki*, vol. 7, SKT no. 87 (Tokyo: Meiji shoin, 1982), p. 1041; Burton Watson, trans., *Records of the Grand Historian of China* (New York: Columbia University Press, 1961), vol. 1, pp. 134–35. This is the first reference to the theme of a strong man humbling himself three times before an older person who seems to be of no consequence. The *Shiji* records the legend that Zhang Lang received the military treatise *San Lue* from the elderly Huang Shi Gong. Zhang encounters an old man along a riverbank, and the old fellow makes Zhang pick up his shoe and help him put it back on. The old man tells Zhang to come to see him again, but he is late to arrive and is ordered to come a third time. The old man then acknowledges that Zhang is worthy of receiving his teachings and hands over the treatise.
21. A mountain in Ōmi near Lake Biwa.
22. Originally from the poem "Fa Mu" in the *Shi Jing* (*The Book of Odes*), "Xiao Ya," sec. 165. The poem is about inviting friends to a party deep in the mountains on a fine spring day. The phrase conjures up a lonely site deep in the mountains and suggests the image of a talented man who has withdrawn from the world. See Arthur Waley, trans., *The Book of Songs* (New York: Garland Press, 1993), no. 195.
23. Described in glowing terms as a skilled swordsman and practiced military strategist in Kurokawa, *Takeda sandai gunki*, vol. 1, ch. 5, pp. 166–71.
24. 181–234. He is also known as Kong Ming. He served the kingdom of Shu during the Three Kingdoms period and is famous as a military strategist. From *Meng Qiu*, "Kong Ming Wo Long," in Hayakawa, ed., *Mōgyū*, vol. 2, pp. 148–49, which describes Kong Ming as an example of the truly wise and virtuous man whose talent only a good ruler or general can appreciate. Zhu Ge Kong Ming was humbly visited three times by Liu Xuan De, king of Shu, before Kong Ming agreed to serve him.
25. From the *Shinchokusenshū*, poem no. 1310, in Matsuzaki Hitoshi et al., eds., *Chikamatsu jōrurishū* (CJS), vol. 2, SNKBT no. 92 (Tokyo: Iwanami shoten, 1995), p. 239, n. 15.
26. There is a tradition of seeing military omens in the movement of clouds.
27. Chikamatsu suggests that Kansuke is a kind of wise Daoist immortal. See the reference in *Love Suicides on the Eve of the Kōshin Festival*, act 1, in which Hanbei relaxes with a pipe (cf. n. 13).

28. Kansuke's words contain an array of suggestive sexual slang.
29. 3.75 kg.
30. A native of Chu in the Zhou dynasty. He found an unpolished precious stone and took it to two successive rulers who didn't recognize its value and had one of his legs cut off each time as punishment for his apparent deceit. Finally Wen Wang recognized its value. This is a metaphor for rulers' inability to discern the worth of a good man and for the necessity for a virtuous man to persevere in the face of adversity. Originally in *Han Fei Tzu*, ch. 13, "Hou Shi," in Takeuchi Teruo, ed., *Kanpishi*, vol. 1, SKT no. 11 (Tokyo: Meiji shoin, 1960, pp. 154–55; Burton Watson, trans., *Han Fei Tzu: Basic Writings* (New York: Columbia University Press, 1964), pp. 80–81; retold in *Meng Qiu*, "Bian He Qi Yu," in Hayakawa, ed., *Mōgyū*, vol. 2, pp. 300–1.
31. *Gikeiki*, ch. 5, "Yoshino Hōshi Chases After Hangan," in Kajiwara Masaaki, ed., *Gikeiki*, NKBZ no. 31 (Tokyo: Shōgakkan, 1971), p. 308; Helen McCullough, trans., *Yoshitsune: A Fifteenth-Century Japanese Chronicle* (Tokyo: University of Tokyo Press, 1966), pp. 190–91. The trick doesn't work for Benkei and Yoshitsune.
32. An allusion to *Tsurezuregusa*. Yoshida Kenkō is discussing the power of language in *waka* poetry and uses this line about a sleeping wild boar as an example of how a line of verse can tame even a fierce animal. See Donald Keene, trans., *Essays in Idleness* (New York: Columbia University Press, 1967), ch. 14.
33. Several images here relate to flies (*hai*), which I have translated as "maggots." The other reference is to the serving of red beans and rice gruel at the Tendai "Daishikō" ceremony on the twenty-fourth day of the eleventh month and its being eaten with twigs. *Hai* is a related word for the "Daishikō" ceremony. See Matsuzaki et al., eds., CJS 2, p. 244, n. 5.
34. 161–223. Hero of Three Kingdoms period as the king of Shu, who humbled himself three times before Kong Ming to persuade Kong Ming to serve him. See Matsuzaki et al., eds., CJS 2, p. 244, n. 6. Chikamatsu again places the tale in the context of the *Romance of the Three Kingdoms*.
35. d. 219. General of the kingdom of Shu, known for his bravery, who served Xuan De. Described in *Wakan sansai zue* (1712), ch. 62, in *Nihon shomin seikatsu shiryō shūsei*, vol. 28 (Tokyo: San'ichi shobō, 1980), p. 852.
36. A reference to an incident in *The Tale of the Soga Brothers*, book 8, in which Nitan (or Nitta) no Tadatsuna kills a huge boar, already pierced by several arrows, that is on the rampage in the midst of the shogun Yoritomo's hunting party. He rides the ferocious animal and finally kills it with his sword in front of Yoritomo, thereby gaining fame and a grant of land from Yoritomo. However, this boar was thought to be a deity of Mount Fuji, and afterward Tadatsuna was accused of treason and killed, seemingly as a result of the god's curse. Kansuke and his fam-

ily are the focus of the tragedy of the play. Kansuke was also reported to have died in the fifth battle at Kawa-nakajima. See Ichiko Teiji, ed., *Soga monogatari,* NKBT no. 88 (Tokyo: Iwanami shoten, 1966), p. 315–16; Thomas Cogan, trans., *The Tale of the Soga Brothers* (Tokyo: University of Tokyo Press, 1987), pp. 206–8.

Notes to Battle at Kawa-jima, act 2

1. From the Chinese poem *Shu Xiang* by Du Fu (710–70). See Kamata Tadashi and Yoneyama Toratarō, eds., *Kanshi meiku jiten* (Tokyo: Taishūkan, 1980), p. 612. Kong Ming was visited three times by Liu Xuan De in order to persuade him to become his military strategist. This incident is recorded in "Chu Shi Biao" in *Gu Wen Zhen Bao Hou Ji,* in Hoshikawa Kiyotaka, ed., *Kobun shinpō goshū,* vol. 1, SKT no. 16 (Tokyo: Meiji shoin, 1963), p. 348.
2. An allusion to the Japanese translation of *San Guo Zhi Yan Yi* (*Romance of the Three Kingdoms*), Ōhashi Shintarō, ed., *Tsūzoku sangokushi* (TS), Teikoku bunko no. 11 (Tokyo: Hakubunkan, 1893), vol. 1, p. 659.
3. Ibid, pp. 666–67.
4. 1294–1336. He fought on the side of Emperor Go-Daigo against the Kamakura government and was known as a clever military strategist.
5. An allusion to Ōhashi, ed., TS, p. 659.
6. I have not indicated all the variations, but these few lines in fact have four different singing styles: *haru fushi, ji, utai,* and *ji iro.* This unusual complexity for so few phrases suggests the chanter's concern with detail in introducing the image of the elderly heroine of acts 2 and 3.
7. An allusion to a phrase in Ōhashi, ed., TS, p. 667.
8. Ibid, p. 668.
9. Shinano Province, modern-day Nagano Prefecture.
10. From the military treatise *San Lue,* "Shang Lue"; see Matsuzaki Hitoshi et al., eds., *Chikamatsu jōrurishū* (CJS), vol. 2, SKNBT no. 92 (Tokyo: Iwanami shoten, 1995), p. 249, n. 19.
11. Taken from *Bi Yan Lu* (J: *Hekiganroku*), sec. 9, a religious treatise important to the Rinzai Zen sect. See Matsuzaki et al., eds., CJS 2, p. 250, n. 2.
12. *San Lue,* "Shang Lue," Matsuzaki et al., eds., CJS 2, p. 250, n. 3.
13. An allusion to Chikamatsu's play *Yuki onna gomai hago-ita* (1708), act 2, in *Chikamatsu zenshū* (CZ) (Tokyo: Iwanami shoten, 1985), vol. 5; Matsuzaki et al., eds., CJS 2, p. 250, n. 5.
14. One *kan* is 3.75kg.
15. It was commonly said in Chikamatsu's time that the bonds of parent and child

last for one life, husband and wife for two lives, and lord and retainer for three lives.
16. A popular saying originally from the Lotus Sutra, ch. 27. See Matsuzaki et al., eds., CJS 2, p. 251, n. 24.
17. A story originally from the *Shiji* (*The Book of History*), "Qi Tai Gong Shi Jia," about Tai Gong Wang Lu Shang. One legend is that he served the king of Yin but left after finding him wanting. Unable to find a lord that he respected, he went to live as a hermit in Zhou, just fishing every day. Another is that he was talented but lived as a hermit, serving no one. He was persuaded to serve the king of Zhou because of his virtue. King Wen supposedly watched him fishing for three days before inviting him to return with him in his carriage. The incident is also mentioned in Ōhashi, ed., TS, p. 672, as well as in *Wakan sansai zue* (1712), sec. 64, in *Nihon shomin seikatsu shiryō shūsei*, vol. 28 (Tokyo: San'ichi shobō, 1980), p. 849. This is another allusion to the theme of being able to perceive a man of virtue, being humble, and respecting others even if at first he seems to be just a nobody.
18. A river in Xian City.
19. Modern Yamanashi Prefecture.
20. This is a travel (*michiyuki*) scene performed as a dance.
21. The notation *shita* is used six times in the first few lines of this section, signaling a threatening style of music and voice.
22. An allusion to lines from the nō play *Futari-Shizuka*, in Koyama Hiroshi et al., eds., *Yōkyokushū*, vol. 1, NKBZ no. 33 (Tokyo: Shōgakkan, 1973), p. 322. The play is set in Yoshino where Shizuka-gozen fled with her lover Yoshitsune, who was pursued mercilessly by the forces of his half brother Yoritomo. Her spirit returns to the place and possesses a woman of the area. In the end, she herself appears, looking exactly the same, and recalls their time as fugitives on a treacherous journey. The line quoted comes at the end of the play and is an allusion to Bai Juyi's poem *Chun Ye* ("A Spring Evening"), which is in the Japanese collection *Wakan rōeishū*. See J. Thomas Rimer and Jonathan Chaves, trans., *Japanese and Chinese Poems to Sing: The* Wakan rōeishū (New York: Columbia University Press, 1997).
23. An allusion to *Ise monogatari*. The poet (Narihira) is fleeing the capital toward the east after committing an indiscretion with a certain court lady and marvels at the sight of Mount Asama, an active volcano. See Helen McCullough, trans., *Tales of Ise* (Stanford, Calif.: Stanford University Press, 1968), sec. 8.
24. An allusion to the nō play *Bashō*. *Bashō* is an evergreen "banana" plant with very large (2 m long) and easily torn leaves. Its flowers are yellowish and large, but the plant does not bear fruit. See Koyama Hiroshi et al., eds., *Yōkyokushū*, vol.

2, NKBZ no. 34 (Tokyo: Shōgakkan, 1975), p. 300; Nippon gakujutsu shinkōkai, ed., *The Noh Drama, Ten Plays from the Japanese* (Rutland, Vt.: Tuttle, 1955).

25. *Kurokami* means "jet black hair."
26. Present-day Aichi and Shizuoka Prefectures.
27. Present-day Nagano Prefecture.
28. Described in ch. 18 of *Tsurezuregusa* (*Essays in Idleness*). The author, Yoshida Kenkō, praises such famous Chinese men of simple tastes, saying that the Japanese do not appreciate such attitudes. Chikamatsu also refers to Xu You in *Lovers Pond*. He is famous as a hermit who refused offers of high office. See Donald Keene, trans., *Essays in Idleness* (New York: Columbia University Press, 1967).
29. 513–482 B.C., Confucius's most able disciple. This quotation, from the Confucian *Analects,* "Yong Ye," sec. 6, describes the pleasures of a simple meal. Confucius held up Yan Hui as an ideal, who lived with the mind of one who has attained enlightenment, finding pleasure in simple things. See Yoshida Kenkō, ed., *Rongo*, SKT no. 1 (Tokyo: Meiji shoin, 1960), p. 134; Arthur Waley, trans., *The Analects of Confucius* (London: Allen & Unwin, 1938), pp. 117–18.
30. Allusions to *Shuo Yuan*, "Jing Shen." Both passages refer to men's change of attitude toward their parents when they become romantically interested in women and eventually have a family. Mencius held up Emperor Shun as the ideal example of one who loved and served his parents throughout his life. See D. C. Lau, ed., *A Concordance to the Shou Yuan* (Hong Kong: Commercial Press, 1992), sec. 10.9, p. 77; *Mencius*, ch. 9, "Wan Zhang Zhang Ju Shang," in Uchino Yūichirō, ed., *Mōshi*, SKT no. 4 (Tokyo: Meiji shoin, 1962), p. 318; D. C. Lau, *Mencius* (London: Penguin Books, 1970), p. 138.
31. *Analects,* "Wei Zheng" sec. 2, last line; Yoshida, *Rongo*, p. 60; Waley, trans., *The Analects of Confucius*, p. 93.
32. Chikamatsu suggests that passion wins out.
33. An allusion to a line in the nō play *Tenko* at the end, when the spirit of Tenkō is relieved of his suffering just as dawn appears. The play is a strong statement against deception and abuse of power by those in positions of authority. The line is also quoted in *Lovers Pond,* act 1. See Sanari Kentarō, ed., *Yōkyoku taikan* (YTK), vol. 4 (Tokyo: Meiji shoin, 1927), p. 2145; Chifumi Shimazaki, trans., *Restless Spirits from the Japanese Noh Plays of the Fourth Group* (Ithaca, N.Y.: Cornell University Press, 1995).
34. Chikamatsu uses this example of military strategy in his *Battles of Coxinga*, act 2. See Donald Keene, trans., *Major Plays of Chikamatsu* (New York: Columbia University Press, 1961).
35. 1538–1614. Lord of the area of present-day Shizuoka Prefecture. After Takeda

Shingen broke an alliance with him, he had the shipment of salt and sea products to Takeda stopped.

36. Chikamatsu takes this "salt embargo" incident from *Takeda sandai gunki*, ch. 12, in Kurokawa Shindō, ed., *Takeda sandai gunki*, vol. 1, Kokushi sōsho no. 22 (Tokyo: Kokushi kankōkai, 1916), pp. 387–90.

Notes to Battle at Kawa-jima, act 3

1. Active in the Spring and Autumn period 770–403 B.C., described in *Xin Xu*, sec. 5, "Za Shi," par. 28, in D. C. Lau, ed., *A Concordance to the Xinxu* (Hong Kong: Commercial Press, 1992), p. 31. This is an analogy for a ruler who says that he wants good retainers but doesn't want a truly talented individual who might contradict him.
2. Chikamatsu suggests the theme that a ruler or leader must both recognize true talent and face up to the demands and criticisms of a truly honorable and principled retainer.
3. From sec. 17 of *Kōyō gunkan*, in Matsuzaki Hitoshi et al., eds., *Chikamatsu jōrurishū* (CJS), vol. 2, SNKBT no. 92 (Tokyo: Iwanami shoten, 1995), p. 262, n. 10, but other quotations in this scene show that Chikamatsu is also using *Tsūzoku sangokushi* (TS) and *Takeda sandai gunki* (esp. ch. 10) as his sources to build the details of the characters and situation, particularly the personality of Terutora as an impatient and fierce warrior, less mature in comparison to Shingen. See the introduction to this play for details about these sources.
4. A *koku* is a measure of rice, about 180 liters. It was the measure of samurai stipends and therefore rank and wealth.
5. d. 189 B.C. A Chinese military strategist under the Han dynasty, described in *Shiji*, sec. 7, "Xiang Yu Ben Ji," as a brave and resourceful man who saves his king from an assassination attempt. See Burton Watson, trans., *Records of the Grand Historian of China, Translated from the "Shih chi" of Ssu-ma Ch'ien* (New York: Columbia University Press, 1961), vol. 1, "Basic Annals of Hsiang Yū," pp. 52–54.
6. d. 168 B.C. A Chinese military strategist under the Han dynasty, described in *Shiji*, sec. 25, "Liu Hou Shi Jia," also referred to in act 1, scene 2. Watson, trans., *Records of the Grand Historian*, pp. 134–51.
7. The creation of Kansuke's filial devotion to his mother is from TS, in which the mother of Xu Shu is represented as a highly principled, samurai type of woman. The introduction of the mother and other two women adds a "private" dimension to the traditional tale of the rivalry between the two famous

generals. Furthermore, the mother, as in TS, becomes the focus of the theme of a truly honorable individual. See Ōhashi Shintarō, ed., *Tsūzoku sangokushi* (TS), Teikoku bunko no. 11, vol. 1 (Tokyo: Hakubunkan, 1893), p. 643.

8. Chikamatsu had earlier, in *Keisei hangonkō* (1708), created a major character (Ukiyo Matahei) with a stutter and used this as a crucial aspect of that drama. See Shuzui Kenji et al., eds., *Chikamatsu jōrurishū*, vol. 2, NKBT no. 50 (Tokyo: Iwanami shoten, 1959).

9. An allusion to a phrase in the nō play *Takasago*, which describes an old couple, the deities of Sumiyoshi and Takasago shrines. See Koyama Hiroshi et al., eds., *Yōkyokushū*, vol. 2, NKBZ no. 34 (Tokyo: Shōgakkan, 1975); Royall Tyler, trans., *Japanese Nō Dramas* (London: Penguin Classics, 1992).

10. A style of calligraphy originating from that of Fujiwara no Yukinari (972–1027) and popular in Chikamatsu's time.

11. All the items (and other puns immediately following) have something to do with "salt," an item that takes on significance at the end of this act.

12. Nagao Terutora served the Ashikaga shogunate as a representative in Kamakura and was given a formal rank in the shogunate government. He is dressed formally as he would have been in that role. The mother realizes who the samurai is.

13. 1294–1336. A famous warrior who fought to protect Emperor Go-Daigo's government against Ashikaga Takauji.

14. An allusion to TS (Ōhashi, ed., TS, p. 643).

15. The mythical Chinese dragon-like figure often used as a metaphor for martial prowess.

16. A flower that supposedly blooms only once in three thousand years, signaling the success of the Buddha. See Matsuzaki et al., eds., CJS 2, p. 269, n. 27.

17. A reference to *Da Xue* (*Great Learning*). This is a complex section on revealing to the world the virtue (Ch: *de*, J: *toku*) that heaven has bestowed on one and on understanding one's role and duty in life and acting on it. See Akatsuka Kiyoshi, ed., *Daigaku*, SKT no. 2 (Tokyo: Meiji shoin, 1967), p. 61; James Legge, trans., *The Chinese Classics* (Oxford: Clarendon Press, 1893), vol. 1, p. 361.

18. An allusion to *Wei Liao Zi*, "Wuyi" sec. 8; see Matsuzaki et al., eds., CJS 2, p. 270, n. 3.

19. *Lun Yu* (*Analects*), ch. 17, "Yang Huo," par. 438. This refers to the tactics suitable for teaching the less educated about the Way. See Arthur Waley, trans., *The Analects of Confucius* (London: Allen & Unwin, 1938), book 3, no. 20, pp. 209–10.

20. Two contemporary sources, *Kawanakajima gokado kassenki* (a manuscript) and

Buhen-banashi kikigaki (1680), each give one half of the name used here for Kenshin's sword. See Matsuzaki et al., eds., CJS 2, p. 270, n. 14.

21. This section is sung to sad melodies in the "*ai no yama*" style used by itinerant women singers. This song section deepens the emotion of the act and contrasts with the intensity of the anger between Terutora and the mother. Further, Okatsu's wish to sacrifice herself for the mother prepares the scene for the tragic climax.
22. The music returns to *gidayū* style.
23. The cadence marker is missing in the text.
24. Most likely a popular song of the time; the source is not known.
25. An allusion to *Shiji*, book 7, "Xiang Yu Benji," a phrase spoken by Fan Kuai, mentioned earlier in this act: "Great deeds do not wait on petty caution; great courtesy does not need little niceties." See Watson, trans., *Records of the Grand Historian*, vol. 1, p. 54.
26. Yoshitsune led a company of three thousand horsemen down the steep mountainside, which was thought to be impossible to cross. His daring tactic at Ichinotani totally surprised the Heike forces, causing their defeat and retreat. See Helen McCullough, trans., *The Tale of the Heike* (Stanford, Calif.: Stanford University Press, 1988), book 9, pp. 310–12.
27. Chikamatsu based the tragedy of this third act on the story from ch. 15 of TS, the Japanese version of the *Three Kingdoms* (ch. 8 of the Chinese original). Xu Shu (Dan Fu) is wooed into the enemy's camp by a similar subterfuge. The use of false letters as a trick appears in other battle tales as well. On learning that he has been taken in by a fake letter from her, Xu Shu's mother immediately rebukes him for his carelessness and kills herself. See Ōhashi, ed., TS, pp. 644–48.
28. There is no cadence marker here, but the next line has *ji haru*, which implies the beginning of a new musical paragraph.
29. It was popularly said that husband and wife were together for two lives. Seven lives was considered the limit of a soul's reincarnation, and therefore, he pledges that they will be together forever.
30. Her reasons contrast with the incident in TS. See n. 27.
31. A phrase from *Tsurezuregusa*, sec. 122. Yoshida Kenkō is describing the qualities that make a gentleman. One of these is the ability to make a tasty meal, since food is precious to humankind and a gift from heaven. See Donald Keene, trans., *Essays in Idleness* (New York: Columbia University Press, 1967).
32. A saying originally from Chinese, explained in *Kango yamato koji* (1691) (Kyoto University, Faculty of Letters Library), vol. 5.
33. From *Kokon chomonjū*, ch. 20, no. 678. Chikamatsu uses this reference to rein-

force the importance of Kansuke's mother in his upbringing. A child first follows his mother's ways and later his father's. See Nishio Kōichi, ed., *Kokon chomonjū*, vol. 2, Shinchō Nihon koten shūsei no. 76 (Tokyo: Shinchōsha, 1986), pp. 362–64.

34. Historical record shows that he cut his hair and took this "priest name," meaning "humility, modesty, and truth, sincerity," in the twelfth month of 1574.
35. Ōhashi notes, in Matsuzaki et al., eds., CJS 2, p. 285, n. 27, that although there are no historical records that Kenshin provided Shingen with salt, such a legend circulated early on and appears in *Takeda sandai gunki*. See Kurokawa Shindō, ed., *Takeda sandai gunki*, Kokushi sōsho no. 22 (Tokyo: Kokushi kankōkai, 1916), vol. 1, p. 390.
36. A series of associations and wordplay center on "*shio*," meaning "salt," "full (tide)," and "warm feelings."
37. A line from the *Kokinshū* poem no. 1097. The Saya Mountain divides the poet from his loved one in Kai. The poem suggests that the mother dies longing to go to Kai, Shingen's territory. See Laurel Rodd with Mary Henkenius, trans., *Kokinshū: A Collection of Poems Ancient and Modern* (Princeton, N.J.: Princeton University Press, 1984); Helen McCullough, trans., *Kokin Wakashū: The First Imperial Anthology of Japanese Poetry* (Stanford, Calif.: Stanford University Press, 1985).

Notes to Battle at Kawa-jima, act 4

1. This seems to have been taken from a popular song of the time and would have had lively shamisen accompaniment, indicated by the notation *ainote* in the text.
2. This act focuses on the relationship between Shingen and his son Katsuyori, whom he has banished because of his elopement with Kenshin's daughter Emon. The image of a deer's love for its child is an important metaphor in the act.
3. Along the borders of Kai, Shinano, and Suruga: the area between the modern prefectures of Yamanashi, Nagano, and Shizuoka.
4. Ōhashi notes the existence of a woodblock, held in Tenri Library, for a printed version of this fourth act alone, which suggests the success of this act in performance, especially for the stage props used to create the autumn mountain scene. See Matsuzaki Hitoshi et al., eds., *Chikamatsu jōrurishū* (CJS), vol. 2, SNKBT no. 92 (Tokyo: Iwanami shoten, 1995), p. 286, n. 14. Chikamatsu refers to the stage prop for Mount Tenmoku in *Love Suicides on the Eve of the Kōshin Festival*, translated in this volume.
5. Chikamatsu is alluding to ideas about the power of poetry espoused in the

opening of the preface to the *Kokinshū*. See Laurel Rodd with Mary Henkenius, trans., *Kokinshū: A Collection of Poems Ancient and Modern* (Princeton, N.J.: Princeton University Press, 1984), p. 35; Helen McCullough, trans., *Kokin Wakashū: The First Imperial Anthology of Japanese Poetry* (Stanford, Calif.: Stanford University Press, 1985), p. 3.

6. An allusion to the preface of the *Kokinshū*. See Rodd, trans., *Kokinshū*, p. 41; McCullough, trans., *Kokin Wakashū*, p. 5.

7. From the *Kokinshū* poem no. 215. Chikamatsu has altered the last two lines of this famous poem, *Okuyama ni / momiji fumiwake / naku shika no / koe kiku toki zo / aki wa kanashiki* (hearing the cry of the stag; how sad is autumn) to *kokoro wa aware to omowazu ya* (don't you feel pity in your heart, [or for its heart]). See Rodd, trans., *Kokinshū*, p. 109; McCullough, trans., *Kokin Wakashū*, p. 55. This intensifies the imagery, emphasizing the heart (*kokoro*) of the deer, and makes it more forceful, questioning whether the listener can feel compassion and pity (*aware*) for the deer. It shifts the poem away from being introspective and self-reflexive, about the sadness of autumn for all humankind, to a focus on human sensitivity to nature and animals. The next lines aim at the heart of the true warrior, who must know compassion (*nasake*), a major theme of the play.

8. An allusion to the opening of the preface of the *Kokinshū*. See Rodd, trans., *Kokinshū*, p. 35; McCullough, trans., *Kokin Wakashū*, p. 3.

9. Ōhashi notes that this may have been an invention of Chikamatsu, as no record of this affair exists. See Matsuzaki et al., eds., CJS 2, p. 288, n. 9.

10. An allusion to *Wenxuan*, ch. 37 "Cao Zijian: Qiu Zi Shi Biao." Cao Zijian is discussing the relationship between a ruler and his ministers or advisers: a ruler must place suitable men in positions of responsibility according to their abilities; men must be able to judge their own abilities and seek positions that fit their skills. In this case, Katsuyori must prove his worth to his father Shingen. See Obi Kōichi, ed., *Monzen*, vol. 5, Zenshaku kanbun taikei no. 30 (Tokyo: Shūeisha, 1975), p. 181.

11. From the Chinese tale about Xuyou and Chaofu, as told in *The Tale of the Soga Brothers*, book 5. The hermit Xu You washed his ears after hearing of the corruption at court. Chikamatsu refers to this earlier in this play as well as in *Lovers Pond in Settsu Province*, act 3. See Thomas Cogan, trans., *The Tale of the Soga Brothers* (Tokyo: University of Tokyo Press, 1987), p. 132.

12. Most of this scene is played as a dance piece. The opening is from a popular song, the source unknown.

13. This section is played by two chanters, indicated in the text by the *shite* (Emon) and the *tsure* (Katsuyori).

14. The passage has complex wordplay, alluding to *Tsurezuregusa*, sec. 62. In a skillful poem, Princess Ensei expresses her love for her father, the retired emperor

Go-Saga. See Donald Keene, trans., *Essays in Idleness* (New York: Columbia University Press, 1967).

15. Emon and Katsuyori vowed (in act 2) to remain apart until the battle between their parents is resolved.
16. Katsuragi Mountain is in the Nara area inhabited by the god Hitokoto-nushi. The god was asked by En no Gyōja to build a stone bridge, but it collapsed in the middle. Legend also holds that Hitokoto-nushi was ugly and therefore worked only at night so no one could see his face. This is an allusion to the *Gosenshū* poem no. 985, in Katagiri Yōichi, ed., *Gosenwakashū*, SNKBT no. 6 (Tokyo: Iwanami shoten, 1990); and to the *Genpei seisuiki*, sec. 28, "En no Gyōja," in Mizuhara Hajime, ed., *Shintei Genpei jōsuiki*, vol. 3 (Tokyo: Shinjinbutsu ōraisha, 1988).
17. A quotation from the nō play *Ukai*, in Yokomichi Mario and Omote Akira, eds., *Yōkyokushū*, vol. 2, NKBT no. 41 (Tokyo: Iwanami shoten, 1960), p. 176; Arthur Waley, trans., *The Nō Plays of Japan* (London: Allen & Unwin, 1921); and a reference to *The Tale of the Soga Brothers*, book 2, "Kanetaka muko ni toru koto"; Cogan, *The Tale of the Soga Brothers*, pp. 56–57. *Ukai* is set in Kai Province, which relates it to the setting of this play. The story is about the sin of killing things, even animals and fish, and the main character is the spirit of a cormorant fisherman. The context of the quotation in the original nō play is ironic in the sense that the lovers look to the moon as a focus for their vow of love, whereas the fisherman sees the moon as a hindrance to night fishing. The second half of the play is about the power of Buddhism to save sinners from the crime of killing.
18. The "burning house" is a metaphor, originally from the Lotus Sutra, frequently used as an image in literature for human passions, delusions, and obsessions.
19. These both refused to become Emperor Yao's successor, preferring to be hermits. When Chao Fu heard that Xu You had come to wash his ears in the stream to clean out such a request from Yao, he led the ox away so that it would not soil the water. See n. 11, and also n. 23 in act 3 of *Lovers Pond in Settsu Province*.
20. There are similar lines in the ballad-drama (*mai no hon*), *Taishokan*, in which the words are used as a description of the power of a woman's love. See Asahara Yoshiko, ed., *Mai no hon*, SNKBT no. 59 (Tokyo: Iwanami shoten, 1994), p. 41.
21. This would normally be a cadence line.
22. The cadence notation is missing.
23. Sarudahiko appears in the *Kojiki* and *Nihonshoki* as a local deity who leads Amaterasu's envoy Ninigi no Mikoto around the islands of Japan. In the *Nihonshoki*, he is described as a fierce god who at first resists the arrival of the heavenly gods. Amaterasu sends the alluring Ame-no-uzume to seduce him. She arrives with breasts exposed and skirt lowered to below her navel. See W. G.

Aston, trans., *Nihongi: Chronicles of Japan from Earliest Times to A.D. 697* (Tokyo: Tuttle, 1972), pp. 76–78.

24. This again alludes to the opening of the *Kokinshū* preface. Chikamatsu suggests that the power of art in general is to make us, even the fierce samurai or demons, human. His phrase here, as at the beginning of this act, is *nasake shiru*, "to know compassion, love." See Laurel Rodd, with Mary Henkensius, trans., *Kokinshū: A Collection of Poems Ancient and Modern* (Princeton, N.J.: Princeton University Press, 1984); Helen McCullough, trans., *Kokin Wakashū: The First Imperial Anthology of Japanese Poetry* (Stanford, Calif.: Stanford University Press, 1985).

Notes to Battle at Kawa-jima, act 5

1. An allusion to *Sunzi* (*Art of War*), "Mou Gong," ch. 3. The original says: "To fight one hundred battles and win one hundred times is not the mark of a good general. A truly good general defeats his enemy without fighting." This suggests Kansuke's strategy. See Roger Ames, trans., *Sun-tzu: The Art of Warfare* (New York: Ballantine Books, 1993), p. 111; Ralph D. Sawyer and Mei-chuen Sawyer, trans., *The Seven Military Classics of Ancient China* (Boulder, Colo.: Westview Press, 1993).
2. The main sources for this act are the manuscript *Kawa-nakajima gokado kassenki*, printed in *Zoku gunsho ruijū*, vol. 21, no. 2 (Tokyo: Zoku gunsho ruijū kanseikai, 1923); and *Kōyō gunkan*, ch. 32, in Sakai Kenji, ed., *Kōyō gunkan taisei*. 4 vols. (Tokyo: Kyūko shoin, 1995).
3. Yamamoto Kansuke is dressed as Shingen.
4. *Hibari* is a skylark with speckled yellow plumage; *hibarige* is a horse with a black mane and yellow-speckled coat.
5. This line revolves on wordplay: *uchiwa* (fan) contains *uchi*, which also can mean "within the house."
6. From the nō play *Takasago*, in Koyama Hiroshi et al., eds., *Yōkyokushū*, vol. 1, NKBZ no. 33 (Tokyo: Shōgakkan, 1973), p. 58; Royall Tyler, trans., *Japanese Nō Dramas* (London: Penguin Classics, 1992).

Notes to Love Suicides on the Eve of the Kōshin Festival, introduction

1. The translation is based on the annotated texts in two volumes: Torigoe Bunzō, ed., *Chikamatsu Monzaemonshū*, vol. 2, NKBZ no. 44 (Tokyo: Shōgakkan, 1975); and Matsuzaki Hitoshi et al., eds., *Chikamatsu jōrurishū* (CJS), vol. 2, SNKBT no. 92 (Tokyo: Iwanami shoten, 1995). *Shinjū yoigōshin* was annotated by Iguchi Hiroshi in the second of these.

2. Yokoyama Tadashi, ed., *Jōrurishū*, NKBZ no. 45 (Tokyo: Shōgakkan, 1971).
3. Tsuchida Mamoru, "Ochiyo to Hanbei," *Ehime Daigaku: Kokugo kokubun* 12 (1962): 3–7.
4. Quoted in Fujii Otoo, ed., *Chikamatsu sewamono zenshū*, vol. 3 (Tokyo: Fūsanbō, 1944), pp. 413–14.
5. See *Gidayū nenpyō: Kinseihen*, 6 vols. (Tokyo: Yagi shoten, 1979); *Gidayū nenpyō: Meijihen* (Osaka: Gidayū nenpyō kankōkai, 1956); *Gidayū nenpyō: Taishōhen* (Osaka: Gidayū nenpyō kankōkai, 1970).
6. See *Kabuki nenpyō*, 8 vols. (Tokyo: Iwanami shoten, 1963); *Shōchiku hyakunenshi*, vol. 3: *Engeki shiryō* (Tokyo: Shōchiku kabushiki kaisha, 1996); *Kabuki-za hyakunenshi*, 3 vols. (Tokyo: Shōchiku kabushiki kaisha, 1998).
7. Yokoyama, *Jōrurishū*, pp. 304, 330.
8. Suwa Haruo, *Chikamatsu sewa jōruri no kenkyū* (Tokyo: Kazama shoin, 1974), pp. 434–40. *Tokugawa jikki*, in the *Kokushi taikei*, vol. 45 (1933; reprint, Yoshikawa Kōbunkan, 1965), pp. 1–358, covers the reign of Yoshimune during Chikamatsu's lifetime. See also Iguchi Hiroshi, *Chikamatsu sewa-jōruriron* (Tokyo: Izumi shoin, 1986), pp. 156–75. The recent long article by Shirase Kōji, "*Shinjū yoigōshin no hōhō*" (parts 1 and 2), *Kokubungaku: Gengo to bungei* 112 (1995): 47–85, and 113 (1996): 95–114, is the most detailed study of this play to date.
9. Translated in Donald Keene, trans., *Major Plays of Chikamatsu* (New York: Columbia University Press, 1961).
10. Ibid.
11. Kubo Noritada, *Kōshin shinkō* (Tokyo: Yamakawa shuppansha, 1956), pp. 19, 83–86, 213–15.

Notes to *Love Suicides on the Eve of the Kōshin Festival*, act 1

1. An old name for Osaka.
2. Ki no Kaion's play, *Shinjū futatsu hara-obi,* based on the same incident, opened before Chikamatsu's version. It also has the first act set in Hamamatsu (Shizuoka Prefecture) in order to establish Hanbei's background as a samurai (see the introduction to this play). This fief was Tokugawa territory.
3. It is clear from various references in this act that Chikamatsu is referring to the shogun Yoshimune's reforms gradually introduced after he became shogun in 1716, and to the martial image of Yoshimune himself. Suwa Haruo documented the political references in this act in his *Chikamatsu sewa jōruri no kenkyū* (Tokyo: Kazama shoin, 1974), pp. 434–40. He shows that each of Chikamatsu's references are to specific Yoshimune actions or policies. The *Tokugawa jikki,* seventh and eighth months of 1716, records that Yoshimune reinstated falconry

as a sport soon after his accession in 1716, after it had been outlawed by Tsunayoshi in 1693. Yoshimune was known to be an enthusiast of all forms of hunting. Since Tsunayoshi was notorious for his laws against killing any animals, Yoshimune's passion for hunting and modesty in all things at the other extreme drew just as much criticism. The *Tokugawa jikki* has numerous references to regulations on falconry as well as to Yoshimune's expeditions. See *Kokushi taikei*, vol. 45 (1933; reprint, Tokyo: Yoshikawa kōbunkan, 1965).

4. A reference to the nō play *Hōkazō*. Two brothers seek to avenge their father's murder. They sing a song in the guise of itinerant performers to lull the victim and catch him off guard. The quotation comes from the end part of their song, just before they attack. In Chikamatsu's play, everyone is lost in a whirlwind of activity in anticipation of the daimyo's return, the reference presaging the disaster to follow. See Yokomichi Mario and Omote Akira, eds., *Yōkyokushū*, vol. 2, NKBT no. 41 (Tokyo: Iwanami shoten, 1960), p. 407; Arthur Waley, trans., *The Nō Plays of Japan* (London: Allen & Unwin, 1921).

5. He is the personal assistant to the master.

6. The description suggests the shogun, Yoshimune.

7. *Tokugawa jikki* notes that from 1717, as an example to others, Yoshimune was known to go on falconry expeditions wearing such modest garments. See Matsuzaki Hitoshi et al., eds., *Chikamatsu jōrurishū* (CJS), vol. 2, SNKBT no. 92 (Tokyo: Iwanami shoten, 1995), p. 309, n. 32.

8. *Tokugawa jikki* notes that even those in the highest positions should have only such a simple meal. *Tokugawa jikki*, sixth month, 1716, in *Kokushi taikei*, vol. 45, p. 14.

9. A Korean embassy came to Japan in 1719 to greet the new shogun Yoshimune. There is a record showing that they were entertained extravagantly at the Osaka headquarters of the Nishi-Honganji sect. See *Kaiyūroku*, fourth day of ninth month; cf. Matsuzaki et al., eds., CJS 2, p. 311, n. 14. Fujiwara Yamakage (824–88) was the founder of the Shijō school of cuisine.

10. *Tokugawa jikki* records an incident when Yoshimune scolded two lords, Abe Bungo no Kami and Hōjō Tajima no Kami, for their extravagant clothes. See Suwa, *Chikamatsu*, p. 438. The edicts that Yoshimune issued on the eleventh of the third month of 1717 call for frugality in all parts of samurai life, including clothes. See *Tokugawa jikki*, in *Kokushi taikei*, vol. 45, p. 62. In the fifth month of the following year, a general edict was issued against extravagance for all Japanese. See ibid., p. 117.

11. *The Tale of the Heike*, book 7, "The Death of Sanemori"; Helen McCullough, trans., *The Tale of the Heike* (Stanford, Calif.: Stanford University Press, 1988), pp. 233–35. Sanemori served Minamoto no Yoshitomo until his defeat in the Hōgen no Ran battle in 1158 but afterward served Taira no Koremori. He is

famous for dyeing his white hair black and wearing fine brightly colored brocade into battle as if he were a young warrior.

12. From the *Azuma kagami*. Like Sanemori, Genzō fought for Yoshitomo in the 1156 Hōgen insurrection but did not abandon the Genji. He lived as a hermit and later helped Yoritomo lead the attack on the Genji. See Matsuzaki et al., eds., CJS 2, p. 312, n. 2.

13. From a proverb meaning that something will change into something unexpected, found in *Sewa yakigusa*, vol. 1; see Matsuzaki et al., eds., CJS 2, p. 313, no. 25.

14. A Chinese sage of the Sui period (581–618) whose real name was Li Hongshui. He was known to be able to blow his metal stick into the air and ride on it and to be able to fashion things with his breath.

15. A measure of weight, 3.5 gm, in this case, of silver. One thousand *monme* equals one *kan*.

16. A measure of weight, 3.5 kg, in this case, of silver.

17. A quotation from the nō play *Funa-Benkei*, which describes the ferocious attack of the avenging ghost of Tomomori on Yoshitsune and his men. Like Yoshitsune and Benkei, Hanbei is unperturbed by the passion of their demands. See Koyama Hiroshi et al., eds., *Yōkyokushū*, vol. 2, NKBZ no. 34 (Tokyo: Shōgakkan, 1975), p. 447; Royall Tyler, trans., *Japanese Nō Dramas* (London: Penguin Classics, 1992).

18. In his late plays, Chikamatsu frequently uses the word *keiyaku* for "vow" or "promise." In most cases, it is denotes a solemn vow that must be upheld even in the face of death.

19. An allusion to a phrase in the kyōgen play *Kaki-yamabushi* describing the action of cowering monkeys: a *yamabushi* ascetic has come down from a mountain retreat after his training and gets caught stealing persimmons. He tries to imitate being a monkey so that the owner will not see that he is a man. The kyōgen makes fun of the image of the brash and strong *yamabushi* ascetic. See Matsuzaki et al., eds., CJS 2, p. 318, n. 11; a different version is translated in Carolyn Morley, *Transformation, Miracles and Mischief: The Mountain Priest Plays of Kyōgen* (Ithaca, N.Y.: Cornell University Press, 1993).

20. From a proverb meaning to have good intentions repaid with spite: "to bring saké and get a kick in the backside."

Notes to Love Suicides on the Eve of the Kōshin Festival, act 2

1. In Seikachō, Sōrakugun, Kyoto Prefecture, midway between the cities of Kyoto and Nara.

2. In *Sanka chōchūka*, the song is a complaint against a lover who has lost interest.

See Takano Tatuysuki, ed., *Nihon kayō shūsei*, vol. 7 (1927; reprint, Tokyo: Tōkyōdō shuppan, 1960), p, 353.

3. Literally "Tamamizu," the name of a village near the setting of the scene.
4. Lines from an Owari boatmen's song "Ochiyo-bushi." Ochiyo is, of course, the heroine's name as well. The song suggests that the lover, once passionate, has lost interest and that the woman is waiting for him to come again. Ochiyo has returned home again and again after being divorced, causing rumors in the village. See Matsuzaki Hitoshi et al., eds., *Chikamatsu jōrurishū* (CJS), vol. 2, SNKBT no. 92 (Tokyo: Iwanami shoten, 1995), p. 322, n. 30.
5. The Kyōhō Reforms encouraged such land reclamation in the Kansai area and around the country, offering incentives and tax relief for a period of time. See *Tokugawa jikki*, in *Kokushi taikei*, vol. 45 (1933; reprint, Tokyo: Yoshikawa Kōbunkan, 1965), p. 240. In 1722, a notice was sent around the country setting out the procedures for reclamation applications for each region. See *Tokugawa kinreikō, goshū*, vol. 1 (Tokyo: Sōbunsha, 1959), p. 116.
6. When a woman married, she became a member of her husband's household and officially was no longer part of her parents' family.
7. Both areas are in Osaka City.
8. From a popular saying at the time. A parent's love for his or her children is a central theme of Chikamatsu's mature period.
9. An allusion to a phrase in the nō play *Kosode Soga*. The Soga brothers Jūrō and Gorō go to visit their mother to ask her to forgive Gorō, whom she has disowned. Jūrō tells Gorō that their mother is in the best of moods after he told her that he was off to avenge their father's murder and that she is likely to forgive him. The play ends auspiciously with the mother forgiving Gorō and seeing the two off on their vendetta. See Koyama Hiroshi et al., eds., *Yōkyokushū*, vol. 2, NKBZ no. 34 (Tokyo: Shōgakkan, 1975), p. 293.
10. A book on arithmetic by Yoshida Mitsuyoshi (1598–1672) published in 1627. The others are famous classical works, all available in English translations. Chikamatsu includes his own play, *Love Suicides at Amijima* (1721), translated in Donald Keene, trans., *Major Plays of Chikamatsu* (New York: Columbia University Press, 1961), among the older classics.
11. A fire at the gate (*kadobi*) was used more often at funerals to see off spirits but was also used for wedding farewells.

Notes to Love Suicides on the Eve of the Kōshin Festival, act 3

1. Ryōkai (d. 1719) was a popular Pure Land priest whose activities in Osaka are recorded in the diary *Ōmu ryōchūki*, in *Nagoya sōsho zokuhen*, vol. 12 (Nagoya: Nagoya-shi kyōiku iinkai, 1967), pp. 171–73.

2. This was a festival on the "kanoe-zaru" day of the month (one day in the sixty-day cycle according to the Chinese lunar calendar) with offerings to the deity Shōmen Kongō, one of the Buddhist guardian gods, depicted as a bluish-green statue standing with one foot suppressing a demon. It was common to have an all-night party the evening before. This seems to have originated in a Daoist belief that if you slept on this night, little creatures that live in our bodies would escape to heaven and report all your evil deeds. Because children conceived on this night were thought likely to be sickly or to become criminals, it was said that couples should not have sex on this night. The festival referred to here was on the sixth of the fourth month, 1722.
3. On this day (calculated according to the Chinese lunar calendar), it was common practice to make an offering of daikon radishes to the deity Daikokuten.
4. New Year's Eve is the final day of reckoning for all accounts and bills, and it is traditionally the busiest day of the year. The home is also supposed to have a top-to-bottom cleaning in preparation for the first week of New Year, and a week's quantity of food for visitors also should be prepared by the end of the day.
5. Murder, theft, lust, lying, drunkenness.
6. Chikugo is the honorary title of Takemoto Gidayū, who had died by the time of Chikamatsu's play *Battles of Kawa-nakajima*, performed in the previous year, 1721.
7. The parents-in-law had the right to divorce a daughter-in-law if the husband had died or had been disowned.
8. Minamoto no Yoshitsune (1159–89) was the famous general who defeated the Heike at the end of the twelfth century. His elder half brother Yoritomo, however, had him hunted down and killed. Therefore, he is a symbol of the underdog or wronged individual.
9. Cadence seems to be missing from the text, or it could be that the chanter wants to extend the tension of the performance.
10. Cadence would seem to be natural here, but there is none in the text.
11. The common proverb—meaning that it is better not to know something and remain in the dark, as if one is a buddha free of any anxieties—has been given an ironic twist here.
12. An allusion to the nō play *Yūgyō yanagi*: the spirit of the ancient willow tree has danced and sheds "jeweled tears" at the final parting. See Yokomichi Mario and Omote Akira, eds., *Yōkyokushū*, vol. 2, NKBT no. 41 (Tokyo: Iwanami shoten, 1960), p. 128; Donald Keene, ed., *Twenty Plays of the Nō Theater* (New York: Columbia University Press, 1970).
13. Kōshin can be pronounced "*kanoe-saru*." "*Saru*" is the monkey sign, but the word also means "to depart" and "to divorce" and is used four times in the next few lines as the pair set off.

14. Although this has echoes of Christianity, the metaphor is an image of being led to death in Buddhism as well. *Kango yamato koji*, book 5 (1691) (Kyoto University, Faculty of Letters Library), a guide to phrases from Chinese and Japanese classics, lists this as a metaphor for *mujō* (transience) and approaching death, originally from the Makamaya Sutra (Ch: Mohemoye) and found in the *Senzaishū* poem no. 1201 and the *Shinkokinshū* poem no. 1933. See Katano Tatsurō, ed., *Senzaiwakashū*, SNKBT no. 10 (Tokyo: Iwanami shoten, 1993); Minemura Fumito, ed., *Shinkokinwakashū*, NKBZ no. 26 (Tokyo: Shōgakkan, 1974).
15. This is performed as a song and dance scene. I have not included the notation that signals different kinds of melodies.
16. The *hototogisu* (translated as cuckoo or nightingale) is known to lay its eggs in other birds' nests, particularly those of bush warblers (*uguisu*). *Wakan sansai zue* (1712), sec. 43, gives a description, in *Nihon shomin seikatsu shiryō shūsei*, vol. 28 (Tokyo: San'ichi shobō, 1980), pp. 592–93.
17. An allusion to the *Kokinshū* poem no. 1013. The *hototogisu* is known as the steward of the fields of the netherworld. See Laurel Rodd, with Mary Henkenius, trans., *Kokinshū: A Collection of Poems Ancient and Modern* (Princeton, N.J.: Princeton University Press, 1984); Helen McCullough, trans., *Kokin Wakashū: The First Imperial Anthology of Japanese Poetry* (Stanford, Calif.: Stanford University Press, 1985).
18. The *hototogisu* is the predominant image for the lovers, now with no home. It was thought that those who tried to imitate its cry would spit blood. *Wakan sansai zue* (1712), sec. 43, has a description of this, in *Nihon shomin seikatsu shiryō shūsei*, vol. 28, p. 592.
19. The following section contains an extensive range of wordplay on vegetables and plants.
20. An allusion to a popular phrase originally in the Confucian *Analects*, pars 234 and 363, in Yoshida Kenkō, ed., *Rongo*, SKT no. 1 (Tokyo: Meiji shoin, 1960), pp. 214, 324; Arthur Waley, trans., *The Analects of Confucius* (London: Allen & Unwin, 1938), pp. 144, 188). Two of a trio of which the third is *jin*, virtue: the virtuous man does not worry.
21. This seems to have been a popular song of the time. Ki no Kaion has a similar song in the *michiyuki* to *Shinjū futatsu hara-obi*, his slightly earlier play based on this incident. See Yokoyama Tadashi, ed., *Jōrurishū*, NKBZ no. 45 (Tokyo: Shōgakkan , 1971), p. 334.
22. An allusion to the *Kokinshū* poem no. 628. Lovers regret that rumors will circulate about them. See Rodd, trans., *Kokinshū;* McCullough, trans., *Kokin Wakashū*.
23. In the south Osaka area of Tennōji.
24. From the *Keitoku dentōroku* (Ch: *Jing De Chuan Deng Lu*) (1004), book 2, a Zen

treatise on the priests who have transmitted Buddhist truth from its origins in India through to China. An edition was produced in 1706 in Japan. See Matsuzaki Hitoshi et al., eds., *Chikamatsu jōrurishū* (CJS), vol. 2, SNKBT no. 92 (Tokyo: Iwanami shoten, 1995), p. 348, n. 17.

25. [風覚冷薫信女]. This is her Buddhist name as recorded in the *Setsuyō kikan* (1833), book 25, and at Ginzanji temple. On her grave at Raigōji temple, the name is [声応貞現信女] "A Laywoman of Modest Heart Who Followed Buddha's Teachings." Both gravestones also list the child simply as a baby boy. See Funagoe Seiichirō, ed., *Naniwa sōsho*, vol. 3 (Osaka: Naniwa sōsho kankōkai, 1927), p. 41.

26. [露秋禅定門]. This is his Buddhist name as recorded in the *Setsuyō kikan*, book 25, and at Ginzanji temple. On his grave at Raigōji temple, the name is [通月融心信士] "A Layman of Pure Heart Gentle as Moonlight." See Funagoe, ed., *Naniwa sōsho*, vol. 3, p. 41.

27. From the *Kanmu ryōju* Sutra (Ch: *Guan Wu Liang Shou Jing*), book 9. See Matsuzaki et al., eds., CJS 2, p. 351, n. 13.

28. The first four are birth, aging, sickness, and death, and to these are added losing a loved one, meeting those one hates, wishing for but not getting something, and the five elements of consciousness and perception becoming painful. The phrase is used as a term for all the sufferings of life.

29. These two poems are recorded in *Setsuyō kikan*, book 25. See Funagoe, *Naniwa sōsho*, vol. 3, p. 42.

30. An allusion to a popular saying, in *Kango yamato koji* (1691) (Kyoto University, Faculty of Letters Library), originally from the Han dynasty text *Lunheng*.

Notes to Tethered Steed and the Eight Provinces of Kantō, introduction

1. The text used for the translation is in Matsuzaki Hitoshi et al., eds., *Chikamatsu jōrurishū* (CJS), vol. 2, SNKBT no. 92 (Tokyo: Iwanami shoten, 1995). I am greatly indebted to Professor Matsuzaki's pioneering work in annotating this play in detail for the first time.

2. The 1890 production was entitled *Sōma Heishi nidai-banashi* and was adapted by Fukuchi Ōchi. A 1970 production under the original title was adapted by Tobe Ginsaku, and the main roles were played by Nakamura Utaemon VI, Nakamura Ganjirō II and Jitsukawa Enjaku III (see figures 58 and 60). There are records of productions in 1922 and 1930, but it has not yet become part of the repertoire. See *Shōchiku hyakunenshi*, vol. 3: *Engeki shiryō* (Tokyo: Shōchiku kabushiki kaisha, 1996); *Kabuki-za hyakunenshi*, 3 vols. (Tokyo: Shōchiku kabushiki kaisha, 1998).

3. Yorimitsu was not, in fact, appointed to the post of shogun but gained such sta-

tus in later legend and literature. Uchiyama Mikiko showed how, over several plays, Chikamatsu transformed, the figure of "Yorimitsu" from being an official under the power of the court in the political structure to a shogun figure in the image of the shogun of the Tokugawa era. See Uchiyama Mikiko, *Jōrurishi no jūhasseki* (Tokyo: Benseisha, 1989), pp. 60–62.

4. Uchiyama Mikiko, "*Kanhasshū tsunagi-uma* to sono shūhen," *Kabuki: Kenkyū to Hihyō* 8 (1992): 3–68; Matsuzaki Hitoshi, "*Kanhasshū tsunagi-uma* ron," *Kabuki: Kenkyū to Hihyō* 19 (1997): 107–24, and "*Kanhasshū tsunagi-uma* Kyakuchū yoteki," *Nihon Bungaku Kenkyū* 31 (1996): 59–70; C. Andrew Gerstle, "Heroic Honor: Chikamatsu and the Samurai Ideal," *Harvard Journal of Asiatic Studies* 57, no. 2 (1997): 307–81; and "Gidayū botsugo no Chikamatsu: *Kokusen'ya kassen, Kanhasshū tsunagi-uma*," in Torigoe Bunzō et al., eds., *Chikamatsu no jidai*, IKKB, vol. 8 (Tokyo: Iwanami shoten, 1998).
5. See further discussion of this play in Gerstle, "Heroic Honor."
6. *Kōyō gunkan*, in Sakai Kenji, ed., *Kōyō gunkan taisei*, 4 vols. (Tokyo: Kyūko shoin, 1995); see also the introduction to the play *Battles of Kawa-nakajima* in this volume.
7. The following contain sections on the powers of supernatural swords: *The Tale of the Heike*, book 11, in Helen McCullough, trans., *The Tale of the Heike* (Stanford, Calif.: Stanford University Press, 1988), pp. 383–86; "Tsurugi no maki," in Takahashi Sadakazu, "Tanaka-bon *Heike tsurugi no maki*: kaisetsu," *Kokugo kokubun*, July 1967, pp. 37–58; *Taiheiki*, book 32, in Gotō Tanji, ed., *Taiheiki*, vol. 3, NKBT no. 36 (Tokyo: Iwanami shoten, 1961), pp. 225–29; and *Genpei jōsuiki*, in Mizuhara Hajime, ed., *Shintei: Genpei jōsuiki*, vol. 2 (Tokyo: Shinjinbutsu ōraisha, 1988), pp. 290–91.
8. Yokomichi Mario and Omote Akira, eds., *Yōkyokushū*, vol. 2, NKBT no. 41 (Tokyo: Iwanami shoten, 1963), pp. 373–76.
9. Itagaki Shun'ichi, ed., *Zen-Taiheiki*, 2 vols., Sōsho Edo bunko series nos. 3 and 4 (Tokyo: Kokusho kankōkai, 1988), esp. chs. 14–17, pp. 271–353.

Notes to Tethered Steed and the Eight Provinces of Kantō, act 1

1. The reference is originally from the *Han Shu* (Collections of Writings on the Han Dynasty), ch. 51, "Mei Cheng Zhuan," a biography of the scholar official Mei Cheng (d. 140 B.C.) who served various lords during the Han dynasty. Chikamatsu would have had easy access to this tale in the popular collection of Chinese writings, *Wen Xuan* (Collection of Refined Literature), ch. 39, in Obi Kōichi, ed., *Monzen*, vol. 5, Zenshaku kanbun taikei no. 30 (Tokyo: Shūeisha, 1975), p. 379. This particular passage comes toward the beginning when Mei

Cheng is trying to persuade the Wu King not to lead a rebellion against the Han. The passage contains a string of parable-like examples trying to convince the king of the wisdom of caution, and explaining how both prosperity and disaster always begin with little things, seemingly too slight to cause great consequences. One becomes either a good or bad person through the accumulation of small deeds that may seem insignificant in isolation. We construct our own fate, even though we may not recognize the significance of particular actions. The king ignores Mei Cheng and leads a rebellion anyway, and it fails. This passage illustrates Mei Cheng's lack of fear in speaking against what he considered his lord's unwise plans.

2. From the Confucian *Analects*, ch. 12, par. 6, "Yan Yuan." When Confucius is asked what true wisdom in a ruler is, he answers that those whose minds are unaffected by the mud of slander or the fire of denunciation are the ones who see with a clear mind and are able to judge people accurately and rule wisely. One must have both the conviction that one's perception is correct and the courage to stick to it. Chikamatsu suggests two themes in these opening lines: one's fortune, ill or good, depends on small, apparently insignificant actions, and therefore it is important to maintain an awareness of cause and consequence; a wise ruler is able to perceive the truth of men's words and actions, to see beneath the surface. See Yoshida Kenkō, ed., *Rongo*, SKT no. 1 (Tokyo: Meiji shoin, 1960), p. 264; Arthur Waley, trans., *The Analects of Confucius* (London: Allen & Unwin, 1938), p. 164.

3. Yorimitsu was not, in fact, appointed to the post of shogun but was given that status in later legend and literature; see n. 3 of the introduction to this play.

4. From the *Shiji* (*The Book of History*), ch. 68, "Shang Jun Lie Zhuan." The passage is taken from a section about the implementation of a new set of laws, which argues that those at the top must abide by the law first as an example to their subjects. In the story, the ruler's heir commits a crime, and although he is not punished, his tutor is, and after that, the people abide by the law; the country has no more thieves; and the nation prospers. See Mizusawa Toshitada, ed., *Shiki*, vol. 8, SKT no. 88 (Tokyo: Meiji shoin, 1990), p. 207.

5. A quotation from *Tsurezuregusa*, sec. 206, another reference to the theme of the importance of accurate perception among rulers. See Donald Keene, trans., *Essays in Idleness* (New York: Columbia University Press, 1967).

6. An incident recorded in *Kokon chomonshū*, book 11, episode no. 384, in Nishio Kōichi, ed., *Kokon chomonjū*, vol. 2, Shinchō Nihon koten shūsei no. 76 (Tokyo: Shinchōsha, 1986), p. 28.

7. A painter active in Tang China. The incident is recorded in *Lie Xian Quan Zhuan*, book 6; see Matsuzaki Hitoshi et al., eds., *Chikamatsu jōrurishū* (CJS), vol. 2, SNKBT no. 92 (Tokyo: Iwanami shoten, 1995), p. 359, n. 25.

8. An incident recorded in *Zen-Taiheiki*, ch. 1, "Tsunemoto shika o uchitamou koto," in Itagaki Shun'ichi, ed., *Zen-Taiheiki*, vol. 1, Sōsho Edo bunko series no. 3 (Tokyo: Kokusho kankōkai, 1988), p. 26.
9. J: Shumisen. In Buddhism, Mount Sumeru is the largest of all mountains and is at the center of the world, beneath the sea. At its peak lives Taishakuten (Sanskrit: Sakro devanam Indrah); at its center the four guardian deities. The sun, moon, and stars revolve around Mount Sumeru.
10. A strong man in service to the decadent emperor Zhou of Yin (ca. 1100 B.C.), described in *Shiji* (*The Book of History*), book 5, as a fierce and devious retainer. See Yoshida Kenkō and Mizusawa Toshitada, eds., *Shiki*, vol. 1, SKT no. 38 (Tokyo: Meiji shoin, 1973), p. 134.
11. See Matsuzaki et al., eds., CJS 2, p. 360, nn. 3, 4, 9, and comment. Matsuzaki's notes on this section show that Chikamatsu bases this scene primarily on the story in *Konjaku monogatari*, ch. 25, episode 6 (in which Yorimitsu kills a fox that has invaded the palace) while also alluding to *Zen-Taiheiki*, ch. 1 (in which Minamoto no Tsunemoto shoots a deer; see n. 8) and *Genpei seisuiki*, ch. 16 (in which Minamoto no Mitsunaka kills the fantastic creature *nue* to create the image of the brave Minamoto line of warriors whose bows and arrows can quell any threat to the imperial court. In particular, the predominant image is of the gods guiding the arrow to the mark. Also see Mizuhara Hajime, ed., *Shintei Genpei jōsuiki*, vol. 2 (Tokyo: Shinjinbutsu ōraisha, 1991), pp. 292–93.
12. A famous Chinese archer of the Chu during the Spring and Autumn era (ca. 770–403 B.C.) In *Genpei seisuiki*, ch. 16, it is said that Yorimitsu had received Yang You's bow. See Mizuhara, *Shintei: Genpei jōsuiki*, vol. 2, pp. 295. In *haikai* poetry, his name is commonly associated with a bow. See Takeuchi Waka, ed., *Kefukigusa*, Iwanami bunko yellow series no. 200-1 (1943; reprint, Tokyo: Iwanami shoten, 1988), p. 85.
13. Itagaki, ed., *Zen-Taiheiki*, ch. 18, vol. 1, p. 365.
14. A quotation from the *I Ching* (*The Book of Changes*), sec. 21, in which the metaphor of the action of the upper and lower jaws—which take in hard, potentially harmful, objects and through the natural function of chewing makes them palatable—is used to explain how a government must use its powers to seek out the reasons of crimes and punish the perpetrators. See Imai Usaburō, ed., *Ekikyō*, vol. 1, SKT no. 23 (Tokyo: Meiji shoin, 1987), p. 456.
15. A falling star is considered a sign that someone will try to usurp the kingdom.
16. *Sōma* contains the character for "horse." Masakado was famous as a horseman and used horses skillfully as part of his military strategy.
17. *Batō* means "horse" or "horse's head."
18. The area of modern-day greater Tokyo.
19. Chikamatsu most likely based the figure Yoshikado on the depiction in the *Zen-*

Taiheiki, ch. 18, in which he leads a rebellion to avenge his father Masakado's death. See Itagaki, ed., *Zen-Taiheiki*, vol. 1, pp. 373–77.

20. Matsuzaki suggests that Chikamatsu is referring to the Tokugawa shogun, who traced his lineage to the Genji. See Matsuzaki et al., eds., CJS 2, p. 362, n. 15.
21. Both these are historical figures, although little is recorded about Yorihira.
22. This name is from a minor figure in the nō play *Tsuchigumo*. See Yokomichi Mario and Omote Akira, eds., *Yōkyokushū*, vol. 2, NKBT no. 41 (Tokyo: Iwanami shoten, 1960).
23. An allusion to the kyōgen play *Tsurigitsune*, in which a fox is tempted by the smell of a cooked mouse placed as bait in a hunter's trap. Kochō imitates the scene in which the fox sneaks closer and closer to the bait. See Koyama Hiroshi, ed., *Kyōgenshū*, vol. 2, NKBT no. 43 (Tokyo: Iwanami shoten, 1961), p. 457; Richard McKinnon, trans., *Selected Plays of Kyōgen* (Tokyo: Uniprint, 1968).
24. A reference to the Tanabata legend in which the lovers can meet only once a year. The allusion is to the *Gyokuyōshū* poem no. 468. The imagery of a boat that takes a man to meet his lover is common in poetry. See Matsuzaki et al., eds., CJS 2, p. 366, n. 15.
25. An allusion to a *gongshi* ("court") verse by the Tang poet Wang Jian (d. 830), in the Tang poetry collection of *Santi Tangshi*, vol. 1. The verse is about the lonely life of a court lady who can meet the emperor only rarely, as in the "Oxherd Boy and Weaver Girl" story. See Murakami Tetsumi, ed., *Santaishi*, vol. 1, Shinchō Chūgoku kotensen no. 16 (Tokyo: Asahi shinbunsha, 1966), p. 29. Also quoted in the jōruri *Genji kachō taizen* (1708), act 3. See Matsuzaki et al., eds., CJS 2, p. 368, n. 5.
26. This "cutting of the cap strings" incident is modeled on a tale originally in the *Shuo Yuan*, sec. 6.11, "Fu En Pian," and also in the *Meng Qiu*, a Chinese collection to which Chikamatsu often refers. King Zhuang of Chu similarly saved a retainer from shame by having everyone in the room cut the strings of his cap after an incident in the dark when one of his consorts was accosted during a banquet. This man then later repaid his debt by fighting fearlessly in battle for his lord. See D. C. Lau, ed., *A Concordance of the Shou Yuan* (Hong Kong: Commercial Press, 1992), p. 42; Hayakawa Kōsaburō, ed., *Mōgyū*, vol. 2, SKT no. 59 (Tokyo: Meiji shoin, 1973), sec. 376, p. 746.
27. An allusion to the last line of the god nō play *Kaname-ishi*, an auspicious drama celebrating the Kashima Shrine. The theme is that the gods protect the court from its enemies within or without and that both learning and the martial arts must be maintained. There is a huge stone (*kaname-ishi*) at the Kashima Shrine that represents the immutable power of the gods. See Nonomura Kaizō, ed., *Yōkyoku nihyaku gojūbanshū* (Kyoto: Akao shōbundō, 1978), p. 79.
28. This was a style of chanting used by mendicant monks. The word means to

strike a bowl as a percussion instrument. The song itself is found in earlier nō and kyōgen plays, as well as earlier jōruri. Matsuzaki suggests that Chikamatsu used a *hachi-tataki* song similar to the one in the kyōgen play *Fukube no shin, tsutome-iri*, the text of which he quotes on p. 493 of Matsuzaki et al., eds., CJS 2. Kintoki appears dressed as a monk. Kintoki is known as a fierce, red-faced, and rough warrior and so would cut a comic figure dressed as a monk.

29. An allusion to the opening line of the demon nō play *Yamamba*. See Koyama Hiroshi et al., eds., *Yōkyokushū*, vol. 2, NKBZ no. 34 (Tokyo: Shōgakkan, 1975), p. 503; Royall Tyler, trans., *Japanese Nō Dramas* (London: Penguin Classics, 1992).

30. *Fukube* is a gourd or pumpkin. The word can also refer to a woman's private parts, originating as a slang word among thieves; further, gourds are often hollowed and dried to hold liquid, such as saké.

31. An allusion to two *Kokinshū* poems, nos. 828 and 645. Both are love poems. The first focuses on the Yoshino River which separates the two mountains, "man" and "woman." The second is about a woman recalling the visit of a lover and wondering whether it was a dream. See Laurel Rodd, with Mary Henkensius, trans., *Kokinshū: A Collection of Poems Ancient and Modern* (Princeton, N.J.: Princeton University Press, 1984); Helen McCullough, trans., *Kokin Wakashū: The First Imperial Anthology of Japanese Poetry* (Stanford, Calif.: Stanford University Press, 1985); also Helen McCullough, trans., *Tales of Ise: Lyrical Episodes from Tenth-Century Japan* (Stanford, Calif.: Stanford University Press, 1968), no. 69.

32. An allusion to the Buddhist poem no. 2620 in the *Gyokuyōshū*, in Matsuzaki et al., eds., CJS 2, p. 371, no. 24.

33. Matsuzaki suggests that Chikamatsu's source for this scene could be *Hatakeyamaki*, sec. 5, which has a similar incident of a man being welcomed into a house as if he is the awaited lover. See Matsuzaki et al., eds., CJS 2, p. 373.

34. From the nō play *Ataka*, in which Benkei reads from the nonexistent "subscription list," making up the text as he goes along, about Buddhism and the plan to rebuild the Great Buddha at Tōdaiji in Nara. The meaning of the quotation is that the world lost its way in darkness after the Buddha passed into Nirvana. Kintoki, too, is improvising the content of his Buddhist chant. See Koyama et al., eds., *Yōkyokushū*, vol. 2, p. 314; Kenneth Yasuda, trans., *Masterworks of the Nō Theater* (Bloomington: Indiana University Press, 1989).

35. From a popular saying as recorded in *Kefuki-gusa*, book 2, "A little knowledge blocks the way to Buddha." See Takeuchi, ed., *Kefukigusa*, p. 91.

36. This metaphor is from the Daoist treatise *Lao Tzu*, sec. 60, in which it is used as an example to show that government should not be overbearing if the populace is to flourish and not be troubled. Tsuna's lecture may be seen as a witty commentary on *Lao Tzu*, and this passage is also a satirical comment on the

Kyōhō Reforms being implemented by the Tokugawa government of the time. See Abe Yoshio et al., ed., *Rōshi, Sōshi*, vol. 1, SKT no. 7 (Tokyo: Meiji shoin, 1966) p. 103; Arthur Waley, trans., *The Way and Its Power: A Study of the Tao Tē Ching* (New York: Grove Press, 1958), p. 215.

37. *Kokinshū* love poem no. 522, the first line of which closes the preceding scene. See Rodd, trans., *Kokinshū*; McCullough, trans., *Kokin Wakashū*; also found in McCullough, trans., *Tales of Ise*, sec. 50.

38. An allusion to the last part of the nō play *Kayoi Komachi* and the image of the obsessed lover, Captain Fukakusa, in that play. See Koyama et al., eds., *Yōkyokushū*, vol. 2, p. 160; Donald Keene, ed., *Twenty Plays of the Nō Theater* (New York: Columbia University Press, 1970).

39. The sources for these robber figures are in *Konjaku monogatari*, ch. 25, episode 7, and *Zen-Taiheiki*, ch. 17. See Matsuzaki et al., eds., CJS 2, p. 375, nn. 22–25.

40. Mencius, "Li Lou," book 4, par. 17. Mencius in fact says that although it is proper for a man not to touch the hand of his brother's wife, if she is drowning, it would be irresponsible not to save her. See Uchino Kumaichirō, ed., *Mōshi*, SKT no. 4 (Tokyo: Meiji shoin, 1962), p. 265; D. C. Lau, trans., *Mencius* (London: Penguin Books, 1970), p. 124.

41. Yasusuke is a comic villain character, tough against those weaker than himself but a coward when it comes to those stronger.

42. This section is a burlesque of earlier "Kinpira" puppet plays in which the heroes Tsuna and Kintoki kill all the villains. In either bunraku or kabuki, this would be played as a bombastic comic scene, with plenty of scope for fantastic theatrics.

43. This phrase is originally from the *Shinkokinshū*, poem no. 1916; see Minemura Fumito, ed., *Shinkokin wakashū*, NKBZ no. 26 (Tokyo: Shōgakkan, 1974). It is common in nō plays such as *Tamura* and *Funa-Benkei*, with the meaning of trusting in Kannon's or Amida's vow to save all those who trust in them. Here, however, the meaning is, rather, trusting in the power of the rightful protectors of the realm. See Koyama Hiroshi et al., eds., *Yōkyokushū*, vol. 1, NKBZ no. 33 (Tokyo: Shōgakkan, 1973), pp. 134–35; Koyama Hiroshi et al., eds., *Yōkyokushū*, vol. 2, NKBZ no. 34 (Tokyo: Shōgakkan, 1975), p. 439; Royall Tyler, trans., *Japanese Nō Dramas* (London: Penguin Classics, 1992).

Notes to Tethered Steed and the Eight Provinces of Kantō, act 2

1. It is conventional to have servants explain the background through lively banter and sexual innuendo.

2. The humor turns on a pun: *komochi* can mean "small rice cakes" or "to be with child."
3. Mortar and pestle were common slang for the sexual organs.
4. "Yema" means "gossamer." This was a story well known in Japan, and Matsuzaki notes that it is found in the encyclopedia *Kōeki zokusetsuben* (1717), sec. 8. See Matsuzaki Hitoshi et al., eds., *Chikamatsu jōrurishū* (CJS), vol. 2, SNKBT no. 92 (Tokyo: Iwanami shoten, 1995), p. 384, n. 10.
5. 695?–775. He went to China to study in 717 and lived there many years.
6. These are legends about the supernatural powers of spiders. The second comes from a poem associated with Princess Soto-ori found in the *Kokinshū* no. 1110. See Laurel Rodd, with Mary Henkensius, trans., *Kokinshū: A Collection of Poems Ancient and Modern* (Princeton, N.J.: Princeton University Press, 1984); Helen McCullough, trans., *Kokin Wakashū: The First Imperial Anthology of Japanese Poetry* (Stanford, Calif.: Stanford University Press, 1985); and explained in *Kōeki zokusetsuben tsukehen* (1719), sec. 6 (Matsuzaki et al., eds., CJS 2, p. 384, n. 11).
7. Kochō is a minor figure in the nō play *Tsuchigumo*. See Yokomichi Mario and Omote Akira, eds., *Yōkyokushū*, vol. 2, NKBT no. 41 (Tokyo: Iwanami shoten, 1960), pp. 373–76, in which a huge "earth spider" (*tsuchigumo*) threatens the imperial court but is defeated by Yorimitsu. Chikamatsu uses the spider imagery to weave together two strands in the play: the revenge of a jealous spirit and the earth spider as a threat to the political realm from insurgents. Private and public revenge are intertwined in the world of stories surrounding Yorimitsu, telling of how he and his men fight off supernatural threats to the realm.
8. This refers to Soto-orihime's poem in the *Kokinshū no.* 1110 (Rodd, trans., *Kokinshū*; McCullough, trans., *Kokin Wakashū*). The relevant line says that the spider's actions signal that her lover will come that evening.
9. Auspicious lines from the nō play, *Naniwa*, also quoted in *Lovers Pond*. See Sanari Kentarō, ed., *Yōkyoku taikan* (YTK), vol. 4 (Tokyo: Meiji shoin, 1927), p. 2333.
10. Masakado is thought to have in fact died in battle at Sarushima in Shimōsa, in modern Chiba Prefecture.
11. The description of Yoshikado comes from the *Zen-Taiheiki*, ch. 18. See Itagaki Shun'ichi, ed., *Zen-Taiheiki*, vol. 1, Sōsho Edo bunko series no. 3 (Tokyo: Kokusho kankōkai, 1988), p. 375.
12. Yoshikado, until this point only a voice from off scene, appears on stage.
13. Two examples of warriors dressing as a woman as a tactic can be found in *Konjaku monogatari*, ch. 25, episode 5, when Taira no Koreshige dresses as a woman; and in ch. 9 of *The Tale of the Soga Brothers*, when Gorōmaru dresses as a woman to try to capture Soga Gorō. This tactic is not considered an honorable way to

fight. See Matsuzaki et al., eds., CJS 2, p. 388, n. 21; Thomas Cogan, trans., *The Tale of the Soga Brothers* (Tokyo: University of Tokyo Press, 1987), p. 243.

14. This scene is highly theatrical, in which puppets are tossed about on stage.
15. A quotation from the last lines of the nō play, *Ataka*, in which wanted as fugitives by the government, Yoshitsune, Benkei, and several other loyal warriors manage to bluff their way through an official barrier. The theme of the power of the human spirit through force of will to overcome death is central to many of Chikamatsu's plays. See Koyama Hiroshi et al., eds., *Yōkyokushū*, vol. 2, NKBZ no. 34 (Tokyo: Shōgakkan, 1975), p. 323; Kenneth Yasuda, *Masterworks of the Nō Theater* (Bloomington: Indiana University Press, 1989).
16. This is performed as a song and dance scene. The title of the scene includes only Eika's name, but Yorihira travels with her. The journey is a trial for an aristocratic lady who has never been outside a palace alone without maids and attendants.
17. *Ise monogatari*, sec. 6. Several of the following lines allude to this section, called "Akuta River," in which Narihira flees with a princess far above his station who is supposedly devoured by a demon in the night but is really taken back to the palace by her brothers. Yorihira has risked his position as a samurai for love of Lady Eika and put her in danger. See Helen McCullough, trans., *Tales of Ise* (Stanford, Calif.: Stanford University Press, 1968).
18. Ibid.
19. An allusion to the *Shikashū* love poem no. 229, with the meaning that even if we are separated for a period, we shall be together again, just as a stream may be separated by boulders and turn into rapids. See Kawamura Teruo, ed., *Kinyōwakashū, Shikawakashū*, SNKBT no. 9 (Tokyo: Iwanami shoten, 1989).
20. These lines are from a song in the *Ginkyoku kokondaizen*, a collection of Osaka songs published between 1716 and 1732. See Matsuzaki et al., eds., CJS 2, p. 392, n. 9.
21. From the *Gosenshū* love poem no. 960. Naniwa is an old name for the area of Osaka, but in the poem, the first syllable suggests "name" or "reputation." The poem was sent by a prince to his lover after their illicit affair became public, to express his pledge to her. Yorihira and Eika's affair is already known in the world, whether or not they meet again. Yorihira makes a pledge that they will be together forever. See Katagiri Yōichi, ed., *Gosenwakashū*, SNKBT no. 6 (Tokyo: Iwanami shoten, 1990).
22. An allusion to the *Shinkokinshū* winter poem no. 565. The image is of deep winter when even the evergreen pine seems lonely on the mountain peak after all the other trees have lost their leaves. See Minemura Fumito, ed., *Shinkokinwakashū*, NKBZ no. 26 (Tokyo: Shōgakkan, 1974).
23. From the *Pillow Book*, sec. 1, in which Sei Shōnagon describes autumn as best

at evening when one by one, the crows fly off to their nests to sleep. Chikamatsu has them waking at dawn. See Matsuo Hitoshi, ed., *Makura no sōshi*, NKBZ no. 11 (Tokyo: Shōgakkan, 1974); Ivan Morris, trans., *The Pillow Book of Sei Shōnagon* (New York: Columbia University Press, 1967).

24. Ichiharano was the site of Captain Fukakusa's spirit's attack on Ono no Komachi in the nō play *Kayoi Komachi* (*Komachi and the Hundred Nights*); see the next note. She promised to meet him if he came to her house one hundred nights in a row, but legend has it that either he died on the last night or his father died, and so his love remained unfulfilled. Chikamatsu places Yorihira in the line of passionate lovers such as Narihira and Captain Fukakusa.

25. Another allusion to the nō play *Kayoi Komachi* (Koyama et al., eds., *Yōkyokushū*, vol. 2, p. 154; Donald Keene, ed., *Twenty Plays of the Nō Theater* (New York: Columbia University Press, 1970).

26. The *michiyuki* scene ends with their arrival in Ichiharano.

27. A famous Chinese warrior from the Qin dynasty (221–207 B.C.), described in the *Shiji* (*The Book of History*), vol. 5, "Qin Benji." In the previous scene, after placing Yorihira in the lineage of the famous passionate lovers Narihira and Captain Fukakusa, he portrays him here as a skillful and fierce warrior. See Yoshida Kenkō and Mizusawa Toshitada, eds., *Shiki*, vol. 1, SKT no. 38 (Tokyo: Meiji shoin, 1973), pp. 186–87.

28. The two most famous Chinese military strategists during the Spring and Autumn period (B.C. 770–403).

29. 770–403 B.C. This is recorded as a practice from even earlier times (Matsuzaki et al., eds., CJS 2, p. 398, n. 20).

30. An allusion to a saying recorded in the Han-dynasty compilation *Huai Nan Zi*, vol. 17, sec. 24, meaning that a person's character is like a clean white thread that may be dyed yellow or black. That is, one decision can sometimes turn a person toward good or evil. See Kusuyama Haruki, ed., *Enanji*, vol. 1, SKT no. 62 (Tokyo: Meiji shoin, 1988), p. 1015; also in *Meng Qiu*.

31. A young villain who attacked Yorimitsu at the battle of Ichiharano and was killed, as is related in various sources, including *Kokon chomonshū*, sec. 9, and *Zen-Taiheiki*, ch. 21, and on which much of this scene is based. Yorinobu replaces Yorimitsu in Chikamatsu's version. See Itagaki, ed., *Zen-Taiheiki*, vol. 2, pp. 18–23; Matsuzaki et al., eds., CJS 2, p. 399, n. 31.

32. The first part of this section is chanted in nō style until after Yorinobu's first speech.

33. This phrase is common in nō plays. Chikamatsu is deliberately giving Yorinobu a sophisticated air.

34. From the *Shinchokusenshū* poem no. 410; see Matsuzaki et al., eds., CJS 2, p. 400, n. 11.

35. An allusion to the *Wakan rōeishū* poem no. 27, about the sadness of the passing of youth while watching the falling cherry blossoms in the moonlight. Here the blossoms become snow. See J. Thomas Rimer and Jonathan Chaves, eds. and trans., *Japanese and Chinese Poems to Sing* (New York: Columbia University Press, 1977).
36. From *Zen-Taheiki*, ch. 21. Chikamatsu has Yorinobu rather than Tsuna notice the animal. The following scene is from the same source. See Itagaki, ed., *Zen-Taheiki*, vol. 2, p. 22.
37. This phrase and others similar to it appear in many of Chikamatsu's late-period plays, including *Heike nyogo shima* (1719), act 2, "Kikai ga shima," when Chidori cries out at the cruelty of samurai who are supposed to understand and be sensitive to human feelings (*mono no aware shiru*) and *Battles at Kawa-nakajima*, which is translated in this volume. See Shuzui Kenji, et al., eds., *Chikamatsu jōrurishū*, vol. 2, NKBT no. 50 (Tokyo: Iwanami shoten, 1959), p. 316; Samuel Leiter, trans., *The Art of Kabuki: Famous Plays in Performance* (Berkeley and Los Angeles: University of California Press, 1979).
38. An allusion to the *Shūishū* love poem no. 750, with the headnote that it was sent to a woman the poet secretly loved. The core image is "tears from a silent stream": the lover has yet to open his heart to the woman. "Otonashi no taki" (Silent Waterfall) is a waterfall in northeast Kyoto. See Komachiya Teruhiko, ed., *Shūiwakashū*, SNKBT no. 7 (Tokyo: Iwanami shoten, 1990).
39. Chikamatsu follows the earlier *Watanabe Tsuna mita-gassen* (1663), act 1, in creating the relations among these three. Tsuna's aunt raised him and then offered him into Yorimitsu's service. One major theme of this play is the role of "private" (*watakushi*) familial relations in the public sphere. See Matsuzaki et al., eds., CJS 2, p. 403, n. 29,
40. This use of "snow" as a symbol appears again in act 3. Yorihira is explaining that once he joined up with Yoshikado against the court, his life was over; his only course to die as an enemy. He explains that the only way to clear his shame is to honor his pledge to Yoshikado, even to death.
41. A symbol of Yorihira's death.
42. These are Buddhist phrases expressing an enlightened mind, but Chikamatsu seems to imply the more mundane sense that it is not always simple or easy to judge actions to be right or wrong, good or evil.

Notes to Tethered Steed and the Eight Provinces of Kantō, act 3

1. The source of this phrase is not known. Chikamatsu quotes a phrase about the cleverness of foxes in the first lines of *Twins at the Sumida River*. Here it refers

to the enemy Yoshikado, but it also carries on from the opening lines of act 1 in suggesting the theme of appearance versus reality.

2. This would seem to refer to Shogun Yorimitsu.
3. An allusion to the *Wakan rōeishū* poem no. 60, which is about the bush warbler's (*uguisu*) and butterflies' confusion over the fact that spring is one month longer because of a leap month in that year, and their reluctance to give up the pleasures of spring. See J. Thomas Rimer and Jonathan Chaves, eds. and trans., *Japanese and Chinese Poems to Sing: The* Wakan rōeishū (New York: Columbia University Press, 1997).
4. An allusion to the *Chuang Tzu*, the beginning of ch. 1, which is about the differing ways that creatures (people) with different experiences of life perceive reality. The point is that perspectives on the world are relative and tend to be determined by one's own experience. Aunt Mita's argument can be read as a commentary on this opening passage from the *Chuang Tzu*. See Abe Yoshio et al., eds., *Rōshi, Sōshi*, vol. 1, SKT no. 7 (Tokyo: Meiji shoin, 1966), p. 137; Burton Watson, trans., 1968. *The Complete Works of Chuang Tzu* (New York: Columbia University Press, 1968), p. 29.
5. *Keiyaku*. This word is used time and again by Aunt Mita and Yorimitsu in this dialogue and is used by Yorihira for his promise to Yoshikado and for Eika's promise to her mother.
6. Tsuna was presented to Yorimitsu's father Mitsunaka (Manjū) in earlier versions in such works as *Zen-Taiheiki*, ch. 14—see Itagaki Shun'ichi, ed., *Zen-Taiheiki*, 2 vols., Sōsho Edo bunko series nos. 3 and 4 (Tokyo: Kokusho kankōkai, 1988)—and in Kinpira-jōruri, such as *Kiyohara no udaishō* (1677), act 1, and *Watanabe Tsuna mita-gassen*, act 1—see Matsuzaki Hitoshi et al., eds., *Chikamatsu jōrurishū* (CJS), vol. 2, SNKBT no. 92 (Tokyo: Iwanami shoten, 1995), p. 413, n. 20.
7. An allusion to *Ise monogatari*, sec. 63, in which a younger man is kind to an old woman who has a passion for him, and Chikamatsu's earlier *Kako no kyōshin nanahaka-meguri* (1701), act 2, in which the once beautiful but now old Komachi is described as an old cherry tree. See Helen McCullough, trans., *Tales of Ise* (Stanford, Calif.: Stanford University Press, 1968); *Chikamatsu zenshū* (CZ), vol. 9 (Tokyo: Iwanami shoten, 1988); Matsuzaki et al., eds., CJS 2, p. 414, n. 9.
8. This is associated with a legend told by Kumano nuns known as *bikuni*. Those who didn't give birth to a child were in the next life condemned to a hell where they dug up bamboo roots with candlewicks. See Matsuzaki et al., eds., CJS 2, p. 415, n. 18.
9. Aunt Mita's nephew Watanabe no Tsuna is famous for cutting off the arm of the Ibaraki demon at the Rashōmon Gate in Kyoto. The legend is that the

demon took the form of the aunt in order to get the arm back. The story was a common element in many versions of this "Rashōmon" story throughout the medieval and Tokugawa eras, including *Heike tsurugi no maki* (a tale that evolved from the section "Ken no maki" in book 11 of *The Tale of the Heike*) and the *otogi-zōshi* story *Rashōmon*. See Helen McCullough, trans., *The Tale of the Heike* (Stanford, Calif.: Stanford University Press, 1988), pp. 383–86. One version of this story is printed in Takahashi Sadakazu, "Tanaka-bon *Heike tsurugi no maki*: Kaisetsu," *Kokugo kokubun*, July 1967, pp. 37–58, Itagaki, ed., *Zen-Taiheiki*, ch. 17, vol. 1, pp. 329–35. Chikamatsu is obviously playing with the legend's metamorphosis theme in having Aunt Mita appear as a male warrior (Matsuzaki et al., eds., CJS 2, p. 415, n. 20).

10. A legendary old hag who strips the clothes from all those who cross into the world of the dead.
11. *Watakushi* (private sphere).
12. *Kokka no seidō*.
13. Confucian *Analects*, ch. 7, par. 10, in which Confucius says that he would not follow someone whose only trait was daring and bravery; he wants the leader also to have a good strategy and the means to carry it through. See Yoshida Kenkō, ed., *Rongo*, SKT no.1 (Tokyo: Meiji shoin, 1960), pp. 158–59; Arthur Waley, trans., *The Analects of Confucius* (London: Allen & Unwin, 1938), pp. 124–25.
14. According to a well-known aphorism, "teetotalers, like ghosts, don't exist." See Takeuchi Waka, ed., *Kefukigusa*, Iwanami bunko yellow series no. 200-1 (1943; reprint, Tokyo: Iwanami shoten, 1988), p. 92.
15. This is a demon related to the "Shutendōji demon" of the legends surrounding Yorimitsu and Watanabe no Tsuna, who slew the demon.
16. The area of modern-day Osaka City.
17. The following speech is in the kabuki style, in which one actor praises another in an exaggerated fashion.
18. Tomozuna compares Eika with famous Chinese beauties whose charms overwhelmed rulers.
19. Like the Chinese examples, all these are famous Japanese beauties of legend.
20. Chikamatsu weaves in phrases from popular songs (*Ochibashū*) and a poem from *Ise monogatari*, sec. 23, to give Tomozuna's language a sensual flavor. See McCullough, trans., *Tales of Ise*.
21. This was a popular story in Chinese and Japanese. *Konjaku monogatari*, sec. 9, episode 11, relates this tale in Japanese. In the original, it is his mother who strikes him.
22. The character [雪] can be read *yuki* (snow), *kiyomeru* (purify), and *susugu* (cleanse).

23. Matsuzaki suggests that Yorihira's anger is aimed at Yorimitsu, who wants him to renege on his promise to Yoshikado. This could therefore be seen an example of the tension inherent in the opposing ideas of the samurai as a loyal bureaucrat versus the ideal of a man willing to die for honor. See Matsuzaki et al., eds., CJS 2, p. 427, n. 19.
24. In earlier Kinpira jōruri plays, Kintoki invariably appears as a brash, simple warrior who attacks his enemy without thinking of the consequences.
25. This is from a kyōgen song, later played to the shamisen as well; in *Shamisen kumi-uta*, "Nanatsuko." See Matsuzaki et al., eds., CJS 2, p. 428, n. 15.
26. Both Fan Kuai and Zhang Liang were famous Chinese military men. Chikamatsu has Aunt Mita mimic a contemporary lively kabuki style of *aragoto* "rough-style" acting.
27. This section begins with the vigorous rhythms of nō music from a banquet scene like that in the nō play *Rashōmon*.
28. Matsuzaki notes that the tale of Lady Kesa, who plotted to sacrifice herself in place of her husband, would have been well known to the audience and that Chikamatsu has used elements of the *ko-jōruri* play *Toba koizuka monogatari* in this scene. See Matsuzaki et al., eds., CJS 2, pp. 431–32.
29. An allusion to the *Shūishū* love poem no. 778 by Hitomaro, which is a lament over how long the night seems when one is waiting for a lover. The metaphor refers to a *yamadori* (copper pheasant) which has a long tail. Mating pairs supposedly sleep apart in different valleys at night, and so for these birds, the night is long like the length of their tails. See Komachiya Teruhiko, ed., *Shūiwakashū*, SNKBT no. 7 (Tokyo: Iwanami shoten, 1990).
30. Both phrases, originally from *The Book of History* (*Shiji*), are explained in *Kango yamato koji* (1691, Kyoto University, Faculty of Letters Library), vol. 1.
31. An allusion to the *Goshūishū* poem no. 939 by Sei Shōnagon. See Kubota Jun, ed., *Goshūi wakashū*, SNKBT no. 8 (Tokyo: Iwanami shoten, 1994).
32. The source for this incident is in the classic Chinese text, *Shuo Yuan*, also in *Meng Qiu*, sec. 376, in which the king of Chu, Zhuang Wang, orders all present to cut their cap strings in order to hide the shame of a retainer's indiscretion toward his mistress in the dark during a party. The man then shows his loyalty by extreme bravery on the battlefield (see n. 26 in act 1).
33. A vast mountain mentioned in Buddhist literature.
34. Chikamatsu here uses the place-names Iwade ("Not to Speak") and Shinobu ("Endure"), which often figure in poetry to express the agony of those now about to part.
35. An allusion to *Kong Zi Jia Yu*, sec. 15 in which Confucius explains how a person is affected by those around him, his parents and friends. See Uno Seiichi, ed., *Kōshi kego*, SKT no. 53 (Tokyo: Meiji shoin, 1996), p. 214; Robert P.

Kramers, trans., *K'ung tzu chia yū*, the School Sayings of Confucius (Leiden: Brill, 1950).
36. A sacred mythical mountain in far west China known for its precious stones.
37. Matsuzaki suggests that this refers to Yoshimune. See Matsuzaki et al., eds., CJS 2, p. 441, n. 37.

Notes to Tethered Steed and the Eight Provinces of Kantō, act 4

1. This refers to seven hermit-sages of the Jin dynasty (265–419) who rebelled against the strict norms of society and relaxed with wine in a bamboo grove. "Bamboo" is an auspicious symbol of longevity; here it also most likely refers to the Takemoto (Bamboo) Theater. There were seven main theaters in Osaka. *Chikamatsu goi* suggests that Chikamatsu was making an offering for the continued prosperity of the Takemoto Theater after his own imminent death. See Ueda Kazutoshi and Higuchi Yoshichiyo, eds., *Chikamatsu goi* (Tokyo: Fuzanbō, 1930), p. 262. The lines also allude to a line in the auspicious *Shūishū* poem no. 1177 by Tsurayuki, celebrating the eightieth birthday of a princess which says that although covered with white snow, the deep green of the bamboo never changes, even over a thousand years. See Komachiya Teruhiko, ed., *Shūiwakashū*, SNKBT no. 7 (Tokyo: Iwanami shoten, 1990).
2. Kakinomoto no Hitomaro (ca. 700) is the most famous poet among those represented in the *Manyōshū* anthology, compiled in 759. Yamabe no Akahito (ca. 725) is also a famous poet represented in this collection.
3. A famous zither player of the Spring and Autumn age (770–403 B.C.), who gave up and destroyed his instrument after his friend died because he believed the friend was the only person who could understand his music.
4. Mount Kazuragi is between Osaka and Nara. It is mentioned here because it is the home of the legendary earth spider (*tsuchigumo*) depicted in the nō play of the same name, which Yorimitsu and his men defeat (see n. 19).
5. The area of Kawanishi City in Hyogo Prefecture. This was the home of Mitsunaka (Manjū), the father of Yorimitsu.
6. An allusion to the *Shinkokinshū* spring poem no. 145. See Minemura Fumito, ed., *Shinkokinwakashū*, NKBZ no. 26 (Tokyo: Shōgakkan, 1974).
7. The chanting style changes from popular song back to *gidayū*.
8. Under the lunar calendar, the middle of the seventh month was close to the end of summer.
9. An allusion to Bai Juyi's (772–846) most famous poem *Cheng Wen Ge* ("Song of Everlasting Sorrow") about the beautiful Yang Guifei, which is translated by

Stephen Owen, in Stephen Owen, ed. and trans., *An Anthology of Chinese Literature* (New York: Norton, 1996), pp. 442–47.
10. Kochō, which means butterfly, is also the name of the woman whose jealous spirit is attacking Iyo.
11. The illustrated text of this play says that this scene was extremely popular. See Matsuzaki Hitoshi et al., eds., *Chikamatsu jōrurishū* (CJS), vol. 2, SNKBT no. 92 (Tokyo: Iwanami shoten, 1995), pp. 490–91.
12. This section is a song that accompanies the display of the different kimonos.
13. An allusion to the *Zokusenzaishū* spring poem no. 196. See Matsuzaki et al., eds., CJS 2, p. 448, n. 20.
14. Mikawa irises is an allusion to a poem in *Ise monogatari*, ch. 9, in which each of the five lines of the poem begins with one of the five syllables of *kakitsubata* (iris); hence the link to "threads of five colors." See Helen McCullough, trans., *Tales of Ise* (Stanford, Calif.: Stanford University Press, 1968).
15. Again, an allusion to the character Kochō, who loved Lady Iyo's husband Yorinobu and was killed in act 2.
16. This is a song and dance scene with spectacular stage tricks.
17. Some rural *obon* festivals still have similar phrases in the songs sung to see off ancestor spirits.
18. The illustrated text of this play notes that this scene was cleverly performed with various stage tricks, and was well received (see n. 11). Two months later, however, on the twenty-first of the third month, Osaka had a great fire in which more than half of the city was destroyed, including the Takemoto Theater. The later text, *Jōruri-fu* (1801), notes that because the first character of "Osaka" is the same [大], rumors circulated that this scene brought bad luck. See Matsuzaki et al., eds., CJS 2, p. 451.
19. Chikamatsu has lifted the minor character Kochō from the nō play *Tsuchigumo* (Earth Spider), reinventing her for the important role of the jealous spirit who attacks her rival. *Tsuchigumo* is one of the plays of the Minamoto Yorimitsu legend. The spider represents the threat to the realm, and Yorimitsu and his men are the vanquishers of the enemy. Here, language from the nō play is woven into this dancelike scene. See Yokomichi Mario and Omote Akira, eds., *Yōkyokushū*, vol. 2, NKBT no. 41 (Tokyo: Iwanami shoten, 1960), pp. 373–76.
20. This section is performed by two chanters, one each for the two women *shite* (first), Kochō; *tsure* (second), Iyo and other women; many of the lines allude to the nō play *Tsuchigumo* (see the preceding note).
21. Her lines are adapted from the nō play *Tsuchigumo* (see n. 19).
22. An allusion to a line in the nō play *Teika*, which is about the passionate love between the poets Fujiwara no Teika and Shokushi Naishinnō. After his death,

Teika's spirit became a vine that wound itself around the grave of Shokushi Naishinnō. In the play, the spirit of Shokushi Naishinnō suffers, unable to be free from the passion of her former life. The quotation is from the lines at the end of the play, just as the spirit of Shokushi Naishinnō disappears with the dew at dawn: the chorus says that the vine now creeps round and round more than ever, smothering the grave. See Koyama Hiroshi et al., eds., *Yōkyokushū*, vol. 2, NKBZ no. 34 (Tokyo: Shōgakkan, 1975), p. 313.

23. An allusion to the nō play *Aoi no Ue*, which focuses on the theme of the destructive jealousy of Lady Rokujō, originally depicted in the *Tale of Genji*. The quotation referred to occurs when Rokujō no Miyasudokoro is expressing her bitterness toward Aoi no Ue, Genji's official wife. Rokujō is jealous of Aoi and Genji's pledge of love, which she likens to the flash of a firefly over a dark, murky pond. The reference is to Genji, the "Shining Prince." Chikamatsu has changed the imagery here. See Koyama et al., eds., *Yōkyokushū*, vol. 2, p. 228; Arthur Waley, trans., *The Nō Plays of Japan* (London: Allen & Unwin, 1921).

24. An allusion to a line in the nō play *Yamamba*, which itself is alluding to the Tang poet Du Fu's "Two Poems on the Recluse Zhang." The image is of intense loneliness and comes at the climax (*kuse*) of the play as the protagonist, an old woman, seeks salvation. See Koyama et al., eds., *Yōkyokushū*, vol. 2, p. 518; Royall Tyler, trans., *Japanese Nō Dramas* (London: Penguin Classics, 1992).

25. An allusion to the nō play *Utaura*, about a wandering Shinto priest who is reunited with his son after eight years. In the second half, he dances and sings a description of hell, going into a fit as if he really is suffering. Finally he emerges from his trance, exhausted, and the play ends auspiciously with father and son returning home. Chikamatsu quotes a phrase from the depiction of fiery hell. See Nonomura Kaizō, ed., *Yōkyoku nihyaku gojūbanshū* (Kyoto: Akao shōbundō, 1978), p. 457.

26. From the nō play *Tsuchigumo*. The spider of Mount Kazuragi, from the legend of ancient times, represents the threat to the imperial government from outsiders. See Yokomichi and Omote, eds., *Yōkyokushū*, vol. 2, pp. 376.

27. Ibid.

28. The spider reappears in the form of Kochō.

29. An allusion to the nō play *Dōjōji*, about the fierce anger of a spurned woman who seeks revenge, turning into a serpent and finally exploding into a raging fire. This quotation comes at the end of the play when the woman's spirit, transformed into a raging serpent, collapses. She faces the bell and lets out a breath of fire, which consumes her, too, and she disappears into the depths of a river. See Koyama et al., eds., *Yōkyokushū*, vol. 2, p. 342; Donald Keene, ed., *Twenty Plays of the Nō Theater* (New York: Columbia University Press, 1970).

30. An allusion to a line in the nō play *Kiyotsune*, about the anger of a wife left behind when her husband goes off to die in battle. The spirit of Kiyotsune comes to his wife in a dream. She is bitter toward him, but then he describes his final battle and death. The quotation comes from the end of the play when Kiyotsune describes his fall into the Shura Realm of Never-Ending Battle. See Koyama et al., eds., *Yōkyokushū*, vol. 2, p. 208; Nippon gakujutsu shinkōkai, ed., *The Noh Drama: Ten Plays from the Japanese* (Rutland, Vt.: Tuttle, 1955).
31. An allusion to the nō play *Funa Benkei*, about the attack on Yoshitsune by the revengeful spirit of Tomomori, who had died in the battle of Dan no Ura. The quotation comes from near the end of the play, just before Tomomori's dance, when he raises a storm to attack Yoshitsune's boat, seeking vengeance. See Koyama et al., eds., *Yōkyokushū*, vol. 2, p. 447; Tyler, trans., *Japanese Nō Dramas*.
32. This sword is described in the *Heike tsurugi no maki*. See Takahashi Sadakazu, "Tanaka-bon *Heike tsurugi no maki*: kaisetsu," *Kokugo kokubun*, July 1967, p. 39.
33. An allusion to the *Shiji* (*The Book of History*), book 3 "Yinji." The king of Yin, Di Taiwu, asks Minister Yi Zhi to explain the strange happening in the palace garden where a mulberry tree and a paper mulberry tree entwine and suddenly grow to a huge size. Yi Zhi answers that supernatural forces cannot win against virtue and suggests that the problem lies with him and his government. He advises him to be more diligent and principled. Di Taiwu follows this advice, and the strange apparition withers and vanishes. See Yoshida Kenkō and Mizusawa Toshitada, eds., *Shiki* vol. 1, SKT no. 38 (Tokyo: Meiji shoin, 1973), p. 125.
34. Several works, including *The Tale of the Soga Brothers*, book 8, and the ballad drama and *ko-jōruri*, *Ken sandan*, record the legends of the magical powers of the Genji sword. See Thomas Cogan, trans., *The Tale of the Soga Brothers* (Tokyo: University of Tokyo Press, 1987), pp. 199–201; Matsuzaki et al., eds., *CJS* 2, p. 456, n. 5.
35. An allusion to the nō play *Zekai*, the tale of a Chinese *tengu* demon Zekai who comes to Japan in order to destroy Buddhism but is ousted by priests from Mount Hiei whose prayers arouse the various gods, including Fudō Myōō and Sannō Gongen, to drive him out of Japan. The quotation is taken from the last lines of the play in which the gods cry out that Zekai is never to return to Japan as he disappears into the clouds. See Sanari Kentarō, ed., *Yōkyoku taikan* (YTK), vol. 4 (Tokyo: Meiji shoin, 1927), pp. 1606–7.
36. From the nō play *Tsuchigumo*. See Yokomichi and Omote, eds., *Yōkyokushū*, vol. 2, pp. 375.
37. An allusion to the Chinese text *Yin Yi Xiao Shuo*. See Matsuzaki et al., eds., *CJS* 2, p. 456, n. 13.

Notes to Tethered Steed and the Eight Provinces of Kantō, act 5

1. From the nō play *Tsuchigumo*. See Yokomichi Mario and Omote Akira, eds., *Yōkyokushū*, vol. 2, NKBT no. 41 (Tokyo: Iwanami shoten, 1960), p. 375.
2. This saying comes from a story about Fujiwara Hidesato shooting a centipede with a spit-tipped arrow. See Matsuzaki Hitoshi et al., eds., *Chikamatsu jōrurishū* (CJS), vol. 2, SNKBT no. 92 (Tokyo: Iwanami shoten, 1995), p. 458, n. 8.
3. This is an extravagantly staged fight scene. Daji enjoyed watching men being tortured to death with fire. Chikamatsu uses her as a symbol of the power of lust in the earlier *Lovers Pond in Settsu Province*, act 2.
4. An allusion to the auspicious final lines of the nō play *Takasago*. See Koyama Hiroshi et al., eds., *Yōkyokushū*, vol. 1, NKBZ no. 33 (Tokyo: Shōgakkan, 1973), p. 65; Royall Tyler, trans., *Japanese Nō Dramas* (London: Penguin Classics, 1992).

Bibliography

Abe Yoshio et al., eds. *Rōshi, Sōshi.* Vol. 1. SKT no. 7. Tokyo: Meiji shoin, 1966.
Akatsuka, Kiyoshi, ed. *Daigaku.* SKT no. 2. Tokyo: Meiji shoin, 1967.
Amano Shizuo, ed. *Sonshi.* SKT no. 36. Tokyo: Meiji shoin, 1972.
Ames, Roger T., trans. *Sun-tzu: The Art of Warfare: A New Translation Incorporating the Recently Discovered Yin-ch'üeh-shan Texts.* New York: Ballantine Books, 1993.
Asahara Yoshiko and Kitahara Yoshio, eds. *Mai no hon.* SNKBT no. 59. Tokyo: Iwanami shoten, 1994.
Aston, William G., trans. *Nihongi: Chronicles of Japan from the Earliest Times to A.D. 697.* Rutland, Vt.: Tuttle, 1972.
Brazell, Karen, ed. *Twelve Plays of the Noh and Kyōgen Theaters.* Ithaca, N.Y.: Cornell University Press, 1988.
Brazell, Karen, ed. *Traditional Japanese Theater: An Anthology of Plays.* Ithaca, N.Y.: Cornell University Press, 1998.
Brewitt-Taylor, Charles H., trans. *San Kuo, or the Romance of the Three Kingdoms.* 1925. Reprint, Rutland, Vt.: Tuttle, 1959.
Chan, Wing-tsit, ed. *A Source Book in Chinese Philosophy.* Princeton, N.J.: Princeton University Press, 1963.
Chikamatsu kenkyūjo jūsshūnenkinen ronbunshū henshū iinkai, ed. *Chikamatsu no sanbyakunen.* Osaka: Izumi shoin, 1999.
Chikamatsu zenshū (*CZ*). 17 vols. Tokyo: Iwanami shoten, 1985–94.
Cogan, Thomas, trans. *The Tale of the Soga Brothers.* Tokyo: University of Tokyo Press, 1987.
Crump, James I., trans. *Chan-kuo ts'e.* Ann Arbor: Center for Chinese Studies, University of Michigan Press, 1996.
Doi Jun'ichi. "Okamoto Ippōshi nenpu." *Nihon ishigaku zasshi* 23 (October 1997): 467–80.

Dunn, Charles, and Bunzō Torigoe, trans. *The Actors Analects (Yakusha rongo)*. New York: Columbia University Press, 1969.
Echigoshishū. 3 vols. Tokyo: Kokushi kenkyūkai, 1923.
Edo machibure shūsei. Vol. 2. Tokyo: Hanawa shobō, 1994.
Essa sōsho. Vol. 5. Tokyo: Essa sōsho kankōkai, 1933.
Fujii Otoo, ed. *Chikamatsu sewamono zenshū*. 3 vols. Tokyo: Fūsanbō, 1944.
Fujii Otoo, ed. *Chikamatsu zenshū*. 12 vols. Osaka: Asahi shinbun, 1923.
Funagoe Seiichirō, ed. *Naniwa sōsho*. Vol. 3. Osaka: Naniwa sōsho kankōkai, 1927.
Gerstle, C. Andrew. "Amateurs and the Theater: The So-Called Demented Art of Gidayū." *Senri Ethnological Studies* 46 (1995): 37–57.
Gerstle, C. Andrew. *Circles of Fantasy: Convention in the Plays of Chikamatsu*. Cambridge, Mass.: Council on East Asian Studies, Harvard University Press, 1986.
Gerstle, C. Andrew. "Gidayū botsugo no Chikamatsu: *Kokusen'ya kassen*, *Kanhasshū tsunagi-uma*." In Torigoe Bunzō et al., eds., *Chikamatsu no jidai*. IKKB. Vol. 8. Tokyo: Iwanami shoten, 1998.
Gerstle, C. Andrew. "Hero as Murderer in Chikamatsu." *Monumenta Nipponica* 51, 3 (1996): 317–56.
Gerstle, C. Andrew. "Heroic Honor: Chikamatsu and the Samurai Ideal." *Harvard Journal of Asiatic Studies* 57, 2 (1997): 307–81.
Gerstle, C. Andrew. "Takemoto Gidayū and the Individualistic Spirit of Osaka Theater." In James McClain and Osamu Wakita, eds., *Osaka, the Merchants' Capital of Early Modern Japan*. Ithaca, N.Y.: Cornell University Press, 1999.
Gerstle, C. Andrew, Inobe Kiyoshi, and William P. Malm. *Theater as Music: The Bunraku Play, "Mt. Imo and Mt. Se: An Exemplary Tale of Womanly Virtue."* Ann Arbor: Center for Japanese Studies, University of Michigan Press, 1990.
Gidayū nenpyō: Kinseihen. 6 vols. Tokyo: Yagi shoten, 1979.
Gidayū nenpyō: Meijihen. Osaka: Gidayū nenpyō kankōkai, 1956.
Gidayū nenpyō: Taishōhen. Osaka: Gidayū nenpyō kankōkai, 1970.
Gidayūbon kōsohen. NSBSS. Vol. 7. Tokyo: San'ichi shobō, 1977.
Goff, Janet. *Noh Drama and "The Tale of Genji."* Princeton, N.J.: Princeton University Press, 1991.
Golownin, Vasilii, M. *Memoirs of a Captivity in Japan During the Years 1811, 1812, and 1813*. London: Henry Colburn, 1973.
Go-Taiheiki. Teikoku bunko series. Vol. 65. Tokyo: Hakubunkan, 1900.
Gotō Tanji, ed. *Taiheiki*. Vol. 3. NKBT no. 36. Tokyo: Iwanami shoten, 1961.
Hara Michio. "*Futago Sumidagawa* shikiron: Oiesōdōgeki to shite no seimitsuka." *Kokugo to kokubungaku* 898 (October 1998): 1–14.
Hashimoto Asao, ed. *Kyōgenki*. SNKBT no. 58. Tokyo: Iwanami shoten, 1996.
Hayakawa Kōzaburō, ed. *Mōgyū*. 2 vols. SKT nos. 58 and 59. Tokyo: Meiji shoin, 1973.

Hirata Sumiko. "*Futago Sumidagawa* ni tsuite—Edo to Chikamatsu." *Bunkyō daigaku kokubun* 13 (1984): 35–46.
Hirata Sumiko. "Takeda Izumo to Chikugonojō." In Torigoe Bunzō et al., eds., *Chikamatsu no jidai*. IKKB. Vol. 8. Tokyo: Iwanami shoten, 1998.
Hokuetsu gunki. Essa sōsho. Vol. 5. Tokyo: Essa sōsho kankōkai, 1933.
Hoshikawa Kiyotaka, ed. *Kobun shinbō goshū.* Vol. 1. SKT no. 16. Tokyo: Meiji shoin, 1963.
Ichikawa Yasushi and Endō Tetsuo, eds. *Sōshi.* Vol. 2. SKT no. 8. Tokyo: Meiji shoin, 1967.
Ichiko Teiji, ed. *Soga monogatari.* NKBT no. 88. Tokyo: Iwanami shoten, 1966.
Iguchi Hiroshi. *Chikamatsu sewa-jōruriron.* Osaka: Izumi shoin, 1986.
Ikeda Hiroshi et al., eds. *Okura, Toraaki-bon: Kyōgenshū no kenkyū.* Tokyo: Hyōgensha, 1973.
Imai Usaburō, ed. *Ekikyō.* Vol. 1. SKT no. 23. Tokyo: Meiji shoin, 1987.
Imamukashi ayatsuri nendaiki. NSBSS. Vol. 7. Tokyo: San'ichi shobō, 1977.
Ishikawa Tadahisa, ed. *Shikyō.* Vol. 1. SKT no. 110. Tokyo: Meiji shoin, 1997.
Itagaki Shun'ichi, ed. *Zen-Taiheiki.* 2 vols. Tokyo: Kokusho kankōkai, 1988.
Kabuki hyōbanki shūsei. Vol. 1. Tokyo: Iwanami shoten, 1972.
Kabuki nenpyō. 8 vols. Tokyo: Iwanami shoten, 1963.
Kabuki-za hyakunenshi. 3 vols. Tokyo: Shōchiku kabushiki kaisha, 1998.
Kaewrithidej, Ladda. "Chikamatsu jōruri ni okeru 'kyōran' no igi: *Futago Sumidagawa* o rei ni." *Kyōto daigaku: Kokubungaku ronsō* 1 (1998): 16–41.
Kajiwara Masaaki, ed. *Gikeiki.* NKBZ no. 31. Tokyo: Shōgakkan, 1971.
Kamakura Keiko. "Chikamatsu jidai jōruri: sandanmekō: *Tsu no kuni meoto ike* o chūshin ni." *Chikamatsu ronshū* 8 (June 1986): 22–31.
Kamata Tadashi and Yoneyama Toratarō, eds. *Kanbun meigen jiten.* Tokyo: Taishūkan shoten, 1995.
Kamata Tadashi and Yoneyama Toratarō, eds. *Kanshi meiku jiten.* Tokyo: Taishūkan shoten, 1980.
Kamiya Katsuhiro. "Chikamatsu to tsūzoku gundan." *Nagoya daigaku: Kokugo kokubungaku* 82 (July 1998): 31–42.
Kamiya Katsuhiro. "Chikamatsu to *Yugu zuihitsu*." *Kinsei bungei* 67 (January 1998): 24–32.
Kanaoka Shōkō, ed. *Chūgoku koji seigo jiten.* Tokyo: Sanseidō, 1991.
Kango yamato koji. Woodblock print edition in Kyoto University, Faculty of Letters Library, 1691.
Kanzawa Tokō. *Okina-gusa.* Nihon zuihitsu taisei no. 3. Vol. 20. Tokyo: Yoshikawa kōbunkan, 1978.
Karlgren, Bernhard, trans. *The Book of Odes.* Stockholm: Museum of Far Eastern Antiquities, 1950.

Katagiri Yōichi, ed. *Gosenwakashū*. SNKBT no. 6. Tokyo: Iwanami shoten, 1990.
Katano Tatsurō, ed. *Senzaiwakashū*. SNKBT no. 10. Tokyo: Iwanami shoten, 1993.
Katō Jōken and Mizukami Shizuo, eds. *Chūgoku koji meigen jiten*. Tokyo: Kadokawa shoten, 1979.
Kawaguchi Hisao and Shida Nobuyoshi, eds. *Wakan rōeishūi, Ryōjin hishō*. NKBT no.73. Tokyo: Iwanami shoten, 1965.
Kawamura Teruo, ed. *Kinyō wakashū; Shika wakashū*. SNKBT no. 9. Tokyo: Iwanami shoten, 1989.
Kawa-nakajima gokado kassen. Zoku gunsho ruijū no. 2. Vol. 21. Tokyo: Zoku gunsho ruijū kanseikai, 1923.
Kazamaki Keijirō, ed. *Sankashū, Kinyōwakashū*. NKBT no. 29. Tokyo: Iwanami shoten, 1961.
Keene, Donald, trans. *The Battle of Coxinga: Chikamatsu's Puppet Play, Its Background and Importance*. Cambridge: Cambridge University Press, 1951.
Keene, Donald, trans. *Essays in Idleness*. New York: Columbia University Press, 1967.
Keene, Donald, trans. *Major Plays of Chikamatsu*. New York: Columbia University Press, 1961.
Keene, Donald, ed. *Twenty Plays of the Nō Theater*. New York: Columbia University Press, 1970.
Kitani Hōgin et al., eds. *Dai Chikamatsu zenshū*. 16 vols. Tokyo: Dai Chikamatsu zenshū kankōkai, 1925.
Kobayashi Yoshinori et al., eds. *Ryōjin hishō, Kanginshū, Kyōgen kayō*. SNKBT no. 56. Tokyo: Iwanami shoten, 1993.
Koizumi Hiroshi, ed. *Hōbutsushū, Kankyo no tomo, Hirasan kojin reitaku*. SNKBT no. 40. Tokyo: Iwanami shoten, 1993.
Ko-jōrurishū kankōkai, ed. *Ko-jōruri shōhonshū: Kaganojōhen*. Vol. 4. Tokyo: Daigaku shoten, 1993.
Kokubungaku ronsō shinshū. Vol. 8. Tokyo: Ōfūsha, 1988.
Kokushi taikei. Vol. 45. 1933. Reprint, Tokyo: Yoshikawa kōbunkan, 1965.
Komachiya Teruhiko, ed. *Shūiwakashū*. SNKBT no. 7. Tokyo: Iwanami shoten, 1990.
Kominz, Laurence R. *Avatars of Vengeance: Japanese Drama and the Soga Literary Tradition*. Ann Arbor: Center of Japanese Studies, University of Michigan Press, 1995.
Koyama Hiroshi, ed. *Kyōgenshū*. 2 vols. NKBT nos. 42 and 43. Tokyo: Iwanami shoten, 1961.
Koyama Hiroshi et al., eds. *Yōkyokushū*. 2 vols. NKBZ nos. 33 and 34. Tokyo: Shōgakkan, 1973.
Kramers, Robert P., trans. *K'ung tzu chia yü, the School Sayings of Confucius*. Leiden: Brill, 1950.
Kubo Noritada. *Kōshin shinkō*. Tokyo: Yamakawa shuppansha, 1956.

Kubota Jun, ed. *Goshūiwakashū*. SNKBT no. 8. Tokyo: Iwanami shoten, 1994.
Kurokawa Shindō, ed. *Takeda sandai gunki*. 3 vols. Kokushi sōsho no. 22. Tokyo: Kokushi kankōkai, 1916.
Kusuyama Haruki, ed. *Enanji*. Vol. 1. SKT no. 62. Tokyo: Meiji shoin, 1988.
Kyōto machibure shūsei, bekkan. Vol. 2. Tokyo: Iwanami shoten, 1989.
Lau, Din Cheuk, ed. *A Concordance to the Shou Yuan*. Hong Kong: Commercial Press, 1992.
Lau, Din Cheuk, ed. *A Concordance to the Xinxu*. Hong Kong: Commercial Press, 1992.
Lau, Din Cheuk, trans. *Confucius: The Analects (Lun Yü)*. London: Penguin Books, 1979.
Lau, Din Cheuk, trans. *Mencius*. London: Penguin Books, 1970.
Legge, James, trans. *The Chinese Classics*. Vol. 1. Oxford: Clarendon Press, 1893.
Leiter, Samuel, trans. *The Art of Kabuki: Famous Plays in Performance*. Berkeley and Los Angeles: University of California Press, 1979.
Lombard, Frank. *An Outline History of the Japanese Drama*. London: Allen & Unwin, 1928.
Markus, Andrew. *The Willow in Autumn: Ryūtei Tanehiko 1783–1842*. Cambridge, Mass.: Harvard University Press, 1992.
Matisoff, Susan. *The Legend of Semimaru: Blind Musician of Japan*. New York: Columbia University Press, 1978.
Matsuo Hitoshi, ed. *Makura no sōshi*. NKBZ no. 11. Tokyo: Shōgakkan, 1974.
Matsuura Tomohisa, ed. *Tōshi kaishaku jiten*. Tokyo: Taishūkan shoten, 1987.
Matsuzaki Hitoshi. "*Kanhasshū tsunagi-uma* kyakuchū yoteki." *Nihon bungaku kenkyū* 31 (1996): 59–70.
Matsuzaki Hitoshi. 1997. "*Kanhasshū tsunagi-uma* ron." *Kabuki: Kenkyū to hihyō* 19 (1997): 107–24.
Matsuzaki Hitoshi et al., eds. *Chikamatsu jōrurishū* (CJS). 2 vols. SNKBT nos. 91 and 92. Tokyo: Iwanami shoten, 1995.
McCullough, Helen, trans. *Kokin Wakashū: The First Imperial Anthology of Japanese Poetry*. Stanford, Calif.: Stanford University Press, 1985.
McCullough, Helen, trans. *The Taiheiki: A Chronicle of Medieval Japan*. New York: Columbia University Press, 1959.
McCullough, Helen, trans. *The Tale of the Heike*. Stanford, Calif.: Stanford University Press, 1988.
McCullough, Helen, trans. *Tales of Ise: Lyrical Episodes from Tenth-Century Japan*. Stanford, Calif.: Stanford University Press, 1968.
McCullough, Helen, trans. *Yoshitsune: A Fifteenth-Century Japanese Chronicle*. Tokyo: University of Tokyo Press, 1966.
McKinnon, Richard, N., trans. *Selected Kyōgen Plays*. Tokyo: Uniprint, 1968.

Minemura Fumito, ed. *Shinkokin wakashū*. NKBZ no. 26. Tokyo: Shōgakkan, 1974.
Miyamori, Asataro, trans. *Masterpieces of Chikamatsu: The Japanese Shakespeare*. London: Kegan Paul, 1926.
Mizuhara Hajime, ed. *Shintei: Genpei jōsuiki*. 6 vols. Tokyo: Shinbutsu ōraisha, 1991.
Mizusawa Toshitada, ed. *Shiki*. Vol. 8. SKT no. 88. Tokyo: Meiji shoin, 1990.
Mori Shū. *Chikamatsu Monzaemon*. Tokyo: San'ichi shobō, 1959.
Mori Shū. *Chikamatsu to jōruri*. Tokyo: Hanawa shobō, 1990.
Mori Shū et al., eds. *Chikamatsu Monzaemonshū*. Vol. 1. NKBZ no. 43. Tokyo: Shōgakkan, 1972.
Morley, Carolyn. *Transformation, Miracles and Mischief: The Mountain Priest Plays of Kyōgen*. Ithaca, N.Y.: Cornell University Press, 1993.
Morris, Ivan, trans. *As I Crossed a Bridge of Dreams*. London: Penguin Books, 1975.
Morris, Ivan, trans. *The Pillow Book of Sei Shōnagon*. New York: Columbia University Press, 1967.
Mueller, Jacqueline, trans. "Goban Taiheiki [1710]." *Harvard Journal of Asiatic Studies* 46, 1 (1986): 221–67.
Murakami Tetsumi, ed. *Santaishi*. Vol. 1. Shinchō chūgoku kotensen no. 16. Tokyo: Asahi shinbunsha, 1966.
Muroki Yatarō, ed. *Kinpira jōruri shōhonshū*. 3 vols. Tokyo: Kadokawa shoten, 1969.
Nagatomo Chiyoji. "Jōruribon: sono juyō to kyōkyū." In Torigoe Bunzō et al., eds., *Ōgun jidai no jōruri*. IKKB. Vol. 9. Tokyo: Iwanami shoten, 1998.
Naniwa miyage. Shin gunsho ruijū. Vol. 6. Tokyo: Kokusho kankōkai, 1907.
Nihon koten bungaku daijiten. 6 vols. Tokyo: Iwanami shoten, 1983.
Nihon shomin bunka shiryō shūsei (NSBSS). Vol. 7. Tokyo: San'ichi shobō, 1977.
Nihon shomin seikatsu shiryō shūsei. Vol. 28. Tokyo: San'ichi shobō, 1980.
Nihon zuihitsu taisei no. 3. Vol. 20. Tokyo: Yoshikawa kōbunkan, 1978.
Niima Shin'ichi, ed. *Chūsei kinsei kayōshū*. NKBT no. 44. Tokyo: Iwanami shoten, 1959.
Nippon gakujutsu shinkōkai, ed. *The Noh Drama, Ten Plays from the Japanese*. Rutland, Vt.: Tuttle, 1955.
Nishio Kōichi, ed. *Kokon chomonjū*. Vol. 2. Shinchō Nihon koten shūsei no. 76. Tokyo: Shinchōsha, 1986.
Nishiyama Matsunosuke et al., eds. *Kinsei geidōron*. Nihon shisō taikei no. 61. Tokyo: Iwanami shoten, 1972.
Nonomura Kaizō, ed. *Yōkyoku nihyaku gojūbanshū*. Kyoto: Akao shōbundō, 1978.
Obi Kōichi, ed. 1975. *Monzen*. Vol. 5. Zenshaku kanbun taikei no. 30. Tokyo: Shūeisha, 1975.
Ōhashi Tadayoshi. "Jōrurishi ni okeru jōkyō ninen." In Chikamatsu kenkyūjo jūsshūnenkinen ronbunshū henshū iinkai, ed., *Chikamatsu no sanbyakunen*. Osaka: Izumi shoin, 1999.

Ōhashi Shintarō, ed. *Tsūzoku sangokushi* (TS). 2 vols. Teikoku bunko no. 11. Tokyo: Hakubunkan, 1893.
Ōmu ryōchūki. Nagoya sōsho zokuhen. Vol. 12. Nagoya: Nagoya-shi kyōiku iinkai, 1967.
Ongyoku kudensho. In Nishiyama Matsunosuke et al., eds., *1972 Kinsei geidōron.* Nihon shisō taikei no. 61. Tokyo: Iwanami shoten, 1972.
Ōshima Akira, ed. *Chūgoku meigen meiku jiten.* Tokyo: Sanseidō, 1998.
Ōta Nanpo. "Zokuji kosui." Nihon zuihitsu taisei no. 3. Vol. 4. Tokyo: Yoshikawa kōbunkan, 1977.
Ōtani Tokuzō, ed. *Yōkyoku nihyaku gojūbanshū sakuin.* 2 vols. Kyoto: Akao shōbundō, 1978.
Owen, Stephen, ed. and trans. *An Anthology of Chinese Literature.* New York: Norton, 1996.
Phillipi, Donald, trans. *Kojiki.* Princeton, N.J.: Princeton University Press. 1968.
Roberts, M., trans. *Three Kingdoms: A Historical Novel.* Beijing: Foreign Languages Press, and Berkeley and Los Angeles: University of California Press, 1991.
Rodd, Laurel, with Mary Henkenius, trans. *Kokinshū: A Collection of Poems Ancient and Modern.* Princeton, N.J.: Princeton University Press, 1984.
Rimer, J. Thomas, and Jonathan Chaves, eds. and trans. *Japanese and Chinese Poems to Sing: The* Wakan rōeishū. New York: Columbia University Press, 1997.
Sadler, Arthur L., trans. *Japanese Plays: No-Kyogen-Kabuki.* Sydney: Angus and Robertson, 1934.
Saiki Kazuma, ed. *Mikawa monogatari, Hagakure.* Nihon shisō taikei no. 26. Tokyo: Iwanami shoten, 1974.
Sakai Kenji, ed. *Kōyō gunkan taisei.* 4 vols. Tokyo: Kyūko shoin, 1995.
Sanari Kentarō, ed. *Yōkyoku taikan* (YTK). 7 vols. Tokyo: Meiji shoin, 1927.
Sawyer, Ralph D., and M. Mei-chuen Sawyer, trans. *The Seven Military Classics of Ancient China.* Boulder, Colo.: Westview Press, 1993.
Seidensticker, Edward, trans. *The Tale of Genji.* New York: Knopf, 1977.
Setsuyō kikan. In Naniwa sōsho. Vol. 3. Osaka: Naniwa sōsho kankōkai, 1927.
Shimazaki, Chifumi, trans. *Kami (god)-noh.* Tokyo: Hinoki shoten, 1972.
Shimazaki, Chifumi, trans. *The Noh (Battle Noh).* Tokyo: Hinoki shoten, 1987.
Shimazaki, Chifumi, trans. *Restless Spirits from Japanese Noh Plays of the Fourth Group.* Cornell East Asia Series. Ithaca, N.Y.: Cornell University Press, 1995.
Shimazaki, Chifumi, trans. *Sanbanme-mono (Woman Noh),* 3 vols. Tokyo: Hinoki shoten, 1976.
Shimazaki, Chifumi, trans. *Warrior Ghost Plays from the Japanese Noh Theater.* Cornell East Asia Series. Ithaca, N.Y.: Cornell University Press, 1993.
Shin gunsho ruiju. Vol. 5. 1906. Reprint, Tokyo: Daiichi shobō, 1976.
Shinshaku kanbun taikei (SKT). Tokyo: Meiji shoin, 1960–.

Shirakata Masaru. *Chikamatsu jōruri no kenkyū*. Tokyo: Kazama shoin, 1993.
Shirase Kōji. "*Shinjū yoigōshin* no hōhō" (parts 1 and 2). *Kokubungaku: Gengo to bungei* 112 (1995): 47–85; 113 (1995): 95–114.
Shively, Donald. *The Love Suicides at Amijima: A Study of a Japanese Domestic Tragedy by Chikamatsu Monzaemon*. Cambridge, Mass.: Harvard University Press, 1953.
Shively, Donald. "Tokugawa Plays on Forbidden Topics." In James Brandon, ed., *Chūshingura: Studies in Kabuki and the Puppet Theater*. Honolulu: University of Hawaii Press, 1982.
Shōchiku hyakunenshi. Vol. 3. *Engeki shiryō*. Tokyo: Shōchiku kabushiki kaisha, 1996.
Shuzui Kenji et al., eds. *Chikamatsu jōrurishū*. Vol. 2. NKBT no. 50. Tokyo: Iwanami shoten, 1959.
Smethurst, Mae. *Dramatic Representations of Filial Piety*. Ithaca, N.Y.: Cornell University Press, 1998.
Suwa Haruo. *Chikamatsu sewa-jōruri no kenkyū*. Tokyo: Kazama shoin, 1974.
Suzuki Ken'ichi. *Kinsei dōjō kadan no kenkyū*. Tokyo: Kyūko shoin, 1994.
Takahashi Hiroshi. "Chikamatsu to *Enki kappō*." *Sugino joshi daigaku*, no. 17 (December 1980): 114–77.
Takahashi Hiroshi. "Chikamatsu to *Kinshūdan*," *Sugino joshi daigaku*, no. 18 (December 1981): 31–48.
Takahashi Sadakazu. "Tanaka-bon *Heike tsurugi no maki*: Kaisetsu." *Kokugo kokubun*, July 1967, pp. 37–58.
Takano Tatsuyuki, ed. *Nihon kayō shūsei*. 12 vols. 1928. Reprint, Tokyo: Tokyo shuppan, 1961.
Takemoto fudan sakura. In NSBSS. Vol. 7. Tokyo: San'ichi shobō, 1977.
Takeuchi Teruo, ed. *Kanpishi*. Vol. 1. SKT no. 11. Tokyo: Meiji shoin, 1960.
Takeuchi Waka, ed. *Kefukigusa*. Iwanami bunko yellow series no. 200-1. 1943. Reprint, Tokyo: Iwanami shoten, 1988.
Teele, Roy, Nicholas Teele, and Rebecca H. Teele. *Ono no Komachi, Poems, Stories, Noh Plays*. New York: Garland Press, 1993.
Tokugawa jikki. In *Kokushi taikei*. Vol. 45. Tokyo: Yoshikawa kōbunkan, 1933.
Tokugawa kinreikō, goshū. Vol. 1. Tokyo: Sōbunsha, 1959.
Torigoe Bunzō, ed. *Chikamatsu Monzaemonshū*. Vol. 2. NKBZ no. 44. Tokyo: Shōgakkan, 1975.
Torigoe Bunzō, ed. *Kabuki to kyōgen: Gengo hyōgen no tsuikyū*. Tokyo: Yagi shoten, 1992.
Torigoe Bunzō et al., eds. *Iwanami kōza: Kabuki, bunraku* (IKKB). 10 vols. Tokyo: Iwanami shoten, 1997.
Totman, Conrad. *The Green Archipelago: Forestry in Preindustrial Japan*. Berkeley and Los Angeles: University of California Press, 1989.
Tsuchida Mamoru. *Kōshō genroku kabuki: Yōshiki to tenkai*. Tokyo: Yagi shoten, 1996.

Tsuchida Mamoru. "Ochiyo to Hanbei." *Ehime daigaku: Kokugo kokubun* 12 (1962): 3–7.
Tsunoda Ichirō. "Jōkyō ninen no Dōtonbori." In Torigoe Bunzō et al., eds., *Chikamatsu no jidai*. IKKB. Vol. 8. Tokyo: Iwanami shoten, 1998.
Tsunoda Ryusaku et al., eds. *Sources of Japanese Tradition*. Vol. 1. New York: Columbia University Press, 1964.
Tyler, Royall, trans. *Japanese Nō Dramas*. London: Penguin Classics, 1992.
Uchino Yūichirō, ed. *Mōshi*. SKT no. 4. Tokyo: Meiji shoin, 1962.
Uchiyama Mikiko. *Jōruri no jūhasseki*. Tokyo: Benseisha, 1989.
Uchiyama Mikiko. "*Kanhasshū tsunagi-uma* to sono shūhen." *Kabuki: Kenkyū to hihyō* 8 (1992): 3–68.
Ueda Kazutoshi, ed. *Naniwa miyage*. Tokyo: Yūhōkan, 1904.
Ueda Kazutoshi and Higuchi Yoshichiyo, eds. *Chikamatsu goi*. Tokyo: Fuzanbō, 1930.
"*Umewaka engi*" *no kenkyū to shirō*. Kokubungaku ronsō shinshū. Vol. 8. Tokyo: Ōfūsha, 1988.
Uno Seiichi, ed. *Kōshi kego*. SKT no. 53. Tokyo: Meiji shoin, 1996.
Wakan sansai zue. In *Nihon shomin seikatsu shiryō shūsei*. Vol. 28. Tokyo: San'ichi shobō, 1980.
Waley, Arthur, trans. *The Analects of Confucius*. London: Allen & Unwin, 1938.
Waley, Arthur, trans. *The Book of Songs*. 1937. Reprint, New York: Garland Press, 1993.
Waley, Arthur, trans. *The Nō Plays of Japan*. London: Allen & Unwin, 1921.
Waley, Arthur, trans. *The Tale of Genji*. London: Modern Library, 1993.
Waley, Arthur. *The Way and Its Power: A Study of the Tao Tē Ching*. New York: Grove Press, 1958.
Watson, Burton, trans. *The Basic Writings of Mo Tzu, Hsün Tzu, and Han Fei Tzu*. New York: Columbia University Press, 1967.
Watson, Burton, trans. *The Complete Works of Chuang Tzu*. New York: Columbia University Press, 1968.
Watson, Burton, trans. *Han Fei Tzu: Basic Writings*. New York: Columbia University Press, 1994.
Watson, Burton, trans. *Records of the Grand Historian of China: Translated from the "Shih chi" of Ssu-ma Ch'ien*. 2 vols. New York: Columbia University Press, 1961.
Yamane Tameo. "Fushizuke to hanpon." In Torigoe Bunzō et al., eds., *Chikamatsu no jidai*. IKKB. Vol. 8. Tokyo: Iwanami shoten, 1998.
Yamashita Hiroaki, ed. *Taiheiki*. Vol. 4. Shinchō Nihon koten shūsei no. 72. Tokyo: Shinchōsha, 1985.
Yamashita Hiroaki, ed. *Taiheiki*. Vol. 5. Shinchō Nihon koten shūsei no. 78. Tokyo: Shinchōsha, 1988.
Yasuda Fukiko. *Kojōruri: tayū no juryō to sono jidai*. Tokyo: Yagi shoten, 1998.

Yasuda, Kenneth, trans. *Masterworks of the Nō Theater*. Bloomington: Indiana University Press, 1989.

Yokoyama Shigeru. "Sekkyō shōhon ni junzuru shōhon." In *Chūsei bungaku: Kenkyū to shiryō* (*Kokubungaku ronshū*, vol. 2). Tokyo: Shibundō, 1958.

Yokoyama Shigeru, ed. *Sekkyō shōhonshū*. Vol. 3. Tokyo: Kadokawa shoten, 1968.

Yokoyama Tadashi, ed. *Jōrurishū*. NKBZ no. 45. Tokyo: Shōgakkan, 1971.

Yokomichi Mario and Omote Akira, eds. *Yōkyokushū*. 2 vols. NKBT nos. 40 and 41. Tokyo: Iwanami shoten, 1960.

Yoshida Kenkō, ed. *Rongo*. SKT no. 1. Tokyo: Meiji shoin, 1960.

Yoshida Kenkō and Mizusawa Toshitada, eds. *Shiki*. 9 vols. SKT nos. 38, 39, 41, 85–90. Tokyo: Meiji shoin, 1973–.

Yoshinaga Takao, ed. *Jōruri sakuhin yōsetsu (3): Chikamatsu Hanji-hen*. Tokyo: Kokuritsu gekijo, 1984.

Zoku gunsho ruijū. Vol. 21, no. 2. Tokyo: Zoku gunsho ruijū kanseikai, 1923.

Glossary of Terms

akagai 赤貝	type of mussel; slang for the female sex organ
ai no yama 合山	musical term denoting a sad song or melody
ainote 合手	musical term denoting shamisen accompaniment
aishō 哀傷	tragic, suffering
Ashikaga 足利	family name of the shogun rulers of the Muromachi era; place-name in northeast Japan
aware 哀れ	aesthetic term for sensitivity to pathos; sadness
Azuma 吾妻、東	eastern Japan, sometimes denoting the area of present-day Tokyo
bu 分	gold coin one-quarter of a gold *ryō*; silver coin one-tenth of a silver *monme*
bunraku 文楽	jōruri puppet theater
bushidō 武士道	way of the samurai
cadence	musical term for the closure of a musical phrase
daimyō 大名	samurai lord
dōguya 道具屋	musical term for a particular melody
Edo 江戸	capital of Tokugawa Japan; former name of Tokyo
e-iri kyōgen-bon 絵入狂言本	illustrated kabuki summary books
ema 絵馬	votive offering at a shrine or temple; sometimes a painting of a horse
fuchi 淵	deep pool; metaphor for the lyrical, song parts of a drama
fushi フシ	melody; notation used to denote a musical cadence

Genji (Minamoto) 源氏 (源)	clan to which the Ashikaga, Takeda, and Tokugawa families claimed lineage
Gidayū 義太夫	name of a jōruri performer; term for bunraku music
gin ギン	high pitch
giri 義理	Confucian term for "reason, rational"; popular term for "duty, responsibility"; used in contrast to *jō* or *ninjō*
gōkan 合巻	early-nineteenth-century illustrated popular fiction
fushigoto 節事	song (in contrast to dramatic) sections of scenes
hachi-tataki 鉢タタキ	popular singing style; the singer accompanies himself by striking a bowl to keep the beat
hakama 袴	Japanese traditional "trousers" worn over a kimono
Heian 平安	era name, 794–1185
hikage-bōkō 日陰奉公	to serve from the shadows, an ideal proposed in *Hagakure*, a treatise on the way of the samurai
hito-kai 人買い	trading in slaves
hizamaru 膝丸	famous sword of the Genji clan
ji 地	sung passages with musical accompaniment
jidaimono 時代物	period (history) plays
jigoto 地事	dramatic (as opposed to song) parts of a drama
ji-iro 地色	sung passages with musical accompaniment
jitsu 実	realistic, realism
jitsuji 実事	realism
jo 序	prelude; slow, measured tempo
jō 情	passion, desire, feelings, often used in opposition to *giri*
jo-ha-kyū 序破急	musical or dance pattern with a slow, measured beginning, followed by increasing tempo and intensity to a climax, and completed by a short, quick-paced conclusion
jōruri 浄瑠璃	term for various kinds of narrative chanting styles; puppet theater, later called bunraku
kabuki 歌舞伎	commercial popular theater that developed from the seventeenth century
kagura 神楽	Shinto music; festival music
Kamakura 鎌倉	capital city and era name, 1185–1333
kami 上	highest pitch
kami u 上ウ	high pitch

kan 貫	3.75 kilograms; measure of silver
kanazōshi 仮名草子	seventeenth-century popular fiction
Kantō 関東	greater Tokyo
karakuri からくり	mechanical devices often used as part of a show
kawara-kojiki 河原乞食	literally, riverbed beggar; derogatory name for actors
kawase 川瀬	rapids; metaphor for the active, quick parts of a drama
keiyaku 契約	promise, vow
kimon 鬼門	"demon gate" placed in northeast corner to ward off demons
ko-jōruri 古浄瑠璃	jōruri plays that predate Chikamatsu's works written for Gidayū
kokka 国家	nation, country
kōshaku 講釈	recitation, performance of classical texts
kotoba 詞	spoken passages without musical accompaniment
kowaka-mai 幸若舞	ballad-drama
kowari コワリ	musical term denoting a threatening melody
kudoki クドキ	musical term denoting an "emotional" sung passage; a term for aria-like songs expressing grief or longing
kumo-kirimaru 蜘蛛切丸	"spider-killing" sword with supernatural powers
kyōgen 狂言	relatively short comic play performed between nō plays; a term for kabuki
kyōka 狂歌	comic *waka* poem
maruhon 丸本	official or authentic jōruri published text that includes the chanter's notation
masaru 魔去る、神猿	monkeys at the Hiyoshi (Hie) Shrine that are messengers of the god; written with characters suggesting they have the power to ward off demons
mawashi 回し	belt worn by sumo wrestlers
michiyuki 道行	lyrical dance scene during which the characters travel
monme 匁	one-thousandth of a *kan*, about 3.75 grams
monogurui 物狂い	fall into a state of madness
Muromachi 室町	area of Kyoto; era name 1333–1573
nagaji 長字	musical term indicating a passage sung with the syllables riding the shamisen notes
nagusami 慰み	give comfort; entertain
nai-yomi 内読	the reading of a new play by the playwright, in front of the senior members of the troupe

nasake 情け	compassion
ninjō 人情	love, compassion, desire; often used in contrast to *giri*
ninjōbon 人情本	nineteenth-century popular romantic fiction
nō 能	Japanese mask music-drama developed from the fifteenth century; a term for nō style of chanting in bunraku plays
nyūdō 入道	lay priest
obi 帯	sash for the kimono
obon 御盆	festival in late summer to welcome home the spirits of ancestors
oiesōdō 御家騒動	disturbance in a grand house; subgenre of drama
okuri ヲクリ	notation; musical cadence signaling the exit of a major character
ōyake 公	public, governmental
reizei 冷泉	term for an elegant melody
renbo 恋慕	love
rōnin 浪人	masterless samurai
rōshō 朗誦	to read aloud, recite, chant
ryō 両	measure of weight, about 17 to 18 grams; a gold coin worth about 10 to 15 *ryō* of silver during Chikamatsu's time.
sanbasō 三番叟	auspicious dance opening a day of performance
sanjū 三重	notation; cadence signaling the end of a scene
saru 猿	monkey
sekai 世界	world or setting of a period play
sekkyō (jōruri) 説教 (浄瑠璃)	religious or miraculous drama
seppuku 切腹	ritual suicide; an honorable method of execution
Settsu 摂津	greater Osaka area
sewamono 世話物	domestic or contemporary-life plays
shamisen 三味線	three-stringed instrument used to accompany singers; the instrument used to accompany bunraku chanters
shimenawa しめなわ	large rope used at shrines to mark off sacred space
shinobu-koi 忍恋	service or love of a master without his knowing of it; an ideal aspect of a samurai as espoused in the treatise *Hagakure*
shōhon 正本	authorized text complete with musical notation

shūgen 祝言	auspicious, congratulatory
shukō 趣向	invention, innovation, technique
shu-goroshi 主殺し	killing one's lord or master
sō-honyomi 総本読	the reading of a new play by the playwright in front of the whole troupe
suete スヱテ	notation; musical cadence concluding a highly emotional paragraph
tengu 天狗	goblin or demon with a long nose; known to live in mountain forests, particularly where cedar (crytomeria) is common
Tokugawa 徳川	family that ruled as shoguns during the Edo period, 1600–1868
torii 鳥居	large wooden gates at Shinto shrines
urei 憂い	pathos, suffering
utai 謡	nō drama chanting, singing
waka 和歌	traditional thirty-one-syllable poem
watakushi 私	private, personal, as opposed to *ōyake*, public
yamabushi 山伏	mountain priests; ascetics
yamamba 山姥	mountain crones; women known to eat children but also to help those in distress; wives of *tengu*
yatsushi やつし	disguise
yomihon 読本	narrative fiction with few illustrations and not overtly influenced by kabuki, jōruri, or other forms of chanted narratives
yoriki 与力	official in the Tokugawa government
yūgen 幽玄	elegant, mysterious, beautiful, deep

Other Works in the Columbia Asian Studies Series

Translations from the Asian Classics

Major Plays of Chikamatsu, tr. Donald Keene 1961
Four Major Plays of Chikamatsu, tr. Donald Keene. Paperback ed. only. 1961; rev. ed. 1997
Records of the Grand Historian of China, translated from the Shih chi of Ssu-ma Ch'ien, tr. Burton Watson, 2 vols. 1961
Instructions for Practical Living and Other Neo-Confucian Writings by Wang Yang-ming, tr. Wing-tsit Chan 1963
Hsn Tzu: Basic Writings, tr. Burton Watson, paperback ed. only. 1963; rev. ed. 1996
Chuang Tzu: Basic Writings, tr. Burton Watson, paperback ed. only. 1964; rev. ed. 1996
The Mahābhārata, tr. Chakravarthi V. Narasimhan. Also in paperback ed. 1965; rev. ed. 1997
The Manyōshū, Nippon Gakujutsu Shinkōkai edition 1965
Su Tung-p'o: Selections from a Sung Dynasty Poet, tr. Burton Watson. Also in paperback ed. 1965
Bhartrihari: Poems, tr. Barbara Stoler Miller. Also in paperback ed. 1967
Basic Writings of Mo Tzu, Hsün Tzu, and Han Fei Tzu, tr. Burton Watson. Also in separate paperback eds. 1967
The Awakening of Faith, Attributed to Aśvaghosha, tr. Yoshito S. Hakeda. Also in paperback ed. 1967
Reflections on Things at Hand: The Neo-Confucian Anthology, comp. Chu Hsi and L Tsu-ch'ien, tr. Wing-tsit Chan 1967
The Platform Sutra of the Sixth Patriarch, tr. Philip B. Yampolsky. Also in paperback ed. 1967
Essays in Idleness: The Tsurezuregusa of Kenkō, tr. Donald Keene. Also in paperback ed. 1967
The Pillow Book of Sei Shōnagon, tr. Ivan Morris, 2 vols. 1967
Two Plays of Ancient India: The Little Clay Cart and the Minister's Seal, tr. J. A. B. van Buitenen 1968
The Complete Works of Chuang Tzu, tr. Burton Watson 1968
The Romance of the Western Chamber (Hsi Hsiang chi), tr. S. I. Hsiung. Also in paperback ed. 1968
The Manyōshū, Nippon Gakujutsu Shinkōkai edition. Paperback ed. only. 1969
Records of the Historian: Chapters from the Shih chi of Ssu-ma Ch'ien, tr. Burton Watson. Paperback ed. only. 1969
Cold Mountain: 100 Poems by the T'ang Poet Han-shan, tr. Burton Watson. Also in paperback ed. 1970
Twenty Plays of the Nō Theatre, ed. Donald Keene. Also in paperback ed. 1970
Chūshingura: The Treasury of Loyal Retainers, tr. Donald Keene. Also in paperback ed. 1971; rev. ed. 1997
The Zen Master Hakuin: Selected Writings, tr. Philip B. Yampolsky 1971
Chinese Rhyme-Prose: Poems in the Fu Form from the Han and Six Dynasties Periods, tr. Burton Watson. Also in paperback ed. 1971

Kūkai: Major Works, tr. Yoshito S. Hakeda. Also in paperback ed. 1972
The Old Man Who Does as He Pleases: Selections from the Poetry and Prose of Lu Yu, tr. Burton Watson 1973
The Lion's Roar of Queen Śrīmālā, tr. Alex and Hideko Wayman 1974
Courtier and Commoner in Ancient China: Selections from the History of the Former Han by Pan Ku, tr. Burton Watson. Also in paperback ed. 1974
Japanese Literature in Chinese, vol. 1: *Poetry and Prose in Chinese by Japanese Writers of the Early Period,* tr. Burton Watson 1975
Japanese Literature in Chinese, vol. 2: *Poetry and Prose in Chinese by Japanese Writers of the Later Period,* tr. Burton Watson 1976
Scripture of the Lotus Blossom of the Fine Dharma, tr. Leon Hurvitz. Also in paperback ed. 1976
Love Song of the Dark Lord: Jayadeva's Gītagovinda, tr. Barbara Stoler Miller. Also in paperback ed. Cloth ed. includes critical text of the Sanskrit. 1977; rev. ed. 1997
Ryōkan: Zen Monk-Poet of Japan, tr. Burton Watson 1977
Calming the Mind and Discerning the Real: From the Lam rim chen mo of Tsoṅkha-pa, tr. Alex Wayman 1978
The Hermit and the Love-Thief: Sanskrit Poems of Bhartrihari and Bilhaṇa, tr. Barbara Stoler Miller 1978
The Lute: Kao Ming's P'i-p'a chi, tr. Jean Mulligan. Also in paperback ed. 1980
A Chronicle of Gods and Sovereigns: Jinnō Shōtōki of Kitabatake Chikafusa, tr. H. Paul Varley 1980
Among the Flowers: The Hua-chien chi, tr. Lois Fusek 1982
Grass Hill: Poems and Prose by the Japanese Monk Gensei, tr. Burton Watson 1983
Doctors, Diviners, and Magicians of Ancient China: Biographies of Fang-shih, tr. Kenneth J. DeWoskin. Also in paperback ed. 1983
Theater of Memory: The Plays of Kālidāsa, ed. Barbara Stoler Miller. Also in paperback ed. 1984
The Columbia Book of Chinese Poetry: From Early Times to the Thirteenth Century, ed. and tr. Burton Watson. Also in paperback ed. 1984
Poems of Love and War: From the Eight Anthologies and the Ten Long Poems of Classical Tamil, tr. A. K. Ramanujan. Also in paperback ed. 1985
The Bhagavad Gita: Krishna's Counsel in Time of War, tr. Barbara Stoler Miller 1986
The Columbia Book of Later Chinese Poetry, ed. and tr. Jonathan Chaves. Also in paperback ed. 1986
The Tso Chuan: Selections from China's Oldest Narrative History, tr. Burton Watson 1989
Waiting for the Wind: Thirty-six Poets of Japan's Late Medieval Age, tr. Steven Carter 1989
Selected Writings of Nichiren, ed. Philip B. Yampolsky 1990
Saigyō, Poems of a Mountain Home, tr. Burton Watson 1990
The Book of Lieh Tzu: A Classic of the Tao, tr. A. C. Graham. Morningside ed. 1990
The Tale of an Anklet: An Epic of South India—The Cilappatikāram of Iḷaṅkō Aṭikaḷ, tr. R. Parthasarathy 1993
Waiting for the Dawn: A Plan for the Prince, tr. and introduction by Wm. Theodore de Bary 1993
Yoshitsune and the Thousand Cherry Trees: A Masterpiece of the Eighteenth-Century Japanese Puppet Theater, tr., annotated, and with introduction by Stanleigh H. Jones, Jr. 1993
The Lotus Sutra, tr. Burton Watson. Also in paperback ed. 1993

The Classic of Changes: A New Translation of the I Ching as Interpreted by Wang Bi, tr. Richard John Lynn 1994
Beyond Spring: Tz'u Poems of the Sung Dynasty, tr. Julie Landau 1994
The Columbia Anthology of Traditional Chinese Literature, ed. Victor H. Mair 1994
Scenes for Mandarins: The Elite Theater of the Ming, tr. Cyril Birch 1995
Letters of Nichiren, ed. Philip B. Yampolsky; tr. Burton Watson et al. 1996
Unforgotten Dreams: Poems by the Zen Monk Shōtetsu, tr. Steven D. Carter 1997
The Vimalakirti Sutra, tr. Burton Watson 1997
Japanese and Chinese Poems to Sing: The Wakan rōei shū, tr. J. Thomas Rimer and Jonathan Chaves 1997
A Tower for the Summer Heat, Li Yu, tr. Patrick Hanan 1998
Traditional Japanese Theater: An Anthology of Plays, Karen Brazell 1998
The Original Analects: Sayings of Confucius and His Successors (0479–0249), E. Bruce Brooks and A. Taeko Brooks 1998
The Classic of the Way and Virtue: A New Translation of the Tao-te ching *of Laozi as Interpreted by Wang Bi*, tr. Richard John Lynn 1999
The Four Hundred Songs of War and Wisdom: An Anthology of Poems from Classical Tamil, The Puranāṇūṟu, eds. and trans. George L. Hart and Hank Heifetz 1999
Original Tao: Inward Training (Nei-yeh) *and the Foundations of Taoist Mysticism*, by Harold D. Roth 1999
Lao Tzu's Tao Te Ching: *A Translation of the Startling New Documents Found at Guodian*, Robert G. Henricks 2000
The Shorter Columbia Anthology of Traditional Chinese Literature, ed. Victor H. Mair 2000
Mistress and Maid (Jiaohongji) by Meng Chengshun, tr. Cyril Birch 2001

Modern Asian Literature

Modern Japanese Drama: An Anthology, ed. and tr. Ted. Takaya. Also in paperback ed. 1979
Mask and Sword: Two Plays for the Contemporary Japanese Theater, by Yamazaki Masakazu, tr. J. Thomas Rimer 1980
Yokomitsu Riichi, Modernist, Dennis Keene 1980
Nepali Visions, Nepali Dreams: The Poetry of Laxmiprasad Devkota, tr. David Rubin 1980
Literature of the Hundred Flowers, vol. 1: *Criticism and Polemics*, ed. Hualing Nieh 1981
Literature of the Hundred Flowers, vol. 2: *Poetry and Fiction*, ed. Hualing Nieh 1981
Modern Chinese Stories and Novellas, 1919 1949, ed. Joseph S. M. Lau, C. T. Hsia, and Leo Ou-fan Lee. Also in paperback ed. 1984
A View by the Sea, by Yasuoka Shōtarō, tr. Kren Wigen Lewis 1984
Other Worlds: Arishima Takeo and the Bounds of Modern Japanese Fiction, by Paul Anderer 1984
Selected Poems of Sŏ Chŏngju, tr. with introduction by David R. McCann 1989
The Sting of Life: Four Contemporary Japanese Novelists, by Van C. Gessel 1989
Stories of Osaka Life, by Oda Sakunosuke, tr. Burton Watson 1990
The Bodhisattva, or Samantabhadra, by Ishikawa Jun, tr. with introduction by William Jefferson Tyler 1990

The Travels of Lao Ts'an, by Liu T'ieh-yün, tr. Harold Shadick. Morningside ed. 1990
Three Plays by Kōbō Abe, tr. with introduction by Donald Keene 1993
The Columbia Anthology of Modern Chinese Literature, ed. Joseph S. M. Lau and Howard Goldblatt 1995
Modern Japanese Tanka, ed. and tr. by Makoto Ueda 1996
Masaoka Shiki: Selected Poems, ed. and tr. by Burton Watson 1997
Writing Women in Modern China: An Anthology of Women's Literature from the Early Twentieth Century, ed. and tr. by Amy D. Dooling and Kristina M. Torgeson 1998
American Stories, by Nagai Kafū, tr. Mitsuko Iriye 2000
The Paper Door and Other Stories, by Shiga Naoya, tr. Lane Dunlop 2001

Studies in Asian Culture

The Ōnin War: History of Its Origins and Background, with a Selective Translation of the Chronicle of Ōnin, by H. Paul Varley 1967
Chinese Government in Ming Times: Seven Studies, ed. Charles O. Hucker 1969
The Actors' Analects (Yakusha Rongo), ed. and tr. by Charles J. Dunn and Bungō Torigoe 1969
Self and Society in Ming Thought, by Wm. Theodore de Bary and the Conference on Ming Thought. Also in paperback ed. 1970
A History of Islamic Philosophy, by Majid Fakhry, 2d ed. 1983
Phantasies of a Love Thief: The Caurapañcāśikā Attributed to Bilhaṇa, by Barbara Stoler Miller 1971
Iqbal: Poet-Philosopher of Pakistan, ed. Hafeez Malik 1971
The Golden Tradition: An Anthology of Urdu Poetry, ed. and tr. Ahmed Ali. Also in paperback ed. 1973
Conquerors and Confucians: Aspects of Political Change in Late Yan China, by John W. Dardess 1973
The Unfolding of Neo-Confucianism, by Wm. Theodore de Bary and the Conference on Seventeenth-Century Chinese Thought. Also in paperback ed. 1975
To Acquire Wisdom: The Way of Wang Yang-ming, by Julia Ching 1976
Gods, Priests, and Warriors: The Bhṛgus of the Mahābhārata, by Robert P. Goldman 1977
Mei Yao-ch'en and the Development of Early Sung Poetry, by Jonathan Chaves 1976
The Legend of Semimaru, Blind Musician of Japan, by Susan Matisoff 1977
Sir Sayyid Ahmad Khan and Muslim Modernization in India and Pakistan, by Hafeez Malik 1980
The Khilafat Movement: Religious Symbolism and Political Mobilization in India, by Gail Minault 1982
The World of K'ung Shang-jen: A Man of Letters in Early Ch'ing China, by Richard Strassberg 1983
The Lotus Boat: The Origins of Chinese Tz'u Poetry in T'ang Popular Culture, by Marsha L. Wagner 1984
Expressions of Self in Chinese Literature, ed. Robert E. Hegel and Richard C. Hessney 1985
Songs for the Bride: Women's Voices and Wedding Rites of Rural India, by W. G. Archer; eds. Barbara Stoler Miller and Mildred Archer 1986
The Confucian Kingship in Korea: Yŏngjo and the Politics of Sagacity, by JaHyun Kim Haboush 1988

Companions to Asian Studies

Approaches to the Oriental Classics, ed. Wm. Theodore de Bary 1959
Early Chinese Literature, by Burton Watson. Also in paperback ed. 1962
Approaches to Asian Civilizations, eds. Wm. Theodore de Bary and Ainslie T. Embree 1964
The Classic Chinese Novel: A Critical Introduction, by C. T. Hsia. Also in paperback ed. 1968
Chinese Lyricism: Shih Poetry from the Second to the Twelfth Century, tr. Burton Watson. Also in paperback ed. 1971
A Syllabus of Indian Civilization, by Leonard A. Gordon and Barbara Stoler Miller 1971
Twentieth-Century Chinese Stories, ed. C. T. Hsia and Joseph S. M. Lau. Also in paperback ed. 1971
A Syllabus of Chinese Civilization, by J. Mason Gentzler, 2d ed. 1972
A Syllabus of Japanese Civilization, by H. Paul Varley, 2d ed. 1972
An Introduction to Chinese Civilization, ed. John Meskill, with the assistance of J. Mason Gentzler 1973
An Introduction to Japanese Civilization, ed. Arthur E. Tiedemann 1974
Ukifune: Love in the Tale of Genji, ed. Andrew Pekarik 1982
The Pleasures of Japanese Literature, by Donald Keene 1988
A Guide to Oriental Classics, eds. Wm. Theodore de Bary and Ainslie T. Embree; 3d edition ed. Amy Vladeck Heinrich, 2 vols. 1989

Introduction to Asian Civilizations

Wm. Theodore de Bary, General Editor

Sources of Japanese Tradition, 1958; paperback ed., 2 vols., 1964. 2d ed., vol. 1, 2001, compiled by Wm. Theodore de Bary, Donald Keene, George Tanabe, and Paul Varley
Sources of Indian Tradition, 1958; paperback ed., 2 vols., 1964. 2d ed., 2 vols., 1988
Sources of Chinese Tradition, 1960, paperback ed., 2 vols., 1964. 2d ed., vol. 1, 1999, compiled by Wm. Theodore de Bary and Irene Bloom; vol. 2, 2000, compiled by Wm. Theodore de Bary and Richard Lufrano
Sources of Korean Tradition, 1997; 2 vols., vol. 1, 1997, compiled by Peter H. Lee and Wm. Theodore de Bary; vol. 2, 2001, compiled by Yŏngho Ch'oe, Peter H. Lee, and Wm. Theodore de Bary

Neo-Confucian Studies

Instructions for Practical Living and Other Neo-Confucian Writings by Wang Yang-ming, tr. Wing-tsit Chan 1963
Reflections on Things at Hand: The Neo-Confucian Anthology, comp. Chu Hsi and L Tsu-ch'ien, tr. Wing-tsit Chan 1967
Self and Society in Ming Thought, by Wm. Theodore de Bary and the Conference on Ming Thought. Also in paperback ed. 1970

The Unfolding of Neo-Confucianism, by Wm. Theodore de Bary and the Conference on Seventeenth-Century Chinese Thought. Also in paperback ed. 1975

Principle and Practicality: Essays in Neo-Confucianism and Practical Learning, eds. Wm. Theodore de Bary and Irene Bloom. Also in paperback ed. 1979

The Syncretic Religion of Lin Chao-en, by Judith A. Berling 1980

The Renewal of Buddhism in China: Chu-hung and the Late Ming Synthesis, by Chn-fang Y 1981

Neo-Confucian Orthodoxy and the Learning of the Mind-and-Heart, by Wm. Theodore de Bary 1981

Yan Thought: Chinese Thought and Religion Under the Mongols, eds. Hok-lam Chan and Wm. Theodore de Bary 1982

The Liberal Tradition in China, by Wm. Theodore de Bary 1983

The Development and Decline of Chinese Cosmology, by John B. Henderson 1984

The Rise of Neo-Confucianism in Korea, by Wm. Theodore de Bary and JaHyun Kim Haboush 1985

Chiao Hung and the Restructuring of Neo-Confucianism in Late Ming, by Edward T. Ch'ien 1985

Neo-Confucian Terms Explained: Pei-hsi tzu-i, by Ch'en Ch'un, ed. and trans. Wing-tsit Chan 1986

Knowledge Painfully Acquired: K'un-chih chi, by Lo Ch'in-shun, ed. and trans. Irene Bloom 1987

To Become a Sage: The Ten Diagrams on Sage Learning, by Yi T'oegye, ed. and trans. Michael C. Kalton 1988

The Message of the Mind in Neo-Confucian Thought, by Wm. Theodore de Bary 1989

GPSR Authorized Representative: Easy Access System Europe, Mustamäe tee
50, 10621 Tallinn, Estonia, gpsr.requests@easproject.com